LIBRARY AND INFORMATION SCIENCE ANNUAL

VOLUME 5

1989

LIBRARY AND INFORMATION SCIENCE ANNUAL

VOLUME 5

1989

Bohdan S. Wynar EDITOR

Ann E. Prentice ASSOCIATE EDITOR
Anna Grace Patterson ASSOCIATE EDITOR

1989

LIBRARIES UNLIMITED
ENGLEWOOD, COLORADO

LIBRARIES UNLIMITED, INC.
P.O. Box 3988
Englewood, CO 80155-3988

ISBN 0-87287-760-4
ISSN 8755-2108

Library and Information Science Annual (formerly *Library Science Annual*) is a companion volume to *American Reference Books Annual.*

Libraries Unlimited books are bound with Type II nonwoven material that meets and exceeds National
Association of State Textbook Administrators' Type II nonwoven material specifications Class A
through E.

Contents

Part III
REVIEWS OF PERIODICALS

Part IV
ABSTRACTS OF LIBRARY SCIENCE
DISSERTATIONS
by Gail A. Schlachter

Publications Cited

FORM OF CITATION	PUBLICATION TITLE
ARBA	American Reference Books Annual
BL	Booklist
BR	Book Report
Choice	Choice
C&RL	College & Research Libraries
CLJ	Canadian Library Journal
EL	Emergency Librarian
JAL	Journal of Academic Librarianship
JOYS	Journal of Youth Services in Libraries
LAR	Library Association Record
LJ	Library Journal
Online	Online
RBB	Reference Books Bulletin
RLR	Riverina Library Review
RQ	RQ
SBF	Science Books & Films
SLJ	School Library Journal
SLMQ	School Library Media Quarterly
VOYA	Voice of Youth Advocates
WLB	Wilson Library Bulletin

Introduction

Volume 5 of *Library and Information Science Annual* brings to a close Libraries Unlimited's effort to establish a standard of bibliographic control and critical analysis of the professional literature of library and information science.

For many years library science literature has been neglected by the reviewing media. Although written matter in library and information science areas seems to have proliferated, only a small portion has been reviewed in professional journals (e.g., *Choice, Library Journal, Wilson Library Bulletin, American Libraries*, etc.). *American Reference Books Annual*, in 1970, began reviewing books in library science published or distributed in the United States, providing more comprehensive coverage than had been offered. In 1987 Donald G. Davis and Charles D. Patterson compiled *ARBA Guide to Library Science Literature 1970-1983*, an endeavor to furnish coverage of the library science field from 1970 through 1983 based on *American Reference Books Annual* 1970-1984. Their work constitutes a first step in a retrospective bibliography of almost 2,000 English-language library science titles published or distributed in the United States during this period. When a volume covering the nineteenth century to 1970 has been completed, the library profession will have produced a broad-coverage bibliographic history, a task it has long performed for and encouraged in other areas of learning.

To provide even more comprehensive reviewing of library science materials, Libraries Unlimited began publication of *Library Science Annual* in 1985. Monographs, reference books, and periodicals have been critiqued. With volume 3, the title was changed to *Library and Information Science Annual* to include the related field of information science and to reflect the expanded scope of the annual. At the same time, Ann E. Prentice, now Vice-President for Library and Information Resources, University of South Florida, agreed to serve as associate editor.

Each year the scope of *LISCA* has broadened to some degree. With every volume the objective has been to review all related monographs and reference books. Volume 1 reviewed 253 titles, primarily titles from the United States and a few from Canada. This has grown each year with more than 500 titles being reviewed in this volume. Volume 5 includes not only titles from the United States and Canada, but titles from Great Britain, Australia, and a few from India.

When *Library Science Annual* began in 1985, the editors' objective was to evaluate as many English-language library periodicals as possible. This goal, with the cooperation of publishers, has been largely accomplished. Coverage includes reviews of national, subject-oriented, and regional journals. The major journals of the United States and Canada with a number from Great Britain and Australia have been reviewed.

To highlight research trends in the profession, Gail A. Schlachter has furnished abstracts of the most significant doctoral dissertations produced each year. Over the last five years, 204 dissertations have been abstracted.

Since publication of this title began, the editors have sought to report on significant trends in the literature through the use of essays by prominent professionals. To illustrate the broad spectrum of coverage, individual publishers of library science materials have been featured over the years beginning with Scarecrow Press in 1985, and this year, Greenwood Press. In 1986, James Rettig wrote an analysis of reference book reviewing, and Gwynneth Evans covered book reviewing in Canada. Collection development in support of education for librarianship was explored by Ann E. Prentice in 1987 as were databases on CD-ROM by Carol Tenopir. Sharon L. Baker and Ronald R. Powell assembled the research mechanisms of major library organizations in 1988 to exemplify how these organizations stimulate research. Trudi Bellardo demonstrated the challenges of keeping current in information science in the same 1988 publication.

In *LISCA 1989*, in addition to the Greenwood Press article by Margaret Brezicki, Marie L. Radford discusses interpersonal communication theory in the library context. Nancy J. Butkovich and Marjorie Peregoy continue their discussion of serials—this year relating to house journals, and Sharon L. Baker and Ronald R. Powell continue their discussion on research efforts of major library organizations. Marilyn Karrenbrock, from the point of view of a children's librarian, enlightens readers on books to add to one's professional bookshelf, and Ann E. Prentice provides insight on the latest in products and services.

With the use of essays; reviews of monographs, reference books, serials, and periodicals; and abstracts of current dissertations, the editors have striven to maintain a permanent record of intellectual activity in library and information science and to impose bibliographic control over the literature.

Certain categories of materials are not covered in *LISCA*. Omitted are specific periodical articles, publications of vanity presses, and in-house publications that are not applicable to other institutions. Research reports of limited distribution and audiovisual materials are also not covered.

A bibliographic summary of the entire history of reviews in library and information science includes:

American Reference Books Annual, Bohdan S. Wynar, ed. Littleton, Colo., Libraries Unlimited, 1971-1983.
Volume 1 included reviews of reference materials in library science. Volumes 2 through 14 (1972-1983) included library science monographs and reference books.

ARBA Guide to Library Science Literature 1970-1983, Donald G. Davis, Jr. and Charles D. Patterson, eds. Littleton, Colo., Libraries Unlimited, 1987.
A compilation of *ARBA* reviews for the inclusive years with approximately 70 additional reviews from selected sources.

Library Science Annual. Volume 1: 1985. Bohdan S. Wynar and Heather Cameron, eds. Littleton, Colo., Libraries Unlimited, 1985.
Beginning where *ARBA Volume 16* (1985) left off, *LSA* became a separate publication with expanded review coverage of reference books, professional books, library periodicals, and library science dissertations.

Library Science Annual. Volume 2: 1986. Bohdan S. Wynar and Heather Cameron, eds. Littleton, Colo., Libraries Unlimited, 1986.
Volume 2 continued coverage of library science materials.

Library and Information Science Annual. Volume 3: 1987. Bohdan S. Wynar and Ann E. Prentice, eds. Littleton, Colo., Libraries Unlimited, 1987.
A new title showed broader coverage to include information science.

Library and Information Science Annual. Volume 4: 1988. Bohdan S. Wynar, Ann E. Prentice, and Anna Grace Patterson, eds. Englewood, Colo., Libraries Unlimited, 1988.
Coverage was increased with the addition of monographs from other English-speaking countries.

Library and Information Science Annual. Volume 5: 1989. Bohdan S. Wynar, Ann E. Prentice, and Anna Grace Patterson, eds. Englewood, Colo., Libraries Unlimited, 1989.
This concluding volume reviews 530 books, 25 journals, and abstracts 45 dissertations.

American Reference Books Annual. Bohdan S. Wynar and Anna Grace Patterson, eds. Englewood, Colo., Libraries Unlimited, 1985- .
Coverage of library and information science reference monographs continues.

REVIEWING POLICY

The editors of *Library and Information Science Annual* have applied the same rigorous reviewing standards for which *American Reference Books Annual* is known. The *LISCA* staff keeps an up-to-date list of well-qualified library educators and practitioners so that books may be appropriately assigned for review. This year *LISCA* has used the services of over 180 librarians and scholars at libraries and universities throughout the United States and Canada; their names are listed following this introduction. Reviews in *LISCA* are signed as a matter of editorial policy.

Standard instructions, prepared by the editorial staff, for *LISCA* reviewers are briefly summarized here: reviewers should discuss the work and provide well-documented critical comments, positive or negative. Such things as the usefulness of the given work; organization, execution, and pertinence of contents; prose style; format; availability of supplementary materials (e.g., indexes, appendixes); and similarity to other works and/or previous editions are normally discussed. Reviewers are encouraged to note intended audience and/or level, but the review need not conclude with specific recommendations for purchase.

All the materials reviewed are given full bibliographic description, and citations to other review sources are given for books.

ARRANGEMENT

LISCA 1989 is arranged in four parts. Part 1 contains six essays contributed by authors well known in Canada and the United States, treating various library and information science publishing areas. Part 2, comprising reviews of books, is arranged into subjects, such as automation, cataloging, comparative and international librarianship, information technology, school library media centers, and special librar-ies and collections. Reviews of periodicals, arranged under the headings of National, Subject-oriented, and Regional, compose part 3. The final part, part 4, has abstracts of 45 dissertations listed alphabetically by author's name.

CLOSING COMMENTS

LISCA was created with the needs of students, researchers, practitioners, and library educators in mind. The editors have always believed that publishers and other information professionals would find *LISCA* important to their interests. Unfortunately, declining market response forces Libraries Unlimited to discontinue *LISCA* with the fifth volume. We look forward to the time we or another publisher will be able to reinstate this important publication for the library profession.

In closing, we wish to express our gratitude to the many contributors, as well as to associate editor Ann E. Prentice, without whose support this fifth volume could not have been compiled. We would also like to thank several people who were instrumental in the preparation of *LISCA*: associate editor Anna Grace Patterson; members of our staff, David V. Loertscher, Judy Gay Matthews, Kay Minnis, Susan Penney, Louis Ruybal, Sharon Kincaide, Gaile Martin, and Patricia M. Leach who copyedited and prepared the author/title index.

Bohdan S. Wynar

Editorial Staff

Bohdan S. Wynar, Editor-in-Chief
Ann E. Prentice and Anna Grace Patterson, Associate Editors

Contributors

Stephen H. Aby, Education Bibliographer, Bierce Library, Univ. of Akron, Ohio.

Donald C. Adcock, Director of Library Services, Glen Ellyn School District 41, Glen Ellyn, Ill.

Chris Albertson, City Librarian, Tyler Public Library, Tex.

Ann Allan, Assoc. Professor, School of Library Science, Kent State Univ., Ohio.

Walter C. Allen, Assoc. Professor Emeritus, Graduate School of Library and Information Science, Univ. of Illinois, Urbana.

Mohammed M. Aman, Dean, School of Library Science, Univ. of Wisconsin, Milwaukee.

James D. Anderson, Assoc. Dean and Professor, School of Communication, Information, and Library Studies, Rutgers Univ., New Brunswick, N.J.

Margaret Anderson, Assoc. Professor, Faculty of Library and Information Science, Univ. of Toronto, Ont.

Susan B. Ardis, Head Librarian, Engineering Library, Univ. of Texas, Austin.

Lawrence W. S. Auld, Asst. Professor, Graduate School of Library and Information Science, Univ. of Illinois, Urbana.

Bill Bailey, Reference Librarian, Newton Gresham Library, Sam Houston State Univ., Huntsville, Tex.

Sharon L. Baker, Asst. Professor, Univ. of Iowa, Iowa City.

Robert M. Ballard, Professor, School of Library and Information Science, North Carolina Central Univ., Durham.

Gary D. Barber, Coordinator, Reference Services, Daniel A. Reed Library, State Univ. of New York, Fredonia.

Sallie H. Barringer, Science Librarian, Trinity Univ. Library, San Antonio, Tex.

Susan S. Baughman, Univ. Librarian, Goddard Library, Clark Univ., Worcester, Mass.

Helen Carol Bennett, Reference Collection Coordinator, California State Univ., Northridge.

Ronald P. Blanford, Project Engineer, TRW Defense Group, Redondo Beach, Calif.

Marjorie E. Bloss, Manager, Resource Sharing, OCLC, Dublin, Ohio.

George S. Bobinski, Dean and Professor, School of Information and Library Studies, State Univ. of New York, Buffalo.

Margaret Brezicki, Managing Editor, Greenwood Press, Westport, Conn.

Robert N. Broadus, Professor, School of Library Science, Univ. of North Carolina, Chapel Hill.

Ellen Broidy, History Bibliographer, and Coordinator of Library Education Services, Univ. of California, Irvine.

Simon J. Bronner, Professor of Folklore and American Studies, Capitol College, Pennsylvania State Univ., Middletown.

Barbara E. Brown, Head, General Cataloguing Section, Library of Parliament, Ottawa.

Judith M. Brugger, Serials Cataloger, City College, City Univ. of New York.

Betty Jo Buckingham, Consultant, Iowa Dept. of Education, Des Moines.

Robert H. Burger, Assoc. Professor of Library Administration, Univ. of Illinois, Urbana.

Debbie Burnham-Kidwell, Owner/Indexer, Burnham-Kidwell, Indexer, Kingman, Ariz.

Nancy J. Butkovich, Science and Technology Librarian, Sterling C. Evans Library, Texas A & M Univ., College Station.

Lois J. Buttlar, Asst. Professor, School of Library Science, Kent State Univ., Ohio.

Daniel Callison, Asst. Professor, School of Library and Information Science, Indiana Univ., Bloomington.

Esther Jane Carrier, Reference Librarian, Lock Haven Univ. of Pennsylvania, Lock Haven.

Joseph Cataio, Manager, Booklegger's Bookstore, Chicago.

Dianne Brinkley Catlett, Graduate Assistant/Teaching Fellow, Dept. of Library and Information Studies, East Carolina Univ., Greenville, N.C.

G. A. Cevasco, Assoc. Professor of English, St. John's Univ., Jamaica, N.Y.

John Y. Cheung, Assoc. Professor, Univ. of Oklahoma, Norman.

Boyd Childress, Social Sciences Reference Librarian, Ralph B. Draughon Library, Auburn Univ., Ala.

Larry G. Chrisman, Technical Services Librarian, Univ. of South Florida Medical Center Library, Tampa.

Pauline A. Cochrane, Acting Dean, School of Library and Information Science, Catholic Univ. of America, Washington, D.C.

Gary R. Cocozzoli, Director of the Library, Lawrence Technological Univ., Southfield, Mich.

Barbara Conroy, Educational Consultant, Santa Fe, N.Mex.

Jean L. Cooper, Technical Services Librarian, Science and Engineering Library, Univ. of Virginia, Charlottesville.

Camille Côté, Assoc. Professor, Graduate School of Library Science, McGill Univ., Montreal, Que.

Nancy Courtney, Reference Librarian, Roesch Library, Univ. of Dayton, Ohio.

Brian E. Coutts, Coordinator of Collection Development, Helm-Cravens Library, Western Kentucky Univ., Bowling Green.

Richard J. Cox, Lecturer, Univ. of Pittsburgh, Pa.

Kathleen W. Craver, Head Librarian, National Cathedral School, Washington, D.C.

Milton H. Crouch, Asst. Director for Reader Services, Bailey/Howe Library, Univ. of Vermont, Burlington.

Donald C. Dickinson, Professor, Graduate Library School, Univ. of Arizona, Tucson.

Carol A. Doll, Asst. Professor, Graduate School of Library and Information Science, Univ. of Washington, Seattle.

G. Kim Dority, Editorial Director, Jones 21st Century, Englewood, Colo.

Judy Dyki, Library Director, Cranbrook Academy of Art, Bloomfield Hills, Mich.

Marie Ellis, English and American Literature Bibliographer, Univ. of Georgia Libraries, Athens.

Evan Ira Farber, Librarian, Lilly Library, Earlham College, Richmond, Ind.

Adele M. Fasick, Professor, Faculty of Library and Information Science, Univ. of Toronto, Ont.

Patricia Fleming, Assoc. Professor, Faculty of Library Science, Univ. of Toronto, Ont.

Elizabeth Frick, Assoc. Professor, School of Library Information Studies, Dalhousie Univ., Halifax, N.S.

Ronald H. Fritze, Asst. Professor, Dept. of History, Lamar Univ., Beaumont, Tex.

Sherrilynnne Fuller, Director, Health Sciences Library, Univ. of Washington, Seattle.

Ahmad Gamaluddin, Professor, School of Library Science, Clarion State College, Pa.

Jack I. Gardner, Administrator, Clark County Library District, Las Vegas, Nev.

Allie Wise Goudy, Music Librarian, Western Illinois Univ., Macomb.

Laurel Grotzinger, Dean and Chief Research Officer, Graduate College, Western Michigan Univ., Kalamazoo.

Blaine H. Hall, Humanities Librarian, Harold B. Lee Library, Brigham Young Univ., Provo, Utah.

Marvin K. Harris, Professor of Entomology, Texas A & M Univ., College Station.

Thomas L. Hart, Professor, School of Library and Information Studies, Florida State Univ., Tallahassee.

James S. Heller, Director of the Law Library and Assoc. Professor of Law, Marshall-Wythe Law Library, College of William and Mary, Williamsburg, Va.

Mark Y. Herring, formerly Library Director, E. W. King Memorial Library, King College, Bristol, Tenn.

Susan Davis Herring, Reference Librarian, Univ. of Alabama Library, Huntsville.

Joe A. Hewitt, Assoc. Univ. Librarian for Technical Services, Univ. of North Carolina, Chapel Hill.

Janet Swan Hill, Asst. Director for Technical Services, Norlin Library, Univ. of Colorado, Boulder.

Shirley L. Hopkinson, Professor, Dept. of Librarianship, San Jose State Univ., Calif.

Helen Howard, Director/Assoc. Professor, Graduate School of Library and Information Studies, McGill Univ., Montreal, Que.

Carmel A. Huestis, Editor, Fulcrum, Inc., Golden, Colo.

William E. Hug, Professor, Dept. of Instructional Technology, Univ. of Georgia, Athens.

Janet R. Ivey, Automation Services Librarian, Boynton Beach City Library, Fla.

John A. Jackman, Entomologist, Texas Agricultural Extension Service, Texas A & M Univ., College Station.

Richard D. Johnson, Director of Libraries, James M. Milne Library, State Univ. College, Oneonta, N.Y.

Thomas A. Karel, Asst. Director for Public Services, Shadek-Fackenthal Library, Franklin and Marshall College, Lancaster, Pa.

Marilyn Karrenbrock, Assoc. Professor, Univ. of Tennessee, Knoxville.

Dean H. Keller, Curator of Special Collections, Kent State Univ. Libraries, Ohio.

Thomas G. Kirk, Library Director, Hutchins Library, Berea College, Ky.

Michael E. D. Koenig, Dean, Graduate School of Library and Information Science, Rosary College, River Forest, Ill.

Shirley Lambert, Staff, Libraries Unlimited, Inc.

Brad R. Leach, Records Technician, 18th Judicial District, Englewood, Colo.

Patricia M. Leach, Staff, Libraries Unlimited, Inc.

Hwa-Wei Lee, Director of Libraries, Ohio Univ., Athens.

Richard A. Leiter, Librarian, Littler, Mendelson, Fastiff and Tichy, San Francisco, Calif.

Elizabeth D. Liddy, Asst. Professor, School of Information Studies, Syracuse Univ., N.Y.

David V. Loertscher, Staff, Libraries Unlimited, Inc.

Elisabeth Logan, Asst. Professor, School of Library and Information Studies, Florida State Univ., Tallahassee.

Sara R. Mack, Professor Emerita, Dept. of Library Science, Kutztown State College, Pa.

Linda Main, Asst. Professor, San Jose State Univ., Calif.

Karen Markey, Asst. Professor, Univ. of Michigan, Ann Arbor.

Judy Gay Matthews, Staff, Libraries Unlimited, Inc.

Susan V. McKimm, Business Reference Specialist, Cuyahoga County Library System, Maple Heights, Ohio.

Margaret McKinley, Head, Serials Dept., Univ. Library, Univ. of California, Los Angeles.

Philip A. Metzger, Curator of Special Collections, Lehigh Univ., Bethlehem, Pa.

Connie Miller, Coordinator, Computer Assisted Information Services, Main Library, Indiana Univ., Bloomington.

Jerome K. Miller, President, Copyright Information Services, Friday Harbor, Wash.

Diane Montag, Coordinator, Library and Media Center, Front Range Community College, Westminster, Colo.

P. Grady Morein, Director of Libraries, Univ. of West Florida, Pensacola.

Lynn Morgan, Software Quality Assurance Analyst, Geac Canada, Markham, Ont.

K. Mulliner, Asst. to the Director of Libraries, Ohio Univ. Library, Athens.

Danuta A. Nitecki, Assoc. Director for Public Services, Univ. of Maryland Libraries, College Park.

Margaret K. Norden, Head of Public Services, Marymount Univ. Library, Arlington, Va.

O. Gene Norman, Head, Reference Dept., Indiana State Univ. Library, Terre Haute.

Marilyn Strong Noronha, Reference Dept., Harleigh B. Trecker Library, Univ. of Connecticut, West Hartford.

Jeanne Osborn, formerly Professor, School of Library Science, Univ. of Iowa, Iowa City.

Berniece M. Owen, Coordinator, Library Technical Services, Portland Community College, Oreg.

Willy Owen, Technical Support Manager, Davis Library, Univ. of North Carolina, Chapel Hill.

Maureen Pastine, Director of Libraries, Washington State Univ., Pullman.

Anna Grace Patterson, Staff, Libraries Unlimited, Inc.

Elizabeth Patterson, Head, Reference Dept., Robert W. Woodruff Library, Emory Univ., Atlanta, Ga.

Susan R. Penney, Staff, Libraries Unlimited, Inc.

Marjorie Peregary, Original Cataloguer, Serials, Sterling C. Evans Library, Texas A & M Univ., College Station.

Dennis J. Phillips, Head Librarian, Library Learning Resource Center, Pennsylvania State Univ., Fogelsville.

Phillip P. Powell, Asst. Reference Librarian, Robert Scott Small Library, College of Charleston, S.C.

Ronald R. Powell, Assoc. Professor, Univ. of Missouri, Columbia.

Ann E. Prentice, Assoc. Vice President for Library and Information Resources, University of South Florida, Tampa.

Marilyn R. Pukkila, Reference Librarian, Colby College, Waterville, Maine.

Richard H. Quay, Social Science Librarian, Miami Univ. Libraries, Oxford, Ohio.

Marie L. Radford, Curriculum Materials Librarian, Sarah Byrd Askew Library, William Paterson College, Wayne, N.J.

Kristin Ramsdell, Reference/Bibliographic Instruction Librarian, California State Univ., Hayward.

Lorna K. Rees-Potter, Asst. Professor, Graduate School of Library and Information Studies, McGill Univ., Montreal, Que.

James Rettig, Asst. Univ. Librarian for Reference and Information Services, Swem Library, College of William and Mary, Williamsburg, Va.

James Rice, Assoc. Professor, School of Library and Information Science, Univ. of Iowa, Iowa City.

Philip R. Rider, Instructor of English, Northern Illinois Univ., De Kalb.

Ilene F. Rockman, Librarian, California Polytechnic State Univ., San Luis Obispo.

Antonio Rodriguez-Buckingham, Professor, School of Library Service, Univ. of Southern Mississippi, Hattiesburg.

JoAnn V. Rogers, Assoc. Professor, College of Library and Information Science, Univ. of Kentucky, Lexington.

David Rosenbaum, Reference Librarian, Education Library, Wayne State Univ. Libraries, Detroit, Mich.

Samuel Rothstein, Professor Emeritus, School of Librarianship, Univ. of British Columbia, Vancouver.

Michael Rogers Rubin, Attorney, United States Dept. of Commerce, Washington, D.C.

Edmund F. SantaVicca, Head, Collection Management Services, Cleveland State Univ. Libraries, Ohio.

Robert W. Schaaf, Senior Specialist in U.N. and International Documents, Serial and Government Publications Div., Library of Congress, Washington, D.C.

Jay Schafer, Librarian, Design and Planning, Auraria Library, Denver, Colo.

Isabel Schon, Professor, College of Education, Arizona State Univ., Tempe.

Anthony C. Schulzetenberg, Professor, Center for Information Media, St. Cloud State Univ., Minn.

LeRoy C. Schwarzkopf, formerly Government Documents Librarian, Univ. of Maryland, College Park.

Ravindra Nath Sharma, Asst. Director for Public Services, Univ. of Wisconsin Libraries, Oshkosh.

Patricia Tipton Sharp, Assoc. Professor of Curriculum and Instruction, Baylor Univ., Waco, Tex.

Gerald R. Shields, Assoc. Professor and Asst. Dean, School of Information and Library Studies, State Univ. of New York, Buffalo.

Marilyn L. Shontz, Asst. Professor, Dept. of Library and Information Studies, Univ. of North Carolina, Greensboro.

Bruce A. Shuman, Assoc. Professor, Library Science Program, Wayne State Univ., Detroit, Mich.

Stephanie C. Sigala, Head Librarian, Richardson Memorial Library, St. Louis Art Museum, Mo.

Susan M. Sigman, Staff, Libraries Unlimited, Inc.

Linda Keir Simons, Reference Librarian, Univ. of Dayton, Ohio.

George M. Sinkankas, Assoc. Professor, Graduate School of Library and Information Science, Univ. of Tennessee, Knoxville.

Robert Skinner, Music and Fine Arts Librarian, Southern Methodist Univ., Dallas, Tex.

Linda C. Smith, Assoc. Professor, Graduate School of Library and Information Science, Univ. of Illinois, Urbana.

Nathan M. Smith, Director, School Library and Information Science, Brigham Young Univ., Provo, Utah.

Mary J. Stanley, Reference Librarian/Liaison to School of Social Work, Indiana Univ.-Purdue Univ. at Indianapolis Libraries.

Patricia A. Steele, Head, Education Library, Indiana Univ., Bloomington.

Norman D. Stevens, Univ. Librarian, Univ. of Connecticut Library, Storrs.

Steven L. Tanimoto, Assoc. Professor, Dept. of Computer Science, Univ. of Washington, Seattle.

Elizabeth Thweatt, Technical Services Librarian/Asst. Professor, Gonzaga Univ. School of Law Library, Spokane, Wash.

Andrew G. Torok, Asst. Professor, Northern Illinois Univ., De Kalb.

Carol Truett, formerly Assoc. Professor, School of Library and Information Science, Univ. of Hawaii, Honolulu.

Dean Tudor, Professor, School of Journalism, Ryerson Polytechnic Institute, Toronto, Ont.

Felix Eme Unaeze, Asst. Professor and Business Reference Librarian, New Mexico State Univ., Las Cruces.

Robert F. Van Benthuysen, Library Director, Monmouth College, West Long Branch, N.J.

Phyllis J. Van Orden, Professor and Assoc. Dean, School of Library Science, Florida State Univ., Tallahassee.

Carol J. Veitch, Director, Onslow County Public Library, Jacksonville, N.C.

Kathleen J. Voigt, Head, Reference Dept., Carlson Library, Univ. of Toledo, Ohio.

Carolyn G. Weaver, Assoc. Director, Health Sciences Library, Univ. of Washington, Seattle.

Terry L. Weech, Graduate School of Library and Information Science, Univ. of Illinois, Urbana.

Jean Weihs, Principal Consultant, Technical Services Group, Seneca College of Applied Arts and Technology, North York, Ont.

Bella Hass Weinberg, Assoc. Professor, Div. of Library and Information Science, St. John's Univ., Jamaica, N.Y.

Darlene E. Weingand, Assoc. Professor and Director, Continuing Education Services, Univ. of Wisconsin, Madison.

Lynda Welborn, Asst. Professor, Educational Technology, Univ. of Northern Colorado, Greeley.

Robert V. Williams, Assoc. Professor, College of Library and Information Science, Univ. of South Carolina, Columbia.

T. P. Williams, Head, Social Sciences Dept., Mississippi State Univ. Library, Mississippi State.

Wiley J. Williams, Professor Emeritus, School of Library Science, Kent State Univ., Ohio.

Glenn R. Wittig, Asst. Professor, School of Library Service, Univ. of Southern Mississippi, Hattiesburg.

Bohdan S. Wynar, Staff, Libraries Unlimited, Inc.

A. Neil Yerkey, Asst. Professor, School of Information and Library Studies, State Univ. of New York, Amherst.

Arthur P. Young, Dean of Libraries, Univ. of Rhode Island, Kingston.

Pamela A. Zager, Instructor and Asst. Acquisitions Librarian, Lamar Univ., Beaumont, Tex.

Anita Zutis, Government Documents Special Collections Librarian, State Univ. of New York Maritime College, Fort Schuyler.

Part I
ESSAYS

Interpersonal Communication Theory in the Library Context
A Review of Current Perspectives*

Marie L. Radford

INTRODUCTION

Interpersonal communication is defined as that communication which takes place between people as they interact on a face-to-face basis.[1] Such communication is an extremely important, though often misunderstood, aspect of the work performed by librarians and information professionals, especially within the context of the reference process. The librarian is the human interface between the library user and the information sources. Although the quality of interpersonal interactions is vital to reference service, it is often overlooked as emphasis is instead placed on the information to be retrieved. This article will provide a brief overview of interpersonal communication in the library context and identify some key sources which have recently centered on this or related issues. Additional sources will be provided for those who may be prompted by this discussion to read further about this timely and interesting topic.

INTERPERSONAL COMMUNICATION

In the discipline of communication studies, interpersonal communication focuses upon the description and explanation of the processes by which people are able to understand each other during one-to-one interaction. Although the situation of "two people talking" may, at first glance, seem to be a relatively simple one, its study involves a wide range of scholarly disciplines, each with a different perspective on the interaction. Advances toward greater understanding of human interaction are also taking place in such diversified fields as sociology, psychology, and linguistics.

Human communication can be studied on a variety of different levels. On the behavioral level, one can study both nonverbal (dress, facial expression, body movement, etc.) and verbal (use of spoken language) expression. Most of the library literature deals with interpersonal communication on this, the behavioral level. However, at more abstract levels, it is also important to understand how meanings are produced, transmitted, and understood via communication. For example, a reference librarian in an academic library was once asked "Where are the *Psychological Abstracts* located?" So, being a good librarian, she in turn, asked "Have you ever used them before?" Receiving a hesitant shake of the head in reply, the librarian then launched into a description of the organization and use of this index, only to be interrupted by the student who impatiently explained that she needed to know the location of the *Psychological Abstracts* because she had been told to meet one of her professors in front of them.

Although this may seem to be merely a simple misunderstanding, it is a good example of how even an apparently uncomplicated query may be misconstrued. The librarian "read into" the location question, *understanding* the unarticulated next step. In most instances, the client would want to proceed to use the index. This student merely needed to know the location, therefore any other information was

*The author would like to acknowledge the reviews and helpful comments of Professor Brent D. Ruben and Gary P. Radford, Rutgers University, New Jersey, and Barbara Bendoritis, Passaic County Library, New Jersey.

superfluous. This is but one example of communication interaction between librarian and client. In more complex question negotiations, where clients may not have a clear idea of the information they seek, knowledge of the workings of the communication process can improve the quality of the interaction as well as the satisfaction of clients.

INTERPERSONAL COMMUNICATION IN THE LIBRARY CONTEXT

It is clear from the library literature that interpersonal communication between librarian and client has been an ongoing concern. Literature reviews, including those of Bunge, Crouch, and Rothstein, trace the historical evolution of writings on the subject.[2] Although some have argued that the librarian provides the critical human interface between the information systems of the library and those who need to use them, the bulk of literature on the reference process revolves around knowledge of sources. Yet, interaction with librarians is an important, perhaps the most important, means by which a client can use the library efficiently and effectively. Many clients do not realize this, or may be afraid to approach the librarian, in some cases perhaps not wanting to appear to be ignorant.[3] There are many interpersonal barriers which clients may be unable to overcome.[4]

There is evidence that library administrators are becoming increasingly aware of the importance of interpersonal communication skills for practitioners. One indication of this can be seen by browsing through advertisements for library and other information-related positions in library journals or newspapers. It is not uncommon to find advertisements which list requirements including both professional credentials and communication skills. For example, a recent issue of *Library Journal* contained advertisements for academic, public, and special librarians and information science professionals which included these desired qualifications: "ability to communicate pleasantly and effectively with the public and library staff, ... excellent communication skills, ... and strong communication and human relations skills."[5] Unfortunately, there is no definitive scholarly research to date which has been able to delineate the exact elements of "excellent communication skills" in the library context, and administrators and librarians alike seem to have operated via "rules of thumb" of what constitutes good communication. Herein lies a major problem, because such "rules of thumb" adopt a model of communication that has its basis in information transfer rather than the equally important human aspects of reference interactions.

Traditionally, the reference interaction as performed by the librarian has been viewed as one which has had content (information delivery) as its primary focus. Emphasis has been placed on the information provider's knowledge of information sources and information systems, recently with increasing emphasis on knowledge of computerized systems. The information user has typically come to the library or information center in search of some piece of information (perhaps exactly understood by the user, or perhaps only hazily conceptualized). The information provider has then been expected to determine exactly what information is needed, and to either find the information for the user or assist the user in finding the information. According to Taylor, discovering the nature of the user's information need is a highly complex communication task, yet the evaluation of professional ability has more or less been structured in terms of "finding the right answer," without taking into account the human element.[6] Many times there may not be a right answer, or information available to fill a request. At these times the librarian must endeavor to explain, to help the client to realize the limits of information systems. Despite this, there continue to be researchers who study the ability of information professionals to properly use the reference sources and to correctly answer questions, neglecting, for the most part, questions on the quality of the interpersonal interaction.[7]

There is no doubt that it is extremely important for information providers to be prepared to use sources and systems correctly in helping to satisfy the requests of users. However, it is equally important for providers to be aware that there is another dimension of this interaction which needs to be considered. Beginning with Taylor's seminal article on question negotiation,[8] interest began to focus upon the realization of the highly complex nature of the reference interaction and on the importance of the interpersonal communication skills for the information professional.

The notion of the crux of the reference process as existing exclusively in the transfer of information is reflective of much popular and academic thinking on the nature of communication. To a large extent this stems from the seminal work of Shannon and Weaver.[9] Shannon and Weaver's view of communication, which looks at issues of fidelity, accuracy, and efficiency of signal transmission in telephone systems, became the basis of many models of human communication. It has, however, been criticized consistently on the ground that interpersonal communication could not be conceptualized as being a simple, linear process. For example Watzlawick, Beavin, and Jackson argued that a linear model based on message transfer missed the subjective, relational aspects of interpersonal communication.[10] The field of interpersonal communication has come gradually to accept a process model of communication, one in which complex, subjective relationships between sender and receiver have a great impact upon the message and its meaning. However, the linear process model of Shannon and Weaver continues to dominate contemporary thinking of communication in the library context, a situation which needs to be reexamined in light of current thinking in the field of interpersonal communication.

In the context of the reference encounter, one implication of this shift in communication theory is a recognition that there may be more than one kind of information being communicated. Professionals need to become aware that in addition to *giving* content information in response to the user's request, they are also *giving off* interpersonal or relational information in their verbal and nonverbal expressions.[11] No information exchange between professional and user is free of relational messages. In the fifth edition of his text on reference services, Katz defines a successful interview as

> one in which the patron feels satisfied that the librarian has given undivided attention and has provided competent services. This may be quite different from what a librarian has traditionally considered successful—that the question has been answered completely.[12]

Katz further points out that

> there is an ample body of scholarly knowledge available to the profession which deals with the reference interview process. However, it remains one of the most overlooked areas within the field of library education. Almost without exception, library education programs completely ignore or minimize the teaching of verbal and nonverbal communication skills within reference courses. In the vast majority of library schools, instruction is the reference books approach ... the traditional reference course provides content but does not provide process.[13]

In view of the increasing complexity and dynamism of today's information environment,

it is becoming more important for information professionals to recognize the value of increased understanding of the process of interpersonal communication both in training future professionals and in improving their professional abilities in interaction with clients.

There is also a need for further research in this area to inform practitioners as well as the scholarly community.[14] The library literature on this topic has predominantly been lacking a research base.[15] There is a need to further explore the interpersonal dimensions of the reference encounter in order to better understand this complex process.

There has, however, been increasing attention to this area in the literature.[16] Presented below is a brief literature review of the work that has been done in this area in recent years, plus suggestions for keeping up with forthcoming literature.

AREAS OF INTEREST

Communication Theory for Librarians

A few articles have been published in the journal literature which have explored the area of communication theory as it relates to the reference process. Dervin challenged the application of information theory to the task of question negotiation in the reference interview.[17] Her article provides a cogent and still relevant discussion of the theoretical issues. Glogoff provides an overview of communication theory and discusses its role in the reference interaction.[18] He encourages librarians to broaden their knowledge of this discipline in order to improve their understanding and ability to communicate effectively with clients. A recent article by Budd clings to the traditional information theory approach to communication and stops short of bringing the discussion to reflect current conceptualizations of the interaction.[19]

For further amplification of communication theory for librarians, see the books by Conroy and Jones, Jennerich and Jennerich, and Mathews, which are discussed in the "Library Literature—Books" section below.

Effects of Automation

Another area of concern expressed in the literature has been the impact of automation upon the interpersonal interactions between information professional and client, and, on a broader level, the impact of automation upon the future of reference service itself. Those interested in this increasingly critical domain should consult Auster, Bonta, Dakshinamurti, Holladay, Kibirige, Nielsen and Baker, and Tenopir.[20]

Auster, for example, provides an overview of the study of online searching with regard to interpersonal concerns, and calls for further research in this area, especially that which links specified searcher behaviors to user satisfaction. A later study found that the quality of the interpersonal aspects of conducting an online search has an impact upon client satisfaction: "The search interview has been confirmed as a malleable factor that affects the quality of the search, as perceived by the user."[21] This was also confirmed by Genova.[22]

Additionally, Kibirige examines the communication barriers which may exist between the user and the intermediary in the typical presearch interview.[23] Auster, Dalrymple, and Porter also discuss the changing role of the intermediary with regard to online searching.[24] Nielsen and Baker investigate the impact upon professionals of the development of online public access catalogs which have been designed to be user-friendly, thus to be used without the assistance of a trained intermediary.[25]

In view of the increasing complexity of the information environment and the swift changes that are taking place in information professions, there are many who discuss the evolution of the role of the information professional. Among those who include interpersonal aspects in their discussion are Bearman, Fayen, Nielsen and Baker, and Surprenaut and Perry-Holmes.[26] In addition, Anthes comments on the need for "high touch," or increased interpersonal involvement, between library user and librarian as systems become more computerized and increasingly complex.[27]

Reference Practices

A recent group of articles examines the conceptualization of reference practices upon the negotiation process. Some describe or recreate the role of the reference librarian in terms of alternative models. Among these are suggestions that the librarian should be viewed as a personal librarian or a teacher.[28] Bechtel suggests that the interaction should be conceptualized as a conversation.[29] Parson suggests adoption of a new paradigm in which librarians make

a radical shift away from their strict identification with the library as an agency or

institution to an identification with the client or library user. Such a shift will enhance the effectiveness of the librarian as an information advocate or information-interpretation agent.[30]

Others have studied the effects of identity, attitude, and priority upon the process, the positive effects of librarian self-disclosure, and the librarian's personality.[31] Durrance, Hurych, and Robbins-Carter investigate the influence of reference practices on the client-librarian relationship.[32] Vathis suggests that from the client's viewpoint there are two components of the transaction—the interpersonal level and the intellectual level.[33] Awaritefe writes on applying psychology to library interactions.[34] Anderson discusses the influence of the choice made between the communication strategies of competition and cooperation.[35] Stein suggests that understanding preferred cognitive styles can improve communication in the library setting.[36]

Recently attention has been focused on the impact of the type and structure of questions asked by the librarian. A doctoral dissertation investigates the effects of "neutral questioning," a type of open ended questioning, upon the reference interview.[37] Cummins also discusses question clarification with regard to the reference interview.[38] Ross and Dewdney provide answers to common questions about communication problems which are encountered by librarians who have attended their workshops on reference interviewing.[39]

Nonverbal Aspects

Some attention has been given to the nonverbal aspects of the reference interaction. One study was conducted with intermediaries in presearch interviews.[40] It sought to determine the nonverbal behaviors which facilitated or hindered the "smooth interaction flow of the interview" and the correlation between these behaviors and the level of satisfaction of user and librarian. Genova found that librarians were generally less satisfied than the users. Additional findings were that (1) when librarians used computer terminals users were most satisfied; (2) librarians were less satisfied with long interviews, or interrupted interviews; and (3) user satisfaction and librarian enjoyment correlated positively. These findings indicate that relational dimensions enter into the process even when computer (information content) output would seem to be the only factor that should affect satisfaction of user or librarian.

Other articles on nonverbal behavior and information professionals have been written by Ellison, Larason and Robinson, and Richardson.[41] In addition, Harris and Michell conducted an experimental study of the effects of gender and communication skill in an observer's evaluation of a librarian and found that "nonverbal warmth displayed by the librarian toward the patron had a significant effect on the observers' ratings of competence and professionalism."[42] Glogoff also includes a discussion of nonverbal communication as it relates to the reference interview.[43]

Intercultural Communication

There has been an increase in the number of foreign students in U.S. universities in recent years, and a corresponding increase in their use of libraries. In interpersonal interactions with people from other cultures, it is highly desirable to be aware of cultural differences. Several articles published within the past few years address this concern within the library setting, and offer concrete information and advice.[44] Lam, for example, discusses the need for better communication between black students and white librarians through an increased awareness on the part of the librarians of black cultural differences.[45] Those interested in further reading on the general area of intercultural communication should see recent bibliographies by Kitano and Kitano.[46]

LIBRARY LITERATURE

Books

In recent years there have been only a few books published which provide overviews of interpersonal communication for information professionals. In 1987, Jennerich and Jennerich published a monograph entitled *The Reference Interview as a Creative Art*.[47] This work is recommended as a readable, practical guide to be used by students as well as practicing professionals to improve their reference interviewing techniques. It also integrates diverse concepts, such as those discussed here, which have been explored in journal articles dealing with the reference interview. An excellent bibliography is included. (See also the review in the 1988 volume of *Library and Information Science Annual*.)

Another fairly recent publication is *Improving Communication in the Library*.[48] Although the primary focus of this book is organizational communication, the human information systems which exist within the library setting, it does contain a section on interpersonal communication and critical communication skills within the library setting.

Anne Mathews's *Communicate! A Librarian's Guide to Interpersonal Relations* is a practical guide to interpersonal communication both with the library clientele and among library staff.[49] Mathews discusses this topic in light of research findings and provides many specific exercises designed to improve the quality of interpersonal interactions. In addition, Katz, in *Introduction to Reference Work*, includes a chapter on interpersonal communication aspects of the reference interview.[50]

Journals

Although there are no journals in the library field which are specifically devoted to the topic of interpersonal communication, some of the general library journals do include articles on this subject fairly frequently. The journals listed below are those which have done so in the past five years. (Those marked with an asterisk have published the most articles in this area.)

Canadian Library Journal
College & Research Libraries
Drexel Library Quarterly (has ceased publication)
Journal of Academic Librarianship*
Library Journal
RQ*
Special Libraries

Indexes

The major indexes to use in identifying articles published on this topic include the following:

Communication Abstracts (Beverly Hills, Calif.: Sage Publications)
ERIC — Resources in Education and Current Index to Journals in Education
Library and Information Science Abstracts (*LISA*) (London: The Library Association)
Library Literature (New York: H. W. Wilson)

ERIC has proven to be the richest index, and use of online or CD-ROM versions is particularly rewarding. ERIC provides excellent subject indexing in library and communications journals.

COMMUNICATIONS LITERATURE

Books

In the area of interpersonal communication a great number of books have been published. For the librarian or information professional who has not been acquainted previously with this area of literature, it would be extremely worthwhile to begin by reading an introductory college text on interpersonal communication. The following titles are recommended:

Deetz, S., and S. Stevenson. *Managing Interpersonal Communication*. New York: Harper & Row, 1986.

Devito, J. A. *Communicology: An Introduction to the Study of Communication*. New York: Harper & Row, 1978.

Devito, J. A. *The Interpersonal Communication Book*. 5th ed. New York: Harper & Row, 1988.

Ruben, B. D. *Communication and Human Behavior*. 2d ed. New York: Macmillan, 1988.

Smith, D. L., and K. Williamson. *Interpersonal Communication: Roles, Strategies, & Games*. 3d ed. Dubuque, Iowa: William C. Brown, 1985.

Wilmot, W. *Dyadic Communication*. 2d ed. New York: Random House, 1980.

Additional recommended titles include *Communication Yearbook*, currently under the editorship of Stanley Deetz and published by Transaction (New Brunswick, Canada). It includes a section on recent research in interpersonal communication. Also important is the *Handbook of Interpersonal Communication*, edited by M. L. Knapp and G. R. Miller and published by Sage (1985). This book is a compilation of scholarly articles.

Journals

Again, there are a number of journals in this area. Many of them are highly sophisticated and some have psychological orientations. Among the more readable for those with a limited knowledge of communication are:

Communication Monographs
Human Communication Research
Journal of Personality and Social Psychology

Those interested in advanced reading should see:

Journal of Applied Communication Research
Journal of Communication
Journal of Nonverbal Behavior
Journal of Social Psychology

NOTES

[1] W. Wilmot, *Dyadic Communication*, 2d ed. (New York: Random House, 1980).

[2] C. A. Bunge, "Interpersonal Dimensions of the Reference Interview: A Historical Review of the Literature," *Drexel Library Quarterly* 20 (1984): 4-23; W. W. Crouch, *The Information Interview: A Comprehensive Bibliography and an Analysis of the Literature* (Washington, D.C.: National Institute of Education, 1979). (ED 180 501); S. D. Rothstein, "Across the Desk: 100 Years of Reference Encounters," *Canadian Library Journal* 34 (1977): 391-97.

[3] See also M. J. Swope and J. Katzer, "The Silent Majority: Why Don't They Ask Questions?" *RQ* 12 (1972): 161-66.

[4] See also E. Mount, "Communication Barriers and the Reference Question," *Special Libraries* 57, no. 8 (1966): 575-78.

[5] *Library Journal* 113, no. 8 (1 November 1988): 114-18.

[6] R. S. Taylor, "Question Negotiation and Information Seeking in Libraries," *College & Research Libraries* 29 (1968): 178-94.

[7] See T. Childers, "The Quality of Reference: Still Moot after 20 Years," *Journal of Academic Librarianship* 13, no. 2 (1987): 73-74; R. Gers and L. J. Seward, "Improving Reference Performance: Results of a Statewide Study," *Library Journal* 110 (1985): 32-35; M. L. Goodyear, "Are We Losing Control at the Reference Desk? A Reexamination," *RQ* 25, no. 1 (1985): 85-88; P. Hernon and C. R. McClure, "Library Reference Service: An Unrecognized Crisis—A Symposium," *Journal of Academic Librarianship* 13, no. 2 (1987): 69-80; W. Miller, "Causes

and Cures for Inaccurate Reference Work," *Journal of Academic Librarianship* 13, no. 2 (1987): 71-73; C. Miller and J. Rettig, "Reference Obsolescence," *RQ* 25, no. 1 (1985): 52-58.

[8]Taylor, "Question Negotiation."

[9]C. Shannon and W. Weaver, *The Mathematical Theory of Communication* (Urbana, Ill.: University of Illinois Press, 1949).

[10]P. Watzlawick, J. H. Beavin, and D. Jackson, *Pragmatics of Human Communication* (New York: W. W. Norton, 1967).

[11]See Watzlawick et al., *Pragmatics*; E. Goffman, *Interaction Ritual: Essays on Face-to-Face Behavior* (Garden City, N.Y.: Doubleday, 1967).

[12]W. Katz, *Introduction to Reference Work*, 5th ed. (New York: McGraw-Hill, 1987), 8.

[13]Ibid., 9.

[14]T. R. Cummins, "Question Clarification in the Reference Encounter," *Canadian Library Journal* 41 (1984): 63-67; P. Dewdney, "User Satisfaction with the Public Library Reference Interview: An Experiment to Determine the Effects of Training Librarians in Communication Skills" (Ph.D. diss., School of Library and Information Service, University of Western Ontario, 1986). (*DAI* 47/10A, 3598).

[15]Crouch, *Information Interview*; Taylor, "Question Negotiation."

[16]J. W. Ellison, "How Approachable Are You as a Public Service Librarian?" *Unabashed Librarian* 46 (1983): 4-6.

[17]B. Dervin, "Useful Theory for Librarianship: Communication, Not Information," *Drexel Library Quarterly* 13, no. 3 (1977): 16-32.

[18]S. Glogoff, "Communication Theory's Role in the Reference Interview," *Drexel Library Quarterly* 19, no. 2 (1983): 56-72.

[19]J. Budd, "The User and the Library: A Discussion of Communication," *Reference Librarian* 20 (1987): 205-21.

[20]E. Auster, "User Satisfaction with the Online Negotiation Interview: Contemporary Concern in Traditional Perspective," *RQ* 23, no. 1 (1983): 47-59; B. D. Bonta, "Online Searching in the Reference Room," *Library Trends* 31,

no. 3 (1983): 401-20; G. Dakshinamurti, "Automation's Effect on Library Personnel," *Canadian Library Journal* 42, no. 6 (1985): 343-51; J. W. Holladay, "The Role of an Academic Librarian in the Information Age," *Special Libraries* 73, no. 4 (1982): 266-69; H. M. Kibirige, "Computer-Assisted Reference Services: What the Computer Will Not Do," *RQ* 27, no. 3 (1988): 377-83; B. Nielsen and B. Baker, "Educating the Online Catalog User: A Model Evaluation Study," *Library Trends* 35, no. 4 (1987): 571-85; C. Tenopir, "Online Databases: Costs and Benefits of CD-ROM," *Library Journal* 112, no. 14 (1987): 156-58.

[21]E. Auster and S. B. Lawton, "Search Interview Techniques and Information Gain as Antecedents of User Satisfaction with Online Bibliographic Retrieval," *Journal of the American Society for Information Science* 35, no. 2 (1984): 90-103.

[22]B. Genova, *Nonverbal Behaviors in Presearch Interviews* (Bethesda, Md.: National Library of Medicine, 1981). (ED 205 188).

[23]Kibirige, "Computer-Assisted Reference."

[24]Auster, "User Satisfaction"; P. W. Dalrymple, "Closing the Gap: The Role of the Librarian in Online Searching," *RQ* 24, no. 2 (1984): 177-83; P. Porter, "'Dear PPO5': Interpersonal Communication and the Computer," *Library Hi Tech* 2, no. 1 (1984): 23-27.

[25]Nielsen and Baker, "Educating the Online Catalog User."

[26]T. C. Bearman, "Educating the Future Information Professional," *Library Hi Tech* 18 (1987): 27-40; E. G. Fayen, "Beyond Technology: Rethinking 'Librarian'," *American Libraries* 17 (1986): 240-42; Nielsen and Baker, "Educating the Online Catalog User"; T. T. Surprenaut and C. Perry-Holmes, "The Reference Librarian of the Future: A Scenario," *RQ* 25, no. 2 (1985): 234-38.

[27]S. H. Anthes, "High Tech/High Touch: Academic Libraries Respond to Change in the Behavioral Sciences," *Behavioral and Social Sciences Librarian* 5, no. 1 (1985): 53-65.

[28]B. Bailey, "The Personal Librarian," *Library Journal* 109, no. 6 (1984): 1820-21; B. Nielsen, "Teacher or Intermediary: Alternative Professional Models in the Information Age," *College & Research Libraries* 43, no. 3 (1982): 183-91; J. Rice, "Library-Use Instruction with Individual

Users: Should Instruction Be Included in the Reference Interview?" *Reference Librarian* 10 (1984): 75-84.

[29]J. M. Bechtel, "Conversation, a New Paradigm for Librarianship," *College & Research Libraries* 47, no. 3 (1986): 219-24.

[30]W. L. Parson, "User Perspective on a New Paradigm for Librarianship," *College & Research Libraries* 45, no. 5 (1984): 370-73.

[31]Evelyn H. Daniel, "The Effects of Identity, Attitude and Priority," *Journal of Academic Librarianship* 13, no. 5 (1987): 76-78; M. J. Markham, K. Stirling, and N. M. Smith, "Librarian Self-Disclosure and Patron Satisfaction in the Reference Interview," *RQ* 22, no. 4 (1983): 369-74; Sandra M. Black, "Personality – Librarians as Communicators," *Canadian Library Journal* 38, no. 3 (1981): 65-71.

[32]J. C. Durrance, "The Influence of Reference Practices on the Client-Librarian Relationship," *College & Research Libraries* 47, no. 1 (1986): 57-67; J. Hurych, "The Professional and the Client: The Reference Interview Revisited," *Reference Librarian* 5/6 (1982): 199-205; J. Robbins-Carter, "Library Consultants: Client Views," *Drexel Library Quarterly* 20, no. 2 (1984): 88-99.

[33]A. C. Vathis, "Reference Transaction and End Product as Viewed by the Patron," *RQ* 23, no. 1 (1983): 60-64.

[34]M. Awaritefe, "Psychology Applied to Librarianship," *International Library Review* 16, no. 1 (1984): 27-33.

[35]D. J. Anderson, "Competition and Cooperation as Communication Strategies for Library Managers," *Drexel Library Quarterly* 20, no. 2 (1984): 73-87.

[36]B. L. Stein et al., "Understanding Preferred Cognitive Styles – A Tool for Facilitating Better Communication," *Journal of Education for Library and Information Science* 27, no. 1 (1986): 38-49.

[37]Dewdney, "User Satisfaction"; see also B. Bervin and P. Dewdney, "Neutral Questioning: A New Approach to the Reference Interview," *RQ* 25, no. 4 (1986): 506-13.

[38]Cummins, "Question Clarification."

[39]C. S. Ross and P. Dewdney, "Reference Interviewing Skills: Twelve Common Questions," *Public Libraries* 25, no. 1 (1986): 7-9.

[40]Genova, *Nonverbal Behaviors*.

[41]Ellison, "How Approachable Are You"; L. Larason and J. B. Robinson, "Reference Desk: Service Point or Barrier?" *RQ* 23, no. 3 (1984): 332-38; J. Richardson, "Evaluating Nonverbal Behaviour in the Reference Interview," *International Library Movement* 7, no. 3 (1985): 117-23.

[42]R. M. Harris and B. G. Michell, "The Social Context of Reference Work: Assessing the Effects of Gender and Communication Skill on Observers' Judgments of Competence," *Library and Information Science Research* 8, no. 1 (1986): 85-101.

[43]Glogoff, "Communication Theory's Role."

[44]I. Hoffmann and O. Popa, "Library Orientation and Instruction for Intercultural Students," *RQ* 26, no. 3 (1986): 356-60; L. Greenfield, S. Johnston, and K. Williams, "Educating the World: Training Library Staff to Communicate Effectively with International Students," *Journal of Academic Librarianship* 12, no. 4 (1986): 227-31; R. E. Lam, "The Reference Interview: Some Intercultural Considerations," *RQ* 27, no. 3 (1988): 390-95; T. A. Mood, "Foreign Students and the Academic Library," *RQ* 22 (1982): 175-80; S. G. Wayman, "The International Student in the Academic Library," *Journal of Academic Librarianship* 9, no. 6 (1984): 336-41.

[45]Lam, "Reference Interview."

[46]K. Kitano and S. Kitano, *Intercultural Communication Bibliography, Pts. 1-3* (Edgemont, Pa.: Chelsen House, 1987). (ED 273 125 and 282 271).

[47]E. Z. Jennerich and E. J. Jennerich, *The Reference Interview as a Creative Art* (Littleton, Colo.: Libraries Unlimited, 1987).

[48]B. Conroy and B. S. Jones, *Improving Communication in the Library* (Phoenix, Ariz.: Oryx Press, 1986).

[49]Anne J. Mathews, *Communicate! A Librarian's Guide to Interpersonal Relations* (Chicago: American Library Association, 1983).

[50]Katz, *Introduction to Reference Work*.

House Journals

Nancy J. Butkovich and Marjorie Peregoy

Serial publications are a varied and often overwhelming part of any library's collection. They come in all sizes, shapes, and colors and are published in an astonishing degree of (ir)regularity and (in)frequency. The *Anglo-American Cataloguing Rules, Second Edition* defines a serial as "a publication in any medium issued in successive parts bearing numerical or chronological designations and intended to be continued indefinitely,"[1] but no definition can take into account the great variety of different types of publications which can be included in the term *serial*.

Although they share common characteristics, these different types are published for different reasons and are often aimed at widely differing audiences. A distinctive type of serial publication, which includes specific differences within its type, is commonly known as the house organ.[2] These publications are also often called house journals, house magazines, company-sponsored magazines, internal publications, internal organs, plant publications, and employee magazines.[3] Regardless of their name, they are defined by the *ALA Glossary* as:

1. A type of periodical issued by a business, industrial or other organization for internal distribution to employees; often concerned with personal and personnel matters. Synonymous with employee magazine and plant publication. 2. A periodical issued for external distribution to dealers, customers, and potential customers; generally including articles on the company's products and on subjects related to the business or industry.[4]

In *Free Magazines for Libraries*, Smith notes that, while most house journals are corporate in origin, associations, individuals, universities, and government agencies may also be considered as sponsoring houses.[5]

In China documents functioning as house journals have been identified dating back to 200 B.C. Internal in nature, they were intended to inform the Imperial Court of the Han Dynasty of court activities.[6] Though modern house journals lack such lengthy publishing histories, they have often been published for long periods of time. Four of the titles included in this study, the *Sulzer Technical Review, Lubrication, Brown Boveri Review*, and *Compressed Air*, have been identified by Drott and Griffith as having long publication histories.[7] Ingersoll-Rand Company's *Compressed Air*, which first appeared in 1896, is currently "the oldest ... [technical house] journal in continuous publication."[8]

Our purpose is to examine selected characteristics of house journals and determine their place in libraries, particularly academic libraries. For this study, thirty-six journals were selected from the serials collection of the Sterling C. Evans Library of Texas A&M University. The Evans Library is a medium-sized academic library of 1.7 million volumes and 14,000 serial titles, and because Texas A&M University is both a Land Grant and a Sea Grant institution, the Evans Library has traditionally been oriented toward technology and the sciences.

In order to keep this study within manageable limits, we included only those house journals which fell within the Library of Congress classification range T-TX. Drott, Bearman, and Griffith have noted that "there is no single source which lists them [house journals] in an accurate and current manner."[9] In an effort to confirm our selection, we checked our list of house journals against several periodical directories and studies in current literature. In these sources thirteen titles of the thirty-six were identified specifically as house journals. Table 1 arranges the journals selected for this study by LC classification and identifies the sources which specifically identified titles as house journals.[10]

Table 1

House Journals by LC Classification*

Classification	Title
T (Technology)	*Hitachi Review*
	Newcomen Bulletin
	Windows
TA (Engineering, Civil Engineering)	*Columbia Engineering Research* (S)
	Cornell Engineering
	Engineering Outlook
	Hydro Delft
	Johns Hopkins APL Technical Digest
	News in Engineering
	SIGDA Newsletter
	Texas Civil Engineer
	Trend in Engineering
TJ (Mechanical Engineering, Machinery)	*Brown Boveri Review* (D)
	Compressed Air (D)
	E-Lab
	Energy Studies
	Heat Engineering (S, U, W)
	Lubrication (D)
	Pipeliner (S, W)
	Sulzer Technical Review (D)
TK (Electrical Engineering, Electronics, Nuclear Engineering)	*Asea Journal* (U)
	AT&T Technical Journal (DBG)
	Atom News
	Communication & Broadcasting
	Electrical Communication
	Ericsson Review (U)
	GEC Review
	Hewlett-Packard Journal (U)
	Philips Technical Review
	Philips Telecommunications Review
TL (Motor Vehicles, Aeronautics, Astronautics)	*Lockheed Horizons*
TN (Mining Engineering, Metallurgy)	*The Lamp* (S, U)
	Mines Magazine
TP (Chemical Technology)	*Resin Review* (W)
TS (Manufactures)	*Svetsaren*

*Confirmation of house journal status from other sources. (DGB) = Drott, Bearman and Griffith, (D) = Drott and Griffith, (S) = Smith, (U) = Ulrich's International Periodicals Directory, and (W) = Working Press of the Nation.

There is an important caveat which must be made concerning our selections. We made no effort to identify and analyze house journals which are received by the Evans Library but are discarded rather than retained. We are not attempting to analyze the collection development policies of a specific library; rather, we are using one library's holdings to determine selected characteristics which might make clear the value of these house journals to our own and other libraries.

Because these publications have some readily identifiable differences in purpose and audience, attempts have been made to categorize house journals. One method, mentioned by King, breaks them down according to the content of the articles contained in the publication. These categories include:

[t]he prestige journal which is equivalent in almost every respect to the standard technical journal ... the magazine ... [which] contains general non-technical information and possibly some mention of company products (but no technical details) ... [and] the periodical catalogue which is similar in all respects to trade literature differing only in that it has a recurrent title as a result of which it may be treated as a periodical.[11]

Orser divides house journals into two categories: internal and external, based on the audience to whom the journal is targeted.[12] Smith defined these two categories and added a third, the combination journal. Internal house journals serve to keep the rank and file members or employees informed of the activities of the company or organization to which they belong. External house journals are intended for audiences outside the company, and combination journals try to combine the functions of both internal and external journals into one publication.[13]

Two classic examples of internal house journals are *Atom News*, sponsored by the United Kingdom Atomic Energy Authority, and *Pipeliner*, the house journal of El Paso Natural Gas Company. *Atom News*, published "for UKAEA employees," is both informal and informative.[14] A full-color tabloid, it contains newsy articles, such as the open house ceremonies for the Winfrith nuclear plant, photographs and write-ups of employee activities, such as the receipt by an employee of the British Empire Medal for 30 years of service, and entertainment in the form of a crossword puzzle contest.[15] A feature that we considered a highlight was the page devoted to full-color reproductions of the winning drawings in the employees' children's Easter egg and bunny coloring contest, complete with thoughtful comments on the artistic merits of the winning entries provided by the judges.[16]

Pipeliner is very similar in scope. One of the issues we examined was the 50th anniversary issue, which provided a fascinating history of the growth of one company, El Paso Natural Gas Company, and its house journal. The president and chief executive officer of El Paso Natural Gas, R. S. Morris, attested to the value of a good house journal when he wrote: "When I joined [the company], ... one of the first recommendations I received was to read the Pipeliner [sic] to find out what was going on in the Company. That advice was sound."[17] Frank Mangan, a retired assistant director of the Public Relations Department which produces *Pipeliner*, summed up the history of this publication and, at the same time, defined the various purposes of internal house journals in general:

[Pipeliner] remained for perhaps half its existence a family-oriented, often folksy magazine. In addition to reporting the news, we ran hundreds of pictures of employee's kids and people holding up freshly killed game or large dead fish.... [It] slowly evolved into a more high-tech vehicle whose primary function was to report on changing policies and problems in today's complicated energy world. It also kept employees in touch with each other.[18]

External house journals often appear not to be house journals at all. Ingersoll-Rand's *Compressed Air*, probably the most obviously external of all the journals we examined, shares many of the characteristics of trade journals. We examined the December 1988 issue, and it contained both outside advertising and reader response cards. Articles tend to be more technical in content, and the journal also has a modest subscription charge.

A more typical example is *The Lamp*, which "is published quarterly for Exxon shareholders. Others may receive it on request."[19] The articles appearing in *The Lamp* are entertaining, informative, illustrated with color photographs, and often concerned with something only peripherally related to Exxon. For example, a summary statement for an article entitled "Australia's Expo 88" read "A world's fair in Queensland is expected to draw some 14 million visitors. Exxon has oil, gas and coal interests in that Australian state."[20]

Combination house journals are the most difficult to identify, since they could arguably be put in either of the other two categories. The *Hewlett-Packard Journal* is probably as good an example as any. This journal "is distributed free of charge to HP research, design, and manufacturing engineering personnel, as well as to qualified non-HP individuals, libraries, and educational institutions."[21] The articles are technical in content and "are primarily authored by HP employees, [however] articles from non-HP authors dealing with HP-related research or solutions to technical problems made possible by using HP equipment are also considered."[22]

Drott, Bearman, and Griffith noted four characteristics of these journals which cause librarians no end of aggravation: "irregularity of title, different journals with the same title, irregularity of publication ... [and] failure to number and/or date issues."[23] With the exception of differing publications sharing a common title, we encountered examples of all these problems in our survey. For example, Asea and BBC Brown Boveri merged in 1987 to form the Asea

Brown Boveri Group. Their journals, *Asea Journal* and *Brown Boveri Review*, naturally merged as well, and the new publication is an excellent example of an irregular name form; its cover title is *ABB Review*, and the title on the inside front cover is *Asea Brown Boveri Review*.[24]

Lubrication, produced by Texaco, is a classic example of the irregularly published house journal. Although its MARC record describes it as being published monthly, irregular annual would be a more apt description, since only one issue was published per year in 1983, 1985, 1986, and 1987. Two issues were published in 1984.[25] El Paso Natural Gas Company's 50th anniversary issue of *Pipeliner* is an example of an unnumbered, undated journal. Fortunately, other issues have both volume and issue numbers. Of particular interest to us was the number of libraries holding these titles. By using OCLC records we were able to arrive at minimum numbers, since not all libraries holding any given title are users of OCLC. The results are presented in table 2.

Table 2

Number of Libraries Holding Titles Included in This Study, Based on OCLC Records.

Number of libraries	Number of journals	Cumulative percent of journals
1-25	8	22.2%
26-50	10	50.0%
51-75	5	
76-100	2	77.8%
101-125	3	
Greater than 125	8	100.0%

Source: OCLC nos. 1537474, 1564586, 1567710, 1567917, 1568199, 1586031, 1643586, 1714876, 1751930, 1755500, 1757541, 1913399, 2052744, 2160976, 2162933, 2240471, 2262081, 2268285, 2350930, 2358621, 2376469, 2446207, 2447377, 2470460, 2510097, 2539662, 2681816, 2898443, 2989213, 3827554, 4272908, 4453108, 4590645, 4597216, 6283189, 6311503, 6321664, 6321702, 6321770, 6471895, 6574640, 7066291, 7367435, 7411450, 8749952, 8799180, 9023273, 10804783, 11037038, 11492357, 12271883, 13443014, 13544546, 14523143, 14702964, 15231704.

The data obtained from OCLC and given in table 2 indicate that half the journals in our survey are found in fifty or fewer libraries in the United States. This would indicate that overall these are not frequently acquired by libraries. Some of the titles, such as *Atom News*, which is held by only one library, are rarely retained. At

the other end of the spectrum are *AT&T Technical Journal*, which has 313 holding libraries, and *The Lamp*, which has 296.[26] As a very general rule, publications aimed at least in part at an audience outside the house tend to be retained more frequently than those that target a purely internal audience.

In the case of the internal publications, local interest is also a criterion to be considered. Because it is published by a major regional company, libraries in Texas and the surrounding states would be more likely to have a local demand for *Pipeliner* than would libraries outside the five-state area. This is confirmed by the OCLC holdings information on this journal. Of the thirteen libraries listed, seven are within the state of Texas, three are in bordering states, and only three are in libraries outside the region.[27] We suspect that this "demographic signature" would also be apparent in the holdings of other purely internal house journals.

A major consideration for retention of house journals should be the availability of bibliographic control over their subject content. Although common sense would indicate that it is usually easy to locate an article published in last month's issue of a given journal, it is much more difficult to accurately remember the citation of an article read two or three years earlier. In fact it is often difficult even to remember in which journal the article appeared. Therefore, the usefulness of house journals is enhanced if they are indexed.

We examined OCLC records and entries in *Ulrich's International Periodicals Directory* and *Irregular Serials and Annuals* in order to determine some quantitative information concerning the indexing of the house journals on our list.[28] Table 3 illustrates the number of indexing and abstracting services covering each journal, while table 4 provides a summary of the number of journals from this study included in each indexing and abstracting service. Data for tables 3 and 4 were derived from these three sources.

Table 3

Number of Indexing and Abstracting Services Covering Each Journal

Number of journals (N = 36)	Number of indexing services in which journals appear
6	0
11	1-5
8	6-10
3	11-15
3	16-20
3	21-25
2	26 or more

Table 4

Number of Journals covered in Each Indexing and Abstracting Service

Number of indexing sources	Number of journals covered by each source
27	1
13	2
2	3
3	4
3	5
5	6
2	7
5	8
2	9
1	12
2	13
1	15
2	16
1	17
1	18

The results of the tabulation of data in table 3 indicate that, of the thirty-six journals in the study, six (16.7 percent) were not covered by an indexing source. These are *Atom News, Columbia Engineering Research, Newcomen Bulletin, E-Lab, Windows,* and *Pipeliner.* On the other hand one journal, *Phillips Technical Review,* was indexed by twenty-eight sources; *Compressed Air* by twenty-six; and *AT&T Journal, Brown Boveri Review,* and *Sulzer Technical Review* by twenty-one to twenty-five sources each.

In table 4 twenty-seven indexing sources each included one of the journals in our study. *Engineering Index* included eighteen journals; *Computer and Control Abstracts* covered seventeen; and *Physics Abstracts: Part A, Science Abstracts* and *Electrical and Electronics Abstracts* each indexed sixteen of our journals. *Chemical Abstracts* covered fifteen titles.

In their 1975 analysis of technical house journals, Drott, Bearman, and Griffith noted that the coverage given house journals by indexing and abstracting sources was "generally low."[29] We tend to agree with their assessment, since almost 17 percent (six titles) of our titles were not indexed and an additional 30.5 percent (eleven titles) were indexed by five or fewer sources; however, we wanted to examine the level of indexing given each title in order to clarify this point.

The 510 field in the MARC record is used to identify indexing sources, and an indicator is used to identify the level of coverage, if known. The levels with which we were particularly interested were 1 and 2, indicating a complete level of coverage, and partial coverage.[30] We found that, in the records containing the 510 field, the vast majority of the journals in our study were selectively indexed.[31] The exceptions were *Electronic Components & Applications, Communication & Broadcasting, Brown Boveri Review, Phillips Telecommunications Review,* and *Ericsson Review,* which were fully indexed by *Computer and Control Abstracts, Electrical and Electronics Abstracts,* and *Physics Abstracts: Part A, Science Abstracts.* Also, *Electronic Communication* was fully indexed by *Applied Science and Technology Index.*

While coverage by indexing and abstracting services produces a means of access to the subject content of journals, we also needed some measure of use by readers. *Science Citation Index* provides one such measure in its *Cited Journal Listing.* Of our thirty-six titles, seven were cited in 1985. These were the *AT&T Technical Journal* (which also had a listing under a former title, *Bell System Technical Journal*), *Brown Boveri Review, Communication &* *Broadcasting, Electronic Communication, Ericsson Review, Hewlett-Packard Journal,* and *Phillips Telecommunications Review.* Of these only the *AT&T Technical Journal* (and its former title) was widely cited, being cited by 486 journals in 1985. *Hewlett-Packard Journal* was a distant second with sixty-two citing journals.[32]

The 1987 *Cited Journal Listing,* covering 1986, was very similar, except that there were no listings for the *Bell System Technical Journal* or *Communication & Broadcasting. AT&T Technical Journal* and *Hewlett-Packard Journal* again lead in the number of citing journals with 418 and 34 respectively.[33]

We were intrigued by the degree of self-citedness in these journals. An extreme example was *Ericsson Review.* In 1985 it was cited forty times by five journals; thirty-five of these citations (87.5 percent) appeared in the *Ericsson Review.*[34] The 1986 results for this title were similar, with forty-four citations appearing in four journals. Thirty-nine (88.6 percent) of these citations were in this journal.[35] Since we had already noted that many of these journals draw on company employees as authors, this level of self-citation should, perhaps, not be too surprising. Nonetheless, it does allow room for a certain possibility of bias in the tone and content of the articles, particularly since many of the journals are written primarily by people working within the organization sponsoring the publication.

AT&T Technical Journal and *Hewlett-Packard Journal* were nearly alone in posting low levels of self-citation. If the old and new titles are combined for the AT&T publication in 1985, this journal had 196 self-citations out of 2,851 (6.9 percent), and the Hewlett-Packard publication had 28 out of 129 (4.8 percent).[36] The 1986 results were also in line with this. *AT&T Technical Journal* had a self-citation percentage of 0.9 percent (20 citations out of 2,180) and *Hewlett-Packard Journal* was not listed as a citing source for itself.[37]

Science Citation Index is unique among technically oriented indexing and abstracting services in that it calculates the impact of a journal compared to other journals. This calculation, known as impact factor, is defined as:

A measure of the frequency with which the "average article" in a journal has been cited in a particular year. The *JCR* [*Journal Citation Report*] impact factor is basically a ratio between citations and citable items published.[38]

Of the titles cited in 1985, *Bell System Technical Journal* had the highest impact factor, 1.09, and *Brown Boveri Review* was second with 0.22. *Electronic Communication* was last 0.02.[39] In 1986 *AT&T Technical Journal* was the highest with an impact factor of 0.34, *Brown Boveri Review* was second at 0.22, and *Hewlett-Packard Journal* and *Phillips Telecommunications Review* tied for last place with an impact factor of 0.04.[40] This, combined with the generally low level of citation (once the self-citations are removed), would indicate that these are not generally sources which contribute directly to scholarly research. Key, Sholtz, and Roland, in an article on controlled circulation journals, stated that they are "seldom quoted in primary scientific journals but may be widely read and used."[41] We believe that this statement is probably applicable to house journals as well.

Our study of house organs has verified for us many of the specific identifiable values of this type of serial to a library's collections. In an academic library the house organ serves many needs. These publications give information about the officers, policies, and personnel of specific companies and industries often available in no other source, which can be of practical help to the graduating senior looking at job prospects as well as to the freshman still wrestling with career choices. Additionally the substantive articles in specific technological areas provide an excellent source of information on the state of current research, product availability, and "state-of-the-art" achievements which can benefit the advanced researcher as well as the beginning student and the general patron.

This often unique combination of company information and current technological advances makes the house organ an extremely useful and sometimes overlooked source of quickly available answers to general reference questions for library patrons. The popular writing style and occasional self-aggrandizing tone of some of the articles should not cause librarians to undervalue the information contained in house journals nor ignore its validity. House organs have a definite place among the standard reference sources in an academic or public library, and it is well worth the time to identify these special titles within a serials collection.

NOTES

[1]Michael Gorman and Paul W. Winkler, *Anglo-American Cataloguing Rules, Second Edition* (Chicago: American Library Association, 1978), 570.

[2]David M. Brownstone and Irene M. Franck, *The Dictionary of Publishing* (New York: Van Nostrand Reinhold Co., 1982), 141.

[3]Ray Prytherch, *Harrod's Librarians' Glossary* (Brookfield, Vt.: Gower Publishing Co., 1984), 358; Adeline Mercer Smith, *Free Magazines for Libraries* (Jefferson, N.C.: McFarland & Co., 1985), 1; Frank Orser, "Selling Readership: An Approach to the Production of the Company-Sponsored Magazine," *Serials Review* 7, no. 4 (1981): 43; Brownstone and Franck, 141; *ALA Glossary of Library and Information Science*, ed. Heartsill Young (Chicago: American Library Association, 1983), 113.

[4]*ALA Glossary*, 113.

[5]Smith, 1-2.

[6]Albert Walker, "House Journals" in *Encyclopedia of Library and Information Science*, ed. Allen Kent, Harold Lancour, and Jay E. Daily (New York: Marcel Dekker, Inc., 1974), 61.

[7]M. Carl Drott and Belver C. Griffith, "Characteristics of Technically Oriented House Journals," *IEEE Transactions on Professional Communication* PC-18, no. 1 (1975): 45.

[8]Ibid., 45.

[9]M. Carl Drott, Toni Carbo Bearman, and Belver C. Griffith, "The Hidden Literature: The Scientific Journals of Industry," *Aslib Proceedings* 27, no. 9 (1975): 377.

[10]*LC Classification Outline* (Washington, D.C.: Library of Congress, 1978), 27-29; Drott, Bearman, and Griffith, 376; Drott and Griffith, 45; Smith, 107-8, 122, 196; *Ulrich's International Periodicals Directory, 1987-1988* (New York: R. R. Bowker Co., 1987), 476, 616, 624, 646, 1323; *Working Press of the Nation: The 1988 Media Encyclopedia, Vol. 5 Internal Publications Directory* (Chicago: National Research Bureau, 1987), 2-10, 2-17, 2-19).

[11]David King, "Market Research Reports, House Journals and Trade Literature," *Aslib Proceedings* 34, nos. 11-12 (1982): 469.

[12]Orser, 43.

[13]Smith, 1.

[14]*Atom News*, no. 320 (1988): 1.

[15]Ibid., 5-7.

[16]Ibid., 8.

[17]R. S. Morris, "[Untitled]," *Pipeliner*, 50th Anniversary Issue [1988]: 1.

[18]Frank Mangan, "[Untitled]," *Pipeliner*, 50th Anniversary Issue [1988]: 24.

[19]*The Lamp* 70, no. 2, back cover.

[20]Ibid.

[21]*Hewlett-Packard Journal* 39, no. 6 (1988): 3.

[22]Ibid.

[23]Drott, Bearman, and Griffith, 379.

[24]*Asea Journal* 60, no. 6 (1987): back cover; *ABB Review*, no. 1 (1988): recto and verso of front cover.

[25]*OCLC*, no. 15231704; *Lubrication* 69, no. 1 (1983): front cover; 70, no. 1 (1984): front cover; 71, no. 1 (1985): front cover; 72, no. 1 (1986): front cover; 73, no. 1 (1987): front cover.

[26]*OCLC*, nos. 1537474, 1564586, 1567710, 1567917, 1568199, 1586031, 1643586, 1714876, 1751930, 1755500, 1757541, 1913399, 2052744, 2160976, 2162933, 2240471, 2262081, 2268285, 2350930, 2358621, 2376469, 2446207, 2447377, 2470460, 2510097, 2539662, 2681816, 2898443, 2989213, 3827554, 4272908, 4453108, 4590645, 4597216, 6283189, 6311503, 6321664, 6321702, 6321770, 6471895, 6574640, 7066291, 7367435, 7411450, 8749952, 8799180, 9023273, 10804783, 11037038, 11492357, 12271883, 13443014, 13544546, 14523143, 14702964, 15231704.

[27]*OCLC*, no. 4453108.

[28]*OCLC* (Dublin, Ohio: Online Computer Library Center), OCLC nos. 1537474, 1564586, 1567710, 1567917, 1568199, 1586031, 1643586, 1714876, 1751930, 1755500, 1757541, 1913399, 2052744, 2160976, 2162933, 2240471, 2262081, 2268285, 2350930, 2358621, 2376469, 2446207, 2447377, 2470460, 2510097, 2539662, 2681816, 2898443, 2989213, 3827554, 4272908, 4453108, 4590645, 4597216, 6283189, 6311503, 6321664, 6321702, 6321770, 6471895, 6574640, 7066291, 7367435, 7411450, 8749952, 8799180, 9023273, 10804783, 11037038, 11492357, 12271883, 13443014, 13544546, 14523143, 14702964, 15231704; *Ulrich's International Periodicals Directory* 476, 616-17, 624, 634, 643-46, 650, 653-54, 661, 674, 1235, 1258, 1323, 1379, 1582; *Irregular Serials & Annuals: An International Directory* (New York: R. R. Bowker, 1987), 348.

[29]Drott, Bearman, and Griffith, 381.

[30]*Online Systems Serials Format, Third Edition* (Dublin, Ohio: Online Computer Library Center, 1986), SER 5:6.

[31]*OCLC*, nos. 1537474, 1564586, 1567710, 1567917, 1568199, 1586031, 1643586, 1714876, 1751930, 1755500, 2052744, 2160976, 2162933, 2240471, 2262081, 2268285, 2350930, 2358621, 2446207, 2447377, 2470460, 2510097, 2539662, 2898443, 2989213, 3827554, 4272908, 4590645, 4597216, 6283189, 6321702, 6574640, 7367435, 10804783, 12271883, 13544546, 14702964.

[32]*Science Citation Index: Journal Citation Reports, Cited Journal Listing*, ed. Eugene Garfield (Philadelphia, Pa.: Institute for Scientific Information, 1986), vol. 19, 1740, 1763, 1805, 1866, 1911, 1925, 1977, 2335.

[33]*SCI* (1987), vol. 20, 1657-58, 1723, 1827, 1840, 1891, 2244.

[34]*SCI* (1986), vol. 19, 1925.

[35]*SCI* (1987), vol. 20, 1840.

[36]*SCI* (1986), vol. 19, 1740, 1763, 1977.

[37]*SCI* (1987), vol. 20, 1657-58, 1891.

[38]*SCI* (1986), vol. 19, 108.

[39]Ibid., 1740, 1763, 1805, 1866, 1911, 1925, 1977, 2335.

[40]*SCI* (1987), vol. 20, 1657-58, 1723, 1827, 1840, 1891, 2244.

[41]Jack D. Key, Katherine J. Sholtz, and Charles G. Roland, "The Controlled Circulation Journal in Medicine: Rx or Rogue?" *Serials Librarian* 4, no. 1 (1979): 17.

Greenwood Press
Twenty Years of Scholarly Publishing

Margaret Brezicki

The placid decade of the 1950s was shaken to its roots by the launching of Sputnik in 1957. Although the United States had previously assumed an air of scientific and intellectual dominance, this event became a catalyst that propelled the nation toward the singular purpose of substantially upgrading its educational facilities in an effort to regain the lead which it had—at least symbolically—lost. President John F. Kennedy declared our intention to put a man on the moon by the end of the 1960s, and with the encroaching involvement in Vietnam, a policy of "guns and butter" was instituted to wage both real war and the war of major societal changes.

Greenwood Press was conceived during this period, and while it is very much the product of its times, it has also been shaped by its founders and by those who guide the press today. With the cry for an improved educational system, Congress made available substantial funds to build college library collections. In general, the American publishing industry was not prepared to deal with these needs, but a small segment of it—the reprint industry—found itself in the enviable position of being poised to meet some of the demands.

The reprint companies of the time were extensions of the antiquarian periodical business, dominated by the Kraus Reprint Company and the Johnson Reprint Corporation. Both Hans P. Kraus and Walter J. Johnson were European immigrants who had escaped Nazi Germany. Both had scientific publishing experience, and when they could not find a used periodical to complete a set, they would not hesitate to reprint it after securing copyright permission. These reprint companies recognized that college libraries, with the infusion of additional funding

by government, would demand large runs of periodical literature either to address lacunae or to expand holdings to support new academic programs. A "contract war" ensued, with each company endeavoring to sign the reprint publication rights to the major and even the more recondite periodicals.

One of Greenwood Press's cofounders, Harold Mason, had for years been a major participant in the growth of Kraus Periodicals, the antiquarian arm of Kraus Reprint. A graduate of Emory University, with a doctorate in library science from Columbia University, Mason left Kraus in the mid-1960s for a brief association with the Walter J. Johnson Company, the antiquarian sister company of the Johnson Reprint Corporation. Mason felt that there were major areas being ignored both by Kraus and Johnson that a newly conceived publishing company could address. A friend of his, Harold Schwartz, who at the time was a marketing executive for Parents Magazine Press, agreed. From this alliance Greenwood Press was born in May 1967.

The two cofounders were clearly different people. Mason, with his antiquarian and library-oriented background, was the major architect of Greenwood's early publishing programs, while the more outgoing, flamboyant Schwartz handled Greenwood's marketing and was primarily responsible for raising the funds necessary for its initial reprint programs. The first program to be initiated was the phenomenally successful *Radical Periodicals of the United States*, some 108 periodicals cited in Walter Goldwater's bibliography of the same title. This quickly led to similar programs encompassing journals on the black experience and radical periodicals of Great Britain.

Contemporaneously with the establishment of Greenwood Press was the publication of the first edition of *Books for College Libraries*. This originally began as a recommended list of monographic titles for the University of California system, but by the time it was published by the American Library Association, it was understood to be a "recommended" list of books for all college libraries. The importance of such a recommendation convinced Greenwood to embark upon an ambitious monographic reprint program. As Schwartz's academic background was in philosophy, Greenwood's initial list of titles was heavily weighted in that area.

By the end of 1968, in a mere one and one-half years, Greenwood had already established itself as one of the preeminent reprint companies. Johnson and Kraus no longer had the field to themselves; in fact, as Carol Nemeyer points out in her 1972 publication *Scholarly Reprint Publishing in the United States*, more than one hundred reprint companies were flourishing.

Greenwood's success did not go unnoticed by Wall Street. Publishing companies were the "hot" properties of the late 1960s; they were the "software" that would drive the computer and microfilm hardware that was being manufactured by many large communications-oriented firms. A very successful public company in its own right at the time, Williamhouse-Regency, Inc., although smaller than some of the firms buying publishing operations, had declared its intention of participating in the new software business and began discussions with the cofounders of Greenwood concerning the acquisition of this still nascent publishing organization. In 1969, Greenwood became part of Williamhouse-Regency, Inc.

Its acquisition by Williamhouse had a profound impact on the press in several ways. As part of a publicly held company, the press was expected to improve its business controls and to "redefine its mission." It could no longer function as a private partnership and efficiently manage its explosive growth. Furthermore, it needed to reassess its publishing directions as there were signs that the government funding which had initially propelled Greenwood and other reprint companies was beginning to dissipate.

Williamhouse made funds available to the press for its expansion plans. Greenwood soon established several different divisions, each relating to its central focus of providing materials to college libraries. With the assistance of Felix Reichmann of Cornell University, Greenwood began a Printed Book Catalog program, producing several major works including

printed book catalogs of the American Antiquarian Society (twenty volumes) and the American Philosophical Society (thirty-eight volumes).

As a natural extension of its reprint activities, the press established a microform division. Among its most ambitious efforts was to produce the entire Congressional Hearings in microfiche. In some three years the press filmed about seven million pages at the Senate Library. A Greenwood Periodicals division was also established. While all the titles this division produced are still published today, the press's periodical publishing inexperience rendered its efforts unprofitable. Therefore this division was dissolved within two years of its beginning.

Probably the most significant experiment undertaken by the press in the late 1960s was to begin its "Contributions" program of original publications. This too was a natural extension of its monographic reprint activities. The Contributions series was designed, initially, to give young scholars a publishing voice. It was perceived that university presses, even the better known ones, were not doing an adequate job in this area. In order to attract young scholars to the press, Greenwood signed several advisory agreements with prominent scholars. Among these were Professor Don Martindale, now deceased, of the University of Minnesota, who directed the Contributions in Sociology series; Professor Paul Wasserman of the University of Maryland for the press's Contributions in Library and Information Science; Professor Robert Walker of George Washington University for Contributions in American Studies; and Professor Jon Wakelyn of Catholic University for Contributions in American History. Happily, the latter three publishing arrangements are still in effect today.

Although by early 1970 several of its new programs were well established, Greenwood was still primarily a reprint company, concentrating on its monographic reprint program based on ALA's *Books for College Libraries*. Greenwood was now producing some 600 monographic reprints each year, this single program accounting for a majority of its sales. The importance of the reprint program to the company's well-being required that one manager be dedicated to its development. Thus, a search was begun for such a person. It was at this time that Robert Hagelstein became a part of Greenwood Press. For the second half of the 1960s Hagelstein had helped to guide the Johnson Reprint Corporation through its explosive expansion, first as its production manager and then as its editorial vice-president. He brought to Greenwood administrative, technical, and editorial skills.

With the onset of the 1970s the tragic human toll extracted by the Vietnam war began to be accompanied by inevitable economic consequences. The "guns and butter" policy of the Johnson administration culminated in the mid-1970s with Ford's "whip-inflation-now" and previously unheard of double-digit interest rates. Greenwood's fortunes began to change in this new environment. The period was not a favorable one for businesses in the United States, and the publishing industry was no exception. Furthermore, there was a winding down of the reprint industry. Reprint companies had been spawned on a regular basis; inevitably, the worthwhile monographs and periodicals had progressed from obscurity to availability, leaving fewer titles for the highly competitive reprint industry to publish. It was at this time that one of the company's cofounders, Harold Schwartz, left the press.

In 1972 and 1973 several other key personnel changes took place which had a lasting impact upon the press. Harold Mason, who had guided the press from its inception, left to pursue one of his main interests, the antiquarian periodicals business. With his resignation in December 1972, Hagelstein was appointed president. The architecture for what Greenwood Press is today was then laid. It was clear that if Greenwood was to flourish and grow, it would have to undergo a radical change, shifting from its reprint roots to becoming primarily a publisher of new materials for the higher education market. Other major reprint publishers who failed to perceive the need for a new publishing strategy, such as Arno Press and Garrett Press, became dinosaurs, doomed to extinction.

In addition to laying plans to expand its Contributions series, Hagelstein identified a void in reference book publishing for specialized works that both university presses and commercial presses had failed to see. Greenwood had successfully published a prototype for this program in 1971, *Biographical Dictionary of the United States Executive Branch*, edited by the well-known scholar and author, Robert Sobel of Hofstra University. (This publication began a long, mutually rewarding association with Professor Sobel, which continues to this day.)

Greenwood's reprint background gave the company an ideal base from which to develop its reference book program. It gave it the expertise to develop a wide range of specialized informational tools across the spectrum of the social sciences and the humanities and it provided a viable backlist. Its approach was in keeping with the theory put forth by the late Curtis Benjamin, former chairman of the McGraw-Hill Book Company. It was Benjamin's contention that the tree of knowledge was "twigging." No longer, for example, was a physician trained merely in general medicine. One was expected to pursue a specialty. The same held true for scholars and teachers working in the humanities and the social sciences. These needs had to be addressed. Essentially, this is the mission Greenwood Press carved out for itself: to provide specialized informational tools. This is still the press's mission today and over the years it has developed a system for first identifying those needs and then finding experts to compile reference works to meet them.

With the departure of Harold Mason and with his time increasingly devoted to general management issues, Hagelstein launched a search for someone to direct the new reference book program. In August 1973, James T. Sabin was hired. In addition to his academic expertise (he has a doctorate from Columbia University in African history), Sabin had a diverse publishing background as a reference editor (Macmillan) and text editor (Litton), as well as a freelance writer (Columbia, Funk & Wagnalls).

In 1974, with the publication of several of Greenwood's reference titles contracted earlier, it was clear that reference publishing would become the company's new primary direction. In particular, the *Biographical Dictionary of American Labor*, edited by Gary M. Fink, proved to be a solid commercial as well as scholarly success. Sales extended to a broad public and secondary school library market—far beyond the company's traditional university audience.

Hagelstein was now able to propose a plan to Williamhouse-Regency to support an ambitious expansion of the original book program and, in 1975, Sabin was put in charge of all book programs. With the company's resources now committed to drastically expanding the original book program, new monograph series were systematically devised to cover the entire range of the social and behavioral sciences as well as the humanities. Over the years more than forty original monograph series were established, most often with academic advisors helping in-house editors to find promising areas of new research and manuscripts. Greenwood, for instance, was an early publisher in the black studies field, an area where the press continues to maintain strong programs. By mid-1988 the 120th title in its Contributions in Afro-American and African Studies program had been issued. With its close ties to scholars and research centers throughout the country, Greenwood has been able to stay attuned to changes in academic emphases. As a consequence, the press established an early presence in now-popular areas such as women's and family studies, popular culture, and science fiction and fantasy criticism. The initial series were intended primarily for research and academic libraries. Not only did they develop strong academic followings, but they were viewed by Greenwood's acquisition editors as fertile grounds for developing needed reference books and possible authors to edit those Greenwood-initiated works.

The rapid editorial expansion of Greenwood meant that the company would soon have to develop a comparable production expertise to bring a wide variety of different types of publications into print. In the early 1970s production work on the company's original books had been handled by Planned Production, a New York-based publishing service organization. Hagelstein felt this was a necessary first step but with the expansion it would be equally necessary to bring copyediting responsibility and typesetting in-house to achieve greater control as well as economies of scale. If the company was to produce a wide range of new publications — while maintaining the highest quality production standards and doing so economically — it would have to develop the same kind of production expertise and productivity as it had established in reprint publishing.

In 1973 Carole Bronson joined the company after several years as a high-ranking executive-branch administrative assistant in Washington, D.C. Given her organizational skills, Bronson was put in charge of the fledgling production department in 1974. Building upon Greenwood's reprint production expertise, she fashioned a department that provided the type of accurate and timely publication required by the diverse original book list that was being developed. In-house production editors coordinated a national network of copyeditors, proofreaders, and indexers, and worked with a three-prong system of in-house compositors, traditional composition vendors, and authors who were able to prepare their own works using personal computer-printer and ultimately the now well-established desktop typesetting systems. Manufacturing was handled through leading printers specializing in university press type publications. Every effort was made to manufacture books of the highest standards, recognizing that libraries, primarily, would be the company's major customers. Ever since Hagelstein's arrival in early 1970, the company has used permanent, durable, low neutral pH paper for its publications.

By the mid-1970s, the initial enthusiasm of media-oriented companies to acquire publishing operations had lessened, and divestitures were becoming common. Williamhouse-Regency also had decided to refocus its attention on its primary business areas, and Hagelstein was asked to seek out a new owner for the press. On August 25, 1976, Greenwood Press merged with the Congressional Information Service, a Washington D.C.-based publisher of abstracts and indexes and microfiche of U.S. government documents.

By the late 1970s a sophisticated academic book program had been put in place. Most monograph series were supplemented by bibliographical and bio-bibliographic series in the same subject areas. This bibliographic program provided prospective authors as well as a promotable "backlist" for the stream of major reference projects that were now being issued; Henry Bowden's *Dictionary of American Religious Biography* and Jon Wakelyn's *Biographical Dictionary of the Confederacy* were selected as 1977 ALA Outstanding Reference Books. A new series devoted to the country's major nonprofit organizations, The Greenwood Encyclopedia of American Institutions, was launched at the same time and, the first volume, Gary Fink's *Labor Unions*, was also selected as an Outstanding Reference Book. The following year saw John Ohles's three-volume *Biographical Dictionary of American Educators* as well as Peter Romanofsky's two-volume *Social Service Organizations*, selected as Outstanding Reference Books as well as the initial two volumes of a new bibliographical series, Contemporary Problems of Childhood: Jean Laubenfels's *Gifted Child* and Beatrice Kalisch's *Child Abuse and Neglect*.

Among the 1978 Outstanding Reference Book awards was also Richard Weekes's *Muslim Peoples: A World Ethnographic Survey*, Greenwood's first major reference project devoted to a primarily non-U.S. topic. During the mid-1970s Hagelstein had been actively constructing a distribution network that could effectively market Greenwood's titles outside of the United States, and with this system now in place, the company was in a position to publish titles that were of primary concern to overseas scholars and research organizations. That distribution system now accounts for some 25 percent of all Greenwood books shipped.

Although Greenwood was well aware of changes in the library community's thinking on collection development — indeed, the press had issued Daniel Gore's *Farewell to Alexandria*, a harbinger of the new approach — it was the enactment of California's Proposition 13 that helped to facilitate the next phase of Greenwood's evolution. In an attempt to rein in what was seen as unchecked government spending,

Proposition 13 and similar measures nationwide called into question state and federal commitments to higher education and library development. As government reexamined its priorities, the publishing industry did likewise. Greenwood's response was, first, to accelerate its publishing programs with international sales potential and to begin to look at areas also requiring specialized information but less vulnerable to the vagaries of public funding.

Second, existing academic series in areas such as criminology and gerontology were broadened to include subjects of concern to professionals in government and the private sector. The third and most crucial component in the strategy to insulate the company from the effects of Proposition 13 was the formation of Quorum Books. This new imprint was devised to reach outside the academic market to professionals and special collections in business, public administration, and the law. Walter Bromberg's *The Uses of Psychiatry in the Law* was published in 1979 and the Twentieth Century Fund's *Abuse on Wall Street* the following year under the Quorum Books imprint. These early successes demonstrated that the press had the marketing expertise to venture outside the academic world; additional editorial resources were therefore dedicated to the new imprint.

Equally momentous for Greenwood was a change in corporate ownership. Elsevier-North Holland, the giant Dutch publisher, had been actively seeking acquisition opportunities in the United States, and in October 1979, it acquired Congressional Information Service, Greenwood's parent company. The purchase of CIS put Elsevier in a position to broaden its role as a major information and electronic publisher in the American market. However, it also found itself the corporate owner of Greenwood, a book publisher with its core markets firmly in the academic library world. As a well-managed academic publisher of specialized informational publications, Greenwood had publication plans in keeping with its new owner's long-term objectives. With the resources of Elsevier behind it, Greenwood was ready to take the next steps toward becoming a major American professional, academic, and reference publisher.

In 1981, Eric Valentine, an experienced business book editor at the American Management Association, joined Greenwood to expand the Quorum Book program. He and his acquisition editors brought steady growth to the imprint, which by the mid-1980s was issuing more than sixty new professional titles a year. The success of Peter Waegemann's *Handbook of Record Storage and Space Management* was the impetus for a new program, Quorum Reports.

Recognizing that books alone could not meet informational needs in the professional market, Quorum Reports was devised to produce newsletters, journals, and other subscription publications where timeliness was crucial. In 1985 the *Records Retrieval Report*, a newsletter aimed at information specialists, was launched, and *Advertising Compliance Service*, a looseleaf service for corporate counsel and marketing managers, was acquired. These publications and the *Journal of Accounting, Auditing, and Finance*, published in conjunction with New York University's Ross Institute, were the core of Greenwood's plans to develop specialized subscription publications in business, law, and information management.

Academic library publishing, nevertheless, remains at the heart of Greenwood's programs, and the 1980s saw steady growth throughout the list. Among the books named Outstanding Reference or Academic Books of the early and mid-1980s were Robert Hogan's *Dictionary of Irish Literature*, Anita King's *Quotations in Black*, Eileen Southern's *Biographical Dictionary of Afro-American Musicians*, the first volumes of The Greenwood Encyclopedia of the World's Political Parties, and the three-volume *American Writers before 1800*, edited by James Levernier and Douglas R. Wilmes. New series were launched to strengthen Greenwood's programs in the humanities. The first volumes in Bibliographies and Indexes in Religious Studies, the Gormans' *Theological and Religious Reference Materials*, were selected as Outstanding Academic Books for 1984 and 1985, while the new Bio-Bibliographies in Music series was inaugurated with award-winning titles in 1984 (JoAnn Skowronski's *Aaron Copland*) and 1985 (Michael Meckna's *Virgil Thompson*).

On the cutting edge of reference publishing, Greenwood issued the pioneering, three-volume *Handbook of Popular Culture*, edited by M. Thomas Inge. While the handbook defined the contours of this new field, individual volumes in the new ongoing American Popular Culture and Bio-Bibliographies in Popular Culture series pointed to their rich research potential. Recognizing that recordings as well as radio and film materials were gaining acceptance as research tools, the press devised discography and performing arts series to help provide better access and documentation of these ephemeral sources. The early 1980s also saw innovative methods in composition, methods without which the press could not have grown. These include cottage-industry keyboarding, author-disk conversions, and off-shore keyboarding. These methods remain an integral part of Greenwood's production techniques.

Throughout the second half of 1985, Greenwood's management was occupied with assessing acquisitions that would cement the press's position as a leading American academic book publisher. Praeger Publishers, which had been controlled by CBS since the mid-1970s, was slated for divestiture along with most of the broadcaster's other publishing operations. Recognizing that the acquisition of Praeger would give Greenwood a strong position in paperback texts and in such academic areas as international relations, psychology, and economics — which were targeted for the next phase of Greenwood's expansion — Hagelstein negotiated a successful acquisition and on January 1, 1986, a contract was signed.

Happily for the press, Ron Chambers, Praeger's editorial director, agreed to stay with Praeger and to manage it on Greenwood's behalf. With nearly twenty years' experience in text and professional book publishing, having been with Macmillan and Prentice-Hall before Praeger, Chambers became an important member of the Greenwood management team. The years following 1986 were a period of challenges for Greenwood as it worked to incorporate the Praeger list into the existing marketing and distribution system. With the stroke of a pen, Greenwood's academic and professional publishing programs had almost doubled from 283 titles in 1985 to 545 in 1986. With Sabin now executive vice-president responsible for coordinating the overall editorial effort of the various imprints, and Bronson now vice-president of production and administration, the various Greenwood imprints, including Quorum and Praeger, were poised for further development.

The press continued to produce a strong list in the humanities and social sciences, with such titles as Robert Gorman's *Biographical Dictionaries of Marxism and Neo-Marxism*, Louise Grinstein and Paul Campbell's *Women of Mathematics*, and Richard Kim's *Dictionary of Asian American History* winning Outstanding Reference or Academic Book awards for 1986 and 1987. Yet another new reference series, this time tracing the key concepts in the major disciplines, was launched, with one of the initial volumes of the series, Harry Ritter's *Dictionary of Concepts in History* recognized as an Outstanding Academic Book for 1986.

In the library and information science area, Michael Buckland of the University of California became an advisor for Greenwood's New Directions in Information Management program in 1986, and in 1987 the press inaugurated another new library series, The Greenwood Library Management Collection, designed to provide professional tools for librarians and information specialists. The initial volumes, Gerard McCabe's *The Smaller Academic Library: A Management Handbook* and Elizabeth Wood and Victoria Young's *Strategic Marketing for Libraries* were well received, and the press intensified its efforts to develop needed handbooks in the area. In addition, in 1987 the press was selected to serve as the official publisher for the Beta Phi Mu monograph series; in the preceding year it had been selected to perform a similar function for the American Society for Information Science.

Even if Greenwood's other vast programs in the humanities and the social sciences did not exist, it would have been a major publisher in its own right solely based on its activities in library and information science. Today the Contributions in Library and Information Science series is entering its twentieth year with more than sixty titles now published. Hence, the press has grown into many new areas while in some respects it has changed in order to remain the same. Underscoring its continuing commitment to the library community, in 1987 it named Nora Kisch director of marketing; she is Greenwood's first marketing director with a master's of library science.

As its twenty-one year history shows, Greenwood has been and remains a constantly evolving press. Initially a reprinter, today reprints comprise little of its overall activities. Greenwood's early efforts in original book publishing focused primarily on American history; today, the program spans the entire range of social and behavioral sciences and the humanities. Tools for the librarian and information scientist have always been at the core of the press's programs; from hardcover and microform reprinting has emerged an array of reference and research series as well as professional books, newsletters, and such subscription-based publications as the *Index to Current Urban Documents* (now also available online) and the *Greenwood Annual Abstract of Legal Dissertations*.

While the press has evolved, it has remained true to several key precepts established in its earlier years. The press remains a publisher without an editorial viewpoint. Conservative as well as Marxist scholarship is presented in its scholarly monograph programs; if a viewpoint can be supported by documentation and scholarly methodology, the work will be considered for publication. Equally important for future evolution is Greenwood's watchfulness for the effects of the "twigging" of the tree of knowledge that will carry the press into the twenty-first century.

Additions to the Professional Bookshelf
Recommendations from a Children's Librarian

Marilyn Karrenbrock

When I was asked to write this article, I was told, "Tell about the books which have influenced you, those you reread, the old books which are too good to forget. Don't limit yourself to books about libraries; include those in related fields which give a new perspective." When I asked for a definition of *old*, I was told, "Oh, about five years." (At my age, that seems like just yesterday!) I have not kept strictly to these guidelines; most of the books I have included are older books, but some are not. Many are not library specific, and some may not appear to have a direct application to libraries at all. Others are well known to librarians; many are classics in our field or in related fields. All are books which have influenced me, ones to which I frequently return for inspiration and revitalization. They are books which have taught me about children, literature, and the interaction between the two.

CHILDREN AND THEIR DEVELOPMENT

One of the most pressing needs of a children's librarian is an understanding of children. No one has done more to help us in that respect than Jean Piaget. In 1981, Getts and Giacoma recommended Piaget's research as a viable basis for library service to children, but stated that: "To date, Piaget's work has not been the subject of significant study by librarians either in printed research or in graduate programs."[1] They mention Dorothy Broderick, who discusses the application of Piagetian theory to library service in *Library Work with Children*.

Today, discussion of Piaget's theory has become more common in library literature, but how it can be applied to children's services is seldom directly addressed.[2] Linda Lucas and I used it as the basis for the discussion of child development in *The Disabled Child in the Library*; we attempted, as did Carol Collier Kuhlthau in a recent article,[3] to relate Piaget's work to library services. Both Lucas and I and Kuhlthau use Piaget's research more to explain and validate practices already current in library services to children than to suggest new or different services based on his theory. Broderick does make such direct applications in her book, as do Giacoma and Getts in another article.[4] The applications in both cases are limited in number, but do suggest ways that the creative librarian could use Piagetian concepts in working with children.

Piaget was a prolific writer, and not an easy one to read or understand. Because of this, many introductions and overviews of his work have been published, and a person who is unfamiliar with Piaget should begin with one of these. Getts and Giacoma, in the first article mentioned above, provide a good bibliography of secondary sources. *Piaget's Theory of Cognitive Development*, by Barry J. Wadsworth, is quite short and exceptionally clear in its presentation. It explains concepts basic to Piaget's system: schema, assimilation, accommodation, equilibrium, conservation; discusses each of his four well-known stages of development: sensorimotor, preoperational thought, concrete operations, formal operations; provides a useful chapter on Piaget's views of adolescence (ages fifteen to eighteen), a subject often ignored in books about Piaget; and adds implications of Piagetian theory for education, a topic which might be extended to children's librarians.

A person who has become familiar with the basic elements of Piaget's theory from this or other secondary sources should graduate to Piaget's own works. His own overview is found in *The Psychology of the Child*, written with Barbel Inhelder. Piaget's research spanned half a century; his books are numerous and cover many topics. A reader will probably choose one based upon his or her own interests.

L. S. Vygotsky, a Russian psychologist who is often compared to Piaget, is less often mentioned in library literature. Vygotsky died in 1934 after only ten years of work, and his writings, although officially banned for many years in the Soviet Union, circulated in scientific circles there, influencing a generation of Russian psychologists. Most of his works are only now appearing in English; for many years, he was best known in the United States for one book, *Thought and Language*. A new and more definitive translation entitled *Thinking and Speech* has recently been published as part of volume I of *The Collected Works of L. S. Vygotsky*, a projected six-volume, English-language edition of all his works.

Piaget and Vygotsky are most often compared in their approaches to thought and language. Both saw these as separate but related processes, and both men were interested in what Piaget called the "egocentric" speech of young children, speech in which children seem to be talking to themselves. One critical component of Piaget's entire theory of child development is egocentrism, in which the young child is at the center of his or her own universe, unable to conceive that another person might have a different point of view. Egocentric speech reflects this orientation; children do not try to be understood because they think that understanding is inevitable. Egocentric speech contrasts with socialized speech, which is used for communicating with others. Socialized speech gradually replaces egocentric speech as children learn to take another person's point of view. Vygotsky disagreed with Piaget's explanation of egocentric speech. He felt that children are social beings who from the beginning use speech to communicate and affect the behavior of others. Gradually they learn to use language to affect their own behavior. Vygotsky found that children are most likely to use egocentric speech when they encounter difficulties; they use speech to reflect upon the situation and "talk themselves through" it. As children mature, egocentric speech becomes more abbreviated, efficient, and internal, until at last it becomes

inner speech. Vygotsky's book, like those of Piaget, requires some intellectual effort, but it is readable, thought-provoking, and has been highly influential in our understanding of children's cognitive development.

Cognitive psychology and linguistics, the study of language, meet in the field of psycholinguistics, of which one aspect is child language acquisition. Roger Brown has perhaps explained interest in this area best: "It is an odd interest, dependent, I suspect, on some rather kinky gene which, fortunately for our species, is not very widely distributed in the population."[5] Although I recommend several books about language development, I do not pretend that it is a subject which has much *direct* application for library services. It does, I think, have numerous implications for our understanding of children. Many aspects of children's behavior which I have long noted have become much more meaningful as I have read about language development.

A person with little background in this field should probably start with a good general overview, such as Dan Slobin's *Psycholinguistics* and Philip S. Dale's *Language Development*. The two books cover the same basic material but have different emphases. Slobin concentrates on the field as a whole, offering within it a very good chapter on language development in the child. Dale concentrates on this latter aspect and discusses psycholinguistic principles in order to explain it. Since both are textbooks, they are relatively easy to understand and are packed with information.

Roger Brown, a prolific author with a career spanning thirty-five years, is an excellent writer who has been called a "standard-bearer ... of simplicity and clarity, of seriousness and humor, of soft-spoken eloquence."[6] Beginning in 1961, Brown and his students at Harvard conducted a study of child language acquisition which is probably the most famous in the field. For five years they recorded, transcribed, and studied the speech of three young children who have become famous as Adam, Eve, and Sarah. From the voluminous amount of data gathered in this project, Brown developed a five-stage theory of language acquisition. He did not try to explain *how* a child acquired language, but instead described the linguistic knowledge which the child possessed, as demonstrated by the child's language performance. Brown originally intended to issue a full report of this study in two volumes, but only one was ever published. The title, *A First Language: The Early Stages*, refers to the fact that Brown was studying the children's native language, the first one they learned. The subtitle indicates that this book covers only the early stages (stages I and II). The stages were based upon mean length of utterance (MLU), the average length of a speech utterance. Stage I indicated an interval with a MLU of 1.0 to 2.0; it started when the child began to produce multiword utterances and lasted until the child's utterances averaged 2.0 words. Stage II was the interval with MLU between 2.0 and 2.5. *A First Language* is a fascinating and significant book, but it is not for the novice reader of language acquisition.

For those not yet ready to try *A First Language*, I recommend Brown's *Psycholinguistics*, which reprints many of the earlier and more easily understood papers about the study. It also contains a section of articles entitled "Psycholinguistic Processes in Adult Life." Two of Brown's most interesting and well-known articles, "How Shall a Thing Be Called?" and "The 'Tip of the Tongue' Phenomenon," are included. A psychologically based review of Nabokov's *Lolita* concludes the book.

Brown was also a highly gifted teacher. *The Development of Language and Language Researchers*, edited by Frank S. Kessel, is a festschrift of eighteen articles contributed by Brown's most famous pupils. These articles often report current research of the authors, but they also trace the writers' development as students and researchers in the field of language acquisition and development. Like their teacher, they are good writers. Most of the articles are not overly technical, and all are a pleasure to read. The book will open many new vistas to the reader, not only in the field of language development but in such varied areas as cognition, socialization, and literary style.

As a librarian and teacher, I had worked with many disabled children, but I became significantly involved in this area through my reading in Piagetian and language acquisition literature. When I learned that a psychologist named Hans Furth was using Piagetian tasks in studying the thinking of deaf children, I read two of his books, *Thinking Without Language* and *Deafness and Learning*, and promptly discovered a new interest.

Upon rereading these books, I find that they are more relevant for their expansions on Piaget than for discussion of deaf children and their education. Furth's primary objective in his experiments was to show that cognitive development was not dependent upon language, an idea inherent in the work of both Piaget and Vygotsky. The general public, and at one time many psychologists as well, often equated lack of language ability with lack of intelligence. Through a series of Piagetian experiments, Furth was able to show that deaf children were capable of logical thought. Until the stage of formal operations, in fact, deaf children were only slightly behind that of hearing children in their development. According to Piagetian theory, this is not surprising, since development at the early stages is primarily based upon sensorimotor and concrete experiences, rather than linguistic ones. When deaf children reached preadolescence, however, they lagged far behind hearing children in reaching the stage of formal operations, which emphasizes theoretical and hypothetical thinking. Furth's experiments showed that this was also true of hearing children from impoverished cultural backgrounds; thus he attributed the deaf child's lag in development less to lack of language than to a culturally impoverished background resulting from inappropriate methods of early education.

When *Thinking Without Language* was written, deaf education was entirely oral, and much of what the book says about it is no longer true. Also, although Furth says that his deaf subjects had no language (either oral or manual), it is not clear whether some of them might have had more knowledge of American Sign Language (ASL) than he realized. By the time *Deafness and Learning* was written, schools for the deaf were developing methods of education which use any means available for communication, including ASL, finger spelling, pantomiming, lipreading, and writing. Furth acknowledged the widespread use of ASL and insisted that it could be considered a language, although he thought it included more mimetic elements and less syntax than it has since been shown to possess.

Several years ago, at an ALA program on library services for the deaf, appreciation was expressed for the work of Ursula Bellugi in proving that ASL was a true language. Bellugi was an early student of Roger Brown and was responsible for recording and transcribing the speech of Adam in the study which Dan Slobin has called the "Garden of Eden."[7] After leaving Brown and his project at Harvard, Bellugi and her husband, Edward Klima, became interested in sign language through an acquaintance with the "signing" chimpanzee, Washoe. They decided to compare how deaf children of deaf parents acquired ASL as a first language with the way hearing children acquired English. They soon found that before they could study acquisition of ASL, they had to learn its linguistic properties. "At the start," Bellugi said, "I had never met a deaf person, had no idea about what it was deaf people did when they gestured to one another, did not know a single sign, and was completely innocent of the many controversies surrounding the language and education of deaf people."[8] Furthermore, no one knew much about the linguistic properties of ASL; it had never been systematically studied. Klima and Bellugi set out to learn about the language first of all, and in the process produced the proof, long desired by the deaf community, that ASL was not simply a simplified and bastardized form of English, but a full-fledged language with its own grammatical structures produced through a visual-spacial mode rather than an acoustic-sequential one. An extended discussion of their findings about ASL is presented in *The Signs of Language*. Not only do they show the properties of signs and the grammatical processes of ASL, but even such language uses as remembering manually (deaf children sign when producing egocentric speech; deaf adults use mental images of their hands in inner speech), wit and verbal play in sign, and signed poetry and song.

For both normal and disabled children, play is a chief means of learning. One of the best books on the subject is *Toys and Playthings in Development and Remediation*, by John Newson and Elizabeth Newson. The Newsons are psychologists at the University of Nottingham who have made an extensive study of the way both disabled and nondisabled children use toys. People are among the baby's first toys; the child watches and reaches for other people, touches them, plays patty-cake and peek-a-boo. Children develop their sensorimotor skills through toys: rattles, mobiles, blocks, push-and-pull toys. Children develop their muscles with balls; playground equipment; and vehicular toys such as tricycles, bicycles, and skateboards. Dolls and stuffed animals satisfy emotional needs, and also serve as props for fantasy play. Miniature worlds can be created with toys, and through games, which have definite rules, the child learns how to get along with others while developing mental and physical skills. For disabled children, toys may provide motivation; act as an aid in sensory, motor, or mental exploration; provide emotional support or serve as a means of expressing negative emotions; or serve as an assessment device used by doctors or psychologists. The reader will be overwhelmed with useful and interesting information and charmed by the enthusiasm with which the Newsons explore the world of toys and children.

Readers who have any interest in children's use of computers have probably already read Seymour Papert's *Mindstorms: Children, Computers, and Powerful Ideas*. Papert, the developer of the LOGO computer language, is another of Piaget's students. *Mindstorms* is not really about computers. It is about children and how they learn, about how adults have hampered and distorted the development of children's natural abilities. Although Papert sets his discussion in the school environment, teachers are not the only people who make the mistakes he describes. Most adults, including parents and librarians, often do the same. They teach children that answers are either right or wrong, that there is only one right way. Consequently, when children make a mistake, they often simply start over again. They do not learn to look for their mistake and correct it; they do not "debug" it. Children must pass through the preoperational stage in which many of their concepts are incorrect. Adults are likely to "force-feed" the correct concept to children, ignoring the fact that children cannot learn things they are not ready to learn; they can only acquire a concept by developing it for themselves. Although adults may try to help the child discover ideas, the child realizes that the adult already knows what will happen. When children and adults work together to write a computer program and make it work, the adult and the child are learning together. The child learns that everyone makes mistakes, and the adult's role is not to hand down the correct answer but to model the role of learner for the child. One reason that I say that *Mindstorms* is not about computers is that unfortunately I do not see much evidence that society is putting Papert's ideas into practice. Nevertheless, the book has a great deal to teach us about children and their needs. And Papert's description of the LOGO teacher seems to me to be an ideal description of a good librarian. The LOGO teacher does not dictate to the child but will "answer questions, provide help if needed, and sometimes sit down next to a student and say: 'Let me show you something.' "[9]

Librarians have always striven to individualize their services, and they long ago began using various media to appeal to different individuals and different kinds of information needs. Most of us, however, have not made much conscious study of what is currently called learning styles. A good starting point from which to study the subject is *Marching to Different Drummers*, by Pat Burke Guild and Stephen Garger. The book is set in an educational environment, but like Papert's book, it suggests many library applications. Guild and Garger define style as one's basic personality pattern and describe four categories of style differences: cognition, conceptualization, affect, and behavior. They discuss six major research models of learning style and give applications for each: Carl Jung's psychological types, Herman Witkin's field-dependence-independence model, Anthony Gregorc's mediation abilities, the learning style elements of Rita Dunn and

Kenneth Dunn, Bernice McCarthy's 4MAT system, and the modalities models of Walter Barbe and Raymond Swassing and of Rita Dunn and Kenneth Dunn. The book concludes with a section on implementing style, and there is an annotated bibliography of further readings. This work discusses not only children's learning styles but also those of teachers (and by extension librarians).

LITERATURE

Most children's librarians read the professional literature regularly and need few suggestions in this area. In this section I want to share some books about literature in general which I think have relevance for those who work with children.

Americans are always intrigued by people, things, or happenings which are highly successful. The best-selling book has been an item of interest since colonial days, and "popular culture" has become not only a common term but an area of study in higher education. Libraries buy materials, mount exhibits, and plan programs based on popular culture. *The Unembarrassed Muse*, by Russel Nye, is an uninhibited exploration of the history of popular arts in America. Until the eighteenth century, there were two artistic traditions, the high art of the elite upper classes and the folk arts of the poor and uneducated. Popular culture is a middle-class culture, one that arose with the great leap in population, rise in urban population and in education, and the development of technology which resulted from the Industrial Revolution. Nye covers a wide range of popular arts: popular novels and poetry; popular theater; dime novels and comics; mysteries, science fiction, and westerns; popular music; and the popular media. *The Unembarrassed Muse* covers both children's and adult materials and is fun to read.

Two other books, James Hart's *The Popular Book* and Frank Luther Mott's *Golden Multitudes*, cover the history of popular books in America through the mid-1940s. Hart's intent is to show the relationship between popular reading tastes and social pressures, while Mott's work is a history of American bestsellers. Hart's chronological account identifies themes for each period in our history, beginning with the piety of colonial days. He discusses only books which were popular at the time they were first published, and the books he discusses were chosen more subjectively than were Mott's. Hart mentions popular children's books, but does not have separate chapters about them as do Nye

and Mott. Mott discusses only bestsellers, which he defined as books whose total sale since the first publication had been equal to one percent of the population of the United States at the time it was first issued. Thus his study, unlike Hart's, includes books that had their greatest popularity years or even decades after their first publication. Two chapters are particularly interesting: "Is There a Best Seller Formula?" and "What Makes a Best Seller Sell?" Both chapters make generalizations which after forty years can still be applied to materials for either children or adults.

One of the glories of children's literature today is the proliferation of wonderful books of folklore. Children's librarians are usually well acquainted with such books, but have not always delved into the equally numerous collections for adults or in the literature *about* folklore. One of the most fascinating books on this topic is Duncan Emrich's *Folklore on the American Land*. It is crammed with all kinds of fascinating information. Intended as an introduction to American folklore for the general reader, it admirably serves its purpose. It provides information *about* folklore as well as examples of many types: proverbs and proverbial speech; American names; children's folklore including riddles, nonsense spelling, and game, autograph album, and book ownership rhymes; street cries and epitaphs; legends and tales; folksongs and ballads; and folk beliefs and superstitions. There are also wonderful black-and-white photographs which invoke the American spirit.

Any book by folklorist Jan Harold Brunvand is worth reading, but *The Vanishing Hitchhiker* is thoroughly delightful. Brunvand has set out to collect urban legends, which he describes thus:

> The story is *true*; it really occurred, and recently, and always to someone else who is quite close to the narrator, or at least "a friend of a friend." ... The legends' physical settings are often close by, real, and sometimes even locally renowned.[10]

The reader will recognize the stories, many times by the title alone: "The Killer in the Backseat," "The Kentucky Fried Rat," "Alligators in the Sewers." The title story is a classic automobile legend of the roadside ghost who is picked up by a motorist but vanishes when its destination is reached. This book is a great source of the scary and sometimes nauseating stories loved by older children and young adults. It could also serve as a starting point for collecting such legends.

Brunvand has followed this book with other volumes of such tales.

Another book that can be read over and over is *One Potato, Two Potato*, by Mary Knapp and Herbert Knapp. The Knapps have collected examples of the folk culture of American children: games, jeers, jokes, rhymes, superstitions, and many more. The book's subtitle, *The Secret Education of American Children*, describes the Knapps' thesis: children learn many cultural elements from other children, elements which teach them the rules of their peer society and allow them to release tensions, distance themselves from the demands of adult society, and overcome their fears through mockery. The Knapps recognize that child life is more regimented and free time less common than a generation ago, but they believe that children's folklore will endure because it is a psychological mechanism necessary for children's development.

For those interested in a more scholarly approach, Alan Dundes's *The Study of Folklore* is a basic collection of readings in the field. The term *folklore* was coined by William Thoms in 1846 in a letter to *The Athenaeum*. Articles that are particularly useful in teaching about folk literature include "Folk Literature: An Operational Definition," by Francis Lee Utley; "The Four Functions of Folklore," by William R. Bascom; and Lord Raglan's classic description, "The Hero of Tradition." Axel Olrik's "Epic Law of Folk Narrative" is the unsurpassed description of folktale elements; Olrik's laws can help children identify these elements more easily, and storytellers will find that they are a great aid in learning stories. The book includes a great many studies of specific stories, themes, and elements.

One area of children's literature that has always seemed to me to be neglected in the professional literature is that of biography. Catherine Drinker Bowen's literate biographies have given me much pleasure. Several years ago, I read her analysis of the subject, *Biography: The Craft and the Calling*, and it has helped me enormously in analyzing and evaluating biographies. Bowen discusses many aspects of the subject: researching the topic, shaping the story, inserting background material, the author's bias, biographical description, and methods of revealing the hero's thoughts. Many of the techniques which Bowen describes have only recently appeared in children's biographies, but a reading of this book followed by that of any well-written, recent children's biography will reveal how her principles are being used today.

One last book which is "too good to be forgotten" is the first edition of May Hill Arbuthnot's *Children and Books*. Many of us grew up with one edition or another of this book. I myself used the first edition as an undergraduate. The differences between this and later editions are minor, but the book just doesn't seem the same. The best thing about the first edition is the extensive discussion of poetry, which occupies seven chapters and 168 pages. There is room for historical information, characteristics, values, and two full chapters on using poetry with children. The three chapters on traditional literature are equally useful, although more of this material has been retained in later editions. Finally, Arbuthnot discusses comics, radio, and media. The inclusion of "illustrative selections" of literature allows the book to serve as an anthology as well as a text. Many wonderful children's books have appeared since this edition was published, and they appear in later editions. Sadly it seems that today's texts give much less room to exploring topics in depth.

CHILDREN, BOOKS, AND READING

Children's interactions with books occur on many levels. One way is simply the physical act of reading. Every children's librarian should know a little of how this occurs. Today, the emphasis is upon "emergent literacy." This concept suggests that literacy develops from very early in the preschool years; that reading and writing are irremediably intertwined and emerge concurrently, rather than reading appearing first; and that literacy is a process which children must develop for themselves — it cannot be handed to them. The approach to reading instruction which is most often advocated today is "whole language instruction," which melds the language arts — reading, writing, listening, and talking — into a unified whole and which, to be truly effective, must permeate the entire curriculum.[11]

Marie Clay is a reading specialist who has used a whole language approach for years to guide reading instruction in New Zealand. Her *Reading: The Patterning of Complex Behavior* is easy to understand, even for someone who has never taken a course in reading education. She makes a strong case for natural language in books rather than controlled vocabulary. She also advocates close observation of the errors that the child makes when beginning to read. Clay has also written other books on the reading and writing of young children.

Another old book which is "too good to be forgotten" is Edmund Burke Huey's *The Psychology and Pedagogy of Reading*, first published in 1908. It has been called "the most readable English work on the reading habit."[12] The first part of the book, which discusses perceptual aspects of reading such as eye movement, inner speech in reading, and reading rate, is not of particular interest to me, although Clay is concerned with similar aspects even today. The sections on history of reading and reading methods, the teaching of reading, and the hygiene of reading will probably interest many readers. Huey's work does not seem out of place in the whole language approach of today.

Librarians may be a little startled when Huey asserts:

> Thus far I have said little about the child's use of *books*, because I think we should be in no hurry to have him use them. The age is over-bookish.... In the schools of the future books will surely be but little used before the child's eighth or ninth year.[13]

It soon is clear, however, that Huey advocates reading to children and encouraging them to read and write their own materials, turning to books only when they are ready to do so spontaneously. In the section on hygiene of books, he discusses such things as the effects of type style and size and paper color.

Case studies of the reading of young children are popular today, and provide valuable insights for children's librarians. Margaret M. Clark's *Young Fluent Readers* discusses her study of thirty-two Scottish children who were fluent readers before beginning school. She found that the children shared warm, accepting, unpressured family environments, and had parents who entered enthusiastically into their interests and often read to them. The accessibility of books was of major importance. More than half the children used the public library, and Clark emphasizes the need to allow children to choose the books they want, without restriction as to type or number.

Marilyn Cochran-Smith's study concerned fifteen children who attended a nursery school in Philadelphia. Her emphasis was upon how the children were socialized into reading through story hours and other prereading activities. Like Clark, she found that a major factor was communication and sharing of experiences connected with stories. She, too, found that libraries were not doing all they could do:

> Nursery-school storyreadings were interactive reader-listener negotiations based on the sense-making of the audience. Library storyreadings, on the other hand,

were one-sided performances of set texts within which the children's participation was not encouraged and, in most cases, not permitted.[14]

If we wish to take advantage of the opportunities offered by the whole language movement, which encourages literature-based reading instruction and self-selection of materials, we must be willing to encourage more freedom in book selection and more use of expressive language, writing, and talking in our libraries.

Another aspect of child/book interaction is the area of reading interests. This is the most studied of all aspects of reading, and there are many articles which summarize and list reading interest studies.[15] One of the largest and most important of all such studies was the one (actually a series of studies) conducted by George Norvell. He collected information on the reading interests of two and a half million students over a period of several decades. Beginning in 1950, the study was reported in three books, with the final report, *The Reading Interests of Young People*, appearing in 1973. Students (grades 7-12) were asked to rate their interest in both independent reading choices and selections read in class. Norvell was particularly interested in ways to make school literature study more appealing, but his findings confirm those of other reading interest studies (which in general have been remarkably consistent across the years and across age levels) and certainly have applications for the choice of library materials. Norvell found that the most important consideration in arousing interest was the sex of the reader. Boys and girls liked different books, and the materials used in literature programs usually appealed to girls much more than to boys. The book is informative and easily read, though Norvell's style is rather quaint at times: he recommends choosing poems that "rollick" and the rejection of "namby-pambyism."[16]

One of the most interesting reading interest studies is F. Andre Favat's *Child and Tale*. Unlike most studies, it is not simply a report of children's likes and dislikes. Favat's purpose was to discuss *why* children liked particular stories. Beginning with the already well-documented fact that young children enjoy fairy tales, he matched a literary "reservoir" consisting of the tales of Perrault, the Grimms, and Andersen with a psychological one, the early work of Piaget. He concluded that fairy tales contain many elements which correspond to the young child's world view: beliefs in magic and animism, a morality that accepts expiatory punishment and adult authority, an acceptance of events without attempting to relate them causally or logically, and an egocentric attitude toward the world. Favat's ideas are provocative and important for those who are interested in the interaction of children with literature.

A third aspect of the child/book interaction is the reader's response to literature. This is currently a very important area of interest. No work in this area has been more influential than Louise Rosenblatt's *Literature as Exploration*, which celebrated its fiftieth "anniversary" in 1988. When one reads the book today, Rosenblatt's ideas seem so right, even so obvious, that it is difficult to remember that they once seemed revolutionary. Rosenblatt sees the literary experience as a transaction between the reader and the text. The reader brings a particular personal and cultural background which shapes what he or she receives from the text, but at the same time, the nature of the text constrains what the reader can take from it. The act of reading is an emotional involvement in which knowledge of life affects one's perceptions of literature even as the lessons of literature are applied to life. Readers change and grow, and no two reading experiences are ever the same. Although Rosenblatt is writing about young adults, her ideas are obviously true at any level. Librarians who have not read this book owe it to themselves to do so.

Another important response study is *The Child's Concept of Story*, by Arthur Applebee. He discusses what he calls the "spectator role." In the spectator role, the reader reacts to a piece of literature which has been constructed out of the author's subjective experience by techniques which Applebee calls "poetic" because poetry is the most complete example of this type. The reader must react to this personal experience as a spectator, taking it in slowly, analyzing the structure and meaning, waiting to make a judgment until the work can be seen as a whole. Applebee examined how children, from age two until adulthood, adopted the spectator role. He found that the developmental stages of literary response corresponded to Piaget's stages. He also determined that the narratives of preschool children could be categorized in a way similar to that used by Vygotsky to categorize children's concept development. Applebee's book is challenging, but like Favat's, it links literature with development in an intriguing synthesis.

Children, books, and the interaction between them: this is still perhaps the chief concern and the chief delight of the children's librarian.

NOTES

[1]Marilyn Getts and Pete Giacoma, "Jean Piaget: An Introduction and Reader's Guide for Children's Librarians," *Top of the News* 37 (Summer 1981): 361.

[2]See, for instance, Claire England and Adele M. Fasick, *ChildView* (Littleton, Colo.: Libraries Unlimited, 1987), 12-14.

[3]Carol Collier Kuhlthau, "Meeting the Information Needs of Children and Young Adults: Basing Library Media Programs on Developmental States," *Journal of Youth Services in Libraries* 2 (Fall 1988): 51-57. Kuhlthau also discusses the theories of Erik Erikson, Lawrence Kohlberg, and Jerome Bruner in this article.

[4]Pete Giacoma and Marilyn Getts, "Children's Services in a Developmental Key," *Top of the News* 41 (Spring 1985): 267-73.

[5]Roger Brown, *A First Language: The Early Stages* (Cambridge, Mass.: Harvard University Press, 1973), 4.

[6]Frank Kessel, "On Words and People: An Introduction to this Collection," in *The Development of Language and Language Researchers: Essays in Honor of Roger Brown*, ed. Frank S. Kessel (Hillsdale, N.J.: Lawrence Erlbaum Associates, 1988), 7.

[7]Dan Slobin, "From the Garden of Eden to the Tower of Babel," in *The Development of Language and Language Researchers: Essays in Honor of Roger Brown*, ed. Frank S. Kessel (Hillsdale, N.J.: Lawrence Erlbaum Associates, 1988), 9.

[8]Ursula Bellugi, "The Acquisition of a Spatial Language," in *The Development of Language and Language Researchers: Essays in Honor of Roger Brown*, ed. Frank S. Kessel (Hillsdale, N.J.: Lawrence Erlbaum Associates, 1988), 157.

[9]Seymour Papert, *Mindstorms: Children, Computers, and Powerful Ideas* (New York: Basic Books, 1980), 179.

[10]Jan Harold Brunvand, *The Vanishing Hitchhiker: American Urban Legends and Their Meanings* (New York: W. W. Norton, 1981), 4.

[11]An entire section of eight articles on whole language and its implications for the library media program can be found in *School Library Media Annual*, volume 6, ed. Jane Bandy Smith (Englewood, Colo.: Libraries Unlimited, 1988), 3-59.

[12]John B. Carroll, "Introduction," in *The Psychology and Pedagogy of Reading*, by Edmund Burke Huey (Cambridge, Mass.: M.I.T. Press, 1968), x.

[13]Edmund Burke Huey, *The Psychology and Pedagogy of Reading* (Cambridge, Mass.: M.I.T. Press, 1968), 329.

[14]Marilyn Cochran-Smith, *The Making of a Reader* (Norwood, N.J.: Ablex, 1984), 122.

[15]One of the best, though now out-of-date, is Alan C. Purves and Richard Beach, *Literature and the Reader: Research in Response to Literature, Reading Interests, and the Teaching of Reading* (Urbana, Ill.: National Council of Teachers of English, 1972). As noted in the subtitle, it also discusses the reader response aspect of child/book interaction.

[16]George W. Norvell, *The Reading Interests of Young People* (East Lansing, Mich.: Michigan State University Press, 1973), 85-86.

REFERENCES

Applebee, Arthur N. *The Child's Concept of Story: Ages Two to Seventeen*. Chicago: University of Chicago Press, 1978.

Arbuthnot, May Hill. *Children and Books*. Chicago: Scott, Foresman, 1947.

Bowen, Catherine Drinker. *Biography: The Craft and the Calling*. Boston: Little, Brown, 1969.

Broderick, Dorothy M. *Library Work with Children*. New York: H. W. Wilson, 1977.

Brown, Roger. *A First Language: The Early Stages*. Cambridge, Mass.: Harvard University Press, 1973.

Brown, Roger. *Psycholinguistics: Selected Papers*. New York: Free Press, 1970.

Brunvand, Jan Harold. *The Vanishing Hitchhiker: American Urban Legends and Their Meanings*. New York: W. W. Norton, 1981.

Clark, Margaret M. *Young Fluent Readers: What Can They Teach Us?* London: Heinemann Educational Books, 1976.

Clay, Marie M. *Reading: The Patterning of Complex Behaviour*. London: Heinemann Educational Books, 1972.

Cochran-Smith, Marilyn. *The Making of a Reader*. Norwood, N.J.: Ablex, 1984.

Dale, Philip S. *Language Development: Structure and Function*. 2d ed. New York: Holt, Rinehart and Winston, 1976.

The Development of Language and Language Researchers: Essays in Honor of Roger Brown. Edited by Frank S. Kessel. Hillsdale, N.J.: Lawrence Erlbaum Associates, 1988.

Emrich, Duncan. *Folklore on the American Land*. Boston: Little, Brown, 1972.

England, Claire, and Adele M. Fasick. *ChildView*. Littleton, Colo.: Libraries Unlimited, 1987.

Favat, F. Andre. *Child and Tale: The Origins of Interest*. Urbana, Ill.: National Council of Teachers of English, 1977.

Furth, Hans G. *Deafness and Learning: A Psychosocial Approach*. Belmont, Calif.: Wadsworth, 1973.

Furth, Hans G. *Thinking Without Language: Psychological Implications of Deafness*. New York: Free Press, 1966.

Getts, Marilyn, and Pete Giacoma. "Jean Piaget: An Introduction and Reader's Guide for Children's Librarians." *Top of the News* 37 (Summer 1981): 360-66.

Giacoma, Pete, and Marilyn Getts. "Children's Services in a Developmental Key." *Top of the News* 41 (Spring 1985): 267-73.

Guild, Pat Burke, and Stephen Garger. *Marching to Different Drummers*. Alexandria, Va.: Association for Supervision and Development, 1985.

Hart, James D. *The Popular Book: A History of America's Literary Taste*. New York: Oxford University Press, 1950.

Huey, Edmund Burke. *The Psychology and Pedagogy of Reading*. Cambridge, Mass.: M.I.T. Press, 1968.

Klima, Edward S., and Ursula Bellugi. *The Signs of Language*. Cambridge, Mass.: Harvard University Press, 1979.

Knapp, Mary, and Herbert Knapp. *One Potato, Two Potato: The Secret Education of American Children*. New York: W. W. Norton, 1976.

Kuhlthau, Carol Collier. "Meeting the Information Needs of Children and Young Adults: Basing Library Media Programs on Developmental States." *Journal of Youth Services in Libraries* 2 (Fall 1988): 51-57.

Lucas, Linda, and Marilyn H. Karrenbrock. *The Disabled Child in the Library: Moving into the Mainstream*. Littleton, Colo.: Libraries Unlimited, 1983.

Mott, Frank Luther. *Golden Multitudes: The Story of Best Sellers in the United States*. New York: Macmillan, 1947.

Newson, John, and Elizabeth Newson. *Toys and Playthings in Development and Remediation*. New York: Pantheon, 1979.

Norvell, George W. *The Reading Interests of Young People*. East Lansing, Mich.: Michigan State University Press, 1973.

Nye, Russel. *The Unembarrassed Muse: The Popular Arts in America*. New York: Dial, 1970.

Papert, Seymour. *Mindstorms: Children, Computers, and Powerful Ideas*. New York: Basic Books, 1980.

Piaget, Jean. *The Child's Conception of the World*. New York: Humanities Press, 1951.

Piaget, Jean. *The Language and Thought of the Child*. New York: Harcourt, Brace, 1926.

Piaget, Jean, and Barbel Inhelder. *The Psychology of the Child*. Translated by Helen Weaver. New York: Basic Books, 1969.

Purves, Alan C., and Richard Beach. *Literature and the Reader: Research in Response to Literature, Reading Interests, and the Teaching of Reading*. Urbana, Ill.: National Council of Teachers of English, 1972.

Rosenblatt, Louise M. *Literature as Exploration*. 3d ed. New York: Noble and Noble, 1976.

School Library Media Annual. Volume 6. Edited by Jane Bandy Smith. Englewood, Colo.: Libraries Unlimited, 1988.

Slobin, Dan Isaac. *Psycholinguistics*. 2d ed. Glenview, Ill.: Scott, Foresman, 1979.

The Study of Folklore. Edited by Alan Dundes. Englewood Cliffs, N.J.: Prentice-Hall, 1965.

Vygotsky, L. S. *The Collected Works of L. S. Vygotsky. Volume I: Problems of General Psychology*. Edited by Robert W. Rieber and Aaron S. Carton. Translated and with an introduction by Norris Minick. New York: Plenum, 1987.

Vygotsky, L. S. *Thought and Language*. Cambridge, Mass.: M.I.T. Press; New York: John Wiley & Sons, 1962.

Wadsworth, Barry J. *Piaget's Theory of Cognitive Development: An Introduction for Students of Psychology and Education*. New York: David McKay, 1971.

What's New in Products and Services
Viewing the Vendor

Ann E. Prentice

In the next year, what should we look for that is new and/or different? Are there topics of new or renewed interest, new formats of existing materials, or new arrangements of information that will substantially enhance its use? These questions were asked of a selection of publishers and vendors who exhibit at national conferences and who represent several aspects of the information marketplace. Their responses show that a number of new and interesting things are happening that merit further exploration. Particularly in the areas of formats and services, there have been a fair number of innovations. In some instances they lead the library world's needs, as in adaptations of materials to CD-ROM formats, and in other instances those who exhibit at professional association meetings lag behind. An example of this is the rapid acceptance of FAX technology by libraries and its somewhat slower appearance in the exhibit hall marketplace.

New formats of existing resources are one of the most exciting developments that affect both collection building and use. Gale Research is moving into CD-ROM products under the imprint *Gale Global Access*. Its first CD-ROM product covers associations and association periodicals and is entitled *Association CD*. *Association CD* offers global access to nearly 100,000 descriptive entries taken from four of Gale's association databases:

- National organizations of the United States

- National organizations outside the United States and international organizations

- Regional, state, and local organizations of the United States

- Association periodicals

Included in the 1988 base price of $2,195 is a six-month update and reliable search software by Knowledge Access International. Among the benefits to users are access to nearly five times as many entries as are currently available online; more search fields; downloading capability to writeable PC-based diskettes; and the ability to print, organize, and rank the results of information searches by numerous criteria.

Gale will continue to publish in traditional formats. Some will be expanded — *The Encyclopedia of Associations* international volume *International Organizations* will include national organizations based in countries outside the United States.

INTERNET (International Network for Technical Assistance) focuses on developing countries and those U.S. organizations most active in technical assistance work in developing countries. INTERNET's 1988 *Profiles of International Development Contractors and Grantees* is a new publication that contains detailed profiles of each of these organizations, including universities, not-for-profit corporations, private voluntary organizations/foundations, and for-profit firms. The profiles are useful to a number of audiences for a variety of purposes:

1. Corporate and academic organizations with interests in economic development issues and activities can find complete,

accurate information about potential collaborators (or competitors) in one volume.

2. Students and others interested in international careers can identify those organizations that fit well with their training and skills. Several indexes make the *Profiles* a useful placement tool.

3. Faculty members and businesses can use the *Profiles* to find partners with whom to apply for matching grants from the U.S. Department of Education's Business and International Education Program. These grants require a cooperative agreement between an educational institution and a business or trade organization engaged in international economic activity. They can be used to internationalize curricula, to establish student and faculty fellowships and internships, or for research and training.

4. Community outreach groups on college and university campuses will find the *Profiles* a useful source to identify organizations and persons who have international experience and who reside in their geographic area. Organizations such as the Small Business Institutes sponsored by the Small Business Administration and many business schools will appreciate the index listing the 182 small/disadvantaged/minority-owned firms in the *Profiles*. Private voluntary organizations, not-for-profit organizations, and universities are also listed by type.

In all, there are six indexes and two appendices included in the *Profiles* to enhance its usefulness. All information needed to contact the organizations included in the *Profiles*, as well as the 500 telephone numbers and names of international donor agency managers in appendix B, is updated every quarter and the update sent to subscribers at no additional cost.

ABC-Clio continues to expand the scope of its reference materials. New titles on managing online and CD-ROM resources and on developing and maintaining video collections in libraries have been added. New series include Social Studies Resources for Secondary School Librarians, Teachers, and Students, devoted to providing one-stop reference resources on economics, geography, U.S. history, U.S.

government, and global issues, all in easy-to-use formats. The year 1989 will see a return of the classic American Library History, a comprehensive guide to literature on the subject, in a new edition to reflect new technologies. The upcoming Older Adults Issues series will address concerns of this rapidly growing segment of our population. Subjects will include legal issues, health care services, housing, and financial planning.

Scarecrow's traditional support for practitioners of the library profession is reflected in a 25 percent increase in library and information science titles published in 1988 over the preceding year. Jane Anne Hannigan has assumed the editorship of Scarecrow's well-known Library Lit series from founding editor Bill Katz. The *Voice of Youth Advocates* has inaugurated the VOYA Occasional Papers Series with Dorothy Broderick as editor. The best-selling Librarian's Helper cataloging software is now available in a new enhanced version, and during the coming year, the image of the "typical" typed Scarecrow book will be modernized as they begin to typeset all their new titles.

SIRS (Social Issues Resources Series, Inc.) has been publishing its collection of volumes of reprinted articles on social issues and science topics for over fifteen years. Since fall 1988 every SIRS supplement and volume includes two formats: the printed articles and microfiche of all articles and indexes. This provides multiple access to more than 10,000 articles. According to publisher Eleanor Goldstein, "the technology of the microfiche reader and printer has improved to the point where it is now feasible to put SIRS on microfiche. Research indicates that 42x magnification is most appropriate for this purpose."

CLSI has announced both a new product (CD-CAT) and a basic change in the LIBS 100™ System. CD-CAT, CLSI's CD-ROM catalog, contains libraries' complete bibliographic information on compact disks, residing on fully independent, self-standing workstation units. Each CD-ROM catalog workstation can be plugged into almost any electrical outlet to provide a cost-effective, comprehensive public access catalog, with powerful keyword and Boolean searching capabilities and procedures for both "easy" and "advanced" search modes. CLSI has also completed the migration of its LIBS 100 System's operating system from a proprietary operating system to the UNIX™ operating system, a standard in computer technology. This major change in product speeds the delivery of new functions and system enhancements to libraries because of the improved productivity of the software development environment and the new system's ability to incorporate various standard software packages for user interfaces, report generation, networking, office automation, and electronic mail.

SilverPlatter Information, Inc. offers over twenty different titles on CD-ROM. SilverPlatter databases cover health, science, safety, business, technology, education, social sciences, agriculture, and more. All of the databases use SPIRS, SilverPlatter's standard search and retrieval software for the PC environment.

In response to the market's requirements for multiple users to access the same or multiple disks from any workstation, SilverPlatter has developed MultiPlatter™. MultiPlatter is SilverPlatter's networking solution for libraries, linking up to twenty-one CD-ROM drives to multiple computers. Multiple users can access any of the CD-ROM databases in the network, or access the same database. Another solution for making multiple databases available is SilverPlatter's daisychaining capability, which connects multiple CD-ROM drives to a single workstation.

To provide the same powerful CD-ROM searching capabilities for Apple Macintosh™ users, SilverPlatter will be releasing Mac-SPIRS™ in the summer of 1989. MacSPIRS combines sophisticated searching capabilities with the friendly, easy-to-use style of the Macintosh. BRS is on the way to becoming a full service information organization, providing not only new kinds of databases such as the AIDS Knowledge Base from San Francisco General Hospital (ASFG), an electronic textbook available only online, but also value-added services such as enhanced networks and fixed-fee searching. For fixed-price searching, BRS has introduced BRS/OnSite for the local operation of information on a customer's computer and After Dark Unlimited, a fixed-fee, unlimited searching package. A new DIALCOM to BRS/MENUS gateway began providing all DIALCOM users with access to BRS in fall 1988. New databases include Scientific American Medicine (SAMM), online exclusively with BRS. A new Table of Contents feature in BRS/Colleague and BRS/MENUS was introduced with AIDS Knowledge Base (ASFG) and is also available in SAMM.

Faxon has recently released MicroLinx Version 3.2 of its PC-based service for automated serials check-in, routing, and electronic claims transfer. Available in single-user and LAN versions, MicroLinx provides libraries with cost-effective, local control of their serials information. The service includes complete training, documentation, and ongoing support and can interface to major Integrated Library systems. Faxon recently announced a new financial management service, SMARTS (Subscription Management and Resource Tracking System). SMARTS gives users a database-on-disk of their subscription list and related information, along with a program for manipulating the information. In this way, SMARTS supports custom-tailored management and reporting tools, both for internal use and for efficient transfer of orders to Faxon. In addition, Faxon now offers a centralized CD-ROM title ordering service, which allows clients to search and order a wide variety of CD-ROM titles from multiple publishers.

Searchware, from a firm in Woodland Hills, California, is an online information retrieval software system to search and access DIALOG. It runs on an Apple or IBM/IBM-compatible personal computer. Three levels of search are possible for novice to experienced users. Its primary features include cost reduction through offline search strategy development, password security, up-to-the-minute cost accounting, and budget control with its online time. A special educational version is available for teaching online searching in a classroom environment.

Information Made Easy (IME) produces its own micro- and minicomputer software for library and other information handling systems. IME's database engine, called TINman, has been in active use since 1984. From TINman, IME has produced TINlib, a fully integrated, complete library system, which now has over 500 installations worldwide. IME sells through its national distributors currently in the United Kingdom, The Netherlands, West Germany, Switzerland, Italy, Sweden, and Australia. It also sells through third-party arrangements. For example, Unisys sells the IME produced PC/PALS and U/PALS worldwide. IME is run by Kate Noerr, out of its London headquarters. It currently employs over thirty professionals in its UK offices.

These vendors exhibit their products and services at most major library and information conferences so that the interested consumer can try them out and test the statements made about them by their sponsors. This initial step toward developing a consumer's guide to the producer's wares is intended to pique interest and to help focus attention on what is happening in the marketplace represented at professional conferences by exhibitors.

The Research Efforts of Major Library Organizations

Sharon L. Baker and Ronald R. Powell

Several national associations have programs to stimulate research for the profession. This article gathers together in one listing the various research mechanisms of these organizations.

THE AMERICAN LIBRARY ASSOCIATION

ALA's Office for Research is directed by Mary Jo Lynch. The functions of the office are: (1) to collect, analyze, and interpret data about the membership of ALA and users of ALA products and services on an ongoing basis for organizational decision making; (2) to collect and/or promote the collection of statistics about libraries and librarians so that ALA and other organizations will have pertinent and consistent data available to them; and (3) to monitor ongoing research related to libraries and disseminate information about such studies to the profession. In carrying out these functions, the Office for Research provides advice regarding research and statistics to the Executive Board, Council, and any other ALA unit which requests this service.[1]

One major function of the ALA Committee on Research is to advise the Office for Research. The committee's other functions are to facilitate research and related activities in all units of the association, to advise ALA's Council and Executive Board on programs, policy, and priorities regarding research, to recommend procedures to achieve expeditious consideration of all ALA unit proposals for research and related activities by the ALA Executive Board, to encourage the establishment of divisional committees for the purpose of stimulating research, to maintain liaison with all units of the association regarding research and related activities in the units, and to identify questions regarding library service which need to be answered through research and promote the conduct of research to answer those questions.[2]

The 1989 chair of the ALA Committee on Research is Janis C. Keene (Tulsa City-County Library System, 400 Civic Center, Tulsa, OK 74103).

Division Research Committees

A number of ALA divisions also have research committees, each with their own charges and activities. The following are the constituted committees with their respective chairs for 1989.

American Association of School Librarians
Research Committee
Chair: Philip M. Turner
Graduate School of Library Service
University of Alabama
P.O. Box 6242
Tuscaloosa, AL 35487-6242

Association for Library Service to Children
Research and Development Committee
Chair: M. Jean Greenlaw
2600 Sheraton Rd.
Denton, TX 76201

Association of College and Research Libraries
Bibliographic Instruction Section
Research Task Force
Chair: Thomas Kirk
Hutchins Library
Berea College
Berea, KY 40404

Association of College and Research Libraries
Research Committee
Chair: Jerry L. Parsons
California State University—Sacramento
    Library
2000 Jed Smith Dr.
Sacramento, CA 95819

Association of College and Research Libraries
Research Discussion Group
Chair: Timothy F. Richards
Vanderbilt University Libraries
Jean and Alexander Heard Library
Nashville, TN 37203

Association of Specialized and Cooperative
    Library Agencies
Research Committee
Chair: Sally J. Drew
Wisconsin Department of Public Instruction
Bureau of ILL and Resource Sharing
2109 South Stoughton Rd.
Madison, WI 53716

Public Library Association
Research Committee
Chair: Carolyn M. Moore
1901 McKinley St.
Clearwater, FL 33575

Resources and Technical Services Division
Cataloging and Classification Section
Policy and Research Committee
Chair: Judith A. Hudson
501 Stratton Pl.
Delmar, NY 12054

Resources and Technical Services Division
Planning and Research Committee
Chair: Pamela M. Bluh
8594 Hayshed Ln.
Columbia, MD 21045

Resources and Technical Services Division
Preservation of Library Materials Section
Policy and Planning Committee
Chair: Margaret M. Byrnes
4603 Highland Ave.
Bethesda, MD 20814

Resources and Technical Services Division
Reproduction of Library Materials Section
Policy and Research Committee
Chair: Nancy E. Elkington
Hatcher Graduate Library
Preservation Office #7
University of Michigan
Ann Arbor, MI 48109

Resources and Technical Services Division
Resources Section
Policy and Research Committee
Chair: Linda M. Pletzke
8214 Beech Tree Rd.
Bethesda, MD 20817

Resources and Technical Services Division
Serials Section
Policy and Research Committee
Chair: John J. Riemer
1554 Pine Creek Way
Lawrenceville, GA 30243

Young Adult Services Division
Research Committee
Chair: Elizabeth McClure Rosen
Clarion University of Pennsylvania
College of Library Science
180 Carlson
Clarion, PA 16214

Round Tables

Library History Round Table
Chair: Gordon Barry Neavill
Graduate School of Library Service
University of Alabama
P.O. Box 6242
Tuscaloosa, AL 35487-6242

Library Research Round Table
Chair: Joe A. Hewitt
University of North Carolina
Walter Royal Davis Library
Chapel Hill, NC 27514-6080

Research Awards

In addition to the various committees, offices, and round tables, a number of awards promote research in the field.

1. (*Carroll Preston*) *Baber Research Award.* This annual award of $10,000 is presented to a person doing research focusing on improved library services, new uses of technology, or cooperative projects. The award is donated by Eric R. Baber and is administered by the ALA Awards Committee. For more information, write Mary Jo Lynch, Director of ALA's Office for Research, at ALA Headquarters.

2. *Association of College and Research Libraries, Doctoral Dissertation Fellowship.* This annual award of $1,000 is presented to a doctoral

student in the field of academic librarianship whose research indicates originality, creativity, and scholarship. The award was designed to foster research in academic librarianship by encouraging and assisting doctoral students with their dissertation research. The award is donated by the Institute for Scientific Information and is administered by ACRL. For more information, write Mary Ellen Kyger Davis, ACRL Program Officer, at ALA Headquarters.

3. (*Frances*) *Henne YASD/VOYA Research Grant*. This annual award of $500 provides seed money for small-scale research projects that will have an influence on library service to young adults. Applicants must belong to the Young Adults Services Division. Grants will not be given for research leading to a degree. The award is donated by *Voice of Youth Advocates* and is administered by YASD. For more information, write to the Executive Director of YASD at ALA Headquarters.

4. (*Samuel*) *Lazerow Fellowship for Research in Acquisitions or Technical Services*. This annual award of $1,000 is given to provide librarians in acquisitions or technical services with a fellowship for research, travel, or writing. Proposals are judged on their potential significance, originality, and clarity. The award is donated by the Institute for Scientific Information and is administered by ACRL. For more information, write Mary Ellen Kyger Davis, ACRL Program Officer, at ALA Headquarters.

5. *Jesse H. Shera Award for Research*. This award of $500 is given annually for an excellent research paper. Entries are judged on definition of the research problem, application of research methods, clarity of the reporting of the research, and significance of the conclusions. The award is administered and donated by the Library Research Round Table. For more information, write to Mary Jo Lynch, Director of the Office for Research, at ALA Headquarters.

6. (*Justin*) *Winsor Prize Essay*. This award of $500 is given to encourage excellence in research in library history. Essays should be original historical research on a significant subject of library history, and should be based on primary source materials and manuscripts if possible. The award is administered by the Library History Round Table. Manuscripts should be forwarded to Justin Winsor Prize, care of John V. Richardson, Graduate School of Library and Information Science, University of California, 405 Hilgard Ave., Los Angeles, CA 90024.

Research is published by ALA in a variety of ways. Some reports are published by ALA Publishing and released as books. Most research is reported in the various journals published by the association, either as research articles or in research columns. Journals which regularly report research findings include *School Library Media Quarterly*, *Library Resources and Technical Services*, *Public Libraries*, and *RQ*.

THE SPECIAL LIBRARIES ASSOCIATION

Founded more than eighty years ago by John Cotton Dana, SLA provides special support, services, and opportunities for special librarians and information managers. The function of the SLA Research Committee is to encourage and promote research and related projects which will increase the understanding of, encourage innovation in, or improve the theory and practice of the special librarian or information professional. The Research Committee encourages the dissemination of the results of any such research, advises the association on research areas that need to be studied, and makes appropriate recommendations regarding these needs. The Research Committee also reviews Special Programs Fund Grant applications (see address below) and makes recommendations to the SLA Board of Directors. The chair of the 1988/1989 Research Committee is Miriam Drake (Georgia Institute of Technology, Price Gilbert Memorial Library, Atlanta, GA 30332).[3]

Grants from the Special Programs Fund support programs and services that will further the scientific, literary, and educational purposes of SLA. The amount of funding available varies from year to year. Special Programs Fund monies have been used to study corporate excellence and education for special librarianship. For more information, write to Tobi Brimsek, Director, Research and Information Resources (SLA, 1700 Eighteenth St. N.W., Washington, DC 20009).

SLA also publishes *Special Libraries*, a quarterly, refereed journal which reports news, trends, and research related to special libraries.

ASSOCIATION FOR LIBRARY AND INFORMATION SCIENCE EDUCATION

The Association for Library and Information Science Education (ALISE) encourages and supports research in a number of ways. Its

Research Committee serves as the coordinator for all research-related activities of the association. The committee is responsible for reviewing any research-oriented programs planned for the annual conference and for recommending to the Board of Directors all awards for research activities. Marion Paris (University of Alabama) is the 1989-1991 chair of the Research Committee.

The Research Interest Group develops research-related programs for the annual conferences of ALISE. Programs regularly include doctoral forums and forums for current research and issues. Both forums provide opportunities for researchers to share their work informally with small groups of colleagues.

ALISE sponsors three annual competitions designed to promote research. Each year the association awards one or more grants, totaling $2,500, to support research broadly related to education for library and information science. The authors of up to two research papers concerning any aspect of librarianship or information studies are given honoraria of $500 and present their papers at the annual conference. (Recipients of these grants and awards must be personal members of ALISE.) The association also sponsors an annual doctoral dissertation competition. Up to two outstanding doctoral dissertations completed during the preceding year are selected for presentation at the annual conference. Each winner of this competition receives a $400 award plus conference registration and personal membership in ALISE.

The *Journal of Education for Library and Information Science* is the official publication of ALISE. Each quarterly issue of the journal regularly includes research articles and other scholarly papers. The journal also contains the "Research Record," a column that focuses on research issues and reports recently approved doctoral dissertations in library and information science. An important source of educational data is the *Library and Information Science Education Statistical Report*, which is published annually by the association.

AMERICAN SOCIETY FOR INFORMATION SCIENCE

The American Society for Information Science (ASIS) engages in numerous activities to promote and honor research efforts in the field of information science. The Research Committee, a standing committee that serves in an advisory capacity to the Board of Directors, bears the primary responsibility within ASIS for assessing the society's role in the evolution of the field and profession, for identifying potential relationships with research foundations and other funding agencies, and for recognizing the role of research and researchers within ASIS and the field of information science. The 1988 chair of the ASIS Research Committee is Dr. Jeffrey Katzer (Syracuse University).

Since 1987, ASIS has sponsored a program, entitled Student Mini-Conferences, for students in graduate programs of library and information science, as well as in related fields in other schools and departments. The annual conferences, which are run by and for the students, provide opportunities for students to share their research and to meet their future professional colleagues. The Student Mini-Conferences are scheduled regionally in the spring.

Other research activities and interests within ASIS are represented by many of the twenty-one ASIS Special Interest Groups (SIGs). Among the SIGs with the greatest research interests are Classification Research, Foundations of Information Science, Arts and Humanities, Medical Information Systems, and Information Generation and Publishing. Many of the other SIGs also foster activities.

Several awards are presented each year to honor research efforts in information science. The Award of Merit, the society's most prestigious award, is presented annually to an individual who has made noteworthy contributions to the field of information science. Though the award is not specifically for research, it frequently honors individuals whose primary contributions have been based on research activities. The ISI Information Science Doctoral Dissertation Scholarship fosters research in information science by encouraging and assisting doctoral students with their dissertation research. The scholarship recognizes outstanding proposals for doctoral dissertations submitted by graduate students who have completed the coursework for their doctoral degrees and consists of a $1,000 scholarship presented to a current doctoral candidate. The Doctoral Forum honors outstanding achievements by information scientists on the completion of dissertation projects and includes the opportunity for them to present their research at the ASIS annual meeting.

The society also offers other students the opportunity to have their work recognized. The Student Paper Award winner receives full conference registration for an annual meeting as well as partial payment of transportation expenses for the conference. The winning paper may be submitted to the *Journal of the American Society for Information Science* to be considered for publication.

Among ASIS's publications are the *Bulletin of the American Society for Information Science*, the *Journal of the American Society for Information Science*, and the proceedings of its annual conference. The *Journal* and the proceedings are more research oriented than is the *Bulletin*.

NOTES

[1] *ALA Handbook of Organization: 1988-1989* (Chicago: American Library Association, 1988).

[2] Ibid.

[3] *Who's Who in Special Libraries, 1988-1989* (Washington, D.C.: Special Libraries Association, 1988).

Part II
REVIEWS OF BOOKS

Reviews of Books

GENERAL WORKS

Biographies and Memoirs

1. Berman, Sanford. **Worth Noting: Editorials, Letters, Essays, an Interview, and Bibliography.** Jefferson, N.C., McFarland, 1988. 176p. index. $18.95. LC 87-43165. ISBN 0-89950-304-7.

If you are sometimes frustrated with the policies and processes of our profession that stifle your ability to give the kind of library services you would like, or if you are one of those who set the policies and develop these processes, you need to read these thirty-odd essays by Berman, head of the Cataloging Department at Hennepin County Library, Minnesota. Whether he demonstrates how inadequately catalogs direct patrons to materials (for lack of sufficient or exact subject headings), shows how service policies and priorities favor elitist patron groups, or how attitudes toward censorship to assure representation of all viewpoints make us irresponsible providers of information, you may find his arguments convincing, irritating, or even angering; but you will not find them dull or irrelevant. His attacks against the inadequacies of subject headings, his letters and reviews on censorship and human rights in America, Europe, and Africa, and his arguments against creationism as a science show his concern with the profession's need to responsibly address issues of civil liberties. Best of all, they show that a literate, informed, and uninhibited librarian can try to improve not only our professional practices, but our attitudes. The collection also includes an informative interview with Berman and a "Select Chronological Bibliography" of his publications.

Worth, like beauty, is, of course, in the eye of the beholder. But I found *Worth Noting* worth my time for its relevance, style, and tone. Recommended for all libraries. [R: BL, 1 Oct 88, p. 217; JAL, May 88, p. 127; JAL, Nov 88, p. 306; VOYA, Dec 88, p. 256; WLB, May 88, p. 90]   Blaine H. Hall

2. Gaver, Mary Virginia. **A Braided Cord: Memoirs of a School Librarian.** Metuchen, N.J., Scarecrow, 1988. 233p. bibliog. index. $25.00. LC 87-12738. ISBN 0-8108-2032-3.

Of the major figures who played important roles in the development of school libraries from 1930 to 1970, Mary Virginia Gaver has been a giant. This autobiographical volume traces Gaver's personal and professional career and, in particular, her contribution to research, national policy of school libraries, and the development of *The Elementary School Library Collection.*

Gaver draws her material from personal journals kept over a lifetime. The narrative is scholarly with personal reflections of friends and people met along the way. Gaver also includes comments and criticism of current trends in the field from her perspective. The importance of the biography is that it documents much of what happened during the flourishing years of school libraries when the work of dedicated professionals paid off as the federal government assisted school districts all over the country to establish libraries, add audiovisual media, and create service-oriented programs. Of value to historians of the field and for those school library educators and practitioners interested in their "roots." [R: BL, July 88, p. 1844; BR, Sept/Oct 88, p. 48; SLJ, Apr 88, p. 46]
David V. Loertscher

3. Gerard, David. **Shrieking Silence: A Library Landscape.** Metuchen, N.J., Scarecrow, 1988. 287p. index. $29.50. LC 87-32248. ISBN 0-8108-2069-2.

Rather surprisingly, the blurb for this book states its raison d'être and chief value wholly accurately: "There is a plethora of books on the theory and practice of librarianship but a paucity of personal witness." The blurb might well have added that there is an even greater paucity of librarians' autobiographies that are candid (rather than merely polite) and that present personal feelings (rather than merely professional experience). Gerard's reminiscences offer both remarkable frankness and a sense of what it actually *felt* like to be a public librarian in Britain.

The book does have some shortcomings. Gerard's strong interest in modern literature has led him to record interviews with a number of literary figures such as Rebecca West and Alan Sillitoe. Transcripts of these interviews occupy a substantial part of the book and, while useful in themselves, they seem out of place in what purports to be a depiction of "a library landscape." The other failing is the matter of accuracy and fairness in reporting. Gerard tends to be rather careless about getting his facts right and he is overly quick, even brusque, in his judgments. Thus his descriptions of the library scene (especially in the United States) are marred by mistakes and by snide remarks that are needlessly wounding.

Gerard's autobiography stops at the point at which he left library practice to take up a career in library education (ca.1967). Perhaps then we may look forward to another memoir like this one—sometimes cavalier and opinionated but also vivid, unusually revealing, readable, and hence, welcome. [R: LAR, 14 Oct 88, p. 601]   Samuel Rothstein

4. McPheeters, Annie L. **Library Service in Black and White: Some Personal Recollections, 1921-1980.** Metuchen, N.J., Scarecrow, 1988. 152p. illus. index. $22.50. LC 88-1979. ISBN 0-8108-2104-4.

This book represents both a journal of recollections and a journey through the southern library world from 1921 to 1980. It is a pilgrimage into professional and personal concerns, bracketed generously with facts of black library history. Beginning with a discussion of public library service for the black population of the Southeast (1900-1959), the settings for the subsequent chapters include Atlanta, Georgia; Greenville, South Carolina; and Georgia State University—with a sprinkling of other locations provided in conjunction with personal high-

lights. This book can readily serve two obvious purposes: as a lens with which to gain insights into the history and development of librarianship in black communities and as a resource for those historians (and people interested in history) who wish to add perspective to overall library history in the United States.

Personal Recollections is an apt subtitle, but the book is much more than that—it is a window into a world which many of us have never clearly seen. Annie McPheeters makes a valuable contribution to understanding the volatile environment of the period covered and the efforts of black librarians to be influential in a major period of this country's history.

Darlene E. Weingand

5. Powell, Lawrence Clark. **An Orange Grove Boyhood: Growing Up in Southern California 1910-1928.** Santa Barbara, Calif., Capra Press, 1988. 80p. illus. $12.95. LC 87-28811. ISBN 0-88496-275-X.

These brief memoirs will be of interest to people who have known the author, or have read his other books, or are familiar with the area around South Pasadena, California. For others the value will be doubtful. It is strange that Powell wrote only sixty-six pages. Most people probably remember more of this kind of trivia. Some of these accounts are interesting (e.g., that one of the Fugit boys was nicknamed Tempus, and that Powell liked to eat library paste); others are not (e.g., that Powell once emptied a pitcher of water on a cousin). The style is rough in places, excellent in others. Its disconnectedness has a certain charm, as one thought suggests another experience of a different year, but at times the reader must make added effort to keep the facts in view. Some of the mentioned names are big (Ward Ritchie, Liberty Hyde Bailey, Herbert Hoover), but others would seem of local interest only and maybe not much of that.

Altogether, a disappointment coming after such a distinguished writing career.

Robert N. Broadus

Essays and Proceedings

6. **Fifth Annual Forum on Federal Information Policies: The Impact on Competitiveness. A Summary of Proceedings.** By Douglas C. Brooks. Washington, D.C., Federal Library and Information Center Committee, Library of Congress, 1988. 33p. free pa.

This summary is an informative overview of the presentations and panel discussions from the forum's daylong session. Unfortunately, there is no indication in this publication as to the specific date or location of the meeting. The missing data was discovered in the *Library of Congress Information Bulletin*: the forum was held at the Library of Congress in March 1988.

The forum addressed the broad issue of competition for technological information and the inadequate state of federal policies in this area. In the words of Peter Hernon, one of the forum participants, "federal information policy remains piecemeal and, at times, incorrect, contradictory, confusing, simplistic, and based on faulty premises." Throughout the forum, the need for a strengthened federal role was stressed by a variety of participants (representing several government agencies, the U.S. Congress, academia, and the corporate sector).

Some of the themes discussed were the conflict between the desire to expand access to information and the need to curtail access for reasons of national security; the impact of recent legislation on the transfer of technology and cooperative research; restriction of foreign access to federal technical information resources; increased governmental efforts to acquire and disseminate foreign information (especially from Japan); the role of libraries as "information providers" and filters of information; the use of gateway systems to democratize access; and global economic concerns (e.g., trade deficits and foreign ownership).

The summaries of each presentation are quite substantial, ranging from two to five pages of text in this pamphlet. An adequate flavor of the proceedings is conveyed to the reader, though access to the complete text of the presentations would be important for most libraries where advanced research is supported.

Thomas A. Karel

7.   Lang, Jovian P., ed. **Unequal Access to Information Resources: Problems and Needs of the World's Information Poor. Proceedings of the Congress for Librarians February 17, 1986.** Ann Arbor, Mich., Pierian Press, 1988. 249p. bibliog. index. $35.00pa. LC 87-34577. ISBN 0-87650-239-7.

This publication of the proceedings of the annual Congress for Librarians held in 1986 at St. John's University, Jamaica, New York, also contains added papers on pertinent topics. The theme of the congress was "Information Poverty," the problem of unequal access to the world's information. The topics of the twenty-five papers cover obstacles to general access to information such as poverty, literacy, and geography and the library's mission in this area. Other topics, such as the complex problems of the Third World and information, the New World Information and Communications

Order, information access and services to children and young adults and the disabled as well as U.S. policies and influences on information access at home and abroad, are presented. In the appendices are found copies of OMB Circular A-130 (which implements the provisions of the Paperwork Reduction Act of 1980), ALA's response to the circular and its documentation of emerging trends entitled "Less Access to Less Information by and about the U.S. Government." A bibliography of important materials relating to unequal access completes the volume. The publication aims at presenting a reference text for the next White House Conference, which has pinpointed "Access to Information" as one of three areas of major concern. Overall the papers are varied in quality and size but ably identify some of the major issues from the American perspective; they also focus on the basic problems of perception and lack of understanding that are obstacles to the appropriate addressing of these issues. The issues raised in this volume are of major concern to the profession. If the broader objective is consciousness raising, this publication should be purchased by more libraries than just those wanting to have a continuing collection of these annual congress proceedings. [R: BL, 1 Oct 88, p. 217; JAL, July 88, p. 176; JAL, Nov 88, pp. 306, 308; LJ, 15 June 88, p. 44]

Lorna K. Rees-Potter

8.   **Lines of Thought: Selected Papers of Maurice B. Line.** L. J. Anthony, ed. London, Clive Bingley/Library Association; distr., Chicago, American Library Association, 1988. 338p. bibliog. index. $50.00. ISBN 0-85157-417-3.

Maurice B. Line is well-known in the world of librarianship in the United Kingdom. During the course of his long career, he served in various positions including Director General for Science, Technology and Industry in the British Library and Deputy Director of Aslib. A prolific author, he wrote over two hundred articles during the past thirty years on most aspects of librarianship. His writings have always been noted for their practical problem solving and their tireless revelation of new problems facing librarianship. Line is extremely conscious of user needs and wants all librarians to be the same way. This collection consists of what the editor considers to be the thirty best of Line's articles. For U.S. readers, this collection of essays will be particularly helpful since many of the articles were originally published in publications not easily available in the United States.

The earliest writings in the collection appeared originally in the mid-1960s although most of the essays come from the late 1970s and 1980s. All of the essays are divided into seven sections: problems of cataloging and classification, user needs, academic libraries, national libraries, document delivery and lending, issues of information availability, and patterns in publishing (particularly electronic). Although the setting of Line's writings is British, he discusses many issues that are relevant to U.S. readers. Furthermore, he does it in a style that is clear and readable as well as often being humorous. Students, teachers, and practitioners of librarianship will all find many essays worth reading in this collection.   Ronald H. Fritze

Festschriften

9. Woodsworth, Anne, and Barbara von Wahlde, eds. **Leadership for Research Libraries: A Festschrift for Robert M. Hayes.** Metuchen, N.J., Scarecrow, 1988. 255p. index. $25.00. LC 88-6634. ISBN 0-8108-2129-X.

This festschrift was prepared to acknowledge the contributions and accomplishments of Robert M. Hayes, who, in 1988, relinquished his administrative portfolio as dean of the Graduate School of Library and Information Science at the University of California, Los Angeles. The editors and nine of the ten authors are drawn from the alumni of the Senior Fellows program sponsored by the Council on Library Resources and shaped by Hayes at UCLA. The program, which is ongoing, is intended to help meet the need for exceptional leadership. In the preface to this volume Warren J. Haas draws attention to the "powerful respect" the alumni have for Hayes. It is unfortunate that the contribution by Dorothy Anderson, Director of the Senior Fellows program, is not the lead piece. She pays tribute to Hayes and describes his outstanding accomplishments as pioneer, scholar, educator, and administrator. The nine other essays in the order of their appearance are "Reexamining the Literature," by Charles B. Lowry; "The Campus Context," by D. Kaye Gapen; "Changes in Library Organization," by Beverly P. Lynch; "Organizational Leadership," by Sheila D. Creth; "Development of Leadership Potential," by James F. Williams, II; "Roles of Schools of Library and Information Science," by June Lester, "Entrepreneurship and Risk Taking," by Keith M. Cottam; "Career Management for Leaders," by Ellen J. Hoffman; and "Organization and Association Leadership," by Dorothy Gregor. The essays vary in quality, both in content and readability. In general they provide a wide-ranging review of the literature on their selected topics, and as may be expected, overlap and gaps occur. A recurring theme is that there

is a lack of research on leadership in library and information science. The volume concludes with Anderson's tribute to Hayes, a bibliography of his publications, a list of the Senior Fellows, 1982-1987, and an index. This volume should help to stimulate thought about and research into leadership needs, especially in research libraries. [R: JAL, Nov 88, p. 319]

Helen Howard

Philosophy and Theory

10. Bromley, David W., and Angela M. Allott, eds. **British Librarianship and Information Work 1981-1985. Volume One: General Libraries and the Profession.** London, Library Association; distr., Chicago, American Library Association, 1988. 363p. index. $80.00. ISBN 0-85365-557-X.

11. Bromley, David W., and Angela M. Allott, eds. **British Librarianship and Information Work 1981-1985. Volume Two: Special Libraries, Materials and Processes.** London, Library Association; distr., Chicago, American Library Association, 1988. 358p. index. $80.00. ISBN 0-85365-538-3.

These volumes are a continuation of a series on British librarianship that began some fifty years ago and has been issued every five years. The first volume focuses on general libraries (national, university, and government) and the library information profession; the second, on specific types of libraries (art, health sciences, map, music, etc.) and library processes (cataloging, preservation, and technology). Each volume contains twenty-two essays covering a full range of topics such as library management, the full gamut of types of libraries, library education, the book trade, staffing, processing, automation, abstracting and indexing, preservation, and access.

The editors of this work make no attempt to avoid the duplication that quite naturally results when forty-four authors write on overlapping topics. If anything, this work is enhanced by the differing treatments of similar topics. A good index (primarily subject) provides cross-references between essays. (The index applies only to essays within that particular volume. There is no one index for both volumes.) A list of acronyms helps sort out the "alphabet soup" of British librarianship. As one who has trouble keeping the library acronyms of her own country sorted out, this reviewer is most grateful to the editors for this inclusion.

As the library world gets smaller as a result of computer networking, a better understanding of library activities in a variety of countries becomes more important. This work provides an excellent overview of the politics, economics, and priorities that drive the library profession in the British Isles which, in many cases, are not that different from those in the United States. Because of the growing interrelationship of all phases of library and information science, the purchase of both volumes is recommended. [R: LAR, 16 May 88, p. 294; RLR, Aug 88, pp. 191-92]   Marjorie E. Bloss

12.   Bundy, Mary Lee, and Frederick J. Stielow, eds. **Activism in American Librarianship, 1962-1973.** Westport, Conn., Greenwood Press, 1987. 207p. illus. bibliog. index. (Contributions in Librarianship and Information Science, No. 58). $37.95. LC 87-236. ISBN 0-313-24602-5.

The 1960s and early 1970s were characterized by public awareness of individual and group rights and by increased social activism on the part of many professions and established institutions. The roles which librarians, library educators, and the American Library Association (ALA) played during this period have been published previously in library journals. In this collection of fifteen essays, such prominent librarians/educators as E. J. Josey, Major Owens, Faye Blake, and Mary Lee Bundy describe how the era's social movements influenced librarianship and different library institutions.

The book is divided into four sections. Part 1, devoted to movements, relates the civil rights, women's rights, Vietnam War, and intellectual freedom issues to the practice of librarianship. Part 2 discusses the institutional responses of academic and public libraries, library science schools, and *Library Journal* to these movements. Part 3, on groups and programs, describes the first four years of the Black Caucus in ALA, the Congress for Change, library outreach programs, development of Hispanic library programs, and the experiences of blacks in predominantly white library schools. Part 4 concludes with a photographic montage of the sixties and an essay that analyzes the impact of the era on the library profession. Seven appendices furnish reprints of important documents and resolutions regarding the events discussed in the essays.

Most of the contributors to this collection were participants in the events they describe. Their recollections of the issues and problems they encountered add a valuable historical dimension to the work. Coverage of the era is surprisingly balanced even though the authors were not confined to specific topics. While there is some overlap in presenting certain issues (e.g., *LJ* editor Eric Moon's publications are discussed

in two separate sections), the book has a unity that succeeds in reconstructing the era.

The essays are almost entirely descriptive. A deeper analysis of the period and its impact on the profession would have been more helpful. However, library educators, students, and sociologists who wish to study a profession's response to such turbulent times will find this collection an excellent resource. [R: JAL, May 88, pp. 110-11; WLB, Apr 88, p. 85]

Kathleen W. Craver

13.   Hall, David D., and John B. Hench, eds. **Needs and Opportunities in the History of the Book: America, 1639-1876.** Worcester, Mass., American Antiquarian Society; distr., Charlottesville, Va., University Press of Virginia, 1987. 281p. $29.95. LC 86-28694. ISBN 0-912296-87-9.

This is one of the firstfruits of the American Antiquarian Society's (AAS) effort to do for "the book in America" what European scholars (with some notable assistance from U.S. scholars) have done for "the book in Europe": that is, to establish the history of the book in the United States as a central field of study. To this purpose the AAS, in 1983, formally launched its "Program of the History of the Book in American Culture" (actually the history of print in U.S. culture from the beginning to 1876). In due course, in November 1984, United States and (a few) European scholars convened at a conference on the needs and opportunities in the history of the book in U.S. culture. Five of the delivered papers, plus a report on the conference comprise the present volume.

The conference and this attendant volume are only a part of the Society's ambitious program. To enumerate, the program has established a number of research scholarships; went on to inaugurate, in 1983, the annual James Russell Wiggins Lecture in the History of the Book; started a free newsletter entitled *The Book*; and for the early 1990s envisions a multivolume, collaborative history of the book in U.S. culture. The present volume with its substantive, well-researched essays is a welcome contribution to the subject and is a foretaste of splendid things to come.

David Rosenbaum

14.   Riggs, Donald E., and Gordon A. Sabine. **Libraries in the '90s: What the Leaders Expect.** Phoenix, Ariz., Oryx Press, 1988. 197p. illus. index. $24.95pa. LC 88-20521. ISBN 0-89774-532-9.

Speculation about the emerging challenges and opportunities of libraries in the 1990s is brought into focus by twenty-five library leaders drawn from all areas of the profession. Their responses to interview questions provided the conversational dialog transcribed for this volume. Library leaders, selected by Riggs and interviewed by Sabine, include William Asp, Patricia Berger, Margaret Chisholm, Richard Dougherty, Kathleen Heim, Frederick Kilgour, Major R. Owens, William Summers, Robert Wedgeworth, and William J. Welsh. Sixteen chapters furnish commentary on such topics as automation, censorship, library education, commercial competition, and leadership. Congressman Owens, Deputy Librarian of Congress Welsh, and OCLC's Kilgour rate chapters of their own. The future as divined by these leaders is generally a linear extension of the present. Full text retrieval, dial access, telefacsimile, cable television, and community information directories should become more cost efficient and widely adopted by the end of the 1990s. Future professional demands will require brighter library school students and more intensive exposure to the new technologies. Three stimulating ideas, not fully developed, are the call for family learning centers by Owens, the proposal for a leadership institute by Dougherty, and the concept of "transformative leadership" outlined by Riggs.

Practitioners, library educators, and students will benefit from reading this glimpse into the next decade. [R: JAL, Nov 88, p. 312]

Arthur P. Young

15.   Winter, Michael F. **The Culture and Control of Expertise: Toward a Sociological Understanding of Librarianship.** Westport, Conn., Greenwood Press, 1988. 154p. bibliog. index. (Contributions in Librarianship and Information Science, No. 61). $37.95. LC 88-174. ISBN 0-313-25537-7.

Winter shows how the sociological study of professionals and occupations can be used to understand librarianship. He ultimately aims to change the way librarians think about their work, and indirectly, the way they work. This study expands and develops an earlier paper, "The Professionalization of Librarianship" (Graduate School of Library and Information Science, University of Illinois, 1983). In the first chapter Winter reviews the social theory of industrial society, the study of professionals and occupations, and the nature and development of librarianship. He then examines three major theories of the sociology of professions: the trait theory, the functional theory, and the occupational control approach. Subsequently he explains the development of the control theory as a response to the perceived inadequacy of the

trait and functional approaches, and then applies the first to librarianship. The control model can be broken into three parts: collegial control, client control, and mediated control (a hybrid in which a third element qualifies the relationship between providers and users of professional services). Winter provides a critical review of the occupation/profession debate as applied to librarianship and suggests there is something to be learned from each of the three models. He presents a composite model where the main areas of convergence are the schools, the associations, and their relationships in the process of providing professional services. The author concludes with suggestions for research on librarianship as an occupation and a bibliographic essay for those who wish to pursue the research and practitioner literature. The author deftly leads the reader to the point of viewing collegial control as a basic problem in all professional occupations, and he shows the way to looking at professional work in the larger context of all kinds of work. [R: JAL, Nov 88, p. 313; WLB, Nov 88, p. 109]

Helen Howard

Reference Works

ABBREVIATIONS AND ACRONYMS

16.   Sawoniak, Henryk, and Maria Witt. **New International Dictionary of Acronyms in Library and Information Science and Related Fields.** Munich, New York, K. G. Saur, 1988. 449p. $88.00. ISBN 3-598-10697-1.

In an age when acronyms are an integral part of language, any 449-page dictionary, international in scope, will be of value to members of a designated profession. This dictionary lists acronyms used in library and information science and related fields of publishing, printing, archive management, journalism, reprography, and some in computer science and management. It includes, in addition to the well-known international languages, the less popular languages of Central and Eastern Europe, Asia, Africa, and Latin America. This new edition includes 28,500 entries, compared to 12,700 in 1976.

It is difficult to understand the logic used in the selection of related fields and terms, as judged by the U.S. listings checked. Another discrepancy noted was the lack of criteria for inclusion of universities (e.g., four of the nine University of California campuses are included and five omitted, as is the University of Southern California). The California state universities are excluded, yet Colorado and Ohio state universities are included. Errors were detected (e.g., American Association of Law Libraries, AALL, is listed as ALL).

Since library acronyms are included in the three-volume twelfth edition of *Acronyms, Initialisms & Abbreviations* (see *ARBA* 88, entry 1), which lists 420,000 entries, most general reference collections would be better served by purchasing one comprehensive, up-to-date source rather than acquiring marginal, specialized resources. [R: RLR, Nov 88, p. 333]

Helen Carol Bennett

BIBLIOGRAPHIES

17. **Current Research for the Information Profession 1987/88.** Pirkko Elliott, ed. London, Library Association; distr., Chicago, American Library Association, 1988. 1v. (various paging). index. $100.00. ISBN 0-85365-838-2; ISSN 0268-7372.

The 1987/88 edition is a hardcover duplicate of the cumulative fourth issue of the journal, *Current Research in Library & Information Science* (London, Library Association, 1983-). The organization is the same—"a main sequence of project entries arranged by the CRG (Classification Research Group) classification scheme like its big sister *LISA*, a name index, and a subject index" (p. a1). The data found in the main entries vary slightly but normally include the subject(s) (based on the CRG scheme), title, research worker(s), project timeline, funding source and amount, an abstract, and a source from whom to request additional information. *Research* is broadly defined to include almost any type of investigation; the number of entries is dependent upon submission of a project entry form by the researcher(s); and although international, the majority of submissions come from the United States, the United Kingdom, Canada, Australia, and West Germany. Research projects often require more than one year to complete and the current editor notes in the introduction that "approximately 350 new projects" are among the 1,271 entries, which means that more than 900 research projects are included from earlier volumes.

One interesting addition to this volume is a preface titled "Communicating Research in the Information Profession: An Essay" by Jane B. Robbins, professor and director of the School of Library and Information Studies, University of Wisconsin at Madison. The essay is one that should be read by newcomers to the profession or those who have little experience with research in that it articulates barriers, existing publishing practices, and the gap between the practitioner and the researcher. Her conclusion, that "the

information field needs to develop a vigorous and rigorous research community, peopled with *both* those who consider themselves primarily researchers and primarily practitioners" (p. a13), is certainly valid but the essay seems out-of-place in a volume used primarily by researchers or practitioners who are already convinced of that fact.

Although compilations of research in progress in our profession are needed, the publication of this particular series raises some questions. As already noted, it is largely a duplicate of the fourth issue of the journal (although the journal cumulation contains, for some reason, one more item than the published volume). The material is also retrievable through DIALOG. Subscribers to the published journal, for approximately twice the cost, can receive the same coverage without paying for this volume. Conversely, for one-half the cost, the purchaser would receive information on new projects several months to a year after they had been listed in the journal issues. In addition, the journal includes a more comprehensive explanation of the classification scheme, a section on sub-doctoral academic work (e.g., theses done at the master's level); a "List of Abbreviations and Acronyms Commonly Used in Current Research"; and an editor's summary analysis or "flavour" of each issue's new projects.

Despite the concerns noted as well as the sporadic, inconsistent, and individually motivated submission of items, the volume does offer a mechanism by which to identify new and on-going library and information research and the researchers involved in several different countries. The latest volume includes a listing by country in the name index to facilitate geographical association as well as by researcher and subject. Each volume had seen an enhancement of its coverage and the publication is readable and easily accessed.

Laurel Grotzinger

18. Swidan, Eleanor A. **Reference Sources: A Brief Guide.** 9th ed. Baltimore, Md., Enoch Pratt Free Library, 1988. 175p. index. $7.95pa. ISBN 0-910556-26-1.

In 1938, the Enoch Pratt Free Library of Baltimore, Maryland, issued *Guide to Reference Books*. Over the past fifty years, the publication has grown steadily in size and value. This latest update, as before, covers general reference books, the humanities, sciences, and social sciences. Now in its ninth edition, it includes, for the first time, computer-readable databases and resources in microform, necessitating a change in title from *Reference Books* to *Reference Sources*. Its stated purpose, however, remains the same: "to help the reader or library user who is bewildered by the staggering array of reference works that confront him on the shelves of the library."

As its title indicates, this guide is meant to be suggestive rather than complete. Part 1, "Reference Sources General in Scope," lists encyclopedias, almanacs, indexes, dictionaries, maps, bibliographies, and government publications. Part 2, "Reference Sources in Special Subjects," is devoted to interdisciplinary groupings in the humanities, sciences, and social sciences, which are appropriately subsumed and subdivided. Part 3 provides a succinct introduction to database research and relates to both parts 1 and 2. As in the past, inclusion is a commendation, and reference materials in medicine, law, and genealogy have been excluded.

To all libraries, public, university, or specialized, that have gotten good use out of previous editions of this valuable reference tool, this latest update can be warmly recommended. [R: JAL, Nov 88, pp. 331-32; RBB, 15 Nov 88, p. 548; WLB, Nov 88, pp. 126-27]

G. A. Cevasco

DICTIONARIES AND ENCYCLOPEDIAS

19. **Encyclopedia of Library and Information Science. Volume 42, Supplement 7.** Allen Kent, ed. New York, Marcel Dekker, 1987. 428p. illus. $65.00. LC 68-31232. ISBN 0-8247-2042-3.

20. **Encyclopedia of Library and Information Science. Volume 43, Supplement 8.** Allen Kent, ed. New York, Marcel Dekker, 1988. 395p. illus. $65.00. LC 68-31232. ISBN 0-8247-2043-1.

The main set as well as several supplements to the *Encyclopedia of Library and Information Science* have been reviewed in *ARBA* as well as *Library and Information Science Annual.* For example, supplements 39, 40, and 41 were reviewed in *Library and Information Science Annual 1987* (see entries 11-13). In that review it is indicated that among other things, the purpose of the supplements is "to update articles in the main set; to add new articles on topics currently important in the field; to include recently deceased prominent librarians; and, finally, to include articles originally commissioned for the main set but not received in time for inclusion." The main set and first two volumes were reviewed in *Library Science Annual 1985* (see entries 6-9). That review incorporated references to previous reviews of individual volumes and also reviewed early supplements.

The two present supplements include a number of interesting articles. Volume 42

contains "Libraries in Denmark," by Preben Kierkegaard and Hans Lemming, and "The United Nations Bibliographic Information," by Nathalie Dusoulier and S. Stein. Articles in volume 43 include "Congressional Research Services," by Robert Lee Chartrand and Sandra N. Milevski; "Copyright and the Information Professionals," by William Z. Nasri; "Information Resource Management," by Eileen M. Trauth; and "Machine-Readable Cataloging (MARC): 1986," by Henriette D. Avram. The articles are thorough and well documented, and the contributors are recognized authorities in their respective fields.

As mentioned in previous reviews, the impact of technology on the field of library science in recent years has been significant, and it is hoped that once the editor and his staff complete the supplements, a new edition of the encyclopedia will be produced.

Bohdan S. Wynar

21. **General Reference Books for Adults: Authoritative Evaluations of Encyclopedias, Atlases, and Dictionaries.** Marion Sader, ed. New York, R. R. Bowker, 1988. 614p. illus. maps. bibliog. index. (Bowker Buying Guide Series). $69.95. LC 88-10054. ISBN 0-8352-2393-0.

Designed as a buying guide for both librarians and lay people, this work contains lengthy comparative evaluations of general reference sources appropriate for adults. (Similar sources for children and young adults are covered in the first volume in Bowker's Buying Guide Series, *Reference Books for Young Readers* [R. R. Bowker, 1988].) The more than 215 titles reviewed include online and CD-ROM products as well as print materials that were readily available in the United States as of April 1988.

According to the editor, *General Reference Books for Adults* is intended to provide "authoritative, comprehensive and objective" reviews of general encyclopedias, atlases, and dictionaries and to "apply consistent standards and criteria in evaluating each work" (p. xiii). To achieve this goal, the evaluations were prepared by a team of librarians and subject specialists, screened by consultants, and verified and revised by editorial staff. Since the final reviews are truly a collaborative effort, they are unsigned.

A lengthy introductory section includes a history of general reference books and outlines factors to consider in choosing reference materials. In addition, it contains a report of a survey in which librarians rated the usefulness of specific reference sources and also provides comparative charts containing statistical data (such as number of pages, number of entries, number of illustrations, and price) on all titles reviewed.

Reviews are organized into four sections: encyclopedias, world atlases, dictionaries and word books, and large-print reference sources. The categories for encyclopedias and atlases are then arranged alphabetically by the titles being reviewed, while the section on dictionaries is subdivided by specific type (e.g., general, etymological, synonym, and antonym). Accompanying each of the first three sections is an introductory essay that provides tips on what to look for in that particular type of reference source and a glossary of specialized terms frequently used in describing such works. In addition, each essay gives an overview of the format followed by all reviews in that section and explains the criteria considered in evaluating each feature. For example, evaluations of atlases are divided into ten categories, including "geographical balance," "scale and projections," and "currency." This consistent structure among reviews of the same type of source facilitates the comparison of specific features.

Reviews vary in length, depending on the type of source being evaluated. For example, reviews of major encyclopedias are generally at least eight pages long, while those of atlases average one and one-half to two pages. A number of reviews include facsimile pages and sample entries, and encyclopedia evaluations provide excerpts from other reviews. Although the reviews generally reflect the editor's concern for consistency and objectivity, in some instances they do not provide the currency necessary in a work of this type. For example, the evaluation of the *Oxford English Dictionary* fails to mention that a totally revised edition incorporating the supplements will be available early in 1989. Moreover, the review of *World Book* indicates that it is based on the 1987 edition, but the statistics cited, the facsimile page, and the format section all refer to the 1988 edition. Since the compilers obviously had access to information regarding the 1988 edition, it is somewhat surprising that the review does not note that the 1988 edition is the most extensive revision of *World Book* in over twenty-five years.

A bibliography near the end of the volume cites additional sources that review general reference materials. In several instances this list does not include the most recent edition of a work. For example, Kenneth Kister's 1981 *Encyclopedia Buying Guide* (see *ARBA* 82, entry 46) is cited rather than his *Best Encyclopedias* (see *ARBA* 87, entry 54). The well-conceived, comprehensive index includes not only the titles of works reviewed (which are distinguished by small capital letters) but also titles of other works referred to within the reviews as well as references to compilers, editors, publishers, and topics.

Librarians who have found Kenneth Kister's buying guides to encyclopedias, atlases, and dictionaries useful will welcome this new source for detailed, comparative reviews of basic reference sources. It should be a valuable selection aid in libraries that serve high school students or adults, particularly where budgetary constraints require stringent acquisition policies. It is also an excellent source for individuals trying to make wise decisions about purchasing reference titles for their home libraries. *General Reference Books for Adults* has the potential to become a standard selection tool if Bowker establishes a schedule of regular and frequent revisions. [R: LJ, Dec 88, p. 94; WLB, Nov 88, pp. 126-27]   Marie Ellis

DIRECTORIES

22. **American Library Directory 1988-89.** 41st ed. New York, R. R. Bowker, 1988. 2v. index. $164.95/set. LC 23-3581. ISBN 0-8352-2462-7; ISSN 0065-910X.

Pertinent factual information on over thirty-four thousand U.S. and Canadian libraries is included in this two-volume biennial edition. Almost every type of library is covered; however, the directory still lacks a listing of school libraries. Entries are comparable to previous editions and provide not only addresses and personnel information, but collection size, expenditures, and a wide variety of other information about the library. Arrangement is by state or province and then alphabetical by city. An index by library name is provided. Information is supplied by the libraries listed.

Special sections give added value to the volumes. Included are lists of networks, library schools (not just ALA accredited), libraries of the handicapped, state libraries, Army libraries, and USIA centers.

Spinoff publications include the entire database available on DIALOG and access to mailing labels from the publisher. Thus, libraries who cannot afford the $165.00 price can access the information contained through electronic means.

ALD is an indispensable and current tool for all who need information about libraries, including library professionals, publishers, and the general public who want to learn about libraries available not only in their local area, but in areas where they will be traveling.

David V. Loertscher

23.   **Directory of Library & Information Professionals.** Woodbridge, Conn., with American Library Association by Research Publications, 1988. 2v. index. $345.00/set. ISBN 0-89235-125-X; ISSN 0894-7031.

This directory was designed by its publisher in cooperation with ALA to replace *Who's Who in Library and Information Services* (1982). The idea was to publish a work that would be not only more comprehensive than its predecessor, but also machine-readable on CD-ROM. Computerization also provided many different access points to the professionals other than by name. The arrangement of volume 1 is alphabetical by the person's name. Volume 2 provides indexes to names by specialty, employer, consulting expertise, and geographical area.

Information was gathered by massive mailings to the professionals of twenty library and information societies. Self-reports included detailed information on education and positions but restricted prolific writers to three publications of interest. A single followup mailing and some telephone solicitation was done to include as many persons as possible. Individual listings were edited by the publisher but were not returned to respondents for proofreading.

The effort to provide a wider listing of professionals is a great one. However, this publication is full of errors and lacks the comprehensive coverage originally intended by its designers. Its cost to produce both in-print and CD-ROM formats is evident from the price, which puts it out of range of most libraries and library professionals in the country. One would almost wish that the alphabetical access to persons in volume 1 had been published as a separate publication at less than half the price with access by other database fields being limited to an online search or to the CD-ROM application alone. Users of volume 2 will quickly come to the conclusion that access by computer and self-reporting of a single item such as library specialty leads to the most confusing maze of terminology for the same specialty. For example, there are at least fifty different titles which school librarians gave themselves, and the computer generates them as reported. Is computer access to a hodge-podge of information of value? This publication is a good example of what computerization is doing to publishing. Quality standards and information access needs should be evaluated before we drown the world in a morass of information from which we may never recover.

Conclusion? If the person you are looking for responded to the questionnaire, the source is valuable, but don't expect miracles. [R: Choice, Nov 88, p. 458; JAL, May 88, p. 111; LJ, 1 May 88, p. 64; RBB, 1 Apr 88, p. 1319; WLB, Mar 88, pp. 96-97; WLB, June 88, p. 124]

David V. Loertscher

24.   **Grants for Libraries and Information Services: Covers Grants to Nonprofit Organizations in the U.S. and Abroad....** New York, Foundation Center, 1988. 64p. index. $40.00pa. ISBN 0-87954-278-0.

This publication covers grants to nonprofit organizations in the United States and overseas: to public, academic, and special libraries; and to archives and information centers for construction, operations, acquisitions, computerization, and education. It is a single source of information relating to grants for all types of libraries making it a unique document. The arrangement begins with an introduction to grant writing followed by recipient, geographic, and subject indexes, and a listing of foundations.

This is a commendable resource for grant writers and development officers as well as library administrators. The only obvious drawback is the text's tiny print which makes reading difficult. Otherwise, it is a valuable document that is highly recommended to all libraries and information centers.   Felix Eme Unaeze

25.   Looney, Jim, and Colleen Smith, comps. **FOCUS: The Directory of Library Services in British Columbia.** 4th ed. Vancouver, B.C., British Columbia Library Association, 1987. 191p. index. $20.00 looseleaf with binder.

This directory is a couple of years overdue, but its quality makes it well worth the wait. To begin with, it is commendably comprehensive, giving listings not only for conventional libraries but also for such organizations as archives, associations and "reading centres." The coverage is particularly good for those notoriously hard to find out about libraries maintained by law firms, companies, and small societies; this directory's net seems to have caught all the fish around.

The editors have also included a number of very useful features not usually found in a regional directory. Detailed information is given for each branch as well as for the parent institution as a whole. The descriptions of collections give not only number of volumes but also indication of nonbook materials in twenty-seven categories. A geographical index provides access by locality (the main listing being alphabetical by official title), and an index by library type enables one to find, say, all the community college libraries in one grouping. ENVOY (the TransCanada electronic messaging system) and FAX numbers are supplied in addition to the usual telephone numbers and postal addresses. The personnel data indicate whether the staff members are professional, support persons, or technicians and show how many of each there are, down to fractions of FTE. And, most helpful for the forgetful, an index of personal names enables you to find out where that person you met at a conference is working.

All this adds up to a remarkable amount of information in one source. Since this information is also presented accurately (no mistakes discovered) in legible and convenient format and at reasonable cost, FOCUS is by every standard a considerable achievement of its kind. Other regional library directories, please imitate! Samuel Rothstein

26. **World Guide to Libraries. Internationales Bibliotheks-Handbuch.** 8th ed. Munich, New York, K. G. Saur, 1987. 1279p. index. (Handbook of International Documentation and Information, Vol. 8). $220.00. ISBN 3-598-20536-8; ISSN 0000-0221.

This work contains a staggering 37,784 current library entries in 167 countries, an increase of 4,000 entries since the seventh edition (3,000 of which are in the United States). Criteria are that special libraries have holdings of five thousand volumes and general libraries thirty thousand volumes; some Third World countries are excepted.

The directory is arranged in order by continent, country, type of library, then city. A typical entry provides data on the size, specialization and accessibility of each library, including library name in the appropriate language and in English, mailing and telegraph addresses, telephone and telex numbers (no telefax), data of founding, name of director, main departments, special collections, statistics on holdings, participation in data networks and/or interlibrary loan programs, and reference number. There is an alphabetical index by library name (unfortunately, by complete name so that, for example, the John G. Shedd Aquarium Library is found under "John" instead of "Shedd"), but no subject index.

Specific personnel information may already be outdated in many cases since the editorial deadline was 5 August 1987, but the directory is valuable in identifying or verifying institutions, especially those outside of the United States. It also has great potential for library trivia, such as that the national library of Kiribati is located in Tarawa and has thirty-five thousand volumes. However, the price will cause many libraries to hesitate before purchasing it. [R: RLR, Nov 88, pp. 334-35] Jay Schafer

HANDBOOKS AND YEARBOOKS

27. **ALA Handbook of Organization 1987/1988 and Membership Directory.** Chicago, American Library Association, 1987. 905p. $10.00pa. LC 80-649998. ISBN 0-8389-5706-4; ISSN 0273-4605.

The 1987/1988 handbook is identical in format to those of previous years. It serves the dual purpose of being an organizational manual and a membership directory. It is arranged in such a way that if size should ever dictate doing so, two separate volumes could easily be produced. The handbook, appendices, and indexes are in the first section of the book. Included in the handbook are the mission statements of the American Library Association and its various components, with names and business addresses of officials. The constitution and ALA policy manual are included in their entirety, as are lists of periodicals published by the association and awards given in 1988. The appendices provide a variety of useful information, including a calendar of events with location and dates of meetings of ALA and other library associations, and membership application forms with the current dues structure.

The index to the membership directory follows the general index. This places it in front of the directory, but causes no apparent difficulty in use. The 1987/1988 membership directory uses slightly larger print than did the 1986/1987 membership directory. The result is a volume which is approximately 15 percent longer in pages, but is definitely easier to read. There is an entry for each of the more than forty thousand personal members of the association. There are few questions about the American Library Association that one could ask which could not be answered by use of this handbook. Robert M. Ballard

28. **The ALA Yearbook of Library and Information Services: A Review of Library Events 1987. Volume 13 (1988).** Roger H. Parent and Helen K. Wright, eds. Chicago, American Library Association, 1988. 419p. illus. index. $80.00. ISBN 0-8389-0489-0; ISSN 0740-042X.

Continuing the series begun in 1976, this year's volume follows very closely the format of recent years: a few feature articles, a number of special reports, a review of the year's library events, and reports from the fifty states. All of this is published in a large volume, attractively designed, with many illustrations. One of the two feature articles, "Libraries and Adult Literacy," is a competent introduction to the subject; the other, "Leadership and the Information Professions," is provocative, but too brief. The fifteen special reports, all one or two pages in length, are on a wide variety of topics: libraries and the AIDS crisis, The Center for the Book's first decade, nontax sources of revenue for public libraries, ACRL Planning Project for Historically Black College and University Libraries, etc. The 130 items that comprise the "Review of Library Events 1987" consist of reports of activities of library and library-related organizations and groups, and topical reports on a range of subjects such as information technology, library press, copyright, library education, and sound recordings—very useful summaries of recent developments. The fifty state reports provide some basic information about each state library association plus a narrative report on library news and activities in the state. There is a name and subject index, and finally a cumulative index to *ALA Yearbook* features (1976-1988). This last index is welcome, but even more welcome would have been the inclusion in that index of the special reports. This reviewer finds those almost always interesting, and often important professional reading. The same is true of many of the items in the review of library events. All libraries should have the *ALA Yearbook*, and make it easily available to staff members, both for reference purposes and for professional reading.

Evan Ira Farber

29.   Kister, Kenneth F. **Kister's Concise Guide to Best Encyclopedias.** Phoenix, Ariz., Oryx Press, 1988. 108p. index. $15.00pa. LC 88-24044. ISBN 0-89774-484-5.

For some reason Kister is in competition with himself. Oryx Press has already published his *Best Encyclopedias* in full panoply (see *ARBA* 87, entry 54). So why a concise edition? Kister says "the guide is designed especially for busy people in search of a quick but authoritative opinion about the many titles available." Then he reduces the number of titles covered in full to thirty-three. For those titles he presents the "facts" followed by an "evaluation." Many of the facts spliced together in complete sentences appear earlier in a two-page comparison chart. Other needless repetition occurs. The *Kussmaul Encyclopedia* entry is a good example; in the space of one and one-half pages the reader is told three times that the encyclopedia is an electronic database, part of the Delphi Information System produced by General Videotex Corporation, and another three times that it is based on the print *Cadillac Modern Encyclopedia*. When comparing encyclopedias Kister repeats the same numerical facts he gives in the aforementioned comparison chart. This makes for tedious reading. Kister also commits one of

the cardinal sins of evaluation; he admonishes the reader that the *Barron's Student's Concise Encyclopedia* "contains some glaring omissions" in the index without naming any of them. After the thirty-three main entries there is an annotated list of some 187 recommended specialized encyclopedias; the guide ends with a short section on recently discontinued or out-of-print works. Purchase the complete 1986 edition and continue to wonder why this one was published. [R: RBB, 15 Dec 88, p. 687]

Bill Bailey

30.   **Library and Information Science Annual 1988. Volume 4.** Bohdan S. Wynar, Ann E. Prentice, and Anna Grace Patterson, eds. Englewood, Colo., Libraries Unlimited, 1988. 325p. index. $37.50. ISBN 0-87287-683-7; ISSN 8755-2108.

Volume 4 of *Library and Information Science Annual*, continuing the basic format of the first three volumes, is divided into four main sections: (1) essays, (2) reviews of books, (3) reviews of periodicals, and (4) abstracts of library science dissertations. The editors have broadened their original objectives by reviewing all English-language (formerly selected) books in library science published in the United States and by extending coverage of Canadian, British, and Australian imprints. The size of the volume has increased considerably, particularly in the book review section, which has doubled from 253 reviews (volume 1) to 549 (volume 4).

By all objective standards *LISCA* is an excellent reference source. It is physically attractive, has sturdy binding, good quality paper, large boldface type, excellent format and arrangement, and separate author/title and subject indexes. A previous reviewer noted a discrepancy in style and quality among the 180 reviewers and suggested that more editing is needed. While this may be true, one could also argue that because the reviews are not "packaged" by professional reviewers but instead are written by librarians and educators with expertise in the subject, the reviews reflect the profession's diversity and therefore appeal to an equally diverse audience, and that stylistic variation makes the reviews more interesting to read. Reviewers are given guidelines and suggested format, but the style is their own. This reviewer has not detected a single bibliographical nor typographical error.

While some of the material in *LISCA* can be located in other sources, this sturdy, one-volume annual compilation of state-of-the-art essays, book and periodical reviews, and abstracts of library science dissertations is an invaluable addition to the literature of our field. [R: LJ, 15 Nov 88, p. 52]

Helen Carol Bennett

31. **Purchasing an En-cy-clo-pe-dia: 12 Points to Consider.** 2d ed. By the Editorial Board of *Reference Books Bulletin*. Chicago, American Library Association, 1988. 40p. $4.95 pa. LC 88-2187. ISBN 0-8389-3351-3.

Except for the twelve points, this work is an almost exact copy of the reviews of the ten major multivolume encyclopedias from the 1 November 1987 "Reference Books Bulletin" section of *Booklist*. The introduction appears to be addressed to parents who wish to buy an encyclopedia for their children, indicating the age level as the first factor to consider. The other points are authority, arrangement, subject coverage, objectivity, recency, quality, style, bibliographies, illustrations, physical format, and special attributes. Each receives a one- or two-paragraph discussion. Yearbooks, alternative formats such as CD-ROM, and reviews are also discussed briefly.

The guide provides clear, brief reviews, touching on the history of the encyclopedia, the type, number and length of entries, the amount of revision, the illustrations, the index, currency, and the formats available. Kenneth Kister's guide to *Best Encyclopedias* (see *ARBA* 87, entry 54) reviews all of the encyclopedias in the ALA guide plus 42 more general encyclopedias and around 450 specialized encyclopedias. The general encyclopedia reviews it contains are longer—over seven pages for *World Book* compared to two pages in this guide, and ten pages for *The New Encyclopaedia Britannica* compared to three in ALA's guide. *Best Encyclopedias* spends more time on the history of an encyclopedia, provides purchasing information, and gives more examples in the evaluation portion of the review.

Libraries subscribing to *Booklist* or owning Kister's guide will not need the ALA guide for their own selection purposes. Libraries wishing a publication easy to check out to or sell to parents, or small libraries without access to other sources will find the low cost of this authoritative guide most appealing. [R: VOYA, Dec 88, p. 257]

Betty Jo Buckingham

32. Wygant, Alice Chambers, and O. W. Markley. **Information and the Future: A Handbook of Sources and Strategies.** Westport, Conn., Greenwood Press, 1988. 189p. bibliog. index. $37.95. LC 87-36063. ISBN 0-313-24813-3.

Naming and packaging are two important components of our late twentieth-century world. With *Information and the Future* we have an interesting example of the uses of both these trends. On the face of it, judging that is from the title and the introductory remarks, one might think that here was a revolutionary new (or at least markedly different) approach to information seeking. Instead, what we have for the most part is today's model clothed in tomorrow's terminology.

This book is basically a guide to using library and other information resources intelligently. This, in and of itself, is admirable. Anyone who works in a library, or indeed has ever needed to use a library, can testify to the need for well thought out, clearly articulated guides to the madness frequently encountered in the "ordered" world of libraries. Unfortunately, this book offers no more (and, to be honest, certainly no less) guidance, advice, strategic planning, etc., than countless other attempts to make the library intelligible to the user. The problem with this particular work is its pretentiousness.

Reviewed for what it is rather than what it purports to be, *Information and the Future* is a decent, if somewhat cumbersome, introduction to research strategies and sources. Designed to address a wide audience (ranging, according to the introductory chapter, from high school students to professional librarians), the book presents exactly the type of information one would (should) expect a book of this nature to present. The obvious statement sums up this work quite succinctly. Greenwood Press is charging almost $40.00 for information available elsewhere. The selections chosen as examples of guides to the literature, encyclopedias, and indexing and abstracting services are predictable. Perhaps the choices were dictated by the authors' efforts to keep to the letter, if not necessarily the spirit, of the title.

The one section that does stand out is part 3, "Applications." Here the authors present two conceptual tools designed to help researchers "learn about, forecast, and influence the process of social change on topics of importance" (p. 119). The two concepts, the "issue emergence cycle" and the "strategic intelligence cycle," are not so much discussed as drawn, presented in, to quote the text, "graphical illustrations." Some of this is fascinating, although two problems emerge. First, the brief introduction may serve to confuse rather than illuminate. And second, there is no clearly drawn connection between these highly theoretical constructs and the rather pedestrian tone of the earlier sections.

Ellen Broidy

INDEXES

33. Library Literature 1987: An Index to Library and Information Science. Cathy Rentschler and Mary M. Brereton, eds. Bronx, N.Y., H. W. Wilson, 1988. 655p. sold on service basis. LC 36-27468. ISSN 0024-2373.

Library Literature, a popular Wilson index, has been reviewed several times in *ARBA* (see *ARBA* 82, entry 155). The most recent review can be found in *Library Science Annual: Volume 1* (Libraries Unlimited, 1985). First published in 1936, this indexing service is well known to the library profession. The 1987 volume indexes 244 periodicals and includes coverage of books, pamphlets, films, filmstrips, microcards, microfilms, and library school theses dealing with library and information science. Monographic material in English is handled quite well, indexing 60 and 70 percent of books and pamphlets published in this country and Canada, respectively. Publications of Eastern Europe and other developing countries are not as well represented.

As noted in previous reviews, a time lag in indexing periodicals is evident, especially with regard to foreign titles. Nationally known periodicals published in the United States (*Library Journal, Wilson Library Bulletin*, etc.) have a time lapse of only one to two months. Regional publications and subject-oriented periodicals published in this country average around six months, and the time lapse for foreign periodicals is more significant at one to three years.

As in previous volumes, entries for book and nonbook materials are arranged in one alphabet by author and by specific subject heading.

A comprehensive, well-executed, and reliable indexing service, *Library Literature* is recommended to all institutions interested in the professional literature of library and information science.   Susan R. Penney

ACQUISITIONS

34. Approval Plans. By Clinton Howard. Washington, D.C., Association of Research Libraries, 1988. 124p. bibliog. (SPEC Kit, No. 141). $20.00pa.

This SPEC Kit on approval plans, based on a June 1987 survey, updates the 1982 survey data contained in SPEC Kit No. 83, *Approval Plans in ARL Libraries* (1982). It also includes, like the 1982 kit, source documents and internal memoranda from selected member institutions. The 1987 data cover points of continuity and consensus in the use of approval plans between 1982 and 1987, the diversity of ways in which librarians assess these plans, and the impact that the recent and rapid increases in the cost of library materials and automation are having on such plans.

The second part of the 1988 kit—source documents and internal memos—contains two examples (the University of Oregon and the University of Waterloo) of questions and criteria for evaluating vendors; five examples (Library of Congress, the University of North Carolina at Chapel Hill, Arizona State University, New York Public Library, and the University of Texas at Austin) of approval plan profiles, descriptions, and guidelines; and three examples (Arizona State University, Indiana University, and the University of Washington) of the processing and review of approval plans. The selected reading list, concluding this publication, lists six periodical and monographic items published from 1980 through 1987.

Beyond the obvious use by libraries having approval plans and those considering them, *Approval Plans* belongs in library/information science collection development collections. [R: JAL, July 88, p. 181]

    Wiley J. Williams

35. Broadbent, Lorna R., comp. Directory of Acquisitions Librarians in the United Kingdom and Republic of Ireland: With Notes on Computerised Acquisitions Systems. Loughborough, England, National Acquisitions Group, 1987. 1v. (unpaged). index. £20.00pa. ISBN 1-87026-901-2.

At first sight, this appears to be rather unpromising as a reference book. But that initial judgment is premature. It is really quite a handy directory of many of the libraries of the British Isles. The 750 entries were compiled from a questionnaire and are organized geographically under England, Scotland, Wales, Channel Island, Northern Ireland, and the Republic of Ireland. Each entry supplies the library's address, telephone and telex numbers, and the names and job titles of staff connected with acquisitions. Sometimes further information is provided concerning the number of volumes purchased annually by the library and if a computerized acquisitions system is being used and what it consists of. There are indexes to individual libraries and the computer systems, hardware, and software listed in the entries. This is not a standard public library or college library reference work, but it will be of great interest to the collections of library schools for use in the study of acquisitions, automation, and comparative librarianship. Publishers marketing directly to libraries in the British Isles might also find it highly useful for their collections.

Ronald H. Fritze

36. Hazen, Dan C., ed. **Latin American Masses and Minorities: Their Images and Realities. Papers of the Thirtieth Annual Meeting of the Seminar on the Acquisition of Latin American Library Materials....** Madison, Wis., SALALM Secretariat, 1987. 2v. illus. maps. $57.50pa./set. ISBN 0-917617-11-8.

Princeton played host to the thirtieth annual Seminar on the Acquisition of Latin American Library Materials in June 1985. Drawing heavily from Latin Americanists in the metropolitan New York area, the meeting focused on the broad theme "Images and Realities of Latin American Masses and Minorities." Participants were drawn from a wide range of disciplines in the humanities and social sciences. While these published proceedings do not exactly mirror the conference, they have been well organized and edited by Hazen, the librarian for Hispanic Collections at Berkeley.

The papers fall into five broad categories. Part 1, "Philosophical and Conceptual Dilemmas in Latin Americanist Scholarship," includes presentations on the roles of the media, individuals, and academics. Part 2, "Sample Inquiries into Latin American Masses and Minorities," includes papers on transitional literature, women, and social change. Part 3, "Images and Realities in Non-Traditional Formats," includes some fascinating presentations on the "fotonovela" and the "tango." Parts 4 and 5, more typical of previous conferences, focus on research libraries and bibliographies and research guides.

The broad scope of recent SALALM meetings suggests that it has become a worthy rival for the annual meeting of the Latin American Studies Association.

Brian E. Coutts

37. Ilgen, William D., and Deborah Jakubs. **Acquisitions Manual: Guidelines for Librarians, Bookdealers, and Publishers.** Madison, Wis., SALALM Secretariat, Memorial Library, University of Wisconsin, 1988. 95p. index. (Seminar on the Acquisition of Latin American Library Materials Bibliography and Reference Series, 21). $18.00pa. ISBN 0-917617-18-5.

A multilingual acquisitions manual for Latin American area specialists, this book grew out of a SALALM (Seminar on the Acquisition of Latin American Library Materials) workshop at Bogota in 1974. Given the importance of Latin American holdings in major academic libraries, this manual is a welcome attempt to systematize the order process.

The sole purpose of this slim volume, according to the preface, "is to facilitate day-to-day communications among librarians, book-dealers, and publishers." The authors and their SALALM colleagues collaborated to produce this manual in three languages: English, Spanish, and Portuguese. The book is divided into two parts, which address "in some detail, the major areas of the acquisitions process, from initial offer to final payment."

This is number 21 in the SALALM Bibliography and Reference Series, an extremely useful group of bibliographies which may be ordered from the SALALM Secretariat at Memorial Library, University of Wisconsin-Madison.

T. P. Williams

38. Lee, Sul H., ed. **Acquisitions, Budgets and Material Costs: Issues and Approaches.** New York, Haworth Press, 1988. 165p. index. (*Journal of Library Administration*, Monographic Suppl. No. 2). $29.95. LC 87-29867. ISBN 0-86656-690-2.

The eight papers in this volume were first delivered at a national conference sponsored by the University of Oklahoma Libraries and the University of Oklahoma Foundation. Four essays examine approval plans from various perspectives. In the longest of these, Dana Alessi of Blackwell North America provides a detailed statistical analysis of approval plan inflation. Tom Leonhardt advocates approval plans when times are lean, Karen Schmidt encourages publisher-based approval plans, and Jean Loup analyzes approval plans in ARL libraries. Edna Laughrey and Fred Lynden look at projecting and managing materials costs. Jennifer Cargill from Rice University reveals new problems in the acquisition of materials in electronic formats. Finally, there is a bibliography on acquisitions, budget, and materials costs prepared by Lenore Clark of the University of Oklahoma. The advice of these library practitioners is sensible and their insights illuminating for librarians in academic libraries. [R: BL, 1 Oct 88, p. 216]

Margaret McKinley

39. **Serials Control and Deselection Projects.** By David Farrell. Washington, D.C., Association of Research Libraries, 1988. 117p. bibliog. (SPEC Kit, No. 147). $20.00pa.

This is a grim instructional manual on the very best ways to decimate a library's serials collection. In a newsletter the Systems and Procedures Exchange Center (SPEC) of ARL's Office of Management Studies called for documentation on serials deselection and followed this up with a mailing to twenty-six member libraries. Responses were received from eighteen libraries, and documentation from thirteen is included in this work. There are copies of actual memoranda addressed to campus administrators, faculty, and staff informing them about budgetary crises, offering insights as to national and international causes, and instructing them on procedures to follow in serials cancellation projects. This will be an extremely useful guide for any library planning a major cancellation project. The examples provided are thoughtful, well written, illuminating, and extremely practical.

Margaret McKinley

40. Stankus, Tony, ed. **Scientific Journals: Issues in Library Selection and Management.** New York, Haworth Press, 1987. 218p. index. (*The Serials Librarian*: Suppl., No. 3). $29.95. LC 87-7047. ISBN 0-86656-616-3.

As new and specialized scientific journals evolve, do midcareer scientists abandon the older and established journals? Do foreign-born and foreign-trained scientists and physicians who immigrate to the United States maintain their loyalty and publication preferences to the journal titles in their countries of origin? These are the types of questions that the four sections of this book attempt to answer. Other topical areas focus on criteria to aid librarians in establishing policy for both selection and deselection of journal titles, ways in which librarians might better assist the younger scientist in the use of the literature, criteria used to evaluate scientific journals and books as reflected in published reviews, and managerial techniques, including the use of citation analysis for determining journal quality.

If there is a critical comment to be made about this book, it is that the four themes could have had more definitive titles. Yet tedious investigation was necessary for the production of the empirical data presented. It includes much for which the possible implications are significant. For an example, the reader will note the trend toward increased publication in English by German basic science publications. The published literature frequently indicates a trend toward publication in a wider variety of languages and languages other than English.

Tony Stankus has firmly established himself as one of the most productive investigators of the use of scientific journals. This book has significance for those who select scientific journals for library collections and for the primary users and producers of the literature as well. More works of this type are needed. [R: LAR, 14 Oct 88, p. 592]

Robert M. Ballard

ARTIFICIAL INTELLIGENCE AND ROBOTICS

Artificial Intelligence

APPLICATIONS

41. Bryant, Nigel. **Managing Expert Systems.** New York, John Wiley, 1988. 180p. illus. bibliog. index. $26.95pa. ISBN 0-471-91341-3.

With the proliferation of literature on expert systems, a good introduction describing what these systems are, how they work, and where to purchase them, is rare. Bryant's book, written in order "to give a readable and realistic view of what expert systems are and how they can be used," fills this gap.

The book's thirteen chapters begin with two introductory sections that describe expert systems and their components. Choice of application, building of an expert system, and maintenance and updating are covered next. Bryant then presents an example knowledge base, examples of other applications, and instructions for choosing a shell. He provides an alternative approach by describing rule-inducing systems, as opposed to systems where rules are generated by an expert and put into a knowledge base. Finally, he presents a list of suppliers of these systems in the United Kingdom and the United States, as well as ways of getting started with the use of these systems. A glossary of terms and an index enhance understanding and provide access to the book's contents.

Bryant writes clearly; his explanations are sufficient and do not overwhelm the reader with suffocating detail. Although written specifically for managers, *Managing Expert Systems* will be of value to anyone involved in purchasing, developing, implementing, and using an expert system.

Robert H. Burger

42. Daly, Donal. **Expert Systems Introduced.** Lund, Sweden, Studentlitteratur and Bromley, England, Chartwell-Bratt, 1988. 192p. with disk. illus. index. £15.95pa. ISBN 0-86238-185-1.

This book is intended to introduce people who have no technical background to the construction and implementation of expert systems. Accompanying the book is a software package which includes documentation and a tutorial. The software is an expert system shell called Crystal from Intelligent Environments of the United Kingdom. A shell provides structured functions and requires only the input of the knowledge base to develop the expert system.

The book is well organized and easy to understand albeit not well written. It begins with a background to artificial intelligence, describes the elements of expert systems, and culminates in a step-by-step approach to developing expert systems. Those who read the book cover-to-cover and use the associated software will, indeed, learn a great deal about expert systems. The software has good documentation and tutorials. From a brief review of its operations, it appears that the author's statement is accurate: "the software provides familiarity with the technology and gets you well on your way to building your own expert system." The book's discussion of other available software appears to be complete.

The quality of the book is diminished by a nearly useless index, very small print, wordy and awkward writing, and the somewhat biased approach of the author who directs an expert systems company. But despite these deficiencies, it is quite recommendable for those wishing to introduce themselves to expert systems using a printed text and a hands-on approach.

James Rice

43.   Edmunds, Robert A. **The Prentice Hall Guide to Expert Systems.** Englewood Cliffs, N.J., Prentice-Hall, 1988. 440p. illus. bibliog. index. $39.95. LC 87-30396. ISBN 0-13-703241-2.

Intended to give a practical insight into expert systems so that business professionals and members of the MIS (Management Information Systems) community would know what they are, how they are used, and what is involved in implementing them, this book will have a much wider audience. It is designed to serve as a permanent reference source with a glossary, list of publishers, periodicals and books, vendors and their products, and an index. It achieves this purpose very well and with surprisingly little jargon discusses the components of an expert system, knowledge engineering, knowledge base implementation, inference and control implementation, and expert systems implementation. Including the case history of the XCON system developed at Digital Equipment Corporation makes it a history book as well, as do the profiles of a vendor (Symbolics, Inc.), a user (Boeing), and a system (TOGA). The section on applications of expert systems technology in science, engineering, education, medicine, business, industry, military, and space are too short perhaps, but the chapter on getting started will be must reading for all who are beginning to imagine their work life affected by this new development.

As a basic source it will not satisfy the knowledgeable student of expert systems, but its readable style, format, and illustrations will prove interesting and helpful for all other readers. Highly recommended for all libraries. [R: Choice, Nov 88, p. 522]

Pauline A. Cochrane

44.   Harmon, Paul, Rex Maus, and William Morrissey. **Expert Systems Tools and Applications.** New York, John Wiley, 1988. 289p. illus. index. $29.95; $22.95pa. LC 87-17608. ISBN 0-471-83951-5; 0-471-83950-7pa.

Seen as a companion volume to the authors' *Expert Systems: Artificial Intelligence in Business* (Wiley, 1985), the audience of this work is the same as for the first: executives, middle managers, and computer system personnel who are concerned with more technical issues, the evaluation of specific expert systems building tools, learning about applications already in practice, and setting up operational expert systems development groups. The book is divided into four sections: an overview of the expert systems market in early 1987; a discussion of a number of expert systems building tools (e.g., simple rule-based tools, inductive tools, etc.); an overview of the expert systems development process; and a catalog of fielded expert systems applications in such areas as management, office automation, manufacturing, science, and medicine. The fielded expert systems are analyzed as to overall size, task paradigm, development software, knowledge representation, function of the system, source of input, delivery hardware, commercial status, and developer. In all, this book is not as readable as *The Prentice Hall Guide to Expert Systems* by Robert A. Edmunds (Prentice-Hall, 1988), but it does serve a purpose in this rapidly growing field.   Pauline A. Cochrane

45.   Hendler, James A., ed. **Expert Systems: The User Interface.** Norwood, N.J., Ablex, 1988. 324p. illus. index. $45.00. LC 87-18675. ISBN 0-89391-429-0.

Expert systems have captured the imagination of researchers, information professionals, product developers, and designers, and while much has been accomplished in the programming of such systems, little attention has been paid to the user interface. This collection of thirteen papers from a 1986 workshop is good background reading for those wishing current information on expert systems (or whatever they will eventually be called). Hendler, professor of computer science at the University of Maryland, brings these different perspectives on user interfaces together, balancing theory and practice, and intends to afford a smoother, easier introduction to these powerful new tools. There are thirteen papers, covering such topics as specification of procedural knowledge, domain specialists, hierarchical knowledge clustering, and related matters. As such paper titles hint, the book, whatever the intended audience, is *not* for the novice, and will not be comfortably accessible to the nontechnical audience. For readers with background in the theory and mechanics of programming and information transfer, however, this collection will have value, and is recommended. [R: Choice, Oct 88, p. 351]   Bruce A. Shuman

46. Hu, David. **Programmer's Reference Guide to Expert Systems.** Indianapolis, Ind., Howard W. Sams, 1987. 338p. illus. bibliog. index. $19.95pa. LC 87-61480. ISBN 0-672-22566-2.

Designed for advanced programmers who are building artificial intelligence or expert systems, and written specifically for users of the IBM PC/XT and /AT and compatible environments, especially those with pulldown menus and windows, Hu's book is intended to provide the knowledge and specifications used to construct and run an expert system.

Hu is a San Francisco-based programmer and writer specializing in artificial intelligence and expert systems, who will shortly publish a series of professional books entitled Expert Systems Management. This book is designed to provide information and step-by-step instruction in such topics as basic concepts of expert systems technology programmers, available hardware and software, and the basic vocabulary of three languages used today to construct artificial intelligence (LISP, PROLOG, SMALLTALK).

The greatest value of the book lies in its careful and clear section on how to build "inferencing capabilities" into conventional programs. In essence, Hu's instructions will permit one to incorporate expert systems components into preexisting programs. Alternatively, one may build one from scratch, but Hu's thrust may be paraphrased by the question, why start all over again when one may piggyback a sequence of instructions onto a program already residing on a hard disk?

Not for the basic programmer, this paperback is well laid out, helpfully illustrated, and highly recommended for the programmer who has the equipment, the prior knowledge, and the time to create a thinking program with decision making capabilities. Who knows? Tomorrow, the world?   Bruce A. Shuman

47. Lindsay, Susan. **Practical Applications of Expert Systems.** Wellesley, Mass., QED Information Sciences, 1988. 181p. illus. index. $34.50. LC 88-11431. ISBN 0-89435-235-0.

This book is an excellent introduction to the application of expert systems for those who have no need for the details. It intentionally avoids the mechanics of the development process and only briefly covers the basic theory of knowledge engineering. Instead the book concentrates on an overview of the way we use expert systems technology.

Well-detailed case studies provide useful examples of successful applications. By placing these applications in the context of the particular business and providing some development background, one gains a good appreciation for them.

While it chronicles the development process from the macro view of a business supervisor, the book provides a glimpse at the personality types needed to develop a system. It is loaded with insight from system developers about corporate politics, business philosophies, and project initiation and completion. Blank pages seem unnecessary at the end of chapters. The glossary and index are nice inclusions, but no references are provided. The writing style is similar to that of a reporter or a reviewer, and in some ways even emulates a historian by stating the project status and future hopes. This is a refreshing style for an area that is usually written by technical specialists.

Overall this is an enjoyable and easy-to-read introduction to expert systems for a business manager. It suffers, however, from lack of details and incomplete descriptions about the technical aspects of expert systems.

John A. Jackman

48. Rauch-Hindin, Wendy B. **A Guide to Commercial Artificial Intelligence: Fundamentals and Real-World Applications.** Englewood Cliffs, N.J., Prentice-Hall, 1988. 523p. illus. bibliog. index. $28.95pa. LC 87-19326. ISBN 0-13-368770-8.

The author, writing in a clear and interesting manner, assumes no prior knowledge of artificial intelligence (AI), though she does assume a working knowledge of conventional computers and software. Beginning with an excellent overview of AI and how it differs from traditional software programs, Rauch-Hindin explains that AI uses a new approach to problem solving called symbolic processing (i.e., the computer is given reasoning capabilities that simulate what a human might do). She goes on to discuss AI application development tools, different AI programming languages, and types of computer hardware needed to run AI systems. She also has a section on natural language processing. One of the best parts of the book is the section on expert systems and how to build one. Ten chapters discuss real-world applications of AI in industry, business and finance, science, medicine, and engineering.

The most useful section for librarians is the step-by-step approach to building an expert system: how to build the knowledge base and develop the inference strategies and rules. Obtaining knowledge for building a knowledge base, a real problem, is many times glossed over. She also discusses micro-based AI tools for building an expert system, a topic that is often set aside in favor of large-scale application development tools. The book concludes with a look at the future of AI where the author sees programs that will learn from experience or analogy. There is a first-class bibliography and a thorough index.

Although it would have made the book even longer, coverage of speech recognition, computer vision, and robotics would have been nice. [R: Choice, May 88, p. 1433]

Linda Main

49. Stock, Michael. **AI Theory and Applications in the VAX Environment.** New York, McGraw-Hill, 1988. 214p. illus. bibliog. index. $39.95; $24.95pa. LC 87-83097. ISBN 0-07-061574-8; 0-07-061573-Xpa.

This book is a guide to computer professionals, managers, and consultants in industry for the development of artificial intelligence (AI) and expert systems in a VAX computer environment. The emphasis is on practical applications of AI for problem-solving applications in industry, such as alarm management in an industrial plant. The author's objective is to outline some scientific methodologies for building intelligent applications on traditional architectures. The first part of the text after a brief introduction to AI covers five approaches to AI applications that could be used in a VAX environment: integrated AI, cooperative expert systems, distributed AI, time-critical AI, and domain-dependent solution shell technology. With each approach the author discusses it in general, the benefits and problems, any unique features in implementation and the tools, and appropriate techniques and methodologies. The second half of the book looks at new methodologies in knowledge engineering and project management, and tool selection methods and applications in the process and general manufacturing industries and in government. The text concludes with a listing of common expert system shells; a glossary of terms; and a basic bibliography of books on artificial intelligence, computer science, and software engineering pertinent to the book's orientation. There are no footnotes within the text itself but a number of figures designed to illustrate particular concepts are interspersed throughout the text. The book is written at a sophisticated level for the architect, designer, and implementer of AI applications in industry. The emphasis is on the practical. As such the book is appropriate for those in industry or working as consultants and familiar with the VAX environment and somewhat familiar with AI applications.

Lorna K. Rees-Potter

COMPUTER VISION

50. Blake, Andrew, and Andrew Zisserman. **Visual Reconstruction.** Cambridge, Mass., MIT Press, 1987. 225p. illus. bibliog. index. (MIT Press Series in Artificial Intelligence). $30.00. LC 87-4079. ISBN 0-262-02271-0.

An important area in artificial intelligence is vision. As a new edition in the MIT Press Series in Artificial Intelligence, this book deals with vision understanding, that is, the reduction of raw image data into recognizable entities. More specifically, this work provides an overview of continuity analysis useful in edge detection, surface reconstruction, and curve description. After a brief introduction of the concept of piecewise continuity, the algorithm and properties of the weak continuity constraints method is presented in detail. The last section deals with a second algorithm, the graduate nonconvexity algorithm. Though technical in nature, the text is easy to read. Most mathematical derivations are removed from the text but supplied as appendices for the serious reader. Numerous practical examples serve to illustrate the presented concepts. The material included in this research monograph is current and of interest to those interested in applying artificial intelligence techniques to vision understanding. This book is highly recommended as reference in graduate or professional libraries. [R: Choice, June 88, pp. 1588-89]

John Y. Cheung

51. Brown, Christopher, ed. **Advances in Computer Vision. Volume 1.** Hillsdale, N.J., Lawrence Erlbaum, 1988. 233p. illus. index. $27.50. LC 87-27282. ISBN 0-89859-648-3.

This book is volume 1 of a series that covers computer vision in depth and should be considered only by a reader with a strong background in mathematics. Familiarity with artificial intelligence (AI) concepts, cluster analysis, and a genuine interest in computer vision applications are also suggested reader criteria.

It was a bit difficult to get an overview of computer vision, although the introduction and parts of the first chapter attempt to provide this perspective. The chapters are long and few, allowing the authors ample space to deliver thorough treatments of current state of the art efforts in computer vision.

Chapter 1 reviews a complete computer vision system with specific examples from the VISIONS system. Chapter 2, "Computation of Intrinsic Images," is a detailed mathematical discussion of handling image data with the goal of interpretation. Chapter 3 continues with the topic by covering the details of image processing with data from multiple cameras and moving images. The mathematics of these two chapters will surpass the capabilities of some readers.

The authors and fellow researchers in computer vision are to be commended for their ability to locate and blend techniques from many areas of computer science, AI, applied mathematics, and neurobiology. This aspect makes this book fascinating reading.

A few small editorial changes could improve the book slightly. There are a few typographical errors scattered throughout. Both the author-year and numerical system for the many references were used, but were consistent within each chapter. A few diagrams are clearly Macintosh creations (e.g., figure 3.1) and would be better with cleaner lines and more judiciously chosen fonts. A glossary would have been a nice addition since much of the terminology is specialized.

The field of computer visions has made great progress recently and this book will likely become a baseline for some topics and a standard reference for other areas. This book must be considered and studied by anyone sincerely interested in computer vision. [R: Choice, July/Aug 88, pp. 1721-22]

John A. Jackman

52. Haton, J. P., ed. **Fundamentals in Computer Understanding: Speech and Vision.** New York, Cambridge University Press, 1987. 276p. illus. index. $39.50. ISBN 0-521-30983-2.

This collection of papers on the design and development of human-machine communication in artificial intelligence is the result of a course held in 1985 and sponsored by the European Economic Community and the Institut National de la Recherche en Informatique et en Automatique. The course was designed to bring together advanced students and researchers interested in the methods and problems of human-machine dialog, specifically in the areas

of speech, vision, and natural language and to compare the different approaches research efforts in these areas are following. The book is divided into three parts. The first deals with general problems and analysis methods in the design of knowledge-based systems and the integration of these methods in what has since come to be called hypermedia systems. The second concerns image analysis and vision and the problems of representation. And the third part concerns speech recognition and understanding. The book is completed by a very brief subject index.

The contributors are all well-known researchers in areas of knowledge-based systems. The volume suffers from the usual problems of such collections of papers: some unevenness in depth and breadth of coverage and the lack of a common thread or approach throughout. The book is oriented to the advanced student, so this is not a major problem. It is unfortunate that a better subject index was not produced; such entries as "natural language" with one page cited are not very useful. In this rapidly moving field it is a shame that it took three years to produce this series of lectures, as it lessens to some extent the timeliness of the papers. Overall, the volume will be of use to university library collections in engineering and computer science who serve graduate students. The volume would also be useful in advanced library and information science collections.

Lorna K. Rees-Potter

THEORETICAL ISSUES

53. Bond, Alan H., and Les Gasser, eds. **Readings in Distributed Artificial Intelligence.** San Mateo, Calif., Morgan Kaufmann, 1988. 649p. illus. index. $29.95pa. LC 88-13475. ISBN 0-934613-63-X.

Over five hundred research papers have already appeared in this broad and interdisciplinary field concerned with (1) "how the work of solving a particular problem can be divided among a number of modules ... that cooperate at the level of dividing and sharing knowledge about the problem and about the developing solution"; (2) and with multiagent systems where intelligent behavior is coordinated among a collection of autonomous intelligent agents. References to about three hundred of these papers appear in a subject-indexed bibliography. Reprinted in this volume are fifty key papers accompanied by an original historical and conceptual survey of the field and section overviews by the editors. The papers are grouped into three sections: orientation; basic distributed artificial intelligence (DAI) problems, approaches, and implementation frameworks; and DAI applications. This allows the editors to present the objects of study from three realms: the natural systems approach, the engineering-science perspective, and the hybrid approach. Complete with a twenty-page index, the only flaw seems to be that the indexer omitted references to the subject-indexed bibliography which would have been useful in putting the selections in the volume in the context of the greater body of research. This should be a valuable volume for researchers and students in cognitive science, DAI, and related fields.

Pauline A. Cochrane

54. Doukidis, Georgios I., and Edgar A. Whitley. **Developing Expert Systems.** Lund, Sweden, Studentlitteratur and Bromley, England, Chartwell-Bratt, 1988. 232p. bibliog. index. £6.95pa. ISBN 0-86238-196-7.

This book is aimed at executives, academicians, and professionals who wish to familiarize themselves with expert systems and begin to develop their own programs. It uses a theory and practice approach by beginning with background and introductory material and concluding with the actual development of expert systems using both shells and programming languages. A shell allows for the development of an expert system by inputting only the knowledge base itself. The shell introduced in this book, PESYS, is designed to develop a rule-based expert system. The book goes on to introduce the development of an expert system using LISP, a common structured expert systems programming language.

The book is not particularly well written but it is clear and fairly readable. It is well organized and has a fine index. From all indications, it is quite authoritative. Therefore, it is recommended for all audiences but postsecondary readers will definitely have an easier time with it. James Rice

55. Pratt, Vernon. **Thinking Machines: The Evolution of Artificial Intelligence.** New York, Basil Blackwell, 1987. 254p. illus. index. $19.95. LC 87-11647. ISBN 0-631-14953-8.

With an intelligence and clarity rarely witnessed in contemporary writing on computers and artificial intelligence, Pratt carefully describes the evolution of the concept of reasoning and the ways in which it gave rise to the notion of artificial thought in the seventeenth century. He traces the evolution of the machines that fed on and supported this intellectual concept, from Leibnitz through Babbage to Turing. His purpose is to give "an account of how the more psychologically sophisticated powers of contemporary machines have come about, in the belief that this helps bring out the nature of what confronts us. I hope thus to contribute to the discussion we must have about how these machines may be of most use to us, and about how best to fight the forces already exploiting their potential to impoverish and constrain."

The book's fifteen chapters are divided into three sections, each covering the "projects" of the three inventors named above. Each chapter is followed by bibliographical footnotes. An index provides adequate access to the book's contents.

Pratt's book is a balanced, well-structured account that places artificial intelligence in its historical and philosophical context as well as gives a detailed account of how the machines associated with this developing concept were actually constructed. Because he has fulfilled his purpose so well, his book should be required reading for anyone interested in artificial intelligence.

Robert H. Burger

56. Vella, Carolyn M., and John J. McGonagle, Jr. **Competitive Intelligence in the Computer Age.** Westport, Conn., Quorum Books/ Greenwood Press, 1987. 189p. bibliog. index. $35.00. LC 86-25565. ISBN 0-89930-169-X.

This book describes what the authors call a "new era of business research," that is, using online databases to find out about business competition. Applications include gathering competitor data for strategic planning, technology exploitation, financial operations, mergers and acquisitions, lawsuits, marketing, and new product development. Most of the book describes what can be done with commercial and technical databases, how to evaluate data, and how to analyze the result of searches. There are also chapters on how to recognize deliberate disinformation, the ethics of information gathering, and how to keep information about your own firm from being discovered.

The authors sprinkle the text with names of databases but do not give enough detail to teach anyone how or what to search. There is nothing about search services or how to learn about databases, and only a few paragraphs on search techniques. The short bibliography is mostly confined to books on competitive intelligence with very little for the reader who wishes to learn any practical application. Although there are plenty of suggestions of what might be done with databases, the book is sparse in telling how. It is aimed more at selling the idea than describing techniques. [R: Online, Sept 88, pp. 94-95] A. Neil Yerkey

57. Waldrop, M. Mitchell. **Man-Made Minds: The Promise of Artificial Intelligence.** New York, Walker, 1987. 280p. illus. bibliog. index. $22.95; $14.95pa. LC 86-22370. ISBN 0-8027-0899-4; 0-8027-7297-8pa.

This book gives an overview of the developments in the field of artificial intelligence (AI) over the last thirty years. Not primarily intended to be a history, the text generally follows a chronology of developments in AI as a specialty area involving the fields of software engineering, computer science, philosophy, linguistics, and cognition. Part 1, "Thinking about Thinking," traces developments since World War II with special emphasis on expert systems, natural language understanding, and vision and image systems. Part 2, "Visions of a New Generation," covers the major developments since 1980, the advent of fifth generation technology, and the development of commercial AI applications especially in the area of expert systems. Part 3, "The Shape of the Future," looks at the potential roles of intelligent machines, first as facilitators to help with complexity, to explore new ideas and heighten creativity, and second as robots and agents which can take action and do routine work.

This book leads the reader to the question "How much responsibility should intelligent machines actually be given?" Thus the book covers not only research and technical development projects in the AI field but also the human, economic, scientific, and ethical implications of this technology. A discussion of the impact of this technology on work life, employment, and industry is given as well as an overview of Japanese, American, and European responses to fifth generation technology. The text is based on a series of articles that appeared in *Science* magazine. Extensive quotations are used from these articles as well as other major sources in the field. These quotations are well documented in a references section at the back of the book. An additional readings section which covers the foundation books in the AI field completes the text.

The author, a senior science writer for *Science*, has produced a clearly written book in what can be an exceedingly complicated field with little dilution of the concepts concerned. Examples from rule based, natural language understanding and other programs are given to demonstrate the concepts and AI projects presented. This book is consequently highly recommended for any computer science/artificial intelligence collection from public libraries to academic research libraries.

Lorna K. Rees-Potter

58. Wilkins, David E. **Practical Planning: Extending the Classical AI Planning Paradigm.** San Mateo, Calif., Morgan Kaufmann, 1988. 205p. bibliog. index. $34.95. LC 88-13044. ISBN 0-934613-94-X.

After a brief review of some of the classical artificial intelligence (AI) planning systems, the author shows just how far the classical approach goes and what can be done if this paradigm is extended by using causal theories, permitting general constraints, and doing interesting replanning. The book is primarily an in-depth case study of SIPE (system for interactive planning and execution monitoring), developed by the author during the early and mid-1980s.

The SIPE planning system provides a domain-independent formalism for describing a domain at different levels of abstraction, including both actions that can be taken and goals that can be achieved. The system can reason about resources, post and use constraints, and employ a deductive causal theory to represent and reason about different world states. SIPE can intermingle planning and execution, and can accept arbitrary descriptions of unexpected occurrences during execution and modify its plan to take these into account. Heuristic adequacy has been one of the primary goals in the design of SIPE and the author defends this goal and others to researchers who prefer formal theories and are often critical of systems that cannot be proven correct and complete. It is asserted that SIPE sets new standards for performance in classical systems, both for execution time on standard problems and for the complexity of problems that can be solved. The heuristics and algorithms in SIPE are explained clearly and in enough detail so that readers can understand their strengths and weaknesses. Comparison is made with other systems.

A basic background in AI is necessary before reading this book, but it would be useful to any one interested in incorporating planning capabilities into AI systems.

Pauline A. Cochrane

59. Wormell, Irene, ed. **Knowledge Engineering: Expert Systems and Information Retrieval.** London and Los Angeles, Calif., Taylor Graham, 1987. 182p. index. $39.00. ISBN 0-947568-30-1.

In December 1986 a NORDINFO seminar took place in Copenhagen at the Royal School of Librarianship. The aim of the seminar was to connect artificial intelligence (AI) and information retrieval (IR) in order to establish a mutual basis for transfer of theories and techniques. This collection serves as a record of that seminar.

All the papers save one were written by Scandinavian authors who have written both about AI applications in IR systems and experiences in the field of IR which builders of expert systems could or should use. Karen Sparck Jones, who presented the keynote paper on architecture problems in the construction of expert systems for document retrieval is from Computer Laboratory at Cambridge University. All the papers are very readable and informative, but two (by Larsen and Sandahl) stand out because, in one case, the author presents a novel concept of "information space zooming" and in the other, the author reviews developments and explains why the migration of expert systems to the production environment has been slow.

The references with each paper and the thorough index make this slim volume much more valuable than the usual proceedings volume. Recommended. [R: JAL, Sept 88, p. 259]

Pauline A. Cochrane

Robotics

60. **International Encyclopedia of Robotics: Applications and Automation.** Richard C. Dorf, ed. New York, John Wiley, 1988. 3v. illus. index. $295.00/set. LC 87-37264. ISBN 0-471-87868-5.

Robotics is a relatively new field. In fact, Isaac Asimov is credited with coining the word in 1942. At that time he assumed it was the "proper scientific term for the systematic study of robots, their construction, maintenance and behavior." It is the goal of this encyclopedia to define the discipline and practice of robotics by bringing together the core knowledge and practice in the field with that from closely related fields. Included are numerous articles associated with theoretical aspects of robotics as well as articles dealing with both present and future applications of robotics in the factory, office, and home.

The encyclopedia is made up of signed articles by respected researchers in the field from both industry and academic, including many from European and Japanese companies or universities. Each article includes a bibliography as well as extensive cross-references to other articles. As behooves any major technical encyclopedia, this one has numerous tables and figures (over two thousand).

The articles are arranged in alphabetical order. For example, an article entitled "End-of-Arm-Tooling" follows an article titled "Employment, Impact." This would cause a problem were it not for an extensive index found at the end of volume 3. The index makes it possible to find all of the articles related to robotic arms, such as geometric design, arm-joints, or manipulators.

This is an attractive encyclopedia on a topic of great interest to many, not all of whom are engineers and computer scientists. The variety and sheer number of topics covered is impressive. The articles "Art, Robotics In," "Kinematics," and "Robots in Japan" are good examples of the variety and depth of the articles found. They also demonstrate the variety of audience that should be attracted to this set. Not only should it be extremely popular, but it also is a good value for the money.

Susan B. Ardis

AUDIOVISUAL TECHNOLOGY

61. Birnhack, Juliette. **Audiovisual Resources in a Hospital Medical Library: Their Organization and Management.** London, Mansell, 1987. 153p. illus. bibliog. index. $48.00. LC 87-24025. ISBN 0-7201-1881-6.

Birnhack, head of the Audiovisual Teaching Unit at the Chaim Sheba Medical Centre in Israel, bases this introductory guide to the planning and management of a medical audiovisual library on her nearly thirty years of experience. Although there are more comprehensive volumes on medical librarianship and on audiovisual resources, this particular work provides a broad overview of the major problems and solutions involved in organizing a medical nonprint collection.

Following a general introduction that emphasizes the use of audiovisual aids and computer simulations in the electronic-age library, there are eight short chapters. The first, a "concept" chapter, contains some basic definitions (e.g., *audiovisual library*), the rationale underlying audiovisual collections, funding problems, users and their needs, and other "pointers for decision-making" (p. 20). The remaining chapters cover (1) location and layout; (2) equipment and materials (with less than a dozen photographs of such basic machines as a slide projector and cassette copier); (3) storage systems (again including a few photographs of basic items); (4) acquisition, selection, and sources; (5) processing; (6) user routines; and (7) promotion of the audiovisual collection. Each chapter has a few references, lists of sources, and examples of forms where appropriate. A very limited bibliography is followed by two appendices (listing medical audiovisual producers and distributors and recommended audiovisual journals) and a three-page index.

As evident from this review, this *is* an elementary text. For the novice placed in charge or assigned the development of an audiovisual medical collection, the work would be a useful guide. For the professional holding a degree or certification, it might well seem to duplicate previous instruction although some of the medical references are not common core knowledge. The book does include U.K. as well as U.S. sources although there are many more of the latter available than are noted (e.g., only three U.S. audiovisual periodicals are cited). In addition, the equipment references are, in general, at the lower end of the technological spectrum and there are minimal references to computer applications and resources. Although the guidelines might apply to any audiovisual collection or user, it should be clear that Birnhack's medical users are those found in teaching hospitals and does not include the patient or others interested in health information. [R: LAR, 15 June 88, p. 352]

Laurel Grotzinger

62. Casciero, Albert J., and Raymond G. Roney. **Audiovisual Technology Primer.** Englewood, Colo., Libraries Unlimited, 1988. 262p. illus. index. (Library Science Text Series). $22.50pa. LC 87-31142. ISBN 0-87287-620-9.

Casciero and Roney have assembled an excellent document, which media librarians will find most useful at the school, public library and academic library levels. This primer is an introduction to basic media production and nonprint utilization, and serves as a companion to the other basic titles in the field: *Instructional Media* (Macmillan, 1985) by Heinich, Molenda and Russell; *Planning and Producing Audiovisual Materials* (Crowell, 1975-) by Kemp; and *The Systematic Design of Instruction* (Scott Foresman, 1985) by Dick and Carey.

Although this guide defines the basic terms and gives the history of several audiovisual equipment systems, it does not cover the rapid changes in the use of the microcomputer in the design and production of graphics. Many of the techniques discussed here are being replaced with laser printers and video imaging for transparencies and slides. Interactive video receives little attention as well. However, the simple drawings and essential background information are very valuable to the beginner in the media field. Organization, classification, and simple in-house production of media are all clearly shown.

An additional chapter providing guidance in the selection of commercially produced materials would increase the book's value. Although a list of the most important selection guides

would be useful, complete discussion of modern electronic databases that lead to the location of nonprint materials would be the most welcome additional information.

Still, this publication has a place in the education of future school media specialists and nonprint collection developers. I plan to use the primer as one of the texts in graduate-level courses involving instructional design and management of nonprint resources and services. [R: EL, Nov/Dec 88, p. 41; JAL, July 88, p. 189; VOYA, Oct 88, p. 208]

Daniel Callison

63. **Educational Media and Technology Yearbook 1988. Volume 14.** Donald P. Ely, Brenda Broadbent, and R. Kent Wood, eds. Englewood, Colo., with Association for Educational Communications and Technology by Libraries Unlimited, 1988. 293p. index. $50.00. ISBN 0-87287-609-8; ISSN 8755-2094.

The *Educational Media and Technology Yearbook* is a useful guide to associations, publishers, and educational programs in the field of instructional systems technology. This fourteenth volume will be added to most collections in universities that have this special degree at either the master's or Ph.D. level. The review by Clark and Sugrue, "Research on Instructional Media 1978-88," is well done and has great merit as a concise piece that covers a decade of educational technology, but most of the other articles are flat and do not add much to the field. One can find much of the same material in current journals of the field and will find much more detail and depth. For the $50.00 price tag on each volume of this yearbook series, I would be willing to think in terms of purchasing every other or every third year for the address updates, and letting the "research" or "state-of-the-articles" slip on by. The biographical sketches on James D. Finn and James W. Brown, two real pioneers in this field, are nicely done and add a bit of something special to this volume.

An extensive mediagraphy is given in the back, and covers such areas as video, photography, and computers. There is also a section on online databases, which I think is a bit out of the instructional technology territory. Why not leave that one to the information science people?   Daniel Callison

64. Miller, Jerome K. **Using Copyrighted Videocassettes in Classrooms, Libraries, and Training Centers.** 2d ed. Friday Harbor, Wash., Copyright Information Services, 1988. 114p. index. (Copyright Information Bulletin, No. 3). $19.95. LC 87-24572. ISBN 0-914143-14-X.

This is a revised edition of a popular source originally copyrighted in 1984. The cassette video recorder has become the most available medium of communication in homes and schools. The use of this equipment has reshaped the use of television for information, education and entertainment. With this popularity, concern and confusion on the part of librarians and educators has grown concerning their rights in the use of videocassettes in classrooms.

The book opens with a disclaimer: "The opinions contained herein reflect the author's informed opinion, but do not constitute legal advice." Throughout the source he cites relevant court cases and provides examples of library, classroom, and private sector situations. Chapter headings are "Proprietor's Rights," "Home-Use Rights," "Educator's Rights," "Librarian's Rights," "Hospital, Church, and Industrial Training Specialist's Rights," "Business-Meeting Exemption," "Copyright Contracts," and "Warning Notices."

No single source is ever complete, but Miller comes closer than others in this area. He challenges industry statements that videocassettes labeled "Home Use Only" may not be used in classrooms and school libraries, arguing that these showings are exempt from licensing requirements by Section 110 (1) of the copyright act. He also challenges the positions taken by Mary Hutchings Reed (American Library Association's attorney) about the legality of showing videocassettes in public library meeting rooms and carrels, arguing that video showings in public libraries now require licenses as a result of recent federal court decisions in *Columbia Pictures v. Redd Horne* and *Columbia Pictures v. Aveco*.

One disappointing omission is the lack of mentioning a notice that librarians could place on video recorders (like on copy machines), as discussed by Mary Hutchings Reed: "Notice: The copyright law of the United States governs the making of reproductions and the performance of copyrighted material; the person using this equipment is liable for any copyright infringement."

This reviewer does not pretend to be a copyright lawyer or an expert on copyright, but the author raises some important points of consideration and backs them with reasonable arguments. This is a must publication for libraries, schools, and other institutions.

Thomas L. Hart

65. Slawson, Ron. **Multi-Image Slide/Tape Programs.** Englewood, Colo., Libraries Unlimited, 1988. 152p. illus. bibliog. index. $22.50pa. LC 88-17746. ISBN 0-87287-647-0.

Useful as a text or basic reference book, *Multi-Image Slide/Tape Programs* is comprehensive, well written, and accurate. The liberally illustrated chapters include planning multi-image programs, types of multi-image machine configurations, production procedures, and suggestions for multi-image presentations. In addition to a bibliography and index, three appendices are included: "Glossary," "Sources of Information on Multi-Image Programs and Production," and "Forms for Planning."

The book is equally useful to those planning one-image, one-projector presentations even though the term *multi-image* suggests a complex of projectors, programmers, and hundreds to thousands of visuals. For example, an excellent, step-by-step procedure is given for creating slides: using the copystand, setting the camera, selecting the film, preparing captions, and the like.

Multi-Image Slide/Tape Programs is written to project an enthusiasm for the dramatic effects that multi-image produces by providing examples of outstanding programs. This is refreshing at a time when many instructional technologists are trying to make the computer do everything and have turned away from simple or complex 35mm slide programs. The book deserves a place in school, university, public, and special libraries and will be valuable as a text for courses teaching the production of simple to complex audiovisual presentations.

William E. Hug

66. Thomas, James L. **Nonprint Production for Students, Teachers, and Media Specialists: A Step-by-Step Guide.** 2d ed. Englewood, Colo., Libraries Unlimited, 1988. 140p. illus. bibliog. index. $23.50. LC 88-26727. ISBN 0-87287-591-1.

This step-by-step guide to media productions includes storyboarding and scripting, computer graphics, transparency lifts and laminations, sound slides and filmstrips, and single-camera television programs. Each of these chapters follows the same outline which includes definitions of terms, materials and costs, operation checklists, production procedures, follow-up activities, suggestions for tapping local resources, and an annotated bibliography.

Thomas's second edition presents many good ideas with accurately written instructions for each production. The sections "Suggestions for Follow-up Activities" and "Tapping Local Resources" of each chapter attest to the extensive, practical experience of the author. Also, the bibliographies are comprehensive consisting of reviews, advanced production techniques, media catalogs, and related topics.

The guide is straightforward and easy to read with simple and clear line illustrations filling the gap between works concentrating on elementary production techniques and more advanced texts and manuals. The work should be of value to schools, teachers, media specialists, and college classes in media production.

William E. Hug

AUTOMATION IN LIBRARIES

General Works

67. Applying Information Technology in Small Libraries. Proceedings of the Nineteenth Annual Conference.... Jane Vanderlin and William Barrows, eds. New York, Association for Population/Family Planning Libraries and Information Centers-International, c1986, 1987. 150p. maps. $15.00pa. LC 87-1061. ISBN 0-933438-12-5.

Applying Information Technology is a one-volume collection of the papers presented at the nineteenth annual conference of the Association for Population/Family Planning Library and Information Centers, held in San Francisco in 1986. The papers range over mini/microcomputer in-house applications, demographic data and news on DIALOG, and computerized information retrieval in "developing" countries (specifically Brazil).

The important thing to remember about this collection of papers is the date: 1986. The papers are now over two years old, and in the rapidly changing field of information technology this is a lifetime. This is best illustrated by the keynote address given by Linda Mullins, "Computers in Small Libraries—Where Do We Go from Here?" Mullins discusses a potential for CD-ROM and expert systems which has already been realized in 1988. Several of the other articles are similarly dated, such as that by Gloria Roberts discussing the setting up of a computerized database in the library of the Planned Parenthood Federation of America. They used a minicomputer based system and ended up transferring the entire project to a microcomputer to take advantage of what was then (1984) a rapidly developing microcomputer market. Today a small library would consider nothing but a microcomputer. The discussion of "Pro Cite" by Susan Pasquariella predates the vastly improved 3.2 version brought out in 1987.

The volume covers APLIC business and board meetings and committee reports for 1986, and includes a directory of members and a list of all the annual conferences. This collection of papers should be seen as what it is, a snapshot of how things were in a few libraries in 1986.

Linda Main

68. Clayton, Marlene. Managing Library Automation. Brookfield, Vt., Gower Publishing, 1987. 239p. index. $53.95. LC 86-25794. ISBN 0-566-03529-4.

This book is intended to serve as a concise, introductory guide to managing automation for the middle-level manager in libraries and information centers. The author regards "managing" in the colloquial sense of "coping with" as well as in the formal sense of controlling and administering. Thus, the book takes a practical and common-sense approach to implementing automation in libraries. Areas covered include planning for automation, technical support functions, standards, software and hardware, communications and networking, choosing and implementing a system, file creation, and managing a working system.

The content is a combination of what might best be described as management tips and basic information about the components of library systems. Somewhat disconcerting is the apparent assumption by the author that readers know absolutely nothing about either libraries or systems. Thus, a good part of the text consists of elementary explanations of related issues, from cataloging codes to programming languages and computer storage devices. The sections on management are excellent, but one wonders about the managers who would need to apply these principles so soon after being introduced to the area of application.

Most of the examples of organizational and bureaucratic dilemmas to be faced in automating libraries arise from U.K. contexts. Nevertheless, many of the management principles described in this work are applicable to other environments. [R: JAL, May 88, p. 104]

Joe A. Hewitt

69. Condon, Jan. Letting the Information World into Your School: The Use of the Modem. London, School Libraries Group, Library Association, 1987. 16p. £1.50pa. ISBN 0-948933-06-2.

In this brief pamphlet the British Library Association's School Libraries Group gives an overview of the use of a modem in a school library. Starting from the philosophy that "... the technology is incidental to the information. So look at syllabuses and the curriculum first and see where the new technology can enhance the learning experience, whilst at the same time introduce a new and useful skill," the author gives several specific examples of online information useful in schools. Most North American librarians will not have much need for this pamphlet because the examples and sources listed are all British, but as a model for a concise introduction of technology it could be useful to individuals charged with producing the same sort of introduction in their jurisdictions, or to associations that want to help school library personnel to justify the need for online services in schools. Adele M. Fasick

70. Kinney, Thomas. **Toward Telecommunications Strategies in Academic and Research Libraries: Ten Case Studies of Decision-Making and Implementation.** Washington, D.C., Association of Research Libraries, 1988. 30p. bibliog. (OMS Occasional Paper, No. 14). $15.00pa.

Tight organization of well-chosen focal points and succinct descriptions of ten case studies of telecommunications choices of academic libraries enable this slim volume to be effective in its goal of helping the library manager become "telecommunications literate" — a challenge faced by many. Focusing on the rationale for decision making rather than on technological details, this overview covers telecommunications applications in the academic library setting for local area networks, the library and the campus network, links and interfaces for bibliographic systems, and alternatives to remote access. Two pages cover factors in telecommunications strategy formulation and developing strategic goals. Eight general references and twenty-two references divided for the four sections are current, relevant, and accessible to the nonspecialist. This is a good introductory source for the busy manager who needs an overview of the current status of telecommunications applications and references for further research. It also provides the library science student with a perspective on the integration of technologies within an institution.

JoAnn V. Rogers

71. Webb, T. D. **The In-House Option: Professional Issues of Library Automation.** New York, Haworth Press, 1987. 166p. bibliog. index. (Haworth Library and Information Sciences Text, No. 1). $34.95. LC 87-127. ISBN 0-86656-617-1.

The central question discussed in this book is: Should a library, when choosing an automated system, select a turnkey system from a commercial vendor with the computer located in the library or use time on a computer belonging to the parent organization? In the latter case, the library system will be only one of many systems on the computer. Computer specialists will maintain the system rather than librarians.

The author presents two case studies. One reports on the Phoenix Public Library, which used ULISYS software running on the city's computer and managed by the city's MIS department. The other case study discusses DYNIX, which was installed at the Joseph E. Smith library, on the Hawaii campus of Brigham Young University. As the author points out, these are only two case studies, and no general conclusions can be drawn. They do not in fact tell us anything new. The Phoenix Public Library had the age-old problem of computer specialists in the MIS department of the city being too removed from the library and its processes. The Smith library case study is critical of DYNIX, but as the concluding section points out, many of the complaints have been resolved. There are new upgrades to DYNIX software, and the company has a larger and better-trained support team.

The strength of this book is in its discussion of other issues central to library automation. There is an excellent section on the computer skills needed by librarians. The author states that librarians currently do not have enough skill to work efficiently with automated library systems when the computer is maintained in-house. It can be argued, in opposition to Webb, that librarians are rapidly becoming less naive users of computers as more and more libraries automate and more and more library schools prepare students to deal with automation. The study also discusses the impact of automation — essentially a practical, high-skill area — on the philosophical principles of librarianship and their concern with theoretical justifications. Webb argues that increased automation skills can only increase professionalism, and that librarians should not be too concerned with theoretical justifications.

This is a well-written, readable study. It has an excellent bibliography and includes a very insightful overview of relevant literature scattered throughout the text. [R: JAL, May 88, p. 128; LAR, 15 Sept 88, p. 521; RLR, Nov 88, pp. 352-53] Linda Main

Databases and Software

72. Anderson, Eric S. **The Wired Librarian's Almanac.** Crystal Lake, Ill., Follett Software, 1987. 205p. illus. $9.95pa. ISBN 0-695-60026-5.

According to the preface, this volume "is a conglomeration of non-library and library software reviews as well as essays written by several well-known librarians" (p. iii). The author is the editor of the *Wired Librarian's Newsletter* (Eric Anderson, 1983-), and most of the software reviews included in this collection first appeared in that publication. The book seems to be directed toward the school and public library market, since the reviews concentrate on instructional programs for children and library-related software for the small to middling collection. There are no references nor bibliographies appended to the essays, nor is there an index for the volume as a whole.

While the essayists' writing styles are straightforward and sometimes interesting, this book demonstrates the unfortunate fact that information about computers is among the most ephemeral in terms of usefulness. The information presented here appears to be dated and, therefore, of limited value to the experienced library computer user. In fact, the original publication dates are impossible to ascertain in some cases, so that the reader has no idea how old the information really is. I found the reviews to be the most useful and interesting section of the book, even though some of the software mentioned may no longer be available. A major problem is that the author deals only with the Apple/Macintosh line of personal computers in libraries, stating: "If you are into MS-DOS, you are on your own" (p. [1]). I do not recommend this title unless you are a total novice in the computer field or you need to fill in your collection with historical materials. [R: BL, 1 Apr 88, p. 1309; WLB, June 88, p. 125]

Jean L. Cooper

73.   Dyer, Hilary, and Alison Gunson, comps. **A Directory of Library and Information Retrieval Software for Microcomputers.** 3d ed. Brookfield, Vt., Gower Publishing, 1988. 75p. index. $41.95pa. LC 87-23646. ISBN 0-566-05586-4.

The most dramatic change in this third edition is the new print format, which greatly improves both readability and searchability. As in past editions, the major portion of the book contains entries listed alphabetically by program name. The degree of detail varies considerably among entries depending upon how much is included in the Notes field; however, no entry contains any type of evaluation. Listings are found for both British (costs in pounds sterling) and U.S. (costs in dollars) products.

Especially useful are the hardware, supplier, and function indexes. These have no page numbers, but since the entries are arranged alphabetically, it is not a serious problem. The hardware index, while certainly helpful, can be misleading. The PC compatibles list contains only a fraction of the listings found under the

IBM PC heading, presumably because the software producers did not think to include this category in their description.

A brief section gives guidelines for choosing software, but although the advice is good, the entries themselves do not contain enough information for making any choices. The book does, however, serve as a good initial reference source.

Despite these few caveats, the book is a good source of basic information on microcomputer software for libraries and information environments. [R: LAR, 15 Sept 88, p. 522]

Elisabeth Logan

74.   **Essential Guide to Apple Computers in Libraries. Volume 4: Software for Library Applications.** By Patrick R. Dewey. Westport, Conn., Meckler, 1987. 153p. illus. bibliog. index. $24.95 spiralbound. LC 86-17929. ISBN 0-88736-077-7.

75.   **Essential Guide to Apple Computers in Libraries. Volume 5: The Library Macintosh.** By Rosanne M. Macek. Westport, Conn., Meckler, 1988. 308p. illus. bibliog. index. $24.95 spiralbound. LC 87-17929. ISBN 0-88736-078-5.

Dewey's brief manual is a guide to various types of software programs that might be useful in the library using the Apple computer. Many types of programs are listed including word processing, accounting, audiovisual management, cataloging, circulation, graphics, inventory, and utilities, just to cite a few. Each program is described briefly but not very critically. Appendices provide vendor information, a bibliography of software sources, and a few microcomputer user groups listed by state. The most valuable appendix is the result of a survey of Illinois librarians by the author. Each library provides a list of software packages being used and a description of the products produced.

The publication has two major faults. Even though the copyright date is 1987, a number of packages and even a mention of the Apple IIGS are missing. The second fault is more critical. Programs are described with such brevity that significant facts are not provided. For example, the valuable program MacroWorks (now merged with AutoWorks) is said to be important for a glossary function and that "any often-used function can be summoned from within the program." Such an abbreviated description does not give sufficient information on what a "macro" is or its potential in saving time.

In contrast to Dewey's brevity, Macek's *The Library Macintosh* is an excellent, perceptive, and informative guide to programs for the

Macintosh that are useful in library applications. Descriptions are not only informative, but actual examples with accompanying screens provide an excellent picture of what each program can do in a library setting. Macek has written a number of chapters about Macintosh hardware, the user interface, word processing, and graphics and integrated software. Other authors have contributed chapters on communications and on databases and have provided two case studies. Appendices of useful information lead the reader to other sources of information. With the emergence of the Macintosh as a serious contender for the library market, Macek's book is must reading. Dewey's volume, however, is not recommended.   David V. Loertscher

76. Essential Guide to the Library IBM PC. Volume 5: Buying and Installing Generic Software for Library Use. By Patrick R. Dewey. Westport, Conn., Meckler, 1987. 111p. illus. bibliog. index. $24.95 spiralbound. LC 85-10535. ISBN 0-88736-037-8.

A part of an extensive series which introduces the personal computer to the library profession, Dewey's guide outlines uses of commercial, shareware, and public domain software for library applications. The type of software reviewed is that which was created usually for business applications such as databases, word processors, and spreadsheets, but can be tailored to library applications quite easily. The bulk of the work lists a particular software package and then describes both its features and possible uses in a library setting. Coverage is excellent for these types of programs as of the publication date (late 1986). Most of the packages described are still in existence as of late 1988, albeit in newer or updated versions. Users of the guide should contact their local computer dealer for details about newer versions which do similar things that Dewey describes. It is hoped this publication will be updated on a regular basis, since it does provide the kernel of possibilities for generic software in libraries. [R: CLJ, Apr 88, pp. 125-26]

David V. Loertscher

77. Essential Guide to the Library IBM PC. Volume 10: Shareware for Library Applications. By Alan R. Samuels. Westport, Conn., Meckler, 1988. 234p. index. $24.95 spiralbound. LC 85-10535. ISBN 0-88736-184-6.

The author's purpose is "to introduce librarians to an untapped source of high productivity, low-cost software usually called 'shareware.'" Shareware as defined by the author falls somewhere between commercial and public domain software. The book is divided into three major sections: "Introduction to Software Alternatives," "Applications," and "The Shareware." The first section provides an overview of software alternatives, lists sources that regularly review shareware, and provides suggested criteria for selecting shareware. The second section offers suggestions for the application of shareware and deals with the concept of small-scale automated information systems in some detail. The final and largest section is a listing of fifty-four (winnowed from over two hundred) shareware titles with lengthy annotations and detailed comments on the strengths and limitations of each title. Also included are prices and the names and addresses of the producers.

It is assumed that the user of this book has some knowledge of computers and the terminology used as no glossary is provided; however, the endnotes after each chapter do provide definitions for some terms. All of the shareware reviewed requires an IBM or IBM-compatible computer with 640K of memory and two floppy disk drives (or one floppy and one hard disk drive). Among the shareware tested and reviewed by the author are programs for cataloging, database management, graphics, word processing, and spreadsheets. The author's discussion of shareware applications, list of shareware with potential use in libraries, and list of often difficult-to-find names and addresses of shareware producers provide a needed resource for users and potential users of shareware utilizing IBM computers or compatibles.

Donald C. Adcock

78. Saffady, William. **The Macintosh as a Library Workstation: A Report on Available Hardware and Software.** Chicago, American Library Association, 1987. 200p. illus. index. (Library Technology Reports, Vol. 23, No. 1). $45.00pa.

This issue of the highly respected Library Technology Reports series presents Macintosh hardware and software as it was in early 1987, that is before the Macintosh SE or Macintosh II. While many of the comments in the opening thirty-page report, "The Macintosh as a Library Workstation," remain relevant, enough has changed to make this insufficient for librarians interested in the current capabilities of Macintoshes. In addition to the changes in the models themselves and accompanying system software (e.g., Multifinder), were the report being written today, certain topics, including digitizing scanners, large screen monitors, document conversion, hard disk storage, and networks, to name a few, would receive much more emphasis.

The majority of the issue is devoted to accurate and thorough reviews of twenty-four pieces of software. Unfortunately, some are no longer available or of much interest (Jazz and Think Tank 512); others have been significantly upgraded (PageMaker 1.2 and Microsoft Word 1.05). Because many libraries will have software of this vintage, the reviews may still be of some use, particularly where manuals have disappeared. One notable class of items not reviewed is graphics applications: where would Macintosh users be without Macpaint or Macdraw and their competitors? Robert Skinner

Library Information Networks and Systems

79. **California Conferences on Networking. Proceedings, September 22-27, 1988.** By California Library Networking Task Force. Sacramento, Calif., California State Library Foundation, 1988. 200p. $15.00pa. ISBN 0-929722-29-9.

Sharing speakers and format, four conferences on multitype library networking were held in four California cities: Oakland, Sacramento, San Diego, and Long Beach. Independent consultant Carolyn Corbin delivered the keynote address, "Looking toward 2000: Strategies for Libraries." Jackuelyn Thresher, director of the Princeton Public Library in Princeton, New Jersey, delivered the conference address, "What Worked ... What Didn't: An Insider's Perspective of Network Participation in Two States." Other speakers summarized library cooperation in California beginning in 1908 and current networking activities. Comments from California librarians who described potential functions and services of a multitype library network were excerpted for the proceedings. There are summations of small group discussions focused on potential benefits of, and barriers to, multitype library networking. The next steps for library networking in California were suggested. There is a conference agenda, lists of the seven hundred participants, and descriptions of recent network grant programs in California. Finally, there are reports from the 1985 California Conference on Networking. This work could be a useful guide for developing similar statewide or regional conferences. Margaret McKinley

80. Corbin, John. **Implementing the Automated Library System.** Phoenix, Ariz., Oryx Press, 1988. 153p. index. $30.00. LC 88-19650. ISBN 0-89774-455-1.

This companion volume to the author's *Managing the Library Automation Project* (Oryx Press, 1985) is a practical guide for integrating an automated system into a library's organizational management and staffing structure and for managing the system during and after implementation. Corbin, an associate professor at the School of Library and Information Sciences, University of North Texas, has produced a clear, well-organized overview of the implications involved in migrating from manual to automated library operations once a system is in place. The opening two chapters give a basic background of automated library functions and an automated integration project, respectively. The remaining nine chapters detail specific steps of the automation project, covering topics such as staffing, space planning, workstations, documentation, database conversion, and computer operations.

Corbin favors a logical approach to the information he presents, often resorting to lists of options or checklists of steps to be taken. Each chapter begins with a brief introductory summary, including a list of points covered, and ends with suggested readings. An adequate index is also included. The information is general enough that it will appeal not only to the library manager intimately involved with an automation project, but also to senior library management who desire to keep abreast of the automated functions which they manage indirectly. Comparatively speaking, this is a reasonably priced addition to an increasingly crowded field. Pamela A. Zager

81. Durance, Cynthia J. **Linking: Then and Now. Le Lien: D'Hier à Aujourd'Hui.** Ottawa, National Library of Canada; distr., Ottawa, Canadian Government Publishing Centre, 1987. 26p. $6.00pa. $7.20pa. (U.S.). ISBN 0-660-53827-X.

This is the second document in the Canadian Network Papers series dealing with the National Library of Canada's (NLC) networking programs. The first was issued in 1984 under the title *Linking: Today's Libraries, Tomorrow's Technologies* (Ottawa: National Library of Canada, 1983). In that volume, specific recommendations were identified for providing future directions for networking development based on the best assessment of the anticipated library and information environment. This volume evaluates the progress made over the last three years and identifies areas that might need adjustment. Durance has been at the heart of NLC's linking activities early on and is eminently qualified to assess NLC's position.

The recommendations made by NLC at the onset of its networking program are evaluated in terms of accomplishments. Rather than reviewing the recommendations in the order that they were originally presented, related recommendations are discussed topically. This makes for a cohesive, well-written document. The major headings in the document include: "Networking Resources," "OSI Protocol Development," "Networking Policy," "Resource Sharing Initiatives," "Value-Added Services and New Technologies," and "Issues for the Future." Three appendices conclude the work: the 1984 recommendations in their original order, development advisory groups, and principles of networking. The document is published in both French and English.

At the core of NLC's networking programs is the implementation of the Open Systems Interconnection (OSI) model. NLC has used OSI specifically for interlibrary loan applications and is the international forerunner in this area. Consequently, any reports updating NLC's activities with OSI should be greeted with considerable eagerness and this work certainly meets these expectations. This document is compulsory reading for anyone even remotely involved with future library developments.

Marjorie E. Bloss

82. Essential Guide to the Library IBM PC. Volume 11: Acquisitions Systems for Libraries. By Norman Desmarais. Westport, Conn., Meckler, 1988. 246p. index. $29.95 spiralbound. LC 85-10535. ISBN 0-88736-185-4.

The purpose of this volume is to study some of the commercially available acquisitions systems for the IBM PC/XT/AT and compatibles. Only those systems that perform more than simply production of purchase orders (i.e., receiving, accounting, claiming) are included.

The author states that the descriptions of the systems are generally based on hands-on study and "accurately represent the modules at the time of writing" (p. xii). Systems included in this study are OCLC/ACQ350, Any-Book, BataSystems, Bib-Base/Acq, Card Datalog Acquisition Module, Sydney Micro System, and Unicorn/Acquisitions Module. Each review includes a discussion of system features, description of documentation, hardware/software specifications, number of installations, price, and help numbers. There is a chapter on electronic ordering. The final chapter compares the systems reviewed to one another.

Information on specific software packages becomes obsolete quickly. The most useful part of this book, the first chapter, titled "Issues," will not. Here, the author discusses at length the questions to ask vendors and the software features to consider when planning for an acquisitions system. The author provides an extensive

"Checklist of Features" that should prove to be invaluable to any library considering automated acquisitions.

The author has been meticulous in presenting details of various commercially available acquisitions systems, and shows his expertise in this area. This book, one of a series on library applications for IBM PCs, will prepare the reader well for internal decision making and dealing with vendors of automated systems.

Diane Montag

83. Fenly, Judith G., and Beacher Wiggins, comps. and eds. The Linked Systems Project: A Networking Tool for Libraries. Dublin, Ohio, OCLC Online Computer Library Center, 1988. 138p. illus. bibliog. (OCLC Library, Information, and Computer Science Series, 6). $13.50 pa. LC 87-35004. ISBN 1-55653-039-0.

It would be difficult to overestimate the importance of the Linked Systems Project (LSP) to the network environment and ultimately to the users of information obtained through libraries and information agencies. The project intended to develop and implement plans to link the disparate computer systems of the major bibliographic utilities, the Research Libraries Information Network (RLIN), the Western Library Network (WLN), OCLC, and the Library of Congress, had its beginnings in the late 1970s with the interest and support of the Council on Library Resources. The project involves two major components, the communications component and the applicaiton component. The development of standards associated with computer links parallels the progress of the LSP project, which is currently operative only in the exchange of authority data among the utilities but will eventually develop mechanisms for the exchange of bibliographic data. The communications component uses standard protocols of the Open Systems Interconnection reference model, and the application component will use standards currently being developed and considered by the National Information Standards Organization Committee Z39. The twelve papers in this volume bring together for the first time authoritative information about the concepts of the project as well as the protocols being used. Background and an overview are provided by Henriette Avram and Sally McCallum of LC, and Ray Denenberg, also of LC, provides a clear explanation of network protocols. Other topics include record transfer, information retrieval, and exchange of authority and bibliographic records.

While some of the information presented here has appeared in professional articles, some of it, such as that contained in the chapter on costs, is not available elsewhere. The coverage is very thorough and clearly presented. Any professional interested in the evolution of network services and the implications of this project for future developments in the field will find this a worthy contribution. [R: LJ, 1 Nov 88, p. 58; WLB, Sept 88, p. 77]

JoAnn V. Rogers

84.   Genaway, David C., comp. and ed. **Conference on Integrated Online Library Systems, September 23 and 24, 1986, St. Louis, Missouri. Proceedings.** Canfield, Ohio, Genaway, 1987. 460p. illus. $39.95pa. ISBN 0-943970-05-9.

This collection of the proceedings of the third National Conference on Integrated Online Library Systems includes eleven plenary sessions papers and panel discussions and twenty-two contributed papers. The theme of the conference has been expanded to include "open" systems and interfacing stand-alone subsystems, an emphasis reflected throughout the papers.

Among the more notable contributions are Richard W. Boss, "Corporate Mergers and Consolidations and Coming Trends in Integrated Online Library Systems"; Richard S. Dick, "Artificial Intelligence: Implications for Bibliographic Utilities, Online Databases, and Integrated Online Library Systems"; Charles R. Hildreth, "Online Public Access Catalogs: Evaluation, Selection, and Effect"; S. Michael Malinconico, "Integrated Online Library Systems—Alternatives"; and Duane E. Webster, "The Impact of Library Technology on Management."

A particular strength of this collection is the balance between papers providing an overview of integrated online library systems and those dealing with applications in specific library settings. Another well-balanced continuum is that between technical and management issues. Weaknesses are those generic to transcriptions of proceedings: unevenness in the quality of the contributions, the informality and occasional disorganized and rambling nature of the presentations, particularly with respect to panel discussions, and the lack of indexes. Nevertheless, this is an interesting collection of information and perceptive professional commentary on integrated online library systems, suitable primarily for selected browsing rather than for straight reading.

Joe A. Hewitt

85.   Harrison, Denise. **The Development of the Administration of Interlending by Microcomputer (A.I.M.) at Sheffield University Library.** Leeds, England, Department of Library and Information Studies, Leeds Polytechnic, 1987. 103p. (MA Occasional Publication, No. 3). £10.00pa. ISBN 0-900738-39-1.

In December 1985, a pilot evaluatory project was initiated at the medical and dental library of Sheffield University in order to determine the feasibility of automating interlibrary lending activities. Microcomputers were to be used for these activities. If the pilot project proved successful, the intention was to expand automated interlending activities throughout the university system. Unfortunately, numerous problems occurred so that implementation still has not taken place. This document traces the project's background, methodologies, evaluation of automated systems in the United Kingdom, and concludes that additional investigation and discussion are required before final conclusions can be made.

In this age of automation, success stories are the norm. It is the rare article or document that chronicles anything less. Based on this alone, this publication makes for interesting reading. Even so, a basic question arises about the hypothesis behind the project: given the dependence of automated interlending on the linking of many different libraries' collections, was it likely that microcomputers could support these activities effectively?

This report has not been typeset and is issued in a plastic binder. These factors could easily be overlooked if the information contained between the covers were of significance. This simply is not the case. As a result, this work is recommended only for collections that have the luxury of purchasing peripheral works. [R: LAR, 15 June 88, p. 349]

Marjorie E. Bloss

86.   Hewitt, Joe A., ed. **Advances in Library Automation and Networking: A Research Annual. Volume 2: 1988.** Greenwich, Conn., JAI Press, 1988. 257p. $58.50. ISBN 0-89232-673-5.

The concerns of this work center on the intersection of traditional and new technologies, communications among library automation and networking, and the broad impact of technology on libraries. The authors of the papers in volume 2 successfully address their topics to the informed nonspecialist.

Described by the editor as an "eclectic coverage of topics" (p. ix), volume 2 has two sets of interrelated papers. The first set addresses the future of library automation. Francis Miksa envisions that libraries will invest less in collection building and more in providing access mechanisms that depend on demand-driven procedures. His call for intelligent systems is taken up by Rao Aluri and Donald E. Riggs who review the application of expert systems to libraries.

Readers who keep Miksa's ideas in mind might find AMIGOS collection analysis processing as a potential strategy for identifying collection strengths on the road to demand-drive information access. Arnold Hirshon's view complements Miksa's and includes administrative vision and effective management of change. J. Drew Racine speculates on the future role of the OCLC Users Council in OCLC governance.

The second set of papers treats library automation systems and management issues. Jerry V. Caswell recommends a strategy for system performance evaluation. Wilson M. Stahl advises library administrators to develop and maintain an ongoing plan for system upgrades. Jaye Bausser provides assistance in the analysis and planning processes related to closing card catalogs. Issues related to the provision of CD-ROM and other databases accessed by microcomputers are described by Carson Holloway. [R: JAL, Nov 88, p. 330]

Karen Markey

87. Kershner, Lois M. **Forms for Automated Library Systems: An Illustrated Guide for Selection, Design & Use.** New York, Neal-Schuman, 1988. 307p. illus. index. $99.95 looseleaf with binder. LC 87-35029. ISBN 1-55570-026-8.

This is a collection of six hundred forms gathered by the author from a variety of libraries and automated library systems vendors, including CLSI, DYNIX, Geac, and Inlex. The main purpose of the collection is to save librarians from the tiresome business of designing forms themselves. The forms are organized in a looseleaf binder covering nine areas: acquisition control, bibliographic database conversion and maintenance, patron registration and patron maintenance, circulation control, patron requests, online reference searching, patron use of microcomputers, automated systems operations, and administration and management reporting. Each of the nine parts begins with a clear, well-written introduction on the tasks for which the forms are needed for the activity covered in that section. There is also an excellent index.

Some of the forms contain information pertinent to the library that designed them. As these are so library specific they are much less useful than the forms which contain no library data. Although some design ideas can be obtained from such forms, the user has to produce a blank copy of the form; thus, more work is required. There is a short discussion of good form design but no evaluation of the included forms based on the principles of good design. There is also no coverage of the important topic of forms control, which is one most libraries urgently need to deal with.

This collection will be a useful tool for librarians, though it does not come cheap. Large library systems that have a variety of activities for which they need forms will profit most. Smaller systems would find it cheaper to design their own if they had access to a Macintosh or Apple IIGS computer.

Linda Main

88. **Not Alone... But Together: A Conference on Multitype Library Cooperation.** Alphonse F. Trezza, ed. Tallahassee, Fla., School of Library and Information Studies, Florida State University, 1987. 144p. $4.00pa.

This collection of sixteen papers delivered at a 1986 conference held at the Florida State University library school is organized into six parts: "Information Resources and Society," "Multitype Library Cooperation," "Role of Libraries in Library Cooperation," "Networks and Technology," "Current Issues in Nationwide Networking," and "Education and Training." The reader looking for new insight into the problems and solutions to multitype library cooperation will probably be disappointed. There is little new research presented, and most of what is presented lacks the necessary supporting documentation. For the most part, the papers describe a particular experience with, or view of, cooperation or networking. Some of the papers focus more on networking in general and refer to multitype cooperation only in passing.

Two of the stronger papers, Blanche Woolls's "School Libraries in Networking" and Brooke Sheldon's "Education for Library Cooperation," focus on the subject of multitype cooperation more than many of the others. One suspects that the best part of this conference, as is the case with most conferences, was the discussions after the papers. Unfortunately, those discussions are not included. There are a few typographical errors, including references to figures 1 through 4 in M. E. L. Jacob's paper on "Changing Roles: National Networks and the Future," but the figures were not included in the published paper.

There are a number of other proceedings of conferences on networking and multitype cooperation that might serve as a better resource for background on the topic, but the price of this compilation is right for those who want a copy for their collection. [R: JAL, Mar 88, p. 58; JAL, Sept 88, p. 242; RLR, Aug 88, pp. 211-12]

Terry L. Weech

89.   Stallings, William. **Local Networks.** 2d ed. New York, Macmillan, 1987. 434p. illus. bibliog. index. $42.25. LC 86-12857. ISBN 0-02-415520-9.

Local area networks (LANs) connect communicating devices within a relatively small area. They permit the sharing of expensive peripherals in addition to enhancing the use of computers, telephones, and other devices on the network. Information about LANs tends to be written for the technical expert and is very difficult for the relative beginner to understand. The author of this work has provided a clear, concise, relatively nonmathematical exploration of the technology and architecture of networks with a focus on common principles underlying design and implementation of LANs. Definitions of each component of the network, with a description of uses, plus a discussion of benefits and liabilities of each, provide a point from which one can begin to gain a working knowledge of LANs.

This is an acronym-laden field. A list of the most common acronyms is on the front flyleaf, a glossary expands the list considerably, while additional acronyms are included in the index. In another context, this might be viewed as an overemphasis, but in the acronym frenzy of LANs, it is useful. Suggestions for further reading are listed at the end of each chapter and in the bibliography. For those who wish to use this as a text, problems accompany each chapter. Graphically, this is a well-produced book with many well-designed diagrams and charts.

Here is the place to start for those who wish to come up to a basic level of understanding quickly and for those who need a reliable referral source for background information.

Ann E. Prentice

90.   Townley, Charles T. **Human Relations in Library Network Development.** Hamden, Conn., Library Professional Publications/Shoe String Press, 1988. 161p. bibliog. index. $25.00. LC 88-2776. ISBN 0-208-02086-1.

The purpose of this book is "to present information on how organization theory and development techniques can be used to improve the effectiveness of library networks." In this tightly written and well-organized text, two short introductory chapters cover networks and organization behavior in general as it relates to networks. The third focuses on organization development. Chapters 4-7 present nineteen case studies of organization development intervention in library networks. The author reports that the cases are based on actual network situations but that the application of intervention techniques is for the most part invented as

network organizations have been slow to seek out consultants or apply the techniques. Techniques are grouped into human processual, technostructural, human resource management, and strategic intervention. With each case description of the problem is limited and the suggested solution through intervention by a consultant is narrow. There is much food for thought here for network managers in spite of the somewhat superficial nature of the cases. Networks are a particular breed of organization, but problem-solving techniques borrowed from other settings can apply as the author tries to demonstrate. [R: BL, 1 Oct 88, p. 217; JAL, Nov 88, p. 328]   JoAnn V. Rogers

Microcomputers in Automation

91.   **Essential Guide to Apple Computers in Libraries. Volume 3: Communications and Networking.** By Richard Fensterer. Westport, Conn., Meckler, 1988. 219p. illus. index. $24.95 spiralbound. LC 88-9064. ISBN 0-88736-076-9.

Compared to other volumes in the series, Fensterer has put together an excellent introductory guide to computer communications and networking. Written in as nontechnical language as possible, the volume covers the concerns of any library staff who have gone beyond the single station Apple or Macintosh microcomputer and desire to link in-house computers together to take advantage of sharing data and connecting computers to expensive laser printers.

Chapters cover modems, bulletin boards, communications software, how networks operate, network design, network hardware and software, and finally, network operation. Fensterer knows his subject. His experience in communications in his own public library is comprehensive and he not only works his own experience into the text, but is at ease describing other systems and configurations. Many commercial products are described and their features compared, and the information is current to its publication date. There are also enough detailed instructions on hooking up the AppleTalk network that the reader can talk intelligently to dealers and understand the basic procedures of hooking up the system (before tackling cryptic documentation provided by the manufacturers). Helpful photographs, resource lists, and a good glossary increase the usefulness of the text. For any librarian ready to link or communicate via telephone lines with Apple or Macintosh computers, this manual is must reading and highly recommended.

David V. Loertscher

92. Intner, Sheila S., and Jane Anne Hannigan, eds. **The Library Microcomputer Environment: Management Issues.** Phoenix, Ariz., Oryx Press, 1988. 258p. index. $27.50pa. LC 87-24723. ISBN 0-89774-229-X.

One never knows what to expect from edited collections in Z678.9, "Microcomputers—Library Applications." The evolution of this particular volume's title from *Managing Microcomputer Software Collections* to *Managing Microcomputer Collections* to *The Library Microcomputer Environment* (p. vi) is one clue. The editors are both luminaries of the technical services and library education fields. The publisher is one of the most respected. And, indeed, the essays are well written, well chosen, and well constellated.

Comprised of introduction, afterword, index, bibliographies, and thirteen essays, the volume manages to touch upon every major area of importance to the automating library. First, microcomputer software is viewed as a traditional thing (information) in a nontraditional package (diskette). How does one collect it, catalog it, use it at the reference desk? Second, the software is looked at as a nontraditional thing (high tech machinage) crashing the tradition-bound gates of the library. This is probably the most written-about aspect of microcomputers for library applications. However, the information presented here is not adventitious. The UNIX essay is particularly interesting. Last, software is examined in a more visionary way, as a continuous future/present, a prelude to other technologies. The CD-ROM chapter here may read the choppiest, but it is still one of the most insightful of the collection.

There are some great and useful lists in this book: Hannigan's "Curve of nonsatisfaction" (p. 216) and Kay Vandergrift's checklist for tutorial evaluations (p. 228). Mastering a microcomputer routine for the circulation desk or the cataloging office cannot become the end of the line. As Roger Wyatt says, "We shape our technologies and they shape us" (p. 171). [R: BL, July 88, p. 1780; CLJ, Aug 88, p. 256; LJ, July 88, p. 58]　　　　　Judith M. Brugger

93. Nelson, Nancy Melin, ed. **Connecting with Technology 1988: Microcomputers in Libraries. Research Contributions from the 1988 Small Computers in Libraries Conference.** Westport, Conn., Meckler, 1988. 85p. index. (Supplement to *Small Computers in Libraries*, No. 8). $29.50. LC 88-13343. ISBN 0-88736-330-X.

Nelson has brought together slightly expanded versions of the papers delivered at the annual conference on microcomputers in libraries. The seven papers represent some well-known names in library automation including Gary Kildall, the inventor of CP/M; Karl Beiser, library automation coordinator for the Maine State Library; Monica Ertel from Apple; Jennifer Cargill from Rice University; Dorice Horne, software editor of *Small Computers in Libraries*; Dan Marmion from AMIGOS; and William Potter from the Library and Information Technology Association.

For those unable to attend the conference, the papers review the uses of computers in the modern library, the state of the technology, and provide some helpful advice to those beginning or already seriously incorporating microcomputers into library tasks. This work is recommended for those who are trying to keep abreast of the developments in this rapidly changing field. For those already keeping up with microcomputers in libraries through regular reading, this publication will add little to their repertoire.　　　　　David V. Loertscher

94. Palmer, Roger C. **Understanding Library Microcomputer Systems.** Studio City, Calif., Pacific Information, 1988. 128p. with disk. illus. (Professional Skills Series). $29.95pa. LC 88-17866. ISBN 0-913203-19-X.

Presented in this work is the process of creating "a book acquisition system for a special library having a staff of three and a limited automation budget" (p. vii). This process is outlined within the framework of a systems development life cycle. The author pays most attention to life cycle steps involving staff requirements for printed forms, reports, and hardware; system design; hardware selection; and systems documentation.

Understanding Library Microcomputer Systems has four related parts: a life cycle description, a system user manual, exercises, and book acquisition system (BAS) software. Suggested reading lists accompany parts 1 and 3. BAS operates in a microcomputer environment with at least an IBM PC or PC-compatible computer with 512 kilobytes of RAM, DOS 2.1, one 360K floppy drive, 10-megabyte fixed disk, and a printer capable of condensed elite and pica printing using the Epson or IBM Proprinter dot matrix character sets.

Library school educators can enlist comprehensive textbooks in library automation, technical services, systems analysis, or library microcomputer applications to give students broad-based knowledge in these areas. They could supplement their teaching with Palmer's book to increase students' understanding of the system development process and to give them hands-on experience using an automated library system and its documentation.

Karen Markey

95. Uppgard, Jeannine. **Developing Microcomputer Work Areas in Academic Libraries.** Westport, Conn., Meckler, 1988. 124p. illus. bibliog. index. (Supplement to *Small Computers in Libraries*, No. 5). $37.50. LC 87-31232. ISBN 0-88736-233-8.

Chapters 1 through 5 of this volume are anecdotal accounts of five libraries' experiences setting up and operating public access microcomputer labs. While each includes details about the physical problems that were encountered and the attempts to resolve these problems, it is the discussion of, the development of, and changes in policies that are most interesting and will attract the most readers to these chapters.

Chapter 6, "A Librarian/Manager's Point of View," complements the first five chapters by rising above local problems and idiosyncrasies, providing a comprehensive overview of the issues and concerns faced by all academic libraries entering the microcomputer era. The chapter discusses such aspects as the institutional culture; the multiple relationships between the library, the computer center, the university administration, and the campus; software acquisition; financial support; and the appropriate use of software and computing. The excellent advice is helpful without being prescriptive.

Chapters 7 and 8, an annotated bibliography and a directory of library microcomputer labs, are becoming dated. [R: LJ, 15 Sept 88, p. 64]

Lawrence W. S. Auld

Online Catalogs

96. **The COOL-CAT Trial: A Report on the Trial of the CAVAL Operated Online Catalogue and Regional Data Access System.** Camberwell, Vic., Aust., CAVAL, 1987. 1v. (various paging). illus. $19.95pa.

Although based upon the 1986 version of the TOMUS modular turnkey system developed by Carlyle Systems, this trial report can serve as a model case study for those libraries attempting to document the implementation of an online catalog. Results indicate that "TOMUS has proved to be a reliable, readily accessible, easy to use, and flexible searching tool" based upon a pilot project of 300,000 MARC records and twenty-six terminals shared by the libraries of the University of Melbourne, La Trobe University, Deakin University, the State Library of Victoria, Melbourne College of Advanced Education, and the National Library of Australia.

The report is arranged into twelve chapters (e.g., database specifications, user response, and publicity) and six appendices (e.g., system description, welcome screen, and matrix of indexing fields). Within each chapter, practical information on project management structure, site preparation guidelines, and stress test procedures is included. Refreshingly candid and realistic descriptions of problem areas—unstable power supplies and shortage of memory space—are provided and not glossed over.

This report will be of maximum benefit to those libraries planning to bring up an online public access catalog in the near future. Despite system modifications which have occurred over the past few years, the work can still prove to be useful, and serves as a worthy complement to *Automation Projects: The Evaluation Stage* (Library Administration and Management Association, American Library Association, 1988).

Ilene F. Rockman

97. Henty, Margaret. **User Response to URICA: A Catalogue Online.** Canberra, Australia, Australian National University Library, 1987. 69p. (ANU Library Occasional Paper, No. 5). $10.00pa. ISBN 0-7315-0055-5.

Besides being a report of user reaction to a new online public access catalog (OPAC) module of URICA (the Australian National University Library's (ANU) integrated library system), this research report also covers reactions of the ANU population to other forms of the library catalog which they still may be using and investigates whether users found the new system easy to operate or whether they encountered problems with it. Eight months after the OPAC module was introduced in February 1986, a mail survey was sent to a stratified random sample of 1,102 library users in the ANU population. Library users were divided into four groups and within these groups into thirteen strata. The groups studied were academic staff, research assistants, postgraduate students, and undergraduates. The questionnaire was designed to assess public acceptance of URICA, to discover any reasons for dissatisfaction or nonuse, and to seek suggestions for improvement to the system. The response rate was 75 percent overall and no group had less than a 72 percent return. The results are reported by means of tables, charts, and records of open-ended remarks. Among other findings, the results show that subject searching is the most frequent problem for all groups. One respondent expressed succinctly the feelings of more than a third of each group who had problems doing subject searching when he said, "Sure, searching is easy—it's finding that's the problem!" The

LCSH microfiche which is available to users was not found to be useful. Besides improvements in this area, suggestions were made about user education programs, improved software design, a pay printer, circulation data, and a break key. A postscript finishes the report and indicates that several changes have been made to respond to the suggestions and problems of users as revealed in the survey, but no help for the subject searcher is in this list of changes.

This report is an excellent example of what a research report should contain and how clearly it should be written. The appendices contain a copy of the questionnaire, standard errors of estimates, and the weighting used to alter the representation of each stratum to make the data aggregated on a group basis representative. [R: RLR, Nov 88, pp. 345-46]

Pauline A. Cochrane

98. Kesselman, Martin, and Sarah B. Watstein, eds. **End-User Searching: Services and Providers.** Chicago, American Library Association, 1988. 230p. bibliog. index. $26.00pa. LC 87-37444. ISBN 0-8389-0488-2.

Information on end-user searching is scattered throughout library, computer, and business literature. The authors of the book shown here have gathered the important details from the broad spectrum of articles, books, and technical documents to provide a useful compilation of information.

Chapters cover both the practical aspects of beginning an end-user searching service, from preparing a proposal through training and evaluation, and summaries and comparisons of major end-user services and software, information which, of course, is already out-of-date. The research is impressive and, as should be expected of an ALA publication, the documentation is excellent. Chapter notes and bibliographies are supplemented by two annotated bibliographies. A directory of online products and services and an index complete the volume.

It must be admitted that most of the information presented here is available elsewhere. What is useful about this book is that it brings together so much information helpful to anyone considering establishing an end-user search program. While it cannot serve as the only, or even the major, source for making such a decision, it can save a great deal of time and provide a firm basis for further research. [R: LJ, Aug 88, p. 86]

Susan Davis Herring

99. **Nationwide Networking. Proceedings of the Library of Congress Network Advisory Committee Meetings July and December 1986.** Washington, D.C., Cataloging Distribution Service, Library of Congress, 1987. 65p. (Network Planning Paper, No. 15). $7.50pa. LC 87-600299. ISBN 0-8444-0573-6.

The Library of Congress Network Advisory Committee devoted four program sessions to issues related to nationwide networking. Network Planning Papers 12 and 13 reported the first two programs. Network Planning Paper 15 reports the proceedings of the final two sessions and represents the culmination of the four-program series.

This planning paper begins with "Library Networking: Statement of a Common Vision," a brief, general statement endorsed by the committee. Henriette Avram recounts events leading to the statement, and Mary W. Ghikas presents a summary report of the Network Advisory Committee action agenda based on the statement of common vision. Background papers presented in these proceedings include "NCLIS: A Look Ahead" by Vivian J. Arterbery, "Linking Systems and Resource Sharing" by David Brunell, "The Role of Standards in Networking" by Sandra K. Paul, "Networks and Public Policy" by Carol C. Henderson, "Economic Issues in Nationwide Networking" by Fay Zipkowitz, and Eric Love's "Education Needs on the Concept of Networking."

The Network Planning Paper series of LC's Network Development and MARC Standards Office is a basic resource for anyone interested in library networks. *Nationwide Networking* is no exception.

Joe A. Hewitt

100. Nicholas, David, Kevin Harris, and Gertrud Erbach. **Online Searching: Its Impact on Information Users.** London, Mansell; distr., Rutherford, N.J., Publishers Distribution Center, 1987. 160p. bibliog. index. (British Library R & D Report, 5944). $45.00. LC 87-18527. ISBN 0-7201-1887-5.

A report of the Information Seeking in an Information Society (ISIS) research project funded by the British Library Association, this book is primarily a series of case studies examining the impact of online searching on the information seeking behavior of workers at Time-Life International, *The Guardian*, a magazine publisher, and a stockbrokerage firm. Due in part to the difficulty of imposing formal evaluation methods on employees in jobs that require variable and often hectic work schedules, the methodology in these studies is primarily informal interviews and observations. The case studies are fascinating, perhaps more for their detailed description of the intricacies of office politics than for revelations about online use. However, there are some interesting insights into pitfalls encountered when attempting to make online access available to end-users. Conclusions point to a general enthusiasm for the concept of online information, but an equally general reluctance to accept online search as a routine method of acquiring information. Since the report covers the time from November 1985 to October 1986 – now more than two years ago – and describes online activities in the United Kingdom, there is a question of how relevant this information may be for readers in the United States. Nonetheless, the insight into information-seeking behavior in some major British companies may well be worth the price of this book.   Elisabeth Logan

101. **Online Information Services for Schools: Implications for School Libraries.** Doubleview, Aust., Western Australian College of Advanced Education, 1987. 93p. illus. bibliog. $7.00pa. ISBN 0-7298-0050-4.

This is a report consisting of a mere ninety-three pages, including appendices. Its emphasis is primarily on the establishment of online search services in school libraries in Australia. It appears that the intended audience are those individuals who have had no experience whatsoever with computers and computer searching. Although covering a wide range of topics, that is, the role of teacher-librarian in relation to information technology and online services and sources, the book gives minimum detail.

For the librarian and the teacher, probably the most useful information is found in the appendices, notably appendices A and B. Appendix A provides several examples of the ways teachers can incorporate online searching into their lesson plans. Appendix B is an annotated directory of search services.

Except for possibly its readers in Australia, those people interested in online services can find more detailed, comprehensive information elsewhere. [R: LAR, 15 June 88, p. 352]
                              Phillip P. Powell

102. **Remote Access to Online Catalogs.** By Jinnie Y. Davis. Washington, D.C., Association of Research Libraries, 1988. 116p. illus. bibliog. (SPEC Kit, No. 142). $20.00pa.

This SPEC Kit contains the results of a survey on remote access to online catalogs. Members of the Association of Research Libraries (ARL) who provided remote access in 1986 were surveyed during the fall of 1987. Remote access was defined as "the availability of the online catalog through terminals or microcomputers" (p. 1) using a modem or a network to contend for computer ports. The survey was designed to address three areas of concern related to remote access: technical topics,

user instruction and services, and management issues.

The kit includes a copy of the survey questionnaire, a summary of responses and list of respondents, three implementation reports or proposals, examples of instructional materials, user aids and user feedback formats, some sample job descriptions, and one policy statement. A selected reading list is also provided. All samples are unedited copies of documents submitted by participating libraries. In places, more samples would have been useful to provide alternative perspectives. However, the survey results reveal that few formal documents and user studies exist. Remote access is a fairly new service and many institutions are approaching it tentatively.

Although rapidly changing technology will make some information obsolete, the kit contains practical solutions that are proven. The samples document the variety of solutions that ARL members have devised to manage remote access issues. This book is suitable for library managers who are planning to offer remote access for the first time or who are considering changes to existing services. [R: JAL, July 88, p. 182]   Lynn Morgan

CAREERS

103. Everett, John H., and Elizabeth Powell Crowe. **Information for Sale: How to Start and Operate Your Own Data Research Service.** Blue Ridge Summit, Pa., TAB Books, 1988. 178p. index. $15.95pa. LC 88-12319. ISBN 0-8306-9357-2.

Everett and Crowe have produced a well-written introduction to the world of the information broker. In layperson's language, they explain both that which can be accomplished and also the pitfalls one can experience when starting and running a data research service. The first chapters are particularly important for both the beginner and the more experienced searcher. They define the role of the information broker and discuss the many details involved in the actual opening of such a business. Subsequent chapters cover the importance of marketing, fees and charges, and legal considerations. The authors spend an even greater portion of the book discussing the technology about which an information professional needs to know, such as CD-ROM systems, gateway services and software, and full-text databases. Also of interest are the chapters which give in-depth information of a sample search and interviews with successful information brokers. The twenty-four-page final chapter is a directory of database services, publications, professional associations, and software plus a bibliography of books and articles concerning for-profit search services.

This book is highly recommended to anyone, beginner or not, who is considering becoming an information broker and needs a well-written source providing solid background information on the topic.

Phillip P. Powell

104. Johnson, Ian M. **The Library School Leavers Handbook.** Newcastle-under-Lyme, England, AAL Publishing; distr., Newcastle-under-Lyme, England, Remploy, 1987. 51p. £6.00pa. ISBN 0-900092-59-9.

A handy handbook of limited usefulness, this pamphlet offers new library school graduates practical advice on how to get a job and how to look at the employment alternatives that exist in the current job market — in England. The job market there is, as here, a mismatch between available jobs and skilled people. Also, there, as here, universities tend not to offer specific library career assistance. So, this publication is informative on job resources, salaries, applications, and interviews in England. The chapter on alternative careers would have been useful elsewhere if treated with greater depth and creativity. Publishing and teaching are not innovative approaches for librarians to regard as alternatives.

Considering the wealth of self-help career planning and job strategies books, as well as other resources available, this would not be worthwhile as an institutional purchase. It would, however, provide a good orientation for a U.S. librarian seeking to relocate to England. [R: RLR, Aug 88, p. 197]

Barbara Conroy

105. **Librarian Career Resource Network Directory.** Chicago, Office for Library Personnel Resources, American Library Association, 1987. 37p. index. $2.00pa. ISBN 0-8389-7205-5.

The aim of this ALA Office for Library Personnel Resources publication is to provide a "list of practicing librarians who have volunteered to answer career related questions." Volunteers are listed in alphabetical order along with particulars concerning their position, address, areas of expertise, and indications of the method of contact they prefer. Geographical and subject indexes are included. ALA/OLPR assumes responsibility for maintaining the directory.

The philosophy behind such a directory is apparently well founded. Certainly it seems reasonable to identify willing experts to guide

other librarians in career choices and explorations. The problem I have encountered with other such directories is that they are often uneven, poorly maintained, and inadequately distributed. Only responses from users and volunteers and time will tell if this effort can escape those pitfalls. The start is adequate and propitious. We hope that the directory will grow and increase in usefulness.

Patricia A. Steele

106. Mount, Ellis, ed. **Alternative Careers in Sci-Tech Information Service.** New York, Haworth Press, 1987. 154p. bibliog. (*Science & Technology Libraries*, Vol. 7, No. 4). $22.95. LC 87-22317. ISBN 0-86656-694-5.

The eight contributors to the alternative careers portion of this book, speaking from their experience in alternative career positions, discuss opportunities for others with a sci-tech background — whether as librarians, scientists, or engineers — to pursue successful careers. Mount, the editor, is assistant professor at the School of Library Service at Columbia University.

The alternative careers described — each in terms of the skills and education needed, working environment, rewards and challenges, and future prospects — are information broker, translator, acquisitions editor for a scientific publisher, information resources manager, research scientist, online database manager, abstractor, and indexer. The remainder of this work (also published as *Science & Technology Libraries*, vol. 7, no. 4, Summer 1987) includes two special papers (one describing an outstanding collection on electricity at the Engineering Societies Library and the other concluding a two-part account on preserving the collections of the Science and Technology Center of the New York Public Library), a collections study (part 1) dealing with the literature and history of CAD/CAM (Computer-Aided Design/Computer-Aided Manufacturing), and "New Reference Works in Science and Technology," a regular feature of *Science & Technology Libraries*.

Library science collections will want this title as either a monograph or a serial publication. [R: BL, 1 Oct 88, pp. 216-17; JAL, Sept 88, p. 244; LJ, July 88, p. 58; WLB, Oct 88, p. 94]

Wiley J. Williams

107. Ritchie, Sheila, Stephen Roberts, and Simon Pugh, eds. **Employers and Self-Employment in Librarianship and Information Work.** Bradford, England, MCB University Press, 1988. 1v. (various paging). index. (*Information and Library Manager*, Vol. 7, No. 5). $59.95pa. ISBN 0-86176-372-6.

This British publication includes an editorial, five papers, and three book reviews. The papers, read at the East Anglican Librarians Consulative Committee (EALCC) Seminar held in Norwich, England, May 1988, are entitled "Alternative Book Selling"; "The Self-Employed Historical Researcher"; "He Is Not Busy Being Born Is Busy Dying"; "Employment Patterns and Curriculum Development"; and "Manpower Planning and Information Work: A Survey and Checklist." The first three of these are based on the nonlibrary experience of former librarians successful in new professions. This issue includes the complete index to volume 7 of the series.

All of the papers give some valuable and interesting information; but, based on the price, the quality of the papers, and the tight budget libraries have, this issue is not recommended for any collections.   Ravindra Nath Sharma

CATALOGING AND CLASSIFICATION

General Works

108. Piggott, Mary. **A Topography of Cataloguing: Showing the Most Important Landmarks, Communications and Perilous Places.** London, Library Association; distr., Chicago, American Library Association, 1988. 287p. index. $27.50. ISBN 0-85365-758-0.

This book is the highly successful first part of an attempt, in two complementary volumes, to explain the nature, processes, and challenges of cataloging and bibliographic control, and to place them in the context of language, information transfer, and client needs. It begins with a clear and convincing rationale for catalogs and bibliographic control. This is followed by an overview of cooperation, automation, and centralization efforts in technical services. The work continues with a definition of standards and the standard-making process and a brief review of the major standards that apply to bibliographic control. Descriptive cataloging is effectively explained. Two chapters give a valuable introduction to language and script and their effect on bibliographic control. Four chapters provide an introduction to subject cataloging, beginning with the analysis of books and proceeding through the construction of classified subject catalogs and their alphabetical indexes, alphabetical subject catalogs, and some of the nature and problems of important tools and techniques used in subject cataloging. The last chapters discuss the dictionary catalog,

current filing codes, and (very briefly) name catalogs.

The author's approach emphasizes definition, rationale, problems, and context. These are handled with clarity and dispatch. Arguments are logical and convincing. Each chapter cards with a carefully chosen list of references. The book seems free of typographical or substantive error. The table of contents includes chapter topic lists, and there is a good index.

There are some minor deficiencies in the book. The chapters on computerization and cooperation would serve North American audiences better if rewritten to place more emphasis on U.S. and Canadian national, regional, and local systems. These chapters also may appear prematurely in that a clear picture of the whole catalog record may not be fixed in the reader's mind before he or she is asked to consider the complex handling of that record in today's library.

On the other hand, the discussion of European classified catalogs and their indexes is one of this book's strengths. It will give valuable perspective to beginners in countries dominated by dictionary catalogs and the *Library of Congress Subject Headings*.

This book adds value to the cataloger's tools and techniques by pointing out their nature, problems, interrelationships, and wider context. When finished, the work should make an excellent text for technical services courses taught from the major cataloging tools and standards. It may be read profitably by both the student cataloger and the student preparing for other roles who needs a clear and convincing account of the part cataloging plays in libraries, and the complexities with which catalogers must struggle. [R: JAL, Nov 88, p. 329; LAR, 16 Nov 88, p. 675]   George M. Sinkankas

109. Taylor, Archer. **Book Catalogues: Their Varieties and Uses.** 2d ed. Revised by Wm. P. Barlow, Jr. New York, Frederic C. Beil, c1986, 1987. 284p. index. $45.00. LC 86-72682. ISBN 0-913720-66-6.

This is a revision of a well-known and oft-consulted text on an important aspect of the history of bibliography. *Book Catalogues*, originally published in 1957, was a ground-breaking publication for its time and remains a standard reference on its topic.

Taylor's opus concerns published European and North American catalogs of books owned by private individuals, institutions, booksellers, and publishers. The volume includes two valuable lengthy chapters on the history and varieties of book catalogs and the potential research uses of the catalogs. The section on their uses is, of course, dated but presaged much of the work that has been done with such catalogs. The book is rounded off with bibliographies of catalogs and a list of catalogs of private libraries recommended for reference use.

This reissuing of Taylor's work has been much improved by Barlow who has included a brief introduction about Taylor and the significance of this volume, as well as extensive corrections and additions to the original text. Every library with holdings on the history of bibliography will wish to acquire this updated edition.

Richard J. Cox

Classification and Classification Schemes

110. Bose, H. **Universal Decimal Classification: Theory and Practice.** New Delhi, Sterling; distr., New York, Apt Books, 1987. 176p. bibliog. index. $25.00. ISBN 81-207-0716-8.

Bose, "an information scientist who has studied at the Universities of Patna, Calcutta, BHU and Delhi ... [and has] worked in technical information centres for three decades" (book jacket), has written this small work to guide classifiers in the application of the recent 1985 "International Medium Edition" of the Universal Decimal Classification, prepared by the British Standards Institution (BS 1000M: 1985; International Federation for Documentation (FID) Publication, No. 571). Bose presents a brief history of the UDC's development and its chief characteristics, with separate chapters focusing on its many auxiliary schedules, the main schedule of classes, a suggested approach to their application, examples and exercises, and methods for preparing alphabetical indexes to classified files. The book concludes with a listing of UDC fascicules published since 1961, a bibliography, and a very brief index (two pages).

While Bose's experience and thought as a long-time user of the UDC is evident, the book suffers from poor editing. There are too many typographical errors, vague references to notation not yet described or defined, errors, and confusing statements. Some examples: "Till this day the division of classes in both the classification systems [Dewey Decimal Classification and UDC] remains unaltered" (p. 46)—I am not sure what this means; both have received extensive revisions. "The DDC has three auxiliary tables" (p. 46)—the eighteenth edition had seven auxiliary tables. "The meaning of 'facet' needs to be made explicit. It may be recalled that the totality of divisions of a basic class according to a single

train of characteristics is said to constitute one of its facets" (p. 89)—not very explicit, at least to me. "The entire exercise of analysis has to be conducted mental on a plane" (p. 96). But more serious in my view is an underlying misconception of the nature of human analysis and indexing. Both experience and research show that much of meaning resides in the mind of the interpreter, and thus it is inevitable and appropriate that different persons will interpret the same text in different ways. Bose disagrees: "But it should not be so because the methodology of classification, when it rests on a sound theoretical base, should yield the same result whoever may classify the document" (p. vii). Nonsense. I cannot recommend this book. [R: JAL, Sept 88, p. 260]

James D. Anderson

111. Burgess, Michael. **A Guide to Science Fiction and Fantasy in the Library of Congress Classification Scheme.** 2d ed. San Bernardino, Calif., Borgo Press, 1988. 168p. (Borgo Cataloging Guides, No. 1). $22.95; $12.95pa. LC 87-6308. ISBN 0-89370-827-5; 0-89370-927-1pa.

This second edition represents a substantial expansion of the original cataloging guide, filling nearly twice the number of pages. Its section 1 list of Library of Congress subject headings is expanded to include all new ones in use through mid-1987, and indicates cancellations or revisions in brackets. Standard subdivisions for authors and for fictitious characters are separately given, using Edgar Rice Burroughs and Tarzan (fictitious character) as examples. A short explanation of usage precedes the excerpted LC classification tables, which have been shifted from the back of the book to section 2. Section 3 gives author main entries, as verified in LC's Name Authority File through the summer of 1987, together with their LC literature numbers. It also shows LC literature table blocks by author nationality and date, and for authors of other nationalities who write in English. It is prefaced by a five-page discussion of the difficulties resulting from the simplifications introduced in AACR2. Next come similar lists of established main entries and LC numbers for artists, for specific motion pictures, for television and radio programs, and for comic strips, in sections 4 to 7. The program and comic strip categories are newly added. We are assured that this, and its companion Borgo Cataloging Guides, will be updated at regular intervals.

Jeanne Osborn

112. Burgess, Michael. **Mystery and Detective Fiction in the Library of Congress Classification Scheme.** San Bernardino, Calif., Borgo Press, 1987. 184p. (Borgo Cataloging Guides, No. 2).

$22.95; $12.95pa. LC 84-12344. ISBN 0-89370-818-6; 0-89370-918-2pa.

Using the format he previously developed for a cataloging guide to LC and AACR2 usage in the field of science fiction and fantasy, Burgess here performs a similar service for catalogers of mystery and detective fiction. The LC subject headings in section 1 cover LC usage through mid-1987, but the standard subdivisions for authors and fictitious characters included in the science fiction/fantasy guide are omitted. Selected LC classification numbers and an index follow in section 2. Sections 3 to 6 are devoted to LC main entries and classification numbers for specific authors, motion pictures, television programs, and comic strips, respectively. The fact that artists are of minor importance in this genre is confirmed in that no list of main entries and individual LC numbers is given for them. Like the other Borgo Cataloging Guides, this one is to be updated at regular intervals.   Jeanne Osborn

113.   Dershem, Larry D., comp. **Library of Congress Classification Class KDZ, KG-KH: Law of the Americas, Latin America and the West Indies. Cumulative Schedule and Index.** Littleton, Colo., Fred B. Rothman, 1988. 642p. (AALL Publ. Series, No. 28). $85.00 looseleaf with binder. LC 88-18256. ISBN 0-8377-0127-9.

According to the publisher's announcement, from 1982 to 1987 Dershem compiled the cumulative index and cumulative schedule to many of the Library of Congress's K (law) schedules. "The present work cumulates Class KDZ, KG-KH Law of the Americas, Latin America and the West Indies and serves the same function as the previous publications." It is the publisher's contention that "by using this new publication, librarians will have at their fingertips a complete and current schedule for Law of the Americas which should save a great deal of time in both finding and assigning call numbers." It is noted that the price covers the main volume and quarterly supplements taken from the *LC Classification Additions and Changes List.*

Little in the way of description can be added to the publisher's synopsis. This is a publication of "convenience" and there will be a difference of opinion as to whether the convenience of using this cumulation justifies its purchase price. It seems unlikely that the time differential between consulting the separate LC class schedules or using this cumulation is significant.   Larry G. Chrisman

114.   Elazar, David H., and Daniel J. Elazar. **A Classification System for Libraries of Judaica.**

2d ed. Jerusalem, Jerusalem Center for Public Affairs/Center for Jewish Community Studies and Lanham, Md., University Press of America, 1988. 214p. index. $28.50. LC 88-82. ISBN 0-8191-6583-2.

The work under review is actually a reprint, with corrections and addenda, of the second edition published in 1979 by Turtledove Publishing. There is a need to keep this classification in print because of its popularity in synagogue, Jewish school, and community center libraries. Several small Judaica college and research libraries employ this classification scheme as well. The fact that a central cataloging service providing Elazar classification numbers has recently become available (see Frischer's article in *Judaica Librarianship* [Association of Jewish Libraries, 1983-], Vol. 4, No. 1, 1988) may further promote this system of arranging Judaica collections.

The Elazar system has a Dewey-like notational structure—a minimum of three digits followed in some cases by a decimal point and additional numerals or occasional alphanumeric subdivisions. There are no separate tables, but the instruction "divide like" is found frequently in the schedules. The entire 000-999 sequence is devoted to Jewish subjects, as opposed to Dewey's 296 for Judaism and a few other numbers for Jewish topics in the language, literature, and history schedules. The Elazar scheme thus offers brevity of notation, but complicates the integration of Jewish and secular collections, which is increasingly being espoused in libraries of Jewish schools.

Interestingly, neither one of the Elazars is a practicing Judaica librarian. This may account for the paucity of addenda to the scheme (two and a quarter pages) and for the fact that errors were not corrected in the revision. Frischer's article contains many more new numbers than this reprint—all of which had been reported to and approved by the authors. They do cite a suggested revision of the Holocaust schedule by Posner (p. 155), but fail to take note of the fact that a conflict between their Holocaust topical and geographic subdivisions had been pointed out in *Judaica Librarianship* (Vol. 1, No. 1, 1983, p. 27). Nor did they include the term *Holocaust* in the addendum to the index, as the same article suggested.

Perhaps responsibility for the Elazar classification scheme should be taken over by a central cataloging service where it is used and monitored on a daily basis. In the meantime, Judaica librarians will have to work with this imperfect reprint edition.

Bella Hass Weinberg

115. Hunter, Eric J. **Classification Made Simple.** Brookfield, Vt., Gower Publishing, 1988. 115p. illus. bibliog. index. $12.95pa. LC 87-21930. ISBN 0-566-05605-4.

This text is intended to be an introductory study for students of information work or library staff and managers who need to know something about classification for information retrieval. It does not replace the more extensive textbooks on the subject. In a little more than one hundred pages the author, a senior lecturer at the School of Librarianship and Information Studies at Liverpool Polytechnic, is able to define classification; explain faceted, hierarchical, and enumerative schemes; describe the advantages and disadvantages of each; and discuss notation, citation order, and other features of classification schemes. He covers what many texts do not, that is, the relationship between classification and the compilation of thesauri. The references are scant, but contain more U.S. authors than is usually the case for a British publication. Recommended for all library school libraries and as a supplementary text for basic cataloging classes. [R: LAR, 16 Nov 88, p. 675]

Pauline A. Cochrane

116. Satija, M. P., and John P. Comaromi. **Introduction to the Practice of Dewey Decimal Classification.** New York, Envoy Press; distr., New York, Apt Books, 1987. 152p. $22.50. LC 86-83124. ISBN 0-938719-15-7.

Developed when the nineteenth edition of the *Dewey Decimal Classification* was just coming into print, the purpose of this slim volume is to teach the novice how to build numbers using both the schedules and the tables within Dewey Decimal Classification. The concept of number building, order of precedence, use of Tables 1-7, and multiple synthesis are covered. Explanations are clear and plenty of well thought-out examples are given so that the beginner can grasp the process of following the number building instructions to the letter. The last chapter provides several hundred examples (e.g., Female Journalists, 070 + 089 [Table 1] + 91412 [Table 5] = 070.089 914 12).

For the beginner or the teacher of cataloging, this book provides some excellent practice problems. The main drawback, however, is that the twentieth edition is about to appear which will affect some of the problems. Not recommended for those learning the abridged edition of *Dewey Decimal Classification*. [R: JAL, Mar 88, p. 58]

David V. Loertscher

Descriptive Cataloging

117. **Binding Terms: A Thesaurus for Use in Rare Book and Special Collections Cataloguing.** By the Standards Committee of the Rare Books and Manuscripts Section (ACRL/ALA). Chicago, Association of College and Research Libraries, American Library Association, 1988. 37p. $10.00pa. ISBN 0-8389-7210-1.

118. **Provenance Evidence: Thesaurus for Use in Rare Book and Special Collections Cataloguing.** By the Standards Committee of the Rare Books and Manuscripts Section (ACRL/ALA). Chicago, Association of College and Research Libraries, American Library Association, 1988. 19p. $9.00pa. ISBN 0-8389-7239-X.

For years most rare book libraries and departments have developed and maintained local files recording examples of various physical characteristics of books and manuscripts found in their collections. With the advent of machine-readable cataloging it became necessary for libraries to express the information in these local files in a uniform way so that this valuable information could be shared by others. In 1979 the Independent Research Libraries Association issued *Proposals for Establishing Standards for the Cataloging of Rare Books and Specialized Research Materials in Machine-readable Form*, which called for a new field to be added to the MARC format for terms indicating the physical characteristics of materials cataloged. At the same time it was proposed that the Standards Committee of the Rare Books and Manuscripts Section of ACRL undertake the development of a thesaurus of such terms. This thesaurus, it was decided, should be issued in separate parts, and the first, *Printing and Publishing Evidence*, was published in 1986. The next two—*Binding Terms* and *Provenance Evidence*—are under discussion here, and other subjects, such as paper and papermaking and type evidence, are being prepared.

The thesaurus for *Binding Terms* is arranged in two parts, an alphabetical list of terms used to describe materials, techniques and styles of bindings, and a hierarchical list which displays the relationships between broader and narrower terms. Many of the terms in the alphabetical list are defined, often with quotations from Paul Needham's *Twelve Centuries of Bookbinding 400-1600* (Pierpoint Morgan with Oxford University Press, 1979), and the introduction contains a list of references useful to the understanding of the terms.

Provenance Evidence is also divided into an alphabetical list and a hierarchical list, with definitions provided in the alphabetical list. It is important to note that " 'provenance' is here interpreted in its broadest sense to refer not only to former owners in the legal sense, but also to any who may have had temporary custody of the material (such as auction houses or library borrowers) and have left their mark in some way on it" (p. 1). A list of works useful for detailed descriptions of provenance evidence is also provided in the introduction.   Dean H. Keller

119.   Dryden, Jean E., and Kent M. Haworth. **Developing Descriptive Standards: A Call to Action. L'élaboration de Normes de Description.** Ottawa, Bureau of Canadian Archivists, 1987. 15p. (Occasional Paper, No. 1). free pa.

Canadian archivists, through the Bureau of Canadian Archivists's Planning Committee on Descriptive Standards, are exploring the issue of uniform standards for describing archival holdings. The committee was created with this goal in mind. This first publication of the committee identifies the benefits that will be realized from descriptive standards, describes the process by which such standards are being developed, and calls on members of the archives community to participate. Two working groups appointed to begin the actual development of standards and rules are preparing further reports.

The Planning Committee on Descriptive Standards was established on the recommendation of the earlier Working Group on Archival Descriptive Standards. In the group's report, *Toward Descriptive Standards* (Ottawa: Bureau of Canadian Archivists, 1985), the scope of the problem was identified and a course was charted that would lead to the development of descriptive standards for archives.

Lawrence W. S. Auld

120.   Kellen, James D. **A Manual of AACR 2 Examples for Liturgical Works and Sacred Scriptures.** 2d ed. Lake Crystal, Minn., Soldier Creek Press, 1987. 50p. illus. index. $12.50pa. ISBN 0-936996-25-0.

Liturgical works and sacred scriptures are among the more mystifying categories of materials to describe, especially regarding choice of access points. This manual is intended as an aid to catalogers who must apply the *Anglo-American Cataloguing Rules, Second Edition* (*AACR2*) to these and other religious works. The first edition was prepared in 1980 as an aid to AACR2 implementation. The second edition has been updated to reflect rule changes and interpretations promulgated between 1980 and late 1987, making it sufficiently up-to-date to be used with the 1988 reprint of the rules. It contains forty examples of liturgical works, sacred

scriptures, and some other types of religious works. Each example consists of a copy of the chief source(s) of information, a card image of the recommended description, cross-references for entry elements, and citations to AACR2 rules that governed choices made. Citations are brief, simply identifying the element of description to which the rule applies. Occasionally a terse explanation (e.g., "enter under denominational body"), or reference to the Library of Congress practice (e.g., "no brackets — LC option") are included. In rare instances, a more substantive explanation appears. There is an index to rules cited. The introduction stresses that since cataloging rules and applications are always evolving, the current validity of any element in an example cannot be assured. Because of its limited content, there is no way that this manual can be useful without *AACR2* open by its side. Within those limits, however, it may be quite useful to beginning catalogers, catalogers unfamiliar with religious materials, and any cataloger who may occasionally be puzzled by the text of a rule, or who may have difficulty visualizing the result of a particular rule's application.   Janet Swan Hill

121.   **LC Rule Interpretations of AACR2 1978-1987. [Second Update]: Covers** *Cataloging Service Bulletins No. 1 (Summer 1978)-No. 37 (Summer 1987)*; **Includes Rule Index to** *CSB*. 2d ed. Sally C. Tseng, comp. Metuchen, N.J., Scarecrow, 1988. 1v. (various paging). $25.00 looseleaf without binder. LC 85-14527. ISBN 0-8108-2102-8.

Scarecrow continues its periodic updates of Tseng's compilation of rule changes, interpretations, and revisions from the Library of Congress. The present revision carries the work through summer 1987, with new material from other issues. The looseleaf format permits filing a new title page, a revised rule index, and new and substitute pages incorporating the changes. New headings and keywords are added in the "Rule Index," with related *CSB* information on special materials cataloging, Canadian headings, the Cataloging Distribution Service, non-roman character sets, minimal level cataloging, and others included at the end. For catalogers accustomed to depending on the earlier compilations, this update will be indispensable.

Jeanne Osborn

122.   Olson, Nancy B., comp. *Cataloging Service Bulletin* **Index: An Index to the** *Cataloging Service Bulletin* **of the Library of Congress: No. 1-40, Summer 1978-Spring 1988.** Lake Crystal, Minn., Soldier Creek Press, 1988. 127p. $20.00 (unbound). ISBN 0-936996-32-3.

Information from the *Cataloging Service Bulletin* is vitally important to catalogers, but it is difficult to keep track of, so indexes to it are greeted enthusiastically. This new index covers the full run of *CSB*, including the entire AACR2 era. It is unbound, and sized to file with the bulletins themselves. Entries file under all important terms (e.g., creating added entries for the name of a manuscript repository is indexed under added entries, repository, and manuscript, and the relevant rule). Coverage is unpredictably incomplete. For example, *CSB* 13, page 7, under AA1.48B, discusses treatment of privately published works, but the occurrence is not indexed, although the previous version in *CSB* 12, page 7, *is*. Cursory checking also found no entries for "Initialisms in title proper" (*CSB* 13, p. 19); for Korean word division (*CSB* 14, pp. 71-78); or for Macroreproductions (*CSB* 14, p. 58) (but the previous version, *CSB* 12, p. 16 *is* indexed). The ease with which these omissions were detected makes more seem likely. Vocabulary is occasionally inconsistent. For example, *CSB* 13, page 27, and *CSB* 14, page 24, contain versions of the same RI, the first indexed as "Series Tracing," the second as "Series Tracing Guidelines." Other entries under "Series Tracing Guidelines" and "Series Tracings" mean that catalogers will need to follow up on multiple citations before being assured of having exhausted the possibilities of the *index*.

Because of omissions, catalogers may never be assured of having exhausted the possibilities of the bulletins themselves. LC's own index to its *Library of Congress Rule Interpretations* (1988) will eventually reduce interest in detailed indexing for much *CSB* content, but for libraries that do not acquire the separate publication, and for all non-*LCRI* items, independent indexes will still have a place. Catalogers will be glad to have this one, but they should be aware of its shortcomings.   Janet Swan Hill

123. Taylor, Arlene G., with Rosanna M. O'Neil. **Cataloging with Copy: A Decision-Maker's Handbook.** 2d ed. Englewood, Colo., Libraries Unlimited, 1988. 355p. illus. bibliog. index. $35.00. LC 88-13840. ISBN 0-87287-575-X.

This book is misnamed. It is an excellent, maybe essential, manual for all librarians seeking to turn collections into coherent information retrieval systems using current practices for description, indexing, and classification. The theme of the book is absolutely true: rules for description, indexing, and classification and their application, no matter how expert, cannot and will not make an integrated, coherent catalog or classified collection. Each catalog surro-

gate and each classified document must be fit into the existing catalog and collection, and it is the care or carelessness with which these fundamental processes are performed that determine the quality of the information retrieval they support. It matters little, in terms of these functions, whether the cataloging data or "copy" comes from inside or outside the library (for example, from the Library of Congress or cooperating libraries via cataloging utilities).

This book emphasizes the integrating function with its step-by-step description and analysis of every consideration, enhanced by numerous illustrations. It is indeed "A Decision-Maker's Handbook." After an opening overview of the whole situation, the handbook takes decisionmakers through each major component of the library retrieval system: document description, choice and form of name, title and subject access headings, classification, and the exceedingly complicated problem of author, title, and issue notation. Subsequent chapters address sources of cataloging information, cataloging media and the impact of computer-based cataloging. The volume concludes with a very brief bibliography and a useful index.

No book, especially one dealing with such a complicated and technical subject, can be perfect, but this book is remarkably problem and error free. In a comparison of journal arrangement by title rather than by classification notation, the need to shift the collection as it grows unevenly across the alphabet is likewise a problem with classified collections (p. 183). In discussing Dewey Decimal Classification notation supplied by the Library of Congress, the claim is made of "the lack of a means of drawing together materials on the same subject" (p. 242). These small quibbles do not measurably affect the value of the book as a whole.

All librarians, and especially administrators and directors, should be required to read at least the first paragraph of the concluding chapter which includes: "It has been shown throughout this book that it is possible to use outside copy exactly as it appears *only* if the library and its users are willing to accept the potential consequences" (p. 3328). Professionals should want to know what these consequences are, and for that, they will have to read the rest of the book.
                                        James D. Anderson

Nonprint Materials

124. Abell-Seddon, Brian. **Museum Catalogues: A Foundation for Computer Processing.** London, Clive Bingley/Library Association; distr., Chicago, American Library

Association, 1987. 224p. index. $30.00. ISBN 0-85157-429-7.

Abell-Seddon's book serves as an excellent introduction for any type of museum that is considering the automation of its collection records. The first five chapters present discussions of items which must be addressed carefully before any automation is undertaken, including nomenclature, classification, textual versus structured records, technical description, controlled vocabulary, lexicons, and conventions. Abell-Seddon then offers a detailed description, explanation, and justification of his own proposed system, REFORM (Reference Framework for Organising Records in Museums), which utilizes what he terms a four-tiered structure for data elements: historical, descriptive, cumulative, and managerial. Chapter 11 covers factors which must be considered regardless of the system used: content of records, ability to search by individual fields, access (confidential versus open), ease of data revision, and format of final product. The last chapter, "Computer Strategy," offers information which will help an individual museum select a system to meet its requirements, including the difference between database management systems and information storage and retrieval systems, pros and cons of free-text searching, advantages of variable length fields, benefits of a dictionary-driven system, and problems of transferring archival data to computer. Although the publication is directed toward museum collections, much of the information will be beneficial to libraries setting up in-house database systems for special collections as well. [R: LAR, 14 Oct 88, p. 602; RLR, Nov 88, p. 337]   Judy Dyki

125. Olson, Nancy B. **Audiovisual Material Glossary.** Dublin, Ohio, OCLC Online Computer Library Center, 1988. 41p. illus. bibliog. (OCLC Library Information and Computer Science Series, No. 7). $8.50pa. ISBN 1-55653-026-9.

This slight volume is a valuable resource, well worth its purchase price. It is not perfect—the title is misleading, there are some structural problems, and it would be a mistake to regard all definitions as authoritative—but for many general catalogers and other librarians faced with handling a variety of nonbook materials, this glossary may be precisely what is needed.

In choosing terms to include, the compiler interpreted *audiovisual* as encompassing virtually everything that is not a printed book of text. Thus atlases, music scores, broadsheets, computer software, and anything that requires special equipment to use are all included. Definitions are taken from various sources, and

attributed when quoted directly or modified within defined limits. Definitions cover only audiovisual materials, sometimes only *some* audiovisual materials (e.g., *sleeve* is defined only for sound recordings and microfiche, *border* is defined only for maps). The impetus for definition modification is not always clear (e.g., *artifact* is changed from the *ALA Glossary's* "made or modified by human workmanship" to "made or modified by man," while the definition for *puppet film*, which defines a film as movement itself rather than as a representation of movement, is unchanged from OCLC's *Audiovisual Media Format*). Coverage seems uneven, being more inclusive, for example, for cartographic than for graphic materials. A network of *see, see also,* and *cf.* references among terms is helpful, but occasionally incomplete (e.g., no references like *puppet film* to *animation*).

Many terms appear in the *ALA Glossary* (see *ARBA* 84, entry 86). Most special format terms can be found in separate manuals, which are themselves more comprehensive for the particular formats (e.g., H. L. Stibbe's *Cartographic Materials: A Manual of Interpretation for AACR2*, ALA, 1982). The *Audiovisual Material Glossary's* strength is combining deeper coverage of audiovisual material than the *ALA Glossary*, gathering major terms for all sorts of audiovisual materials into a single place, and including terms which have only recently come into library usage (e.g., *optical disc*). Another asset is the presence of drawings to augment certain definitions (e.g., *isometric view, stereograph reel,* etc.).

Janet Swan Hill

126. Olson, Nancy B. **Cataloging Microcomputer Software: A Manual to Accompany AACR 2: Chapter 9, Computer Files.** Englewood, Colo., Libraries Unlimited, 1988. 267p. illus. bibliog. index. $23.50pa. LC 88-8457. ISBN 0-87287-513-X.

With the 1987 publication of *AACR2 Chapter 9: Computer Files, Draft Revision* (American Library Association, 1987), existing instructional materials for cataloging computer files were rendered to some degree outdated. If this present manual covered only application of the new rules for description, it would be worth acquiring. In fact, it covers much more, from circulation decisions to preservation issues, to description, subject analysis, and MARC tagging, and it does so in a clear and well-organized manner. Inclusion of the text of the *AACR2* rules, as well as relevant Library of Congress and Sears subject headings, excerpts from the Library of Congress and Dewey Decimal

Classification schedules, and lists of established forms of names for program, computer, and operating systems, means that many catalogers may be able to catalog microcomputer software with the aid of this tool alone. One hundred examples of (untagged) catalog records for software packages are also provided, as well as a glossary, an index, and two bibliographies. A chronology of the development of the rules for cataloging computer files should be of interest to those who are curious about how cataloging standards may be developed and revised. There are some weaknesses: when the rules, headings, and classification numbers are revised (as they inevitably will be), catalogers who use this manual as a self-contained tool will begin to produce cataloging records that diverge from the national standard; and catalogers who follow Olson's suggestion to provide both general and specific subject headings for the same work will produce records at odds with Library of Congress practice. Notwithstanding these caveats, the work is both useful and usable, and well worth the purchase price.

Janet Swan Hill

127. Olson, Nancy B. **A Manual of AACR 2 Examples for Microcomputer Software with MARC Tagging and Coding.** 3d ed. Lake Crystal, Minn., Soldier Creek Pass, 1988. 75p. illus. $17.50 spiralbound. ISBN 0-936996-34-X.

This work reviews the rules of descriptive cataloging for microcomputer software. It also addresses some areas not unique to cataloging software, such as the rules for abbreviating states. Rules regarding the choice of entry and added entries are also covered. The author provides helpful additional information such as the need to differentiate between new versions of software versus revised versions of the operating system. Even though one recent example of LC cataloging from OCLC lacks a title page, all other examples include the title page screen. It is very helpful that serial as well as monographic formats are covered. This work should be purchased by library schools with advanced cataloging or nonbook cataloging courses. Technical service operations processing software will also find it helpful.　Ann Allan

Subject Headings

128. Bratcher, Perry, and Jennifer Smith, comps. **Music Subject Headings.** Lake Crystal, Minn., Soldier Creek Press, 1988. 323p. $50.00 pa. ISBN 0-936996-31-5.

This volume of music subject headings compiled from the *Library of Congress Subject*

Headings is a tool long overdue. Its contents reflect LC subject headings as of September 1987, so headings are those from the tenth edition, plus updates listed in the *Music Cataloging Bulletin* (Music Library Association, 1970-). The subject headings are, however, listed in the thesaurus format of the eleventh edition of the *Library of Congress Subject Headings*. In addition to listing the subject headings, the authors have provided an excellent introduction which offers guidance in using the subject headings. Topics covered in the introduction include general principles in assigning headings for musical works, pattern headings, a list of subdivisions, and the explanation and assignment of ethnic headings. The authors have also noted some significant changes in the subject headings.

This new resource will certainly be valuable to music catalogers. The authors have indicated that they feel that their publication will be useful to libraries involved in retrospective conversion of their music collection. Public service music librarians as well, may find that it is handy to have a copy at their public catalogs. Hopefully the authors will compile a new edition periodically to reflect changes in headings and policies made at the Library of Congress.

Allie Wise Goudy

129. **Canadian Thesaurus 1988: A Guide to the Subject Headings Used in the** *Canadian Periodical Index* **and** *CPI Online.* **Thésaurus Canadien 1988.** Robert Lang and others, eds. Toronto, Info Globe, 1988. 465p. $85.00 spiralbound. ISBN 0-921925-04-2; ISSN 0838-3553.

This thesaurus "is designed to facilitate retrieval of material when searching the *Canadian Periodical Index* online or in print." *CPI* indexes more than 375 periodicals, including those in the French language and the eighteen U.S. titles most commonly found in Canadian libraries. This "bilingual list of over 35,000 terms covering all major subject areas and emphasizing Canadian topics ... reflect[s] the content of magazines indexed in *CPI*. The level of specificity given to each subject corresponds to the level of detail found in the periodical literature." The fact that the publisher, Info Globe, is owned by the *Globe and Mail*, an influential Toronto-based newspaper available throughout Canada, gives this list authority.

The *Canadian Thesaurus* can also be used as an adjunct to *Canadian Subject Headings*, second edition (Ottawa, National Library of Canada, 1985) and to *Répertoire de vedettes-matière*, ninth edition (Québec, Université de Laval, 1983). Its value to catalogers lies in the provision of subject headings not found in either of the two subject heading lists used by most Canadian libraries. Catalogers in bilingual libraries will find the French-English equivalencies very helpful.

This work is a recommended purchase for large cataloging departments or those that do in-depth cataloging, and for reference departments where *CPI* is consulted frequently. Updated and revised editions are planned for the future.

Jean Weihs

130. Dickstein, Ruth, Victoria A. Mills, and Ellen J. Waite. **Women in LC's Terms: A Thesaurus of Library of Congress Subject Headings Relating to Women.** Phoenix, Ariz., Oryx Press, 1988. 221p. $28.50. LC 87-34766. ISBN 0-89774-444-6.

This thesaurus is a guide to the Library of Congress's (LC) subject headings used for and about topics dealing with women. The terms included in this work are taken from the 1983 microfiche update of the *Library of Congress Subject Headings* (*LCSH*). Also included are any new or changed headings beginning with the word *women* from the tenth edition of *LCSH*.

The thesaurus begins with an alphabetical listing of all included terms. Following this are individual chapters organized by specific topical terminology relating to women. Chapters include "Communication and Information"; "Economics and Employment"; "Education"; "History and Social Change"; "International Women"; "Languages"; "Literature"; "Religion and Philosophy"; "Law, Government, and Public Policy"; "Health and Biological Sciences"; "Natural Science and Technology"; "Social Science and Culture"; and "Visual and Performing Arts." Introductory scope notes begin each chapter.

Four appendices describe the subdivisions used with LC subject headings. The fifth appendix provides a listing of LC call numbers assigned to women and topics relating to them.

The intended users of this thesaurus are researchers and librarians using subject catalogs and indexes when researching women's studies materials as well as librarians who catalog and index such materials. Unquestionably this work will provide significant value for its audience as it is well organized, complete, and serves as a springboard to other related indexes and databases pertaining to this growing interdisciplinary field. [R: LJ, July 88, p. 58; RBB, 1 Sept 88, p. 57]

Marjorie E. Bloss

131. Woods, William E. **Manual and List of Subject Headings Used on the Woods Cross Reference Cards.** 6th ed. Evergreen Park, Ill.,

Woods Library Publishing, 1987. 132p. $7.95 pa. ISBN 0-912304-09-X.

This manual and list of subject headings is a clear and well-written guide for those making use of cross-reference cards in their card catalogs. After an explanatory introduction, there is a list of all the subject headings and their related *see* references which are found in the Woods set of cards.

This sixth edition is based on the thirteenth edition of the *Sears List of Subject Headings* (H. W. Wilson, 1986). The layout is clear and easy to understand. The cross-reference cards accompanying the volume are ready for filing into the card catalog. The options of filing all the cards at once, involving some blind references, or of carefully revising them to show only the subject headings actually in use (which entails updating from time to time) are carefully explained. The terms or letters indicating the type of reference are *see*, *see also*, *x* and *xx*. These have been dropped by the Library of Congress in favor of *use*, *used for*, *broader term*, *narrower term*, and *related term*.

Since most of the larger libraries use the Library of Congress subject headings and have an online catalog, this manual and set of cards would be of no use to them. It will, however, be of interest to small libraries using card catalogs and the Sears subject headings.

Barbara E. Brown

CHILDREN'S LITERATURE
General Works

132. Gallagher, Mary Elizabeth. **Young Adult Literature: Issues and Perspectives.** Haverford, Pa., Catholic Library Association, 1988. 214p. bibliog. index. $20.00pa. ISBN 0-87507-038-8.

Intended as a college text for classes in young adult literature, the work succinctly reviews: (1) the physical, sexual, intellectual, social, emotional, and moral growth and development patterns of young adults; (2) their literacy needs for lifelong learning across a broad range of reading interests and levels; (3) the historical development of the production, promotion, advocacy, and censorship of young adult literature; (4) the methods of bringing the literature to its intended audience—booktalks, reading aloud, sustained silent reading, and programming by teachers, librarians, and parents; and (5) young adult literature itself, from the historical highlights of its beginnings in the 1930s to a discussion of the major authors and works of various types of literary genres—problem novels, romance and sexuality, history, science fiction and fantasy, adventure and mystery, and religion and philosophy. Each chapter includes bibliographies of books and other materials on the topics covered. It also includes appendices on materials selection resources and a professional reading list, a glossary, and an index.

The typescript format is strictly utilitarian, but the work provides a good overview of young adult literature and lists the resources useful in pursuing the subject in greater depth. Librarians, teachers, parents, and others interested in promoting leisure and recreational reading among young adults will find its succinct coverage of the major issues involved in understanding this important subject its greatest value. [R: BL, 1 Oct 88, p. 259] Blaine H. Hall

133. Lees, Stella, ed. **Track to Unknown Water. Proceedings of the Second Pacific Rim Conference on Children's Literature.** Metuchen, N.J., Scarecrow, 1987. 406p. index. $32.50. LC 87-12852. ISBN 0-8108-2006-4.

This collection of papers from the Second Pacific Rim Conference on Children's Literature is loosely divided into six parts, each of which focuses on minority groups in the countries of the Pacific and their particular needs in the area of children's literature. The sections are "The Pacific: The Children and the Cultures"; "Minorities: The Cage of Ignorance"; "The Children: In Their Own Words"; "The Children: In Need of Special Care"; "The Oral Tradition: A Rhythm That Dances"; and "A Minority of One: Transitions and Meeting Points."

The countries represented in the collection are Canada, the United States, Mexico, New Zealand, Fiji, Indonesia, Papua New Guinea, Japan, and Australia. Twenty-two of the thirty-eight contributors are from Australia. The papers deal with a variety of topics. Several are concerned with the treatment of Pacific minority groups in children's literature such as the Maori in New Zealand, aborigines in Australia, and the Korean and Ainu peoples living in Japan. Others deal with literature and library service for minority children including blind, mentally handicapped, and physically handicapped children. Several papers contain useful bibliographies of children's books.

Among the contributors are Betsy Byars, a well-known author of books for children including *The Pinballs* and *The 18th Emergency*, and Sheila Egoff of Canada who edited the collection of papers from the First Pacific Rim Conference. As the second conference was held in 1979, some of the material on children's reading interests and current trends in children's

literature may be slightly dated. [R: BL, 1 Apr 88, p. 1357; BR, May/June 88, pp. 46-47]
Nancy Courtney

Bibliographies

GENERAL WORKS

134. Booth, David, Larry Swartz, and Meguido Zola. **Choosing Children's Books.** Markham, Ont., Pembroke, 1987. 176p. index. $9.95pa. ISBN 0-921217-12-9.

This new annotated bibliography of books for children up to age 14 is an endeavor of three devotees of children's literature who have selected these titles on the basis of their experience with children. The list is divided into four age groups (birth-5, 5-8, 8-11, and 11-14). The authors have attempted to group the books within the age divisions by genre or theme, as well as give a section of read-aloud books. Books typically read by adults to children are arranged alphabetically, while those read by children on their own are given in order of difficulty. The variety of organizational aspects proves both useful and confusing. With only an author index, a user could search several sections before locating a title whose author is not remembered.

Some choices of groupings are obviously arbitrary. Why should *Tex* by S. E. Hinton be included in the section for young adolescent "Reluctant and Remedial Readers" instead of "Fiction for Developing Readers" or the theme section "Relationships"?

Annotations are concise and helpful, and each is followed by titles of other books by the same author, sequels to the listed book, and other books in the series. The strongest feature of this bibliography is the quality of the literature recommended. As a source for choosing good books to share with children, this book is useful. For ease of use, this source has limitations. Patricia Tipton Sharp

135. **Bowker's Forthcoming Children's Books. Volume 1, Number 4: September 1987-January 1988.** New York, R. R. Bowker, 1987. 273p. $49.95pa. ISSN 0000-0965.

This bimonthly serial companion to *Children's Books in Print* and *Subject Guide to Children's Books in Print* (see ARBA 88, entries 21 and 22), begun in 1987, gives bibliographic information on over eighteen hundred juvenile titles. Access is by separate subject, author, and title listings, with a final section on publisher information. The subject headings are based on *Sears List of Subject Headings* (see ARBA 87, entry 595), with additional terms taken as needed from the *Library of Congress Subject Headings*. The copy reviewed also contained a special section with an article on Jean Fritz's *Shh! We're Writing the Constitution*, and other short articles relevant to the children's book industry.

Included in this issue are titles from the previous twelve months as well as expected titles for the following five months. All the information is supplied by publishers, which means that some authors are listed in several places due to variant forms of the names. Yet another addition to the growing collection of Bowker bibliographic tools, this issue is attractively produced on a better quality paper than one is accustomed to in the Books in Print series, with slightly larger type and better contrast, making it easier to read. While there is some overlap between this and *Forthcoming Books in Print*, it is minor. Those who work with children's books will be pleased to have this publication to alert them to what is on the way in the world of children's literature.   Marilyn R. Pukkila

136. **Children's Books of the Year.** 1988 ed. New York, Child Study Children's Book Committee, Bank Street College, 1988. 55p. illus. index. $4.00pa.

Any number of organizations publish brief lists of books of the year for various age groups. These include state library associations that involve students in making their choices, and national associations that issue brief lists of best books selected by librarians and teachers. There are fewer organizations which offer frequently published, inexpensive lists of children's books. Among those that are still available are the Association for Childhood Education International's list (now quadrennial) and the annual list from the Library of Congress.

This offering has been an annual publication for fifty years, making it one of the most reliable lists. It includes some six hundred books published in 1987 or late 1986, whittled down from three thousand reviewed. They are grouped for ages five and under, ages five through eight, ages eight and up, and special interests. These categories are further divided by type of book for the age level categories, and by broad subject areas for special interests.

Entries are in alphabetical order by title, with author, illustrator, publisher, price, and a brief annotation given. There are indexes of titles, authors, and illustrators, and a list of publishers. The publisher's list seemed short, but all the publishers whose entries were checked were on the list. The committee is "a voluntary group of about thirty parents, teachers, librarians, writers, illustrators, and psychologists" who review books using criteria based on "suitability of text and illustrations for the age for which the book is intended; the author's sincerity and respect for the young reader; the credibility of characterization and plot; the authenticity of background of time and place; the treatment of ethnic and religious differences; the absence of race, sex, and age stereotypes; and the quality of writing" ("About This List"). This year the committee is offering a separate *Paperback Books for Children through Age 14*.

The *Children's Books of the Year* list has the advantage of being an annual upon which one can depend. The criteria are appropriate. Many of the authors and illustrators are standard entries on children's book lists. It would be nice to have a clear designation of the affiliation of the group of reviewers, but fifty years have brought them wide acceptance and have given this document a solid position among annual reviews of children's literature.

Betty Jo Buckingham

137. Gagnon, André, and Ann Gagnon, eds. **Canadian Books for Young People. Livres Canadiens pour la Jeunesse.** 4th ed. Cheektowaga, N.Y. and Toronto, University of Toronto Press, 1988. 186p. illus. index. $14.95pa. ISBN 0-8020-6662-3.

With the increasing number of Canadian children's books published in recent years, André Gagnon and Ann Gagnon faced a formidable task in updating the 1980 edition of this work, but they have succeeded in producing a valuable selection aid. In this edition they have compiled a selective list of more than twenty-five hundred titles, both English and French, with brief annotations in the language of publication. The annotations are concise and most are entirely descriptive, although occasionally an evaluative comment slips in. Within each language section, the arrangement is by subject: picture books, science, arts, fiction, and so forth. The age range covered is from preschool to eighteen, and each title is assigned an approximate age level. There are separate sections for professional media in each language as well as useful listings of award books, periodicals, and publishers' series. The three indexes—author, title, and illustrator—integrate the two languages. Information given for each item includes ISBN and price, thus making the book useful as a buying guide, although the short in-print life of Canadian children's books will make disappointments inevitable. The double-column pages and small but legible type, as well as the line drawings used to separate sections, make for an attractive, compact compilation of information which will be helpful for children's librarians and others who wish to build a collection of Canadian children's books.

Adele M. Fasick

138. Lipson, Eden Ross. **The New York Times Parent's Guide to the Best Books for Children.** New York, Times Books/Random House, 1988. 421p. illus. bibliog. index. $22.95; $12.95pa. LC 87-40587. ISBN 0-8129-1649-2; 0-8129-1688-3pa.

A selective guide to nearly one thousand of the best books for children published in the United States, the volume includes "a mixture of classic, standard and distinguished new titles.... Some are noble classics, some are just fun; others may be helpful directly or indirectly as they address real issues children face" (p. xii).

The main titles are numbered consecutively and grouped according to text level from wordless through books for middle and advanced readers. Books are listed alphabetically by title within each section. For each title, the following bibliographic information is provided: author, illustrator, publisher in hardcover and paperback, date of original publication, and a notation of awards, if any. As the author is Children's Book Editor of *The New York Times*, she has included mention of *The Times* Best Illustrated winners. The annotations, highly colored by Lipson's "own tastes and enthusiasms" (p. xiv), are very brief, usually only a sentence or two. A unique feature of the book is the variety of indexes; there are title, author, and illustrator indexes; "Age-Appropriate Indexes"; "Read-Aloud Index"; and "Special Subject Indexes," with categories such as "Adoption," "Biography/Autobiography," and "Growing Up."

The author's admittedly subjective selection criteria have produced a collection in which the balance is slightly skewed. Most recognized titles are included, but a few are not. As for authors included, Lipson makes some interesting choices. William Steig has ten titles; Dr. Seuss only seven. Beverly Cleary has only four titles; Lorna Balian none at all. Jane Yolen rates seven. Barbara Cooney has only one, and that not one of her best. In view of the fact that more objective selection criteria were not applied, buyers should be aware that this is really *"Eden Ross Lipson's Parent's Guide to the Best Books for Children."*

Carmel A. Huestis

139. Lukenbill, W. Bernard, and Sharon Lee Stewart, comps. and eds. **Youth Literature: An Interdisciplinary, Annotated Guide to North American Dissertation Research, 1930-1985.** New York, Garland, 1988. 466p. index. (Gar-

land Reference Library of Social Science, Vol. 400). $65.00. LC 87-38077. ISBN 0-8240-8498-5.

Youth Literature is a selective interdisciplinary guide to youth literature from 1930 to 1985. It is intended as an update and expansion of the 1972 work *A Working Bibliography of American Doctoral Dissertations in Children's and Adolescents' Literature, 1930-1971* (see *ARBA* 74, entry 1292) by Lukenbill. This present volume gives titles and annotations for over fifteen hundred doctoral studies conducted at major North American universities on the subject of youth literature.

The editors broadly define "youth" as the period of life from preschool to about age eighteen. The wide range of topics covered (e.g., social attitudes and values, minority cultures, and political environment) illustrates the interrelatedness of youth literature to such disciplines as sociology, psychology, anthropology, and history. Generic studies about reading and reading environments, types of literature, and literary criticisms are also included.

Dissertation Abstracts International (*DAI*) is the primary source for titles selected. The arrangement is simple with just two major divisions—part 1 lists the titles and annotations arranged alphabetically by author, and part 2 is a subject index to the dissertations listed. Cross-references are provided.

The bibliographic citations for each title include author, title of dissertation, university accepting the dissertation, date of degree, and *DAI* reference number. The annotations, based on *DAI* abstracts, are clear and concise, range in length from about twenty to one hundred words, and are descriptive rather than critical. A few titles (less than 10 percent) have no annotations because they were not given in *DAI*.

This work is useful to anyone interested in youth literature. Those planning a study dealing with this literature have in one source a variety of research designs from which to choose.

Dianne Brinkley Catlett

140. **Reference Books for Young Readers: Authoritative Evaluations of Encyclopedias, Atlases, and Dictionaries.** Marion Sader, ed. New York, R. R. Bowker, 1988. 615p. illus. index. (Bowker Buying Guide Series). $49.95. LC 87-38234. ISBN 0-8352-2366-3.

This first entry in Bowker's Buying Guide Series meets the need for critical information necessary to evaluate and select encyclopedias, atlases, and dictionaries for children and young adults. An additional section on large print reference materials is included. To help readers make sound choices of reference works, *Reference Books for Young Readers* discusses the effective use of reviews and gives detailed criteria for evaluating reference works.

In preparing this guide, a national survey was conducted in which public and school librarians were asked to evaluate and rate encyclopedias, dictionaries, and atlases. The questionnaire used a list of general reference works in the three major review categories and the frequency of their use by elementary, middle school, and high school students. The results of this survey provide accessible, detailed information for any school or public librarian working with children or young adults.

Comparative charts provide basic factual information about every reference book or set evaluated. Sources are current. The charts are followed by chapters containing detailed evaluations of approximately two hundred encyclopedias, atlases, dictionaries and word books, and large print reference books. Reference is made to online formats as well as CD-ROM. Specific titles are discussed, and there is generous use of facsimiles. Appendices include a selected bibliography and a list of publishers. The index is the weakest feature of this book; for example, it includes no references to online systems or CD-ROM.

This is a long needed reference source for librarians, library school students, and the general public. It provides accurate information in a clear format. [R: LJ, 15 Oct 88, p. 84; RBB, 1 Sept 88, p. 56; RLR, Aug 88, pp. 183-84; VOYA, Dec 88, pp. 257-58; WLB, June 88, pp. 143-44]   Lynda Welborn

141. Williams, Jane A. **Who Reads What When: Literature Selections for Children Ages Three through Thirteen.** Placerville, Calif., Bluestocking Press, 1988. 60p. index. $3.95pa. LC 87-27854. ISBN 0-942617-01-0.

This bibliography of children's books was compiled using literature recommendations from the Textbook Evaluation Reports, private school recommended reading lists, and the author's own favorites for parents to use in helping their children choose books. There are three lists of indexes: age, title, and author. Unless parents have read the introductory section, they will be rather confused by the format of the indexes. The age index lists selections at suggested age levels for reading. Several of these indicated reading levels seem inappropriate (e.g., *Freckles* and *Island of the Blue Dolphins* for a nine-year-old). The number following the titles in the other indexes refers to the age level rather than a page number. As the author indicates, many of the titles are out-of-print and may not be accessible. There are many important authors and titles missing from this compilation, especially

at the lower level (Carle, Keats, Zion). Nancy Larrick's *A Parent's Guide to Children's Reading* (see *ARBA* 84, entry 608) contains many of the same selections and is much easier to use. Many of the titles included in *Who Reads What When* are not found in either *Children's Catalog* or *The Elementary School Library Collection*, which are basic standards for book selection. No list is all-inclusive, and this should be used only as a supplement if additional reading lists are desired. Not recommended as an important tool. [R: JAL, Mar 88, p. 45; LJ, 1 Apr 88, p. 83]   Mary J. Stanley

142. **Your Reading: A Booklist for Junior High and Middle School Students.** 7th ed. James E. Davis and Hazel K. Davis, eds., and the Committee on the Junior High and Middle School Booklist, NCTE. Urbana, Ill., National Council of Teachers of English, 1988. 494p. index. $12.95pa. LC 88-25148. ISBN 0-8141-5939-7.

In the seventh edition of *Your Reading*, the National Council of Teachers of English continues its practice of evaluating, recommending, and annotating books of interest to students in the fifth through ninth grades. Although aimed primarily at students, this now-standard reference source is valuable as a selection aid for teachers, librarians, and parents who need help in sifting through the myriad of new titles for this age group that appear each year.

After considering approximately six thousand books published between 1983 and 1987, NCTE's Committee on the Junior High and Middle School Booklist chose almost two thousand titles for inclusion. Selection was made on the basis of both audience appeal and literary merit, with books of exceptional literary merit receiving a special annotation. The titles are grouped by subject and literary type or both into sixty-one highly diverse categories (e.g., "Abuse," "Picture Books for Older Readers," "Historical Novels," "Computers," "Death and Dying," "Dating and Love," "Fantasy," and "Trivia"). Within each category the books are arranged alphabetically by author. Each entry provides author, title, publication, collation, and ISBN information, and is briefly, yet effectively, annotated. In keeping with the focus of the book, these annotations are written to appeal directly to the student reader, not the adult; and in most cases they succeed remarkably well. The book is concluded by an author index, a title index, and a directory of publishers.

Concise, accessible, and well arranged, this latest edition of a standard juvenile reference work should be welcomed both by students and interested adults and deserves a place on the reference shelves of most junior high and middle school libraries.

Kristin Ramsdell

SPECIAL INTERESTS

143.   Books for the Gifted Child. Volume 2. By Paula Hauser and Gail A. Nelson. New York, R. R. Bowker, 1988. 244p. index. (Serving Special Needs). $32.95. LC 79-27431. ISBN 0-8352-2467-8.

Building on the model of a previous volume, Hauser and Nelson have assembled a list of 195 beginning, intermediate, and advanced titles published in the 1980s for the gifted reader. Titles have been selected based on their potential to challenge readers with abstractions, ambiguities, and other reasoning tasks. In addition, books eliciting an emotional or an imaginative response were included. The books are arranged alphabetically by author and contain lengthy descriptive annotations. There is a title, level, and subject index. Chapter 1 of the book provides an essay on the gifted student and describes various types of literature of interest to this group.

While the titles seem to have been selected carefully, the book suffers from a flawed structure. If the book had been arranged by theme, or if there had been an extensive theme index (the subject index is too brief), and if the annotations would have suggested uses of the book with the gifted reader (only a few comments of this nature are given occasionally), the book would have been a better prescriptive source. As structured, the annotations are too long, and the user has to spend an inordinate amount of time reading before the volume can serve the needs of a teacher of the gifted or a librarian short on time.

Recommended as a checklist against the current collection if the library can afford it.

David V. Loertscher

144.   High Interest Easy Reading for Junior and Senior High School Students. 5th ed. By Dorothy Matthews and the Committee to Revise *High Interest-Easy Reading* of the National Council of Teachers of English. Urbana, Ill., National Council of Teachers of English, 1988. 115p. index. $6.25pa. LC 88-1430. ISBN 0-8141-2096-2.

The fifth edition of this booklist for adolescents who are not eager readers describes 367 fiction and nonfiction titles published between 1984 and 1986. Some classic favorites published earlier are also included.

The National Council of Teachers of English has established a committee, chaired by Matthews, to revise and update *High Interest Easy Reading*. Teachers, school media specialists, parents, public librarians, and students themselves can rely on this popular selection tool for identifying books that have particular appeal to students and are useful in completing assignments in various areas of the curriculum. According to the introduction (p. vii), books included here are either exciting stories, contain "suspenseful action, likeable characters," or are concerned with topics that are part of the young adult's everyday life and culture.

Entries are arranged alphabetically by author under twenty-three subject headings, some of which are fantasy and science fiction, love and friendship, real people, sports, technology, ghosts and the supernatural, mystery, how-to books, and humor. Each entry includes complete bibliographic description (including total page numbers) and International Standard Book Number for ease in ordering. Annotations always indicate the age of the leading character(s) and provide a brief summary of the story or subject content. [R: BR, Sept/Oct 88, p. 50; RBB, 1 Sept 88, pp. 48, 50; VOYA, Aug 88, pp. 153-54]

Lois Buttlar

145.   Horner, Catherine Townsend. The Single-Parent Family in Children's Books: An Annotated Bibliography. 2d ed. Metuchen, N.J., Scarecrow, 1988. 339p. index. $29.50. LC 87-26403. ISBN 0-8108-2065-X.

The single-parent family has always been represented in children's literature. Prior to the 1960s, the cause of single parenthood in books was invariably widowhood or orphanhood with a single guardian (e.g., Sydney's *Five Little Peppers* and Hergan's *Mrs. Wiggs of the Cabbage Patch*). With the sexual revolution of the 1960s and 1970s, a leap in the divorce rate, and the emergence of the popular psychology movement eventually came the publication of books that deal realistically with death, divorce, separation, desertion, remarriage, binuclear families, and never-married mothers. Today there are a wealth of books that deal with these topics multidimensionally and provide literary expression in the popular children's genres of mystery, adventure, fantasy, contemporary realism, humor, topical books, science fiction, and historical fiction.

Horner's comprehensive bibliography annotates and rates 596 fiction and 26 nonfiction titles published between 1965 and 1986 that pertain to families fractured by divorce, desertion, separation, or the death of a parent; unmarried mothers or other single adults as heads of households; and the protracted absence of one parent from a traditional two-parent home. Some modern classics and old favorites published prior to 1965 are also reviewed.

The bibliography is intended for professionals and lay persons interested in identifying a variety of reading materials for children from nontraditional homes. Clearly annotated and arranged, the bibliography provides valuable access to titles that speak to the need of millions of children and their families now living in single-parent households in the United States. [R: BR, Nov/Dec 88, p. 47; RBB, Aug 88, p. 1907; VOYA, Dec 88, p. 257]

Debbie Burnham-Kidwell

146. Howard, Elizabeth F. **America as Story: Historical Fiction for Secondary Schools.** Chicago, American Library Association, 1988. 137p. index. $15.00pa. LC 88-3453. ISBN 0-8389-0492-0.

Designed to assist teachers and librarians in selecting novels which will stimulate students' interest in history, this guide identifies over 150 novels, most published in the last twenty years, which portray the experiences and feelings of ordinary people living through key periods in American history. An emphasis is placed on themes involving the experiences of fictional young people, such as "building a sod house on the Nebraska prairie, following the North Star with a bold band of escaping slaves, or parachuting into enemy territory after a B-17 is shot down" (p. xii).

The book is arranged in seven broad chronological/topical categories: colonial America; the American Revolution and the new nation; the Civil War and Reconstruction; westward expansion and the native American response; immigration, industrialization, and urbanization; the jazz age and the Depression; and America in the modern world. Entries consist of the title of the book and its imprint, indication of the reading level, a short annotation introducing the plot, a comment on historicity, and suggestions for reports or activities. As the author indicates, the suggested activities are just that—suggestions. Teachers, librarians, and students are expected to devise additional follow-up activities.

Some of the standard bibliographies consulted by the author were H. W. Wilson's *Senior High School Catalog* (see *ARBA* 88, entry 640) and *Junior High School Catalog* (see *ARBA* 86, entry 596), *The American History Book List for High Schools* (National Council for the Social Studies, 1971), the National Council of Teachers of English lists for junior and senior

high schools, and *Books for the Teen Age* (see *ARBA* 87, entry 618). Additional titles were suggested by quite a few "knowledgeable" individuals named in the acknowledgments section. Because the guide focuses on more recent books, generally 1940 to 1986, some of the older classics such as *Uncle Tom's Cabin* have been omitted. However, a sampling of the material includes such works as *Johnny Tremain, Across Five Aprils, My Antonia, The Jungle, The Grapes of Wrath,* and *The Bridges at Toko-ri,* as well as the even more recent *1787, Roots: The Saga of an American Family, Bold Journey: West with Lewis and Clark, The Tempering,* and *A Woman of Independent Means.* This would be a useful tool for teachers and librarians who want to bring the social studies curriculum to life by showing students through contemporary literature that history is the story of real people's lives. [R: BL, 1 Oct 88, pp. 259-60; RBB, 15 Nov 88, p. 550]

Susan R. Penney

147. Marantz, Sylvia S., and Kenneth A. Marantz. **The Art of Children's Picture Books: A Selective Reference Guide.** New York, Garland, 1988. 165p. index. (Garland Reference Library of the Humanities, Vol. 825). $27.00. LC 88-1704. ISBN 0-8240-2745-0.

This annotated 451-item bibliography provides selected primary and secondary sources on the art and illustration of children's literature. Most of the sources have been published within the past twenty-five years, with emphasis on the more recent sources located in the United States. The sources listed include books, periodicals, articles, videotapes, films, filmstrips, and dissertations and theses. The subjects presented in the bibliography are the history of children's picture books, how a picture book is made, criticism of children's picture books including their use with children, anthologies of artists, information on individual artists, guides and aids to further research, and locations of some collections and archival materials on picture books and their creators. Artist, author, and title indexes provide easy access to the information. This will prove to be an excellent resource for those with special interests in the art of children's literature.

Marilyn Strong Noronha

148. Nakamura, Joyce, ed. **High-interest Books for Teens: A Guide to Book Reviews and Biographical Sources.** 2d ed. Detroit, Gale, 1988. 539p. index. $95.00. LC 81-6889. ISBN 0-8103-1830-X.

Over thirty-five hundred fiction and non-fiction titles by two thousand authors, of special interest to junior and senior high school students, with sources of critical reviews about them are listed in this reference tool aimed at librarians, classroom teachers, and reading tutors. This second edition updates and expands the first edition published by Gale in 1981.

Titles included have been recommended in reading lists by educators, librarians, and publishers as especially appropriate for enticing students with learning disabilities, or those who need to improve their reading skills, to read. They have been identified as "high interest/low-readability level" materials and include both contemporary works and favorite classics by familiar authors.

In the main body of the work, "Guide to Book Reviews and Biographical Sources," entries are arranged by author (or pseudonym), with dates of birth and death (if applicable) indicated. At least one citation to a source of further biographical information follows. For individual books by each author, a list of citations to evaluations of the title in reviewing periodicals is provided. Subject headings and cross-references to name variants/pseudonyms, co-authors/adapters or authors of adapted works under which other books have been written and reviewed are also indicated. Two brief sections, "Book Review Sources Cited" and "Biographical Sources Cited," give complete names of biography and review sources indicated by abbreviations or codes in the entry. In addition to a title index, the second edition has included a very useful subject index with over 500 categories popular with young adults, such as adventure stories, mystery and detective stories, sports, occult sciences, motorcycles and motorcycle racing, rock music and musicians, and family life and family problems. Subject headings are those used by the Library of Congress and also from the *Sears List of Subject Headings.*

While recommended lists for students whose chronological age exceeds their reading ability are not hard to find, a tool that identifies in one place all sources of reviews for each title is a definite asset. [R: RBB, Aug 88, p. 1903; VOYA, Aug 88, p. 153]

Lois Buttlar

149. **The Newbery & Caldecott Awards 1988: A Complete Listing of Medal and Honor Books.** Chicago, Association for Library Service to Children, American Library Association, 1988. 40p. index. $5.00pa. ISBN 0-8389-7209-8.

This work is a useful compilation of the Newbery and Caldecott award winners and runners-up from the inception of each award through 1988. Listings for each award are in reverse chronological order and include title, author, illustrator (for Caldecott books), and publisher. A brief history of the award precedes the chronological list.

Although this information is available in many children's literature textbooks, purchasing guides, and professional journals, this is still a useful booklet. Unlike *Hornbook Magazine's* Newbery and Caldecott Medal series, which includes acceptance speeches, book notes, excerpts, illustrations, and other useful information, *The Newbery & Caldecott Awards* is just a list. This is the information most requested by students, parents, and other laypersons. It is exactly the type of material classroom teachers, children's literature professors, and librarians working with children use most often. Recommended.

Carol J. Veitch

150. Roberts, Patricia L. **Alphabet Books as a Key to Language Patterns: An Annotated Action Bibliography.** Hamden, Conn., Library Professional Publications/Shoe String Press, 1987. 263p. index. $27.50. LC 87-3216. ISBN 0-208-02151-5.

This reference source focuses on language patterns in alphabet books. After a comprehensive introduction to language patterns and their efficacy for children's language, literacy, and learning skills, Roberts analyzes nearly five hundred alphabet books for language patterns. The introduction addresses research findings about language patterning, then discusses numerous types of language patterns and patterns as a means of playing with language, making oral responses, writing, etc. This introduction is both useful and well organized.

The bibliography is organized into categories by the language patterns used in the book. Each entry is by author's last name, has an annotation, and gives the suggested age level. Annotations typically describe the book's approach, provide response activities, and specify the language pattern used. Some titles are designated "Recommended." An index of authors and titles is also included.

Having the source be inclusive means that some entries are not outstanding literary or artistic examples, and books which use the alphabet merely as a vehicle for organization are also included (*Ancient Egypt from A to Z, The Smurf ABC Book*, etc.).

This resource is an excellent source for the wide variety of alphabet books available, and it is an interesting application of language patterns. [R: BL, 1 Oct 87, p. 327]

Patricia Tipton Sharp

151. Schon, Isabel. **A Hispanic Heritage, Series III: A Guide to Juvenile Books about Hispanic People and Cultures.** Metuchen, N.J., Scarecrow, 1988. 150p. index. $17.50. LC 88-18094. ISBN 0-8108-2133-8.

Once again Isabel Schon has produced a quality guide to assist librarians and teachers in developing and broadening the reading interests of children and young adults, particularly in the selection of literature about the Hispanic culture. This work contains evaluative, not merely descriptive, annotations of hundreds of fiction and nonfiction (including biographies) books arranged by specific country or geographic region. Users can quickly locate books about Argentina, Nicaragua, Spain, or the United States through the table of contents. Separate author, title, and subject indexes round out the work.

Entries include "most in-print books in English published since 1984 in the United States," and noteworthy titles are designated with an asterisk. Citations include standard bibliographic information, as well as price and grade/audience level designations. Schon includes refreshingly candid, clearly written, personal comments to describe the books, and does not hesitate to state strengths and weaknesses. Her insights range from "this is an excellent tribute" to "this is definitely the wrong book to introduce children to Mexico."

Although entries are not numbered, the arrangement of the book is logical and easy to use. Excellent as a collection development tool, this is an affordable book which will be useful to academic, school, and public libraries.

Ilene F. Rockman

152. Wear, Terri A. **Horse Stories: An Annotated Bibliography of Books for All Ages.** Metuchen, N.J., Scarecrow, 1987. 277p. index. $27.50. LC 87-13050. ISBN 0-8108-1998-8.

Over fifteen hundred titles dealing with equine fiction are arranged here according to age group. The compiler has interpreted "horse stories" quite broadly, and thus includes fiction on donkeys, mules, merry-go-round horses, rocking horses, and toy horses. She excludes unicorns and most Westerns, arguing that the latter "usually are not horse stories" (p. vi). On the other hand, books such as *The Mammoth Hunters, The Good Master,* and *Madeleine in London* are included, while McKinley's *The Blue Sword* and *The Hero and the Crown* are excluded, thus proving that one person's horse story may be ignored by another horse lover. The one-sentence summaries for each entry are concise but thorough. Some especially helpful features include information on series and se-

quels and a mention if the book was still in print as of November 1986. There are no notations of Newbery or other award winners, and an author index would have been a useful addition to the title and subject indexes since the entries are by age group, but these are minor quibbles. Public librarians will find this a useful and reasonably priced tool for helping patrons of any age who are looking for another good horse book. [R: BR, May/June 88, pp. 48-49; RBB, 1 May 88, pp. 1486-87; RLR, Nov 88, pp. 333-34; VOYA, Oct 88, p. 210]

Marilyn R. Pukkila

153. Wilson, George, and Joyce Moss. **Books for Children to Read Alone: A Guide for Parents and Librarians.** New York, R. R. Bowker, 1988. 184p. index. $32.95. LC 88-10430. ISBN 0-8352-2346-9.

Over four hundred books have been listed and annotated for the child in grades 1 through 3 to use for independent reading as opposed to a list of books to be read to a child. The list is arranged by reading level in seven chapters, starting with wordless books and continuing by half grade levels through grade 3. Each chapter is further arranged by easy, average, and challenging for that level (for example, books for the first half of grade 1, readability: 1.0-1.4). Titles are listed first for easy reference and then each title is listed with a descriptive paragraph, followed by its genre and subject headings.

The authors note that while the list is arranged by reading level (Spache and Fry), they did consult with children about the titles and tried to take their suggestions. However, this is the point at which the list fails. If librarians and children waited to enjoy the books listed until they had gained the recommended reading level, they would miss many good titles, and many more would no longer be of interest. For example, the list recommends waiting until the second half of grade 3 before reading *Where the Wild Things Are, The Biggest Bear,* and *Jumanji.* Waiting until the first half of grade 3 is recommended before reading *Stone Soup, Strega Nona,* and *Lyle, Lyle, Crocodile.* While the advocates of teaching reading through literature could use this list because of the good titles it contains, the grade level structure would have to be ignored. As librarians know, children will rise to meet more difficult vocabulary when the interest level in a book is high.

Other features of the book are flawed. The subject headings suggested for the items are too much like *Sears* and too little like Bowker's excellent *A to Zoo* list, which bring out story themes. Likewise, the alphabetical listing of authors puts Dr. Seuss in the "Ds."

The list has some good titles and one could argue about many which were excluded, such as *Green Eggs and Ham*. Overall, the list is useful for its inclusions, but should not be used as the authors have structured the list. [R: LJ, Dec 88, p. 96]   David V. Loertscher

Biographies

154. Bingham, Jane M., ed. **Writers for Children: Critical Studies of Major Authors since the Seventeenth Century.** New York, Scribner's, 1988. 661p. index. $90.00. LC 87-16011. ISBN 0-684-18165-7.

"A critical guide to selected classics in children's literature ... important writers from the seventeenth century to the first part of the twentieth century. It includes eighty-four original critical essays, alphabetically arranged with selected bibliographies" (introduction). Beginning with Louisa May Alcott and ending with Charlotte Mary Yonge, each essay is by a named, often noted, contributor, and while entries vary in length, most cover the subject quite fully.

There are a listing of contributors with their backgrounds and credentials and a full index of important persons, titles, and events mentioned.

This extremely interesting and well-written reference work is aimed at scholars and critics in the field of children's literature, and is obviously of great interest and value to children's librarians, students, and researchers in the field as well as those who are concerned with this delightful and important area of literature. Useful (maybe even essential) for academic libraries as well as public and school libraries of any size. [R: Choice, Feb 88, p. 890; WLB, Jan 88, pp. 98-99]   Eleanor Elving Schwartz

155. Rollock, Barbara. **Black Authors and Illustrators of Children's Books: A Biographical Dictionary.** New York, Garland, 1988. 130p. illus. bibliog. (Garland Reference Library of the Humanities, Vol. 660). $25.00. LC 87-25748. ISBN 0-8240-8580-9.

Black authors and illustrators (115) from the United States, Africa, Canada, and Great Britain whose works have been published in the United States are profiled in this biographical dictionary. Intended to "represent those black authors who have made or are making literary history in the world of children's books" (p. xi), the collection includes subjects whose works were published as early as the 1930s, although most are from the 1970s and 1980s.

Each profile includes a biographical sketch plus a bibliography of the subject's work for

children. The sketches range in length from about 30 to 350 words; most are very brief. "Bibliographical Sources and References" (p. xiii) lists seventeen sources for more information. Also included in the collection are fifty-one black-and-white photographs of people and book covers.   Nancy Courtney

156. **Something about the Author: Facts and Pictures about Authors and Illustrators of Books for Young People. Volume 49.** Anne Commire, ed. Detroit, Gale, 1987. 310p. illus. index. $68.00. LC 72-27107. ISBN 0-8103-2259-5; ISSN 0276-816X.

Following the tradition of earlier volumes, *Something about the Author* (*SATA*) contains both personal and professional material about authors of children's literature. Generously illustrated articles enable children and young adults to learn more about their favorite authors. Continuing the format of long biographical features, brief entries, and obituary notices, Commire has added to this edition full biographies of Frank Bonham, Chester Gould, and Leon Uris, among others. Among those included with brief entries are Jan Andrews, Tamore Pierce, and Agnes S. P. Szudek. Obituaries include Elizabeth Coatsworth, Paul Galdone, and Jane Quigg. With effort made for complete coverage, each biographical entry contains correct name, personal information, career facts, writings and information concerning them, any adaptations, sidelights, and references to other sources. Few changes have occurred since *SATA* was last reviewed (see *ARBA 85*, entries 1026-1029) and it continues to be recommended as an excellent source for children and young adults seeking biographical information on authors.   Anna Grace Patterson

Dictionaries and Encyclopedias

157. **Children's Britannica.** 4th ed. Margaret Sutton, James Somerville, and others, eds. Chicago, Encyclopaedia Britannica, 1988. 20v. illus. (part col.). maps. index. $299.00/set. LC 87-81078. ISBN 0-85229-206-6.

Children's Britannica supersedes *Britannica Junior Encyclopaedia for Boys and Girls*, edited by Marvin Martin and published in fifteen volumes from 1934 to 1984. *Britannica Junior Encyclopaedia* was reviewed in *ARBA 82* (see entry 47) and *ARBA 78* (see entry 64).

Similar to *Britannica Junior*, the text of *Children's Britannica* is written in a simple, straightforward manner that is easy for children to understand. Like its predecessor, this twenty-volume set is curriculum-oriented and designed for use by elementary school students. Although the *Children's Britannica* is prepared under the supervision of the *Encyclopaedia Britannica*, it is a separate entity and should not be considered on the merits of the parent encyclopedia.

Under the editorial direction of Margaret Sutton with senior editor James Somerville and five associate editors, *Children's Britannica* employs a good system of cross-referencing that guides the student to related articles. The illustrations are quite adequate, with many black-and-white and several four-color illustrations. The text is often accompanied by line drawings and maps.

Volume 20 contains an analytic index to the encyclopedia that serves as the key to all information contained in the set. Also listed in volume 20 are advisors and authors contributing to this edition, plus some helpful instructions for its use. Readers are advised to consult volume 20 first, which is a very valid recommendation. For example, if the reader wishes to obtain information on the goldfinch, he or she will not find a separate article on this bird under "G" in volume 8. This is because the goldfinch has been classified as a member of the finch family, and hence, is treated under the single article of that title. The index serves to direct the reader from "Goldfinch" to "Finch Family." The same is true of cross-references listed at the end of longer articles. Many children will use them, but for most readers it is simpler to use the index, which connects interrelated topics.

The structure, content, and style of the articles reflect the encyclopedia's focus on elementary level students. For example, a two-page article on the letters of an alphabet explains that letters are actually signs which stand for sounds. The definition is followed by a brief paragraph covering early writings, and another on writing with an alphabet. To assist students in further research, the article concludes with a leading statement on the phonetic alphabet and directs the reader to an article on "Phonetics." Accompanying the article are illustrations showing some of the stages in the development of the English alphabet. One illustration shows Arabic characters, Russian letters, Chinese characters, etc., unfortunately with explanations that are at times inadequate. A string of characters is provided as an example of the various forms of the alphabet, but no translation is provided.

A much longer article has been written on American literature in volume 1, with cross-references to drama, poetry, and prose. It is well written and covers such topics as the Revolutionary period, the early nineteenth century, the New England poets, the poetry revival, the interwar period, the Southern literature renais-

sance, and the period since World War II. The article ends with comments about playwrights such as Tennessee Williams, Arthur Miller, and William Inge, and indicates that many of the writers mentioned in the article are covered in separate biographical sketches.

All in all, *Children's Britannica* is essentially a well-edited encyclopedia for elementary students. The format is attractive, and the cross-references and index are quite adequate. The 1988 edition was substantially revised and contains not only many longer articles but also six thousand short "capsule" entries. These brief entries give the reader instant facts which in many cases will be very helpful in the school curriculum. *Children's Britannica* is an accurate and reliable school encyclopedia and can be safely recommended for its intended audience. [R: WLB, Nov 88, pp. 121-22]

Bohdan S. Wynar

158.   **The Children's Encyclopedia and Atlas.** London, Treasure Press; distr., Toronto, Doubleday Canada, c1981, 1987. 1v. (various paging). illus. (col.). maps. index. $24.95. ISBN 1-85051-213-2.

This encyclopedia and atlas is an attempt to organize information that would appeal to youngsters, although there is no introduction or suggestion of purpose or use of the work. The fifteen topics of the encyclopedia include the universe, the Earth, plant world, history of man, etc. An index is provided to the encyclopedia and maps. The atlas index is complicated to use and, in the copy reviewed, was missing pages 54 and 55. The work is in full color and makes liberal use of diagrams, illustrations, and photographs.

Children would find the work interesting as a picture book but would have difficulty reading the fine print used in the maps. The text is clear and easy to read, albeit uninteresting. The encyclopedia would have value to parents as a source for reading to and talking with young children about the pictures and topics. Because of the organization and the limited index to the encyclopedia, the work has only marginal value as a reference tool.   William E. Hug

159.   Paton, John, ed. **Picture Encyclopedia for Children.** New York, Grosset & Dunlap/Putnam, 1987. 380p. illus. (part col.). maps. index. $19.95. LC 86-81788. ISBN 0-448-18999-2.

The *Picture Encyclopedia* covers some 750 subjects in brief, attractively illustrated articles on animals, places, people, history, and science and technology. It is arranged in alphabetical order, in a two-column format. Many articles include references to other entries, in capital letters in a different type style. In addition, an index covers over twenty-seven hundred topics including the main entries. The reading and interest level would probably range from grades 3 to 6.

This encyclopedia has many more illustrations per page than multivolume encyclopedias, nearly all in color. However, larger encyclopedias cover thousands more articles. For example, the letter "H" takes 12 pages and 27 entries in *Picture Encyclopedia*, but 428 pages with over 1,000 entries in the 1988 *World Book* (see *ARBA* 88, entry 52).

In a spot check of entries, some problems were found. The article on presidents of the United States lists all presidents, but only six have separate entries and only those six appear to be in the index. The only Protestant group that rates an entry is the Quakers, although five other groups mentioned in the article on Protestants are indexed. There is a brief entry for each state, including the capital, the state flower, etc., and a drawing of the United States with the state highlighted. Canadian provinces are covered in separate articles but there is only one map, under Canada. Some cities such as London, New York, and San Francisco are included separately, while others, such as Los Angeles, Miami Beach, and Minneapolis, are not. In a similar fashion, some countries, such as Argentina, Belgium, and China, are included, but others, such as Algeria, Colombia, and Ethiopia, are not. The article on flags includes national flags for seventy-eight countries, with no explanation why others are missing.

While a person wishing to find a comprehensive encyclopedia would need to look further, this is an attractive book which should appeal to younger children and give them opportunities to look things up in alphabetical order and to use indexes and cross-references. It also is much more affordable for family purchase than multivolume encyclopedias. [R: SLJ, May 88, p. 32]   Betty Jo Buckingham

160. **Raintree Children's Encyclopedia.** Milwaukee, Wis., Raintree, 1988. 11v. illus. (part col.). maps. index. $240.00/set; $180.00/set (schools and libraries); $145.93pa./set; $109.45 pa./set (schools and libraries). LC 87-16543. ISBN 0-8172-3050-5; 0-8172-3051-3pa.

The first edition of this set was published by Macmillan of London in 1974, with the second in 1980 and the third in 1986. All three previous editions were published under the title *Macmillan Children's Encyclopedia.* Unfortunately, this British encyclopedia was never reviewed in *ARBA*, nor was it reviewed in Kister's *Best Encyclopedias: A Guide to General and*

Specialized Encyclopedias (see *ARBA* 87, entry 54).

Each of the ten volumes of the encyclopedia covers a different topic, with volume 11 serving as an index volume and brief reference section. The topics covered include people, animals, plants, Earth and beyond, famous men and women, travel and communications, modern world, countries and customs, arts and entertainment, and sports and recreation.

Perhaps the strongest point of *Raintree Children's Encyclopedia* is its illustrations, which are well executed, colorful, and blend with the text. The text, however, is less than satisfactory. For example, a very brief entry on Roman Catholics reads:

> Early Christians belonged to the one "catholic" (world-wide) Church. In time, they divided into the Roman Catholic Church and the Eastern Orthodox Churches. The head of the Roman Catholics is the Pope, the Bishop of Rome. Roman Catholics must keep the Church's rules, confessing their sins and going to the service called mass each Sunday. They believe that Christ's mother, the Virgin Mary, and the saints can help them when they pray to God.

Treatment of Protestants, Quakers, Presbyterians, and Mormons is just as brief and inadequate, and is indicative of the type of coverage provided for other subjects. An article on Roman Catholics in *Children's Britannica* (Encyclopedia Britannica, 1988) is much more extensive and includes information on Roman Catholic beliefs, worship, origins, and history.

Considering the price of *Raintree Children's Encyclopedia*, it seems to us that *Children's Britannica* or even *Young Students Encyclopedia* (Weekly Reader, 1982) would be a wiser investment. [R: RBB, 1 Sept 88, p. 55]

Bohdan S. Wynar

Handbooks

161. Adamson, Lynda G. **A Reference Guide to Historical Fiction for Children and Young Adults.** Westport, Conn., Greenwood Press, 1987. 401p. bibliog. index. $49.95. LC 87-7533. ISBN 0-313-25002-2.

This comprehensive, historical fiction guide describes the works written since 1940 of eighty award-winning authors. Main entries are accessible alphabetically by the author's last name. Specific titles, main characters, historical personages, places, and important historical aspects of several novels can be found via a similar alphabetical progression. Within each author's entry are a bibliography of the author's works, a description of his or her honors, a lengthy annotation of each cited title, and a summary of the author's general themes and style. Two useful appendices provide access by classifying titles according to historical periods and by Fry Readability levels. In addition, there are two appendices: a bibliography on writing historical novels by writers cited in the guide, and a secondary bibliography about the authors and historical novels cited in the guide.

The integration of author, people, place, historical event, and main character entries is disconcerting. The guide would be improved by listing, for example, characters in a separate part of the book. Coverage of these entries is also somewhat uneven. For example, a paragraph is devoted to Lindisfarne, while there are no entries for Confucius, Buddha, or Adolph Hitler. These flaws are minor, however, when considering the potential use for this book. The titles cited are covered more thoroughly than in Nilsen and Donelson's *Literature for Today's Young Adults* (2d ed., Scott Foresman, 1985), Irwin's *Guide to Historical Fiction* (see *ARBA* 73, entry 1252), the *Children's Catalog* (see *ARBA* 86, entry 821), and *Senior High School Library Catalog* (see *ARBA* 88, entry 640). The book is a valuable resource for teachers, parents, and school and public librarians who wish to compile bibliographies and reading lists or simply acquire more knowledge about historically based fictional works. [R: RBB, 15 Feb 88, pp. 984, 986; RQ, Spring 88, pp. 433-34]

Kathleen W. Craver

162. Gillespie, John T., with Corinne J. Naden. **Juniorplots 3: A Book Talk Guide for Use with Readers Ages 12-16.** New York, R. R. Bowker, 1987. 352p. index. $24.95. LC 87-27305. ISBN 0-8352-2367-1.

Juniorplots 3 is similar in format to *Juniorplots* (Bowker, 1967) and *More Juniorplots* (Bowker, 1977) although this work does not include any introductory material on booktalking techniques. Instead, it refers the reader to several resources on the topic.

Juniorplots 3 gives detailed plot summaries of eighty books which have proven popular with adolescent readers (grade 6 through high school). The selected titles have been recommended in at least two standard reviewing sources and meet the interests and needs of young adults of different reading levels and developmental stages. Titles were grouped into eight subjects/genre: teenage life and concerns, adventure and mystery stories, science fiction

and fantasy, historical fiction, sports fiction, biography and true adventure, guidance and health, and the world around us. The first category contains the largest number of titles.

As with the previous *Juniorplots*, a detailed plot summary is followed by an enumeration of primary and secondary themes. Suggestions are given for booktalks, including paginations for selections to read aloud. Six to eight related titles are briefly described, with bibliographic data also provided. When biographical data were found on the author of the featured book, appropriate citations are provided for follow-up research.

This is a welcome addition to the professional collections of public and school librarians working with young adults. Highly recommended. [R: RBB, 1 June 88, p. 1659; SLJ, Sept 88, p. 126]

Carol J. Veitch

163. Hendrickson, Linnea. **Children's Literature: A Guide to the Criticism.** Boston, G. K. Hall, 1987. 664p. index. (Reference Publication in Literature). $35.00. LC 86-19455. ISBN 0-8161-8670-7.

This guide to criticism in the field of children's literature demonstrates the extent to which the field has gained stature as an academic discipline during the past fifteen years. No specific dates of coverage are given, but the number of articles from the 1970s and 1980s indicates the growth in the field. Few of the books analyzed were published earlier than 1960, although a few classics such as those by Paul Hazard (1944) and Lillian H. Smith (1953) are included. The compiler states that "the starting point ... was the critical sources." Journals and books were examined to find books and articles that "provide insight into the work or topic discussed" and "say something significant or enlightening." In addition to books and journal articles, a number of unpublished dissertations and ERIC documents are listed. The bibliography is divided into two sections: "Authors and Their Works," and "Subjects, Themes and Genres." Indexes to authors, titles, subjects, and critics are also included, thus providing easy access for almost any purpose. Annotations are brief and descriptive, indicating the scope of the item but not evaluating its contribution. A six-page appendix lists reference works and journals in children's literature. Students of children's literature, teachers, and librarians will find this a compact, useful guide to a variety of critical articles. [R: Choice, May 87, p. 1380; RBB, 15 June 87, p. 1576]

Adele M. Fasick

164. Jones, Dolores Blythe. **Children's Literature Awards and Winners: A Directory of**

Prizes, Authors, and Illustrators. 2d ed. Detroit, Neal-Schuman with Gale, 1988. 671p. index. $92.00. LC 84-643512. ISBN 0-8103-2741-4; ISSN 0749-3096.

The second edition of this work is divided into four parts: directory of awards, authors and illustrators, selected bibliography, and indexes. Four types of indexes are offered: award, subject index of awards, author/illustrator, and title.

The directory of awards includes the name and address of the sponsoring organization, purpose and history of the award, frequency, selection criteria, award categories, rules and regulations, and form of award. Award recipients are listed from the award's inception to 1987, and entries include author, title, illustrator, translator, publisher, and date of publication. Awards that have been discontinued are included in the list.

The most important tools for the reader are the indexes. The newly added author/illustrator and title indexes are straightforward and easy to use, yet the reader may encounter difficulties using the award index and subject index of awards, the latter also being new to this edition. These two would benefit from more extensive cross-referencing to bridge the disparity between official title and commonly used titles, such as the Sequoyah Children's Book Award versus the Oklahoma Sequoyah Children's Book Award.

Further, the subject index of awards should be more comprehensive. There is no access by state to all the awards originating in that state. For example, the Charlie May Simon Award, if placed under the heading of Arkansas, would be easier for the reader to locate than under the Children's Choice subject heading. Perhaps a fifth index of awards by state could be created for successive editions.

Children's Literature Awards & Winners is more extensive than its counterpart, *Children's Books: Awards & Prizes*, compiled by The Children's Book Council, though it is also more expensive. Each is published periodically. For the library who can afford the price, its collection will benefit from having this reference source. [R: RBB, 15 Dec 88, p. 688]

Susan M. Sigman

165. Kobrin, Beverly. **Eyeopeners! How to Choose and Use Children's Books about Real People, Places, and Things.** New York, Viking Penguin, 1988. 317p. illus. bibliog. index. $16.95; $7.95pa. LC 88-40115. ISBN 0-670-82073-3; 0-14-046830-7pa.

"Are you a parent, a grandparent, a teacher, a librarian, a friend of one, about to become one, or any combination thereof? If so, this book is a bundle of ideas just for you—a passel of persuasive prose about the pros of children's nonfiction books" (p. 1). Thus the author gives her own best summary of what the book is about and whom it is for. Over five hundred trade books (i.e., not textbooks and not fiction) are organized by subject, with a more detailed subject index and an index of authors, titles, and illustrators to provide still more thorough access. Every entry is vividly discussed, and frequently accompanied by tips for projects to link the books to children's everyday experiences. Kobrin's material is gender inclusive and sensitive to the issues of race, disabilities, and nontraditional families. She includes books for "difficult" topics such as death, alcoholism, sex, and divorce, as well as the more standard fare of dinosaurs, lasers, cars, grandparents, music, zoos, outerspace, etc. All materials mentioned were in-print and available as of the beginning of 1988.

The first portion of the work is a handbook addressed to the various types of adults who bring children and books together. In this section, Kobrin's energetic creativity shines forth with suggestions that are stimulating and relevant. She reminds adults to teach children to read critically, to be aware of points of view, dates of publication, and potential biases. She reminds teachers to consult with librarians before giving out assignments, and offers librarians suggestions on how to encourage reading.

Kobrin is dedicated to the notion that both nonfiction and fiction together comprise literature, and her enthusiasm is infectious. This book is more than just a bibliography or a handbook; it is a celebration of the very best that can happen when children and books are brought together. [R: BL, 1 Oct 88, p. 331]

Marilyn R. Pukkila

166. Polkingharn, Anne T., and Catherine Toohey. **More Creative Encounters: Activities to Expand Children's Responses to Literature.** Englewood, Colo., Libraries Unlimited, 1988. 116p. illus. bibliog. index. $17.50pa. LC 88-8892. ISBN 0-87287-663-2.

This is a continuance of a title issued in 1983 entitled *Creative Encounters* which provided activities for literature used with children. In this new title, fifty-one children's books have been selected and activities developed around these titles that will require ordinary classroom materials. These activities enrich the literature they represent. A summary of the story is included as well as materials required, step-by-step activities, patterns to use, and other related titles or titles by the same author. The activities presented allow the children to use their creativity and express themselves in the situation. The note section varies the activity depending on the ages of the children involved in it.

The authors' focus is on the relationship of readers to the content of the book and how they can share their response with others. Books have been carefully chosen and encompass many subjects that readers will be able to identify with and respond to with their imagination and own experiences. These selections include familiar favorites as well as new titles, and represent authors such as Tomie de Paola, Eric Carle, Lorna Balian, and William Pène du Bois. This title stands apart from its predecessor and provides opportunities for the teacher and the librarian to effectively use with good children's literature. Using these activities with the literature will promote pleasurable reading experiences for the child as well as developing thinking, listening, and communicating skills. This will be an excellent resource for public and school libraries.　　　　　Mary J. Stanley

167. Reed, Arthea J. S. **Comics to Classics: A Parent's Guide to Books for Teens and Preteens.** Newark, Del., International Reading Association, 1988. 121p. illus. $8.95pa. LC 88-10171. ISBN 0-87207-798-5.

This is a practical, commonsense guide to young adult literature. Like Jim Treleases's *Read Aloud Handbook*, it provides a basic introduction for parents who are interested in their children's reading. The first chapters of Reed's book discuss the physical and emotional development of preteens and teenagers. Chapters 6 and 7 are annotated bibliographies of books which should appeal to most adolescents. They are arranged by topic and coded for reading interest levels. Chapters 8 and 9 discuss ways to share books with young people and include a discussion of the positive and negative effects of television on the reading of adolescents. The last section of the book includes book selection tips, sources for buying and borrowing books, and a bibliography of books and magazines about adolescents.

This book is a good introduction to the topic of books and the adolescent reader. Parents will find it both interesting and useful. It could also be used as a supplementary textbook in young adult literature courses. Both public and school libraries will find it a valuable addition to their collections. [R: BL, 15 Nov 88, p. 516]　　　　　Carol J. Veitch

168. Spirt, Diana L. **Introducing Bookplots 3: A Book Talk Guide for Use with Readers Ages 8-12.** New York, R. R. Bowker, 1988. 352p. index. $39.95. LC 87-37513. ISBN 0-8352-2345-0.

Librarians, teachers, and other adults looking for books suitable for children in grades 3 to 6 (ages eight to twelve) will find many excellent suggestions in this collection by Diana Spirt. Like her previous books, *Introducing Books* (see *ARBA* 71, entry 136) and *Introducing More Books* (see *ARBA* 79, entry 235), this volume concentrates on quality books and groups them thematically under headings such as "Making Friends," "Developing Values," "Forming a View of the World," and "Understanding Social Problems." Books are arranged alphabetically by author within each section, but additional guidance is given by a "Reading Ladder" section in which titles are arranged by age level and difficulty. There are also author/title/illustrator and subject indexes. For each of the eighty-one featured books the author provides a lengthy plot summary. The pattern is to start with a paragraph about the author's previous works, describe the book cover and illustrations, and then move to a summary of the plot. Occasionally these summaries are confusing (see "The Boy and the Devil," p. 82), but most of them give a clear account of the book. A thematic analysis of each book and suggestions about how to discuss it as well as a listing of related materials are included. Since the books were published between 1979 and 1986, many of the titles will be new to librarians, especially those working in small libraries. This book could be used as a selection aid as well as a booktalk guide in many libraries. [R: RBB, 1 Sept 88, pp. 50, 52; SLJ, Sept 88, p. 126]　　　　　Adele M. Fasick

169. Walker, Elinor, comp. **Book Bait: Detailed Notes on Adult Books Popular with Young People.** 4th ed. Chicago, American Library Association, 1988. 166p. index. $10.95pa. LC 88-987. ISBN 0-8389-0491-2.

The fourth edition of this excellent young adult readers' guide is based upon ninety-six selections made by a group of fifteen teenagers in grades 7 through 9. Books include works of fiction, biography, autobiography, and nonfiction. Each "main entry" contains a three-quarter page summary of the book, a paragraph highlighting its notable qualities, passages recommended for booktalking, and brief annotations of additional genre titles. The selections retain some entries from the third edition, such as *Ann Frank: The Diary of a Young Girl*, but most titles, such as *Into the Mouth of the Cat: The Story of Lance Sijan, Hero of Vietnam*, are new recommendations. Spanning a spectrum of fifty subjects from adventure, civil rights, courage, danger, and fantasy to the generation gap, minorities, sex, suspense, and women's rights,

Book Bait provides school and public librarians with a wealth of popular, appealing young adult books to booktalk and recommend to adolescents. The annotations are carefully written and related titles are well chosen. Objectionable language and sex scenes are also appropriately noted for specific titles. Also included are a subject index of main entries and a title index. This new edition should be considered an essential purchase for all public and secondary school libraries. [R: BL, 1 Oct 88, p. 259]

Kathleen W. Craver

Indexes

170. Shields, Nancy E. **Index to Literary Criticism for Young Adults.** Metuchen, N.J., Scarecrow, 1988. 410p. $32.50. LC 87-37. ISBN 0-8108-2112-5.

Geared toward the novice researcher, this index lists four thousand plus authors who are covered in a small selection of standard library reference books. *British Writers* (see *ARBA 88*, entry 1199) and *Nineteenth-Century Literature Criticism* (see *ARBA 86*, entry 1086) are examples of the reference books chosen for availability and wealth of information.

Contemporary authors as well as those of the past are indexed alphabetically, with book, volume, and publisher information following in an abridged form, discarding awkward abbreviations and keys. Cross-references aid the researcher with pseudonyms and variant name spellings, but authors with multiple pen names have all books listed for each. In special cases subject headings and page numbers are provided.

It should be kept in mind that this book provides a starting place for research. The researcher's success will result from following the bibliographical map provided in the reference books indexed. [R: RBB, 15 Sept 88, pp. 138, 140; VOYA, Dec 88, p. 259; WLB, Sept 88, pp. 95-96]

Patricia M. Leach

171. Smyth, Margaret, comp. **Picture Book Index.** Newcastle-under-Lyme, England, AAL Publishing; distr., Newcastle-under-Lyme, England, Remploy, 1987. 50p. illus. £9.95. ISBN 0-900092-65-3.

Intended as a companion to the fifth edition of *Junior Fiction Index* by the same publisher this title provides subject access to children's picture books. The emphasis is on recent books and those titles identified as standard. There is a strong British bias as shown in subject terms such as *comfort blanket*, *bunyip*, *dustmen*, and *jumble sales*. The index terms selected were based on Smyth's experience and the books themselves. A partial list of "special situation" subject headings (e.g., adoption and stepfamilies) is given, but most terms are found by browsing. A complete list of terms or the use of standardized subject headings would have been more efficient. Also, an author/title index would have been helpful, especially in identifying multiple titles by a single author. The book itself is strictly an index, giving a citation for each title included—but no annotations indicate if entries are fiction or nonfiction.

Picture Book Index is potentially useful for those libraries with strong collections in British picture books. Carolyn Lima's *A to Zoo: Subject Access to Children's Picture Books* (2d edition, R. R. Bowker, 1986) is quite extensive, and Sharon Dreyer's *The Bookfinder* (3d edition, American Guidance Service, 1985) indexes books for specific situations, such as sibling rivalry. Both should be considered for purchase before Smyth's index. Furthermore, both *Children's Catalog* and Lois Winkel's *Elementary School Library Collection* provide some subject access. This work is not a top priority purchase.

Carol A. Doll

172. **Young Adult Book Review Index 1987.** Barbara Beach and Beverly Anne Baer, eds. Detroit, Gale, 1988. 451p. $85.00. ISBN 0-8103-4373-8; ISSN 0897-7402.

This new annual incorporates all the review citations for books and periodicals from *Book Review Index* that at least one reviewer recommended for persons ages eleven through seventeen (16,800 review citations from about sixty-three hundred books and periodicals). It also contains citations for books if the targeted audiences overlap each end of the range, and books originally written for adults, but evaluated for young adults by one or more reviewers. *Book Review Index* now indexes more than 465 periodicals.

Each entry includes the author's or editor's name in boldface type; the title; the illustrator in parentheses; an abbreviation of the reviewing source with the date, volume number, and page on which the review appears; and a letter code identifying the type of book being reviewed, if appropriate (c = book for children ten and younger, a = adult, y = young adults eleven and older, r = reference work, and p = periodical).

Endsheets give a listing of the periodical abbreviations. A name and address list of publications indexed as well as illustrator and title indexes are included.

This is a good, single, concise source for needed information on young adult literature. Libraries already owning *Book Review Index* may not want to purchase this specialized title unless they have a separate department for young adults.   Kathleen J. Voigt

CHILDREN'S SERVICES

173. Bell, Irene Wood. **Caldecott Search-a-Word Learning Guide.** Englewood, Colo., Libraries Unlimited, 1988. 257p. illus. bibliog. index. $19.00pa. LC 88-779. ISBN 0-87287-592-X.

This title contains 144 puzzles based on 35 books that have won the Caldecott medal. Students must circle the correct word (arranged horizontally, vertically, or diagonally, spelled forward or backward) located in an array of camouflaging letters. There are four sections in this book. Two sections give students lists of words to locate—one set in an array approximately fifteen letters by fifteen letters, the other in a thirty letter by thirty letter square. In the other two sections students must generate the word list by answering clues.

Since the puzzles are based on Caldecott-award-winning titles, the books used for the puzzles are likely to be available in most communities. Although there are 144 puzzles, the same word lists and the same clue lists are used for both the small and large letter squares. For example, the first items on the list for both *Make Way for Ducklings* puzzles are "public garden," "ducks," "waddle," and "dither." The sections with the small letter arrays are labeled "word comprehension"; those sections with the large letter squares are labeled "thought comprehension." Although the puzzles can be entertaining and can develop word and letter *recognition* skills, circling given words or answering clues by recalling words or facts are not comprehension skills. Permission is given for teachers and media specialists to make multiple copies of these puzzles for classroom use, but some of the larger puzzles will not photocopy well because they are too light and/or letter quality is poor. Finally, there is an appendix of book report forms which seems unrelated to the rest of the book. For example, there is a book report sheet for biographies, but none of the thirty-five Caldecott titles used is a biography.

Puzzles can and should be used to promote classroom learning. The price of this volume seems high, given the content.

Carol A. Doll

174. Bodart-Talbot, Jon, ed. **Booktalk! 3: More Booktalks for All Ages and Audiences.** Bronx, N.Y., H. W. Wilson, 1988. 371p. bibliog. index. $28.00pa. LC 88-17284. ISBN 0-8242-0764-5.

This is a collection of about five hundred booktalks, arranged alphabetically by title. The talks, ranging in length from two sentences to almost two pages, were written by Bodart-Talbot and 160 contributors. Indexes allow access by age of potential reader and theme or genre. Intended as a companion volume to *Booktalk! 2* (H. W. Wilson, 1985), there is also a cumulative index to booktalks in both volumes.

There is good variety in the titles included here. Booktalks are suitable for all ages, as the titles range from picture books, such as *Ira Sleeps Over*, to adult books, like *The Shining* by Stephen King. Titles represent many genres, including contemporary realism, science fiction, fantasy, mystery, informational, and biography. While most are copyrighted in the 1980s, older titles such as Lois Lenski's *Strawberry Girl* and Mark Twain's *The Adventures of Tom Sawyer* can be found. In general, the booktalks do capture the mood or esscence of each title, tend to be enthusiastic, and would pique the interest of listeners.

At the same time, this title is narrow in focus, being a collection of booktalks only. If public, school, or academic libraries can afford the price, the book is generally well done. [R: BL, 1 Oct 88, p. 259]   Carol A. Doll

175. Irving, Jan, and Robin Currie. **Full Speed Ahead: Stories and Activities for Children on Transportation.** Englewood, Colo., Teacher Ideas Press/Libraries Unlimited, 1988. 244p. illus. bibliog. index. $21.50pa. LC 88-29540. ISBN 0-87287-653-5.

Similar in format and purpose to Library Unlimited's *Mudluscious: Stories and Activities Featuring Food for Preschool Children* (1986) and *Glad Rags: Stories and Activities Featuring Clothes for Children* (1987), this teacher resource is a practical and creative way to share literature with children. Through the helpful program planning suggestions, quality picture books and enrichment activities can be easily targeted to preschool and primary age children. Through the transportation theme, children are exposed to a wide variety of stories about travel—on water, in the air, or on land. Books about magic carpets, carousels, and roller skates are not overlooked, nor are those on various cultures (Eskimo dog sleds) and occupations (truck drivers).

Arrangement is by eight thematic chapters that follow a similar organization: purpose, initiating activity, annotations, literature activities (e.g., flannel board stories, storytelling, and fingerplays), participatory games, crafts, and take-home activities. The work concludes with a resource bibliography, skills list (e.g., word recognition and group cooperation), and an index of authors and titles.

This nominally priced sourcebook is sure to be a big hit with elementary school teachers, child caregivers, children's librarians, curriculum developers, and parents.

Ilene F. Rockman

176. MacDonald, Margaret Read. **Booksharing: 101 Programs to Use with Preschoolers.** Hamden, Conn., Library Professional Publications/Shoe String Press, 1988. 236p. illus. bibliog. index. $32.50. LC 87-35777. ISBN 0-208-02159-0.

Children's librarians are always looking for new and different program ideas to use with small children. *Booksharing* is an excellent collection of 101 complete forty-five-minute programs. While each program is thematic, the author stresses that good programming should begin with the books themselves, then work on the creation of a total program. Each story time program has been used with children ranging from age two through age six. Plans include several books, songs, crafts, films, creative dramatics, fingerplays, and poems which provide a comprehensive learning experience for the child. Craft ideas and follow-up activities are described, but there are no detailed instructions or patterns. There are two series of programs which focus on art and music as well as the more traditional holiday, seasons, or concept programs.

A complete bibliography which includes reference to the program(s) where the items was used is provided, as is an index of recommended films. The musical notations which are included are handwritten and sometimes difficult to read. They are, however, still useful to the program planner. Recommended. [R: BL, 1 Apr 88, p. 1356; JOYS, Summer 88, p. 464; SLJ, Aug 88, p. 48]

Carol J. Veitch

177. Waddle, Linda, ed. **Library Services to Youth: Preparing for the Future.** Champaign, Ill., Graduate School of Library and Information Science, University of Illinois, 1988. 114p. (*Library Trends*, Vol. 37, No. 1). $15.00pa.

This issue is essentially a collection of papers written by youth advocates on various aspects of library services to youth, which in this case includes twelve- to eighteen-year-olds. According to the issue editor, young adult services are not a high priority in the library world. Since 1968 there has been a steady decrease in both the resources and staff in public libraries to serve these young people. Waddle, School Library Media Specialist at Cedar Falls High School, Iowa, has decided that there is a definite need for the profession to examine its current state and begin to make plans for the future. She has secured the services of youth advocates to produce eight papers, each of which deals with a special aspect of the problem.

Because youth have little authority in the institutions which govern their lives, Judith Flum suggests ways in which young adults can gain power so that their library and information needs can be met on a local, state, and national level. Charles Harmon and Frances Bradburn attack the problem of reading and information needs of youth and conclude that young adult librarians must understand, accept, and meet these needs and interests. Information access is the concern of Frances McDonald, who desires to remove the barriers of physical as well as intellectual access. Giving young adults freedom to use all materials no matter where they are located will alleviate the former, while an educational process may have to be used on the latter. Doris Epler describes how one state is solving the problems of access set forth by McDonald. Access Pennsylvania will eventually give the citizens of the state access to the resources of any library in the state which cooperates in the project. Her article addresses specifically the integration of online searching into the school library media curriculum and the bringing of schools into the resource sharing network. New information skills and processes must supplant the traditional skills taught in schools if we are to prepare young adults for the information age, advises Leah Hiland, while Barbara Baskin, Betty Carter, and Karen Harris insist that the literary experience gives readers the values they are seeking. Hispanic young adults bring a different set of problems to the librarian attempting to adequately serve them. Adela Artola Allen presents her thoughts and practical suggestions to meet the needs of the underserved ethnic individuals. Finally, Gerald Hodges uses research methods and data to focus on decision making for young adult services in public libraries.

These papers not only present an excellent overview of the problems that exist but also set forth cogent solutions which appropriate members of the profession should examine carefully so that the necessary steps will be taken to prepare our youth to function in the current information age and be ready for the future. This issue should be required reading for library directors, young adult librarians, and library and information science students who are interested in serving young adults. [R: LAR, 15 July 88, p. 409; RLR, Aug 88, pp. 193-94]

Sara R. Mack

COLLECTION
DEVELOPMENT

178.   Corrall, Sheila, ed. **Collection Development: Options for Effective Management. Proceedings of a Conference of the Library and Information Research Group, University of Sheffield, 1987.** London and Los Angeles, Calif., Taylor Graham, 1988. 155p. illus. $34.00 pa. ISBN 0-947568-25-5.

The twelve papers in this collection were presented at a 1987 conference sponsored by the (British) Library and Information Research Group. The authors hold positions in university research libraries, polytechnics, and industrial and public libraries. The papers present various strategies and techniques for collection management, and examine national issues and initiatives in Great Britain. Paper titles include "The Industrial Information Service," "Periodicals Reviewing by Voting," "Journal Acquisition versus Article Acquisition," and "A Review of Relegation Practice" (relegation is the process of selecting titles for placing in storage). Most of the papers include bibliographical references.

Articles on collection development and management have been rare in British library literature, so this collection improves the situation somewhat. More British studies are likely to follow and will most likely stem from the national collection development initiatives described herein. U.S. librarians could gain valuable insights from their British colleagues, but they will no doubt balk at the price of a 155-page softcover book printed in typescript.

Gary D. Barber

179.   Scholtz, James C. **Developing and Maintaining Video Collections in Libraries.** Santa Barbara, Calif., ABC-Clio, 1989. 196p. illus. index. $35.00. LC 88-16871. ISBN 0-87436-497-3.

Scholtz has prepared a concise guide for librarians of public libraries planning to establish video collections of varying sizes. He discusses the history and recent developments in the commercial side of the video industry, and he describes the mechanics and electronics behind basic hardware. The major portion of his text is devoted to collection development including strategic planning, public-interest surveys, technical processing, policy development, and selection and evaluation. Selection and maintenance of equipment is covered, and a chapter is devoted to copyright, loan fees, and access by minors. Collection sharing among libraries and the future of the video industry is also discussed, although Scholtz does not

mention instructional use, foreign videos, non-commercial documentaries, and high-tech installations. There is a brief bibliography of video reference tools.

This book would be best utilized by a librarian in a public library for which a modest collection of commercially-produced videotapes, with minimal on-site use, is wanted.

Margaret McKinley

180.   Valk, Barbara G., ed. **Collection Development: Cooperation at the Local and National Levels. Papers of the Twenty-Ninth Annual Meeting of the Seminar on the Acquisition of Latin American Library Materials....** Madison, Wis., SALALM Secretariat, 1987. 146p. bibliog. $36.50pa. ISBN 0-917617-10-X.

The twenty-ninth annual meeting of the Seminar on the Acquisition of Latin American Library Materials (SALALM) was held at the University of North Carolina, Chapel Hill, in June 1984. The major theme of the meeting was "Collection Development Cooperation at Local and National Levels." The papers from this meeting have been capably edited and organized by Valk of UCLA's Latin American Center. The papers are organized under five broad categories: "Latin American Studies and Cooperative Collection Development," "Specialized Research Collections—Legal Resources," "Collection and Organization of Primary Resource Materials," "Collection Techniques—Foreign Acquisition Trips," and "Bibliographies and Reference Aids." There is a list of panels and workshops and a list of contributors at the end of the volume, which is unindexed.

Among the many interesting presentations were Deborah Jakubs's "National Level Cooperation...," which describes the pros and cons of the RLG conspectus; Selma Cervetti de Rodriguez's "Latin American Legal Materials," which provides detailed lists of Latin American legal publishers; and "Book Buying Trips to Latin America," by Tulane's Thomas Niehaus, in which he provides useful suggestions for such trips. This volume, as have others in the series, should prove a boon to all librarians involved in Latin American collection development.

Brian E. Coutts

181.   Van Orden, Phyllis J. **The Collection Program in Schools: Concepts, Practices, and Information Sources.** Englewood, Colo., Libraries Unlimited, 1988. 347p. bibliog. index. $24.50. LC 87-33892. ISBN 0-87287-572-5.

The purpose of this book is to provide an overview of the processes and procedures used to develop and maintain a building-level media collection. The three main sections deal with the setting of the school library media center, the selection of materials in the collection, and administrative concerns of acquisition, maintenance, and evaluation.

The principal strength of this title is that it brings together in one place bits and pieces of traditional library courses. For example, concerns about bias in informational books can be a part of children's literature; selection bibliographies and tools are covered in reference courses; evaluation of nonbook media may have its own course; policy development is part of administration; and working with jobbers and weeding are covered in a collection development course. In addition, educational philosophy and styles of teaching are included. It is beneficial for readers to see the various elements of these courses integrated into collection development.

This strength of the book also causes its main weakness. So many topics are covered that few are treated in depth. For example, when discussing evaluation, Van Orden states that "through carefully worded surveys," (p. 263) it is possible to determine user perceptions of the collection. This is a true statement, but there is no discussion about how to write good survey questions. Nor are there sources given in the bibliography of that chapter on questionnaire development. At the same time, the section on weeding the collection has a good bibliography and an enlightening discussion of concerns media specialists express in opposition to weeding.

While many topics are covered, there is no discussion of copyright regulations. Given the current concerns about copyright law, especially in terms of television broadcasts and microcomputer software, this topic should have been included. Also, it would have been helpful to have at least some discussion on using microcomputers to help with administrative tasks. There is no material on management systems, word processing, or spreadsheets. Given the current use of this type of software, and the fact that this use will continue, this topic should have been addressed. Furthermore, there is no mention of the *Pico v. Board of Education Island Trees Union Free School District No. 26* case in the intellectual freedom section. This should have been included, since it did eventually go to the Supreme Court.

Overall, the fact that this book pulls together information from so many different areas of librarianship and education compensates for its weaknesses. [R: BL, July 88, pp. 1823-24; BL, July 88, p. 1845; BR, Sept/Oct 88, p. 49; SLJ, Oct 88, p. 44; VOYA, Oct 88, pp. 209-10]   Carol A. Doll

COLLEGE AND RESEARCH LIBRARIES

General Works

182. Armsby, Allen, and others. **Library & Learning Resources Management: Current Trends.** Blagdon, England, Further Education Staff College, 1987. 1v. (various paging). (Coombe Lodge Report, Vol. 19, No. 9). £3.75pa.

The Coombe Lodge Reports, new to this reviewer, are issued by the Further Education Staff College and treat various aspects of further education. This number contains seven short papers (about seventy pages altogether) that consider recent changes in the practice and theory of further education, and especially their implications for librarians. Topics covered include curricular developments, open learning, student-centered learning, information technology, management and organization, staffing and funding, and finally, the need for evaluation. Some of the situations and concerns are familiar (especially for community college librarians) and there are a number of interesting comments and bits of sage advice; however, because the British system of public higher education is so different from that of the United States, including the expectations for librarians, the report is of very limited value for most U.S. college and university librarians.

Evan Ira Farber

183. **The Automation Inventory of Research Libraries 1988.** Maxine K. Sitts, ed. Washington, D.C., Association of Research Libraries, 1988. 1v. (various paging). $30.00pa. ISBN 0-918006-57-0.

This fourth annual *Automation Inventory* provides profiles and analyses of the state of automation in 117 academic and research libraries in the United States and Canada as of summer 1988. As previously, it has been generated from a database maintained by the Office of Management Services's Systems and Procedures Exchange Center (SPEC). The database is available for online searching and on floppy disk. For the first time this title contains some analysis of aggregate data. It is based on data from 1987 and 1988 and focuses on changes in operating status and vendors as profiled in public access and technical services bibliographic functions. Because of the deadline for publication, the analysis is limited; but the intention is to extend it in the future. In the tables and listings, data are provided on nineteen library functions according to six descriptive factors:

operating status, extent of system, computer ownership and use, public access, number of workstations, and name of the vendor. The volume also includes a list of vendors for selected functions; information on related SPEC Kits; the cost of back issues of *Automation Inventory*, of floppy disks, and of online searches; the names of individuals contacted to provide data; and an appendix containing the instructions sent to each participating institution. This edition has been improved by pagination and its value enhanced by some interpretation of the data. Further analysis over time should provide considerable insight into trends in the automation of ARL member institutions.

Helen Howard

184. Breivik, Patricia Senn, and Robert Wedgeworth, eds. **Libraries and the Search for Academic Excellence.** Metuchen, N.J., Scarecrow, 1988. 213p. index. $25.00. LC 88-15855. ISBN 0-8108-2157-5.

In March 1987 Columbia University and the University of Colorado sponsored an invitational symposium on the role of the academic library in higher education. The seventy-two participants received ten background papers that served as the basis for discussion at the conference. This volume includes these papers as well as the texts of two speeches delivered by Ernest Boyer and Major R. Owens and summary comments by Frank Newman. The major theme of the volume is that although the condition of education in the United States has served as the basis for a number of studies since the early 1980s, the role of academic libraries has been ignored. The papers seek to remedy that omission and raise the consciousness of participants. Inspecting the list of those attending, one senses the sermon is being given to those already converted. Papers present testimony on how academic libraries have met the needs of non-traditional and minority students, how they can assist in the education of teachers, how they serve to foster research in their institutions, and how they aid regional economic development. Two papers address technology in libraries and their participation in electronic networks. One paper on curriculum change in higher education (reprinted from another volume) is interesting reading but not directly related to the symposium's theme. Newman's concluding address, evidently a transcript of his relatively informal remarks, presents many excellent insights and questions; however, his comments are poorly organized and edited. A series of action recommendations on how the effectiveness of academic libraries can be improved conclude the volume. Readers will encounter few new thoughts

or ideas in this book, and it serves mainly as a consolidation of academic library issues and concerns at the end of this decade.

Richard D. Johnson

185. Oberembt, Kenneth J., comp. **Annual Reports for College Libraries.** Chicago, Association of College and Research Libraries, American Library Association, 1988. 135p. illus. (CLIP Note, No. 10). $20.00pa. ISBN 0-8389-7219-5.

This is the latest addition to the CLIP (College Library Information Packet) Note series published by the Association of College and Research Libraries. It reports the results of a survey of how 191 small college and university libraries prepare and use annual reports. Usable responses from 128 questionnaires provide information about preparation, structure, production, distribution, and value of annual reports. In addition, five complete annual reports as well as selected annual report data-gathering forms and graphics are included.

The selected data-gathering forms clearly demonstrate that we are well versed in counting and measuring; the consistency in types of data reported is obvious and it is interesting to see the similarities in reporting forms. In contrast, the wide variety of graphics used is clearly a result of local staff skill and/or interest rather than conformity to national reporting requirements.

Anyone concerned with annual report preparation in a small academic library should find something of interest in this volume, whether it be confirmation of current local practice or new or improved ideas for presentation of materials. [R: JAL, Nov 88, p. 338]

Susan S. Baughman

186. **OMS 1987 Annual Report.** Washington, D.C., Association of Research Libraries, [1988]. 53p. illus. free pa.

The Office of Management Studies (OMS) has been serving research and academic libraries for almost two decades and reports annually on its activities. In customary OMS fashion this report highlights the year's activities, services, and products under a central theme, then concludes with a roster of priorities for the next year. The theme for the 1987 report is managing technology in the scholarly environment.

OMS programs are discussed in detail under four major categories: applied research and development, academic library program, Systems and Procedures Exchange Center, and organizational training and staff development. Priorities are also listed under these general headings. Appendices include a list of articles and presentations by OMS staff, brief biographical sketches of OMS staff, publications, order forms, and prices.

Librarians and scholars interested in the numerous activities and ventures of the Office of Management Studies would find this compact summary very useful. Copies are available from the office at no cost.   P. Grady Morein

187. Person, Roland Conrad. **A New Path: Undergraduate Libraries at United States and Canadian Universities, 1949-1987.** Westport, Conn., Greenwood Press, 1988. 160p. bibliog. index. (New Directions in Information Management, No. 17). $29.95. LC 87-29553. ISBN 0-313-25303-X.

Person has written a remarkably inconclusive study of undergraduate libraries which never convincingly accomplishes the objectives listed in the preface. The book's arrangement is confusing, beginning with a nondescript account of undergraduate libraries, then proceeding through one half of a literature survey, sections on unsuccessful and successful libraries, the other half of the literature survey, and finally a concluding chapter. A major failing is the lack of a clear definition of undergraduate libraries; even the definition the author appears to prefer is referenced but never fully paraphrased. The conclusions appear to be without solid support; all descriptions and evaluations are based on subjective opinions. And, as Person admits, "the evidence, or lack of it, revealed in this study does not permit one to say undergraduate libraries are or are not justified" (p. 128). On the plus side, the book includes an interesting historical survey and an extensive bibliography.

Overall, this is a book which might be of interest to a specialist in this facet of library history. It would be appropriate in a comprehensive library science collection. [R: JAL, July 88, p. 182; LJ, Aug 88, p. 86; WLB, Oct 88, p. 95]   Susan Davis Herring

188. Schwartz, Ruth. **Multicampus Libraries: Organization and Administration Case Studies.** Metuchen, N.J., Scarecrow, 1988. 262p. bibliog. index. $27.50. LC 88-21910. ISBN 0-8108-2173-7.

The nearly frenetic growth of American higher education following World War II produced a pattern of organization that has become known as the multicampus university system. Geographically separated libraries on the multiple campuses of a university became, in turn, the multicampus libraries of today. While these libraries share the same goals and problems of single-campus libraries, they face some unique issues: the degree of centralization versus local autonomy, the nature of power and control exercised by the parent institution, and the organization of the libraries.

Drawing upon the seminal assessment of the multicampus university configuration by Eugene C. Lee and Frank M. Bowen in 1971, the author examines the structure, governance, and processes of the multicampus university library. Three multicampus universities, two private and one semipublic, located in the northeastern United States, were selected for investigation using the case study method. Two types of library administration are represented: decentralized authority—campus libraries which have local autonomy, and centralized authority—campus libraries which function within a centrally controlled library system. University identities are not revealed.

Tentative conclusions derived from the analysis indicate that the proximity of the campus library to the central libraries influences the level of autonomy and that resident faculty and students promote strong libraries. Creation of campus libraries may be described as the "action of entrepreneurism and expedience" rather than proper planning. Libraries are often neglected in the institutional planning process, and it is the institutional leadership which most heavily sets the library program.

Although more concisely delineated hypotheses would have been preferred, this study does successfully illuminate issues and trends for more general treatment in the future.

Arthur P. Young

189. Seibert, Warren F., and others. **Research Library Trends, 1951-1980 and Beyond: An Update of Purdue's "Past and Likely Future of 58 Research Libraries."** Springfield, Va., National Technical Information Service, 1987. 181p. (Lister Hill Technical Report, LHNCBC 87-2). $18.95pa.

This study serves to expand upon the original Purdue studies, published between 1965 and 1973, by describing library growth during the thirty-five-year period from 1951 to 1985. It also serves as a validation study of Purdue's growth forecasts published in 1965 and revised in 1971. The report provides fascinating data on a variety of growth factors. The view of the dramatic changes in growth that occurred beginning in 1971 is particularly interesting. Those interested in research libraries will find this work of value for the data and interpretation it provides, for the excellent introduction giving a succinct review of growth studies and the relevant literature, and particularly for the detailed descriptions of further studies which are suggested by the data.

A couple of these studies are worth mentioning. One encourages the investigation of new measurement factors in a technologically advancing environment. Certainly the contributions of new technologies to the service configuration must be explored. The authors also point to study of the process by which operational changes related to new technologies are adopted by library constituencies—a sensitive and thorny area.

The reader will find this study useful reading on a number of levels. It will be important to the library growth literature.

Patricia A. Steele

190. **User Surveys.** By Pamela Noyes Engelbrecht and Mel Westerman. Washington, D.C., Association of Research Libraries, 1988. 119p. bibliog. (SPEC Kit, No. 148). $20.00pa.

This monograph is one of the Systems and Procedures Exchange Center's (SPEC) Kits (a full subscription covers ten monographs [issues] per year). This particular issue focuses on user surveys. Beginning with a much-too-brief introduction to the topic (two pages), which attempts to highlight rationale, strategies, and methods, this monograph continues with SPEC survey results of libraries with user study experience. Brief library reports follow, with the bulk of the monograph dedicated to examples of general and targeted user surveys.

Models can be useful so that the "wheel" is not continually being reinvented. With this concept in mind, individual libraries must decide whether this access to sample questionnaires constructed and implemented in major ARL libraries is a desirable investment.

Darlene E. Weingand

Bibliographies

191. **Books for College Libraries: A Core Collection of 50,000 Titles.** 3d ed. Virginia Clark, ed. Chicago, Association of College and Research Libraries, American Library Association, 1988. 6v. index. $500.00/set. LC 88-16714. ISBN 0-8389-3353-X.

The first edition of this title was published in 1967 to replace Charles B. Shaw's *List of Books for College Libraries* which was published in 1931. The first edition of *Books for College Libraries* (*BCL1*) had a cut-off date which coincided with the beginning of *Choice*, with the hope that the journal could be used as a complementary, on-going revision and supplement. This did not materialize however. Periodic reassessments that included categories not covered by *Choice* were necessary, and *BCL2*

appeared in 1975 (see *ARBA 76*, entry 141). In 1985 work began on *BCL3*. The current edition recommends approximately fifty thousand books based on college library standards revised in 1985 (one hundred faculty members per one thousand students in ten fields of study would require 104,000 volumes). With half that number recommended by *BCL3*, a small college library would have flexibility to fill needs not included in the basic subject areas. The volume distribution related to subject areas is basically the same as with the earlier editions although there is a small increase in the number of titles in the areas of psychology, science, technology, and biography (up 17 percent from 14 percent).

Still arranged in six basic volumes with the sixth volume serving as an index to the remaining five, *BCL3* has broad subject arrangement by humanities (volume 1); language and literature (volume 2); history (volume 3); social sciences (volume 4); and psychology, science, technology, and bibliography (volume 5). Within each volume, entries are arranged in Library of Congress call number order. The title selection mirrors the qualifications of the more than five hundred college faculty and collection development librarians of the United States and Canada. Those involved in the compilation of *BCL3* included teachers in the field, reference librarians, and the referees who were chosen for their knowledge in collection development and in the various subject areas.

Entries that were listed in *BCL2* are noted with an asterisk. Although they are not annotated, entries include fairly complete bibliographic information except for price and the title's availability. Although it is understandable that an out-of-print book would be an excellent choice in a particular collection, it is also necessary that the user of this text be aware of whether it is in-print.

Effort to maintain currency is apparent; most titles in the computer area have publication dates in the 1980s, with a few earlier publications. More titles have been added to QH (natural history, biology) and Z678-686 has a totally new bibliography, the lack of which was mentioned in the review of *BLC2*. As with any undertaking of this size, one may differ with the choices of titles included, but for a basic guide this continues as a standard.

Anna Grace Patterson

192. **Recommended Reference Books for Small and Medium-sized Libraries and Media Centers 1988.** Bohdan S. Wynar, ed. Englewood, Colo., Libraries Unlimited, 1988. 261p. index. $32.50. LC 81-12394. ISBN 0-87287-682-9; ISSN 0277-5948.

Bohdan S. Wynar, editor and publisher of *American Reference Books Annual* (*ARBA*), has selected 517 "original and unabridged" reviews from the 1988 volume of *ARBA* for this eighth annual volume. Two criteria apply: the reference work must be recommended, and it must be appropriate for small and medium-sized libraries. While many would concur with most of the choices, inevitably, some appear to be rather esoteric for such libraries, for example, *Administrative and Financial Terms* issued by the Food and Agriculture Organization of the United Nations.

Reviews, including standard citations; codes for college, public, and school libraries; and references to other reviews in standard library review media, are arranged by author, editor, or title (not AACR2 main entry) within classes based on broad subject and form (not Dewey). Among the four broadest categories, 39 reviews fall under "General Reference," 217 under "Social Sciences," 185 under "Humanities," and only 76 under "Science and Technology." Reviews are signed, and reviewers, with affiliations, are listed at the front of the volume.

Additional access is provided by an author/title index and a rather skimpy subject index. Since the main arrangement provides broad subject access, the index ought to provide more specific access. It frequently fails. Reference works on the Bible, the saints, Christianity, the Catholic Church, liturgy, and worship may be found only under "Religion," even though there is at least one reference book on each of these topics. *Women in Science* is not listed under "Women's Studies." The entry for "mushrooms" refers to "fungi," but there is still no entry for *Wild and Exotic Mushroom Cultivation in North America*. The next edition of this standard work needs a new indexer!

James D. Anderson

Catalogs and Collections

193.   **The Center for Research Libraries Handbook 1987.** Chicago, Center for Research Libraries, 1987. 161p. index. $10.00pa.

This is the irregularly published (since 1969) guide to the contents of the Center for Research Libraries. It represents a convenient overview of the collections if the center's *Catalog* is not available or as the only access to certain classes of material not included in the center's *Catalog*. Now thirty-eight years old, the center is a cooperative venture of 150 research libraries across the United States. From a collection of 3.5 million volumes, it lends to its members, which are of three types: "Voting," "Associate,"

and "User." (The *Handbook* states "any institution supporting research or having a research library is eligible to join." Users of the *Handbook* should write to the center at 6050 South Kenwood Avenue, Chicago, IL 60637 for membership information.)

The *Handbook* is a descriptive listing which characterizes the nature and size of the major components of the collection. The listings are arranged under major subject and form categories (e.g., "Africa," "Art and Architecture," "Microfilm and Reprint Collections," "Underground Press") with a slightly more detailed subject index. The volume concludes with a statement of the collecting, deposit, and loan policies of the center.

The collections (according to the *Handbook*) are strong and continue to be built in the areas of publications from the Academy of Sciences of the USSR, foreign doctoral dissertations, foreign newspapers, U.S. newspapers, state government documents of the United States, and materials from Africa and East, South, and Southeast Asia. This is an important guide for libraries that do heavy interlibrary loan in support of faculty research, but those who use the center frequently should also have its *Manual of Interlibrary Loan Policies and Procedures*.

Thomas G. Kirk

COMPARATIVE AND INTERNATIONAL LIBRARIANSHIP

General Works

194.   Hu, James S. C., ed. **Library and Information Science Education: An International Symposium. Papers Presented at the International Conference on Library and Information Science Education Sponsored by ... National Taiwan University November 29-30, 1985.** Metuchen, N.J., Scarecrow, 1987. 277p. maps. $27.50. ISBN 0-8108-2111-7.

These seventeen conference papers address the past, present, and future of education for library and information professionals, with most of the papers by deans and faculty from the United States and the Republic of China (Taiwan). Single papers are offered from Canada (Norman Horrocks, Dalhousie University), England (Peter Harvard-Williams, Loughborough University of Technology), Germany (Rupert Hacker, Bavarian Civil Servants' College), and Japan (Yoshinari Tsuda, Keio University). An editor's introduction and a "welcome address" by the university president precede the papers, and the conference program concludes the volume. The papers are arranged thematically from past to future, with considerable attention focused on curricula and course outlines. Especially interesting, because the topics have received less international attention are the papers by James S. C. Hu and Harris B. H. Seng detailing the development of library science as a discipline in China. Beyond the papers from Taiwan educators, the volume is most useful as a summary of some current thinking on library and information science education from selective international perspectives.

K. Mulliner

195.   Kawatra, P. S., ed. **Comparative and International Librarianship.** New York, Envoy Press; distr., New York, Apt Books, 1987. 216p. index. $30.00. LC 87-80656. ISBN 0-938719-22-X.

This collection of fifteen essays addresses a variety of topics in the area of comparative and international librarianship. Recognized leaders in the field from different parts of the world consider problems and prospects in five categories: perspective, national libraries and bibliography, academic and special libraries, professional education, and information services. Data on both historical and current developments in world librarianship are included.

In the introduction to the volume, Kawatra indicates that it is not possible to cover all countries or subject areas and he does not attempt to do so. The index does pull together data on several major subjects and helps to fill the gap in quality English-language literature on foreign libraries. Individuals interested in developing an awareness of the library profession on an international scope will find this volume an important complement to other titles on comparative librarianship. [R: JAL, Mar 88, p. 43]

Ahmad Gamaluddin

Africa

196.   Sitzman, Glenn L. **African Libraries.** Metuchen, N.J., Scarecrow, 1988. 486p. illus. bibliog. index. $49.50. LC 87-35658. ISBN 0-8108-2093-5.

Sitzman's book contains both factual and impressionistic information about libraries in Africa. Part 1, "Buildings and People: A Photographic Sampling," contains ninety numbered black-and-white photographs with corresponding annotations that represent libraries in thirteen countries in west, central, southern, and eastern Africa. The pictures are grouped by library type: public, children's and elementary school, secondary school, academic, special,

and cultural. Also included in part 1 is a brief section about the development of African institutions of library education. From the information presented in part 2, "Chronology of Library and Related Events, 1773-1984," the author concludes that "the history of modern African libraries stretches backward almost two hundred years ... that something was happening all along for most of that period," and that "the chronology confirms what scholars have said repeatedly, that the first libraries established in an African country have usually been scientific and government department libraries" (p. 82). In part 3, "Development of Library Literature, 1950-1980: A Bibliographic Essay," the extent of evolving activities related to African libraries is clearly demonstrated as the increasing number of paragraphs and pages reported on library events grows from year to year. Part 4, entitled "Angola to Zimbabwe: A Nation-by-Nation Survey," offers entries which cover the most important events in each country arranged by type of library. The last part, "Bibliography of African Librarianship," lists approximately 2,700 titles with no annotations. If used with other books on library development in Africa, such as Wilfred J. Plumbe's work *Tropical Librarianship* (Scarecrow, 1987), Sitzman's book should enrich a person's reading and research on libraries in the African experience. [R: WLB, Dec 88, pp. 104-5]

Mohammed M. Aman

Australia

197.   Bundy, Alan, and Judith Bundy, comps. and eds. **Australian Libraries: The Essential Directory.** Blackwood, S.A., Aust., Auslib Press, 1988. 61p. $16.00pa. ISSN 1031-5187.

For those looking for a comprehensive and inexpensive source of brief information that will furnish them with the simple facts about almost any Australian library, *ALED 88* is a useful source. It is more comprehensive although not as detailed as the *Directory of Australian Academic and Research Libraries* (4th ed., 1988), the *Directory of Australian Public Libraries* (2d ed., 1987), the *Directory of Australian Special Libraries*, or the *Directory of Library Suppliers Used by Australian Libraries.* In fact its entries for academic/research libraries and public libraries are derived from those first two directories supplemented by information about a range of special libraries, library suppliers and databases obtained from responses to a questionnaire. Only school libraries are omitted.

All entries are arranged alphabetically by the name of the institution, with appropriate cross references, and there are no indexes. Each entry includes, where it is available, the following information: name, postal address, telephone, fax, telex, and/or electronic mail numbers, chief librarian, number of branches, number of volumes, number of current serial titles, number of staff (full-time equivalent), and type of library. The entries for suppliers are listed in the same alphabetical sequence but are boxed to highlight them. Scattered throughout are brief entries on the current status of such things as directories of Australian libraries, library education, statistics and surveys, and the like.

For most Australian libraries this directory, which is scheduled to be published biennially, should prove to be a useful first source of basic information. It is useful for libraries in the United States and other countries only if they need directory type information for a greater range of Australian libraries than may be found in the *World of Learning* and other general international directories.

Norman D. Stevens

198. **Libraries Alone: Proceedings of the Rural and Isolated Librarians Conference, Wagga Wagga, July 1987.** James Henri and Roy Sanders, eds. Wagga Wagga, N.S.W., Aust., Libraries Alone, 1988. 153p. maps. $25.00pa. (U.S.). ISBN 0-7316-1776-2.

Small, often isolated, rural libraries have in recent years been identified as a special class of libraries with special needs. In the United States the Center for the Study of Rural Librarianship, under the direction of Bernard Vavrek at Clarion State University in remote western Pennsylvania, has become the focal point for the study and support for such libraries. It is fitting, therefore, that Vavrek served as the keynote speaker and summarizer for the July 1987 Rural and Isolated Librarians Conference held at Wagga Wagga, Australia, as it addressed the concerns of such libraries in Australia and New Zealand where they are even more common, and more isolated, than in the United States. These proceedings represent one of the first sources of detailed reporting on the special needs and concerns of rural libraries; as such, these papers will be of considerable interest and value to all who work in such libraries. Many of the twenty-four papers in this volume speak to specific aspects of the Australian and New Zealand experience, such as networking in those countries and service to aborigines, but a number of them address more general issues such as staff development, training of paraprofessional staff, political and financial management, and the use of volunteers. Primarily of

value, therefore, to librarians in Australia and New Zealand, they do still have a good deal to offer to librarians in the United States and elsewhere who work in similar settings. Like most conference proceedings, the results are uneven and often deal in broad generalities; however, given the lack of other materials on this subject, this volume is a useful addition to the literature of librarianship.

Norman D. Stevens

199. Naude, Sandra, and Laurel A. Clyde. **The Library at St. Hilda's Anglican School for Girls, Perth: A Case Study in School Library Automation.** Doubleview, Aust., Western Australian College of Advanced Education, 1987. 35p. illus. bibliog. $7.00pa. ISBN 0-7298-0059-8.

A girls' school in Perth, Australia, is the focus of this case study showing a library's efforts to automate operations in the face of rapid growth in student enrollment and library collections. Early on, the authors have attempted to avoid making this a how-to book. Instead, they have shown that a school with limited resources can establish an automated environment in its library.

The thirty-five-page study first gives the reader background information about the school and the library, but, as hoped, it is the integrated online system and its applications which receive primary emphasis. The clearly written and profusely illustrated book discusses the software and hardware, the online catalog, cataloging, circulation, inventory, statistics, and accounting capabilities of the system. In addition, there are brief discussions on teaching students how to use the catalog and on other computer applications in the library such as online searching and word processing. One criticism does arise. There is little or no mention of the money involved in acquiring and maintaining such a system. Even if the figures were to be in Australian dollars, this type of information would be pertinent.

For those librarians who are in the beginning stages of considering full-scale automation in their school library, this would be a very good introduction.

Phillip P. Powell

200. Oley, Elizabeth, and Julie Badger, comps. and eds. **Bibliography of Education Theses in Australia: A List of Theses in Education Accepted for Higher Degrees at Australian Universities and Colleges in 1985.** Hawthorn, Aust., Australian Council for Educational Research, 1987. 109p. index. $25.00pa. ISSN 0811-0174.

Published annually since 1978, this bibliography provides the only systematic bibliographic accounting of master's theses and doctoral dissertations in the field of education, including library science, awarded by colleges and universities in Australia. Prior to 1978, partial coverage, in much less detail, was provided by the *Australian Education Index*. In addition, other separately published bibliographies have been compiled (primarily by the Australian Council for Educational Research) which document theses and dissertations completed as far back as 1919. The preface of *Bibliography of Education Theses in Australia* (*BETA*) provides detailed listings of all previous compilations. Neither *Masters Abstracts International* nor *Dissertation Abstracts International* (both published by University Microfilms International) provides coverage, with few exceptions, of Australian theses and dissertations.

Of the 471 entries in this edition of *BETA*, 188 are to master's theses, primarily dealing with elementary and secondary education-related subjects. Eighty-nine entries are for the Ph.D., with the remaining ciations scattered over a variety of master's in specialized areas such as library science or curriculum studies.

BETA is arranged alphabetically by author, with most abstracts running from 150 to 500 words in length. *BETA* also includes a subject index, with most entries being assigned from five to ten subject headings. Considering the moderate length of the abstracts, most are well written and convey the critical elements, especially methodology and conclusion. This edition of *BETA* contains a very interesting doctoral dissertation, a history of the Library Association of Australasia from 1896 to 1902.

I could not locate an online or CD-ROM database which included the information in this bibliography.   Richard H. Quay

201.   Whyte, Jean P., and Neil A. Radford, eds. **An Enthusiasm for Libraries: Essays in Honour of Harrison Bryan.** Melbourne, Ancora Press, Graduate School of Librarianship, Monash University, 1988. 288p. bibliog. index. $36.00. ISBN 0-86862-010-6.

Unlike most North American library festschriften, this one, in what might be regarded as typical Australian fashion, has some real bite to it as well as some unity of purpose. These eleven essays by colleagues of Harrison Bryan, who has been perhaps the most important contemporary Australian librarian, all speak directly—and often critically—of the various roles he has played in the dramatic development of librarianship in Australia since 1945. Best of all the editors have allowed Bryan in a concluding

essay to offer "some comments and an occasional rejoinder" to what his friends have had to say about his work. All of this makes for lively and entertaining reading even though the significance of the issues may be beyond the knowledge and scope of interest of most of us. The various essays deal with his career as a librarian, his work as a bibliographer and printer, and various specific library issues in which he has played a leadership role including library history; education for librarianship; public service and statistics in academic libraries; building research collections; technical services; library buildings; library cooperation and politics; and the development of the Australian National Library. While by no means a major work, this collection of essays is an important contribution for those interested in the growth and development of librarianship in Australia.

Norman D. Stevens

China

202.   Wei, Karen T., comp. **Library and Information Science in China: An Annotated Bibliography.** Westport, Conn., Greenwood Press, 1988. 273p. index. (Bibliographies and Indexes in Library and Information Science, No. 3). $39.95. LC 88-17767. ISBN 0-313-25548-2.

This comprehensive bibliography lists 991 books, chapters in books, periodical articles, conference papers, theses, dissertations, and ERIC documents on all aspects of library and information science in pre-1949 China, the People's Republic of China, and the Republic of China. The scope is broad, covering books and printing; the history of Chinese libraries; national, college and university, public, special, school and children's libraries and archives; cataloging, classification, Chinese collections, and acquisition; automation and information services; education for librarianship; publishing and trade; international exchange and activities; librarians; copyright laws; library associations; and research librarianship.

Most of the cited works are in the English language. A few important Chinese, French, German, and Japanese works have been included if they are accompanied by a translation or an abstract in the English language. Almost all of the titles are twentieth-century works, although a very small number date from the late nineteenth century. About 96 percent of the entries have descriptive annotations which are well written and effectively summarize the contents and indicate the scope of the work. Entries are arranged in ten subject categories with a section on bibliography and reference works, which contains forty-four entries. Rapid reference access is provided by author and subject indexes. This compilation, the only comprehensive bibliography on the subject to date, will be an extremely useful research aid for students of the field and for scholars generally.

Shirley L. Hopkinson

Great Britain and Ireland

203. Bromley, David W., and Angela M. Allott, eds. **British Librarianship and Information Work 1981-1985. Volume One: General Libraries and the Profession.** London, Library Association; distr., Chicago, American Library Association, 1988. 363p. index. $80.00. ISBN 0-85365-557-X.

British Librarianship and Information Work is a continuation of a series on British librarianship that began some fifty years ago and is issued every five years. Two volumes cover the years 1981-1985. This first volume focuses on general libraries and the library information profession. It includes twenty-two essays covering a full range of topics such as government and libraries, library management, various types of libraries (national, university, polytechnic and college, metropolitan, city, and county), education, staff, history, and archives. The second volume of the set will include the broad topics of special libraries, materials, and processes. It, too, will contain twenty-two essays.

The editors of this work make no attempt to avoid the duplication that quite naturally results when forty-four authors write on overlapping topics. If anything, this work is enhanced by the differing treatments of similar topics. A good index (primarily subject) provides cross-references between essays. A helpful list of acronyms sorts out the "alphabet soup" of British librarianship.

As the library world gets smaller as a result of computer networking, a better understanding of library activities in a variety of countries becomes more important. This work provides an excellent overview of the politics, economics, and priorities that drive the library profession in the British Isles. One can assume that the second volume of this set will live up to the high standard established by the first.

Marjorie E. Bloss

204. Coombs, Douglas. **Spreading the Word: The Library Work of the British Council.** London, Mansell, 1988. 298p. bibliog. index. (Information Adviser Series). $63.00. LC 87-31231. ISBN 0-7201-1955-3.

Nearly fifty-five years ago the British Council was created by R. A. Leeper. His foreign office memorandum was entitled simply "Cultural Propaganda," and his contention was that the British government should do something to counter the rapid growth of state-subsidized propaganda from other countries. Much of it, he believed, was designed to damage Great Britain's political or commercial influence. The idea of "the establishment of English libraries" was a pivotal feature of cultural propaganda activity. While the history of the British Council was well documented in Frances Donaldson's book, *The British Council: The First Fifty Years* (London: Cape, 1984), Donaldson makes little mention of libraries. Coombs capitalizes on this weakness by devoting the entire volume to a well-documented description of the development of the library work of the British Council from its inception in 1934 to the 1980s. A nonlibrarian himself, Coombs reveals how the British Council has at times shown more enthusiasm for libraries than for librarianship. For example, British Council librarians have seen themselves as "poor relations." This is evidenced by the fact that "to this day no distinguished figure from the library world or librarianship has been invited to sit on the governing body of an organization which spends ... *one fifth* of its budget on books, library and information work" (p. vii). Coombs's history credits some of the librarians, with their missionary zeal and their faith in the free public library system, as a mighty weapon in the struggle against ignorance, poverty, and tyranny. Coombs's objective to contextualize the efforts of the librarians "to propagate this gospel under the banner of 'library development'" (p. ix) has been dutifully met.

The book provides interesting and enjoyable reading that restores one's confidence in the library profession and the importance of the printed word. The book gives due credit to the international network of the British Council librarians who have done so much to foster the development of public libraries in developing countries, as well as other aspects of library services (e.g., library education).

Mohammed M. Aman

205. Day, Alan. **The British Library: A Guide to Its Structure, Publications, Collections and Services.** London, Library Association; distr., Chicago, American Library Association, 1988. 190p. bibliog. index. $27.00. ISBN 0-85365-628-2.

For many people, the British Library is simply the British Museum's library renamed. However, this change that took place in 1973 was more than a mere change of name. A new and complex institution came into being that combined the venerable British Museum Library with a number of other institutions. It provided Great Britain with an up-to-date national library and information service. The purpose of Day's excellent book is to give a brief, descriptive overview of the history and the functions of the British Library. Part 1 is concerned with humanities and social sciences collections such as printed books, Western manuscripts, newspapers, and sound recordings. It will be of interest to many researchers who are planning to visit England and use these famous collections. Parts 2 through 4 describe the bibliographic services, science and technology collections, and the research and development department of the British Library. Those interested in learning more about the development of these sorts of national library services in Great Britain will want to read these sections. Part 5 discusses plans for future developments, including the somewhat stalled plans for a new building at St. Pancras in London. Five appendices supply information on the various library publications, cultural events sponsored by the British Library, supporters' clubs, addresses of various divisions of the library and admissions policies, and a select bibliography of recent publications on the British Library. All of the world's great research libraries should have a guide that is as clear and useful as this one.

Ronald H. Fritze

206.   Harrold, Ann, ed. **Libraries in the United Kingdom and the Republic of Ireland 1988.** 14th ed. London, Library Association; distr., Chicago, American Library Association, 1988. 170p. index. $23.00pa. ISBN 0-85365-897-8.

Like its predecessors, the fourteenth edition of this excellent reference tool is an accurate listing of the major libraries and schools of librarianship serving the United Kingdom and Ireland. The libraries included are of four categories: public, academic, governmental, and schools of librarianship. The information pertaining to each type of library includes a name of person in charge; telephone, telex, and fax numbers; and full street address. Within these major categories, the libraries are organized by major regions of the countries. An index of library names and regions at the end of the book helps to retrieve the necessary information. Under "Public Libraries" are listed all headquarters and central libraries as well as the major branches of public library systems, while under "All University and Polytechnic Libraries" are listed most of these libraries as well as site libraries and those in major academic

departments. Included also are a selected number of government, national, and special libraries considered to be the major libraries in their own fields. The book is highly recommended for any large academic, public, or special library with international interests. [R: RLR, Aug 88, p. 182]

Antonio Rodriguez-Buckingham

207.   **The Library Association Yearbook 1988.** R. E. Palmer, comp. London, Library Association; distr., Chicago, American Library Association, 1988. 403p. $40.00pa. ISBN 0-85365-578-2; ISSN 0075-9066.

This sturdily bound yearbook provides current information about the Library Association of the United Kingdom. It is arranged in three parts. Part 1 contains pertinent information about the staff and officers of the association, its branches, special interest groups, publications, grants and awards, and other organizations affiliated with the association. Part 2 contains documentary sources such as the Royal Charter, the bylaws, regulations, and code of professional conduct. Part 3 is an alphabetical listing of its members as of February 1988.

This carefully wrought work is a useful reference source for all library professional collections. [R: LAR, 14 Oct 88, p. 614]

Robert H. Burger

India

208.   **Handbook of Libraries, Archives & Information Centres in India. Volume 4: Asia-Pacific Cooperative Information Systems, Networks and Programmes.** B. M. Gupta and others, eds. New Delhi, Information Industry Publications; distr., Columbia, Mo., South Asia Books, 1987. 323p. index. $48.50. ISBN 81-85112-04-5.

209.   **Handbook of Libraries, Archives & Information Centres in India. Volume 5: Information Technology, Industry and Networks.** B. M. Gupta and others, eds. New Delhi, Information Industry Publications; distr., Columbia, Mo., South Asia Books, 1987. 290p. illus. index. $48.50. ISBN 81-85112-05-3.

Volumes 4 and 5 of the proposed eight volumes of *Handbook of Libraries, Archives & Information Centres in India* are full of information for researchers. Both volumes fill a major gap in the library literature.

Volume 4 deals with Asian Pacific cooperative information systems, networks, and programs. There are thirty-six chapters written by many well-known authors and specialists. The articles cover many topics including "Regional Networks for the Exchange of Information and Experiences in Asia and the Pacific"; "Regional Cooperation in Agricultural Fisheries"; "Medical Information in Asia"; "Asian Institute of Technology"; "UNESCO Educational Documentation and Information Service for Asia and the Pacific"; "Documentation Centre for the Non-Aligned Countries—Colombo"; "Development of Information Network on South Asia"; and "Asia Pacific Information Network in Social Sciences." All articles contain important information and will be very helpful to researchers. There is a useful index.

Volume 5 deals with information technology and networks in India. There are twenty-four chapters in this volume, with articles on topics such as "Information Technology in the 80s"; "INDONET: A National Computer Network"; "Videotex and Teletext"; "Satellite Telecommunications: Its Special Applications"; "Reprography and Printing Industry in India"; "An Introduction to Online Networks and Services"; "Computer Software for Libraries and Information Work: Problems and Prospects for India"; "Microcomputer-based Information Storage and Retrieval System;" and many other research articles. In short, the book deals with cultural, economic, and social aspects of developments in information technology and industry and online access to international databases. Both volumes are highly recommended for libraries, librarians, and researchers interested in Asia and especially in the development of Indian libraries, archives, and information centers. Ravindra Nath Sharma

210. Majumder, Uma. **India's National Library: Systematization and Modernization.** Calcutta, National Library, 1987. 244p. bibliog. index. price not reported.

This publication is based on the author's dissertation entitled "Guidelines for the Development of the National Library of India in the Light of the British Library Experience" submitted at the Department of Information Studies, University of Sheffield, in 1984. The main intention of the publication is to suggest streamlining the library operation and management of India's National Library. After discussing the concept of a national library in chapter 1, there is only enough of a historical perspective to achieve some statistical comparisons within India and with the British Library in chapters 2 and 3. The thirty pages which make up chapter 4 contain guidelines and recommendations for acquisition, book exchange, reader services, information services, and related bibliographical activities. Computerization and cooperation are

dealt with in sufficient detail to be called a "blueprint." This book should rightfully take its place on the shelf with other books on national libraries around the world. It was carefully written to provide past, present, and future views of India's National Library.

Pauline A. Cochrane

Islamic Countries

211. Sibai, Mohamed Makki. **Mosque Libraries: An Historical Study.** London, Mansell; distr., Rutherford, N.J., Publishers Distribution Center, 1987. 174p. index. bibliog. (Libraries and Librarianship in the Muslim World). $49.00. LC 87-24036. ISBN 0-7201-1896-4.

Despite the fact that Muslims are frequently referred to as the "Ahl al-Kitāb" (People of the Book), this being a reference to the *Quran*, and that the mosque is *the* central institution in Muslim society, there has not previously appeared in any language a detailed account of the history and development of mosque libraries. This work, drawing upon both Arabic and Western sources, both classical and modern, makes a very good attempt to fill that gap.

As a piece of historical writing, the work is developed soundly and logically beginning with an examination of the role of the mosque in Muslim society: first as a place of worship, then as a community center filling social, political, and educational roles. Sibai moves on to discuss the emergence of books in Muslim society, and only after setting out the full background does he proceed with the history of mosque libraries per se. The beginnings, the operation, and the decline of mosque libraries also receive treatment.

While a first attempt at providing this type of historical overview, the work is more descriptive than analytical. The author himself says "there is still much more to be said about the historical development of mosque libraries as well as of their influence by and contribution to Muslim Learning and scholarship" (p. 125). This book represents a good beginning to a valuable and interesting part of Islamic history. [R: LAR, 15 July 88, p. 409; RLR, Aug 88, pp. 203-4] Margaret Anderson

Malaysia

212. **Formulating a National Policy for Library and Information Services: The Malaysian Experience.** Oli Mohamed, ed. London, Mansell; distr., Rutherford, N.J., Publishers Distribution Center, 1988. 130p. illus. index. $42.50. LC 88-10032. ISBN 0-7201-1951-0.

"Policy by itself will have little effect if it is not backed by the necessary allocation of resources, both human and material," cautions the director general of the National Library of Malaysia, D. E. K. Wijasuriya, in the preface. Containing papers delivered to a seminar on national policy for library and information services in 1984, this volume concludes with a postscript summarizing a 1987 report of a task force, led by Wijasuriya, to draft a national policy. Unfortunately, no mention is made of the extent to which resources have been (or can be expected to be) allocated. Still, the twelve papers presented by Malaysian librarians, educators, and government officials (and one by a UNESCO consultant) provide a detailed examination of major issues to be addressed in a Malaysian national policy. The topics covered include reading programs, resource sharing, automation and telecommunications, finances, coordination, and staffing, among others. Especially noteworthy is the paper on access to government information, a sensitive issue in Malaysia and in many developed as well as other developing nations. While the delay in publication leaves one wondering what has happened since the papers were presented in 1984, this compilation affords important insights (grounded in Malaysian realities rather than purely theoretical prescriptions) into the variety of issues to be addressed by a national policy—a lesson relevant to many countries around the world.

K. Mulliner

Portugal

213.   Buller, Nell. **Libraries and Library Services in Portugal.** Halifax, N.S., School of Library and Information Studies, Dalhousie University, 1988. 121p. illus. bibliog. (Occasional Papers Series, No. 46). $16.00pa. ISBN 0-7703-9722-0.

This is number 46 in a continuing and useful series of short monographs issued by the School of Library and Information Studies of Dalhousie University of Canada. Previous volumes have covered a wide variety of topics but have included a number of works on libraries and library development in other countries. Even though this is a general survey, or introduction, to libraries and librarianship in Portugal, it is useful because so little is available in English.

The mimeographed typescript volume is divided into a number of short chapters that present the basic facts about the various types of libraries in Portugal. Two introductory chapters provide a brief historical context to the factors

that have affected the development of the country's current political, economic, and educational situation. The chapters on libraries are basic descriptions of the national library, university libraries, state public libraries, municipal libraries, private libraries, and foreign and special libraries. Each of these chapters is then broken down into individual descriptions of major libraries. These descriptions vary slightly, depending on the author's view of the importance of the library, but generally present a thumbnail sketch of the history of the library, staffing, collections, accessibility to users, funding, and services. While libraries throughout Portugal are covered, the emphasis is on those in Lisbon, the capital city. A variety of appendices give useful information and photographs of several libraries. The most useful is appendix 19, which is a summary table of services provided by the libraries described in the volume.

By the author's own admission, this is a survey of the topic. It is based on her nine-month visit to Portugal and is heavily dependent on interviews and English-language sources. As a descriptive survey of individual libraries it is a good one, and a prospective visitor to any one of the libraries described here would find it to be a useful introduction. While the author does occasionally go beyond description of individual libraries to comment on both the causes as well as the future prospects for library development for a particular type of library or library service, anyone expecting an analytical treatment of any of these topics will be disappointed. Her bibliography of sources, while useful for general description, is also limited for additional analytical work. Despite these problems, the volume is a good beginning-level treatment of the topic and will be useful to a wide variety of readers interested in Portugal specifically, and library development in other countries in general.

Robert V. Williams

Underdeveloped Areas

214.   de Horowitz, Rosario Gassol. **Librarianship: A Third World Perspective.** Westport, Conn., Greenwood Press, 1988. 140p. bibliog. index. (Contributions in Librarianship and Information Science, No. 59). $37.95. LC 87-17741. ISBN 0-313-25507-5.

The author hypothesizes that planning and developing educational programs for librarianship can be understood only within a perspective of the contextual dimension (the country's style and circumstances of development) and the conceptual dimension (the worldwide professional paradigm). To support her hypothesis, de Horowitz, professor of library and information science at Venezuela's Banco del Libros, relies on historical and contemporary evidence. Her book is divided into three thematic parts. Part 1, "The Issues of National Development," is based on the premise that an educational program in librarianship should respond to the real needs of the community or nation. De Horowitz examines how, in the Third World, planners of library and information services are confronted with issues related to overcoming underdevelopment. In part 2, "The Theoretical Foundations of Librarianship," she investigates worldwide contemporary library thought as it is being altered by advancements in knowledge and technology. The author believes that professionals from developing countries should cooperate in the effort to coordinate library information systems, not only locally and nationally, but also on regional and international levels. In part 3, "Synthesis and Interpretation," a programmatic relationship is established between the two preceding sections and a theoretical framework is advanced. The implications for curriculum design are discussed. Although the majority of cases and examples used to support the author's hypothesis are derived from her Latin American experience, her observations and findings can be extended to other Third World countries. Issues discussed of interest to national development planners include: technology transfer and selection, literacy and adult education, information services, and regional and international cooperation. The author's analytical and descriptive approach in creating a theoretical framework for planning and design programs in library and information studies in the developing world is unusual. This work is highly recommended reading for all librarians, development planners, educators, and Latin American specialists. [R: JAL, Sept 88, p. 246]

Mohammed M. Aman

215. Parker, J. Stephen. **Asking the Right Questions: Case Studies in Library Development Consultancy.** London, Mansell; distr., Rutherford, N.J., Publishers Distribution Center, 1988. 239p. index. (Information Adviser Series). $54.00. LC 87-24670. ISBN 0-7201-1898-0.

Certainly Parker has established his place in the field of international librarianship and, in particular, the emerging and very important area of consultant work for developing nations. Himself a teacher and consultant, Parker presents a series of actual case studies carefully selected to provide a varied and profound picture of the problems encountered in attempting to analyze, identify, and recommend key ac-

tions needed in any area of development. As the founding proprietor of Library Development Consultants in Great Britain, the author has drawn on a variety of projects from the public systems, to national information systems, to database creation, to the planning of buildings serving university- and national-level services. Couple this work with his previous efforts published by Mansell, *Information Consultants in Action* (1986) and *Aspects of Library Development Planning* (1983) and one has the basis for a very effective course in international consultancy (not to mention library development). And very likely to be overlooked are the values found herein for the foreign agency contemplating using consulting services for library and information service planning. The work is redolent with practicality and a good deal of the detraction necessary to understand that the glamour often associated with consultancy by the outsider has its limits. For the record the areas covered in the case studies include Jordan, Qatar, Libya, Brazil, Portugal St. Kitts-Nevis, and the British Virgin Islands. [R: LAR, 14 Oct 88, p. 601]

Gerald R. Shields

216. Partridge, W. G. McD. **Low Budget Librarianship: Managing Information in Developing Countries.** London, Library Association; distr., Chicago, American Library Association, 1988. 93p. $16.95pa. ISBN 0-85365-618-5.

As the title suggests this is a book about librarianship in its most modest form. There are no glamorous subjects like computerization, high technology, or complex fiscal management. It is a down-to-earth treatment of the subject of how to develop and nourish modest public, school, and academic library services in poor countries. Among the topics Partridge addresses in his short, lighthearted fourteen chapters are information needs in developing nations, requirements for library work in the Third World, considerations for technical innovations, basic preservation techniques for tropical climates, library architecture in tropical climates, promotion reading, and opportunities for professional development. Most of the author's examples are taken from African countries or Australia, his own country.

This is valuable reading to library science students, librarians in general, and library consultants to developing poor countries in particular.

Mohammed M. Aman

COMPUTERS

General Works

PHILOSOPHY AND THEORY

217. Bosshardt, Chris A. **Hard Disk Smarts: Everything You Need to Choose and Use Your Hard Disk.** New York, John Wiley, 1988. 305p. illus. index. $21.95pa. ISBN 0-471-63847-1.

Unlike many computer books that assume a good deal of computer literacy on the part of the reader, this one is written in a clear and easy-to-comprehend manner. It offers carefully detailed step-by-step procedures for the assessment of hard disk needs, the installation of a hard disk, and the preparation of a newly installed hard disk for use. In addition, the author outlines daily operations such as organizing subdirectories, backing up hard disk data, and transporting a computer with a hard disk. Closing chapters take the reader past the rudimentary material to more sophisticated hard disk usage, including a discussion of various tools and "power user" techniques, such as third party backup programs, disk defragmenting, disk testing, and data security.

The book is written for persons using an IBM PC, XT, AT, or Portable, a Compaq, or a compatible computer with an operating system of PC-DOS or MS-DOS, version 2.0 or higher. There is an adequate index as well as a very detailed table of contents. Each of the early chapters covering the more basic material begins with a section entitled "Do You Need to Read This Chapter,"which allows readers to evaluate the chapter in relation to their knowledge, much in the manner of a self-paced tutorial. The language throughout is readable and easily understood, and the book is especially recommended for the relative novice who wants to acquire a basic knowledge of hard disk operations as well as a quick reference to commands and power user techniques.   Pamela A. Zager

218. Hutchison, David, and Peter Silvester. **Computer Logic: Principles and Technology.** Chichester, England, Ellis Horwood; distr., New York, Halsted Press/John Wiley, 1987. 265p. illus. index. (Ellis Horwood Series in Computers and Their Applications). $53.95. LC 87-21356. ISBN 0-470-20988-7.

This excellent book, aimed primarily at first and second year students in computer science or electrical engineering, is an updated version of Hutchison's *Fundamentals of Computer Logic* (Halsted Press, 1981). Not only does this revision include new developments that have occurred over the past several years, but it also includes new chapters on VLSI (very-large-scale integration) circuit design and new computer architectures. The work consists of eight chapters devoted to such topics as the structure of computers, logic building blocks, combinational and sequential logic, logic circuits in practice, von Neumann computer architecture, and the hardware-software interface. Furthermore, a ten-page annotated bibliography of works, arranged by chapter topics, gives the student guidance for further reading. Three appendices provide additional printed information. Appendix 1 gives sample literature from a semiconductor manufacturer; appendix 2 is an example of a data sheet available to designers using programmable logic devices; and appendix 3 presents brief details of four VLSI design systems. An index provides adequate access to the book's contents.

The authors' work is valuable on many counts: its structure, which introduces progressively complicated topics; its clear straightforward prose; and the fact that only a familiarity with binary numbers and "an acquaintance with the notion of programming" are noted prerequisites. Nonengineering students who have an interest in computer hardware will find that this book will meet their needs as well.

Robert H. Burger

219. Karin, Sidney, and Norris Parker Smith. **The Supercomputer Era.** San Diego, Calif., Harcourt Brace Jovanovich, 1987. 313p. illus. (part col.). index. $19.95. LC 86-32005. ISBN 0-15-186787-9.

This is a well-written treatise that functions as a primer and a handbook to the emerging field of supercomputing. What might be a mystifying subject for some readers is made enjoyable in this easy-to-read introduction. The author describes a supercomputer as "the most powerful computer at any given time"; it has ten times the performance of the largest mainframe, and one thousand times greater performance than a personal computer. Supercomputers are designed for those applications which require extensive calculations. The size of a supercomputer is measured not in bytes of memory or of storage capacity, but in "mflops" (megaflops) which are how many millions of calculations ("*flo*ating *p*oint calculations") per second. In the near future, as this technology matures, the measurements will be in gigaflops, which are billions of calculations per second.

The center sections of the work outline how supercomputers are being used today in physics, medicine, aviation, engineering, geosciences, meteorology, and graphics and the arts. There is also speculation on the future configurations of the machinery and the proposed potential uses and projects for advanced generations of the machine. Some additional material includes appendices describing the "bewildering" array of models available and existing sites of super-computers in operation and how to get access to them. There is a short bibliography, notes are provided for each chapter, and there is an index.

Highly recommended for any situation where there is an interest in computers, from secondary school level on up.

Gary R. Cocozzoli

220. Lancaster, F. W., ed. **What Is User Friendly?** Champaign, Ill., Graduate School of Library and Information Science, University of Illinois, 1987. 121p. index. (Clinic on Library Applications of Data Processing: 1986). $15.00. ISBN 0-87845-072-6.

Everyone dealing with information has envisioned a comprehensive information system, which would not only do what we told it to do, but would do exactly what we *want* it to do (with a minimum of effort and aggravation on our part). Most of us would settle for a system that did not actively seem to get in the way during our search for information, one that understood enough of our information problem to know when to help and when to leave us alone.

There is a scale of possible responses to automated information systems ranging from "user-intimate" to "user vicious," says Lancaster, and the condition of being "user friendly" is only a middling degree of "human-ness" in a system. Questions may be asked: Does the system respond to human language? Does it communicate well? Is it accommodating? Personable? Logical? Forgiving? Easy to use? For an online commercial information utility or a library's online catalog, the same questions pertain.

This book contains the proceedings of the twenty-third annual Clinic on Library Applications of Data Processing, held at the University of Illinois in April 1986. Why it took two years for this book to be available for reviewing is not explained, but in the fast-changing and continuously evolving library/information world, the sooner the information is published, the better. Nonetheless, there is a gold mine of good information here as a collection of library/information practitioners and educators discuss the topic.

What is really good about these papers is the variety of perspectives from which the above questions are approached: psychological, social, economic, technical, and even international.

Papers from such library luminaries as Ken Dowlin, Michael Gorman, Christine Borgman, and Linda Smith (whose article with concluding thoughts on the future applications of user friendliness in information systems is a gem) make this book highly interesting and useful for all concerned with improving the interface between technical services and a demanding public in libraries. [R: JAL, July 88, p. 186; JAL, Nov 88, pp. 308-9; LJ, 15 June 88, p. 44]

Bruce A. Shuman

221. Nurminen, Markku I. **People or Computers: Three Ways of Looking at Information Systems.** Bromley, England, Chartwell-Bratt, 1988. 202p. illus. bibliog. index. £15.75pa. ISBN 0-86238-184-3.

Computing is a basic tool that has invaded science, business, education, and most other aspects of our life and work. Initially computers were very expensive and understood by only a few specialists. As they proliferated, a number of approaches to dealing with their effect on society have emerged. The system theoretical approach views all information as exact and able to be processed by the machine. Humans serve the machine, which is the ideal bureaucrat, dictating in a consistent manner action to be taken based on objective input. The sociotechnical approach links humans and machines in an organizational structure that integrates both social and technical needs, while the human approach places the machine at the service of humans. The author moves step by step to develop each perspective, showing how concepts and their implications affect the management of information and the management of people. Although the author labels the system theoretical approach the ideal approach, he raises important questions about the interaction of humans and machines that deserve wide discussion. The author presents his ideas clearly and in a well-organized progression. His presentation is not particularly easy to read. It is, however, well worth the effort.

Ann E. Prentice

222. Zuboff, Shoshana. **In the Age of the Smart Machine: The Future of Work and Power.** New York, Basic Books, 1988. 468p. illus. index. $19.95. LC 87-47777. ISBN 0-465-03212-5.

Zuboff has written a carefully researched and detailed study of the nature of work and the effect of computer technology on it. She artfully combines an historical narrative about work and a clinical examination of several contemporary settings that have adopted computer technology in order to point out the potential disasters and benefits that can ensue. Her book's twelve chapters are divided into three sections: "Knowledge and Computer-Mediated Work"; "Authority: The Spiritual Dimension of Power"; and "Technique: The Material Dimension of Power."

The author's main argument is that an organization can automate—"replace the human body with a technology that enables the same processes to be performed with more continuity and control"—or informate—"increase the explicit information content of tasks and set into motion a series of dynamics that will ultimately reconfigure the nature of work and the social relationships that organize productive activity." "Informating derives from and builds upon automation." Recognition of how to informate an organization is the key not only to success, but also to a more humane and fulfilling work environment.

The book contains an index, as well as endnotes and two appendices. It is a scholarly treatment of a topic that has defied simplification and easy answers. Zuboff's work is a carefully wrought study that deserves careful examination by anyone concerned with the world of work and the effects of computer technology on it.

Robert H. Burger

REFERENCE WORKS

223. **Computing Information Directory: A Comprehensive Guide to the Computing Literature.** 5th ed. Darlene Myers Hildebrandt, comp. and ed. Federal Way, Wash., Pedaro, 1988. 893p. index. $139.95pa. ISBN 0-933113-03-X; ISSN 0887-1175.

The main impetus of this reference guide is to list bibliographical data on over fifteen hundred computer publications. The computer industry has blossomed in the last two decades, as has the amount of literature published in the field. This book provides the tools to survey the extent of literature available. The bulk of this guide is an exhaustive listing of computer journals. The vast number of computer titles is cross-referenced to guide users to titles in similar and related areas. An exhaustive collection of computer-related items is also provided, including university computer center newsletters, computer books, dictionaries and glossaries, indexing and abstracting services, software sources, review sources, hardware sources, directories, encyclopedias and handbooks, and computer languages. Also included are six appendices dealing with Association for Computing Machinery (ACM) Special Interest Group (SIG) Proceedings from 1969 to 1985; historical guides to the computing literature; a

bibliography of career and salary trends in the United States 1970-1986; expansion to the Library of Congress classification schedules QA 75 and QA 76, 1986 draft; and subject, publishers', and master indexes. This is a comprehensive guide to where computer information can be found. This book can be considered as a resource tool and is highly recommended as reference material for college and professional libraries.

John Y. Cheung

224. **Encyclopedia of Computer Science and Technology [Volume 19] Supplement 4.** Allen Kent and James G. Williams, eds. New York, Marcel Dekker, 1988. 390p. illus. $115.00. LC 74-29436. ISBN 0-8247-2269-8.

As with previous volumes, the editors have assembled experts to summarize what is currently known about computers and high technology across a wide spectrum of interest. Articles are written for those already knowledgeable in the field, not the novice. Many articles require advanced programming knowledge to understand.

Topics of broad interest include database design, local area networks, optical character recognition, and decision support systems. Advanced topics include analytic hierarchy process and symbol manipulation packages.

For libraries already owning previous volumes and finding them of use to their patrons, volume 19 should be added as a matter of course. For libraries considering a first purchase, the sophisticated nature of the articles as a match for patron needs should be ascertained before purchase. The encyclopedia is an attempt to bring together what is known at a particular point in time, realizing full well that the material is outdated the minute it is committed to print. If a library has need of that type of source, this is a good purchase.

David V. Loertscher

225. **A Glossary of Computing Terms: An Introduction.** 5th ed. Edited by Glossary Working Party, British Computer Society. New York, Cambridge University Press, 1987. 73p. index. $3.95pa. LC 86-20738. ISBN 0-521-33261-3.

This volume's main distinction is that it presents entries not in alphabetical sequence, but rather within fifteen categories: applications, communications, data representation and structure, documentation, input and output, computer personnel, computers, programming languages, storage, operational processes, programming, machine architecture, systems software, truth tables and logic gates, and units (e.g., *giga*). An index in the front takes one to the relevant section, in some cases from like terms which are not actually included but whose definition is related to the term defined. Unfortunately, the index is not complete. For example, ASCII is mentioned in the entry for character codes but not directly in the index. Definitions are terse, sometimes, as the book itself admits, making them of "limited use." (For example, the programming language LISP is defined as "used for list processing," with no indication of its wide employment in artificial intelligence.) In spite of this, the low cost of the book together with the topical arrangement makes it a satisfactory introduction or review for the major areas of computer science.

Robert Skinner

226. LaGasse, Charles E. **The Computer Resource Guide.** 1988 ed. Concord, Mass., Computer Insights, 1987. 84p. index. $24.00pa. LC 87-70697. ISBN 0-942199-00-6.

The guide serves as a first reference point for computer-related information, listing 240 primary computer resources under eighty-five subjects. Criteria for inclusion are as follows: subject areas must relate to computer systems, hardware, software, or services; resources chosen are unique, comprehensive, or well known. The list is intended to either locate the appropriate resource or assist the reader in finding it.

Resources are grouped by type (e.g., books, magazines, newsletters, catalogs, conference/exhibits, sourcebooks) under alphabetically arranged subject headings. These resources may be from public or private organizations, which can be for profit or nonprofit. Entries are briefly annotated.

Three alternative indexes list computer resources by type, vendor, and computer resource (to answer the question "Is a certain resource included?"). A special features section offers guidelines and advice as to recommended acquisitions, resources, and associations to join. A preview of the planned 1989 edition is provided, promising expanded subject areas and resource types, as well as the addition of more product-specific resources and U.S. government publications.

Cross-referencing among the subject areas would also be a valuable feature to consider, as more and more terms are used in computer jargon, and more assistance is needed to locate the desired item. [R: RBB, 1 June 88, p. 1654]

Anita Zutis

227. Lynch, Don B. **Dictionary of Computer and Information Technology Terms.** Bromley, England, Chartwell-Bratt, 1987. 225p. illus. £7.25pa. ISBN 0-86238-128-2.

Lynch, senior lecturer in computer studies at Bourneville College of Further Education Birmingham, has compiled a dictionary containing over twenty-five hundred common computer and information technology terms, codes, acronyms, and abbreviations. The terms are listed alphabetically, followed by clear, informative, and precise definitions. Each alphabetical section is preceded by a list of acronyms, abbreviations, and other words which have become part of computer technology jargon and are often confusing for beginners. The page layout is suitable for a dictionary of this type. The appendices contain the following useful information: common codes, metric unit prefixes, logic functions and symbols, Huffman code, flowchart symbols, and powers of two. Because the dictionary is directed toward the nonexpert, it is most suitable for students of computer information technology and for those exposed to computer technology either through personal computing or employment-related experiences. A most valuable addition to both an individual's or library's reference collection.

Mohammed M. Aman

228. **McGraw-Hill Encyclopedia of Electronics and Computers.** 2d ed. Sybil P. Parker, ed. New York, McGraw-Hill, 1988. 1047p. illus. index. $75.00. LC 87-37592. ISBN 0-07-045499-X.

A one-volume encyclopedia composed of 520 articles, selected from the sixth edition of the *McGraw-Hill Encyclopedia of Science and Technology* (see *ARBA* 88, entry 1448), concentrating on electronics and computers. The subject matter ranges over diverse topics in these fields such as fabrication methods for integrated circuits, the flow of electricity through semiconducting materials, electromagnetic pulse, and the use of computers in areas such as robotics, data management systems, communications, and consumer products. This second edition contains 45 new and 120 revised articles (about a quarter of the articles appearing in the first edition). The articles are organized in alphabetical order with many keyword subheadings and numerous illustrations, photographs, tables, line drawings, and diagrams. The articles are clear although technically written and most contain references to other articles in the volume and selected bibliographies. There is a useful index to the detailed contents of the articles at the back of the volume. The articles are written by noted authorities in these fields.

This encyclopedia is intended for the technically oriented lay or professional reader and will serve as a useful first reference source for technical terms and concepts. [R: RBB, 1 Oct 88, pp. 242-43]   Lorna K. Rees-Potter

Access Control

229.   Baskerville, Richard. **Designing Information Systems Security.** New York, John Wiley, 1988. 247p. illus. index. (John Wiley Information Systems Series). $49.95. LC 87-31959. ISBN 0-471-91772-9.

Information systems security is a newly emergent field of study that is concerned with the protection of information within an organization. Although in many organizations the emphasis is on the computer and computer security, the trend is toward looking at the larger issues of who has information, who needs information, and how to prevent access to those who should not have certain information. The author describes in relatively nontechnical language security analysis and design methodologies that can be applied to the entire organization. Within the larger context, he focuses on computer security and protection of information. This begins with accurate data input and continues throughout the usable life span of the information. Potential threats to information security such as fraud, theft, computer viruses, and fire and water damage are described as are means to limit identifiable threats.

Whatever systems and methodologies are put into place, appropriate access must be allowed for those who own the system, those responsible for working with the information, and those whose business or personal lives, or both, are affected by the information and its use. Issues of privacy and the ethical uses of information must also be considered. The author successfully introduces this field of study and brings together the technical, managerial, and ethical issues. References at the end of each chapter are useful as are the descriptions of the methodologies for structured information systems analysis and the systems engineering approach, and a case study describing applications.   Ann E. Prentice

230.   Gasser, Morrie. **Building a Secure Computer System.** New York, Van Nostrand Reinhold, 1988. 288p. illus. bibliog. index. $34.95. LC 87-27838. ISBN 0-442-23022-2.

In the past, computer security meant physical control of the equipment; but with easy access to microcomputers and floppy disks, security has become more difficult and complicated. Gasser has written a technical reference work on how to build a secure computer system, covering both internal security controls within

the hardware and software and external controls—physical, personnel, and procedural security.

The book is divided into three parts. Part 1 is an overview discussing why systems are not secure, general concepts, and design techniques. Part 2 covers detailed concepts: principles of a security architecture, access control and multilevel security, viruses, and covert channels. Part 3 deals with implementation and covers hardware security mechanisms, security models, security kernels, specifications and verification, networks, and distributed systems. Each chapter concludes with a reference list and a short bibliography ends the book.

The book is clearly written but is aimed at the computer analyst. The most useful sections for librarians are the discussion on controlling access to data and software instead of restricting access to the hardware and the section on customizing passwords for individual users, specific terminals, specific applications, or any combination of these. Gasser also shows how password routines can disconnect a person attempting to enter the system after a limited number of unsuccessful tries. The coverage of "Trojan Horse viruses"—programs or subroutines that masquerade as friendly programs—is also relevant for librarians.

Linda Main

231.   Schweitzer, James A. **Protecting Information on Local Area Networks.** Stoneham, Mass., Butterworths, 1988. 138p. illus. index. $24.95. LC 87-17219. ISBN 0-409-90138-5.

In a competent, no-frills style Schweitzer introduces business managers to the need for security on computer information networks. He first outlines how the networks operate, allowing people near and far to use information stored in computer databases. He follows this with a survey of the problems a company may experience if competitors or other unauthorized users read or alter such files. He concludes with practical suggestions to businesses, both profit and not-for-profit organizations, for protecting themselves from electronic "raids."

Schweitzer is systems security technology manager for Xerox Corporation and has published several other books and articles on security management. He writes for managers with little expertise in the technical aspects of computer science, and he does so without being condescending. Throughout the book he offers very specific and workable ideas on data security measures that any company can use. For example, appendix A, "A Management Task List," includes such questions as whether the business has "defined its critical information base and identified the value of information elements therein." There is a short bibliography of references.

This is a brief, but well-organized and well-written survey of a topic with which any manager who has people talking to computers that are talking to other computers must deal.

Berniece M. Owen

232. Turn, Rein, ed. **Advances in Computer System Security. Volume III.** Norwood, Mass., Artech House, 1988. 376p. illus. (Artech House Telecommunications Library). $60.00pa. LC 81-65989. ISBN 0-89006-315-X.

The year 1988 was notable for computer security issues. We saw the first trial of a person for allegedly placing a virus in a business computer system as well as a virus that tied up academic, research, and defense computer systems throughout the country. Such issues are not new, as is demonstrated by this third volume in a series devoted to computer security threats. While the majority of this work is technical, portions of several articles in the opening section ("Computer Security Environment") are accessible and make good background reading on computer viruses. The five other sections cover approaches to security technology, trusted operating systems and architectures, database security, and database communications security. Articles are taken from a variety of sources which appeared between 1984 and 1987 including most notably *Computers & Security* (Elsevier Science Publishing, 1982-), *IEEE Transactions on Software Engineering. Proceedings* (IEEE Computer Society Press, 1975-), *IEEE Symposium on Security and Privacy. Proceedings* (IEEE Computer Society Press, 1980-), and the proceedings of the ninth and tenth National Computer Security Conferences. A number of authors treat the development of security policies during this period including the National Computer Security Center's "Orange Book." While this volume is important, libraries for whom the purchase is marginal may want to consider whether they own the original titles from which the articles were extracted.

Robert Skinner

Databases

233. Bremner, Joe, and Peggy Miller. **Guide to Database Distribution: Legal Aspects and Model Contracts.** Philadelphia, National Federation of Abstracting and Information Services, 1987. 93p. $160.00 spiralbound. ISBN 0-942308-22-0.

Written for the business person or lawyer unfamiliar with database contracts, this book reviews the process of licensing machine-readable databases. The context is the negotiation of an agreement between a database producer and an unrelated online vendor. Because databases differ from other types of property or other intellectual works, licenses are necessarily unique and complex. A complete sample agreement is provided as an appendix, and each of the sixteen chapters covers terms and provisions of that license. Each chapter also addresses an important issue or concept, such as fair use, data handling, royalties, copyright and trademark protection, and marketing. The discussions are clear, well written, and relatively free of legal jargon. A separate chapter presents the results of an informal survey of leaders in the database industry commenting on the most pressing licensing issues. The problem areas are royalties, downloading, gateways, cross-file searching, and whether the Uniform Commercial Code, dealing with the sale of goods, also applies to online searching. This book should be most helpful to those involved in negotiating contracts. Even for those not involved, it gives an interesting overview of business issues in the database world.

A. Neil Yerkey

234. Fidel, Raya. **Database Design for Information Retrieval: A Conceptual Approach.** New York, John Wiley, 1987. 232p. illus. index. $29.95. LC 87-12967. ISBN 0-471-82786-X.

By employing an extended case-study approach, Fidel's book "explains how to perform data requirements analysis and how to represent the outcome of this analysis in a formal and comprehensive model that is useful for software and hardware considerations." The work consists of eight chapters: "Introduction," "Methods of Collecting User Requirements," "Requirements Analysis," "Data and Operations Dictionaries," "The Entity-Relationship Model," "The Integration of Schemata," "Preparation for Data Collection," and "Evaluation." A glossary of frequently used terms and a brief index accompany the work. Fidel's step-by-step approach works well and no prior knowledge of systems analysis or computer programming is necessary. A database of restaurant information in Seattle is used to illustrate design principles and processes.

The book is well structured and enables the novice to learn sound principles of database design in the absence of an existing process. This is the work's strength. It would be useful for anyone facing the frustrating and tedious task of creating a database from scratch.

Robert H. Burger

235. Gaydasch, Alexander, Jr. **Effective Database Management.** Englewood Cliffs, N.J., Prentice-Hall, 1988. 239p. bibliog. index. $37.33. LC 87-19364. ISBN 0-13-241472-4.

This excellent book covers database technology and administration with an emphasis on database management systems (DBMS) for large-scale, multi-user, multiprocessing applications using mainframe computers. Very little is given about microcomputer DBMS. Making effective use of databases in a large, complex organization requires both business and technical skill. This book is almost evenly divided between the two. Business aspects include how to decide if a DBMS will help solve data management problems, choosing a system, cost issues, planning, development, and administration. Technical issues include data models, normalization, database design, redundancy problems, indexes, pointers, searching, and the like. The technical chapters should be especially helpful to anyone trying to learn or broaden their understanding of mainframe DBMS. Technical terms and concepts are clearly explained and illustrated. The author does not try to sell DBMS as the cure for every ill, but realistically presents the problems and potentials of database management. The book is well written in an informal, sometimes anecdotal, style. Illustrations are clear and helpful, being simple enough to grasp, but complex enough to provide realism. There are numerous checklists and summaries, a quality index — a rarity among computer-oriented books, a good glossary, and a very short bibliography.

A. Neil Yerkey

236. Hartley, Jill, Amanda Noonan, and Stan Metcalfe. **New Electronic Information Services: An Overview of the UK Database Industry in an International Context.** Brookfield, Vt., Gower Publishing, 1987. 147p. $38.95pa. ISBN 0-566-05489-2.

This report of a study by the Technical Change Centre in London offers a look at the database industry in the United Kingdom as of 1984. Short sections cover Japan, the United States, and the European Economic Community, and discuss an international perspective to what is primarily an assessment of the role of the United Kingdom in database production and use. Tutorial chapters in market and database economics, the structure of the online industry, government information policy (both U.S. and U.K.), and information technology are the foundation upon which the final conclusions are based. Although the overview nature of the tutorials leads to some misleading oversimplifications (e.g., free text searching *can* be used to

advantage in bibliographic files), and there are a number of annoying typographical errors, this book summarizes the British database industry and explores its relative international position. Although U.S. readers might do well to be aware of the international issues raised here, the focus of the book means it is likely to have a limited appeal for them. [R: LAR, Apr 88, p. 236]

Elisabeth Logan

237. Jones, Paul E., Jr., and Robert M. Curtice. **Logical Data Base Design.** 2d ed. Wellesley, Mass., QED Information Sciences, 1988. 265p. index. $39.95. LC 88-11385. ISBN 0-89435-232-6.

Database construction presents challenging physical and logical design considerations, and even though homegrown databases may be as unlike as fingerprints, certain universal and axiomatic principles should be understood *before* one writes the first instruction. The first edition of this title, published by Van Nostrand Reinhold in 1982, listed Curtice as the principal author, then Jones. Presumably, despite such changes, this edition is intended to update the previous work, yet, curiously, no mention is made of its predecessor. That mystery aside, chapters address logical database design, the logical design process, data elements, advanced notation, and documentation, with examples and case studies sprinkled throughout. Illustrations consist mostly of standard flowcharts, and the notation should present no particular difficulties to those familiar with the subject.

The work is full of commonsense advice to the database designer, including some experiential (and sometimes overlooked) rules. A warning: much of this material is quite technical, and the novice student of databases may be confused, even lost, by the time the later chapters roll around. At the very least, one using this book as an aid to database construction needs a solid grasp of logic, flowcharting, and standard engineering design notation. A good subject/author index rounds out this attractively and sturdily bound book, with good-quality, glare-resistant paper. The advice is sound, the text is readable, and the diagrams are clear and helpful, so what more could you ask? Recommended, but those new to database design will find more of what they are looking for in simpler treatments.

Bruce A. Shuman

238. Rogers, Helen, comp. **Canadian Machine-Readable Databases: A Directory and Guide. Bases de Données Canadiennes Lisibles par Machine.** Ottawa, National Library of Canada, 1987. 134p. index. $12.50pa.; $15.00pa. (U.S.). ISBN 0-660-53734-6.

This publication is a bilingual (English and French) directory of approximately 450 databases in machine-readable form created and produced in Canada. The databases listed cover all disciplines from the humanities to the sciences. They may be textual, statistical, or videotex in nature and may be publicly accessible or not. The restriction is that they must be produced by a Canadian organization, firm, or individual. The preface indicates that the directory information is current as of June 1987 and will be updated with future editions. The directory is intended as a reference tool for the Canadian information industry, information scientists, and librarians in particular.

It is organized primarily in alphabetical order by the database name, with subject, database producers, online and offline service vendors, and database name reference lists. Each entry gives full information on the content and scope, coverage, language, updating, access conditions, and notes any print equivalent. The coverage appears excellent to this reviewer, listing a number of databases not publicly accessible that are often not found in such directories. It might be more useful in future editions to include some indication of the size and growth of the databases covered. There are some typographical errors in the text such as a duplication of index information in the subject index under "Leisure," and a transposition of some index entries under "Law" to "Library Catalogues." Hopefully the next edition will eliminate these errors through better editorial review. Recommended for libraries that provide online search services, especially if Canadian information is required.

Lorna K. Rees-Potter

239. Tenopir, Carol, and Gerald Lundeen. **Managing Your Information: How to Design and Create a Textual Database on Your Microcomputer.** New York, Neal-Schuman, 1988. 226p. illus. index. (Applications in Information Management and Technology Series, No. 5). $37.50pa. LC 87-34894. ISBN 1-55570-023-3.

The authors, educators, and database professionals explain the design, creation, and operation of microcomputer-driven, in-house databases, which will have most of the characteristics and perform most of the functions of large, commercial database systems. Among covered topics in this work are feasibility studies, planning factors, costs, design considerations, selection of software, and evaluation of systems. Tenopir and Lundeen go easy on the technical jargon which tends to creep into books in this genre, and succeed in presenting a very readable do-it-yourself guide. In tone, the book

is addressed to a readership of intelligent, but not necessarily advanced, students.

Information on such important matters as updating, maintenance, backup, and quality control is included, as well as a brief, intriguing chapter on the future of homegrown databases and equipment. Illustrations, few in number, are mostly simple charts and diagrams, and in this respect, one might wish for more. Each of the eleven chapters concludes with a further readings set of recent references and citations on the topics presented. Appendices include a detailed case study concerning the design of a database, names and numbers for ordering selected software packages (without annotation or evaluation), and some software reviewing sources. A six-page glossary concludes the work, along with two very thorough indexes. This paperback seems a bit expensive, but solely considering content and presentation, what's not to like? [R: LJ, July 88, p. 58]

Bruce A. Shuman

240. Wiederhold, Gio. **File Organization for Database Design.** New York, McGraw-Hill, 1987. 619p. illus. bibliog. index. $40.95. LC 87-2675. ISBN 0-07-070133-4.

This author has written a number of books on the topic of database design and implementation. He writes clearly and puts complex topics into a well-organized and readable text. The book begins with a general introduction to its scope and purpose, along with definitions of terminology and various distinctions that are necessary to prevent confusion. The author then embarks on a thorough analysis of transaction oriented file organization. *Transaction* here means the completion of a program which performs some operation (e.g., updating, records management, or information retrieval) on a file. The principles presented are not specific to files alone, but can and should be considered in any significant software design project.

There are many graphics illustrating points made. Formulas for decision making are included and exercises are provided at the end of each chapter to test the reader's understanding. The topic is presented in the context of centralized as well as distributed processing, and data processing as well as knowledge engineering. A very extensive bibliography and a general index are included at the end.

This is an excellent book which should be used in conjunction with other texts on database design and implementation. It is a useful presentation of an important topic in an up-to-date and very readable fashion.

James Rice

Microcomputers

241. Brey, Barry B. **Microprocessors and Peripherals: Hardware, Software, Interfacing, and Applications.** 2d ed. Columbus, Ohio, Merrill Publishing, 1988. 525p. illus. index. $37.95. LC 87-63189. ISBN 0-675-20884-X.

Although the author indicates that this book is appropriate for use in undergraduate engineering classes, it will also be of value to the practicing engineer/programmer. It provides a detailed description of the architecture of two of the most important processors used in today's microcomputers, the Intel 8085A (an easily programmable student version of the 8088 chip used in the IBM PC) and the Motorola MC6800 used by Apple. Readers will need a solid background in electronics and some assembly-language programming experience; this volume is not intended for the novice or amateur.

Introductory chapters detail the development of microprocessors and present the fundamentals of the Intel and Motorola designs. Subsequent chapters explain the interfacing of the microprocessors with memory devices and input/output systems, including keyboards, CRTs, and serial communication ports. Two chapters new to the second edition, and reflecting its extended emphasis on peripherals, describe interfaces to disk systems (floppy, hard, and optical) and to printers. Two final chapters illustrate practical applications: routines are included, for example, to program point-of-sales terminals and traffic light controllers.

The textbook orientation is reinforced by a format that includes learning objectives, chapter summaries, and review questions. However, the wealth of circuit, timing, and pinout diagrams, many provided by the manufacturers themselves, makes this a useful technical reference for programmers who work directly with microprocessors and I/O systems.   Willy Owen

242. Dewey, Patrick R. **Interactive Fiction and Adventure Games for Microcomputers 1988: An Annotated Directory.** Westport, Conn., Meckler, 1988. 189p. illus. index. $39.50 pa. LC 87-16473. ISBN 0-88736-170-6.

The microcomputer revolution occurred at the time when the video game phenomenon was hitting the United States. It was only natural that programmers would create for the home computer market what was available in the video arcade. To some extent, the adventure game is a direct competitor with the video game. However, a new genre appeared for microcomputers which no video game could duplicate. This new genre was interactive fiction. The best known program of this type is "Zork," which can take an individual weeks or months to solve.

Dewey's purpose seems to be twofold. He attempts to list most of the adventure and interactive fiction for microcomputers. Those games he is personally familiar with, he describes in detail, and reviews their strengths and weaknesses. He does this with skill and provides perceptive analyses. For the games he is not familiar with, he quotes or paraphrases the information given on the game box. Thus, the user can expect two completely different types of coverage.

General information given for each game includes name, producer, cost, hardware, grade or difficulty level, type, and a description. Coverage is excellent up to the end of 1987 and even includes publishers' descriptions of some games coming out in 1988.

Dewey's book is for game enthusiasts who want to build their repertoire, libraries which try to serve parents of game enthusiasts, educators who need to choose the best of interactive fiction, and computer stores who want a quick lookup reference for their computer customers. [R: JOYS, Spring 88, p. 365; RBB, 15 Sept 88, p. 140]

David V. Loertscher

243. **Encyclopedia of Microcomputers. Volume 1: Access Methods to Assembly Language and Assemblers.** Allen Kent and James G. Williams, eds. New York, Marcel Dekker, 1988. 434p. illus. $160.00. LC 87-15428. ISBN 0-8247-2700-2.

Designed as a companion to *Encyclopedia of Computer Science and Technology* (Marcel Dekker, 1975-), the intention of this encyclopedia is to produce a comprehensive work covering at least five hundred articles in ten volumes. The definition of *microcomputer* was a problem for the editor, since the distinction between microcomputers and mainframe computers has almost been erased.

The coverage is to include "the broad spectrum of microcomputer knowledge ... and is aimed at the needs of microcomputer hardware specialists, programmers, systems analysts, engineers, operations researchers, and mathematicians." Some of the articles are to be readable to the novice, others to the specialist.

An examination of the entries shows many entries on computer companies (most of which have been in business less than ten years) and technical articles such as "Aerospace Digital Crewstations," "ALGOL," and "Analytic Hierarchy Process." Very few of the entries would be of interest to the typical user of microcomputers who uses application programs or tries to keep up with trends in the field.

Recommended as a source for more technical articles.   David V. Loertscher

244. **Encyclopedia of Microcomputers. Volume 2: Authoring Systems for Interactive Video to Compiler Design.** Allen Kent and James G. Williams, eds. New York, Marcel Dekker, 1988. 452p. illus. $160.00. LC 87-15428. ISBN 0-8247-2701-0.

Volume 2 of the multivolume *Encyclopedia of Microcomputers* covers twenty-five topics. Five profile computer companies or computer-related organizations: Burroughs, C. Itoh, CCITT, Century Analysis, and Commodore. Nine relate to programming, from the system level to authoring systems, including videodisc authoring systems, automated program generators, BASIC, benchmarking programming languages, BIOS, COBOL, command languages, Common LISP, and compiler design. Eight concern themselves with applications: automated forecasting, automated material handling, automated office information systems design, bilingual language processors, CAD/CAM from a management viewpoint, chemical engineering, civil engineering, and client-centered information processing. The three remaining entries cover microprocessor circuits, image data compression, and bibliographic control of microcomputer software.

Entries are signed and range from two pages to almost sixty. On the whole, they do an adequate job of covering their subjects for persons with only a moderate amount of computer literacy. Most authors have provided bibliographies, some with over one hundred items; however, citations are almost entirely before 1986 and this also reflects the currency of the entries themselves. There are a number of charts and a few photographs. The volume shows some problems in proofreading. Librarians familiar with the Dekker sets *Encyclopedia of Computer Science and Technology* (for reviews of vols. 2-6, see *ARBA* 78, entry 1523) and the *Encyclopedia of Library and Information Science* (for reviews of vols. 39-41, see *ARBA* 87, entries 578-580) will have a good idea as to what to expect from *Encyclopedia of Microcomputers.*   Robert Skinner

245. Naiman, Arthur, ed. **The Macintosh Bible: Thousands of Basic and Advanced Tips, Tricks and Shortcuts Logically Organized and Fully Indexed.** 2d ed. Berkeley, Calif., Goldstein & Blair; distr., Emeryville, Calif., Publishers Group West, 1988. 759p. illus. index. $28.00pa. ISBN 0-940235-01-3.

Having had the opportunity to use the first edition of this work extensively, I was not surprised to find that the second edition is even better. It is a testament to the thoroughness of the original authors (Dale Coleman and Arthur Naiman) that the first edition remains useful today, almost two years after publication—not a short time in the volatile areas of microcomputer hardware and software. It is also helpful that readers receive two free updates as part of the purchase price. In addition to the usual tips for users of specific programs and peripherals, new Macintosh users will find a good deal of useful information in the first hundred pages or so. If you purchase machine-specific books for your library, this should be one of them. (Incidentally, the book is also available for $79.95 accompanied by three disks which constitute *The Macintosh Bible: STAX! Edition.* The HyperCard version, which was not available for review, excerpts information from the printed volume.)   Robert Skinner

Online Searching

246. Armstrong, C. J., and J. A. Large, eds. **Manual of Online Search Strategies.** Boston, G. K. Hall, 1988. 831p. illus. index. $57.50. LC 87-22882. ISBN 0-8161-1885-X.

More than three thousand databases are now available for searching, each different in content. This manual provides searchers who already have some skill with additional information to assist them in conducting more successful online searches. After an overview of search strategy in general, the body of the book consists of chapters devoted to databases in particular subject areas. For each subject there is a discussion of the special characteristics of the literature, coverage of databases, description of fields, comparisons of coverage and choice of host, plus search examples to clarify strategy. Additional chapters provide an overview of citation indexing with discussion of the purposes of citation analysis, a review of databases such as BRS Afterdark intended for the individual who is not an information professional, and descriptions of quick reference databases. The final chapter provides an update on electronic journals. The appendix includes a list of all databases mentioned in the text and their hosts plus a brief bibliography.

The chapters are written by expert searchers representing educators, database managers, librarians, and consultants from the United States and Europe. Coverage is thorough and the information up-to-date. Useful bibliographies are found at the end of each chapter.

Anyone doing or teaching reference services will find this a most valuable resource; the online searcher will find it close to indispensable. [R: JAL, Mar 88, p. 52; LAR, 15 June 88, p. 353; Online, Sept 88, pp. 92-93]

Ann E. Prentice

Software

247. Brown, C. Marlin "Lin." **Human-Computer Interface Design Guidelines.** Norwood, N.J., Ablex, 1988. 236p. illus. bibliog. index. (Human/Computer Interaction). $32.50; $45.00 (instituions). LC 87-14473. ISBN 0-89391-332-4.

This text is full of practical suggestions and guidelines to aid designers of the interface between computers and their users. The author has developed from a number of sources the guidelines which include evidence from experiments, predictions from theories of human performance, principles of cognitive psychology, principles of ergonomic design, and evidence gathered through engineering experiences.

The first chapter summarizes general human-computer interface concepts such as mental processing requirements, consistency, physical analogies, and design for novices, experts and intermittent users while the remainder of the work provides more information in specific areas. Detailed guidelines are given on designing display formats, effective wording, color, effective use of graphics, dialog design, data entry control and display devices, and error messages and online assistance. A final section provides useful information regarding implementation of human-computer interface guidelines including knowing the users, prototyping and user testing, and designing by iterative refinement. The guidelines are presented in outline form and illustrated by example applications. Much of this work consists of common sense, but, nevertheless, useful rules of thumb. The extensive bibliography provides useful access to relevant research findings which are scattered throughout many disciplines. A checklist of guidelines summarizes the work and provides a useful overview of recommendations. An index of concepts completes the work.

The application of design guidelines such as these provides a systematic approach which, hopefully, will promote consistency among designers responsible for different parts of the system's user interface. This book should be required reading for designers of library systems. For librarians who more and more frequently are participating not only in the design of screens for online catalogs but also in the development of in-house software programs and the selection of computer systems this work should provide excellent evaluation benchmarks in the areas of user friendliness, consistency, and effectiveness.

Sherrilynne Fuller

248. Christian, Kaare. **The C and UNIX Dictionary: From Absolute Pathname to Zombie.** New York, John Wiley, 1988. 216p. $29.95; $16.95pa. LC 88-14208. ISBN 0-471-60929-3; 0-471-60931-5pa.

This book is a useful collection of terms that are unique to the C and UNIX environment. The author has done a good job of selecting the terms to include in the text and has provided useful definitions and explanations of these terms. The examples of codes included are concise and effective. Few terms of general use to other areas of computer science have been included. I would prefer to have more items included that are UNIX and C jargon, such as *bang* (the exclamation mark), *white book* (the K&R text), *Dennis* (Dennis Ritchie), and *death-star* (an AT&T logo).

A few definitions exhibit small problems: the *MERT* definition is not complete; there was a backslash missed in the *backslash* definition; describing *lex* as a lexical analyzer is not very helpful; and the *lint* definition has a wording problem. Some alternative definitions should be included, such as *strip* (to turn the eight bit off), *port* (an input/output hardware connection, often a RS232 coupler), and *code generator* (also an application generator).

Some UNIX gurus may consider things like *backspace, bell, form feed,* and *carriage return* to be escape sequences. However, they are treated as ASCII characters on many systems. I think that the escape sequence definition should be restricted to sequences like those that control printers and screens and actually contain an escape that the programmer must enter.

This is a very useful book for beginners in UNIX and C and useful as an occasional reference for experienced UNIX users.

John A. Jackman

249. Dumas, Joseph S. **Designing User Interfaces for Software.** Englewood Cliffs, N.J., Prentice-Hall, 1988. 174p. illus. bibliog. index. $31.00pa. LC 87-7178. ISBN 0-13-201971-X.

It has been said that most systems are designed by geniuses to be run by idiots. True or not, this idea gains credence as many intelligent people become unglued when confronted with sophisticated computer programs, or go through trauma when obliged to read user's manuals. Dumas, a psychiatrist with the American Institute for Psychological Research, works in human factors research and development, which gives him the credentials to write about automation from the point of view of the user. His principal motifs are that computer software must be designed with the user's limitations and attitudes in mind, and the screens one must wade through to get into programs ought to speak plainly.

Dumas focuses on "the user-software interface" (already with the jargon!). Specifically, he offers rules for raising the comfort level of those who will page through introductory screens in search of whatever benefits the program holds. He preaches psychological understanding of human reactions, user behavior, and how much information normally can be absorbed at one time. Written for the novice, this book is illustrated with cartoon figures showing, just as examples, how one creates a manual, when and where to use menus, and how to organize lists. Think like a user, Dumas reminds the programmer frequently, and screens will be lucid, readable, and unambiguous. All of the advice in this book is well intended but some of it seems obvious (e.g., using common, short English words that clearly describe the action that the command will carry out and choosing words that are distinctive from one another). Still, anyone creating software for use by others, or writing a user's manual to accompany a program, should memorize these rules, instructions, and models of clarity.

Bruce A. Shuman

250. Hernon, Peter, and John V. Richardson, eds. **Microcomputer Software for Performing Statistical Analysis: A Handbook Supporting Library Decision Making.** Norwood, N.J., Ablex, 1988. 311p. illus. bibliog. index. (Information Management Policy and Services Series). $29.50; $45.00 (institutions). LC 88-6360. ISBN 0-89391-376-6.

These two respected library educators have written and compiled a text intended for librarians and library school students, encouraging them to use their IBM or IBM-compatible personal microcomputers—already present in their libraries—for statistical analyses. They also believe the book will interest library science educators for use in their research methods courses. The authors list six objectives for their book: (1) "assist ... in selecting software that analyzes data and reports the application of statistical tests"; (2) "identify and discuss important issues related to the selection and application of microcomputer statistical analysis software"; (3) "identify uses of statistical analysis software and offer recommendations about the use of such software for decision

making"; (4) "place statistical analysis packages in proper context—their relationship to other types of software"; (5) "guide libraries in the use of selected statistics, the interpretation of computer generated printout, and the presentation of data for effective planning and decision making"; and (6) "identify selected writing concerning statistical analysis software and the effective presentation of data" (p. xi).

These objectives have been achieved. The book is quite free from jargon, considering the topic, and most of the information should be easily understood by the uninitiated. Selecting the StatPac statistical package to illustrate the manipulation of data was a good choice by the authors because its menu program makes it easy to follow and use. Most libraries already possess some software and the book shows how to use it for statistical analysis and report writing. The generic and specific types of software discussed include: spreadsheets (Lotus 1-2-3); database managers (Reflex); word processors (WordStar Release 4 and WordPerfect 4.2); and grammar checkers (RightWriter). An appendix lists and evaluates a number of statistical software packages. The bibliography has breadth and cites many current sources, an important feature for this volatile subject.

Nathan M. Smith

251. Jameson, Alison. **Downloading and Uploading in Online Information Retrieval.** Bradford, England, MCB University Press, 1987. 64p. bibliog. (Library Management, Vol. 8, No. 1). $83.95pa. ISBN 0-86176-299-1.

Downloading and Uploading is another in the excellent series put out by MCB. They consistently publish scholarly but still useful and informative material.

The work was submitted in partial fulfillment for a master's degree at University College London, and has a definite British/European bias. It discusses several systems and services not easily accessible from the United States, namely BLAISE, PRESTEL, ESA, and DIMDI.

The book covers exactly what it says it does: software for downloading and uploading, technical developments relevant to downloading and uploading, applications and legal aspects of downloading and uploading. The author also reports briefly on three case studies (all conducted in London libraries).

The work was completed in 1987, and as a result parts of the text are a little out-of-date (e.g., the section on costs and the discussion of CD-ROM). There have also been some changes in the software packages discussed since the work was written. The most useful chapters are the ones which succinctly discuss the applications of downloading and uploading (temporary storage, editing and reformatting retrieved records, database creation, etc.). I also found that the chapter on the legal aspects of downloading gave a lot of information very quickly on the bibliographic utilities, abstracts, copyright law, licensing, contract law, and fair use (Great Britain and the United States).

The 168 references provide excellent source material on downloading and uploading, though nothing more recent than 1986 is included. [R: RLR, Feb 88, pp. 34-35]

Linda Main

252. Mills, Harlan D. **Software Productivity.** New York, Dorset House, 1988. 274p. index. $25.00pa. LC 88-5099. ISBN 0-932633-10-2.

Mills is a mathematician who is currently director of the Information Systems Institute in Vero Beach, Florida. This volume contains twenty papers on software engineering he has written (and presumably given) over the past two decades or so. Some, the foreword tells us, were previously unpublished while others are no longer accessible; but now they are brought together and conveniently located in a single source. Because it is Mills's fundamental premise that one must have a good handle on the mathematics of programming in order to design and produce good software, he uses mathematical notation, a mathematician's smorgasbord of formulaic expressions, Greek letters, and superscript numbers, liberally, which will create a serious stumbling block for many readers. Curiously, while the book bears a 1988 copyright, the nineteen papers reprinted here date from 1967 to 1981, with approximately 60 percent of them predating 1970. As so much as happened in the intervening years, the lack of currency may render many of these papers obsolete, and useful primarily as studies in the development of programming theory, practice, language, and principles.

This book's appeal will be understandably limited, and the insubstantial index offers the browser little in the way of finding specific nuggets of information. The papers entitled "How to Buy Quality Software" and "How to Write Correct Programs and Know It," while possessed of a certain timeless truth, are fifteen years past currency, and offer little that cannot be found in any competent programming text. Worst of all, almost none of Mills's papers discuss PC applications of programming, for obvious reasons. Libraries striving for complete collections in the area of computer programming may want to acquire this one. Those seeking modern, accessible, and PC-relevant

treatments, however, will be disappointed, and are advised to give this a miss.

Bruce A. Shuman

253. Simpson, W. Dwain. **New Techniques in Software Project Management.** New York, John Wiley, 1987. 250p. index. $34.95. LC 87-20286. ISBN 0-471-85551-0.

The author describes this book as "a collection of the best new contributions to software project management—both programs and techniques—while at the same time providing an up-to-date general view of software program development." It is a systematic and comprehensive guide for managing the development of new software from initial design through beta testing with particular emphasis on methods for monitoring and maintaining control of the project, ensuring complete documentation, and evaluating the final product.

In spite of the wide range of materials covered, the text is quite easy to read. The intended audience includes experienced project managers who wish to sharpen their skills as well as new managers in need of guidance on how to approach projects of this sort. Considerable prior knowledge is assumed, so that specific techniques are described only in sufficient detail for review and to determine their place in the overall process.

This book's primary value as a reference work will be to the project manager who keeps a copy on hand for private use in the office. For more complete descriptions of the various techniques, other more detailed sources must be consulted. The merit of this book is that it brings the various techniques together in an integrated process. The casual user will find the index troublesome with some topics directly accessible while others of equal importance are accessible only as subheadings.

Lawrence W. S. Auld

254. **Software for Schools 1987-88: A Comprehensive Directory of Educational Software Grades Pre-K through 12.** New York, R. R. Bowker, 1987. 1085p. $49.95. ISBN 0-8352-2369-8; ISSN 0000-099X.

An indispensable tool for educators, *Software for Schools* provides access to computer software for educational as opposed to recreational needs. The bulk of the tool is divided into two major sections. The first is an extensive listing by machine, then by subject and grade level. The second is an alphabetical listing of software by title with extensive bibliographic information, including a brief description of the package.

The subject index (by machine) provides educators with an excellent tool when searching for a specific application. This listing is worth the price of the tool, since it takes much of the guesswork out of software identification. By cross-referencing the title found in the subject index with the alphabetical indexing, enough information is provided to order the product on preview.

Other useful but briefer sections include an educational computer periodicals directory, a publishers' index, an index to professional software of use to educators in managing educational operations, and a few introductory articles about computer education in the schools. Compared to *T.E.S.S.* (see *ARBA* 88, entry 392) guide to computer software, this directory is not as comprehensive, but provides much more detailed information and indexing access. Every school/school district with heavy investments in computers and computer education should own this tool. It is well worth the price. [R: JOYS, Spring 88, p. 366; RBB, 15 May 88, p. 1588]

David V. Loertscher

255. Stark, Robin. **Encyclopedia of Lotus 1 2 3.** Blue Ridge Summit, Pa., TAB Books, 1987. 484p. index. $29.95; $19.95pa. LC 87-19839. ISBN 0-8306-7891-3; 0-8306-2891-6pa.

In spite of strong competition from other spreadsheets, Lotus 1-2-3 is probably the program most associated with the IBM personal computer. Such popularity has spawned numerous cottage industries ranging from templates, software enhancements, and, of course, books explaining how to get the most out of the program. Stark's work is "A complete cross-reference to all macros, commands, functions, applications, and troubleshooting." The book begins with a short introduction to Lotus, followed by 200 pages on commands, 150 on functions, 50 on macros, and a short section on companion programs that accompany Lotus, as well as the widely used HAL. Following this is a useful "Troubleshooting Guide" covering some of the frequently encountered error messages or questions. Explanations are clear and there are numerous examples. The author has gone out of his way to provide cross-references and there is a good index (in a spot check of the index, the only omission I discovered was the function @LOG(x), but there was an entry to the proper page under the term *logarithms*). Lotus users, and they are legion, will find this book a helpful tool.

Robert Skinner

Systems

256. Adrian, Merv. **The Workstation Data Link.** New York, McGraw-Hill, 1988. 240p. illus. index. $24.95pa. LC 87-83100. ISBN 0-07-000474-9.

The intent of this book is to present authoritative information and to offer helpful guidelines on transferring data files in different formats between small and large computer systems. The work consists of sixteen chapters that are arranged into three parts. In part 1 (chapters 1-5) the author presents a fundamental model of a workstation data link, data architectures and extraction engines, mainframe communication standards and protocols, and the OSI (Open Systems Interconnection) model and LAN (local area network) protocols. Part 2 (chapters 6-8) is devoted to basic telecommunications concepts and the description and implementation of links. Part 3 (chapters 9-16) covers several managing methodologies and recent (1988) developments including Microsoft, Ashton-Tate, and others. The book contains a glossary of commonly used terms, as well as an index.

The author, who is a communications manager at Shearson/American Express, writes often for professional and trade journals. His book is aimed at both the nontechnical manager concerned with productivity and the computer expert in a corporate environment. Although the book's information is accurate and its overall structure sound, the author does not always successfully bridge the gap between the varying levels of his audience's expertise.

Robert H. Burger

257. Blokdijk, André, and Paul Blokdijk. **Planning and Design of Information Systems.** Orlando, Fla., Academic Press, 1987. 578p. illus. index. $65.00. ISBN 0-12-107070-0.

An information system is a computerized bookkeeping and management system that helps a company to carry out its regular business. It usually involves data on product orders, accounts payable and receivable, project tasks, employee profiles, customer profiles, and any other data needed to run the business. In the past, information systems were usually developed by experienced analysts who based a new design on a closely matching previous one. In this book, however, a new, more theoretical approach is recommended in which a theoretical model is first developed, followed by a detailed design. The authors do not advocate one theory or model; they offer a smorgasbord. The book is written clearly and it reads easily. The authors have forty years of experience in the field, and they are employees of IBM in Belgium. The book should prove useful to someone who wants to know what is involved in designing and setting up a computerized information system for a business, government office, or other institution.   Steven L. Tanimoto

258. Dicenet, G. **Design and Prospects for the ISDN.** Norwood, Mass., Artech House, 1987. 288p. illus. index. $60.00. LC 87-73182. ISBN 0-89006-269-2.

This is an excellent addition to the publisher's series on telecommunications. The Integrated Services Digital Network (ISDN) approach has progressed recently into an important factor in the telecommunications industry. This all-digital, common-channel signaling system has become widely accepted due to its ability to handle a broad and diversified range of services needed for office automation and modernization. This book is written as a definitive guide to all aspects of ISDN by a group of ten engineers of the National Center for Telecommunication Research in France. (G. Dicenet is a pseudonym denoting them in French.) This book is the summary of their research contributions for the past two decades. The first part deals in general with the basic principles and definition of ISDN. Topics include ISDN characteristics, services, user-network interfaces, transmission, protocols, terminals, user installations, switching, operation, and maintenance. The last part of the book deals specifically with the implementation of ISDN in France and broadband ISDN. Instead of just presenting the detailed specifications of ISDN, the authors concentrate on the design philosophy and rationale, thus providing the necessary insights to those not particularly familiar with the ISDN approach. A list of acronyms and abbreviations is extremely helpful to the readers. An exceptionally detailed index is provided making this book an excellent reference for professionals and practicing engineers in the telecommunications industry. This book is highly recommended for college and professional libraries.   John Y. Cheung

259. Emery, James C. **Management Information Systems: The Critical Strategic Resource.** New York, Oxford University Press, 1987. 341p. illus. index. (Wharton Executive Library). $17.95. LC 87-7922. ISBN 0-19-504392-8.

The aim of this book is to tell managers what they need to know in order to play a leadership role in the deployment and operation of an effective information system. The book is an addition to the Wharton Executive Library, a new series sponsored by the University of Pennsylvania's Wharton School. Each book in the series is supposed to be up-to-date, authoritative, brief, nontechnical, practical, and compact. Emery, professor of decision sciences at the Wharton School, devotes the early chapters to a presentation of the technology (programming languages, transaction processing, decision support systems, application software, and high productivity development tools) and the latter chapters to relevant managerial topics (economics of information, system concepts, planning and implementing a successful management information system). He addresses senior managers who know how organizations work, but who may know little about computers, and provides them with the insights necessary to assess their options. He has accomplished his task with distinction; a lot of technical information has been presented in a clear, readable fashion.

A minimum of line drawings, but no halftones, are incorporated in several chapters. New terms are introduced in the text in boldface type and are then fully defined in the glossary. Annotated lists of references appear at the close of each chapter, and a detailed index appears at the back of the book.   Glenn R. Wittig

260. Gill, Suzanne L. **File Management and Information Retrieval Systems: A Manual for Managers and Technicians.** 2d ed. Englewood, Colo., Libraries Unlimited, 1988. 221p. illus. bibliog. index. $26.50. LC 87-32474. ISBN 0-87287-625-X.

This text is intended for students who may be expected to design, implement, or maintain filing systems in real-life situations. It emphasizes creation of a procedures manual and practical, rather than theoretical, organization of material. The history of business records, beginning with clay tablets and concluding with computers, is outlined. In providing guidance for the development of a procedures manual, there are detailed analyses of filing and classification methods in which many alternatives are presented, but one is given preference over any other. A single exception is made for filing word-by-word. There are detailed instructions for preparing materials for filing and for filing them. Records retention, circulation procedures, equipment and supplies, and centralization versus decentralization are discussed in individual chapters. Three paperless storage methods are described: micrographics, computers, and optical disks. There are also four case histories, three of them computer-based, in which currently functioning records management systems are described in detail. There is a glossary. An astonishing amount of instructional material is covered in this relatively short book. After completing this text, including the exercises, a student could probably design and implement a filing system. [R: Online, Nov 88, p. 95]   Margaret McKinley

261. Gosling, Jane. **SWALCAP: A Guide for Librarians and Systems Managers.** Brookfield, Vt., Gower Publishing, 1987. 129p. illus. bibliog. index. $43.95. ISBN 0-566-03539-1.

This work of about one hundred pages (excluding appendices) discusses the history and systems of a cooperative automation network in the United Kingdom. Beginning in 1969 as a research project investigating the feasibility of such an endeavor, initially with four universities in the southwest of England, it evolved into a private limited company in 1986. The South West Academic Libraries Cooperative Automation Project has twenty-three members who use the cooperative system for cataloging (all but one) and for circulation (all but six). Most are academic libraries such as the universities of Bristol, Exeter, Reading, and Southhampton and polytechnic institutions such as Bristol, Plymouth, and Trent. In 1983 the organization agreed to develop a new stand-alone integrated system. Most of the volume discusses capabilities and limitations of the two subsystems prior to the development and implementation of the new integrated system, which as of October 1986 consisted of circulation, cataloging, and public access facilities, with acquisitions under development and serials control and ILL in the planning stage.

The discussion of the cataloging and circulation systems is on a level of interest to the librarian user of the system. Many figures illustrate the results of various inquiries or transactions performed. The descriptions cannot be generalized to other systems, although system designers may find them of some use. The new integrated system, Libertas, is outlined in six pages following the more thorough explanation of the older system. Some evaluation is given in a short conclusion which states that the systems are well suited to the members' needs as a result of the involvement of library staff in the design of the system.   JoAnn V. Rogers

262. Held, Gilbert. **Communicating with the IBM PC Series: Concepts, Hardware, Software, Networking.** New York, John Wiley, 1988. 314p. illus. index. $34.95. LC 87-29595. ISBN 0-471-91667-6.

From the title, I expected a step-by-step primer for the novice PC user who wants to call up another computer. This book is much

more—a technical, yet very readable, treatment of the various methods of communications with the IBM PC. It provides the details of hardware and software connections and includes information on the theory and background of communications.

The treatment of topics is a little uneven. The eighty-page chapter on fundamental concepts jumps into the details of telephone companies, character coding, and other topics that are too tedious to appreciate before the PC is ever mentioned. The chapters on PC hardware are very detailed with diagrams of the computer case and even the locations of screws. The PC software discussion is also easily followed. Other sections are more technical, such as the discussion of packet-switching networks and local area networks (LAN). Some topics included are slightly out-of-date (e.g., acoustic couplers). The emphasis is mainly on IBM mainframe connections to PCs although most options are mentioned. The book is written from the perspective of a corporate PC manager rather than a hobbyist. And many PC users would not use information on packet-switching networks, hardware connection options, and LANs. I was surprised by the lack of discussion of bulletin boards which certainly will be the main use for many PC users new to communications.

The book seems free of errors (only a handful of typographical errors have crept in) and the author certainly has a thorough grasp of the topic. The figures and tables are direct, simple, and to the point. The lists of vendors and PC products are by no means exhaustive in this rapidly changing field.   John A. Jackman

263. Knightson, K. G., T. Knowles, and J. Larmouth. **Standards for Open Systems Interconnection.** New York, McGraw-Hill, 1988. 388p. illus. index. $39.95. LC 87-26068. ISBN 0-07-035119-8.

The concept of Open Systems Interconnection (OSI) has gained wide acceptance in recent years. This book is one of the first to clearly explain the principles and utility of the OSI standards. As such, it is an invaluable companion to the standards themselves.

The book is logically divided into five sections. The first part gives an introduction of standards organizations and the reference model. The second part deals with the interconnection of open systems, that is, the physical layer, the data link layer, the network layer, and the transport layer. The third part deals with communication between open systems, that is, the session layer, the presentation layer, and the application layer. The fourth part discusses specific services dealing with file transfer and job transfer. The last part touches on wider issues such as management, security, and conformance. The material stresses the underlying principles of the OSI system and presents these concepts in great detail. No special mathematical background is required to understand the book, but basic knowledge of computer networks is helpful to appreciate the breadth of the presentation.

This book is an indispensable reference for professionals in the computer network environment, particularly those involved in the design and implementation of OSI systems. It is also a useful guide for managers who wish to gain a basic understanding of OSI systems. Highly recommended for professional libraries.

John Y. Cheung

264.   Layzell, P. J., and P. Loucopoulos. **Systems Analysis and Development.** 2d ed. Bromley, England, Chartwell-Bratt, 1987. 232p. illus. bibliog. index. £8.50pa. ISBN 0-86238-156-8.

The complexity of contemporary information systems and the availability of new technologies give rise to new approaches in systems analysis. This textbook examines new developments and techniques. The first few chapters introduce information systems, describe more traditional approaches, and explain a case history which is used throughout the book. Since existing development methodologies are too numerous to discuss in one textbook, a classification scheme is presented as a way of approaching the topic on a conceptual level. Then, the text discusses specific techniques for selected methods. Chapters 3 through 5 cover various aspects of analysis including problem determination and fact gathering, system specification, and data analysis. Chapters 6 through 9 cover design topics including process, data and interface design, and automated system design. The final chapter addresses issues of system testing and control.

Technical descriptions of analysis techniques such as modeling, data flow diagrams, and data dictionaries are concise and clear. Illustrations and charts are used liberally to clarify the text. A lengthy list of references and a bibliography organized by name of systems development methodology point the reader in the direction of additional reading material. This text offers a well-written discussion of systems design techniques and issues.   Lynn Morgan

265.   Lorin, Harold. **Aspects of Distributed Computer Systems.** 2d ed. New York, John Wiley, 1988. 339p. bibliog. index. $42.95. LC 88-14905. ISBN 0-471-62589-2.

This book was written in order "to describe the state of the art and the underlying issues [of distributed computer systems] as they are currently understood." The work's sixteen chapters and appendix are divided into three parts. Part 1, "Overview and Examples," provides a general introduction to distributed computer systems with examples. Part 2, "Hardware and Software Issues in Distributed Systems," covers software systems, structures, interconnection, data and its distribution, distributed databases, and distributed functions. Part 3, "Organization and Economics," deals with the various costs associated with these systems and includes a discussion of a management style for distributed processing. The work is supplemented with a bibliography and a well-constructed index.

Lorin's book is well structured and clearly written. He has updated the examples used from the first edition. The contents will be useful both for the student learning about these systems for the first time and for the experienced manager who needs a cogent overview of this complex topic.   Robert H. Burger

266.   Modell, Martin E. **A Professional's Guide to Systems Analysis.** New York, McGraw-Hill, 1988. 317p. illus. index. (McGraw-Hill Software Engineering Series). $34.95. LC 88-8885. ISBN 0-07-042632-5.

Organizations grow and change in their functions and may change in direction or purpose. The art of systems analysis is applied to assure that the organization operates with maximum efficiency to achieve its objectives. From two decades of experience with a major consulting firm, the author has assembled a wealth of practical information on how to conduct a systems analysis. Based on lecture notes for an internal company training course, it is both a comprehensive introduction for the beginning analyst and a reference source for the more experienced.

Techniques for analysis are the same regardless of the level of automation in the organization or the extent to which data analysis is automated. Once the general purpose and function of the organization is understood, appropriate analysis techniques can be applied. The author describes data gathering techniques, including interviewing and modeling. Charts illustrating various modeling techniques are useful extensions of the text. Analyses of functions, processes, tasks, and data are described and means of validating results indicated.

Modell's approach to systems analysis is particularly useful to a wide audience because it is nontechnical; provides step-by-step assistance in conducting various analysis tasks; and most important, emphasizes the need to understand the organization being studied, why one enters the analysis process, and what its purpose is.

Ann E. Prentice

267. Reed, Daniel A., and Richard M. Fujimoto. **Multicomputer Networks: Message-Based Parallel Processing.** Cambridge, Mass., MIT Press, 1987. 380p. illus. index. (MIT Press Series in Scientific Computation). $40.00. LC 87-22833. ISBN 0-262-18129-0.

An excellent addition to the Scientific Computation series by MIT Press, this text provides a comprehensive and definitive treatment of a rapidly evolving area in computer architecture dealing with message-based multicomputer networks with no shared memory. Major architectural issues are presented in this monograph, including analytic models of interconnection networks, VLSI constraints and communication, communication paradigms and hardware support, multicomputer operating systems, applications in distributed simulation and partial differential equations, and performance analysis of commercial hypercubes. The presentation is void of architectural and analytic details. This provides for clear, easy reading. Emphasis is placed on presenting the crucial points on the conceptual level and richly illustrating them with realistic examples. Extensive references are given at the end of each chapter for further reading. This text is ideal as a reference guide for those interested in computer network processing and is highly recommended for acquisition in college and professional libraries. [R: Choice, July/Aug 88, p. 1722]

John Y. Cheung

268. Ronayne, John. **The Integrated Services Digital Network: From Concept to Application.** New York, John Wiley, 1988. 230p. illus. index. $34.95pa. ISBN 0-470-21025-7.

This book guides the user to technical bulletins and more comprehensive literature on Integrated Services Digital Networks (ISDN). The book is very well written and apparently flawlessly edited; the diagrams are clean, neat, and consistent throughout; and the delivery is insightful because it treats many issues from historical and political perspectives while concentrating on the technical details. Two strong points are the figures used extensively and the international flavor of the coverage, making the book more comprehensive and interesting. One should take time to study the figure because the text acts as glue to link the technical details presented in these figures. The references are clearly indicated throughout the work to allow the reader a rapid path to the technical bulletins

that complete the ISDN description. A nice glossary is included, a necessity for the "alphabet soup" that makes up the jargon of communications.

I highly recommend this book to anyone who is interested in the technical details of ISDN. It should be especially useful for the novice and also provides perspective and a handy technical reference for the hardware and software designer of ISDN.

John A. Jackman

269. Saunier, Fredric. **Marketing Strategies for the Online Industry.** Boston, G. K. Hall, 1988. 224p. illus. index. (Professional Librarian Series). $36.50; $28.50pa. LC 88-1227. ISBN 0-8161-1863-9; 0-8161-1879-5pa.

Technological "gee whiz" will no longer sell online information products and services. Managers must devote more attention to marketing if they hope to reap a profitable share of an increasingly competitive field. The author examines fifty samples of online industry advertising campaigns. The advertisements are shown, sometimes as they evolved, and then analyzed from the standpoint of explicit copy (what it says), implicit copy (images, styles, colors, etc.), and audience factors. The approach is both analytical and prescriptive. There is ample discussion of the theory and practice of marketing, buyer motivation, and advertising efficiency and creativity. The author explains what is right and wrong about the illustrative advertisements and gives specific advice about how to sell an online product or service. This book is intended for information managers who have a product or service to sell. Libraries and information agencies looking for better ways to serve their clients may find some useful advice here, but the thrust is on selling, not serving.

A. Neil Yerkey

270. Schatt, Stan. **Understanding Local Area Networks.** Indianapolis, Ind., Howard W. Sams, 1987. 276p. illus. bibliog. index. $17.95 pa. LC 87-62168. ISBN 0-672-27063-3.

Libraries are making increasing use of local area networks (LANs), both through participation in connecting units of an organization by LANs where the library is a part and through installation of a LAN within the library. This tutorial book offers an introduction to the technology and its application together with descriptions of LANs available from major vendors (IBM, Novell, ThreeCOM, AT&T, Corvus). Five of the eleven chapters deal with how LANs and the various hardware and software components work in general, and the remainder focus on specific system descriptions.

With one exception (Corvus), only networks of IBM and IBM-compatible microcomputers are considered.

The format of the book is well suited to self-study. The book has good definitions and descriptions of concepts and devices, making effective use of numerous illustrations. A glossary brings together many of the definitions especially helpful in interpreting the many acronyms, and the index allows quick location of specific topics in the text. Additional useful features include explanations of the advantages of networking versions of certain categories of software (word processing, spreadsheets, database management systems, accounting) and a detailed outline of RFP (request for proposal) development for acquiring a LAN. The brief bibliography lists little more than the documentation made available by various LAN vendors. The book emphasizes office applications, so the reader will have to look elsewhere for discussions of specific library applications. Nevertheless, many of the issues discussed, such as network security, standards, and gateways to other networks, are important in a library setting.

Linda C. Smith

271. Tanenbaum, Andrew S. **Computer Networks.** 2d ed. Englewood Cliffs, N.J., Prentice-Hall, 1988. 658p. illus. bibliog. index. $50.00. LC 88-16937. ISBN 0-13-162959-X.

The author has organized this second edition like the first. Its basic framework is the Open Systems Interconnection (OSI) reference model. Because so much has changed in the telecommunications field over the past decade, this new edition is, for all intents and purposes, a new book. The work is divided into ten chapters and an appendix. Chapter 1 deals in a general way with the uses of computer networks, network structures and architectures, the OSI reference model, services, standardization, and some sample networks (e.g., ARPANET, BITNET). Chapters 2 through 9 provide detailed coverage of the seven layers of the OSI reference model (chapters 2 and 3 cover the physical layer). Each of these chapters ends with a summary of the material and several problems directly related to the concepts introduced. Chapter 10 presents an annotated bibliography of works that could be used in obtaining more detailed information about the material appearing in chapters 1 through 9. The appendix introduces the reader to queueing theory and its applications. An index provides adequate access to the book's contents.

This excellent work would be appropriate for use as a textbook for students in computer, information, or library science or as a reference

guide for the experienced professional. The text, written in a clear, no-nonsense style, is well illustrated with charts, diagrams, tables, and examples of protocol algorithms. Any inquisitive reader, having a knowledge of high school algebra, will find the book comprehensible and complete.

Robert H. Burger

272. Weinberg, Gerald M. **Rethinking Systems Analysis & Design.** New York, Dorset House, 1988. 193p. illus. bibliog. index. $26.50pa. LC 88-5083. ISBN 0-932633-08-0.

Systems analysis and design is a carefully structured approach to the review of existing systems and the design of more efficient systems. Weinberg, who has written widely on this subject, cautions the reader that in addition to the often-described structured approach to systems analysis and design there are numerous nonquantifiable variables that must be considered. He looks at the preparation of the systems person and calls that individual a generalist who specializes in systems. This person can be part of any discipline, an individual whose skills and experience go far beyond academic preparation as a systems analyst. Using fables, anecdotes, and other attention-getting techniques he urges the analyst to be a careful observer of how the organization really works, to look for the right question, and to listen to what people say. Considerable attention is given to exploring the way systems analysts think and to urging that they come to their task with an open mind, examine what an organization is, how it behaves, and how it reached its current status before making changes.

The presentation is light and often humorous with a style of writing unusual to this topic. Advice derived from experience is given to the analyst and to those contemplating hiring one. It is a useful supplement to texts that present systems analysis and design as a rigid formula for achieving the right answer. There is a brief annotated bibliography.

Ann E. Prentice

273. Weinberg, Gerald M., and Daniela Weinberg. **General Principles of Systems Design.** New York, Dorset House, 1988. 353p. illus. bibliog. index. $27.00pa. LC 88-3904. ISBN 0-932633-07-2.

Most books about systems design are guides to a methodology with examples of applications. This work's much broader approach, written by an anthropologist and a computing expert, provides a set of general principles and does not emphasize methodology. The authors combine the views of their disciplines and look at larger issues such as the interplay between systems and people, the abstract and concrete, and the theoretical and practical. Principles of systems design are explained in terms of their relevance to science and social science. Questions for further research are posed in various settings from artificial intelligence, to zoology, to economics. Because of the wide range of applications of systems theory, this publication could be used as a textbook for use in a variety of courses. Students in any environment would learn underlying principles that apply to all aspects of our world. At times the multiple tracks of mathematics, social sciences, and systems theory become very complex and require careful reading and rereading.

The authors' style is light and sometimes humorous with a large number of quotations from literature (especially from Lewis Carroll's *Alice* books which the authors suggest as recommended reading). Never dull, sometimes very complex, the book bears evidence of a global view in which systems design is a means of organizing ideas, structures, things, and experience. The bibliography representing many disciplines and many views expands on the text.

Ann E. Prentice

Video Display Terminals

274. Galitz, Wilbert O. **Handbook of Screen Format Design.** 3d ed. Wellesley, Mass., QED Information Sciences, 1988. 307p. illus. bibliog. $39.95. LC 88-15849. ISBN 0-89435-258-X.

The third edition of Galitz's handbook is itself a model of good design and clear writing. Because he recognizes that "the most common communication bridge between a person and a computer system is a visual display terminal," his book's appropriate purpose is to "assist a designer in developing an effective screen interface between a program and its users." He accomplishes this modestly stated goal in thirteen information-packed chapters.

Galitz begins by focusing on the user and the physical and psychological factors that impede optimum use of computer systems. After considering characteristics of any computer system that affect the user, he covers several types of screens (e.g., data-entry, inquiry, multipurpose, question-and-answer, and menu), color-in-screen design, graphics, and source documents, and concludes with a chapter on screen design steps. A ten-page list of references provides access to the research that stands behind the author's crisply stated design principles.

The writing is simple and direct; principles are stated clearly, followed by justification for

them. Not only should Galitz's handbook be on the reference shelf of anyone who designs a computer screen display, it could also be useful for those who are concerned about human factors in efficient information processing.

Robert H. Burger

275. Scalet, Elizabeth A. **VDT Health and Safety: Issues and Solutions.** Lawrence, Kans., Ergosyst, 1987. 143p. illus. index. $35.00. LC 87-12756. ISBN 0-916313-13-1.

VODS — video operator distress syndrome — has been of major concern to industry and business for several years. Increasingly, however, libraries have had to address this concern, especially as the pace of automation increases. *VDT Health and Safety* is an excellent source book answering any conceivable question that might arise.

The book starts with an overview of health concerns, followed by chapters on VDTs and radiation, eyes and vision, strain and injury, stress, pregnancy and reproduction, and policy and regulation issues. The chapters on radiation and eyes and vision are particulary good, explaining the problems and concerns simply, and at the same time destroying many of the fallacies that float around concerning VDTs and what you can "catch" from them. The chapter on strain and injury contains excellent guidelines for setting up workstations. It includes some very well-laid-out diagrams.

Each chapter has a further reading section which is annotated. There is a useful glossary at the end of the book.

Linda Main

CONSERVATION AND PRESERVATION

276. Banks, Joyce M. **Guidelines for Preventive Conservation. Directives Régissant la Conservation Préventive.** rev. ed. Ottawa, National Library of Canada, 1987. 45p. $3.50pa.; $4.20 pa. (U.S.). ISBN 0-660-53823-7.

The second edition of conservation guidelines prepared for Canadian federal government libraries aims to help librarians develop local conservation policies, plan in-house conservation programs, and train staff in proper handling of materials. The book also provides a model policy for preventive conservation that can be adapted for local use. The book starts with a definition and eight principles of preventive conservation. Each principle is then expanded upon with prescriptives/recommendations, published standards if available, and recommended reading. Both American (ANSI) and Canadian standards are included. The last section presents a model preservation policy that incorporates many of the earlier recommendations. The book includes the usual directives on environment, storage, and lighting, but it also deals with compact shelving, book supports, microform housing, disasters, and other topics. Recommendations are quite specific, especially with regard to the handling of books. This is a well-organized volume. The bibliographies contain items published through 1986. Both text and bibliographies appear in English and French. Regrettably, there is no index. but the table of contents serves to guide the reader to the appropriate section. Although not a substitute for more comprehensive treatments of conservation such as Susan Swartzburg's *Conservation in the Library: A Handbook of Use and Care of Traditional and Nontraditional Materials* (Greenwood Press, 1983), it is a good addition to conservation collections. Because of its low cost and brevity, it could be used with library staff in a conservation awareness program. [R: CLJ, Oct 88, pp. 335-36]

Linda Keir Simons

277. Cunha, George Martin. **Mass Deacidification for Libraries.** Chicago, American Library Association, 1987. 1v. (various paging). illus. bibliog. index. (Library Technology Reports, Vol. 23, No. 3). $45.00pa.

This report, carefully documented, follows the tradition of excellence established by the Library Technology Reports series. Cunha, an authority in the field of preservation and conservation, presents a study on mass deacidification and the development of methods, with the costs and safety. He investigates at length two processes: DEZ from the Library of Congress and the WEI T'O System from the Canadian Library. The Canadian process used in the National Library and the Public Archives is based on magnesium alkoxides and alkoxy carbonates dissolved in mixtures of methanol and freons. The DEZ process (diethyl zinc) used by the Library of Congress, claims to be a complete and safe process for books. It is accomplished in three phases: preconditioning, permeation, and postconditioning. Five thousand books can be processed in one cycle for fifty to fifty-five hours at the cost of two to three dollars per book. The WEI T'O System requires screening of books before the treatment and a postdeacidification period and the unit cost is in the range of $3.95 to $6.60 per volume.

There is a lack of information on the impact of this process on library operations (e.g., staff, budget, etc.). Both systems presented in this report are good, and both have advantages

and shortcomings. Only experience can prove their efficiency, safety, and real costs.

Camille Côté

278. England, Claire, and Karen Evans. **Disaster Management for Libraries: Planning and Process.** Ottawa, Canadian Library Association, 1988. 207p. bibliog. index. $20.00pa. ISBN 0-88802-197-6.

The Canadian Library Association has published an excellent manual on all aspects of disaster preparedness. The text goes beyond its title topic to deal with the problems of slow paper destruction resulting from bad environmental conditions and acidic materials. This well-organized book is divided into three parts. The first gives a short history of library disasters in Canada and discusses organizational issues in disaster planning, including developing a disaster manual, organizing staff, and purchasing insurance for library collections. The second section gives advice to follow when faced with a disaster resulting from fire or floods. A separate chapter gives directions for working with fungicides and other chemicals used in preservation and salvage work. The third section of the book discusses the "quiet disaster," ongoing decay of library materials. In this section the authors argue persuasively that preservation and disaster preparedness are two parts of the larger field of collection management. Its chapters deal with managing preservation, environmental preservation of collections, and an excellent literature review. The book concludes with a fire safety self-inspection form, a form for a directory of preservation personnel, a bibliography, and an index.

This book could be used by anyone interested in establishing and maintaining programs of library disaster preparedness and preservation. Clearly, the authors have read widely and selected well for their bibliography. They have succeeded in synthesizing today's research and practice into a useful manual for administrators and conservators alike. [R: CLJ, Dec 88, p. 398; LJ, 1 Sept 88, p. 148]   Linda Keir Simons

279. Fox, Lisa L., comp. **A Core Collection in Preservation.** Chicago, Resources and Technical Services Division, American Library Association, 1988. 15p. $5.00pa. LC 88-12102. ISBN 0-8389-7224-1.

This useful work lists and annotates books, journal articles, government reports, and audiovisuals dealing with materials preservation which "have been judged accurate, useful, and especially significant" by members of the Preservation of Library Materials Section of ALA's

Resources and Technical Services Division. Only English-language works are included, and highly technical works have been excluded. Pricing and acquisition information is given for all but a few items, although that information will date quickly. The bibliography is divided into nine sections. The general works section is followed by works on paper and the environment, repair and conservation treatments, library binding, microfilming and copying, nontextual materials, emergency preparedness, and planning and organization. The last section lists serial publications of interest to conservators.

The committee has made an excellent selection of basic materials including works by such noted experts as Pamela Darling, Carolyn Clark Morrow, George Cunha, Susan Swartzburg, and Peter Waters. The bibliography draws from archival and museum publications where appropriate, and includes materials from Canada and other countries. Annotations are brief but helpful. A library wishing to start or to expand its preservation collection will find this book immensely useful. It will also be of help to librarians and others wishing to do some basic reading in either the general field of conservation or in one of the specific areas such as emergency preparedness.   Linda Keir Simons

280.   Palmer, R. E., ed. **Preserving the Word: The Library Association Conference Proceedings, Harrogate 1986.** London, Library Association; distr., Chicago, American Library Association, 1987. 147p. $27.50pa. ISBN 0-85365-847-1.

The twenty papers collected here were presented at the 1986 Library Association Conference at Harrogate and they address the broad topic of preservation and conservation of library material. Most of the experts are from institutions in Great Britain and the examples and points of view are predominantly British, although the presence of Americans Sandy Dolnick, Joseph W. Price, and David Stam on the program does bring an international flavor to the proceedings. Questions about what should be preserved, how, and at what cost are examined from the points of view of academic, public, and special libraries and from the unique positions of the national libraries of England, Scotland, and Wales. Experts also discuss different approaches to protecting, repairing, and replacing library material, and the education of those involved in preservation and conservation activities is also discussed. Other papers are on fund raising, paper conservation, publishers' bindings, storage options, and cooperation among libraries. There are two historical articles on lessons learned from the flood in Florence,

Italy, in 1966. The essays vary in length, detail, and documentation, but together they provide a useful overview of the problem and what is being done about it in Great Britain. [R: LAR, 16 May 88, p. 294; RLR, Aug 88, pp. 204-5]
                Dean H. Keller

281.   **Preservation Education Directory.** 5th ed. Susan G. Swartzburg, comp. Chicago, Resources and Technical Services Division, American Library Association, 1988. 30p. index. $5.00 pa.

The main body of this work, now in its fifth edition, lists preservation programs and courses offered at accredited library schools in the United States and Canada and preservation components in other library school courses. The only preservation degree program listed is at Columbia University, where students may earn either an M.S.L.S. or an advanced certificate in preservation. Both programs are described. Many library schools now offer individual courses in preservation. Schools are listed alphabetically by name, and each entry describes the course content and, usually, the number of course credits given. Schools which incorporate preservation information into other courses, such as rare books, history of books and printing, and collection management, are also listed with briefer entries. A second section of the book lists institutes and associations in North America which offer courses or workshops on preservation. Section 3 describes five conservation training programs for conservators who perform hands-on restoration work. Section 4 tells the reader how to acquire information about programs abroad from the International Centre for the Study of the Preservation and the Restoration of Cultural Property in Rome. It is followed by a geographic index for the institutions in the United States and Canada. This book will be useful to individuals who wish to study preservation management or conservation techniques. And since it lists which library schools in each state offer preservation courses, it can also help library administrators recruit preservation/conservation specialists for their staffs. It should be available to both library staff and patrons.   Linda Keir Simons

282.   **Preservation Planning Project Study Team Final Report.** Pittsburgh, Pa., University of Pittsburgh; distr., Washington, D.C., Association of Research Libraries, 1987. 98p. $15.00 (unbound).

This is the final report of a fourteen-month study undertaken by the University of Pittsburgh Libraries to develop a five-year preservation plan. The study team was broken into five task forces, which surveyed and reported on the following conservation areas: condition of the collections, environmental conditions, organization of the preservation process, resources/ instruction (education of staff), and disaster planning. Most of this volume deals with the summary reports of these task forces as well as an executive summary. The reports are necessarily quite specific to the University of Pittsburgh, and another library would not adopt the recommendations without a study of local conditions. Nor is the book a manual of preservation practice. Its value lies in the appendices, which contain the charges to the study team as a whole and to each task force. A library administrator wanting to undertake a similar study could adapt the specific charges easily. Not all libraries have the personnel resources that Pittsburgh has, but even smaller institutions could use some of the ideas on organization and objectives. The volume is stapled with paper covers and will have to be protected if it goes into any collection except that of a private office. [R: JAL, Sept 88, p. 269]

Linda Keir Simons

COPYRIGHT

283. Hébert, Françoise. **Photocopying in Canadian Libraries: Report of a National Study. La Photocopie dans les Bibliothèques Canadiennes.** Ottawa, Canadian Library Association, 1987. 75p. $55.00pa. ISBN 0-88802-233-6.

This study of photocopying practices in Canadian libraries was conducted to "help librarians to make informed judgements about photocopying under the Copyright Act, to negotiate and deal effectively with reprography collectives, and to better represent the interests of libraries and library patrons at a time when legislation regarding photocopying is being revised in Canada." The investigators sent questionnaires and log sheets to a national sampling of academic, public, and special libraries inquiring what was being photocopied and for what purposes. The findings give an interesting picture of library practice: overall, patrons made 41 percent of all copies while staff made 59 percent; 54 percent of exposures were from published works and of these 23 percent were from books (the rest from periodicals, newspapers, etc.). Only 2 percent of the exposures were from published works in the public domain. Half of the published works copied were from U.S. sources while 34 percent were Canadian. While this study cannot determine precisely how much photocopying falls under fair usage and how

much would be liable for payment to a reprography collective, it does present the first well-documented indication of the extent of photocopying in libraries. Most Canadian libraries will find this study useful, and many American libraries will be interested also.

Adele M. Fasick

284.   Henn, Harry G. **Copyright Law: A Practitioner's Guide.** 2d ed. New York, Practising Law Institute, 1988. 844p. illus. bibliog. index. $85.00. LC 87-63438.

As the most comprehensive analysis of the Copyright Act of 1976 and in addition to explaining the act section by section, the author, an expert in copyright, trademark, and patent law, increases the reference value of his book by including important documents for easy access: the copyright laws of 1976 and 1906, rules and regulations (including the CONTU guidelines), Copyright Office forms and circulars, and congressional committee reports. The guide ends with a good bibliography, which is an expanded and updated version of the one included in the first edition of this guide, published in 1979 and entitled "Copyright Primer." Important new chapters in this latest edition are "Semiconductor Chip Products" and "Satellite Cable Programming." An outstanding reference feature is its use as a citator, enabling users to locate relevant court cases and additional federal legislation, enacted and proposed. The author's explanations of legalities are easily understood; his comments given in extended footnotes serve to clarify difficult problems and often contain practical examples.

The guide is beautifully printed, and an attractive format and complete table of contents serve to simplify access to information. The index is complete. Librarians may be disappointed not to find included in the appendices examples of specific library policies regarding copyright. An excellent compilation of these may be found in the Association of Research Library's *University Copyright Policies in ARL Libraries* (1987). Mary H. Reed's *The Copyright Primer for Librarians and Educators* (American Library Association, 1987) contains many more explanations relevant to libraries. Henn's guide is intended for all practitioners, including lawyers, and is a most useful guide to include in academic and special library collections.

Milton H. Crouch

285.   **Intellectual Property Rights in an Electronic Age. Proceedings of the Library of Congress Network Advisory Committee Meeting April 22-24, 1987.** Washington, D.C., Cataloging Distribution Service, Library of Congress,

1987. 66p. (Network Planning Paper, No. 16). $7.50pa. LC 87-600457. ISBN 0-8444-0592-2.

As the title indicates, this book contains the proceedings of an April 1987 meeting of the Library of Congress Network Advisory Committee. As such, it comes complete with a copy of the meeting's agenda, a list of attendees, a summary of the committee's business session, and the text of five papers presented at the meeting, each of which in some way addresses the question of the ability of copyright law to adapt to emerging information technologies.

The heart of the book is the five papers, which include (1) "The OTA Report on Intellectual Property Rights," by Linda Garcia; (2) "The End of Copyright," by Robert J. Kost; (3) "The Copyright Law: Can It Wrap Itself around the New Technologies?" by Ralph Oman; (4) "Current Bibliographic Database Ownership Issues and the Protection of Non-Traditional Formats—One User's Point of View," by W. David Laird; and (5) "ACS Chemicals Journals Online: Is It Being Downloaded, Do We Care?" by John A. Hearty and Barbara F. Polansky. There is nothing startling in any of these papers, but taken together the papers do competently present a summary of the dilemma that the copyright law now faces. As such, the book is worthy of attention as a handy reference to explain this public policy issue. [R: LAR, 14 Oct 88, p. 598]　　　Michael Rogers Rubin

286.　Sinofsky, Esther R. **A Copyright Primer for Educational and Industrial Media Producers.** Friday Harbor, Wash., Copyright Information Services, 1988. 236p. bibliog. index. (Copyright Information Bulletin, No. 4). $29.95. LC 87-15423. ISBN 0-914143-12-3.

A Copyright Primer is intended as an introduction to copyright issues for "educators, industrial trainers, and other amateur and small producers, including producers of programs for local-access cable TV channels" (p. xi). Part 1 of the book discusses key sections of the U.S. Copyright Act, including what types of works are copyrightable; who owns copyright; fair use and other exemptions; and copyright notices, deposit, and registration requirements. Part 2 provides an overview of selected production issues, including a checklist of basic legal procedures for producing copyrightable materials; protecting scripts, titles, and characters; copyrighting dramatic and visual works; ownership rights in printed materials, music, photographs, and other visual arts; and public domain materials.

As is the case with so many works dealing with copyright, the appendices make up a substantial portion of the work. The appendices include reproductions of the fair use guidelines for print materials, music, and off-air taping; several Copyright Office circulars; and selected Copyright Office regulations. Readers should pay close attention to Sinofsky's disclaimer that her opinions do not constitute legal advice. She ably meets her stated goal of providing readers "a glimmer of some of the key copyright issues you should encounter during a production" (p. xi), and wisely suggests that producers discuss these matters with an attorney. In view of the complex nature of copyright law and the author's purpose of providing only an introduction to copyright issues affecting media producers, the cautious reader will heed her suggestion.

This work is recommended for libraries in institutions offering media services support, as well as for media producers. Also recommended for such libraries are Sinofsky's *Off-Air Videotaping in Education* (R. R. Bowker, 1984), *Modern Copyright Fundamentals*, by Weil and Polansky (Van Nostrand Reinhold, 1985), and *The Copyright Primer for Librarians and Educators* (American Library Association, 1987). [R: LJ, 15 Sept 88, p. 75]

James S. Heller

287.　**University Copyright Policies in ARL Libraries.** Washington, D.C., Association of Research Libraries, 1987. 118p. illus. bibliog. (SPEC Kit, No. 138). $20.00pa.

The author has compiled a useful collection of copyright policies and related documents issued by several universities. They include policies for copying journal articles for class distribution, performance rights (for music and audiovisual works), library photocopying, interlibrary loan, etc. The volume also includes three policies reserving legal rights to the university for computer programs and other items produced by faculty and staff. Included are several items that are not policies, but which are appropriate to the book. These include copyright information pamphlets distributed to faculty, purchase orders for nonprint media that include the right to duplicate the product, and so forth.

This collection of useful documents is offered without commentary. It is recommended for university and college libraries, but should be used in conjunction with a slightly older work, Charles W. Vlcek's *Copyright Policy Development: A Resource Book for Educators* (Copyright Information Services, 1987). Vlcek offers criteria and procedures for preparing copyright policies, plus six outstanding school and university copyright policies. [R: JAL, Mar 88, p. 50]　　　Jerome K. Miller

DATA COMMUNICATION

288. Binkowski, Edward. **Satellite Information Systems.** Boston, G. K. Hall, 1988. 213p. bibliog. index. (Professional Librarian Series). $38.50; $29.95pa. LC 88-16455. ISBN 0-8161-1856-6; 0-8161-1880-9pa.

Whenever we make a telephone call, watch television, or access various information networks, chances are excellent that satellite information systems are involved. These "interconnected systems of artificial satellites in earth's orbit that gather, receive, process, and transmit data and communication for use on the surface" have, in the past thirty years, become essential to daily life. The author provides a brief overview of the development of satellites from both a technological and an economic viewpoint. In the United States the involvement of various interests, including the military, the Federal Communications Commission, AT&T, and other commercial groups has resulted in a complex mix of regulations, ownership, and access to the present systems.

The author's descriptions of the economic, technical, and political issues provide a cogent picture of the current state of satellite systems. User issues such as deregulation of access, privacy of communication, speed of technology, and confusion over public and private access are explored. Issues for those developing and operating systems include cost, the difficulty of putting satellites in orbit, and uncertain political climates. Global issues include the limited number of prime locations for satellites, the need to network among systems, and the increasing need to explore national interests and their relation to international interests. Directories of publications and associations relevant to this new and rapidly evolving subject are provided, as is a bibliography arranged by format: books, periodicals, newspapers, and documents. This is an excellent place for the intelligent consumer to become aware of the state and status of satellite information systems.

Ann E. Prentice

289. Chorafas, Dimitris N. **Electronic Document Handling: The New Communications Architecture.** Princeton, N.J., Petrocelli Books, 1987. 253p. illus. index. $24.95pa. LC 86-30428. ISBN 0-89433-281-3.

This book deals with the complex and timely topic of designing networks and large computer systems that provide the most efficient hardware and software for exchanging and processing information. The author discusses data processing in the context of national as well as international systems; information in the form of data, text, graphics, image, and voice; and architectures including single workstations, local area networks, and large-scale timesharing systems. Issues such as system compatibility, open systems, file transfer protocols, and database standards are all discussed.

The author has a broad knowledge of a wide variety of international standards and practices. He includes many charts, tables, graphics, and figures to illustrate and supplement the text. He writes clearly and succinctly. The book is preceded by a good table of contents and followed by an adequate index. A list of acronyms is also included at the end.

This book is recommended for anyone involved in design aspects of microcomputer utilization in any institution. It is equally recommended for libraries serving such people.

James Rice

290. Martin, James, with Joe Leben. **Principles of Data Communication.** Englewood Cliffs, N.J., Prentice-Hall, 1988. 346p. illus. maps. index. $33.00. LC 87-7289. ISBN 0-13-709891-X.

Although written as a technical book "intended for programmers, analysts, managers, and telecommunications staff members who require an introduction to data communication facilities," a programming background is not required and only a general understanding of data processing fundamentals is assumed. Many illustrations, graphs, and charts make for easy readability.

This book is a worthy addition to Martin's line of computer-related texts. The first edition was published in 1972 and given the considerable technological change since that date, a revised work is certainly overdue. The book is divided into five major parts, with an additional prologue explaining computer architectures and terminology and an epilogue focusing on Integrated Services Digital Network (ISDN) technology. Part 1 consists of three chapters on communication channels, transmission facilities, and the telecommunications industry. Part 2 includes chapters on terminal equipment, modems and line drivers, and line control equipment. Part 3 deals with controlling transmission, data link protocols, access methods and teleprocessing monitors, and personal computers. Part 4 focuses on the Open Systems Interconnection (OSI) model, IBM's systems network architecture, public data networks and information utilities, and local area networks (LANs). Finally, part 5 considers application design, user interface design, response time requirements, and network design. An excellent glossary and index complete the work.

This book is must reading for those persons involved with selecting and implementing library automation systems. It will make communication with data processing people and vendors *much* easier!

Darlene E. Weingand

291. Zureik, Elia, and Dianne Hartling. **The Social Context of the New Information and Communication Technologies: A Bibliography.** New York, Peter Lang, 1987. 310p. (American University Studies. Series XV: Communications, Vol. 2). $35.00. LC 87-3450. ISBN 0-8204-0413-6.

In this bibliography the editors have attempted to provide a major tool for bibliographic control of the rapidly expanding literature on the social context of information and communications technology. No one can fault them for lack of ambition nor the importance of their topic. Indeed, the social consequences of the new information and communications technologies may well turn out to be of far greater significance than any of the technologies themselves. The editors devised eighty codes to classify the more than six thousand entries in this book, which are from an electronic database at Queen's University.

Entries are arranged alphabetically by author, with these one- to two-letter codes preceding them. Codes cover such topics as artificial intelligence; computer-assisted design and manufacturing; copyright and patenting; computer crime; office, home, and factory work; robotics; unions; transborder data flow and funds transfer; women; and national distinctions (e.g., Canada, Western Europe, Third World). Entries may be assigned more than one code although the majority have only one or two.

Criticisms of this bibliography relate to organization, entry contents, and the coding system. Organization by author, while a common arrangement, does not seem practical given the lack of subject or category index. If one wanted all citations on artificial intelligence, one would have to manually search every single page of the book. A second criticism relates to the lack of annotations for entries. While other bibliographic data are complete, the lack of content summary for citations seems a fairly serious omission. This would, in fact, seem to be what could have distinguished this work from any other mere listing of bibliographic citations.

Finally, the subject access which the editors attempt is disappointing on several counts. First, the categories are often too broad to be helpful in locating specific information. For example, banking, insurance, financial institutions, and commerce are all lumped together. Privacy (freedom, data protection, surveillance, etc.) comes before patents in the code list, which is confusing, and while one assumes this includes privacy of information, this is not indicated. Some codes, such as that for science fiction, seem out of place in the list, and a final criticism relates to the fact that science fiction (its code is HO, which is used for two entirely different subjects) is entirely out of order alphabetically and the code S which is used in the bibliography appears nowhere in the coding list. One could assume, since three citations by noted science fiction writer Arthur C. Clarke on page 61 have this S designation, that it is perhaps an error and should be something else, but one is not sure. Perhaps the category was an afterthought.

In summary, if one can overlook the overly broad categories, the inefficient organization, and the fact that most citations fall within a narrow range of years (mid- to late 1970s up to the early 1980s), one could find this bibliography useful. However, online searching by keywords or descriptors would probably be much quicker and more expedient and result in a more current bibliography for those who need references on the social implications of the new technologies. One must still applaud the efforts of these editors, because any large-scale bibliography is a tremendous amount of work and adds to bibliographic control of important topics such as this.

Carol Truett

EDUCATION AND TRAINING

292. **ALISE Library and Information Science Education Statistical Report 1988.** Timothy W. Sineath, ed. Sarasota, Fla., Association for Library and Information Science Education, 1988. 252p. $30.00pa. ISSN 0739-506X.

This is ALISE's ninth annual compilation of statistics relating to North American library schools, their faculty, students, curricula, financial situation, and continuing education activities. Because a major purpose is to create a longitudinal database, substantial comparability of data is maintained from year to year. In addition to the five subject sections, a "Summary and Comparative Analysis" outlines notable trends and conditions. Because sections are prepared by different authors, they differ in approach, comprehensiveness, and presentation. Data are supplied by ALISE-member schools responding to questionnaires. Respondents this year included most ALA-accredited programs and some non-ALA programs (for which data are charted separately). There is much information presented, but there is much information not covered. Under "Faculty," the number, age, sex, and salary of full-time faculty are covered, but not specializations. Adjunct faculty are simply enumerated. Under "Curriculum," total hours required for degrees is given, but not distribution among subjects. Courses added or discontinued by schools are listed, but there is no way to determine the resulting curricula. Under "Students," there is enrollment information about full and part-time students, divided by degree pursued, sex, ethnic and national origins, but nothing about the background and aspirations or students.

The report is a valuable and tantalizing source of information, focused on library schools in an administrative sense. To gain a more complete picture of education for librarianship, the reader must consult additional information sources, such as the directory issue of the *Journal of Education for Library and Information Science*, library school catalogs, and a 1988 study of the collective library-school student body, preliminarily reported in *Librarians for the New Millenium* (American Library Association, 1988).   Janet Swan Hill

293.   Chirgwin, F. John, and Phyllis Oldfield. **The Library Assistant's Manual.** 3d ed. London, Clive Bingley/Library Association; distr., Chicago, American Library Association, 1988. 118p. illus. maps. bibliog. index. $18.00. ISBN 0-85157-420-3.

This is a very British book. The reference tools described are British, the laws those of the United Kingdom, and only British books are cited in the bibliography. Because of this, it may have limited use outside the British Isles, particularly for the audience to whom the authors have directed it: library assistants, "those engaged upon in-service training courses, and people contemplating a career in libraries," and those seeking "a simple introduction to libraries and librarianship."

This work is not suitable for use in the education of library technicians for two reasons. First, North American library technicians are not the counterparts of British library assistants. Second, an "introduction to libraries and librarianship" in 112 pages is too brief an overview of general library procedures to be useful in library technician programs. However, the book does have value for non-British readers as an introduction to British libraries and librarianship.

The work originally "arose out of a course preparing candidates for the Library and Information Assistant's Certificate of the City and Guilds of London Institute." This genesis is reflected in the list of assignments at the end of each chapter. This third edition has been revised and updated and some older material deleted. New sections on electronic mail, data protection, the Open College, and the General Certificate of Secondary Education have been added.

Jean Weihs

294.   Moen, William E., and Kathleen M. Heim, eds. **Librarians for the New Millennium.** Chicago, Office of Library Personnel Resources, American Library Association, 1988. 109p. $10.00pa. ISBN 0-8389-7259-4.

This volume is a compilation of papers addressing some of the problems and issues (e.g., salary, working conditions, attitudes, etc.) associated with the recruitment of library personnel. Prepared by the ALA Office for Library Personnel Resources Advisory Committee, the papers were presented at an invitational preconference held in New Orleans, July 1988. Personnel shortages, both present and projected, are discussed in order to remind those now in the profession that recruitment of capable people to the field should be an ever present concern for information professionals at all levels.

The papers focus on recruitment by specialization (e.g., cataloging, science librarianship, etc.), library type (e.g., academic, school, or special), and population (e.g., minorities). Also discussed is an anticipated shortage of library school entrants. A 1988 ALA survey of library student attitudes, featured in the final paper, gives clues to both the interests and expectations of those who are preparing to enter the profession and thereby provides a framework for future planning and profiling.

The papers, written by library practitioners and library educators, are informative, well written, and generously documented.

Dianne Brinkley Catlett

295.   Paris, Marion. **Library School Closings: Four Case Studies.** Metuchen, N.J., Scarecrow, 1988. 168p. bibliog. index. $20.00. LC 88-7276. ISBN 0-8108-2130-3.

Twelve graduate library programs ceased operations in the decade prior to the author's study. Given new occupation categories in information services, and at least the potential for all library education programs to enlarge "their frame of reference," Paris seeks to answer the question "Why?" Using the case study approach, the author investigated the circumstances which led to closings at four universities. For the sake of anonymity, they were designated as Alpha University, the University of Beta, Gamma University, and the University of Delta. Two were public and two were private universities.

Alpha faculty members in mathematics, computer science, and business were apparently offended at the intent of the library school to become the College of Information Management. Beta faculty in the School of Business determined that library education courses encroached upon their turf in management information systems. Only at Beta was loss of accreditation an issue. Nor did reaccreditation help matters. Financial difficulties were a concern at all four universities and were the initial cause for scrutiny, but appear not to have been the underlying cause for closings. Library school executives and faculty were viewed as being socially and academically isolated from their peers. Executives lacked credibility with university administrators and thus lacked the ability to alter misconceptions. As the universities redefined their missions or restructured course and program offerings, the closings were political decisions and accomplished with relative ease. Originally the author's doctoral dissertation, this book should be read by all library school faculty and administrators. [R: JAL, Nov 88, pp. 314-15; LJ, 15 Sept 88, p. 64; WLB, Oct 88, p. 95]   Robert M. Ballard

INDEXING AND ABSTRACTING

296. Rowley, Jennifer E. **Abstracting and Indexing.** 2d ed. London, Clive Bingley/Library Association; distr., Chicago, American Library Association, 1988. 181p. illus. bibliog. index. $27.50. ISBN 0-85157-411-4.

First published in 1982, this work by Jennifer Rowley, senior lecturer in information technology at the Department of Library and Information Studies, Manchester Polytechnic, has been updated for students of library and information science, including new chapters on the role of computers and natural language indexing. The actual processes of abstracting and indexing are given little attention, reflecting the little we really know about these intellectual processes. The bulk (and the strength) of the book is an overview of the context and purpose of indexing and abstracting, the systems and approaches used by indexing and abstracting services, and underlying theoretical concerns. Back of the book indexing is hardly mentioned, but issues such as specificity, exhaustivity, and especially vocabulary control are given appropriate attention. String indexing per se is largely ignored, but PRECIS, a prominent example, is described in some detail. Descriptions and

explanations are generally clear and straightforward, but some needed illustrations are lacking. Errors are rare, but the statement "in contrast to specificity, exhaustivity increases precision at the cost of recall" (p. 56) is a particularly glaring one. The same paragraph goes on to say, quite properly, that "recall is improved by high exhaustivity," clearly a contradiction to the previous statement.

Nevertheless, this is a good overview of the role of indexing and abstracting in information retrieval and the various approaches that may be taken.

James D. Anderson

INFORMATION SCIENCE

General Works

297. Cawkell, A. E., ed. **Evolution of an Information Society.** London, Aslib; distr., Medford, N.J., Learned Information, 1987. 289p. illus. $59.00. ISBN 0-85142-211-X.

The social and human elements of the information age are often lost among the technological developments of bigger and faster machines that store, calculate, and transmit information. This anthology of classic articles that have shaped our information society gives equal attention to both. The distribution of information among rich and poor countries, national differences in approaching solutions to information questions, the implications of an information economy, and the future of our information society are among the issues discussed. On the technology side, articles from H. G. Well's 1937 proposal for a world encyclopedia and a world brain, and Shannon's theory of communication to current innovations in information transmission describe the technical, while raising human and social issues. A final article by Bodin on the social implications of intelligent machines rounds out the anthology.

The emphasis is on U.S. and U.S. writers, and the major themes are social. Claims that technology is changing our world are reviewed over a fifty-year span of articles and it is possible to see trends and to place in context the implications of the latest technological breakthrough. The emphasis of the articles, all required reading for anyone who would understand the times in which we live, is on society and the role of technology in society. It is required reading not just for those concerned with technology but also for those of us wishing to survive and to benefit from it.

Ann E. Prentice

298. Debons, Anthony, Esther Horne, and Scott Cronenweth. **Information Science: An Integrated View.** Boston, G. K. Hall, 1988. 172p. illus. index. (Professional Librarian Series). $38.50; $29.50pa. LC 88-12666. ISBN 0-8161-1857-4; 0-8161-1877-9pa.

An introductory text to information science emphasizing a systems perspective and the interdisciplinary character of the field, the stated objective of the book is to explore the nature of information and the laws and principles that govern these systems. The text covers information professionals, their work and education, the tools and methods of the discipline, systems theory, the technology of information systems, and the technology of communications systems. Information system synthesis is discussed outlining different approaches or models to the interface between components of information systems, including human components. A chapter on social and moral issues explores the impact of information systems particularly on individual rights. The text concludes with a brief section on the future role of information systems and of those who practice the science. Intended "for those who are unsure about what information science is," perhaps the book more aptly presents a traditional information systems approach to information science.

The text is aimed at the introductory level, is clearly written, and gives highly selected references at the end of every chapter to principal works of the authors noted. The more advanced student will have to go elsewhere for more in depth or up-to-date information. Some sections of the text are particularly weak: for example, the communications technology chapter covers communications, networks, and the various individual technologies in eleven pages. Two pages in the chapter on systems theory and information science are given to expert systems.

There is not a large body of literature outlining in introductory form the theories in this field. With the above limited qualifications the title will be useful to library and information science collections. [R: WLB, Nov 88, p. 109]

Lorna K. Rees-Potter

299. Dyer, Hilary, and Gwyneth Tseng, eds. **New Horizons for the Information Profession: Meeting the Challenge of Change. Proceedings of the Annual Conference of the Institute of Information Scientists, University of Warwick, 1987.** London and Los Angeles, Calif., Taylor Graham, 1988. 225p. $34.00pa. ISBN 0-947568-32-8.

This compendium of conference presentations addresses changing patterns of work at both the corporate and individual levels. The identified themes of the papers include pricing of information services and the barriers to information access; the increasing use of information technology by professionals in a spectrum of fields and the consequent need for user-friendly access; the issues concerning quality and value-added information services; the social and political implications of new technologies; the tension between information flow and confidentiality/secrecy; the need for continued education of people of all ages in order to keep pace with technological developments; and the challenges of corporate information systems and integrated approaches to information supply.

The major divisions of the text are "New Horizons for the Information Profession," "Future Implications of Corporate Information Systems," "Applications of Technology," "Student Session," "Question Time," "Implications of Technology," the Institute of Information Scientists Presidential Address ("Science and Myth Information"), and "Social and Professional Implications of Technology."

While having appropriate roots in the environment of the United Kingdom, the concepts and research presented in this text have international implications. Definitely recommended for collections related to information technologies.

Darlene E. Weingand

300. **Future Trends in Information Science and Technology. Proceedings of the Silver Jubilee Conference....** P. A. Yates-Mercer, ed. London and Los Angeles, Calif., Taylor Graham, 1988. 123p. $35.00pa. ISBN 0-947568-20-4.

These eight papers, in celebration of the London City University's Department of Information Science, were originally presented at that location on 16 January 1987. Four papers treat information technology and four papers discuss its social and professional aspects. Within the first group are "Online Library Catalogues and Information Retrieval Systems: What Can We Learn From Research?" by Charles R. Hildreth; "Practical Applications of Optical Disk Image Systems in Document Management," by Terry Plume; "Network Technology—Current and Future," by Barry Mahon; and "Intelligent Interfaces for Information Retrieval Systems: Architecture Problems in the Construction of Expert Systems for Document Retrieval," by Karen Sparck Jones. Within the second group are the following: "The Future of Information Science as a Profession," by Elspeth J. Scott; "The Politics and Power of Information," by Duncan Campbell; "Future Trends in Information Science Education," by A. J. Meadows; and "Online Information: A Ten-Year Perspective and Outlook," by Stephen E. Robertson. Each paper presents an overview of the topic, is solidly written, and is fully documented.

Recommended for professional reading for those whose work environments and reading interests focus on these issues, and for those with an interest in international and comparative librarianship.   Edmund F. SantaVicca

301.   Gray, John. **National Information Policies: Problems and Progress.** London, Mansell; distr., Rutherford, N.J., Publishers Distribution Center, 1988. 143p. bibliog. index. (Library Management in Context). $45.00. LC 88-13480. ISBN 0-7201-1994-4.

Information policy covers a wide range of issues and problems and although the context may change, the elements to be addressed are similar in all countries. Education at all levels, the information industries, information professionals, and users have a stake in policy development. The author, who has been involved with information policy for more than two decades, discusses the development of national information policy and the problems policymaking bodies address. He cites information policy decisions and activities to illustrate the ways that nations have developed their policies. Areas of common agreement, areas of potential conflict, and restraint on the development of policy are discussed generally and then made specific through examples. In developing countries which typically lack good educational systems, libraries, information services, and the money to provide any of these infrastructures, the problems are exaggerated.

In this presentation, the reader receives an overview of what national information policy is and why it is important. With this as background, one's own national information policy can be better understood and assessed. The author understands his subject and writes well. The bibliography provides useful additional sources with international coverage.

Ann E. Prentice

302.   Hernon, Peter, and Charles R. McClure. **Public Access to Government Information: Issues, Trends, and Strategies.** 2d ed. Norwood, N.J., Ablex, 1988. 524p. bibliog. index. (Information Management, Policy, and Services). $60.00; $29.95pa. LC 88-19249. ISBN 0-89391-522-X; 0-89391-523-8pa.

Each chapter of the second edition of this important work first published in 1984 has been thoroughly updated and reorganized to reflect recent trends in federal information policies and services. It is the first issue-oriented book in the field that addresses trends and strategies relating to public access to government information. Over 35 percent of the volume represents new material. The work focuses on the federal depository library system and the publications printed by or under contract to the Government Printing Office (GPO) distributed or sold by the superintendent of documents.

However, the book takes a much broader approach not only with respect to government information, but also by documenting librarianship. The authors analyze issues related to the broader spectrum of federal government information policies including non-GPO publications, technical report literature, nonprint formats, online databases, and other new or emerging technologies. Separate chapters discuss exploiting state and local government information sources and access to information from international governmental organizations. Documents librarianship is examined within the context of a library's total collections and its reference and technical services. It advocates greater integration of government publications, both bibliographically and physically, to bring them into the mainstream of a library's services and collections. Separate chapters are devoted to public access to government publications and information held in depository collections; federal information policies and their impact on public access; microforms and access to government publications; processing depository publications; education of the government information professional; and restructuring the GPO's depository library program, to name several examples. The authors throughout the volume critically assess current practices and traditional assumptions within the broad context of librarianship and information policy, and evaluate current and needed research in the field. They also offer solutions and practical recommendations to make government information policy and services more effective.

LeRoy C. Schwarzkopf

303.   Katz, Raul Luciano. **The Information Society: An International Perspective.** Westport, Conn., Praeger/Greenwood Press, 1988. 168p. illus. bibliog. index. $35.95. LC 87-25884. ISBN 0-275-92659-1.

This book examines how the employment and utilization of information workers are influenced by the economic and political forces in developed and developing countries. Emphasis is on developing countries, but a substantial foundation is laid in chapter 1 by examining processes in developed countries for purposes of comparison. A major hypothesis of the book is that politics has a heavier influence on growth of the information society in developing countries than previously recognized. There is ample documentation throughout and tables and figures allow easy summarization of arguments. A minor distraction is that some figures have been overly reduced and often require careful scrutiny to decipher them. This is a good scholarly work and should be of interest to any academician investigating this area. Ideas abound and the bibliography and index are useful as well.   Marvin K. Harris

304. Lesko, Matthew. **Information USA Workbook: Sources, Techniques and Tools for Coping with the Information Explosion.** Chevy Chase, Md., Information USA, 1988. 485p. $95.00pa.

The primary purpose of this workbook is to introduce the reader to the various unusual and nontraditional sources of information. In particular, the workbook discusses the details and lists the information sources for market studies, company information, demographics and statistics, experts, industry sources, technology, government databases, online databases, legislation, and foreign markets. Most of the sources listed in this workbook lie in the public sector and often are the same sources for the popular commercial ventures. The volume provides the name, address, and telephone number of the agencies responsible for the particular information in question. These entries are usually arranged alphabetically or by state for quick reference. This workbook is a good tool for those in need of information, but uncertain what is available and where to get it. It is recommended for any libraries used by the public.
          John Y. Cheung

305. Sardar, Ziauddin. **Information and the Muslim World: A Strategy for the Twenty-first Century.** London, Mansell; distr., Rutherford, N.J., Publishers Distribution Center, 1988. 186p. bibliog. index. $45.00. LC 87-28295. ISBN 0-7201-1728-3.

Developed from the concepts put forward in the keynote address presented to the second Congress of Muslim Librarians and Information Scientists held in Malaysia in October 1986, this work focuses on the role of information in Muslim societies and on the relevance of information science to the needs and requirements of these societies. Also of concern is the role of information in development.

Sardar begins by challenging the idea that the "information revolution" offers humanity the means for a better society. Muslim countries, who are concerned with preserving their culture and values while urging their scholars to develop new disciplines (such as Islamic

economics, political science, and science), need to develop an infrastructure for generating their own information, thus enabling them to become research-oriented and knowledge-based societies. Sardar covers such topics as the Islamic heritage, the development function of information, information and cultural subversion, information and the quality of life, and developing national information systems. He also examines the transfer of information and the communication of knowledge within the scholarly community, and discusses the responsibilities of Muslim librarians and information scientists as the "Gate-Keepers and Purveyors of Ideas." His concluding chapter, "Building Blocks of an Islamic Information Policy," outlines the features he sees necessary for a sensible information strategy for the Muslim world in the twenty-first century. These include the generation of a knowledge base, the development of an appropriate information structure, the role of Muslim librarians and information scientists, and meeting the needs of Muslim scientists, technologists, and scholars.
          Margaret Anderson

306. Schement, Jorge Reina, and Leah A. Lievrouw, eds. **Competing Visions, Complex Realities: Social Aspects of the Information Society.** Norwood, N.J., Ablex Publishing, 1987. 167p. index. (Communication and Information Science). $29.50. LC 87-14318. ISBN 0-89391-402-9.

This book examines the social and communication aspects of the information-oriented industrial society. It begins with three theoretical chapters giving very different views of what the information society means and what it is. The next six discuss how education, communication, law, ethics, and business will affect, and be affected by, a society and economy increasingly dependent upon information. A final chapter develops an agenda for communication research, proposing six research topics which include examining information as a commodity, social and work changes in the new age, and the relationship of information to public value and policy. Like most books with multiple authors, this contains a mix of interesting and not-so-interesting chapters. The most useful are the editors' own chapters and summaries, plus one or two chapters on communication patterns, one on legal issues, and a description of the entrepreneurial spirit in the Silicon Valley. The latter raises interesting questions about the diffusion of such work practices and ethics into the rest of society. In all, this is an important book for understanding some of the social/communication issues of the information age.   A. Neil Yerkey

307. Turner, Christopher. **Organizing Information: Principles and Practice.** London, Clive Bingley; distr., Chicago, American Library Association, 1987. 158p. illus. bibliog. index. $17.50. ISBN 0-85157-379-7.

The organizing of information is fundamental not only to traditional librarianship, but also to a variety of new "advice agencies": governmental, business, and social offices such as Britain's National Association of Citizen's Advice Bureaux. Recognizing that many of these contemporary agencies are managed by subject experts with a limited understanding of basic information retrieval systems, Turner has produced this basic guide to organizing information. While covering many of the topics included in the standard cataloging texts, this is not a primer or manual. It assumes a more philosophical posture, concentrating on presenting rationale and context for determining correct approaches to organizing information.

This engaging publication is succinct yet thorough. There are seven chapters, a selective bibliography, and a brief index. Chapters include material on catalogs and cataloging, the subject approach to information, selected classification schemes, alphabetical subject approaches, computerized retrieval systems, and the management of information retrieval systems. Within these broad topics are detailed discussions of such issues as precoordinate indexes, cycled and rotated indexes, permutated indexes, postcoordinate indexes, chain indexing, PRECIS indexing, and catchword indexing.

While philosophical in nature, the book is also very practical. For instance, in discussing citation indexes Turner explains, "although totally beyond the scope of a small information unit to produce, their availability through online database hosts such as Lockheed Dialog means that searchers need to be aware of their capabilities" (p. 138). Turner not only identifies important questions, but also presents a means of answering them. Moreover, he makes generous use of examples including reprints from important information sources such as the *Cumulative Book Index*, the *British National Bibliography*, and the *ERIC Thesaurus*.

Another attractive feature of the book is that it is very pleasant to read. In dealing with intricate, complex issues the writing style is unpretentious and refreshing. Turner is a knowledgeable, forceful writer. Librarians and information workers in all types of information units will find this publication useful and appealing.

P. Grady Morein

308. Young, Paul. **The Nature of Information.** Westport, Conn., Praeger/Greenwood Press, 1987. 192p. bibliog. index. $35.00. LC 87-6953. ISBN 0-275-92698-2.

Young's goal in this publication is to define information in mass energy terms, "not only making possible a unification of mind and matter, but enabling us to approach the universe in its entirety as a wholly mass-energy system" (pp. ix-x). He proposes a theory based upon facts, postulates, and speculation, which he acknowledges cannot now be proved right or wrong but which offers value in "its attempt to sketch an account of the world as an entirely physical phenomenon" (p. 147).

The book consists of a brief introduction, five chapters, a section of notes, a bibliography, an index and a paragraph about the author. In chapter 1 Young examines the historical and current meanings of information as used in everyday affairs, as well as in scientific settings such as computer science, physics, and biology. He then analyzes form and its relation to mass energy in chapter 2. Chapter 3 returns to the subject of information and describes it as a form phenomenon. In chapter 4 the author addresses the question of mind and the brain-mind barrier. The final chapter is entitled "Coda," but is less a summation than an explanation of the philosophical and behavioral implications of this theory.

Young presents a bold theory which he recognizes will require analysis and scrutiny. It is an intriguing book which should be of considerable interest not only to students of information, but also to a wide range of scholars in the humanities and the social sciences as well as the physical and biological sciences. [R: RLR, Nov 88, p. 355]

P. Grady Morein

Information Management

309. Allred, John, with others. **Managing Information in Educational Guidance.** Leicester, England, National Institute of Adult Continuing Education, 1988. 120p. illus. £6.50pa. ISBN 0-900559-68-3.

One might appreciate the helpful list of sources in *Managing Information*, once one overcomes the poor editing. This volume, especially in its introductory sections, is replete with the latter; bad grammar, possibly offensive metaphors, and jargon tarnish the pages. There are some interesting, if not insightful, diagrams on page eight that are repeated on later pages. And the sample evaluation forms feature unexplained acronyms.

It comes as a surprise, then, that chapter 3, "Sources of Information," and chapter 5, "The Information," are really very good. The authors of this volume are all connected with the Unit for the Development of Adult Continuing Education, based in Leicester, England. And the information sources that they deal with are, unsurprisingly, British. In chapter 3 an annotated bibliography of printed sources is followed by detailed descriptions of various databases and adult education projects, including hardware requirements and corporate addresses where necessary. Chapter 5 shows how to construct entries for a local information file, and sample entries are provided. Indexing and access techniques are discussed.

The information in the book might prove less useful for Americans; and British readers may have to do much sifting through the text. [R: LAR, 15 July 88, p. 409]

Judith M. Brugger

310. Flood, Stephen. **Processing Words: The Information Manager and Word Processing.** London, Aslib; distr., Medford, N.J., Learned Information, 1987. 97p. illus. $25.00pa. ISBN 0-85142-216-0.

Stephen Flood postulates that word processing is underutilized by organizations because it is viewed as "the simple automation of a clerical task" (p. 1). He argues that the information in documents becomes more valuable if it is subject to standards similar to those used for data processing. His comparison between word processing and database manipulation indicates that a close relationship, which has largely been ignored, exists. Lack of document standards and audit trails, poor security practices, inappropriate management control, and inconsistent handling of documents are key problem areas for word processing. The book argues that data processing and records management concepts applied to textual documents provide new applications and expanded potential for word processing.

The nature of word processed documents has led information managers to ignore the need for compliance with data protection legislation. In a discussion of the United Kingdom's Data Protection Act and the individual's right of access to personal files, Flood demonstrates why managers need to change their attitude toward word processing. This slim volume offers practical advice to managers and users in addition to examining the more theoretical aspects of text manipulation. For example, one chapter is devoted to a comparison of the capabilities between dedicated word processing machines and software for microcomputers. The section

devoted to the selection and implementation of word processing systems offers a refreshing outlook. This book provides an enjoyable and thoughtful examination of word processing.

Lynn Morgan

311. Hall, V. J., and J. W. Mosevich. **Information Systems Analysis: With an Introduction to Fourth-Generation Technologies.** Scarborough, Ont., Prentice-Hall Canada, 1988. 417p. illus. index. $15.00pa. ISBN 0-13-464363-1.

This is a textbook for students of systems analysis in the corporate business setting. The goal is to create an understanding and an ability to use systems analysis to produce software appropriate to this environment. The emphasis is on business processes rather than on technical computer processes. The traditional structured analysis method using data flow diagrams is followed. The book is organized into three parts. Part 1 looks at the corporate setting of information systems, systems life cycle, the corporate data model, the relational model, and data management using data dictionaries. Part 2 covers the structure analysis process and data flow diagrams as well as strategies to use in considering economic feasibility using cost/benefit analysis. Part 3 discusses fourth-generation languages and uses NOMAD2 as an example. Set up as a textbook, each chapter has a series of exercises for discussion or assignments, and the appendices give guidelines for student projects and a number of case studies. The text is nontechnical and appropriate to undergraduate business students.

Lorna K. Rees-Potter

312. Holloway, Simon. **Data Administration.** Brookfield, Vt., Gower Publishing, 1988. 151p. illus. bibliog. $49.95. LC 87-28913. ISBN 0-291-39765-4.

Holloway has prepared a "simple guide to the concepts involved in data administration." He includes definitions, objectives, planning, organizational roles and relationships, tools and techniques, database design and documentation, and privacy and security issues. There are also a sample data administration plan and a plan for a data administration department. Holloway addresses business or commercial applications for data administration rather than bibliographic or text processing applications. He has, indeed, set forth understandable, succinct concepts and methodologies for planning, executing, and maintaining a data management system in an organization. His discussion of legislation applies to the United Kingdom only; however, while many software names and techniques have the same limitation, this book would be a useful supplementary text for students being introduced to systems analysis in business situations. Margaret McKinley

313. Kesner, Richard M. **Information Systems: A Strategic Approach to Planning and Implementation.** Chicago, American Library Association, 1988. 263p. index. $30.00pa. LC 88-10371. ISBN 0-8389-0493-9.

This book is aimed at information professionals, archives administrators, librarians, and other records managers who wish to plan and implement information systems. With each new book on this subject, one must look more and more carefully at whether or not a significant contribution to the literature is being made. The author states in his introduction that this book is "the intellectual heir" to his book, *Automation for Archivists and Records Managers: Planning and Implementation Strategies* (American Library Association, 1984). This book attempts to build on the former text and present some specific, tried and tested tools for planning, selection, implementation, and evaluation of systems. It is this reviewer's opinion, however, that the author has failed in his stated objectives.

The book is well organized and reasonably well written, albeit somewhat wordy and vague. On the one hand, it deals with the general subject matter at a very fundamental level, and on the other hand, it attempts to do so much that it does not do any of it really well. The author presents a number of topics such as "Preparing a Request for Proposal," "The Planning Matrix," "The Action Plan," and others which are covered in a page or two and leave much to be desired.

All of the specific information contained in the book is available in other sources. The author cites several texts, aimed at his audience, which are superior to this book in meeting certain of the objectives he has set for himself. In short, if one wishes to plan an information system, one may learn something from reading this source, but one would be well advised to consult other sources. After so doing, this book will be of little value. [R: LJ, 15 Nov 88, p. 52; WLB, Nov 88, p. 110] James Rice

314. Loehlein, Patricia. **Management Information Systems: An Information Sourcebook.** Phoenix, Ariz., Oryx Press, 1988. 219p. index. (Oryx Sourcebook Series in Business and Management, No. 13). $55.00. LC 87-38194. ISBN 0-89774-375-X.

This book is a very useful and rather extensive compendium (over 600 items plus a useful list of other sources) in an area that is of growing importance. There are, however, a number of ways in which the book could be substantially improved. First, the scope of the book could be expanded. For example, there is very little coverage of the burgeoning area of information systems and competitive advantage. Only one of the well-known trilogy of "Information Archipelago" articles in the *Harvard Business Review* by McFarlan and others is actually included. The other two appear only as mentions (without adequate citations) in the annotation to the first.

Second, the indexing leaves much to be desired. There are no index entries under "productivity" or related terms, despite the fact that there is a section entitled "Labor Productivity/Programming Activity." That section is again indicative of the rather narrow scope of the book; the emphasis is upon the productivity of the creators of MIS systems, not upon the much more important aspect of the productivity of the users of the MIS system. In addition, Keen's important book, *Competing in Time: Using Telecommunications for Competitive Advantage* (Ballinger Publishing, 1986), fails to appear under "Competitive Advantage," nor is the "information archipelago" concept retrievable in any fashion from the subject index.

Finally, the annotations could be much improved; they are too often descriptive rather than substantive. The annotation for "Research in Management Information Systems: The Minnesota Experiments" (*Management Science* 23 (9): 913-23, May 1977) tells us "the results were significant," but not why, nor much less what, they were. One gets the impression that the annotations were in many cases created by people who could have benefited by a better knowledge of the field as a whole and a greater awareness of the key issues and of the relative importance of topics and findings.

In summary, the book contains a wealth of useful information and is of great utility to anyone interested in the topic. Browsing in the book is almost sure to be rewarding. As mentioned, however, the book could use a great deal of improvement. It appears to have been assembled with plenty of good, hard work, but apparently without adequate subject expertise, and therefore, without proper attention to the hot topics in the field and to the terminology currently in use.

Michael E. D. Koenig

315. Rabin, Jack, and Edward M. Jackowski, eds. **Handbook of Information Resource Management.** New York, Marcel Dekker, 1988. 567p. illus. index. (Public Administration and

Public Policy, 31). $99.75. LC 87-18922. ISBN 0-8247-7739-5.

Information resource management (IRM), the application to information of the same management skills used in the control and supervision of such other resources as money, personnel, and facilities, is a rapidly developing field. The handbook under review is a highly successful attempt to present "an encyclopedic treatment of the major areas in information systems and data administration."

The handbook is divided into four units, each of which has four to five topically related chapters authored by experts in the field. The units are (1) "Theoretical/Technological Developments and Their Pedagogic Underpinnings," (2) "Elements in Information Systems and Data Administration," (3) "Information Systems Architecture," and (4) "Data Administration." Although the chapters relate closely to one another, each one is structured to stand independently. References are provided at the end of each chapter.

The contributions are generally well written, although the prose occasionally is dense and jargon-ridden. There is a subject index, but it is inadequate for a work of this length and importance. Overall, however, the handbook will prove to be useful as we grope our way into the information future. [R: RLR, Aug 88, p. 219]
Robert H. Burger

316. Robek, Mary F., Gerald F. Brown, and Wilmer O. Maedke. **Information and Records Management.** 3d ed. Mission Hills, Calif., Glencoe Publishing, 1987. 580p. illus. index. $23.95. ISBN 0-02-820590-1.

This book deals with organizing and arranging records information so as to yield the maximum records accessibility at minimum cost. The creation, active life, and final end of a record are considered as the authors link traditional manual systems with the latest in office technology. The explosion in technology prompted the publication of this third edition, which includes three new chapters on computerization and microimagery. Also added are corporate records case studies at the end of every major section and short paragraphs called "Trends" sprinkled throughout the text, pointing out tendencies in records management.

A scholarly treatment of the subject matter meets guidelines for records management established by ARMA (Association of Records Managers and Administrators). In fact, the book is often used as a college text as well as a reference book in the field. A student workbook and an instructor's manual are available and both expand on the discussion points, the case

problems, and the suggested projects found at the end of each chapter in the text. Helpful summaries conclude each chapter. An index, a glossary, and several appendices covering records associations and publications are provided at the end of the book.

Not only will the records manager find this title invaluable, but so too will any person in charge of organizing records of any sort. The text is written in a straightforward manner and subjects can be easily identified. The book not only furnishes overall theory, but many of the small details such as purchasing equipment or estimating space. This book is not quite a how-to beginner's book, but for the professional it is a written, updated memory.   Brad R. Leach

317. Roberts, N., and D. Clarke. **The Treatment of Information Issues and Concepts in Management and Organizational Literatures.** Sheffield, England, Department of Information Studies, University of Sheffield, 1987. 130p. bibliog. (CRUS Occasional Paper, No. 15; British Library R & D Report, 5951). £10.00pa. ISBN 0-906088-34-8.

This technical report presents a review of 255 items drawn from management and organizational literature to establish the treatment accorded information issues and the development of information concepts from the perspective of information studies. General treatment of organizations as information entities, information activities associated with planning and strategic issues, and the handling of information ideas in relation to business success and failures are examined critically. Proposals are made for the cooperative development of information concepts and research ideas between management, organizational, and information specialists.

The report stems from a growing interest in organizational issues displayed by management and the information disciplines with the possibility of unplanned convergence. That is, can information concepts and research from one area be employed usefully in another? In addressing this question the authors have confined their review to the role external information plays, both to place a limit on the study as well as the assumption that the properties of internal (within an organization) information are better understood. Some of the basic information concepts reviewed include uncertainty and the amount of information, formal and informal channels of communication, and information overload.

The authors conclude that information interests do overlap in some areas, are complimentary in others, and totally distinct in yet others.

Problems arise in that many of the information concepts lack operational definitions, a problem that might be solved by the development of a common information vocabulary. This book will be interesting reading for managers and information specialists, librarians, and students.

Andrew G. Torok

318. Schmidt, Janet. **Marketing the Modern Information Center: A Guide to Intrapreneurship for the Information Manager.** New York, FIND/SVP, 1987. 193p. illus. bibliog. $95.00 looseleaf with binder. ISBN 0-931634-73-3.

The aim of this volume is "to provide a strategy by which the corporate librarian may parlay his status into an important managerial position enabling him to better satisfy the increasingly complex demands of the company he serves" (pp. 4-5). Corporate librarians are admonished to strike the words *library* and *librarian* from their vocabulary, to be proactive in developing, marketing, and providing a wide range of information services, and to transform the information center into a center for generating new ideas. The author takes a very upbeat approach to the new era in which information is considered to be a valuable commodity.

The first half of the volume presents selected aspects of a survey carried out by FIND/SVP in 1983. This New York-based firm, which provides information services and publications worldwide, gathered data through telephone interviews with a stratified random sample of five hundred of their clients. It is important to note that this sample is a very select group of active information users and that the term *end-user* is used to describe clients who contact FIND/SVP directly. The objectives of the survey were to identify demographic and other characteristics, determine the users' principal information needs and how they are being fulfilled, determine what the users use information for and why they use an information "retailer" like FIND/SVP, and to identify unfulfilled needs. The second half contains three chapters: "Marketing the Information Center," "Promoting the Information Center's Product," and "Current Issues and Future Trends." The volume concludes with reproductions of brochures from two information centers and a seven-page bibliography.

The attempt to expand the reporting of the survey project into a guidebook falls short of the mark. The *why*, *what*, and *how* of marketing are crammed into some eighty double-spaced pages. Although this volume seems to be the first devoted entirely to market corporate information services and is written with the greatest enthusiasm, it is not comprehensive.

Physically it is awkward, a looseleaf binder with double-spaced typed pages. An information manager will benefit from reading this volume once but is not likely to consider it a guidebook. [R: RLR, Aug 88, p. 209]

Helen Howard

319. Thierauf, Robert J. **Effective Information Centers: Guidelines for MIS and IC Managers.** Westport, Conn., Quorum Books/ Greenwood Press, 1988. 263p. index. $39.95. LC 87-32602. ISBN 0-89930-308-0.

The author's definition of an information center is "a place where end users in an organization go to obtain information primarily about microcomputer hardware and software." Using this very specific definition, the author discusses how to develop and manage this type of center. Each chapter is introduced with a list of issues to be explored and concludes with a summary statement and a generous number of additional references. Appearing in several chapters are sections of a questionnaire whose purpose is to gather information useful to the development of a center. Relevant concepts are described, purposes of particular questions are discussed, and questions are prepared. Difficulties in establishing centers are explored, particularly those resulting from an anticipated resistance to change.

This could have been a more useful exploration of the uses and management of this type of center. The author's consistently negative comments about resistance to change by existing management groups, such as those involved in management information systems, and by employees unwilling to learn to use computing, detract from the presentation. Most questions in the questionnaire include subjective statements that often result in subjective responses. The style of writing is difficult. Careful editing to ensure clarity of thought and correct construction would have improved the presentation. The style of writing and the pervasive negative attitude toward many of the potential users of such centers detract considerably from what might otherwise have been a useful text.

Ann E. Prentice

320. Wetherbe, James C. **Systems Analysis and Design.** 3d ed. St. Paul, Minn., West Publishing, 1988. 395p. illus. index. $37.00. LC 88-102. ISBN 0-314-73098-2.

321. Wetherbe, James C. **Cases in Systems Analysis and Design.** 3d ed. St. Paul, Minn., West Publishing, 1988. 1v. (various paging). illus. $24.95pa. LC 88-5511. ISBN 0-314-73038-9.

The third edition of *Systems Analysis and Design*, which "attempts to integrate the new techniques into the system development process," consists of sixteen chapters divided into three sections. Section 1, "Conceptual Foundations," presents concepts, themes, and frameworks used throughout the book. Section 2, "Techniques and Technologies for Systems Analysis and Design," covers a wide range of systems analysis techniques that deal with problem recognition, information systems design, selection of technology and personnel, implementation and evaluation, and a newly included chapter on project management for systems development. Section 3, "Strategic, Administrative, and Higher-level Concepts and Techniques," discusses such topics as systems administration strategic planning, analysis and design of decision support systems, end-user computing, and a concluding chapter on future considerations of systems analysis. Each of the book's chapters includes a summary, exercises, and a list of selected references. An index is provided, which, although adequate in length and precision, lacks sufficient proper cross-referencing.

The book is well illustrated, provides unambiguous diagrammatic explanations of key concepts, and is obviously based on both sound theory and broad practical experience. Although the examples used are those of business and industry, any organization could profit from the book's contents. An accompanying casebook presents five problems for developing system design specifications.   — Robert H. Burger

Information Technology

322. Batt, Chris. **Information Technology in Public Libraries 1987.** Winchester, England, Public Libraries Research Group, 1987. 115p. £8.50 spiralbound. ISBN 1-870917-01-4.

Surveys were conducted in 1985 and 1987 by the Association of London Chief Librarians to collect data on use of new technologies in U.K. public libraries. Results of the two surveys (based on the same questionnaire) provide an overview of libraries incorporating information technologies into their operations. With an emphasis on hardware, the author has summarized its availability and its use in library operations. Supporting the summary are appendices which include a copy of the questionnaire, raw data in tabular form, and a list of all individuals contacted. The list is useful to those wishing to know exactly what their colleagues are doing while the summary is useful to those desiring a general overview. It is often difficult to present the results of a study in a way that will satisfy both audiences. The author has done that very

well and in addition has raised issues requiring thoughtful consideration: the ways in which use of information technology in libraries builds relationships to the wider information infrastructure; and the need for librarians to become more extroverted with their information partners across the information spectrum. This is an excellent report that does what such a report should do—summarize data, reach both specific and general conclusions, and provide the reader with new and useful information and insights. That it is well written is an added bonus. [R: LAR, 15 Sept 88, p. 521; LJ, Aug 88, p. 86]

Ann E. Prentice

323. **Campus of the Future: Conference on Information Resources, Wingspread Conference Center, June 22-24, 1986.** Dublin, Ohio, OCLC Online Computer Library Center, 1987. 145p. illus. bibliog. (OCLC Library, Information, and Computer Science Series). $9.00pa. ISBN 1-55653-010-2.

The creation of the Higher Education Policy Advisory Committee of OCLC in 1984 marks the beginning of the series of events that culminated in the Conference on Information Resources for the Campus of the Future. Held at Racine, Wisconsin, in 1986, the purpose of the conference was to consider the next generation of university information systems and the resources that will be required to provide such systems. The activities of the conference are organized in the book under four categories: a summary of the proceedings, the papers presented, the universities' summaries of their information services and activities, and four appendices including one on issues for future discussion.

The quality of this book is best represented by the papers from the conference: the implications of the technological revolution for higher education presented by Richard M. Cyert; Maurice Glickman's paper on the creation, communication, and conservation of knowledge as the goals for higher education; the changing scene of American higher education by Evelyn Daniel; and D. E. Van Houweling's paper on the information technology environment of higher education. The book is highly recommended for special and academic libraries.

Antonio Rodriguez-Buckingham

324. Crawford, Walt. **Current Technologies in the Library: An Informal Overview.** Boston, G. K. Hall, 1988. 324p. index. (Professional Librarian Series). $38.50; $29.95pa. LC 88-21226. ISBN 0-8161-1886-8; 0-8161-1888-4pa.

Most professional librarians try to keep themselves up-to-date by reading the professional journals. This usually suffices for trends in the field, but the world of technology has come upon us so rapidly that even the most faithful journal reader has a hard time staying knowledgeable about so many technologies developing simultaneously.

For the busy librarian, Crawford has prepared an excellent short encyclopedia-type reference book that spans the various technologies impacting library work. Each article is brief, provides an excellent historical timeline of the technology, and is written as if Crawford were giving a personal, brief "scoop" from the insider's point of view. This book will fill in many a gap for the person somewhat conversant with technology (and if you read it in the next year, you will be very current).

The list of technologies covered is impressive. The first section concerns publishing media and consists of the printed page, microform, analog audio, digital audio, videocassettes, videodiscs, CD-ROM, digital publishing and optical storage, software for lending, and preservation. The second section covers computers and communications and consists of computers, input and display, printers, graphics and speech, magnetic storage, telecommunications, teletext and videotex, electronic mail and telefacsimile, and local area networks.

A must for the beginning professional and all the rest of us who want to be "up" on the latest. [R: LJ, 15 Oct 88, p. 62; WLB, Nov 88, p. 110]   David V. Loertscher

325. **Encyclopedia of Information Systems and Services, 1988: [In Three Volumes: United States Listings, International Listings, and Indexes]: An International Descriptive Guide to Approximately 4,100 Organizations, Systems, and Services....** 8th ed. Amy Lucas, Annette Novallo, and Nan Soper, eds. Detroit, Gale, 1988. 3v. index. $400.00/set. ISBN 0-8103-2532-2; ISSN 0734-9068.

This compendium is indeed very useful, though encyclopedic it is not. Realistically in this age of convergence when the boundaries of librarianship, information service, and virtually everything else are becoming increasingly more porous and diffuse, what compendium really can be encyclopedic? Volume 2, *International Listings*, in particular is weak. For example, there is no mention of the Gulf States Documentation Center in Baghdad, though this center is quite active in the field of petroleum literature and other areas of interest to the Arab countries. When turning to a country with which one is familiar, one is struck by the absences. There are only three listings for Argentina and apparently no mention of CONICET (Consejo

Nacional de Investigaciones Científicas y Technicas), a rather major organization, or any of the information services it supports.

The U.S. listings were far better — when looking up services or organizations of interest (Telebase Systems; Personal Library Software; Geographic Data Technology, Inc.), I found almost everything I sought.

The index volume is on the whole well done. It will take the reader from Easynet to Telebase systems, or from CLASE (Citas Latinoamericanas en Sociologia, Economia y Humanidades) to CICH (Centro de Informacion Cientifica y Humanistica). There are some definite oversights, however. "Mapping Systems: Digital" takes one to Petroleum Information Corporation, but not to the equally relevant Geographic Data Technology, Inc. To be fair however, the indexing on the whole is much better than in some other indexes and is vital, since you will not find CICH under CICH or Centro, but under National Autonomous University of Mexico of which it is a subunit.

Although the entries rely heavily upon organization-supplied data, they tend to be rather more complete than in many other reference volumes. Thus, the encyclopedia is a very useful supplement to the *Directory of Online Databases*, edited by Carlos Cuadra, and the other online database directories, particularly if information is needed on organizations.

A real benefit of the product is that it has tried very hard to be current and to incorporate new technologies and the organizations and services associated with them. It is therefore a useful alternative to other products when pursuing new technology. That emphasis upon currency, certainly to be applauded, leads to the obvious question of the availability of the data file on CD-ROM, online, or some version more timely than the printed form.

Another question we may ask is, what level of completeness can one reasonably expect in a product like this? On the domestic side, the volume serves quite well. On the international side, we should probably expect more, but be grateful for what we have.   Michael E. D. Koenig

326. **ESPRIT '88: Putting the Technology to Use. Proceedings of the 5th Annual ESPRIT Conference, Brussels, November 14-17, 1988.** Edited by Commission of the European Communities, Directorate-General Telecommunications, Information Industries and Innovation. New York, Elsevier Science Publishing, 1988. 2v. illus. index. $223.75/set. ISBN 0-444-87145-4.

These proceedings are from the fifth conference sponsored by the European Strategic

Programme for Research in Information Technology (ESPRIT). At the 1988 conference 125 research papers reported on various technical projects grouped into two areas: (1) advanced microelectronics, VLSI technologies, software technology, and advanced information processing; and (2) office systems, computer integrated manufacturing, and information exchange systems. These two volumes document the cooperation between several hundred large and small information technology companies and research institutions throughout the twelve countries of the European Economic Community. Indexes in volume 2 help the reader find reports on various projects by author, project number, acronyms, and keyword.

This set is a valuable and timely record of European progress in the areas covered.

Pauline A. Cochrane

327.   Jones, C. Lee, ed. **Directory of Telefacsimile Sites in Libraries in the United States and Canada.** 3d ed. Buchanan Dam, Tex. C B R Consulting Services, 1987. 128p. $18.00pa.

This edition lists close to seven hundred sites in the United States and Canada that have reported the use of telefacsimile equipment to the editor. A brief introduction describes how this information was obtained and contains a summary by manufacturer of the hardware installed in the participating libraries.

The directory is organized by state or province (separate sections) and lists libraries alphabetically within each section. Each entry contains the name of the institution or library, address, fax telephone number, contact person, voice telephone number, and equipment used. Three indexes supplement the main directory. These indexes provide access to the entries by state and city, by institution, and by fax telephone number beginning with the area code. The institution and fax telephone number indexes would be more useful if they provided geographic information so that the reader could go directly to the desired entry in the main directory.

Although its value is limited by the rapid growth and changes occurring in telefacsimile services, this type of book is needed by libraries involved in the technology.

Dennis J. Phillips

328.   Lynch, Don B. **Information Technology Dictionary of Abbreviations and Acronyms.** Bromley, England, Chartwell-Bratt, 1988. 349p. £8.50pa. ISBN 0-86238-153-3.

The proliferation of information technology in recent years has spawned an even greater explosion of technical jargon, especially abbreviations and acronyms, most of which are confusing to all but the specialists. Even specialists may not recognize abbreviations beyond their fields of expertise. This dictionary exemplifies the problem. The author has collected more than six thousand common abbreviations and acronyms associated with information technology, yet with striking mistakes and omissions. The author's British background is evident in the entries included and omitted. An example of the mistakes is the definition of UNISIST as "United Nations Information Systems in Science and Technology," while UNESCO, who coined the term, insists UNISIST is not an acronym but stands for "World Information Systems for Science and Technology" or, more recently as "Intergovernmental Program for Co-Operation in the Field of Scientific and Technological Information." Examples of the many inconsistencies in selecting entries follow: CATLINE (Catalog On-line, National Library of Medicine) is included but not MEDLARS (Medical Literature Analysis and Retrieval System) or MEDLINE (MEDLARS On-line); AGRIS (International Information System for the Agricultural Sciences and Technology) but not INIS (International Nuclear Information System); TELENET (Telenet Communications Corp.) but not TYMNET (TimeShare, Inc. Network); and INSPEC of the United Kingdom but not COMPENDEX (Computerized Engineering Index) or CAS (Chemical Abstacts Service) of the United States. In addition to mistakes and omissions, the definitions are too brief to be really useful. Giving the full name of an abbreviation or acronym is informative only to those already familiar with the meaning. These shortcomings leave the publication of limited reference value despite its claim to the contrary.   Hwa-Wei Lee

329.   **National Online Meeting. Proceedings—1987, New York, May 5-7, 1987.** Martha E. Williams and Thomas H. Hogan, comps. Medford, N.J., Learned Information, 1987. 506p. illus. index. $50.00pa. ISBN 0-938734-17-2.

These seventy papers are a potpourri of diverse topics addressing information accession and utilization, held together by the fact that the computer is an essential component of each topic. By my evaluation, there are twenty-nine papers from a library perspective, twenty-one on business aspects, twenty on technical aspects, five of a review nature, and four not categorized. The book mirrors the frustrating nature of the information stampede the authors are trying to harness, in that reading it is like browsing through an eclectic unrefined database. Everyone it seems is either building or accessing a database, and many are trying to find someone to buy their products. There is wide variation in sales and revenues estimates from the database industry among authors (compare pp. 3, 35, and 152). Public policy on information access (p. 433) is a serious issue that is well treated. Surprisingly to me, no papers addressed security and sabotage involving "viruses" or other problems. The index is useful but many papers lack references and contain typographical errors, and nothing can provide coherence to the overall work. Future offerings would benefit from better organization, editing, and rigorous review.

Marvin K. Harris

330. Rowley, Jennifer E. **The Basics of Information Technology.** London, Clive Bingley; distr., Chicago, American Library Association, 1988. 146p. illus. index. $20.00. ISBN 0-85157-396-7.

Because it is a straightforward primer on information technology written for information managers, this work underscores the "technology" rather than the "information" aspect of this field. It is concerned with the tools themselves: computers, software, and telecommunications, instead of their application in any specific environment. Not all applications are excluded, however. To stress the point that information technology is ubiquitous in libraries and to give it a wider perspective, the author includes a selection of application examples that would interest students of library and information studies. Information management is introduced only briefly because it is assumed that the reader is familiar with topics such as organizations, management, information retrieval, and systems design.

Written in understandable language, and assuming no previous knowledge of computers or mathematics, this work reflects the impact computers are having on our visual world, learning, creativity, problem solving, and the general understanding of humanity. The book is a must for all academic libraries and should be on the shelves of every educated person from artists to philosophers. [R: LAR, 15 June 88, p. 352; RLR, Aug 88, pp. 219-20]

Antonio Rodriguez-Buckingham

331. Simpson, Henry, and Steven M. Casey. **Developing Effective User Documentation: A Human Factors Approach.** New York, McGraw-Hill, 1988. 290p. illus. bibliog. index. $39.95. LC 87-29690. ISBN 0-07-057336-0.

User documentation is as important as the software to those using computers. It is the

guide linking users to the software and its uses. Writing documentation is a learned skill different from the skills required to write software. Typically, a team approach is followed, with one group preparing software and a second group writing manuals, tutorials, and other aids. The authors have provided an overview of the several types of user documentation and detailed instructions on how to prepare documentation appropriate to user and use. They warn against writing documentation that is too technical for the intended user, uses inconsistent terminology, or is written by several individuals with differing styles.

The book itself is tightly structured and clearly written, following the guidelines for documentation writing. Numerous charts and diagrams are used to illustrate concepts. Each step from identifying potential users, developing appropriate documentation, designing the documentation, to determining graphic presentation is carefully described. Those developing documentation or evaluating existing documentation will find this a useful text and guide. Although *human factors* is in the subtitle of the book, there is little evidence that human factors are of primary importance other than in the recognition that different types of users need different types of instruction.

Ann E. Prentice

332. Wood, Lawraine, and Richard Haigh, eds. **The Future of Industrial Information Services. Proceedings of the Library Association Industrial Group 1987 Annual Study Weekend, High Wycombe.** London and Los Angeles, Calif., Taylor Graham, 1987. 97p. maps. $24.00 pa. ISBN 0-947568-29-8.

Several topics are of particular concern to librarians regardless of the positions they hold. At the top of the current list are such hot subjects as planning, managing change, development and use of new technology, and the role of education in preparing librarians to succeed in their own roles. The papers selected from those given at the Library Association Industrial Group's Annual Study Weekend in March 1987 address each of these topics. The paper on how one plans for information service and then executes the plan is particularly useful.

These papers serve as a useful update on subjects of current interest, but there is little here that is new or that differs from similar information in a variety of other sources. [R: LAR, 15 June 88, p. 351]

Ann E. Prentice

INTELLECTUAL FREEDOM AND CENSORSHIP

333.   Bosmajian, Haig A., ed. **Freedom of Expression.** New York, Neal-Schuman, 1988. 117p. index. (First Amendment in the Classroom Series, No. 3). $29.95. LC 87-28131. ISBN 1-55570-003-9.

Edited by a University of Washington speech communications professor, this volume focuses on "how first amendment rights apply to the classrooms of a free society." Other volumes in the series discuss censorship, freedom of religion, academic freedom, and the freedom to publish.

The full texts of twenty Supreme Court and lower court decisions issued between 1943 and 1986 are reprinted in this one handy volume. Freedom of expression issues include refusing to salute the flag in the classroom, wearing armbands or buttons, or displaying signs on campus based upon religious or political beliefs. Each case is preceded by an introductory paragraph delineating the facts, arguments, and conclusions of the court. A subject index rounds out the work.

With a foreword by Alan H. Levine, civil rights attorney and president of Advocates for Children, a New York-based educational advocacy and student rights organization, this brief volume will be useful to students, parents, and school administrators. It is especially welcome in smaller collections which may not contain extensive legal holdings such as codes and statutes. As a quick overview of a timely, continuing controversial topic, the volume presents a helpful synthesis for interested lay readers. [R: BR, Nov/Dec 88, p. 51]   Ilene F. Rockman

334.   Reichman, Henry. **Censorship and Selection: Issues and Answers for Schools.** Arlington, Va., American Association of School Administrators and Chicago, American Library Association, 1988. 141p. illus. bibliog. $12.95 pa. LC 88-16815. ISBN 0-8389-3350-5.

This practical manual for school librarians includes background information on the definition of censorship, the motives of censors, and the extent of the problem and the content areas subject to question. Ways in which librarians can defend themselves and their collections against attack are also suggested. A chapter on the issues in dispute gives examples of attacks based on concerns about sexuality, sex education, secular humanism, creationism, and other sensitive content. Knowing what has happened in other schools should help educators to be prepared for local struggles; unfortunately, as the author points out, knowing the sensitive issues has sometimes led librarians and principals to become overly cautious in selection, thus becoming their own censors. A chapter on developing a selection policy should help librarians prepare for possible trouble, and a chapter on what can be done after an attack occurs gives realistic suggestions for coping. The book also contains a chapter explaining relevant legal decisions in censorship cases and concludes with a dozen appendices of helpful documents and sample forms. Because censorship incidents have been increasing for the past ten years or so, schools will want to take advantage of the guidance offered in this book.   Adele M. Fasick

335.   West, Mark I. **Trust Your Children: Voices against Censorship in Children's Literature.** New York, Neal-Schuman, 1988. 176p. illus. bibliog. $19.95pa. LC 87-31452. ISBN 1-55570-021-7.

Interviews with ten authors, three people involved in publishing children's books, and five anticensorship activists make up the text of this book. The authors of often-censored books, including such well-known writers as Judy Blume, Norma Klein, Robert Cormier, and Roald Dahl, describe the ways in which censorship problems have affected their work. All of the interviewees speak out against people who would restrict the rights of children to read about characters who use the vulgar language that real children use, characters who are sexually active, or those who behave in ways disapproved by adults. Some of the most disturbing statements in the book are about quiet, often hidden, censorship. Robert Cormier writes: "I recently met a teacher ... who wants to teach *The Chocolate War*, but her department head is afraid that the book would cause trouble and won't order it. The book ... wasn't thrown out of the classroom; it was simply prevented from ever entering it." And Billy Miles describes how she once lost a book club sale because she refused to change a twelve-year-old character's reference to a nightgown from "sexy" to "snazzy." This book will provide librarians and teachers with concrete examples and apt quotations about the censorship controversy which has grown to alarming proportions during the 1980s. [R: BL, July 88, 1780; BL, July 88, p. 1824; SLJ, May 88, p. 51]

Adele M. Fasick

INTERLIBRARY LOANS

336.   Cornish, Graham P. **Model Handbook for Interlending and Copying.** Paris, UNESCO

and Wetherby, England, IFLA Office of International Lending, 1988. 79p. bibliog. £5.00pa. ISBN 0-7123-2045-8.

This handbook, originating in a project of the IFLA Section on Interlending and Document Delivery, is designed to provide a useful checklist of possibilities and a comprehensive list of questions that should be considered by library staff writing or rewriting a staff manual on interlibrary lending. It does not intend to give detailed instructions on how to operate interlibrary loans in a particular situation, but aims to outline what the steps in the procedure are, to look at the various problems which may be encountered, and to identify the decisions which need to be made. Very clear and concise information (frequently in question form) is outlined under the following headings: "General Information," covering definition, policy, general principles, staff, keeping up-to-date, equipment, publicity, user education, basic considerations, files, statistics, legal requirements, and finance and accounting; "The Requesting Library," covering requesting policies, user interview, verification, sources for document supply, selecting a source of supply, policies of supply sources, preparing the request for transmission, procedures following dispatch of request, receipt of material requested, passing material to the user, materials returned by user, returning materials to the supply source, and negative replies; "The Supply Source," discussing supplying policies, receiving a request, processing a request, checking material before despatch, despatch of material requested, returned materials, and negative response; and "International Requests." The appendices include a select bibliography, model national interlibrary lending code, and principles and guidelines for procedure in international lending.

Not everything in this handbook will be relevant to every library, but the detailed listings of interlibrary loan procedures offer suggestions from which interlibrary loan librarians can pick and choose to suit their needs. This very practical guide should be useful to a department preparing its own handbook or, when a local detailed handbook is unavailable, for orienting librarians new to the interlibrary loan process. [R: JAL, July 88, p. 190; LAR, 14 Oct 88, p. 608]   Esther Jane Carrier

337. Morris, Leslie R., and Patsy Brautigam. **Interlibrary Loan Policies Directory**. 3d ed. New York, Neal-Schuman, 1988. 781p. index. $87.50pa. LC 87-35001. ISBN 1-55570-024-1.

This third edition of the standard interlibrary loan policies directory provides the most current printed information available for over fifteen hundred academic, public, and special libraries in the United States, plus a few Puerto Rican and Canadian universities. (Inevitably a few libraries are omitted.)

Arranged alphabetically by state and then by name of library or institution, the information received in response to a survey questionnaire includes ILL address and telephone number; acceptable methods of transmission; average turnaround time; policies regarding the loan of books, periodicals, newspapers, doctoral dissertations and master's theses, government documents, technical reports, microforms, audiovisual materials, and computer software; photoduplication services; billing procedures; packing requirements for mailing; time service is suspended during Christmas holidays; lending policies to foreign libraries; and groups of libraries for which fees are waived. Several of the categories are new to this edition.

Also included are three useful indexes: name of library/institution index with state identification, an index to libraries with facsimile transmission and receiving capabilities (with fax number when supplied), and an index to those libraries that charge for loaning books (fees range from $0.75 to $15.00). Unfortunately, the number of libraries charging for book loans is growing. All blank or indefinite ("varies") responses were considered as "No."

This directory should be very useful to all librarians working with interlibrary loans. Although some of this information is available in OCLC's online interlibrary loan file, the policies of many more libraries are included here, and frequently more detailed information is listed. Although all prices and policies are subject to change, for the present this is a very convenient and comprehensive directory. [R: WLB, Oct 88, p. 110]   Esther Jane Carrier

LIBRARY FACILITIES

General Works

338. Tucker, Dennis C. **From Here to There: Moving a Library**. Bristol, Ind., Wyndham Hall Press, 1987. 179p. illus. bibliog. index. $34.95; $24.95pa. LC 87-28061. ISBN 0-55605-027-5; 0-55605-028-3pa.

The folksy presentation of this volume belies the comprehensive and useful coverage of its topic: moving a library. The author's premise is that most librarians who are responsible for moving a library have not had the benefit of previous experience. He, therefore, successfully attempts to provide a practical and easily understood manual which will take the place of first-hand experience.

"The secret for a successful move is found in the key word — 'planning'." This sets the theme of *From Here to There*. Planning a move begins before the architect starts the new facility. Weeding, cleaning, fumigating, and deacidifying the collection in conjunction with a move are thoughtfully covered. A detailed discussion presents the advantages and disadvantages of the different methods of moving: on book trucks, on trays or troughs, in boxes (including choosing a box), or as loose books. Easy formulas for spacing books and periodicals show how to allow for expansion of the collection. Furniture, equipment, and computers receive specific attention.

The text concludes with chapters on what to do after moving day: the importance of shelf reading, rewarding the workers, and dedicating the new facility. A comprehensive bibliography and index are provided along with a list of professional library moving companies. Anyone who is moving a library for the first time and those who have had unsuccessful previous experiences will find this easy-to-read and understand book extremely useful if not indispensable. [R: BL, 1 Apr 88, p. 1310; LJ, 1 Apr 88, p. 64]   Jay Schafer

Buildings

339.   Adaptation of Buildings to Library Use. Proceedings of the Seminar Held in Budapest, June 3-7, 1985. Michael Dewe, ed. Munich, New York, K. G. Saur, 1987. 254p. illus. (IFLA Publications, 39). $34.00. ISBN 3-598-21769-2.

These proceedings of the seventh Seminar on Library Buildings, jointly organized by the IFLA Section on Library Buildings and Equipment and the Association of Hungarian Librarians, reflect a worldwide trend of reusing and adapting existing buildings to house libraries. At a 1975 IFLA seminar, the consensus was "that a librarian must never accept an old building which has previously been used for other purposes." Economics and a renewed interest in historic preservation have reversed this belief.

The proceedings are divided into three parts: (1) formal papers presented at the seminar which address the functional, technical, financial, and aesthetic issues involved in the adaptation of existing buildings, including specific case studies; (2) short reports of experience with a variety of adaptation projects; and (3) information concerning actual adaptation projects which were visited during the seminar.

The case study approach to presenting this international view of reusing buildings for public, school, and academic library purposes is both informative and interesting. The proceedings are weak in information about persons giving presentations, reproduction of some drawings and plans, and absence of an index. The text is completely in English, but the use of the metric system may be a challenging inconvenience for American readers. [R: LAR, 16 May 88, p. 296]

Jay Schafer

340.   Dahlgren, Anders C., ed. Library Buildings. Champaign, Ill., Graduate School of Library and Information Science, University of Illinois, 1988. 1v. (various paging). illus. bibliog. (*Library Trends*, Vol. 36, No. 2). $10.00pa.

Dahlgren presents a collection of thirteen essays (plus an introduction and a selected bibliography) on trends in the design of library buildings. Four essays are on types of libraries (public, academic, school, special); the others are on lighting, mechanical systems, environmental design, staff furnishings, output measures and space planning, alternatives to a new building, revitalizing existing space, financing public libraries, and a look at the library building of tomorrow. The authors include practicing librarians, a number of building and design consultants, architects, and an engineer.

This reader came away with many nuggets of information and with a number of interesting suggestions and observations. Because so many aspects are treated, no one topic can be discussed thoroughly. If there is any one overall impression, it is that library design is in a stage of transition, that because of technology's impact, many standards no longer hold and there are few traditional assumptions that still go unquestioned.

As Dahlgren notes in his introduction, there is not space enough in this issue to explore all the factors affecting library buildings, so the authors "have tried to identify some current concerns." The issue cannot serve, in other words, as a manual for a librarian planning a building. On the other hand, students of library design or those interested in planning a building can profit from this book's ideas and observations and the obvious wealth of its authors' experiences. [R: JAL, May 88, p. 133; LAR, 15 Sept 88, p. 528]

Evan Ira Farber

Space Utilization

341. **Building Use Policies.** By Patrick Coyle. Washington, D.C., Association of Research Libraries, 1988. 113p. bibliog. (SPEC Kit, No. 144). $20.00pa.

Like other volumes in the series, this one contains a collection of policy statements related to an academic library activity or administrative concern. *Building Use Policies* covers "Food and Drink Policies," "Smoking Policies," "General Building Use Policies," and "Library Aesthetics." In all there are forty different statements grouped under these four headings. In addition to the policies there are the results of a brief survey conducted by the publisher in 1986, and a five-item selected reading list.

The policies included are dated between 1982 and 1986, and are based on the 1986 survey. A two-page summary of the policies is also included. While there are no very recent ones, the selection of policies include a range of philosophies about each issue. For those currently considering a building policy in one of the four areas, this is a good source for examples of policy statements. It is not, however, a useful source for an analysis of the issues nor a bibliographic entreé to the literature.

Thomas G. Kirk

342. Revill, Don, ed. **Working Papers on Building Planning.** Oxford, England, Council of Polytechnic Librarians, 1987. 201p. illus. £10.50pa. ISBN 0-907130-13-5.

Another in the council's series of working papers, this one contains a collection of internal documents from eleven polytechnic libraries which were planning or building libraries. It is, then, not a reference work; the contents are highly specific to the situations of the eleven institutions. The documents range over twelve years (1974-1986) and are organized into three groups—arguments for space, studies in space usage and occupancy, and architects' briefs and schedules of accommodation—and they include numerous tables, diagrams, charts, and questionnaire forms. While the quality of reproduction leaves something to be desired, and the information is sometimes confusing or irrelevant for U.S. readers due to different measurement systems, building codes, and space standards, the collection could be useful to those planning to write a building program. After all, their and our needs and problems are not very different so that the strategy used to justify a new building, or the format of the reports, or even the use of figures or of language, can provide helpful suggestions.

Evan Ira Farber

LIBRARY HISTORY

343. Achilles, Rolf, comp. and ed. **Humanities' Mirror: Reading at the Newberry, 1887-1987.** Chicago, Newberry Library, 1987. 124p. illus. (part col.). $16.95pa. LC 87-62235.

In 1987, Chicago's Newberry Library celebrated its centennial. The library is unique in that it is a privately endowed research library with its primary collections in history and the humanities. This book historically reflects on the library through a series of essays. Each author is affiliated with the Newberry in some way and brings a different perspective to this work.

Each essay is well written and informative. "A History of the Newberry Library," "Building the Collection," and "The Newberry Library Today" all trace the development of the library to where it is today. "Collecting in the Second Century" examines the directions for the Newberry's second hundred years. "The Newberry Experience" recounts the impact of the library on six researchers who have used some of the Newberry's vast resources. The essays are far from objective, as can be expected under the circumstances.

Scattered throughout the text are handsome picture reproductions of items found in the Newberry. These are briefly described in what could be considered an appendix. Unfortunately, these plates are the closest the book comes to including some concept of the Newberry's treasures. Although the historical chronology is most informative, a partial listing of works found in the Newberry itself would have provided an additional depth to this commemorative volume. Even so, the overview of this great library makes for excellent reading by professional librarians as well as anyone else who is a lover of knowledge. [R: WLB, Mar 88, p. 86]

Marjorie E. Bloss

344. Frisbie, Margery. **This Bookish Inclination: The Story of the Arlington Heights Memorial Library 1887-1987.** Arlington Heights, Ill., Friends of the Arlington Heights Memorial Library, 1987. 240p. illus. index. $10.00. ISBN 0-9617830-0-1.

This chatty chronicle about a medium-sized public library in suburban Chicago relates one hundred years of community library services to the people and village of Arlington Heights, Illinois. In the spirit of any number of such works (e.g., *The Story of a Small Town Library* by Frances Rogers [Overlook Press, 1974]), this volume is descriptive rather than interpretive in style. Although certain to be of great interest to anyone associated with this library no significant insight into the issues and themes of American public library history is afforded. This is recommended only for those exhaustively collecting local library histories or who may have a personal interest in Arlington Heights.

Chris Albertson

345. Wiegand, Wayne A., and Dorothy Steffens. **Members of the Club: A Look at One Hundred ALA Presidents.** Champaign, Ill., Graduate School of Library and Information Science, University of Illinois, 1988. 30p. (Occasional Papers, No. 182). $3.00pa.

This is an excellent study of the first one hundred presidents of the American Library Association covering the period 1876-1986. It deals with many characteristics of past presidents, including their gender and racial composition, marital status, politics, religion, place of birth by geographic region, highest nonlibrary degree earned, regional location of institutions granting nonlibrary degree, terminal library degree earned, administrative position held, and geographic region of employer of all presidents.

The text is supported by many tables (by type of activity). It shows that 75 percent of the first one hundred presidents have been men, but 60 percent of the last ten presidents have been women. Only two presidents have been black. The study reveals that before 1976 only whites occupied the office of president. Only four Catholics and two Jews have been elected president, as compared to forty-two Protestants. Data on other presidents' religions are not available. The study shows that a majority of librarians holding administrative positions in large academic or public libraries or library educators serving as deans or directors were elected to the office. It also shows that a woman holding a top administrative position in a library school had a better chance of election to the office as compared to academic or public library directorship.

Comparing all regions, the study shows that all regions have been well represented with the exception of the West Coast. Only five presidents have been elected from the West and eight received their library degrees in the western United States. The research shows that three lawyers, one medical doctor, and a minister have been elected to the office. Six presidents had doctorates, less than half had no formal library education, and eleven did not graduate from college.

The study tables give information by sex and years, showing that no school librarian, reference librarian, cataloger, Hispanic, Oriental, or native American has ever been elected to the office. According to the authors, there are significant gaps and bias toward the dominant group in the association. Many interesting questions have been raised and the authors have concluded that "the American Library Association has not been in the vanguard of social changes at any time in its history."

An added attraction of the book is an appendix with a list of the first one hundred presidents from Justin Winsor to Beverly Lynch, with their dates in the office. This is an excellent study and recommended for all librarians, library educators, library historians, and all types of libraries. [R: JAL, Sept 88, p. 247]

Ravindra Nath Sharma

346. Young, Arthur P. **American Library History: A Bibliography of Dissertations and Theses.** 3d ed. Metuchen, N.J., Scarecrow, 1988. 469p. index. $39.50. LC 88-10072. ISBN 0-8108-2138-9.

Every new edition of *American Library History* is a significant improvement of an already useful reference book. This third edition was long overdue, since the second was published in 1974. The current work is a bibliography of 1,174 items, of which 964 are annotated listings of doctoral dissertations and master's theses and 210 are unannotated listings of unpublished reports and papers. The book begins with a brief chapter describing and listing the various reference sources for American library history. These items are not numbered. The second and main part of the book is the bibliography of dissertations and theses, which is divided into fourteen sections. Each section concerns a type of library (e.g., public, school, etc.) or a topic (biography or education). The annotations are basically descriptive and range from 40 to 120 words in length. Enough information is provided to indicate whether the item is of interest for further study, although no critical evaluation is provided. Part 3 is a listing of unpublished papers and reports, largely organized in the same manner as part 2. Separate indexes to authors and subjects are provided. Amazingly, no one apparently had written a thesis or dissertation on the Allen County Public Library of Fort Wayne, Indiana! All library schools, education programs, history departments, and individuals studying American library history should acquire or have access to this useful publication. It provides the invaluable service of locating materials that are difficult or impossible to find. Professor Young deserves our gratitude. [R: JAL, Nov 88, p. 314]

Ronald H. Fritze

LIBRARY INSTRUCTION

347. **Biblio-Tech: Survival Skills for the Information Age: A Handbook of Research Skills— Both in and out of the Library, for Use in College—and Long Afterward.** rev. ed. Waterbury, Vt., Community College of Vermont, 1987. 66p. illus. bibliog. index. $7.50pa.

This book is a bibliographic instruction manual for college students. In separate chapters it covers a definition of information, plagiarism, the research process, library and community resources (the later including government offices, professional societies, businesses, and so on), interlibrary loan, computers, reference departments, and government documents. Appendices include one on footnotes and bibliographic entries, an annotated bibliography of research guides, a glossary of library terms, an outline of the Dewey and LC Classifications, and a condensed version of Benjamin Bloom's Taxonomy of Cognitive Objectives. The information contained in the book is for the most part accurate and helpful although the authors could show more awareness of the fast-changing computer technology in libraries. They do not mention CD-ROM databases and discuss computer catalogs only briefly. Contrary to their assertion, some libraries do permit the public to use OCLC. Chapters on government documents and reference are short and not as useful as they could be. The documents chapter mentions SuDocs numbers, for example, but does not explain what they are or give examples of them. But the major complaint with this book stems from its stated audience and use. Its information is sometimes too generalized (i.e., not specific to a certain library) and sometimes too detailed to be used as a quick reference. At the same time the book is not a course textbook to take the place of a composition textbook for an English class. It could serve as a text for a semester class in library skills, although it would have to be supplemented by local information, especially if the library had a computer catalog. Most teachers in other college courses have so much content to teach that they refuse to spend much time on library skills. They prefer to see a chapter or two incorporated into a class text such as James P. Farrelly and Lorraine M. Murphy's *A Practical Guide to Research Papers* (Harcourt, Brace, Jovanovich, 1988) or the *Prentice-Hall Handbook for Writers* (10th ed., 1988). A student will be better served by a good book on writing research papers and a copy of the local library's handbook.

Linda Keir Simons

348. Frick, Elizabeth, ed. **A Place to Stand: User Education in Canadian Libraries.** Ottawa, Canadian Library Association, 1988. 356p. bibliog. $30.00pa. ISBN 0-88802-231-X.

This collection of original essays on bibliographic instruction (BI) in Canada has a nationalistic intent—to focus "the hot spotlight of serious concern on our experience" as opposed to what is happening in the United States, Great Britain, and other Commonwealth countries. The essays (1) survey BI instruction in Canadian academic, public, government, and school libraries; (2) address user education for online public access catalogs; and (3) look at the problems of administration of BI, covering the management and support of BI and training librarians to teach. The final essay is an annotated bibliography of 196 sources on Canadian library user education, listing materials appearing in Canadian sources (whether by Canadians or others), materials about Canada (published anywhere), or materials by Canadians (published anywhere).

Most of the essays introduce and define their province; address related literature, theory, and methodology; and report survey findings (often institution by institution) and discuss the implications of the results.

Reading this collection not only provides a good sense of BI in Canadian libraries, but also gives an overview of universal BI issues. The cited survey results obviously reflect only Canadian experience, but the repeated references to standard U.S. (and occasionally British) BI publications and practitioners and the asserted similarities of the Canadian experience and practice to those elsewhere suggest that the findings are similar to our own practice and experience. Highly recommended for Canadian librarians, but useful for anyone interested in both the historical and practical aspects of library user education. [R: JAL, Nov 88, p. 321]

Blaine H. Hall

349. Hendricks, William. **Library Studies: Suggested Activities to Motivate the Teaching of Library Skills.** Stevensville, Mich., Educational Service, 1987. 219p. illus. index. $6.95pa. ISBN 0-89273-141-9.

This handy collection of library-oriented classroom ideas and projects will be welcomed by elementary and junior high school teachers and librarians who are looking for additional ways to teach library skills to their students and to encourage library use in general.

More than 175 activities are grouped into seventeen chapters, covering library organization, library conduct, the library catalog, reference, fiction, nonfiction, biographies, periodicals, dictionaries, media, research, motivating students to use the library, alphabetizing and spelling skills, book reports, bulletin boards, the book, and the librarian. Each activity lists an appropriate grade level range and includes sections defining purpose, materials, and procedure; sections providing variations on activities or suggestions for relating these projects to other school activities are sometimes included.

The selected activities range from simple to complex, and while many may already be familiar, most teachers will find a number of new, workable, and adaptable ideas. The suggestions aimed at the librarian show a similar range. For example, most experienced librarians will not need suggestions on how to arrange a book truck for easier shelving, but there are a number of other ideas that might well prove useful.

The book concludes with an "Easy Reference Index" which is simply a duplicate of the table of contents with the grade levels for each activity indicated. While somewhat useful, this listing could have been made even more so had it been arranged by grade level (e.g., with all activities appropriate to the fourth grade in one list).

All in all, *Library Studies* is a concise, nicely done compilation that will be a useful addition to the faculty reference shelf in most elementary and junior high school libraries.

Kristin Ramsdell

350. Penchansky, Mimi B., Evelyn Apterbach, and Adam Halicki-Conrad, comps. **International Students and the Library: An Annotated Selective Bibliography on the Theme of the LACUNY 1988 Institute.** Flushing, N.Y., Library Association of the City University of New York, 1988. 29p. $3.00pa.

This bibliography provides a brief guide to significant information on orienting foreign students to the college or university library. It covers books, journal articles, reports, and studies. Organizations that work with international students are included, as well as tips on helping these students use the library. It must be emphasized that it is a selective bibliography – coverage is somewhat limited – but each entry has a long, detailed annotation that is particularly helpful. While it would hardly be an exhaustive source for the subject, this work would help librarians who are faced with serving a large population of international students begin to familiarize themselves with the issues of this area. Also, the section of tips on helping foreign students in the academic library would be

useful for those librarians looking for immediate ways of better serving this special group of library users. In short, almost everything included could be found by searching recent volumes of *Library Literature* or ERIC, but for a minimal price, the Library Association of the City University of New York has done it for you.

Sallie H. Barringer

351. Stripling, Barbara K., and Judy M. Pitts. **Brainstorms and Blueprints: Teaching Library Research as a Thinking Process.** Englewood, Colo., Libraries Unlimited, 1988. 181p. bibliog. index. $19.50pa. LC 88-12821. ISBN 0-87287-638-1.

Designed for secondary school teachers (content specialists) and media specialists (process specialists), the book suggests strategies (brainstorms) and processes (blueprints) for teaching library research as a thinking process. Underlying the approach are two taxonomies: research (levels of thought: fact finding, asking/searching, examining/deliberating, integrating/concluding, and conceptualizing) and REACTS (levels of reaction: recalling, explaining, analyzing, challenging, transforming, and synthesizing).

The authors offer many practical suggestions and provide handouts to guide the process. The research process is explored in terms of choosing a broad topic; obtaining an overview; narrowing the topic; developing a thesis (purpose); formulating questions; planning for research and production; finding, analyzing, and evaluating sources; evaluating evidence; taking notes; compiling bibliographies; establishing conclusions; organizing information into an outline; and creating and presenting the final product. Also covered are preparing students and implementing and evaluating the program. The appendices include a philosophy and goals statement skills continuum for grades 7 through 12.

School library media specialists not engaged in such activities could share the ideas with one or more teachers for the exploration and experimentation. Others will find additional suggestions for integrating such programs into the curriculum. With the increasing access to electronic databases, the limited coverage of this topic (one page) may not be sufficient.

Phyllis J. Van Orden

352. Svinicki, Marilla D., and Barbara A. Schwartz. **Designing Instruction for Library Users: A Practical Guide.** New York, Marcel Dekker, 1988. 249p. index. (Books in Library and Information Science, Vol. 50). $55.00. LC 87-22502. ISBN 0-8247-7820-0.

A guide to teaching library skills in a university setting, this work is a tasteful blending of theory and practice. Svinicki and Schwartz give just enough information about learning principles. learning objectives, sequencing, motivation, and evaluation to provide even the novice program planner with a framework on which to build realistic programs of instruction. The authors advocate informed decision making as a basis for planning relevant library programs.

Almost a third of the book is devoted to library instruction case studies. The authors apply decision-making principles in each of the case studies as they consider some major constraints (objectives, students, situation, and instructor) in order to arrive at teaching options (direct, semidirect, or indirect), teaching methods, and the sequence of instruction. Various teaching/learning options are explored on the premise that "just as different bibliographic tools have different purposes and approaches, so different instructional tools have different purposes and approaches" (p. 6).

Charts and graphs are used generously to illustrate main concepts. Major points are highlighted in the table of contents. There is an adequate index.

This book is a must for college and university library program planners, both new and experienced. It may also serve as a textbook for library schools that incorporate bibliographic instruction in the curriculum. [R: CLJ, Oct 88, p. 334; LJ, 1 May 88, p. 64]

Dianne Brinkley Catlett

LIBRARY RESEARCH

353. Felknor, Bruce L. **How to Look Things Up and Find Things Out.** New York, Quill/ William Morrow, 1988. 290p. index. $22.00; $9.95pa. LC 87-22096. ISBN 0-688-07850-8; 0-688-06166-4pa.

As its title indicates, this book was written more for the inexperienced information seeker than for seasoned researchers. Yet there is information to be gleaned here by anyone who has ever experienced frustration with libraries and reference materials, whatever the reason. Writing in a friendly, conversational style, Felknor offers both encouragement and advice to would-be information seekers. He begins by identifying finding devices that are common to most reference books. He then provides clues to obtaining information about people, places, and various subject fields (e.g., geography, history, the arts, religion, science, mathematics, the social sciences, medicine, technology)—the major portion of the work. Although there are

some recommended titles given in each subject category, this is not a bibliography per se.

Included in the volume is a concise yet informative chapter on computers and computer databases. And there is an index complete with cross-references.

The real "hero" of the book, however, is the reference librarian, whom the author both implicitly and explicitly advises the reader to seek anytime help is needed. This practical advice comes from Felknor's own experiences with libraries and research. [R: LJ, 1 Feb 88, p. 60; WLB, Apr 88, p. 102]

Dianne Brinkley Catlett

354. Lutzker, Marilyn. **Research Projects for College Students: What to Write Across the Curriculum.** Westport, Conn., Greenwood Press, 1988. 141p. bibliog. index. $35.00. LC 87-37549. ISBN 0-313-25149-5.

Librarians and instructors will find this book intriguing: it presents very useful term projects yet falls just short of meeting needs adequate for use as a textbook. As presented, the suggestions and ideas will be welcomed by innovative educators who are willing to break from the traditional term paper concept and encourage student creativity.

This textbook-type volume is aimed at a concept termed "writing across the curriculum." Conceived in London in the late 1960s, writing across the curriculum was introduced in the United States in 1977. The program is intended to teach writing for students enrolled in any curriculum, and this book intends to provide suggestions on how students can utilize a variety of resources to develop research papers they want to write and teachers will enjoy reading. Suggested sources for topic development include several librarians will easily recognize: *American Diaries* (Gale, v. 1, 1983; v. 2, 1987), *State Censuses* (B. Franklin, 1969-), and the *Index to Current Urban Documents* (Greenwood Press, 1972-). The main part of the book is divided into five chapters centered around these different types of primary sources and includes newspapers, legal cases, and annual reports. In all, this is a unique book for today's teachers, and although it only scratches the surface of sources available in most college and university libraries, it is a book that still should be considered for text adoption. Boyd Childress

355. **The Role of the Librarian on a Research Team. Papers Presented at a Program ... at the NYLA Annual Conference, Lake Placid, N.Y., October 23, 1987.** James K. Webster, ed. New York, New York Library Association, 1988. 32p. $5.00pa. ISBN 0-931658-25-X.

These papers were put together in this slender volume to help librarians understand that they can have very significant roles on research terms, but not if they refuse to change their traditional ways of interacting with clients. Neway's article on the team approach stresses that information is power and as such, should be used by the librarian in a participatory context. This will enhance his or her value to the team. Bill Rae argues that although the librarians's willingness to "do something for nothing" is laudable, it diminishes the professionalism inherent in paying for quality. James Webster offers advice on how librarians can join research teams and how they can successfully contribute to the process.

Those who view librarianship with a something-for-nothing approach will object to Rae's argument. But his advice is well taken. The other two authors also provide useful advice on guiding librarians into the helpful world of scholarly research.   Mark Y. Herring

356. Skapura, Robert, and John Marlowe. **History: A Student's Guide to Research and Writing.** Englewood, Colo., Libraries Unlimited, 1988. 1v. (various paging). illus. bibliog. $10.00pa. LC 88-8799. ISBN 0-87287-649-7.

357. Skapura, Robert, and John Marlowe. **Literature: A Student's Guide to Research and Writing.** Englewood, Colo., Libraries Unlimited, 1988. 1v. (various paging). illus. bibliog. $10.00pa. LC 88-8513. ISBN 0-87287-650-0.

From choosing a report topic to term paper formatting, Skapura and Marlowe have written succinct, step-by-step guides to enable students to succeed in accomplishing historical or literary research and writing. Both guides address a variety of typical report writing concerns: beginning research; taking notes; organizing notes and outlining; writing the report; and formatting in an acceptable bibliographic citation style. Each guide includes a respective list of historical/literature reference books that provide a general overview of topics. Students do not devote much time to reading materials regarding report writing, and what distinguishes these guides from others are their clear approach and outline format. Students could probably read and begin following the outlined steps within an hour. Several styles and examples of note-taking which give students an excellent choice depending upon the nature of the reading material are provided. The authors' selection of the internment of Japanese-Americans during World War II as a sample historical research topic is logically supported with note-taking examples throughout the historical guide and is developed

into a concise thesis statement. Although there are similar titles in print concerning report writing (e.g., Nancy Everhart's *So You Have to Write a Term Paper* [Watts, 1987]) all are more serviceable as a class text for a course in research and writing than are these two volumes.

The flaw with these guides concerns their considerable text overlap. Differences exist in only two areas: a different subject example for note-taking is presented in each guide; and the recommended reference books are subject-specific to each guide. Otherwise, there are no significant textual differences.

Either guide is a useful resource for students. At the cost, however, librarians might purchase only one since the texts are duplicative. A capable librarian could easily adapt either guide to suit the other subject area. [R: BR, Nov/Dec 88, pp. 48-49]

                Kathleen W. Craver

358. Tudor-Šilović, Neva, and Ivan Mihel, eds. **Information Research: Research Methods in Library and Information Science. Proceedings of the International Seminar on Information Research, Dubrovnik, Yugoslavia, May 19-24 1986.** London and Los Angeles, Calif., Taylor Graham, 1988. 261p. $46.00pa. ISBN 0-947568-26-3.

This book prints fifteen papers given at the May 1986 conference on information research held at the Inter-University Centre of Postgraduate Studies in Dubrovnik, Yugoslavia. Contributors from a number of countries, principally Yugoslavia and Great Britain, discuss a wide variety of research topics. The papers are divided into two main groups. The first group deals with cases and issues in research and the dissemination of its results. The second group treats various research methods and results. Paper topics include: the history of the Council on Library Resources; a rationale for professional involvement in research; the difficulties of introducing new information technologies to a reluctant staff; research methods in human interaction with information systems; citation analysis; and an explanation of market research. As with most conference proceedings, the papers are rather mixed in terms of style and interest to the reader. Some of them may suggest topics for further investigation to researchers. Others will be of interest to librarians trying to establish systems to document current research and its results. The collection's usefulness is enhanced by the fact that it is indexed in *Library Literature.* [R: LAR, 15 Sept 88, p. 526; LJ, 1 Sept 88, p. 148; RLR, Aug 88, pp. 212-13]

                Linda Keir Simons

MANAGEMENT

General Works

359. Bradley, Jana, and Larry Bradley. **Improving Written Communication in Libraries.** Chicago, American Library Association, 1988. 364p. illus. bibliog. index. $26.50. LC 88-10059. ISBN 0-8389-0497-1.

Jana Bradley, at one time an editor, is now a librarian very skilled in giving workshops on written communication and publication. Larry Bradley is an English professor. In this book they pool their expertise to create a clear and useful reference tool for librarians covering a variety of topics from composing memos to writing for publication. Its design allows the user to read only areas of interest and to concentrate on the level of instruction needed.

Librarians are called upon to write for many audiences. These authors help direct writing to the proper audience in the appropriate context. The checklists, skills tests, and other study aids are particularly valuable as one approaches this work. The book certainly fills a need in the library literature for guidance expanded beyond the focus of "getting published." Theory, practicality, and interest combine to fashion a book librarians will want on their personal reference shelves. [R: LJ, 15 Nov 88, p. 52]   Patricia A. Steele

360. **Cambridgeshire Library and Information Plan 1987-1992 Written Statement.** By Capital Planning Information Limited. Cambridge, England, Cambridgeshire County Council, 1987. 59p. maps. £2.50 spiralbound. ISBN 0-902436-457.

Several years ago the Library and Information Services Council of England recommended the preparation of library and information plans throughout the country. The *Cambridgeshire Library and Information Plan 1987-1992* is the first such plan to be published and is thus a pioneering document.

Prepared by a consulting firm on behalf of the Cambridgeshire County Council, this volume sets forth goals and objectives, assesses the strengths and weaknesses of the existing situation, identifies the various problems which confront the library services, and analyzes the merits of the strategies which might be employed to resolve the problems and attain the goals. Ultimately, the authors of the plan recommend the adoption of the so-called "partnership option," a form of cooperation which would have "local government changing its role away from being a provider of services towards being a catalyst and facilitator ..." (p. 3).

Though Cambridgeshire is a small, semi-rural county of no great intrinsic importance, this library plan deserves considerable attention. As the first of its kind in England, it is of historic interest to British librarians. As an example of how a plan is done and done well, it is of value to public librarians everywhere.

Samuel Rothstein

361. Cargill, Jennifer, and Gisela M. Webb. **Managing Libraries in Transition.** Phoenix, Ariz., Oryx Press, 1988. 201p. bibliog. index. $29.50. LC 87-24703. ISBN 0-89774-302-4.

The authors of this book state that it "should be especially useful for those administrators who find themselves hired into traditional organizations where changing expectations and environments have been largely ignored" (p. vi). They also offer the hope that the book will be helpful to those administrators brave enough to initiate changes in libraries and add to their understanding of the change process. Unfortunately this work falls far short of its objectives. The titles of the three parts incorporating nine chapters are promising: changing organizational environments, changing organizational roles, and using human resources to implement and manage change. The content is disappointing, however. The treatment of these key areas is carried out at a superficial level; unsupported generalizations abound: "Productivity of workers will increase with the assumption of a responsibility for the tasks to be performed" (p. xiii). There appears to be an underlying attitude of "we/they" (i.e., librarians/managers). Short cases inserted throughout the text include questions designed to make the reader focus and analyze a variety of plausible work situations. A bibliography of some eighty journal articles and monographs includes some of the classics in the field but concentrates on literature published in 1986. A separate section for audiovisual materials does not fare as well: more than half of the twenty-eight items were produced in the 1970s. An appendix on staff management tools includes examples of training programs, staff recognition programs, and staff evaluation forms. [R: BL, 1 Apr 88, p. 1309; JAL, May 88, p. 133; JAL, Nov 88, pp. 305-6; LJ, 15 Oct 88, p. 62; WLB, Apr 88, p. 86]

Helen Howard

362. Euster, Joanne R. **The Academic Library Director: Management Activities and Effectiveness.** Westport, Conn., Greenwood Press, 1987. 149p. bibliog. index. (New Directions in Information Management, No. 16). $35.00. LC 87-8375. ISBN 0-313-25789-2.

What is the state of leadership in academic libraries? How is the library director viewed internally by staff and externally by colleagues and administration? Euster explores the academic library director's activities and effectiveness in the context of the literature of leadership, organizational structure, and organizational effectiveness. Directors of forty-two academic libraries in the United States participated in the study. They, their staff, and peers in the university administrative structure responded to questionnaires describing the various facets of the director's activities and the extent to which they were performed. Four groups of leaders, identified as "Energizers," "Sustainers," "Politicians," and "Retirees" were then profiled and their prevalence in the sample indicated.

Who would benefit from reading this carefully crafted and well-written study of those holding leadership positions in academic librarianship? Search committees would benefit from learning what the library director does or should do and from identifying the various characteristics of the type of leader they wish to hire. Students who aspire to such positions would receive career guidance. Library staffs would better understand the possibilities and limitations of the position. Library directors would gain important insights into how peers have described and are performing their role, which in turn could be related to how they are functioning.

The organization of the study follows the standard dissertation format. The crisp style of writing moves the reader along. Of particular benefit are the review of the literature and the questionnaires which could be used by readers to examine their own academic environment. [R: JAL, May 88, pp. 116-17; LJ, 15 June 88, p. 44; WLB, May 88, p. 91]   Ann E. Prentice

363.   Jacob, M. E. L., ed. **Planning in OCLC Member Libraries.** Dublin, Ohio, OCLC Online Computer Library Center, 1988. 133p. bibliog. (OCLC Library, Information, and Computer Science Series, No. 9). $16.50pa. ISBN 1-55653-051-X.

Although this book primarily analyzes the results of a 1987 survey of OCLC-member libraries which addressed planning activities, it also serves as a primer on the concepts and processes of strategic planning. The survey questionnaire developed by the OCLC Office of Library Planning in conjunction with the OCLC Users Council Planning Committee was completed by over 2,200 libraries. Together with the planning documents of 236 libraries, these responses were analyzed and summarized into

most of the topics which comprise this book's eight chapters. Chapter 1 offers an overview of OCLC, networks, and the Users Council Planning Committee's roles and planning processes. Chapter 2 discusses in detail institutional and library planning processes, with an in-depth, illustrated overview of strategic planning. Chapter 3 outlines sources of statistical and planning data relating to libraries and includes results of a 1986 OCLC planning and budgeting study. Chapters 4-7 review the survey results and plans by library type, specifically by academic and research, state, public, and special libraries. Chapter 8 presents a summary of the major findings, identifies unanswered questions, and suggests future research topics. The appendices include a list of the Users Council Planning Committee members from 1983 to 1988, a reprint of the survey letter and questionnaire, and a list of institutions submitting plans. A short glossary and a bibliography conclude the volume.

As a reference tool, this monograph offers research data and insightful conclusions which provide a baseline for describing the state of planning among libraries in the late 1980s. Use of charts, figures, and tables, boldface subheadings, and organization by library type facilitate access to this information. The strategic planning process is well described through a clearly written text, examples, and summary charts and figures. This text is recommended for anyone interested in planning activities in general and in libraries specifically, for the library administrator seeking an introduction to the strategic planning process for staff or planning advisers, or for the observer of how decisions in libraries might be directed.   Danuta A. Nitecki

364.   Katz, Bill, ed. **The How-to-Do-It Manual for Small Libraries.** New York, Neal-Schuman, 1988. 387p. bibliog. index. $39.95pa. LC 87-12390. ISBN 1-55570-016-0.

In this volume thirty-four practitioners give practical advice to librarians who are responsible for small libraries. An introductory section of five chapters discusses different types of small libraries—public, school, four-year college, two-year college, and special. The next four sections present separate chapters grouped by function—administration, collection development and technical services, public services, and computers. A bibliographic essay describing literature of the last decade and a general bibliography conclude the volume. Emphasis is on practical information and is current as of mid-1986. Because of the multiplicity of authors, there is some duplication of information. Through its Small Libraries Publications series, ALA provides a similar service in a group of separate pamphlets; however, the present volume brings all the needed data together under one cover. Much of the information is valuable to all libraries regardless of size, and some chapters present a relatively painless introduction to various specialties. [R: BL, 1 Jan 88, p. 747; BR, May/June 88, p. 43; CLJ, Dec 88, p. 395; JAL, May 88, p. 133; LJ, 15 Mar 88, p. 42; VOYA, Dec 88, p. 257; WLB, June 88, pp. 124-25]   Richard D. Johnson

365. Lancaster, F. W. **If You Want to Evaluate Your Library....** Champaign, Ill., Graduate School of Library and Information Science, University of Illinois, 1988. 193p. illus. bibliog. index. $34.50. ISBN 0-87845-078-5.

Although Lancaster designed this book primarily as a text for students, its value will be felt far beyond the confines of a classroom. The introduction defines the context: "The library ... can be looked upon as an interface between the available information resources and the community of users to be served. Therefore, any evaluation ... should be concerned with determining to what extent it successfully fulfills this interface role." The author then proceeds to describe the elements which can be evaluated—document delivery services and reference services—and other aspects of evaluation including resource sharing as well as cost effectiveness and cost-benefit studies. The various methods used for evaluation are described and analyzed, with numerous examples drawn from research studies. The methodology of each is described clearly and succinctly, with the weaknesses and strengths carefully explained. The result is a book which will help students to understand the process of library activities and help librarians to monitor and measure the value of their work. At the end of each chapter Lancaster lists a handful of study questions designed for classroom use. Some questions are specific and relate directly to the text, whereas others, such as "What are the benefits of a school library? How would you conduct a cost-benefit study in this environment?" could lead to a lifetime of research. This is an important book for the field. [R: BL, 1 Oct 88, p. 217; JAL, Nov 88, p. 320; WLB, Sept 88, p. 76]   Adele M. Fasick

366. McCabe, Gerard B., ed. **The Smaller Academic Library: A Management Handbook.** Westport, Conn., Greenwood Press, 1988. 380p. bibliog. index. (Greenwood Library Management Collection). $49.95. LC 87-23655. ISBN 0-313-25027-8.

This handbook is intended for librarians who work in smaller academic libraries which serve student populations ranging from several hundred to seventy-five hundred. Contributors were selected from smaller academic library settings to ensure familiarity with the issues and problems. Divided into seven parts and thirty chapters, the volume covers general administration, personnel, budgets and finance, collection, user programs and services, technical services, and physical plant. A bibliographic essay supplements chapter references.

The presence of so many contributors almost guarantees an uneven product, and this volume suffers accordingly. Chapters by Fred Heath on administration; Murray Martin on the budget; Kathryn Soupiset, Craig Likness, and Richard Werking on the materials budget; Susan Grigg on archives administration; Frederick Smith on collection size management; and Daniel Vann on students, stand out for their clarity, logical presentation, and knowledge of the relevant literature. Lower grades must be accorded to the redundant chapter (13) on library budgeting and fiscal management, the chapter (19) on improving reference service, and the inadequately developed chapter (24) on managing library automation.

This handbook contains a few solid essays, many average contributions, and a few marginal entries. Perhaps contributing to the variability is the lack of a sound premise. The editor never defines the smaller academic library except by enrollment, and most of the contributors do not consider the problems of the smaller environment. Overall, smallness rarely serves as a definition which includes or excludes processes and services. Readers should consult the general literature; the issues are generic and applicable to all libraries. [R: CLJ, Dec 88, p. 400; JAL, July 88, p. 182; LJ, 15 May 88, p. 64; WLB, Oct 88, p. 95]   Arthur P. Young

367. Murphy, Marcy. **The Managerial Competencies of Twelve Corporate Librarians: A Validation Study of New Directions in Library and Information Science Education.** Washington, D.C., Special Libraries Association, 1988. 37p. (SLA Research Series, No. 2). $7.00 spiralbound. ISBN 0-87111-332-5.

This research report, by Professor Murphy, of the School of Library and Information Science, Indiana University, attempts to analyze the competencies—"knowledges, skills, and attitudes"—of a sample of corporate library managers. For this purpose, the investigator identifies four objectives: (1) identifying the competencies of twelve library managers or supervisors (unnamed) in seven corporate libraries in companies (named) located in Michigan, Indiana, and the Denver area; (2) comparing and contrasting these competencies with those reported in *Special Librarian Competencies* by King Research (available from ERIC as ED 265 857); (3) investigating the means (self-education, intra- and extra-corporation) by which librarians in rapidly changing corporate environments keep themselves up to date; and (4) replication of King's critical incident methodology of gathering data on the behavior of high achievers.

In connection with the second objective, Murphy notes the controversy surrounding the multivolume King project (which was funded by the U.S. Department of Education) from its very beginning, then remarks that because it proved necessary to wait until the King report was published, "this study also assumed the character of a validation" (p. 4). With respect to the fourth objective, the investigator calls attention to having adopted and used the King interview questionnaire with one major modification — adding a question asking interviewees to describe both recent negative incidents as well as recent positive ones, in order to identify competencies they lacked as well as those that seemed to be well developed.

As it turns out, because of "time and space constraints" (p. 8), answers to only selected questions are addressed. The full questionnaire, however, is given as Appendix 1. Appendix 2 lists representative examples of respondents' good incidents (or successes) and bad incidents (or failures). Appendix 3 lists the seven clusters of "knowledges" set forth in the King report.

The first five chapters discuss the problem to be researched, the methodology, the results, how corporate library managers keep up to date, and the study's summary and conclusions. The sixth chapter ("References") frequently annotates the notes in chapters one through five. This chapter and the implications for education for corporate library managers and for special librarianship given in chapter five are likely to be the most useful portions of this report for library educators and practitioners alike.   Wiley J. Williams

368.   Revill, Don, ed. **Working Papers on Objectives and Planning.** Oxford, England, Council of Polytechnic Librarians, 1987. 145p. £8.00 pa. ISBN 0-907130-14-3.

Modeled on the "SPEC Kit" collection published by the Office of Management Studies, Association of Research Libraries, this series includes material on more than ten topics of particular interest to British and European academic libraries. Building planning, automation, staff training, and organizational charts are some of the topics. Operating under the direction of the Council of Polytechnic Librarians,

the purpose of the program (as with the "SPEC Kits") is to provide documents that suggest new ideas and fresh approaches for dealing with current problems.

This particular work addresses the issue of formulating objectives and planning for their attainment. The volume begins with a brief introduction to the topic that defines various terms associated with planning. This preface is followed by four sections of documents, each dealing with a specific element of planning: (1) overall library aims; (2) policies; (3) policies/ library liaison; and (4) plans and objectives. (Sample documents were furnished by various polytechnic institutions in Great Britain.) The documents provide a broad perspective on British library policies and practices. While the print in some of the documents lacks a degree of quality, the cost is relatively moderate. Library schools and librarians with an interest in international librarianship would find this particular volume useful.   P. Grady Morein

369.   Salter, Charles A., and Jeffrey L. Salter. **On the Frontlines: Coping with the Library's Problem Patrons.** Englewood, Colo., Libraries Unlimited, 1988. 170p. bibliog. index. $19.50. LC 88-8805. ISBN 0-87287-658-6.

It is no secret that many large libraries in the 1980s have become daytime shelters for the homeless and mentally ill. Library staff now need to know more than the latest CD-ROM search techniques or how to use *Science Citation Index*; they also need to be experts in the control of "problem patrons." The authors' book is especially designed to assist library staff in the identification of tricky situations and to effectively defuse patrons with a wide range of behaviors.

To help in the analysis of potentially dangerous situations, twenty-four case studies are presented documenting exhibitionism, paranoia, schizophrenia, drunkenness, drug use, and mental retardation. Each case is amplified with discussion questions, an outcome statement, an analysis, tips, and short bibliography. These cases make up the 107 pages of part 1 and make this volume suitable for classroom use. Part 2 discusses strategies for coping with problem patrons. Short sections on the causes of mental illness and types of common illnesses are a prelude to practical advice for preparing for and confronting a troublesome visitor. Documentation, staff training methods, selection of security forces, and dealing with other agencies are covered. Appendices offer a library preparation checklist, samples of documentation, and an extensive bibliography. Seasoned librarians may not need to read this book because they have seen the problems firsthand, but new public service librarians should study this volume thoroughly. [R: LJ, 15 Nov 88, p. 52; WLB, Dec 88, p. 105]

Stephanie C. Sigala

370.   Thompson, James, and Reg Carr. **An Introduction to University Library Administration.** 4th ed. London, Clive Bingley/Library Association; distr., Chicago, American Library Association, 1987. 265p. bibliog. index. $40.00. ISBN 0-85157-398-3.

This enlarged and largely rewritten fourth edition of *An Introduction to University Library Administration* is intended to address overall changes in managerial strategy necessitated by changing circumstances (reductions in library funding and increased emphasis on performance) within the university community since the issue of the third edition (1979).

Chapters are provided on general functions of the university library, staff, reader services, processes and routines, library buildings, and cooperation. The authors' counsel is based largely on British libraries and librarianship. Individuals interested in a brief, well-documented overview of administrative concerns and those looking for an introduction to British university library administration will find this title of greatest interest. Others may find that information provided on reader services, staff recruiting, finance, etc., may serve as a springboard for development of ideas more practically applied to libraries outside Great Britain.

Extensive chapter-end bibliographies and a good index also serve to enhance the value of this volume. [R: RLR, Feb 88, pp. 45-46]

Ahmad Gamaluddin

Personnel

371.   Alvarez, Robert S. **Library Boss: Thoughts on Library Personnel.** South San Francisco, Calif., Administrator's Digest Press, 1987. 317p. $19.95. LC 87-70126. ISBN 0-9618247-0-0.

Alvarez, who started *Library Administrator's Digest* in the 1960s, has taken selections from it to create *Library Boss*. Although the digest covered all topics related to libraries, this book is limited to personnel issues: selection and training; relationships with the staff, nonprofessionals, library board, and community; retirement; having the right attitudes; openness to new ideas; and quality of service. The digest and the book contain the author's musings resulting from personal experience—the book is not a report of research. It is helpful, however,

reminding one of basic principles that may occasionally be forgotten in the press of daily routines. [R: BL, 1 Jan 88, p. 747; CLJ, Apr 88, p. 121; JAL, Sept 88, p. 242]

Nathan M. Smith

372.   Blanksby, Margaret. **Staff Training: A Librarian's Handbook.** Newcastle-under-Lyme, England, AAL Publishing; distr., Newcastle-under-Lyme, England, Remploy, 1988. 58p. £8.95pa. ISBN 0-900092-68-8.

While Blanksby does not declare a purpose in producing this handbook, it appears the author's aim is to provide an introductory primer to library staff training rather than an explicit training manual. The work contains ten brief chapters including a list of five additional readings and an exhibits section composed of fifteen sample documents. Emphasis is given to identifying training needs and to considerations and methods for satisfying training needs. Blanksby classifies training methods into two categories: "at work" opportunities and "away from work" activities. She stresses "at work" opportunities which include expanded assignments, performance review, coaching, exposure to higher levels of management, and others. "Away from work" activities consist of such applications as courses, seminars, conferences, and guided reading. Perhaps the most useful part of this book is the exhibits. Rather detailed examples are presented on topics ranging from job description and personnel specification to task analysis and training audit. In addition, Blanksby provides a number of graphic illustrations on issues such as training cycles, variables in learning, and the growth process.

Since the tone of presentation is definitely British, some of the concepts may be new to readers unfamiliar with British personnel practices. For example, Blanksby presents a "faults analysis" technique in which a problem, fault, or failure of some kind is explored through a series of structured questions. The book is interesting and presents useful information for both line and staff managers in libraries. However the price is somewhat high for such a modest publication. [R: LAR, 15 June 88, p. 349]

P. Grady Morein

373.   **Performance Appraisal in Research Libraries.** Washington, D.C., Association of Research Libraries, 1988. 100p. bibliog. (SPEC Kit, No. 140). $20.00pa.

This SPEC Kit from ARL's Systems and Procedures Exchange Center (SPEC) in the Office of Management Studies updates earlier kits on performance appraisal from 1974 and 1979. A short 1987 questionnaire to ARL members, eliciting seventy-one responses, is summarized in a two-page SPEC flyer inserted as a first item. The bulk of the kit consists of photocopies of fifteen documents from fourteen university libraries of procedures and policies used. They are grouped in three sections: an overview of procedures, peer review, and merit increase review. The flyer, prepared by Allen B. Veaner, gives a good summary of the questionnaire responses as well as the documents themselves — variations in procedures followed, heavy reliance on qualitative judgment in establishing criteria, flexible and open character of guidelines, considerable variation in formation and structure of peer review bodies, and a general trend to spell out performance policies and procedures in great detail. A short bibliography concludes the kit. The quality of photocopies varies (with several pages of the Stanford document almost illegible). The kit can prove a useful source for libraries implementing or reviewing their own performance appraisal procedures. [R: JAL, Mar 88, p. 51; LJ, 15 Apr 88, p. 62]   Richard D. Johnson

374. Person, Ruth J., and George Charles Newman. **Selection of the University Librarian.** Washington, D.C., Association of Research Libraries, 1988. 23p. bibliog. (OMS Occasional Paper). $15.00pa. ISBN 0-918006-56-2.

Recognizing the importance of the appointment of a new library director and the increasingly complex process for selecting administrators in higher education, the authors undertook a study to identify characteristics that contribute to a successful search for a university librarian. They examined the literature, then conducted in-depth interviews with participants in the search process for a library director at five large universities. Questions consisted of nineteen items covering such topics as how the persons serving on the search committee were selected; what previous experience did they have with search/screen processes; what were their responsibilities; what criteria were used to screen applicants; why was the particular person chosen; and what special problems were encountered in the selection process. Interviewees included the university president/chancellor, provost/vice-president for academic affairs, chairperson of the search committee, members of the search committee, and affirmative action officer.

This concise publication summarizes the study, reports literature findings, and describes the results of the analysis. A section titled "Common Themes for a Successful Search" defines four elements that appear to contribute to a successful search. In their conclusion, the authors discuss the role of outsiders (i.e.,

nonlibrarians), the assertive search, and questions for future study.

Funding for the research was provided by the Council on Library Resources as part of a Faculty/Librarian Cooperative Research Project Grant. Academic librarians, faculty, and administrators involved in a search for a library director would find this inexpensive publication useful. Students of librarianship would also acquire worthwhile information from this work. [R: JAL, May 88, p. 117]
P. Grady Morein

375. **Search Procedures for Senior Library Administrators.** By John Ulmschneider. Washington, D.C., Association of Research Libraries, 1988. 107p. bibliog. (SPEC Kit, No. 143). $20.00pa.

Recruitment and retention of library directors is increasingly viewed by universities as a major decision affecting services to scholars and teachers in all disciplines. Within research libraries, there is considerable attention devoted to the identification and hiring of associate/assistant directors who are largely responsible for the direct administration of many library functions.

To ascertain search procedures for these positions, this SPEC Kit summarizes the findings of a fifty-eight-library survey and furnishes eighteen supporting documents. It is based on a review of 60 director searches and 176 associate-/assistant-level searches over the past decade. Results indicate that procedures for the selection of library directors have become more formal, utilize national searches, apply rigorous evaluation, and attract major participation by institutional officers. Searches usually produce a suitable pool of candidates and searches are rarely reopened. National advertising and the use of personal and professional contacts are commonplace. Search committees are generally used for both types of positions. Parent institution administrators participate broadly in director searches, whereas associate-/assistant-level searches are usually considered internal library matters.

Policy, procedure, and screening statements are appended from such institutions as Cornell University, University of Alabama, University of Connecticut, and Southern Illinois University at Carbondale.

This SPEC Kit ably distills essential trends and furnishes supporting materials about a significant personnel activity which has long-term implications for the library's direction and the institution's vitality. [R: JAL, Sept 88, p. 270]   Arthur P. Young

Public Relations

376. Canoles, Marian L. **The Creative Copy-cat III.** Englewood, Colo., Libraries Unlimited, 1988. 207p. illus. bibliog. index. $19.50. LC 87-29851. ISBN 0-87287-576-8.

The basic intent of this book is to promote reading by using bulletin boards to advertise individual books. The 120 fiction titles featured range from picture books through high school classics and popular fiction. Animal stories, fantasy and science fiction, historical fiction, mysteries, realism, and romance-adventure stories are represented by twenty titles in each chapter. Each entry includes a suggested bulletin board; author, title, and quote from the book; directions and necessary materials for construction; a list of related display items; and pertinent subject headings.

There is nice variety in the books included in terms of genre, reading levels, and interest levels. The quotes chosen to represent each title are pertinent and often enticing, which can be helpful in reading guidance. Patterns included in the appendix could be helpful, and the bibliographies of books used, suggested sources for titles, crafts, and supply catalogs are useful.

It takes quite a bit of time to construct bulletin boards. It would seem that such an investment in time would be better spent in other promotional activities that can "advertise" more than one book at a time — such as booktalks — unless student aides or other volunteers actually do the work. While the idea of using bulletin boards as book billboards is interesting, the time involved seems high, especially without research to show exactly how effective the procedure actually is. There are a few format and editing problems. The bulletin boards are designed for a space 60 by 60 inches, but the sample boards shown are rectangular. The idea of including photographs of the boards is a good one in principle, but the picture quality is not good, details are hard to see, and the photographs do not closely match the corresponding drawing. Cynthia Voigt's name is misspelled.

Overall, this title contains some standard bulletin board ideas. The quotes used to represent each title are generally well done, but the suggested technique of one book per bulletin board is too time consuming. [R: BL, July 88, p. 1822; BL, July 88, p. 1844; VOYA, Aug 88, pp. 152-53]   Carol A. Doll

377. **Great Library Promotion Ideas IV: JCD Library Public Relations Award Winners and Notables 1987.** Sandra A. Scherba and others, eds. Chicago, American Library Association, 1988. 57p. illus. index. $11.95pa. ISBN 0-8389-3363-7.

The Library Administration and Management Association (LAMA) of ALA has compiled a series of books which highlight the winners of the John Cotton Dana Library Public Relations Award for each year since 1984. This is the fourth book of the series.

A slim paperback, it is divided into general subjects including planning, fund raising, summer reading programs, and short-term events. Generally, there are at least five libraries included under each subject. Although public libraries predominate, academic and military libraries are also mentioned. Each entry describes a library's particular public relations idea, its objectives, a description of the activity, funding sources, a description of the community, and the name and address of a contact person. Included with some entries is a black-and-white facsimile of a poster or a pamphlet used in that particular public relations event.

The preface and introduction give the reader helpful information concerning the John Cotton Dana awards and the selection process for these awards. The only indexing is a geographic index which is adequate considering the size of the book.

This book would be most appropriate in a library's professional collection. Also, it might be helpful to other organizations of an educational or a public service nature that are trying to enhance their own public profiles.

Phillip P. Powell

378. Leonard, Carolyn, and Marian Colclasure. **Print Shop Graphics for Libraries. Volume 5: States and Politics.** Englewood, Colo., Libraries Unlimited, 1988. 36p. with disk. illus. maps. $25.00pa. LC 88-8653. ISBN 0-87287-726-4.

This book is one volume in a series of graphics data disks for use with Print Shop and similar computer programs. All titles in the series are available for Apple computers, volumes 1 and 2 have an IBM version, and volume 4 a Macintosh version.

Side one of this volume's disk provides graphics of all the states, areas of the country, and the continental United States and North America, although apparently not to the same scale. For example, Rhode Island seems about the same size as South Dakota. In addition, side one has fifteen pictures relating to the November 1988 Presidential campaign, and other symbols relating to the federal government complete the one hundred images. The flip side of the disk provides fifteen high-resolution panels. A third of these are of President Reagan and the presidential candidates. The others include the U.S. flag, the Statue of Liberty, the Capitol, and similar patriotic sites and emblems. A manual with facts about the states and each president, and some information on the two finalists in the 1988 presidential election accompany the disk. The electoral college votes for 1900-1984 are charted on maps not included on the disk. On the whole, the emphasis on the 1988 campaign cuts into the publication's usefulness for libraries or social studies classes since the election is over. The graphics of national buildings and symbols could be of use to libraries or classrooms for celebrating patriotic occasions. The use of state information and maps, which most people in a library would not seek in a computer program manual, seems more problematic.

The high-resolution graphics are of good quality. But the higher-quality graphics now available for the Mac and some other computers will challenge the quality of the graphics in this program.   Betty Jo Buckingham

379. Leonard, Carolyn, Marian Colclasure, and Mark Loertscher. **Print Shop Graphics for Libraries. Volume 2: Perpetual Calendars.** Englewood, Colo., Libraries Unlimited, 1987. 52p. with disk. $23.00pa. LC 87-16799. ISBN 0-87287-606-3.

Perpetual Calendars is volume 2 of Libraries Unlimited's series on Print Shop Graphics for libraries. Sold as a 5¼-inch microcomputer disk with a fifty-two-page book to accompany it, this volume contains data for forty-eight different monthly calendars in four subject areas: children's literature, young adult literature, adult literature, and library history. Each of the calendars contains names, birth dates, and famous works of notable authors. The twelve library history calendars also include significant dates in the development of libraries around the world. The disk is only a data disk, however, and must be used with a separately purchased calendar-generating program from Broderbund Software called Print Shop Companion. In addition, users must have a microcomputer from the Apple II series or one of the IBM PC group, as well as a printer that will produce graphics and can be configured to the Print Shop Companion.

The accompanying book contains chronological listings by subject area of all the dates, names, and titles found in the calendar disk files. The Print Shop Companion program does permit either temporary or permanent modifications to the files allowing users to add dates and events of local interest—such as the birth date, name, and book title of a local children's

author. The program does not allow for merging two or more months from the separate subject areas. The only index to the names and titles included in the calendar files is found on the disk. (The Apple version requires the use of another separate program, AppleWorks, to access the index.)

Although the written documentation and directions are not as thorough as beginning users might like, the convenience of having all the author data collected, input, and ready to use will be appealing to those already familiar with Print Shop Companion. The publishers do provide a telephone number for user assistance and free replacement of defective disks.

Marilyn L. Shontz

380. Leonard, Carolyn, Marian Colclasure, and Mark Loertscher. **Print Shop Graphics for Libraries. Volume 3: Books and Fonts.** Englewood, Colo., Libraries Unlimited, 1988. 12p. with disk. illus. $21.50pa. LC 88-2305. ISBN 0-87287-659-4.

This third volume of Libraries Unlimited's Print Shop Graphics series consists of a twelve-page softcover book and a 5¼-inch floppy disk to be used with the Apple II+, IIe, or IIGS microcomputer and a graphics program. The first several pages of the book contain illustrations of the 100 graphics and the 15 different fonts found on side 1 and 2 of the disk, respectively. The remainder of the text lists ideas for using the fonts and graphics. The disk and book are "designed for librarians and teachers who are interested in promoting reading and books" (p. 1). Users should note that the disk requires separate purchase of a graphics program such as Print Shop, PrintMaster Plus, or Print Magic. The authors also warn that some early versions of Print Shop may not work with this volume's disk. For those who may have difficulty using the disk, the publishers offer a telephone number for help and free replacement of defective disks.

Of the graphics included, all use a book motif and most are intended for children and young people—there are a lot of animals and story characters. "Time to Read," "Celebrate Reading," and "Books are Too Good to Miss" are examples of the logos included with the graphics. The fifteen different styles of lettering come in several sizes and (helpfully) include numbers and punctuation marks. The variation in letter sizes increases the usability of the Print Shop program which limits letter size to the user's font choice.

At the end of the book fifty projects are briefly described. Ideas for using the graphics include bookmarks, awards, signs, labels, name tags, mobiles, and book jackets.

　　　　　　　　　　　　Marilyn L. Shontz

381.　Matthew, Howard. **Community Information: A Manual for Beginners.** Newcastle-under-Lyme, England, AAL Publishing; distr., Newcastle-under-Lyme, England, Remploy, 1988. 40p. bibliog. £6.00pa. ISBN 0-900092-62-9.

This monograph—in reality, more a pamphlet in format—is a rather neat introduction to the providing of community information. Although published in Great Britain, with numerous references to agencies and publications that are decidedly British, this work can be easily generalized to any country's situation. Beginning with a definition of community information and a discussion of political context, the author proceeds to create a methodology that addresses the evaluation of needs, staff concerns, and types of materials. Once the system is in place, further sections focus on presentation, promotion, and evaluation.

For those librarians who are just beginning to pull together community information and wish to do so in an organized and effective way, this booklet can provide much that is useful in terms of ideas and strategies. A quick read—but filled with thoughts to ponder and stimuli for action. [R: LAR, 15 Aug 88, p. 472; RLR, Aug 88, p. 204]　　　　Darlene E. Weingand

382.　Matthews, Judy Gay, Michael Mancarella, and Shirley Lambert. **ClipArt & Dynamic Designs for Libraries & Media Centers. Volume 1: Books & Basics.** Englewood, Colo., Libraries Unlimited, 1988. 193p. illus. bibliog. index. $25.00pa. LC 87-33877. ISBN 0-87287-636-5.

There is something for just about everyone in this clip art collection designed especially to promote books and libraries. Part 1 is for the novice. It discusses the techniques, materials, and equipment needed to create attractive, professional looking visuals. Part 2, "Clip Art," begins with a section of very simple projects which use some of the clip art from the book to demonstrate how a design can be trimmed, combined with other images, and used in a variety of printed materials. The rest of part 2 is more clip art. For ease in locating a specific type of design, the authors have divided the art into thirteen sections: "Very Simple Projects"; "Books, More Books, and Still More Books"; "Doing It in the Library"; "Holidays & Monthly Potpourri"; "Party Animals"; "People & Books"; "Out in the Open" (outdoor and sports); "Storybook Characters & Fancy Creatures"; "Pretty Boxes" (borders); "Attention

Getting Doo-dads"; "You Oughta Be in Pictures"; "Maps and Grids"; and "Headlines."

The work also contains a bibliography of other clip art and related books. A glossary defines all the technical terms from part 1. An index is provided.

Librarians in all types of libraries will find this book a useful one for their graphic arts collections, and judging from the title, additional volumes will be forthcoming. Recommended. [R: BL, 1 Apr 88, p. 1337; BR, Sept/Oct 88, p. 49; VOYA, Apr 88, p. 51]　　　Carol J. Veitch

383.　Matthews, Judy Gay, and others. **Print Shop Graphics for Libraries. Volume 4: Dynamic Library Graphics.** Englewood, Colo., Libraries Unlimited, 1988. 52p. with disk. illus. $24.00pa. (Apple version); $23.50pa. (Macintosh version). LC 88-8644. ISBN 0-87287-690-X (Apple version); 0-87287-691-8 (Macintosh version).

This booklet is designed as a manual to accompany either the Apple or Macintosh versions of a computer graphic designs disk for use with the program Print Shop. The designs are intended to be particularly useful for illustrating and enhancing library newsletters, bookmarks, and other projects and publications. Library public relations personnel will find the pictures a welcome and lively addition to their PR bag of tricks. The introduction to each version tells users the details of software and hardware requirements.

Beyond the software, however, the authors provide readers with some helpful, general hints about printing and publicity projects for libraries or other "do-it-yourself" agencies. Matthews and her colleagues condensed material from their book *ClipArt & Dynamic Designs for Libraries & Media Centers* (Libraries Unlimited, 1988) to suggest production techniques for amateur editors and printers. They include a list of useful supplies as well as a discussion of layouts and printing, binding, and folding requirements.

Even if one does not have a computer and the Print Shop program, this will be a useful manual. Together users will have an invaluable tool for producing interesting and eye-catching library handouts.　　　Berniece M. Owen

384.　Weingand, Darlene E. **Marketing/Planning Library and Information Services.** Littleton, Colo., Libraries Unlimited, 1987. 152p. illus. bibliog. index. $23.50. LC 87-22653. ISBN 0-87287-516-4.

Weingand's discussion focuses on the essentials of marketing and planning. No space is wasted on detailed explanations and examples;

issues are presented succinctly, almost in outline form. Some readers may be annoyed by the staccato writing style. Many administrators will have to turn to introductory texts for the background they may need to take full advantage of this important discussion. And this is an important book for all library administrators to review. The author's concern is that librarians are not prepared to face the future realistically because they do not know the needs of users and she warns, "librarians who have historically devoted their talents and skills to a service ethic that has been admirable now find this ethic to be increasingly unworkable in a time of economic constraints." For the author, the concepts of marketing and planning are interrelated. Emphasis is placed on the marketing audit—assessing library user needs and a library's capabilities for meeting those needs. A major portion of the book is devoted to system design and includes practical information on creating the planning team, setting goals, identifying unique services, and measuring costs.

Each chapter ends with a "Scenarios for Further Thought" section. These will help the more perspicacious reader, but many readers might need controlled classroom instruction or discussion to get the most from them. Illustrations contribute to an understanding of the text. The bibliography is highly selective and unannotated. [R: CLJ, Aug 88, p. 254; JAL, May 88, p. 120; RLR, Nov 88, p. 353; WLB, Apr 88, p. 86]   Milton H. Crouch

385. Wood, Elizabeth J., with Victoria L. Young. **Strategic Marketing for Libraries: A Handbook.** Westport, Conn., Greenwood Press, 1988. 214p. index. (Greenwood Library Management Collection). $37.95. LC 87-15022. ISBN 0-313-24405-7.

Wood, an assistant professor at Bowling Green State University, has written an unusual book which combines the use of marketing libraries with strategic planning. She begins the first section of the book by explaining the principles of marketing, including the elements of the marketing mix—product, price, place, and promotion. She discusses the idea of product life cycles and media selection, and she enumerates the steps in the marketing process. The book deals with the importance of gathering and analyzing environmental and organizational data in order to identify opportunities, user needs, and constraints. The author provides the rationale for identifying target markets, and she discusses the marketing system.

The second part of the volume covers principles of strategic planning with a detailed discussion of the mission, goals, objectives, and strategies. The author notes several growth strategies that can be considered for expanding and diversifying markets, and she concludes the book by presenting and illustrating portfolio analysis and management, a technique that can be used as a guide to supplement administrative experience and judgment. Wood also includes sample strategic plans and bibliographies.

The book offers a new and stimulating approach to marketing libraries by integrating it with the planning process of management. It goes beyond Joseph P. Grunenwald's *Developing a Marketing Program for Libraries* (Center for the Study of Rural Librarianship, Clarion State College, 1983), which was designed primarily for small public libraries. Wood's book frequently offers information and examples for public, academic, and special libraries, and it provides an in-depth discussion of marketing libraries and strategic planning. It is a useful tool for the experienced administrator and the library science student. [R: BL, 1 Apr 88, p. 1310; JAL, May 88, p. 120; WLB, May 88, p. 91]   O. Gene Norman

Time Management

386. Berner, Andrew. **Time Management in the Small Library: A Self-Study Program.** Washington, D.C., Special Libraries Association, 1988. 102p. illus. bibliog. $125.00 spiral-bound.

The first in a series of self-study programs launched by SLA, this course is available in three formats: IBM disk, Apple disk, and a manual version. (The manual version and the IBM disk were used for this review.) The manual is a combination of text and a small amount of programmed instruction. Of the 102 pages (the cover is counted as page one), over one-third are blank or contain only a section heading. The purpose of the "course," finally revealed on page 81, is "to provide you with the basic precepts of time management so that you can make specific applications of these precepts to your own small library." The volume is divided into two sections: program text and supplemental material. The first covers time management basics, using time effectively, turning goals into reality, and turning theory into practice by putting time management to work. The supplemental material consists of a daily time log, a reprint of the author's fall 1987 article in *Special Libraries*, a bibliography of thirty-three items, a statement indicating that this course earns three CEUs, and a two-page course evaluation form. The content of the manual is slight and achieves its purpose only to a very limited extent. The IBM disk is basically a replication of the manual, although the program section provides an additional opportunity for interaction via questions. The price for this course seems exorbitant. It is unfortunate that SLA's self-study program has made such a feeble beginning. Helen Howard

NEW TECHNOLOGIES

General Works

387. Cone, Robert J. **Key to High-Tech: A User-Friendly Guide to the New Technology.** Rochester, N.Y., Galcon Press, 1987. 153p. index. $10.95pa. LC 87-81270. ISBN 0-943075-17-3.

This guide seeks to explain in layperson's language a number of high technology topics. Brief chapters are given to each main topic, with a second section of the book covering other topics, such as holography, in lesser detail. To use this work, one must know the name of the technology involved. For instance, compact disks are under "Optical Data Storage" and under "Laser," but there is no indexing to tell the user this. Since this is written for people with no specific scientific training, this format could be a drawback. Each chapter gives a brief description of the term, tells several commercial applications, and may tell some background or how the technology works. The explanations are understandable by an intelligent adult, and compress a great deal of information into very few words. There are other technical dictionaries and encyclopedias on the market that are aimed at technical personnel, and therefore do not really compete with this title. This is a useful source for those needing a little background on basic topics, but it is not comprehensive, and is not a substitute for a dictionary. Also, to really understand many of these topics requires more discussion and detail than are given here. [R: RBB, 1 Oct 88, p. 242; SBF, May/June 88, p. 271] Susan V. McKimm

388. **How to Find Information on Emerging Technologies.** By Washington Researchers Publishing. Washington, D.C., Washington Researchers, 1987. 85p. index. $50.00pa. LC 86-51629. ISBN 0-934940-49-5.

Readers will pay a lot (probably too much based on how fast the information will be out-of-date) but they will get a conveniently organized, fact-filled, if not fancy, package. This publication "identifies the federal government offices that play key roles in technology development, support, and regulation," describes the activities of these offices, and tells who to contact for more information. For example, the names and telephone numbers of the Consumer Assistance and Small Business Division of the Federal Commerce Commission, the addresses for all the laboratory representatives who participate in the Federal Laboratory Consortium for Technology Transfer, and the names and contact points for congressional committees, subcommittees, caucuses, and clearinghouses that deal with science or technology are included. Under the listing for each government agency or office, in addition to addresses, names, and telephone numbers, descriptions of role, purpose, and publications are found. A sample tracer bullet—which is a scientific name for information pathfinder—is included under the Library of Congress, for example, along with a list of additional bullet topics. One look at the tracer bullet will leave you hungering for more. Washington Researchers Publishing has pulled together an interesting and useful compilation of information. Specialized science and engineering libraries, however, are the only ones likely to pay the high cost. Connie Miller

389. **Image Understanding Workshop. Proceedings of a Workshop held at Cambridge, Massachusetts, April 6-8, 1988.** San Mateo, Calif., Morgan Kaufmann, 1988. 2v. illus. $40.00pa./set. ISBN 0-934613-68-0.

Image understanding is a branch of artificial intelligence concerned with extracting meaningful information from images. This workshop covers the latest techniques employed in prototype vision systems for manufacturing, navigation, cartography, and photointerpretation. Directed primarily toward scientists working in image understanding, the workshop reviews the latest research results in the Defense Advanced Research Projects Agency (DARPA) image understanding research program keeping researchers abreast of evolving technology and promoting cross-fertilization of ideas and techniques among various programs.

The proceedings include overviews of the research in progress at eight major universities and five corporate research laboratories, and technical reports describing major results that have been achieved. The contents are all related by a common theme of parallel architectures and algorithms. The technical articles represent the cutting edge of research, while the overview articles provide a conceptual framework and broad references to past work in the field.

This compilation would be a valuable addition to any technical collection. It serves as a reference work in its own right, as an index to other resources, and as an introduction to the expanding field of image understanding.

Ronald P. Blanford

390. Veith, Richard H. **Visual Information Systems: The Power of Graphics and Video.** Boston, G. K. Hall, 1988. 321p. illus. bibliog. index. (Professional Librarian Series). $36.50; $28.50pa. LC 87-31265. ISBN 0-8161-1861-2; 0-8161-1881-7pa.

Veith's book characterizes a new kind of information system, the so-called visual information system, in which the primary messages carried by the system are visual images. He divides the visual experience into elements— color, form, motion, video—which are put together by tools (e.g., icons) to produce an object (e.g., a stored picture, a CAD system). The book discusses the technology of computer graphics and video and the increasing interaction between the two. Veith covers bit mapping, display memory, visual display devices, graphics applications (spreadsheets, games, CAD, etc.), graphics interface design (pop-up menus, dialog boxes, etc.), graphics standards, laser and video discs, and expert systems. He sets it all within a framework drawn from physiology and psychology, namely, how people actually "see" and "perceive."

The book is scholarly and well written, though occasionally the layout is confusing. Chapter 5 seems to follow more logically from chapter 3. The bibliography is extremely useful. The core of the book is the use of graphics to present and manipulate information, but its appeal to librarians may be limited. It will be most useful to those librarians who need a definition of a particular term or to those—still small in number—actually involved in the design of graphics software. The majority of librarians currently are concerned with the use of graphics software, and the demand is for practical, skill-building information. There is no mention of HyperCard—surely a good example with its designing features and dialog boxes and buttons—nor of Hypertext—the linking of text and graphics. There is no discussion of applications such as Thunderscan or Computer Eyes in the sections on digitizing. A useful textbook, but with limited appeal for working librarians. [R: LJ, 1 May 88, p. 64; Online, Nov 88, pp. 94-95; WLB, Nov 88, p. 110]   Linda Main

CAD/CAM Systems

391. Cox, John, Peter Hartley, and Doug Walton. **Keyguide to Information Scources in CAD/CAM.** Lawrence, Kans., Ergosyst, 1988.

257p. bibliog. index. $65.00. LC 88-9185. ISBN 0-916313-15-8.

Although there have been at least two other bibliographies written about portions of CAD/CAM (computer-aided design/computer-aided manufacture) literature, this work appears to be the first to provide background and directory information plus listings of print and electronic sources discussing CAD/CAM.

The guide is divided into three parts: survey of CAD/CAM and its information sources, bibliography, and directory of organizations. At the beginning of the book, the authors have included a glossary of terms and initialisms, appropriate for the novice and experienced user alike. Part 1 is a series of lengthy historical and bibliographic essays covering such topics as the history of CAD/CAM, CAD/CAM's scope, libraries and information services, online information sources, and audiovisual material, just to name a few. The extensive critically annotated bibliography in part 2 lists indexes and abstracting services, books, journals, information services, handbooks, conference proceedings, newsletters, reports, yearbooks, and directories that range from general to specific. Like everything else in the guide, the sources reported are international in scope, both English and non-English. Part 3, the annotated directory of organizations, is a list reporting the scope and interests of international, national, and regional organizations from the likes of the United States, United Kingdom, and the Soviet Union, to Paraguay, Sri Lanka, and New Zealand—any country which has an interest in CAD/CAM issues.

The authors have compiled an impressive list of sources for the researcher. The annotations, which describe virtually every entry, are clearly written. The index gives easy access by author, title, and subject. This work would be an appropriate addition to any collection of high-tech resources.   Phillip P. Powell

392. Stark, John. **Managing CAD/CAM: Implementation, Organization, and Integration.** New York, McGraw-Hill, 1988. 189p. index. $34.50. LC 88-8903. ISBN 0-07-060876-8.

This is the second volume in the McGraw-Hill Manufacturing and Systems Engineering series. The author is director of Coopers and Lybrand Associates, a firm of European CAD/CAM and CIM management consultants. According to the publisher, this series is "designed for upper- and middle-level managers of manufacturing companies and for design, drafting, and manufacturing engineers." This is a timely book on a timely topic. Several articles in recent journals have discussed the increasing use of

CAD/CAM and its effect, or lack thereof, on productivity. A major assumption of any CAD/CAM installation is that it will have a positive effect on productivity, and increasing productivity is one of the stated objectives of this book. Consequently, the book describes activities that must be undertaken if the dream of increased productivity is to be realized. While covering some theory, the primary goal of this book is a practical discussion of CAD/CAM purchasing, system implementation, and management. As a result, a fairly large section of the book is devoted to "people" issues, including the attitudes of accountants, managers, electronic engineers, purchasing agents, and draftspersons. However, omission of either chapter references or suggested readings limits the strength of the title.　　Susan B. Ardis

CD-I Technology

393. Compact Disc-Interactive: A Designer's Overview. Edited by Philips International. New York, McGraw-Hill, 1988. 239p. illus. index. $39.95. LC 88-2735. ISBN 0-07-049816-4.

As the preface to its second edition states, this book is not a designer's guide to producing an interactive compact disk (CD-I). An insufficient body of knowledge and experience exists to allow such a guide to be published: as of December 1987, only two CD-I disks had been publicly displayed. By providing what it can provide — an overview rather than a step-by-step guide — Philips International hopes, through its "interactive" volume, to stimulate the imaginations of potential designers and to contribute to the growth of CD-I understanding and development.

Compact Disc-Interactive moves a reader from basic to complex concepts, from introductory to technical levels. References to related sections and chapters, which appear in the book's margins, pull various concepts together. For example, marginal references in the second chapter, which describes the background of CD-I, refer a reader to a typical CD-I application in chapter 6, to a discussion of National Television Broadcast Standards in chapter 3, and to a detailed look in an appendix at compact disk real-time operating systems (CD-RTOS). While the sections on design briefs, storyboards, design mechanics, disk structure, file managers, and synchronization and control may provide more technical detail than many readers need, librarians will want to pay particular attention to the chapters on what CD-I can do, and how, specifically, it can be applied (e.g., a Grolier multimedia encyclopedia, a

French phrase book). Those who wish to have some influence on the products available to library users must understand the technology on which the products will be based.

A detailed table of contents, an index, and a glossary of terms make the work convenient to read from cover to cover or selectively. Even libraries with this volume's first edition will find the substantially revised second edition worth adding to their collections.　　Connie Miller

CD-ROM

394. Holtz, Frederick. CD-ROMs: Breakthrough in Information Storage. Blue Ridge Summit, Pa., TAB Books, 1988. 215p. illus. index. $22.95; $14.95pa. LC 88-9424. ISBN 0-8306-1426-5; 0-8306-9326-2pa.

Holtz's book is no particular breakthrough itself, but it does gather into one handy volume most of the basics required by anyone trying to cope with compact disk technology. Sprinkled through the book — especially in the sections on multimedia CD-ROM, companion technologies, and past, present, and future developments — are essays by experts in technology, education, and information science. These essays not only contribute valuable content, they also add breadth and depth to Holtz's practical reference tool. Chapters and appendices describe and list CD-ROM drives and drive manufacturers, CD-ROM products and product suppliers, and some of the better known system integrators, like SilverPlatter Information Services and Reference Technology. The standard for the structure of compact disks and their files, first developed by the High Sierra Group and revised by the European Computer Manufacturers Association, is reprinted in full. An index and a detailed table of contents make *CD-ROMs* easy to consult as well as to read from cover to cover. Holtz's book will not add a great deal that is new to library collections where information on compact disks has been fastidiously collected. On the other hand, it is a one-volume source of most of what is essential for those using or helping others use the technology.

Connie Miller

395. Miller, David C. Special Report: Publishers, Libraries & CD-ROM: Implications of Digital Optical Printing. Benecia, Calif., DCM; distr., Chicago, Library and Information Technology Association, American Library Association, 1987. 99p. $12.00pa.

This work's size (5½ by 8½ inches with less than 100 pages) is deceptive. This sixth special report for the Fred Meyer Charitable Trust provides more than enough information to equip a reader to discuss and make decisions about compact disks as a publishing medium. Economy in size results, in part, from Miller's knowledge of the subject. His name will be familiar to attendees of conferences or to readers of collections such as *CD-ROM: The New Papyrus* (Microsoft Press, 1986) that focus on optical technology. But expertise alone did not produce the report's readability. Miller extracts the essentials and explains them, with humor and clarity, in ways that make even complex concepts accessible. He argues convincingly that, at a cost of $0.02 per page, CD-ROM publishing is economically inevitable. He addresses the copyright "jungle" by drawing on the Office of Technology Assessment's *Intellectual Property Rights in an Age of Electronics and Information* guidebook, and discusses CD-ROM publishing, writing, and editing. Librarians who have already been struggling to incorporate compact disks into their collections and services for some time may find the section examining CD-ROM in a library context of least use. But the idea that CD-ROMs, compared to books, are "repertoires" and that their users are "converters" rather than readers should stimulate some serious consideration about the future design of information services.

Two appendices list the highlights of the Microsoft Second International Conference on CD-ROM held in March 1987 in Seattle, and describe the new optical media such as compact disk interactive (CD-I), WORM, or DRAW disks, and erasable optical disks. This small, interesting, enjoyable, and informative report is worth every penny of its relatively small price. [R: JAL, Mar 88, p. 35]   Connie Miller

396. Oppenheim, Charles, ed. **CD-ROM: Fundamentals to Applications.** Stoneham, Mass., Butterworths, 1988. 308p. illus. index. $95.00. LC 88-19386. ISBN 0-408-00746-X.

This is a collection of essays written by both Europeans (primarily British) and North Americans who are active in the CD-ROM field. The essays cover a wide range of topics. Following the introduction to the various optical storage media available, topics discussed include CD-ROM products, CD-ROM and publishers, technology and applications, and case studies. Each of the twelve essays, averaging twenty-six pages in length, is detailed and often profusely illustrated with charts, tables, and facsimile search screens found on different systems. In addition to the essays covering CD-ROM technology are case studies describing the ways this technology is being utilized at ADONIS, an Amsterdam-

based documentary delivery service, and by Pergamon, a major scientific publisher. This practical information seems to balance the preponderance of technical information presented.

The title of the book may be deceiving to the reader who is seeking a good general work on CD-ROM technology. It appears to be aimed rather at informing potential producers of CD-ROM systems instead of potential users. And this it does very well. Public and academic librarians wishing to learn about particular systems providing bibliographic information and their applications would do well to look elsewhere.   Phillip P. Powell

397. Sherman, Chris. **The CD ROM Handbook.** New York, McGraw-Hill, 1988. 510p. illus. index. $59.95. LC 87-83103. ISBN 0-07-056578-3.

This is an exceptionally thorough and comprehensive introduction to the history, technology, and manufacturing of CD-ROM disks, although it also covers software, hardware, and applications. Its seventeen chapters written by "more than twenty authorities in the field" are grouped into parts which take an in-depth look at this new technology by covering the following topics: an introduction (the CD-ROM industry, applications, and CD-ROM publishing); the CD-ROM format (hardware and device integration); advanced CD-ROM formats (compact disk-interactive, digital video interactive, and future possibilities of CD-ROM); information storage and retrieval (designing a CD-ROM information structure, data conversion, and full text indexed retrieval systems); and creating a CD-ROM (data preparation and premastering, CD-ROM mastering, and manufacturing).

Two particularly noteworthy features are the final two chapters, 16 and 17, which present a selected bibliography of CD-ROM articles, books, and ERIC documents, and a discography of CD-ROM titles published as of April 1987, respectively. The former concludes with a very brief list of CD-ROM databases, which seems a bit redundant since chapter 17 lists thirty pages of disks, including most, but not all, of these same databases. The latter also appends an additional brief list of "Undocumented CD-ROM Applications" cited in the literature but not yet verified. The full CD-ROM list is alphabetical by title, with no subject index.

Focusing primarily on the technical aspects of CD-ROM, this work provides a very thorough look at the technology. There are excellent and very clear diagrams throughout the book illustrating much of the technical material discussed in the text. The editor plainly states that the work is aimed at actual developers of CD-ROM who "must have a thorough, intimate understanding of CD ROM technology." This is definitely state-of-the-art material, and while everyone does not need this much detail, it would be hard to find more comprehensive coverage of the topic.

The book is recommended for special libraries, library information and computer science collections, and engineers and others needing a comprehensive work on CD-ROM technology, but not necessarily a comprehensive listing of available disks.   Carol Truett

Optical Storage Devices

398. Crowell, Peter. **Authoring Systems: A Guide for Interactive Videodisc Authors.** Westport, Conn., Meckler, 1988. 168p. illus. index. (Supplements to *Optical Information Systems*, 2). $29.95. LC 86-12496. ISBN 0-88736-084-X.

For several years now, Meckler has been providing librarians with a valuable service by publishing extensively and promptly in areas of automation likely to be of interest to them. Its several journals and the annual Small Computers in Libraries conference provide useful forums for the exchange of information. The only significant weakness in this program is that it attempts to address participants at all levels of knowledge and skill. That problem plagues this slim volume, and many readers will veer from boredom to befuddlement in scanning its pages.

Crowell presents an elementary introduction to the available means of producing interactive video systems for instructional purposes. Individual chapters discuss general software issues, the type of authoring systems available, the use of programming languages as an alternative to authoring systems, the capabilities of HyperCard, and the use of graphics in the authoring environment. The discussions are often brief to the point of being perfunctory, yet larded with technical terms the novice may not understand. The book's best feature is the chapter which provides an authoring systems information database. A series of tables compares features of nearly sixty products; their usefulness would have been enhanced, however, by a brief caption or title for each table characterizing the features being compared. In general, this title is best suited for someone with a good grasp of microcomputer operations and no experience with authoring systems or videodiscs.
        Willy Owen

399.   Feitelson, Dror G. **Optical Computing: A Survey for Computer Scientists.** Cambridge, Mass., MIT Press, 1988. 393p. illus. bibliog. index. $39.95. LC 87-35704. ISBN 0-262-06112-0.

Being the first attempt of its kind (according to the author), this is a general survey of the field of optical computing written by a computer scientist mainly for other computer scientists. The emphasis of the book is not on optical techniques and devices, but on applications and implementations of computer concepts. Beginning with a general overview, the book is divided into three parts. Part 1 deals with special-purpose optical processors, moving from a general description of optics to discussions of analog image processing, numerical processing, and hybrid systems. Part 2 explores the possibilities of a general-purpose digital-optical computer, surveying nonlinear optics, optical approaches to computer components, and the types and feasibility of such technology. Part 3 discusses the impact of optical computers and their prospects. This publication is basically designed as a textbook for upper-level undergraduate or graduate courses in computer science. As such, it is well written, well organized, and provides extensive annotations and bibliographic references for future reading. Its only real problem is its irritatingly poor print quality, since it was photographed directly from the author's typewritten copy. For the librarian or information professional with a good background in computer science who wants a (relatively) nontechnical monograph on optical computing, this would be an excellent choice. It is not, however, a good introduction to the field for the uninitiated.   Sallie H. Barringer

400.   **Optical Publishing & Storage: Products That Work. Proceedings of Optical Publishing & Storage '87....** Joe Bremner, Fran Spigai, and Carol Nixon, comps. Medford, N.J., Learned Information, 1987. 197p. illus. $50.00pa. ISBN 0-938734-22-9.

This book contains twenty-nine articles reproduced from camera-ready copy that are based on papers presented at the second annual conference on the optical publishing industry sponsored by Learned Information. The theme of this meeting was "real-life applications of optical information systems in the fields of publishing and archival storage of information." As with the 1986 conference, participants came from the government, academia, and industry, with university representatives considerably more in evidence. Many of the academic group's papers describe individual library's initial experiences with CD-ROM or specific CD-ROM products, and although all have useful points, much of this by now has been fairly well covered elsewhere. Two papers concerning more sophisticated uses of optical disk technology in libraries are one on a hybrid system at the National Library of Medicine and Richard Sweeney's description of the model electronic library.

Nonlibrary applications described in other articles are often specialized: for example, "CD-ROM for the Trial Lawyer" and a description of the retrieval system used at Hewlett Packard. Because a number of the articles are targeted toward special interest groups, the proceedings as a whole are not as valuable to a general audience as the earlier volume. Nevertheless, those looking for specific examples of how some components of industry and education have used CD-ROM will find this set of proceedings useful.

Robert Skinner

401.   The Optical Publishing Directory 1987. By Richard A. Bowers. Medford, N.J., Learned Information, 1987. 199p. bibliog. index. $45.00 looseleaf with binder. ISSN 0893-0317.

The optical publishing industry is making rapid advances in libraries and information-dependent enterprises. The industry, however, is not without its casualties. The first edition of this directory contained listings of forty-two products. Eighteen of those did not make it into this updated edition, which contains eighty-four titles currently available.

The directory has several sections. A "State of the Art" essay provides the reader with background information on CD-ROM and the impact of optical publishing on information markets. Extensive definitions of key terms and concepts associated with optical publishing are provided in a glossary. The "Product Profiles" section comprises nearly half the volume. Each profile includes information about the manufacturer, print equivalent, bibliographic type, optical format (CD-ROM, WORM, videodisc), product description, hardware specifications, software, and price. This section is arranged by name of the product.

An applications index groups entries by general subject, for example, business, medicine, etc. A product type index lists titles according to their format such as bibliographic, reference, statistical, etc. Additional information is provided on hardware vendors, CD-ROM manufacturers, videodisc players, and Write-Once vendors. A general index appears at the end of the book.

This directory contains a variety of valuable and difficult-to-find information about optical publishing. It is a welcome addition to the literature. [R: RBB, 1 Mar 88, pp. 1114-15]

Dennis J. Phillips

402.   Saffady, William. Optical Storage Technology 1988: A State of the Art Review. Westport, Conn., Meckler, 1988. 155p. illus. bibliog. index. $39.50pa. ISBN 0-88736-344-X.

This is the fourth in a series of annual state-of-the-art surveys of the optical disk industry. It is directed at data processing administrators, systems analysts, and other information specialists, as well as librarians. It reviews products introduced in 1988. Organized along the lines of previous issues, it is divided into two sections: reviews of read-only optical disks, such as CD-ROM; and reviews of read/write (e.g., erasable, optical disks). The first of these two sections is likely to be the more useful for librarians, since it contains long, detailed descriptions of the CD-ROM industry and current products available. The orientation is generally towards evaluation of hardware rather than the contents and organization of individual data disks. The second half of the book, reviewing read/write optical disks, describes products that are as yet more appropriate for business and industry than libraries. The technology to support such systems is simply not available for most institutions. It does offer a fascinating glimpse into the possible future of these systems and what uses libraries might have for this technology. There is an excellent bibliography of reviews of individual products and a complete list of the addresses (but not telephone numbers) of all manufacturers and vendors whose products are mentioned. The major fault of the book, for most librarians, is that it tends to be rather technical; however, it does offer a very good and very complete overview of current developments in this rapidly evolving field.

Sallie H. Barringer

403.   Schwartz, Ed. The Educators' Handbook to Interactive Videodisc. 2d ed. Washington, D.C., Association for Educational Communications and Technology, 1987. 151p. bibliog. $22.95pa. LC 85-71983. ISBN 0-89240-049-8.

Although I did not have access to the first edition of the handbook, the foreword states that the book has gone through "extensive changes, clarifications, and corrections." The majority of this book is devoted to descriptions of laser videodisc players (home and industrial), video monitors and projectors, interfaces to connect a player to a computer, authoring software for developing instructional units using videodiscs, and, most extensively, a listing of available videodiscs of interest to educators. This latter section is divided into approximately sixty sections ranging from aeronautics to vocational education-telemarketing. In addition to a brief description of the videodisc's program, system requirements, publisher, and price are also indicated. For the earlier equipment sections, technical specifications are provided but no comparisons.

General information in a variety of areas relating to videodiscs and their control and playback is provided in the first seventeen pages. Persons unfamiliar with the technology will find these discussions useful, but will have to look elsewhere for in-depth treatments. The information on specific players and discs is helpful to have in one place, although I found several available pieces of equipment unmentioned (most notably the Macintosh and its videodisc controller software). Robert Skinner

404. Souter, Gerald A. **The DISConnection: How to Interface Computers and Video.** Boston, G. K. Hall, 1988. 193p. illus. bibliog. index. (Video Bookshelf). $45.00. LC 87-17235. ISBN 0-86729-218-0.

DISConnection is a very informative work on the current status of laser disc technology from the standpoint of a video producer. The historical background in the introduction sets the tone of the book and eases the reader into the modern technology discussed. Uncluttered with technical details, the book is spaciously formatted, written with a rich vocabulary, and carefully edited. It is loaded with photographs of actual equipment and diagrams of key concepts. Souter, who certainly has done his homework on the subject, gives a wonderful overview of the technical aspects of laser discs. His experience and philosophy about the production and uses of videodiscs are freely shared, and he provides some important points to consider before developing a system of one's own. The author has made a small and common mistake assuming that HyperCard is hardware; it is all software. The work has a glossary loaded with terms unique to film editing and video production. The fact that technology is changing rapidly makes this book valuable for anyone trying to understand laser discs. John A. Jackman

PERIODICALS AND SERIALS

405. **Advances in Serials Management: A Research Annual. Volume 2: 1988.** Marcia Tuttle and Jean G. Cook, eds. Greenwich, Conn., JAI Press, 1988. 212p. $58.50. ISBN 0-89232-672-7.

Despite an optimistic title, this second volume in the series demonstrates that serials librarians are still gnashing their teeth over a predictable group of problems. Dual pricing structures, vendors, and the serials department

in the academic hierarchy are all topics discussed in volume 1 that reappear in volume 2.

This volume contains nine articles that treat serials from a number of perspectives and levels. Two historical views are significant. One is a well-researched comparison between serials problems in the 1930s and the 1980s; another is a description of the effects of AACR2 on serials management. More basic are the introductory articles "Subscription Agents and Libraries" and "Serials Control from an Acquisitions Perspective," neither of which offers anything new to the practicing serials librarian. Among substantive articles completing the volume are works on the serials conversion project at the University of North Carolina at Chapel Hill, the role of the serials librarian in academic libraries, and an overview of serials automation.

The contributors to this volume are primarily academic librarians who administrate technical services or serials departments. Their articles constitute a useful textbook for students on the issues facing serials librarians in the 1980s. Few advances are documented here, however, so the practicing librarian will find no new weapons in the battle for serials control. Stephanie C. Sigala

PUBLIC LIBRARIES

General Works

406. Fox, Beth Wheeler. **The Dynamic Community Library: Creative, Practical, and Inexpensive Ideas for the Director.** Chicago, American Library Association, 1988. 138p. illus. bibliog. index. $17.50pa. LC 88-10057. ISBN 0-8389-0496-3.

The promotional sheet for this text describes it as "a tool-kit for the director of the small library, covering everything from publicity, to training volunteers, to planning programs and services." This is an apt description, for the scope of its coverage indeed does cover the waterfront. It is important to recognize, however, that this coverage does not allow for depth of treatment.

With this caveat in mind, the reader is encouraged to actively examine Fox's hints and ideas for managing the small library. While the author skips merrily along from topic to topic, the topics she has chosen are critical to effective library management, and this book provides an excellent introduction to these concepts. Topics covered include volunteers and other components of the "reserve team," analyzing the community, fund raising, the library's image, promotional activities, presentations, and planning. While this reviewer would argue with this arrangement of topics and would begin with the chapter on planning, there is certainly no quarrel with the relevance and importance of the ideas presented. In addition, an appendix contains some very useful illustrative documents, such as intellectual freedom documents, sample policies and bylaws, and sample forms.

This is a clearly written text, covering areas of primary concern, and should be on the reading list of every director of a small community library. [R: WLB, Dec 88, p. 105]

Darlene E. Weingand

407.   **The Future of the Public Library: Conference Proceedings.** Dublin, Ohio, OCLC Online Computer Library Center, 1988. 150p. illus. bibliog. (OCLC Library, Information, and Computer Service Series, No. 8). $13.50pa. ISBN 1-55653-050-1.

This work summarizes the important proceedings of the conference held in March 1988 at OCLC headquarters in Dublin, Ohio. At the conference, distinguished librarians and library educators from more than fifty institutions discussed technological, economic, and societal issues that may affect the public library environment in the year 2000 and beyond. Major issues included are the future of resource sharing and interlibrary cooperative relationships; new methods for providing access to information, resources, and knowledge; and the need for the new attitudes and skills in the public library environment.

Included in the text are three papers by Thomas H. Ballard, Linda Crismond, and Kathryn Stephanoff. Two formal reactions to each paper and summaries of small group discussions are also included. Ballard's presentation is the most provocative in that he successfully challenges our basic assumptions about library networking and resource sharing.

Also included are the conference keynote address and the closing remarks by Robert Olson of the Institute for Alternative Futures, and a summary of the closing session panel discussion between a public library director, a library school dean, a state librarian, and a library science educator from the United Kingdom. In addition, photographs from the conference, a list of conference participants, and a list of selected readings appear in the monograph.

This is one of the most important monographs on public libraries in recent years and should be read by all persons involved with public libraries. [R: WLB, Dec 88, p. 105]

George S. Bobinski

408.   Gervasi, Anne, and Betty Kay Seibt. **Handbook for Small, Rural, and Emerging Public Libraries.** Phoenix, Ariz., Oryx Press, 1988. 196p. index. $27.50pa. LC 86-42966. ISBN 0-89774-303-2.

This handbook is intended, in the authors' words, to provide a "single source that would introduce lay people to the breadth of library service in a way that opens doors and explains rather than a way that closes doors and confuses" (preface). It succeeds quite well as an overview of how to establish and administer a small public library.

The book is divided into three sections. The first section is addressed to those who want to establish a small or rural public library, and the second is directed to library boards. The audience for the third section is the library director. The seventeen chapters discuss a wide range of topics, including evaluating community needs, legal issues, fund raising, space planning, hiring practices, outfitting the library, collection development, public and technical services, and cooperative services.

The authors readily acknowledge that their coverage of these topics is not deep; their goal is to provide a broad overview of the issues that need to be addressed in creating and running a small or rural library. They get quite specific in stating how certain library functions should be performed, however, which is the primary shortcoming of the book. Because of the intentional lack of depth, I would feel a little more comfortable with the book had the authors spoken in more general terms about running a small or rural library. I am troubled by statements such as "periodicals are not cataloged" and by the authors' acceptance of the notion that the public catalog must necessarily be a *card* catalog.

Notwithstanding these criticisms, the handbook clearly meets a need in library literature. It should not be used alone, however, but rather in conjunction with other books such as Katz's *The How-to-Do-It Manual for Small Libraries* (Neal-Schuman, 1988). Gervasi and Seibt's handbook is recommended for librarians and trustees of small or rural libraries. [R: CLJ, Dec 88, p. 395; WLB, June 88, pp. 124-25]

James S. Heller

409.   Jones, Derek, ed. **The Impact of Charges in the Public Library Service. Proceedings of a Seminar ... at the London International Book Fair, 29 March 1988.** London, Library Association; distr., Chicago, American Library Association, 1988. 39p. $13.00pa. ISBN 0-85365-938-9.

The seminar focuses on proposed legislation enabling local governments to charge fees for all categories of library service. These published proceedings contain four formal presentations and brief statements from dozens of librarians attending the seminar. Speakers review the text of the legislation and point to latitudinal phrasing. Overall, speakers support the discretionary nature of the legislation but oppose mandatory charges. Two speakers do not believe extra fees will result in increased funding for libraries. A county librarian reviews the arguments for and against fees; a university librarian discusses possible implications for academic and public libraries; and a conservative administrator presents arguments supporting the new legislation. The formal presentations are well organized and ideas expressed are not foreign to most North American librarians.

The most vexing issue recognized by all speakers, including the conservative speaker, centers on interlibrary loan. The proposed legislation suggests that lending libraries charge for loans and would allow borrowing libraries to charge the primary user for all direct costs plus service fees. This possible combination of costs would make the system too expensive for individuals and if the lending library did not charge, but the borrowing library did, it would be inequitable for the lending library not to pass on administrative costs. The question of uneven information service to users, especially the poor, is another major concern.

Attendees realize the need to reach agreement on what should be considered free basic library services, but there is little discussion of this important question. Then too, there is no fully developed discussion about library cooperation if legislation is passed unchanged. Possible use of money realized from additional fees is a stated concern but little discussion is included here.

This full-blown discussion of fee-based versus free library services will interest librarians throughout the world.   Milton H. Crouch

410.   A Marketing Study for Five Public Libraries: The Cooperative Community Awareness and Marketing Project. Chicago, Carroll Group, [1987?]. 249p. $29.95 spiralbound.

This monograph is the output of a grant-funded project by the Illinois State Library, which had as its self-stated purpose "to find ways to apply marketing principles and practices to a library environment." In examining the report, this reviewer must conclude that the effort was partially successful.

The approach taken in this study places primary emphasis on market research—a valuable

and essential first step in engaging in a marketing effort. The study also devotes considerable attention to the final marketing step: promotion. Focusing on these two aspects, the project has produced a range of ideas and suggestions that should prove to be useful to library managers, regardless of type of library.

However, the critical middle steps of developing library goals and objectives in tandem with product, price, and distribution decisions have been given only tangential attention. Although focus groups composed of community members and staff considered some problem-solving strategies (and although there was a heavy emphasis on books—particularly from staff), the actual implementation of the middle steps is glossed over enroute to discussion of promotional techniques. Despite this major flaw, this report would be helpful to library managers as they design a full marketing/planning process—provided that it is used as supplementary to a text that considers the entire process.

Structurally, this monograph is a spiral-bound reproduction of typed copy, 8½ by 11 inches. It is double-spaced and quite legible. [R: LJ, 1 Apr 88, p. 64]   Darlene E. Weingand

411.   Murison, W. J. The Public Library: Its Origins, Purpose, and Significance. 3d ed. London, Clive Bingley/Library Associations; distr., Chicago, American Library Association, 1988. 251p. index. $49.00. ISBN 0-85157-430-0.

The third edition of Murison's book contains an introductory description of the public library followed by coverage of the public library movement with respect to origins, purpose, and social background and the current status of the British public library with respect to education, information, and recreation. Other chapters cover the library in other social fields; the limitations of books as opposed to communication via nonprint media; the Public Lending Right Act of 1979 (a chapter new to the third edition); and the significance and limitations of the public library. With the exception of the inclusion of the new chapter mentioned above and the exclusion of one entitled "Payment to Authors," chapter titles remain the same from one edition to the next.

The definition of the role of the public library from the 1985 IFLA standards for public libraries is used for the first time in the third edition. The historical chapters include a minimal amount of revision, but the chapter "The British Public Library Today" lists events that have transpired since the second edition: the local government acts that reorganized boundaries and services in England, Scotland, and Wales;

the changing economic conditions; and the Library Association guidelines establishing the relationship between the public and private sectors' services.

A new topic raised in "The Library for Education and Information" is that of the almost universal role of national governments assuming responsibility for public libraries. With outstanding cooperation among British libraries, the local authorities do not, for the most part, seem willing to relinquish their jurisdiction to the central government.

Finally, Murison emphasizes an important change in the librarians' role from one of passive service to a more active involvement in societal problems and needs. Librarians are meeting these situations with the most current technological means of providing information, news, education, and entertainment of high quality whether in library buildings or other nontraditional settings. The underprivileged, the elderly, minorities, immigrants, prisoners, and the hospitalized continue to receive attention in the third edition.

Lois Buttlar

412. **The Second Young Adult Program Guidebook.** Compiled by Young Adult Program Guide Committee, New York Library Association. New York, New York Library Association, 1987. 80p. illus. bibliog. $15.00pa. ISBN 0-931658-20-9.

As a compilation of up-to-date programming ideas for young adults, this work arranges programs alphabetically by type (e.g., arts and crafts). For each program the following sections are included: "Intended Audience," "Preparation," "Description," "Evaluation," and "Program Planner." The descriptions of the programs are concise and informative. Readers are encouraged to contact the program planner (addresses and telephone numbers are provided) for additional information and resources for young adult programming. This guidebook also includes copyright-free clip art, sample pamphlets and public relations material, information on booktalking, graphics, and how to set up a program. The program checklist and worksheet would be helpful for anyone planning programs, whether they be juvenile, young adult, or adult. An additional bibliography on programming for young adults and an index conclude this useful and handy volume.

Janet R. Ivey

413. Williams, Patrick. **The American Public Library and the Problem of Purpose.** Westport, Conn., Greenwood Press, 1988. 144p. bibliog. index. (Contributions in Librarianship and

Information Science, No. 62). $37.95. LC 88-16382. ISBN 0-313-25590-3.

This is an interesting and well-written historical essay which attempts to trace the problem of finding the right place for the public library in society. The right place is defined as developing an idea of purpose that identifies a distinctive and valuable contribution that the public library could make within resources provided by society.

The author starts his analysis with the opening of the first public library in Boston in 1854 and ends optimistically with the publication of *Planning and Role Setting for Public Libraries* by ALA in 1987. In between he describes various public library attempts at finding a purpose as seen through the following chapter headings: "The Fiction Problem, 1876-1896"; "The Library Militant, 1894-1920"; "Adult Education, 1920-1948"; "The Public Library Inquiry, 1948-1950"; "Folklore and Public Relations, 1950-1965"; and "Information for the People, 1965-1980." Wilson believes that the public library's purpose should be as an institution of informal self-education for those who seek it but not for the masses who have other distractions and commitments. Education is what the public expects of the library and that is what they will support.

This is an important addition to the literature of public library history. At the same time one can argue with the author's approach and interpretation. Public library history did not begin with the establishment of the Boston Public Library but rather with social libraries that existed in the United States from 1750 and that formed the basis for public libraries. Public libraries are local institutions, each with its own sense of purpose. There is no national policy for public libraries. As a result there is a wide spectrum of public library purposes and practices depending on the characteristics of each community.

In spite of the struggle for purpose as described by the author, the public library has developed into a strong and widespread intitution. From one public library in 1854 we now have 8,865 individual public libraries with an additional 6,350 branches and 55,000 other outlets, such as bookmobile stops and deposit collections, serving 98 percent of the U.S. population through a network of public library systems. Public library expenditures and usage continue to rise. New buildings are being built. The public library is alive and well even without a unified sense of purpose.

George S. Bobinski

Adult Education

414.   Fisher, Raymond K. **Library Services for Adult Continuing Education and Independent Learning: A Guide.** London, Library Association; distr., Chicago, American Library Association, 1988. 108p. bibliog. index. (Library Association Pamphlet, No. 40). $19.00pa. ISBN 0-85365-608-8.

This volume addresses well the growing needs of British libraries as they respond to increasing pressures from adult learners. It specifies concisely the types of needs adult learners have as they engage in formal education or informal independent learning. Then, with a section for each type of library, guidelines outline the kind of information and services required and, in some cases, ways to obtain the information or establish the services. The volume is indexed and includes a bibliography of mostly British titles.

In the United States the wide spectrum of adult learners has long preoccupied public libraries. The Adult Independent Learning Project in the 1970s was an exciting initiative and has had a lasting effect on the perspective of librarians. Now adult learners are considered a major factor in designing, revitalizing, and marketing library services.

Many ideas and working tools came from that project, yet little reference is made to any U.S. materials or experiences. The insular approach of this work offsets its advantage of a coherent and concise set of guidelines. Thus, it is a helpful handbook for assessing one's current library but not much assistance in planning and adapting that library to better meet adult learner needs.   Barbara Conroy

Budgeting

415.   Norton, Bob. **Charging for Library and Information Services.** London, Library Association; distr., Chicago, American Library Association, 1988. 59p. (Viewpoints in LIS, 1). $11.00pa. ISBN 0-85365-818-8.

Because the debate over charging for library service has technological, social, and economic roots, it is not limited by national boundaries. Focusing on public libraries in the United Kingdom, Norton asks many of the same questions librarians in the United States ask. Is the public library still relevant, given the many sources of information now available? What implications does competition with profit-making rivals have for survival? What steps must the public library take to ensure a relevant future?

The author stresses the need to move away from traditional thoughts and actions and to see the library with a fresh, realistic perspective. An outline for conducting a market audit and discussion of pricing and its limitations are followed by questions that various stakeholders, such as the online industry, libraries, and funding agencies, need to answer. The political nature of the decisions to be made is emphasized.

The bibliography of resources, most of which refer to recent newspaper and journal articles, provides timely references. The Library Association guidelines for public and private sector relationships presented in the appendix are one response to the debate.

Although the social and historical context differs and the governmental authority over public libraries is more centralized in the United Kingdom, the issues are similar, although proposed solutions are not necessarily those that would be acceptable in the United States. Much of the discussion is helpful and with its different perspective permits new insights. [R: LAR, 14 Oct 88, p. 613]   Ann E. Prentice

Collection Development

416.   Gutierrez, David, and Roberto G. Trujillo, comps. **The Chicano Public Catalog: A Collection Guide for Public Libraries.** Encino, Calif., Floricanto Press, 1987. 188p. index. $39.00pa.

The compilers state that this core bibliography "represents a solid, basic collection in Mexican American Studies" (p. i). It includes 487 titles of Chicano materials almost exclusively in the English language in such fields as social science, language, literature, and history. Even though most academic areas of Mexican-American studies are well represented in this work, many important areas such as education are virtually ignored. The most glaring omission in this core bibliography, however, is in the area of fiction. One must question the inclusion of only two novels, a few short stories, and a few plays in what is supposed to be a collection guide for public libraries. [R: Choice, Feb 88, p. 882; WLB, Apr 88, pp. 98-99]   Isabel Schon

417.   **Hennepin County Library Collection Maintenance Manual.** rev. ed. Minnetonka, Minn., Hennepin County Library, 1988. 51p. $7.50pa.

This manual is a weeding document for the twenty-six branches of the Hennepin County Library system. It includes collection policies for community (branch) libraries; weeding schedules for both juvenile and adult books;

criteria for replacing weeded volumes; binding guidelines; a section on "merchandising" or promoting books within each branch; and a listing of Hennepin's collection development and maintenance training sessions. The bulk of the book addresses the various fiction and nonfiction categories for both adult and juvenile books and directs staff how to weed. For some subjects very specific advice is given. For example, real estate examination books are to be kept for only three years while history of real estate can be kept up to ten. Despite these specifics, however, the individual branches are allowed to exercise a considerable amount of judgment. Many categories say to weed on condition and use. Within the Dewey Decimal Classification, the individual topics treated reflect public library concerns and topics (e.g., auto repair, crafts, numismatics, and stamp catalogs) rather than academic or special library topics. The guidelines reflect a rigorous determination to present only up-to-date and attractive material to the clients of the Hennepin system.

Hennepin's marketing approach to public library collections and its manual could serve as a guide for any public library wishing to improve the quality of its collections through a weeding program. The book is of less interest to academic libraries who often must use criteria other than currency and attractiveness to judge the value of books on their shelves.

Linda Keir Simons

418. Mason, Sally, and James Scholtz, eds. **Video for Libraries: Special Interest Video for Small and Medium-sized Public Libraries.** Chicago, American Library Association, 1988. 163p. index. $14.50pa. LC 88-22235. ISBN 0-8389-0498-X.

Mason and Scholtz asked subject experts to submit lists of instructional, informational, or otherwise educational videocassette titles that they would recommend for a public library collection. Working with these lists, Mason and Scholtz compiled the present guide arranging one thousand entries in broad Dewey Decimal Classification categories. Each entry includes title, variant title, series, release date, producer and distributor, running time, price, availability of public performance rights, Library of Congress subject headings, Dewey Decimal Classification numbers, and brief annotation. Videos for children are listed separately. There are cross-references within the guide and a general index. Most videos listed have been distributed since 1982. Feature films recommended for a core collection are listed separately and include titles alone. Names and addresses of producers, distributors, wholesalers, and retailers are pro-

vided in appendices. Well-organized, carefully edited, and literate, this guide will be a pleasure to use. The editors recognize that prices and other information will be out-of-date soon. One can only hope that new editions will appear in the future.   Margaret McKinley

419. **University Press Books for Public Libraries.** 10th ed. New York, for Public Library Association, American Library Association by Association of American University Presses, 1988. 87p. index. free pa. ISSN 0731-2857.

The latest edition by the Public Library Association's Small and Medium-Sized Libraries Section highlight the 1987 offerings of university presses. Judged by eleven public librarians, this work continues the practice of the ninth edition in excluding university press journals and serials. Each entry, arranged in Dewey Decimal Classification order with an author and title index, is annotated with liberal quotes from the reviewing media. Still useful for the smaller library wanting guidance in selecting titles from the annual university press output.

Chris Albertson

420. **Young Adult 1987 Annual Booklist.** Los Angeles, Calif., Adult Services, Los Angeles Public Library, 1987. 71p. $5.00pa.

Published by the Los Angeles Public Library, this thin 8½-by-11-inch stapled paperback lists books published in 1985 and 1986 that the Los Angeles adult services staff judged would be of interest to young adults. The list is divided into twenty-three pages of fiction entries and eight pages of nonfiction entries with brief annotations, an unannotated list of twenty-two career titles and two songbooks; fifteen pages of unannotated listings of "Adult Books Having YA Interest and/or Assignment Value"; and twenty-one pages of unannotated listings of "Selected Uncataloged Paperbacks."

This is not an essential purchase for any selector. Most individuals selecting young adult materials would have already been aware of these items from reviews, while those inexperienced selectors may seek help directly from the annual "Best Books" lists of the American Library Association's Young Adult Service Division or the H. W. Wilson catalog series (*Junior High School Catalog* [see *ARBA 86*, entry 596] or *Senior High School Catalog* [see *ARBA 88*, entry 640]).   Chris Albertson

Trustees

421. Baughman, James C. **Trustees, Trusteeship, and the Public Good: Issues of Accountability for Hospitals, Museums, Universities,**

and **Libraries.** Westport, Conn., Quorum Books/Greenwood Press, 1987. 187p. index. $35.00. LC 86-25574. ISBN 0-89930-195-9.

Citing data and actual cases from court records, newspaper and professional literature as well as from interviews, the author presents a thought-provoking account of the deeds and misdeeds of those in charge of charitable trusts (10 percent of the nation's wealth). Baughman's thesis is that there are basic misunderstandings concerning charitable organizations, not only among the public but also among governing boards. He claims that trustees of nonprofit organizations are generally not aware that they are fully accountable to the public whom they serve. He also points out that attorneys general, with the support of the courts, have gone so far as to take over and operate nonprofit organizations or have removed from office trustees who have not fulfilled their duties or who have misbehaved.

Although only one chapter out of seven deals with libraries there is much pertinent and useful information for those interested in trustees and libraries. This well-written work will be of interest to managers, directors, and trustees of nonprofit organizations as well as to volunteers of these organizations and the interested public. [R: RQ, Summer 88, pp. 590-91]

George S. Bobinski

422.   Bruce, Lorne, and Karen Bruce. **Public Library Boards in Postwar Ontario, 1945-1985.** Halifax, N.S., School of Library and Information Studies, Dalhousie University, 1988. 149p. (Occasional Papers Series, 42). $16.50pa. ISBN 0-7703-9717-4.

This monograph is very interesting and is both well written and well researched. The text is supplemented by useful tables and statistical data. Lorne Bruce is Public Services Librarian at the McLaughlin Library of the University of Guelph. He has written several articles on public library history in Ontario and previously held positions as chief librarian at the Hanover Public Library and at the King Township Public Library. Karen Bruce is a trustee of the Tecumseth Library Board in Ontario.

The main message of this work is that, despite the great expansion of public libraries in Ontario, these libraries have maintained their equilibrium because of the fundamental continuity in the thinking and practices of public library government. The authors predict that the library boards will continue as an established form of library government at the local level in Ontario because they fulfill community needs. Their study shows how systematic agreements on several topics — the practices of appointed

library boards, the political aspects of board representation, influence, power, authority, public participation, accountability, intergovernmental relationships, and professional administration — all have guided the working relationships by which library services are provided throughout the province.

This publication is quite specialized but will be of interest to those concerned with public library management, public library history, and Canadian librarianship. It would also be useful reading to public library trustees in the United States.

George S. Bobinski

423.   **Trustee Tool Kit for Library Leadership.** By California Association of Library Trustees and Commissioners. Betty Bay, ed. Sacramento, Calif., California State Library Foundation, 1987. 425p. maps. bibliog. $25.00pa.

This is an exemplary reference guide for public library trustees and commissioners in California prepared jointly by the California Association of Library Trustees and the California State Library. Much of the information would be useful for public library trustees anywhere. Indeed, this guide should be emulated by other states.

Chapters include "Statutory Authority"; "Library Funding"; "Legal Duties, Liabilities, Rights"; "Effective Board Organization"; "Systematic Planning Process"; "Policy Setting/Budget-Making"; "Public Community Relations"; "Working Relationships"; "Library Advocacy"; "Special Challenges" (e.g., selecting a head librarian, and censorship attacks); and "Helpful Organizations."

There are numerous, useful appendices which include items such as California public library statistics, a handy list of library terms and acronyms, various ALA policy statements, and information and maps on California's fifteen cooperative public library systems.

A bibliography and a reading list are also included at the end of the volume. Unfortunately the reading list of major monographs is very dated and does not include many important books on public libraries published since 1980.

But as a whole this is an excellent compilation of very helpful and practical information for both trustees as well as staff in public libraries of California with 75 percent of the contents being useful anywhere else in the United States. [R: BL, 1 Jan 88, p. 748]

George S. Bobinski

424.   Young, Virginia G. **The Library Trustee: A Practical Guidebook.** 4th ed. Chicago, American Library Association, 1988. 230p. bibliog. index. $25.00. LC 88-6313. ISBN 0-8389-0495-5.

Virginia Young's books directed toward library trustees have been seminal works in trustee literature. This fourth edition continues that tradition. The original edition in 1964 addressed topics such as duties and responsibilities, qualifications and appointment, organization, the trustee as policymaker, relationships with librarians and staff, law and finances, building problems, the political process, ALA standards, library systems, public relations, the friends of libraries groups, and associations. This latest edition does this—and much more.

Each chapter is authored by one or more individuals well-known in library and information science circles. Law and finances, once combined in one chapter, now require individual chapter treatment. The political process has also been subdivided into chapters on the state library, the federal government, and the National Commission on Libraries and Information Science. New areas covered are labor-management relations; planning; trustee education; gifts, grants, and bequests; buildings; advocacy; intellectual freedom; and volunteers. It is obvious that Young updates her work in a timely way. Useful appendices focus on orientation, ALA policy statements, sample library policies, budget checklist, bylaws, evaluation, statements on preservation, rules for volunteers, and forming a friends group.

This book is must reading for trustees, both new and continuing. It should be part of every public library's professional collection. [R: BL, 1 Oct 88, p. 217]   Darlene E. Weingand

User Studies

425. Powell, Ronald R. **The Relationship of Library User Studies to Performance Measures: A Review of the Literature.** Champaign, Ill., Graduate School of Library and Information Science, University of Illinois, 1988. 41p. (Occasional Papers, No. 181). $3.00pa. ISSN 0276-1769.

Concern with library effectiveness (particularly in public libraries) has grown tremendously in recent decades. When concern grows, so too does the literature, often with overwhelming results. This little monograph is a scholarly effort to tame and understand the literature dealing with the needs of users.

Powell's organization is straightforward: For each of the three methodologies involved (user studies, performance measures, and performance measures based on user studies), he examines four aspects of the approach. He has sections on the previous literature on the topic, what data collection techniques have been used,

possible benefits of the methodology employed, and the limitations of the methodology. He finishes with his own summary and conclusions and provides an extensive list of references.

For each methodology, the literature of past studies, both methodological and applied, is well explained and documented. Definitions are laid out. A tremendous amount of information is mustered, analyzed, and synthesized in these sections. In subsequent sections the advantages suggested for each methodology are summarized, documented, and explained. Powell describes how each of the methodologies has fallen short of the fully desired outcome.

In his conclusion, Powell suggests that "what libraries should be most concerned with measuring is their ultimate product—performance or effectiveness and that the best indicators of their level of performance are, or should be, based on user data such as satisfaction." He advocates one possible approach involving "user-oriented performance measures."

Powell has performed a genuine service for scholars, students, and practitioners by bringing together and analyzing an often confusingly diverse literature, giving it focus and direction. Highly recommended for professional schools examining the assessment of library services and for libraries planning such assessments. [R: JAL, May 88, p. 119]   Elizabeth Frick

PUBLISHING

General Works

PHILOSOPHY AND THEORY

426. **Book Industry Trends 1988.** 12th ed. By the Center for Book Research. New York, Book Industry Study Group, 1988. 197p. $200.00pa. ISBN 0-940016-28-1.

This work is a storehouse of statistical information pertinent to publishing, the publishing industry, and libraries. In variance with the previous annual editions, this is the product not of one, but of many individuals: industry experts, analysts at the Center for Book Research, and faculty at the University of Scranton. Appearing for the first time is an introductory section of text that presents overviews of the U.S. economic outlook through 1993 and of the book industry; consumer profiles; and profiles of markets in various types of books. Library acquisitions and publishers' manufacturing expenditures are also profiled. However, the main corpus of the work is composed of three seemingly endless tables and their subtables. Major sections of tables include: "Estimated Publisher's Book Sales—By Type of Book and Market, 1982-1991" (fifty-six subtables), "Estimated Book Sales by Wholesalers and Jobbers—By Type of Book and Market, 1982-1991" (twenty-seven subtables), "Estimated Consumer Expenditures—By Type of Book and Market, 1982-1991" (twenty-nine subtables).

Although not as lengthy as the previous three sections, sections that follow include significant information useful for collection development, and for budget and other long-range planning initiatives in libraries. These include: "Estimated Materials Acquisitions by U.S. Libraries, 1982-1991," "Estimated Average Unit Cost of Materials Acquired by U.S. Libraries, 1982-1991," "Estimated Acquisitions by U.S. Libraries of Domestically Published Books, 1982-1991," "Estimated Average Unit Cost Incurred by U.S. Libraries for Domestically Published Books, 1982-1991," and "Estimated Publishers' Manufacturing Expenditures, 1982-1991."

The main text is supplemented by a list of sources, definitions, and a description of methodologies used to compile all information. Finally, an index to book-type categories, allowing the reader to locate pertinent information within the three major tables, is presented.

Highly recommended for academic, public and school library administrators involved in budget and acquisitions planning, collection development, and fundraising, this should provide solid and instructive data for funding sources, both internal and external to the library.   Edmund F. SantaVicca

427.   Cole, John Y., ed. **Books in Our Future: Perspectives and Proposals.** Washington, D.C., Library of Congress, 1987. 399p. bibliog. index. $16.00. LC 87-600047. ISBN 0-8444-0554-X. (For sale by the Superintendent of Documents, GPO, Washington, D.C.).

Featuring essays by such well-known "bookish" figures as Jacques Barzun and Kenneth E. Dowlin, this book is a supplement to the report of a former Librarian of Congress, Daniel J. Boorstin, to the U.S. Congress in 1984 on the Books in the Future Project. The project considered the role of books and reading in society, and project advisers contributed to this supplement. Cole served as project director.

The book is a representative sample of current thinking by individuals and by professional groups, such as the National Commission on Excellence in Education, about the place of the printed word in a technological and computer-driven age. Authors express their concerns about a wide range of book-related topics

including illiteracy, the future of libraries, free access to information, preservation of old books, and future production of the printed word. Cole introduces each article with comments about the author's place in the world of books. He concludes with excerpts from Boorstin's report, a positive statement that we must "use all our technologies to make the most of our inheritance [active reading] to move toward an American renaissance of the culture of the book." [R: JAL, Nov 88, p. 308; LJ, 1 Apr 88, p. 64; WLB, Mar 88, pp. 85-86]

Berniece M. Owen

428.   Feather, John. **A History of British Publishing.** New York, Croom Helm/Routledge, Chapman & Hall, 1988. 292p. bibliog. index. $72.50. ISBN 0-7099-1067-3.

Feather (senior lecturer in the Department of Library and Information Studies, Loughborough University) states in the preface that this book is a history of British publishing over the last five hundred years, and not a history of the book trade or of the book in Great Britain. To this end, after an introduction on the book trade before printing (e.g., from the fourteenth century to 1476), Feather traces British publishing within the framework of four chronological periods. The first, 1476-1695, is the history from the introduction of printing into Great Britain to the end of strict government control of publishing, principally through the Stationers's Company. The second period goes from 1695 (the lapse of the Printing Act) to 1800, by which date publishing was a modern industry with the functions of printer, publisher, and bookseller clearly differentiated and a variety of serial publications (e.g., newspapers and periodicals) had appeared. The third part, 1800-1900, discusses the period when publishing became a full-fledged industry. The last section is devoted to the trade in the twentieth century.

This well-written, easy-to-read text concludes with: (1) extensive notes on each chapter; (2) a selective bibliography of titles, primarily from the twentieth century (with a few from the nineteenth century); and (3) an author, title, and subject index (the latter being especially helpful because of numerous subentries). Inexplicably, the bibliography does not include such titles as Nicholas Barker's *The Oxford University Press and the Spread of Learning, 1478-1978* (Oxford, 1978), or Robin Myers's bibliographical guide, *The British Book Trade* (Gower, 1973).

Feather's general history of British publishing, of course, will not replace larger standard histories like *Mumby's Publishing and Bookselling* by Frank Mumby (Bell and Hyman, 1982) or Stanley Unwin's *The Truth about Publishing*

(8th ed. Allen and Unwin, 1976). Still, library science collections may want this work because of its recency.

Wiley J. Williams

BIBLIOGRAPHIES

429. **Bookman's Price Index: Subject Series. Volume 1: Modern First Editions.** Daniel F. McGrath, ed. Detroit, Gale, 1987. 1154p. $125.00. ISBN 0-8103-2535-7.

This work is essentially a list of the current (mid-1980s) U.S. market values (prices) of collectible twentieth-century U.S. and British novels, plays, and books of poetry. Some thirteen thousand titles (some titles have multiple entries so that the total number of entries is about thirty thousand) are listed alphabetically by author. Each entry has been taken directly from the 1984, 1985, or 1986 catalog(s) of one (or more) of 178 U.S. and/or British bookdealers specializing in collectible twentieth-century fiction and thus consists of both basic card catalog information and a detailed description of the physical condition of the book. Coverage is strongest for collectible twentieth-century U.S. novels and weakest for science fiction and fantasy titles. Since there is no way of knowing if these titles actually sold at their listed catalog price or were eventually sold at a lower price to another dealer, collectors must also consult the yearly *Book Auction Records*, keeping in mind that auction prices are usually lower (when there is no competition for a given title) or higher (when there is a bidding war for a given title) than catalog prices.

Since the last edition of Van Allen Bradley's *The Book Collector's Handbook of Values* (see *ARBA* 83, entry 864) was published six years ago, and since Mildred Mandelbaum's *The Used Book Price Guide* is only published every five years and tends to list the less expensive fiction titles, there is no real competitor to this work save the yearly *Bookman's Price Index*, which is based on fewer dealer catalogs. It is to be hoped that future editions of this time-saving work will expand its coverage of science fiction, fantasy, and mystery titles and include auction prices (when available) of titles whose catalog value exceeds $500.00.

Joseph Cataio

430. Melanson, Holly, comp. **Literary Presses in Canada, 1975-1985: A Checklist and Bibliography.** Halifax, N.S., School of Library and Information Studies, Dalhousie University, 1988. 187p. bibliog. index. (Occasional Papers Series, 43). $16.50pa. ISBN 0-7703-9717-4.

Holly Melanson, Coordinator of Collections Development at Dalhousie, defines a literary press "as one that is created solely to encourage and provide a forum for new Canadian poets, novelists, dramatists and other creative artists" (p. i). Her directory has entries for 240 English Canadian presses active during the eleven years following publication of Grace Tratt's standard *Check List of Canadian Small Presses, English Language* (Halifax: Dalhousie University Libraries and School of Library Service, 1974). This bibliography is similar in format to the original with arrangement by name of press and entries consisting of ISBN, full postal address if available, names of founders, dates of operation, literary publications by year, and bibliography of articles about the press. There are two indexes: regional by province and nominal for the founders. Unfortunately, there is no index to the more than 4,000 literary press publications included as part of the entries. Apart from a few problems with margins, the format and production are equal to the careful work of compilation.

Patricia Fleming

431. Morton, Herbert C., and others. **Writings on Scholarly Communication: An Annotated Bibliography of Books and Articles on Publishing, Libraries, Scholarly Research, and Related Issues.** Lanham, Md., with American Council of Learned Societies by University Press of America, 1988. 151p. index. $27.50; $14.75pa. LC 87-32931. ISBN 0-8191-6825-4; 0-8191-6826-2pa.

This bibliography seeks to suggest the range of published materials on the topic of scholarly communication in the humanities and social sciences. Writings in the sciences and the professions are excluded. Works selected for inclusion are intended as illustrative of the literature, not a definitive listing; nor do the authors claim they have systematically combed the literature. The work includes lengthy abstracts of eighty-seven journal articles, books, and reports, followed by citations (at times with annotations) to 146 related publications. They are arranged in eleven chapters according to broad subjects (e.g., book publishing, libraries and computing, scholars and technology). An author index completes the volume. Morton's excellent introductory bibliographical essay provides a good overview of the following sections. The work has its principal value as a guide for the individual seeking an introduction to the literature on this amorphous subject, not the researcher seeking detailed information on specific subjects.

Richard D. Johnson

432. Wagner, Henry R., Eleanor Bancroft, and Ruth Frey Axe. **A Check-list of Publications of H. H. Bancroft and Company 1857 to 1870.** Berkeley, Calif., Friends of the UCLA Library and Friends of the Bancroft Library, 1987. 85p. index. $10.00pa.

The original compilers of this list of Bancroft publications, Henry R. Wagner and Eleanor Ashby Bancroft, died within six months of each other in the mid-1950s, leaving the work unfinished. Only recently has the work surfaced, and it is presented here with additions and revisions. Wagner was a collector, bibliographer, and historian, and Bancroft was assistant to the director of the Bancroft Library. H. H. Bancroft is best known as a historian, but he and his brother Albert were successful publishers (1857-1886) until a complete breach ended the relationship. Axe sketches the history of the two main Bancroft imprints (H. H. Bancroft and Company and A. L. Bancroft and Company); Bancroft-Whitney, founded by A. L. in 1886, and the Bancroft Company, founded by H. H. in 1887, are not considered here. In her introduction Axe also discusses the reasons for the break (a disastrous fire in their underinsured building seems to have been the last straw in a long-simmering feud). There are 212 entries, arranged chronologically. Bibliographic and copyright data are given. Locations in dozens of libraries are noted in addition. Valuable for students of Western publishing history.   Walter C. Allen

DIRECTORIES

433. Advertising and Publicity Resources for Scholarly Books. New York, Association of American University Presses, 1988. 864p. index. $200.00pa. LC 87-73317. ISBN 0-945103-00-X.

Published as an aid to marketing scholarly books, this directory provides a listing of scholarly periodicals worldwide in which a publisher might advertise or send review copies of publications. Accordingly, the periodicals (and other publications of value in marketing scholarly books) are grouped by subject, such as "African Studies," "Agriculture," "History," "Oceanography," etc. Each entry provides the title, address, and telephone number of the periodical, subjects covered, types of articles, audience, language, date begun, frequency, circulation, and what percent of the circulation is in the U.S. and what percent is to individuals as opposed to institutions. Names of key contacts, such as the book review editor, are noted, as well as availability of the mailing list and whether advertising is accepted. Advertisement specifications and rates are also listed.

This work is only a starting point; it is no substitute for careful research. For example, many of the subject areas contain questionable inclusions, such as *Western Horseman* (primarily a popular periodical) under "Agriculture and Animal Science," when *Equus*, a far more scholarly periodical, is omitted. Many periodicals included in Katz, *Magazines for Libraries*, 5th ed. (see *ARBA* 87, entry 80), have been missed, but *National Librarian*, with a circulation of 400, has been included. *Emergency Librarian* is included, but not *The Book Report*.

Much of the information was supplied directly by the publishers, but unfortunately, no attempt was made to fill the gaps. The uneven coverage detracts greatly from this work's value; *The Serials Directory* and *Ulrich's International Periodicals Directory* (are much more complete. [R: LJ, July 88, p. 71]

Shirley Lambert

434. American Book Trade Directory 1988-89. 34th ed. New York, R. R. Bowker, 1988. 1812p. index. $159.95. LC 15-23627. ISBN 0-8352-2461-9; ISSN 0065-759X.

This directory, now in its thirty-fourth edition, provides users with a convenient compilation of current information about American and Canadian booksellers. Arranged first by state, then by city, each book outlet is described as to size of stock, telephone number, specialties, name of owners and buyers, chain affiliation (if any), and SAN (Standard Address Number). In the case of antiquarian dealers, the directory indicates the number of catalogs issued annually. The newest version of the directory lists 25,395 retailers and wholesalers, an increase of 1,423 names over the previous year. Since information is gathered annually by questionnaire and telephone inquiry, accuracy is one of the volume's hallmarks. In addition to the listing of book outlets, one can use the directory to locate addresses of bookstore chain and franchise headquarters, wholesalers of books and magazines, auctioneers and appraisers of literary property, foreign-language specialists, and exporters and importers. The main section of the book is followed by a topically divided index enabling the user to locate dealers who specialize, for example, in dolls, dance, or railroadiana. The *American Book Trade Directory* gives the user the benefit of Bowker's many years of publishing experience. No public or academic library should be without this thorough and well-organized volume.

Donald C. Dickinson

435. BookGuide 1988-89: Ontario Sellers of Used & Rare Books. Cobalt, Ont., Highway

Book Shop, 1988. 146p. maps. index. $5.95pa. ISBN 0-88954-324-0.

This is a nicely executed, moderately priced guide to some 312 used bookdealers, antiquarian print and map dealers, and comic book dealers in Ontario, Canada. The first section lists 93 dealers in Toronto, the second 120 dealers in southwestern Ontario, the third 56 dealers in southeastern Ontario, the fourth 26 dealers in Ottawa, and the fifth 17 dealers in northern Ontario. These lists are either alphabetical by the name of the bookstore or alphabetical by city. Up to nine items of information are provided for each dealer, including name, address, telephone number, hours open, name of proprietor, subject specialties, size of book stock, special services (catalogs and search service), and the names of accepted credit cards. There are also a fifteen-page essay on bookselling and book collecting, a two-page calendar of events, and alphabetical and subject specialty indexes. The identification of dealers who issue catalogs along with their subject specialties makes this guide a valuable tool for the specialized collector who buys primarily from catalogs. There is no equally inexpensive, equally up-to-date, and equally detailed guide to the used book, map, and print dealers of Ontario; and any collector, dealer, or library seeking new sources of these items would be well advised to purchase it.

Joseph Cataio

436. **Cassell & The Publishers Association Directory of Publishing 1988.** 13th ed. London, Cassell; distr., Philadelphia, Taylor & Francis, 1987. 387p. index. $55.00pa. ISBN 0-304-31442-0.

This directory, now in its thirteenth edition, provides facts on over eleven hundred publishing firms, with the majority located in the United Kingdom and the Commonwealth. Firms in the United States are excluded. Users of this directory can obtain for each firm, the address, telephone number, description of publishing specialty, number of titles published annually, number of employees, and names of chief officers. In addition to the identification of publishing firms, the directory supplies lists of author's agents, trade and professional societies, book clubs, remainder houses, literary and trade events, and periodicals of the trade. All this is drawn together by a thorough listing of publishers by field of activity and an index of personal names. This useful volume should be purchased by any academic or public library that is involved in overseas purchasing or whose staff needs to answer reference questions on overseas publishers. The directory will serve as a supplement to *Books in Print* and has a greater variety of information than is found in *British Books in Print*.

Donald C. Dickinson

437. **Directory of Book, Catalog, and Magazine Printers.** 4th ed. By John Kremer with others. Fairfield, Iowa, Ad-Lib Publications, 1988. 191p. illus. bibliog. index. $15.00pa. ISBN 0-912411-13-9; ISSN 0895-139X.

This directory lists almost one thousand printers of books, catalogs, magazines, and other bound publications, including annual reports, calendars, journals, newsletters, yearbooks, etc. Along with the alphabetical listing of printers are included a how-to-use section, how to request printing quotations, tips for saving money on printing, how to read the printer listings, working with overseas printers, list of overseas printers, and appendix material that provides print-user survey results, resource guides, recommended reading, and indexes— many of them: by main focus, by printed items, by in-house binding capabilities, services offered, optimum print runs, Canadian and foreign printers, and an alphabetical index of all printers listed in the directory.

Each listing includes company name, address, telephone number, print runs preferred, binding capabilities, other services offered such as typesetting, color separations, and fulfillment, size of printing presses, typical turnaround times for printed material, and terms of payment.

The directory material is also available as a database program for IBM-PC compatible and Macintosh computers. Advertisements are sprinkled throughout, which is somewhat distracting.

A disclaimer is included in the foreword: "Most of these listings are based on the printer's self-report and some printers are not above exaggerating their capabilities, services, and turnaround times." Amen! Getting reliable quotations for printing takes time and using this book and some of its specialized sections will certainly help maximize your efforts.

Judy Gay Matthews

438. **The International Directory of Little Magazines and Small Presses.** 24th ed. Len Fulton, ed. Paradise, Calif., Dustbooks, 1988. 887p. index. $35.95; $22.95pa. ISBN 0-916685-05-5; 0-916685-04-7pa.

The twenty-fourth edition of this directory continues to grow in volume and stature. It is of inestimable value to writers, scholars, and librarians as it is the most up-to-date source on those difficult to find little magazines and small presses. Listings are of three kinds—magazines, presses (book publishers), and cross-references— all arranged in one alphabet. For magazines, entries include title, name of press, editor(s), address, telephone number, date founded, type of material published, information on contributors, frequency of publication, number of issues published in 1987 and anticipated issues for 1988 and 1989, subscription price, average number of pages, page size, production method, length of reporting time on manuscripts, payment rates, copyright arrangements, number and type of reviews, advertisement rates, and membership in small magazine or press organizations. Press listings include similar information. This 887-page paperback provides detailed information on over forty-six hundred markets for writers and is updated by new listings which appear in the *Small Press Review*. It is of particular value to academic and large public libraries with special collections of contemporary fiction, art, and poetry; women's studies; countercultures; ethnic or minority studies; science fiction and/or fantasy; and the avant-garde. But any library, any writer, anyone interested in the new, the unusual, trends and developments in the literary and artistic worlds, etc., will find this publication fascinating and valuable in tracing the nontraditional, out of the mainstream periodical publication. The subject index ranges from little magazine and small press publications on African literature, Americana, book reviewing, classical studies, comics, futurism, and gardening to the occult, visual arts, the West, women, and Zen. A regional index covers little magazines and small presses by state and country. This directory of little magazines and small presses continues to be a "must" for every library of any size. Maureen Pastine and Martha S. Perry

439. **LMP 1988: Literary Market Place: The Directory of American Book Publishing with Names & Numbers.** New York, R. R. Bowker, 1987. 1181p. index. $85.00pa. LC 41-51571. ISBN 0-8352-2391-4; ISSN 0075-9899.

Several minor changes have occurred with the publication of the forty-eighth edition of *LMP*. Indexes, now appearing in the back of *LMP*, are "Names & Numbers," "Publisher Toll Free Directory" (new with this edition), "Index to Sections," and "Index to Advertisers." Another new section is "Magazines" (73), which lists not only periodicals that carry book reviews, but also those that excerpt and serialize books as well as those that are vehicles for book trade advertising.

For inclusion in *LMP*, entrants and nominations for new entrants are sent questionnaires. Those who do not respond and who cannot be verified by public sources or who fail to meet entry criteria are then dropped. *LMP 1988*

contains "11,757 total entries, 24% of which are new," according to the preface.

LMP is divided into fifteen general areas with each subcategory assigned a section number. Among the major groups are "Book Publishing," "Book Clubs," "Literary Awards, Contests & Grants," "Radio & Television," and "Newspaper & Magazine Publishing." Entries provide, along with other information, name, address, telephone number, key personnel, brief statistics, and descriptive annotations.

As Dority pointed out in her review (see *ARBA* 86, entry 609), there is no substitute for the breadth of coverage that *LMP* provides. It remains a necessary and recommended tool in spite of its new increased price ($85.00 for the 1988 edition compared to $54.95 for the 1985 edition). Anna Grace Patterson

440. Robinson, Ruth E., and Daryush Farudi, comps. **Buy Books Where—Sell Books Where 1988-1989: A Directory of Out of Print Booksellers and Their Author-Subject Specialties.** 6th ed. Morgantown, W. Va., Ruth E. Robinson Books, 1988. 274p. index. $29.75pa. ISBN 0-9603556-7-7.

This directory lists the subject and author specialties of over twenty-one hundred American used book dealers. Section 1 gives the names and addresses of dealers specializing in specific authors, ranging from Edward Abbey to Stefan Zweig. Section 2 supplies the names and addresses of dealers specializing in specific subjects, ranging from the Adirondacks to zoology. Section 3 lists dealers who are generalists. The geographic section lists dealers alphabetically by state (and alphabetically by city within the given state) and is particularly helpful because it also identifies those dealers who issue catalogs. The main weakness of this helpful directory is its omission of major specialty dealers. Under Chicago, for example, no mention is made of the main dealer in Chicagoana, Chicago Historical Bookworks in Evanston, Illinois. Similarly, the listings under "Literature, Modern" and "First Editions, Modern" fail to include two of the finest dealers: Joseph the Provider and Serendipity. A third example of what could be a much longer list is the omission of Articles of War Bookshop under "Military History." In addition to improving its comprehensiveness, future editions of this directory could be improved by including the size of the book stock, the telephone number, and the name of the proprietor.

Joseph Cataio

HANDBOOKS

441. The Bowker Annual of Library and Book Trade Information 1988. 33d ed. Filomena Simora, comp. and ed. New York, R. R. Bowker, 1988. 743p. index. $99.95. LC 55-12434. ISBN 0-8352-2468-6; ISSN 0068-0540.

The thirty-third edition of the *Bowker Annual* continues its important role of providing librarians and booksellers with essential information on both fields. Coverage and structure are the same as in previous editions, including, for example, "Reports from the Field"; "Legislation, Funding, Grants"; "Library/Information Science Education, Placement, and Salaries"; "Research and Statistics"; "Reference Information"; and "Directory of Organizations." Special topics of value in this edition are reading and literacy, the U.S.-U.S.S.R. Agreement on Library Cooperation, and a report on the progress of the sex versus salary/position issue. Important bibliographies such as "The Librarian's Bookshelf" are more up-to-date than in previous editions and statistics are current through 1987.

Because of varying features edition to edition, it is still a good idea to keep the last five volumes at one's fingertips. With such a battery of information at the reference librarian's disposal, it remains the preeminent handbook for librarians and booksellers. Indispensable. [R: LJ, 15 Oct 88, p. 62]   David V. Loertscher

442. Xerox Publishing Standards: A Manual of Style and Design. New York, Watson-Guptill, 1988. 1v. (various paging). illus. bibliog. index. $35.00. LC 88-26078. ISBN 0-8230-5964-2.

Organized in four major parts (on the publishing process, document organization, writing and style, and visual design), this book was "specifically developed to meet the needs of people who produce documentation with electronic and desktop publishing products. These products include personal computers, workstations, electronic typewriters, printers, computer-aided design systems, facsimile devices, and networks, as well as the multitude of software packages that work with them" (p. xvii). The first part of the book is management and process oriented (thirty-five pages); the next three parts are increasingly more technical. Appendices include Xerox document categories and contents, Xerox word list, standard units of measurement, glossary, bibliography, and index. When using this book one should always remember that it was designed specifically for Xerox and is only a guideline for other corporations to consider. Portions of the appendix

material are so specific to Xerox that they may have little application outside its hallowed halls.

Chapters in part 1 include material on document planning, research and design, writing and editing, production, distribution, updating, and storage. Part 2 includes discussion of structure, access, cross-references, front matter, subject matter, back matter, legalities, and document revision. Part 3 encompasses the meaning of style, content, bias-free writing (we can all learn something from this), multilingual communication, paragraph and sentence structure, grammar and usage, spelling, punctuation, capitalization, abbreviations, numerals, and editorial and proofreading symbols. Part 4 (the largest at seventy-eight pages) addresses page specifications, column layout, and design considerations in all its aspects (typeface, graphics, page elements, front and back matter, binding types and specifications, and cover considerations).

To describe the physical layout of this massive undertaking, one could fall upon the actual guidelines outlined in the chapter on design rationale: "The principal goals of page layout are visual recognition and legibility. These goals are accomplished through consistent typography, effective use of white space and graphics, and controlled use of rules." The Optima typeface chosen serves well; without obvious serifs, it is clean and easy on the eyes. Line leading is very adequate and use of white space allows for scanning or reading extensively without excessive eyestrain. The bright white, heavy paper is the perfect foil for the many crisp illustrations. There is little to criticize in this presentation. Cost of production does not appear to have been a consideration; many pages contain only a short paragraph, and graphics are uncrowded, often consuming only one third of a page, allowing the eye to luxuriate in the wide margins and uncluttered presentation.

There are a number of books available that address all the issues involved in electronic production, and among the most timely are *Looking Good in Print: A Guide to Basic Design for Desktop Publishing* (Ventana Press, 1988) and *Computer Typesetting* (Van Nostrand Reinhold, 1988). Anyone that needs standardized presentations that share a consistent visual logic and style will find *Xerox Publishing Standards* essential. It takes much practice and study to produce documents with the tight specifications that Xerox demands and this type of excruciating attention to detail in its most minute aspects is laudable. It behooves all of us to take a very close look at their suggestions and make a serious attempt to standardize and achieve the professional "look" that is so necessary in the business world.

This book is unique and is the leader in its field at this time. A definitive source.

Judy Gay Matthews

Desktop Publishing

443. Bold, Mary. **The Decision to Publish.** Oviedo, Fla., Bold Productions, 1987. 1v. (various paging). bibliog. index. $14.95 spiral-bound. LC 87-30904. ISBN 0-938267-01-9.

Winner of the 1987 Special Book Award of the National Association of Independent Publishers, this is designed for writers who are contemplating publishing their own books, need a user-friendly explanation of desktop publishing, and want to explore nontraditional as well as traditional publishing options (back cover). This comb-bound paperback simply and clearly presents the facts that all self-publishing authors need regarding realistic expectations and careful planning.

Material is presented in ten very informative chapters covering, among others, "The Publisher's Perspective," "The Writer's Perspective," "The Planning Stage," "The Distribution Stage," "Publicity," "Desktop Publishing," and "Resources." Strangely there are no page numbers in the table of contents, but each page is individually numbered by chapter (i.e., I-2, I-3). It is difficult to get instant access through this page numbering system. It would have been very helpful to have the subheads of the main chapters listed in the table of contents, as it is impossible to find the specific subheads in the chapters without flipping through the entire book. I would hate to miss "The Bottom Line" on page I-12, which discusses the economics of self-publishing and anticipated rewards from sales! Who can resist "Agents and Publisher Scum" (pages II-6 and II-7) for a good, honest read?

Full-sized examples of press releases and business cards are included, as is an entire chapter on desktop publishing. Chapter 10 is likely to be a favorite as it addresses the burgeoning area of desktop publishing and includes information on industry standards, printers, monitors, scanners, software, page make-up programs, electronic paste-up programs, and hardware. A list of the author's equipment is appended and leads one to suggest that this was produced on a desktop system.

The resources chapter includes desktop publishing magazines (two), a paragraph on books on publishing (nine), library references (seven), newsletters (three), and postcard printers (photographic postcards) (two), among other information. A six-page glossary and a simple index are included as well.

Limited-run publishing has its place in providing a channel for many good books to be seen and appreciated in the public sector. The homework needed to learn all that is necessary for a successful self-publishing venture is tedious at best. This book can help in this endeavor, and linked with the proper computer equipment, the independent publisher may be able to turn a manuscript into a successful book. Recommended.

Judy Gay Matthews

444. Carson, James. **Desktop Publishing and Libraries.** London and Los Angeles, Calif., Taylor Graham, 1988. 81p. illus. bibliog. $24.00 pa. ISBN 0-947568-34-4.

Carson presents a general summary of use of personal computers in preparation of library publications (i.e., desktop publishing) from a British viewpoint. His 1987 survey of British public libraries revealed interest in the subject, but the vast majority (77 percent) had no plans to implement desktop publishing. Only 4 of the 133 respondents actually were using it, and the author briefly describes their activities. (On the basis of correspondence he also reports on some U.S. experiences.) Cost is the principal factor limiting its adoption, although Carson lists the numerous advantages of desktop publishing: professional appearance of publications, economies, flexibility in operations, and as a tool in marketing library services. He concludes that desktop publishing possesses exciting potential but is "a technology waiting in the wings." A short bibliography (including both British and U.S. titles), a copy of the survey form, and several unimpressive examples of library desktop publishing conclude the volume. The volume's chief aim is to encourage use of this new technology, but it lacks the detail that would make it a useful guide for a library in implementing and using desktop publishing. [R: LAR, 14 Oct 88, p. 588]

Richard D. Johnson

445. Jones, Robert. **dtp: The Complete Guide to Corporate Desktop Publishing.** New York, Cambridge University Press, 1988. 132p. illus. bibliog. index. $39.50; $19.95pa. ISBN 0-521-35179-0; 0-521-35973-2pa.

Although many books cover the general field of desktop publishing in business, Jones's guide is targeted at corporate users. The author begins with rudiments of desktop publishing and page makeup, followed by advice on hardware and software. After these fairly generic treatments are sections specifically on running a desktop publishing system in a corporate environment. The book ends with a bibliography (which omits the magazine *Publish!* [PCW Communications, 1986-]), a list of products and manufacturers, and a glossary.

Although well-written with numerous illustrations, Jones's intended audience is not always clear. Some sections are obviously meant as an overview for managers who need to gain a feel for what will be involved in setting up a desktop publishing system (three short case studies are included). Other sections are aimed directly at the practitioner, but without the numerous examples of page layout and make-overs found in design books. A better title would have been *dtp: An Introduction to Corporate Desktop Publishing*. Readers on this side of the Atlantic will encounter only a few problems with differences between British and U.S. terminology, the most notable example of which is "grams per square metre" as the standard unit for measurement of paper weight.   Robert Skinner

446. Kleper, Michael L. **The Illustrated Handbook of Desktop Publishing and Typesetting.** Blue Ridge Summit, Pa., TAB Books, 1987. 770p. illus. bibliog. index. $49.95; $29.95pa. LC 86-23149. ISBN 0-8306-2700-6; 0-8306-0700-5pa.

Klepper's book runs to almost eight hundred pages and is a sourcebook on every aspect of desktop publishing. There are chapters on type and typesetting, and coverage of representative word processing programs for a variety of machines, telecommunications (for transfering text), converting data formats, typesetting tools, desktop publishing programs, and output devices ranging from dot matrix printers through laser printers and phototypesetters. A discussion of additional applications relates to the typesetting business and desktop publishing. An appendix covers helpful sources of information, such as computer-to-typesetting interfaces and used-equipment dealers. Although the book contains a wealth of useful information, enhanced by numerous illustrations, I found the choice of many of the word processing programs covered difficult to justify in terms of what is most used today (WordStar is there but not Word Perfect which many feel is the leading wordprocessor in the IBM world). The index also is not complete: there are several entries for Microsoft Word but not one for the main discussion of the program. In spite of these cavils, the sheer range of topics treated as well as the author's knowledge of the subject makes this a worthy purchase for most libraries.
          Robert Skinner

447. MacDougall, Alan, ed. **Electronic Publishing and the Librarian: Developments and Implications.** Loughborough, England, East Midlands Group, Library Association, 1987. 30p. £5.00pa. ISBN 0-947696-032.

This short volume includes four papers presented at a 1986 seminar at Loughborough University on developments in electronic publishing. Robin Williamson proposes an imaginative national archive of publications and data in electronic format, which he names the "knowledge warehouse." Adam Hodgkin briefly describes his views of the exciting impact electronic publishing (primarily databases) will have on scholarship. In their paper Hazel Woodward and John Wilson provide a useful summary of a Loughborough project to evaluate different kinds of journal provisions for libraries and whether hard copies of journals can be replaced by electronic journal articles. No clear-cut answers are presented except that in economic terms and given the present state of technology the electronic journal article would have to be very cheap in order to dispense with the journals themselves. In the final paper A. J. Meadows summarizes factors arising from the preceding papers that will influence future developments: technological factors, politico-legal factors, and economics of reader access. These proceedings resemble a slim issue of a periodical with each paper a different article and minimal linkage among them. The Woodward-Wilson report gives further publicity to the Loughborough study, and Williamson's dreaming may serve as the basis for a new kind of storage library.
          Richard D. Johnson

448. McClelland, Deke, and Craig Danuloff. **Desktop Publishing Type & Graphics: A Comprehensive Handbook.** San Diego, Calif., Harcourt Brace Jovanovich, 1987. 265p. illus. $29.95pa. LC 87-8585. ISBN 0-15-625298-8.

Font and graphic capabilities for desktop publishing systems seem endless; guides such as this one that answer vital questions about which tools and abilities are available and how they can be used quickly and effectively are invaluable. No attempt is made to teach graphic design, page layout, or composition; the guide suggests possibilities and points out pitfalls which result in needless trial and error. The book itself was produced using Apple's Macintosh computer and imageset on a Linotronic L100. It represents visually a very fine grasp of layout techniques; the print quality and readability are excellent.

Chapters include discussions of type style, typefaces, type sizes, letter spacing, leading, line length, and text relationships. Illustrations and examples of text material being explained are abundant, well placed, and boldly presented. In the graphics section are text and graphics depicting lines and shapes in all their variations of height and width. Squares, rectangles, circles, and ovals are also discussed and shown in illustrations that suggest unique uses. A twenty-page section of bit-mapped "clip art" is provided as an example of the exciting variety of drawings and graphics that are becoming more widely available. The book ends with information about the typefaces used in this volume, how to enlarge type sizes and some conversion tables, proofreader's marks and two examples of marked copy, and a very interesting section visually comparing dot matrix printout with laser printer output. The difference in quality and readability of these examples is truly astounding and encouraging for those of us who can see the future coming in desktop publishing, but have not quite reached it yet.

There is no index so the table of contents must be relied upon and then it is necessary to scan a page to find specific examples of needed information. However, this is not a serious drawback to enjoying this well-done volume. It is an important book to have handy if you are involved with or considering purchase of a desktop publishing system.

Judy Gay Matthews

449. Miles, John. **Design for Desktop Publishing: A Guide to Layout and Typography on the Personal Computer.** San Francisco, Calif., Chronicle Books, 1987. 103p. illus. index. $18.95 spiralbound. ISBN 0-87701-479-5.

The promise of desktop publishing technology has now given way to the disaster of desktop design: few, if any, of us have the requisite design sense to create layouts that do justice to the information we are presenting. Enter John Miles's *Design for Desktop Publishing.*

The handbook leads off with a chapter on identifying a publication's audience, what they need from the document, and how they will use it. Armed with these facts, the reader is then moved by Miles through basic design considerations (typefaces, typesetting, page grids, symmetry versus assymetry, type and layout, illustration, cover design, color, etc.), exploring the consequences of various choices, and learning how to implement those choices. A four-page glossary of printing and typesetting terms, a very brief, unannotated list of works for further reading, and a one-page index conclude the book. The writing style is crisp and practical. The book's layout carries through the design messages with boxed text and colored type

highlighting noteworthy materials; clear, helpful graphics illustrate major points throughout. Although Miles is British, there is little noticeable British slant to the text or examples used.

For the sake of all of us who read desktop-produced materials, every desktop publisher should have to read Miles's section on "Emphasis" (e.g., "Underlining is a clumsy hangover from the typewriter and should be used only if nothing better is available"). This is a useful book and will help anyone involved in desktop publishing who does not have a background in design and layout.

G. Kim Dority

450. Negru, John. **Computer Typesetting.** New York, Van Nostrand Reinhold, 1988. 185p. illus. index. $39.95pa. LC 88-2367. ISBN 0-442-26696-0.

Presented in a step-by-step format and designed for hands-on use, this book offers pertinent information necessary to answer fundamental questions regarding the latest innovations in computerized typesetting, options to consider in hardware and software, and how to typeset using personal computers. The text is presented in a two-column format, making it very easy to read and browse. Lots of white space; good, strong running heads; nontechnical language; and crisp typeface and illustrations are a plus.

The book covers a broad range of material and is arranged in a systematic fashion, progressing logically through fundamentals (parts of a character, typeface identification, families, specimen books); arithmetic (points and picas, vertical spacing, horizontal spacing); basic type specification (presentation of copy, point size, leading, justified and unjustified copy); working with type (kerning, footnotes, runaround, bullets, type modification); aids to type specification (copyfitting, layouts, tabular composition); typographers (service, editing and proofing, interfacing, graphics); typographic design (principles, legibility, readability); principles of computerized typesetting (systems, how it all works, laser typesetting, front-end systems); interface to typesetting (cable connect, telecommunications, protocols); and output options (for conventional output, laser printers). Included also are eight appendices covering terms and conditions of sale, periodicals, books, professional associations, and more. Discussion of metal typography, history, writing styles, editorial processes, grammar, and graphic design are not included unless specifically related to the typesetting function.

Books of this type are invaluable for understanding and utilizing the new technology. While a novice can learn from this effort, the seasoned professional will also find much of interest. The author has succeeded in developing a very readable and informative book that will help others to grasp the many ins and outs of computerized typography. Highly recommended.   Judy Gay Matthews

451.   Parker, Roger C. **Looking Good in Print: A Guide to Basic Design for Desktop Publishing.** Chapel Hill, N.C., Ventana Press, 1988. 224p. illus. bibliog. index. $23.95pa. LC 87-051149. ISBN 0-940087-05-7.

This "graphic design primer" for the desktop publishing professional is presented in three major sections. Section 1 introduces elements of design, with instructions and examples on choosing the typeface; use of white space; presenting photographs and illustrations; use of bullets, boxes, and rules; and a problem-solving discussion entitled "10 Common Design Pitfalls and How to Avoid Them." Section 2 presents actual examples of projects that have been redesigned using the basic techniques presented in the first section. Section 3 is project-specific and presents "tips and tricks" for improving everything published on a desktop system. The book concludes with a bibliography and source list, a list of seminars and workshops, an index, a reader survey to be completed and mailed back to Ventana Press, and some order forms for additional copies of the book.

There are some very nice touches in the presentation of the material. Most pages are divided by a heavy vertical rule; the left side presents a capsule remark in bold typeface to draw attention to the salient points of the immediate discussion. Several of these highlighted sentences can occur on one page. The actual text and any illustrations are presented to the right of the rule and are given plenty of white space to aid in skimming. The total effect invites an unhurried reading of the entire page, and the eye sweeps naturally from the highlighted material to the text and illustrations.

Parker writes in an easy, relaxed style. It is casual and friendly. The table of contents and index combine to give good access to the many topics of interest. Most chapters have very specific subheads to guide the reader to the desired material. However, chapter 1, "Beginning Observations," is a bit more esoteric. Subheads such as "Direction," "Surprise versus Boredom," "Never Lose Sight of the Total Picture," and "Restraint" do not tell one much about the actual text material. This chapter (seventeen pages) requires a thorough reading. Index entries are more specific than the subheads in the table of contents. For example, in the index "Restraint" is listed as "Restraint, as

design element," but the table of contents lists only "Restraint." Using the index for complete access is critical.

Two other books that also offer suggestions for using desktop publishing more effectively are *The Art of Desktop Publishing* (Bantam Books, 1987) and *Desktop Publishing Type & Graphics* (Harcourt Brace Jovanovich, 1987). If you already have the basics of desktop publishing under control, this book will be invaluable to assist you toward creating better-looking reports, advertisements, newsletters, and other printed material.   Judy Gay Matthews

452.   Stockford, James, ed. **Desktop Publishing Bible.** Indianapolis, Ind., Howard W. Sams, 1987. 470p. illus. index. $24.95pa. LC 87-81109. ISBN 0-672-22524-7.

Written in clear, concise language, and directed at the literate computer user, but novice at desktop publishing, Stockford (a member of the Waite Group) has brought together a variety of important topics in this book. The first section covers the basics of publishing, presents how the world of print worked before the introduction of computers, and gives an overview of the possibilities now that desktop publishing systems have arrived. The second section covers systems and hardware, documenting the needs of both the Macintosh and the IBM clone world. Choosing a computer, monitors, printers, scanning, and necessary workstation components are just a few topics in this section. The third section covers the software that is necessary for desktop publishing including graphics, page layout, and PostScript, and gives examples of software currently available (as of the publication date). The final section relates uses of desktop publishing such as newsletters, magazine layout, cartooning, and work with music.

As an introduction to desktop publishing, this book is highly recommended. As with other books the Waite Group produces, revised editions are likely to be available at regular intervals as the technology is updated. [R: Online, Sept 88, pp. 93-94]   David V. Loertscher

453.   Tilden, Scott W., with Anthony J. Fulginiti and Jack R. Gillespie. **Harnessing Desktop Publishing: How to Let the New Technology Help You Do Your Job Better.** Pennington, N.J., Scott Tilden, 1987. 70p. illus. index. $25.00pa.

According to the news release accompanying the review copy of this slim paperback, the material included is designed to provide information about desktop publishing for managers, publication designers and editors, and all microcomputer users. There is no introduction to pave the way and prepare one for what is included, but there is a brief index at the end that will be essential in trying to locate specific information since there is no table of contents. The fundamentals of desktop publishing are probably here, but how do you get to them? By browsing, of course. Beginning with a few brief paragraphs on DTP in general and a historical overview, the book moves rapidly (too rapidly) into statistics and forecasts about the future of desktop systems, applications and solutions for corporate use situations, "good news/bad news" scenarios which address some of the advantages and drawbacks, the quality of typography, basic design considerations, page layout, and a one-page discussion about self-mailers—all this in sixty-six pages! Nothing is covered in any depth. Special tips and techniques (presented as key phrases) are highlighted in large display typefaces, and most pages have an illustration. The material is not built around any specific software package or computer system and there is a strong emphasis on using this text to "sell DTP to the CEO" (news release), which probably explains the use of such a brief overview of the various aspects of desktop publishing. Just how much information is needed to "sell" someone on DTP is unknown, but two titles that are recommended for an in-depth understanding of what DTP involves are *Desktop Publishing from A to Z* (Osborne/McGraw-Hill, 1986) and *Art of Desktop Publishing* (Bantam Books, 1987). At $25.00 you can forget this one.

Judy Gay Matthews

Library Publications

454. **Library Publications Programs.** By Monica L. Knudsen. Washington, D.C., Association of Research Libraries, 1988. 117p. bibliog. (SPEC Kit, No. 145). $20.00pa.

In response to a survey initiated in November 1987, 105 ARL libraries indicated that they operated some sort of publication program. Some were centralized and highly organized, some were decentralized, and some programmatic. Forty libraries were asked to respond to a more detailed questionnaire; of the twenty-six who responded, sixteen were analyzed for this SPEC Kit. An introduction describes the surveys, the nature of publication programs, their goals, the advantages and disadvantages of centralized programs, distribution and marketing, development of programs, and a number of related issues. The body of the work is made up of analyses of the surveys; examples of position descriptions; questionnaires and surveys;

reports on and descriptions of publications programs; and policies, procedures and guidelines. Documents from Brown University, Columbia University, and the University of California at Berkeley seem to be the most detailed and useful. There is a short reading list. [R: JAL, Nov 88, p. 334]

Walter C. Allen

Private Presses

455. Bigham, Julia. **An Introduction to the Golden Cockerel Press.** London, Victoria and Albert Museum, 1987. 28p. illus. bibliog. £1.95 pa. ISBN 1-85177-035-6.

456. Fish, Wendy. **An Introduction to the Gregynog Press.** London, Victoria and Albert Museum, 1987. 22p. illus. bibliog. £1.95pa. ISBN 1-85177-005-4.

These two handsome pamphlets join a group of others from the Victoria and Albert Museum in providing short introductions to fine private presses in modern Britain. The pamphlets give a brief history of each press, describe the kinds of publications they issue, and include excellent illustrations from these publications. The pamphlets conclude with a list of the press's publications in the National Art Library and a short bibliography. Presses covered in other pamphlets from the museum include Beaumont, Doves, Ashendene, Essex House, Kelmscott, and Nonesuch. These pamphlets will be useful additions to comprehensive collections on the history of printing, but the smaller library will be as well served by such a title as the second edition of Roderick Cave's *The Private Press* (Bowker, 1983).

Richard D. Johnson

457. Hoy, Peter, and others. **Private Press Books 1981-1984.** Pinner, England, Private Libraries Association, 1987. 235p. illus. index. $42.00pa. ISBN 0-90002-15-8.

458. Hoy, Peter, and others. **Private Press Books 1985-1986.** Pinner, England, Private Libraries Association, 1988. 115p. illus. (part col.). index. $24.00pa. ISBN 0-90002-35-2.

This series of volumes has been published annually since 1959; the collection of four years' worth of material in the 1981-1984 volume appears to be the result of difficulties in keeping an editor. Private press publications are listed alphabetically by the name of the press, with a name-title index providing further access. (A geographical index would be helpful, too.) A small section at the end lists literature about private presses. Obviously a labor of love by the compilers, the works are carefully printed and contain illustrations taken from some of the books listed. Neither of the terms "private press" nor "book" is defined, but the usage appears to include what is commonly (at least by persons interested in the subject) understood. Publications from commercial private presses (e.g., Arion Press) as well as those by more traditional hobby presses (e.g., Aliquando Press), are described rather fully in terms of their physical characteristics. This series of volumes is the main source of information on the private press output in the English-speaking world, and is indispensable to libraries interested in such material. [R: LAR, 15 Mar 88, p. 170]   Philip A. Metzger

459.   Woolmer, J. Howard. **The Poetry Bookshop 1912-1935: A Bibliography.** Revere, Pa., Woolmer/Brotherson, 1988. 186p. illus. (part col.). index. $75.00. LC 87-51103. ISBN 0-913506-19-2.

Small, private, financially precarious publishing houses have generally been the outlets for twentieth-century poetry; few commercial presses will bother with it because it seldom sells well enough to justify the costs of publication. One of these small publishers was The Poetry Bookshop, established by poet Harold Monro in 1912 and remaining in business until 1935. Although the quality of both its poetry and its printing was seldom as great as that of Virginia Woolf's Hogarth Press, the Poetry Bookshop did publish Robert Graves's first work (*Over the Brazier*) as well as books by Charlotte Mew, Frances Cornford, Richard Aldington, Ford Madox Hueffer (Ford), and others.

J. Howard Woolmer has produced bibliographies of several of these private presses, basing them on his own extensive collection of their works. The present bibliography describes, in separate sections, books, "rhyme sheets" (broadsides), pamphlets, Christmas cards, periodicals (the Bookshop published two—*Poetry and Drama* and *The Chapbook*), books from other publishers distributed by the Poetry Bookshop, ephemera, and ghosts. A useful secondary bibliography is appended; the index is thorough and accurate. Full bibliographical details are provided for each item. There are many photographs (some in color) of title pages and covers. Facsimile reproductions of a rhyme sheet and a Christmas card are tipped in.

Collectors and scholars alike will welcome this attractive book. It does much to further our knowledge of a small but important corner of the publishing world.

Philip R. Rider

REFERENCE SERVICES

460.   **Fee-Based Services: Issues & Answers. Second Conference on Fee-Based Research in College and University Libraries: Proceedings....** Anne K. Beaubien, comp. Ann Arbor, Mich., Michigan Information Transfer Source, University of Michigan Libraries, 1987. 82p. bibliog. index. $28.00pa. LC 87-34900. ISBN 0-9619861-0-7.

The first conference on fee-based research in college and university libraries was held in 1982. In the five years since then, there have been many developments that justified this second conference. The field of fee-based information services is growing rapidly and this volume should be useful to anyone interested in the topic.

The talks cover aspects of fee-based services such as targeting the audience, selling and promoting the service, financial considerations of operating the service, information brokering, quality control, copyright laws and regulations, and policy-making for the service. The speakers are all very qualified and the papers are well organized and informative. Several existing fee-based services are discussed as examples or for the purposes of illustration.

The book includes a bibliography and a general but fairly useful index. All in all, this source is recommended for those interested in this specialized topic. [R: JAL, May 88, p. 118; JAL, Nov 88, pp. 304-5]   James Rice

461.   Grogan, Denis. **Grogan's Case Studies in Reference Work. 1: Enquiries and the Reference Process.** London, Clive Bingley; distr., Chicago, American Library Association, 1987. 80p. index. $16.95. ISBN 0-85157-364-9.

462.   Grogan, Denis. **Grogan's Case Studies in Reference Work. 2: Encyclopedias, Yearbooks, Directories and Statistical Sources.** London, Clive Bingley; distr., Chicago, American Library Association, 1987. 170p. index. $24.95. ISBN 0-85157-412-2.

463.   Grogan, Denis. **Grogan's Case Studies in Reference Work. 3: Bibliographies of Books.** London, Clive Bingley; distr., Chicago, American Library Association, 1987. 84p. index. $16.95. ISBN 0-85157-413-0.

464.   Grogan, Denis. **Grogan's Case Studies in Reference Work. 4: Periodicals and Their Guides.** London, Clive Bingley; distr., Chicago, American Library Association, 1987. 114p. index. $19.95. ISBN 0-85157-414-9.

465. Grogan, Denis. **Grogan's Case Studies in Reference Work. 5: Dictionaries and Phrase Books.** London, Clive Bingley; distr., Chicago, American Library Association, 1987. 153p. index. $24.95. ISBN 0-85157-415-7.

466. Grogan, Denis. **Grogan's Case Studies in Reference Work. 6: Biographical Sources.** London, Clive Bingley; distr., Chicago, American Library Association, 1987. 154p. index. $24.95. ISBN 0-85157-416-5.

This publication represents a genuine rarity in reference literature: an attempt to describe and analyze the actual process of answering reference questions. Grogan's accounts of how 536 inquiries have been dealt with in real-life library situations offer the reader a chance, so to speak, to look over the shoulders of experienced librarians as they go about their work, thereby obtaining not only a good idea of the "feel" and conduct of reference work but also sage commentary on their strategy.

Grogan limits his cases to those questions answerable by the use of general reference sources and, with the exception of the first, each of the six volumes is devoted to a single type of reference source. This approach is orderly and has the advantage of allowing the purchase of volumes on an individual basis.

A few drawbacks should be noted. The price seems steep: the set totals only 755 pages but costs $128.70. The cases all occur in British libraries and the sources used include a good many unfamiliar to North American librarians; some of the accounts will thus be of doubtful applicability in the United States and Canada. Last, it should be pointed out that, while the cases are all new, the text itself is largely the same as Grogan's two previous volumes of reference case studies (1967; 1972). This is a new edition, not a wholly new book.

These drawbacks should not be seen as challenging the essential merit of Grogan's publication. He has chosen his cases aptly—they are often of intrinsic interest as well as of pedagogical value. His commentaries are perceptive and instructive. The tone is just right, neither patronizingly simple nor taking too much for granted. To paraphrase an old advertising slogan, for the person who wants to see and understand how questions are handled over the reference desk, this is the next best thing to being there. [R: LAR, 15 July 88, p. 406; RLR, Feb 88, pp. 31-32]

Samuel Rothstein

467. Katz, Bill, and Robin Kinder, eds. **Current Trends in Information: Research and Theory.** New York, Haworth Press, 1987. 305p.

(*The Reference Librarian*, No. 18). $34.95. LC 87-17724. ISBN 0-86656-574-4.

This book examines research and theory and their impact on current reference service practices and orientation. Contributors to the book's twenty articles consist of researchers, library school faculty, and reference practitioners. One of the editors (Katz) introduces the volume in the first chapter, "The Influence of Theory and Research in the Practice of Reference Services."

The articles are organized into four sections. "Theory and Research," the first section, contains eight articles, including Neill's review of what constitutes a theory in "Can There Be a Theory of Reference?"; Mansfield's exploration of the relation of other disciplines toward information in "The Wider Scope of Information Research"; McClure and Hernon's examination of unobtrusive testing; Harmon's review of expert inquiry systems; and Hafner's philosophical interpretation of "Public Libraries and Society in the Information Age." Four articles constitute the second section, "Influence of Theory and Research Practice"; among these are Miller and Tegler's thoughtful reconsideration of the role of instruction among librarians, and Rodger and Goodwin's description of "a Cooperative Do-It-Yourself Reference Accuracy Study." Section 3, "Theory," includes descriptions of an application of finite difference calculus (by Pearson), a metatheoretic research approach (by Stanoulov), and a literary analysis (by Walsh). The last section, "Practice: Online," contains five articles which consider online services from the perspective of education of librarians (Krieger), development (Levine), applications (Buchann, Atkinson and Knee), and a specific case study review of WESTLAW (Irving and Mendelsohn). Bibliographies of related works and well-cited references are included throughout the book. The lack of a subject index hinders reference use of this book, but a detailed table of contents assists the reader to locate concepts within each article.

This is recommended reading for reference librarians and managers. It gives theoretical insight, documented research, and practical direction to improve reference services and does so in a variety of ways ranging from humorous and clever metaphoric comparisons to systematic and practical methodological descriptions. The range of perspectives parallels the complexity of reference activities and the mindsets of those involved with reference services. [R: LAR, 14 Oct 88, p. 587]   Danuta A. Nitecki

468. Katz, Bill, and Ruth Fraley, eds. **International Aspects of Reference and Information**

Services. New York, Haworth Press, 1987. 244p. (*The Reference Librarian*, No. 17). $34.95. LC 87-11846. ISBN 0-86656-573-6.

Katz, in the introduction, points out that the papers presented here concentrate almost exclusively on the sciences and the social sciences, and that very little is mentioned about literature and the humanities. The two central problems with information dissemination outside of the United States (excluding perhaps Great Britain and Germany), according to Katz, is the lack of systematic cooperation among nations and the control of information within countries by private versus state agencies. The latter is a problem we are beginning to see in the United States with substantial budget cuts within the Government Printing Office.

The nineteen essays are divided into three main sections. The first section contains five essays, each devoted to defining the problem and placing it into a proper context. Among the most commonly cited problems were the lack of language skills (especially in the United States), weak or nonexisting bibliographic control (mainly non-European countries), lack of funding (and sometimes interest) for the collection of foreign-language materials in the United States, and missing controls relative to the identification and review of reference materials within individual countries. The second section contains six essays discussing the extent of awareness of international information dissemination and exchange within the United States. Two solid essays are included in this section: one by Gary W. North and Nancy B. Faries dealing with the structure of research dissemination by the U.S. Geological Survey and another by Jack C. Wells on the history of overseas collection development by the U.S. Library of Congress. The third section contains eight essays documenting what is currently being done in various regions of the world about the development of national information services. Edwin Cleaves's article on key Latin American reference sources is of particular value, yet the remaining essays are somewhat disappointing both by reason of content and breadth of coverage.

This work is a fair start toward eliminating a surprisingly scant literature base on international and comparative information services. [R: LAR, 14 Oct 88, p. 605]

Richard H. Quay

469. Prytherch, Ray. **The Basics of Readers' Advisory Work.** London, Clive Bingley; distr., Chicago, American Library Association, 1988. 102p. illus. bibliog. index. $17.95. ISBN 0-85157-389-4.

Including "most aspects of public work in a library or information department" within his definition of readers' advisory work, Prytherch provides a general discussion of ways to handle and improve upon many of the public service/reference operations of libraries of various types. The scope of the book is indicated by its chapter titles: "First Catch Your Reader," "Who Are Your Readers?" "Answering Readers' Questions," "Community Information," "Keeping Track," "Publicity and Promotion," and "Staff Training for Readers' Advisory Work." It provides information on everything from making your library more appealing and attractive to the public to training your staff members in basic interpersonal skills. A brief bibliography and an index conclude the work.

Although the information is basic and useful, North American librarians should be aware that the British usage of the term *readers' advisory* is much broader (and somewhat different) than what they might expect, and those anticipating a book on how to advise readers in their literary or recreational reading pursuits will be disappointed. (In fact, the subject is barely mentioned.) *The Basics of Library Public Services and Reference Work* would actually have been a more appropriate and accurate title for those of us on this side of the Atlantic.

However, once this misunderstanding has been clarified and the British orientation of the work recognized, those interested in improving their public services operations should find much in this concise, yet readable, work to recommend it. Basic, practical, and brief. *The Basics of Readers' Advisory Work* provides a good beginning place for librarians who are considering either beginning new or reassessing existing public services programs. [R: LAR, 16 May 88, p. 295; RLR, Aug 88, p. 206]

Kristin Ramsdell

SCHOOL LIBRARY MEDIA CENTERS

General Works

PHILOSOPHY AND THEORY

470. Eble, Mary M., and Jeanne Renton. **New Dimensions in School Library Media Service.** Metuchen, N.J., Scarecrow, 1988. 468p. illus. index. $39.50. LC 88-4230. ISBN 0-8108-2115-X.

This practical guide offers easy-to-duplicate curriculum units that are designed to reinforce and enhance seventh through twelfth grade students' reading, writing, and research skills. Chapter 1 describes in detail a paperback reading program which can include an entire school. It includes copies of student book reviewing and evaluation forms for different grade levels and specific procedures for designing the program. Chapters 2 through 16 contain individual teaching units on student book reviewing, film and book evaluation, thematic identification, book discussion clubs, independent study projects, library research skills, and photograph-essay production. Chapter 17 presents library skills units targeted for each grade level. All chapters are characterized by extensive quotations from various notables about reading, literature, knowledge, and education. Most lessons are accompanied by an annotated list of titles related to different themes and subjects. The appendix provides users with an additional annotated list of appropriate fictional titles and the index permits access by idea, author, and title. For librarians searching for ideas for integrating literature appreciation units into the curriculum, this guide is a recommended purchase.

Kathleen W. Craver

471. Hannesdóttir, Sigrún Klara, comp. and ed. **The School Library: Gateway to Knowledge. International Association of School Librarianship 16th Annual Conference ... Proceedings.** Kalamazoo, Mich., International Association of School Librarianship, 1988. 280p. illus. $15.00 spiralbound.

This title is the published proceedings of the sixteenth annual conference of the International Association of School Librarianship. Topics of the fourteen published papers and two panel discussions range from computers in school libraries, to book selection, to school libraries in South Africa. Minutes of the business meeting and a list of conference participants are also included.

There is value in information about school libraries in other countries. Some things librarians do are universal, such as collection development. Ylva-Lindholm Romantschuk's comments on selecting books in small countries can be of interest to school librarians in both large and small countries. Another advantage of the international viewpoint is that it can help school librarians find a new perspective on familiar library activities. Sharing information can lead to growth, development, and improvement of school libraries. This publication helps to promote such sharing.

This title is spiralbound, possibly in an attempt at speedy publication. However, the printing is crisp, clear, and easy-to-read. It

would have been helpful if the nationality of each author were given, along with the article title. Also, some brief comments about an author's background, work experience, and other credentials would be helpful. Overall, this title is appropriate for academic libraries and those interested in international librarianship.

Carol A. Doll

472. Jay, M. Ellen. **Motivation & the School Library Media Teacher.** Hamden, Conn., Library Professional Publications/Shoe String Press, 1988. 201p. illus. $29.50; $21.50pa. LC 87-37933. ISBN 0-208-02171-X; 0-208-02172-8pa.

This book is based on the author's premise that "[s]chool library media teachers who are alert to motivational theory and its applications will be able to have positive effects on [their] students' desire to learn" (p. 1), and presents her own tried and true activities designed to increase student motivation. The first chapter deals with that perennial student bugaboo, the book report, presenting innovative ways to spice up this traditional classroom activity, while "Writing Spinoffs" and the chapter "Involvement Bulletin Boards" will surely provide even seasoned veterans with some fresh ideas, ranging from activities about Benjamin Franklin to map reading activities around the world. Two particularly noteworthy chapters which could tie nicely into library public relations projects are "Thinking Skill of the Month," which seems particularly relevant given today's current emphasis on this area, and "All-School Contests and Activities." Decorating your door as a book jacket and a new radio drama, "As the Book Returns," sound like fun ways to encourage reading and the language arts, respectively.

The pluses of this work are that it provides some new thoughts on some old topics (e.g., mini-teaching units, a "Jeopardy" game to teach the Constitution, etc.) as well as some new areas such as computer education. And, while some chapters seem somewhat brief, others appear especially well developed and their contents detailed enough to be both useful and replicable.

On the minus side would be the fact that more experienced librarians simply might not need more bulletin board or mini-unit ideas, preferring their own carefully developed ones refined after many years' use. Also, in a few instances at the beginning, poor proofreading marred the author's otherwise clear and concise prose. [R: BL, 1 Apr 88, p. 1356; VOYA, June 88, p. 105]

Carol Truett

473. **Reference Books in the Secondary School Resource Centre.** Nottingham, England, Education Library Service, 1988. 37p. index. £1.00pa.

This annotated guide for secondary school libraries was produced in England by an editorial team. The list includes general and specific reference books for single and double volumes only, excluding multivolume encyclopedias. Most of the books annotated were published in the 1980s, making it interesting for students and increasing the current value of the materials listed. The list is arranged by Dewey Decimal Classification order and includes a title index at the end. For each item, the bibliographic information includes title, author, publisher, date, ISBN, price annotation, and assessment. Small encyclopedias, dictionaries, thesauri, atlases, digests, and companions to literature are included, covering a wide range of topics in the humanities and sciences. Targeted age groups are indicated also.

The list is basic and one could expect perhaps a more comprehensive list for secondary school libraries; but this guide is easy to use and its simple approach should encourage students to use the reference collection often and ask for more guides similar to this. Hopefully the editors will enlarge this booklet in the future.   Camille Côté

474. Turner, Philip M., ed. **A Casebook for "Helping Teachers Teach."** Englewood, Colo., Libraries Unlimited, 1988. 161p. illus. $17.50pa. LC 88-22978. ISBN 0-87287-615-2.

This is a useful guide to planning lessons, and any school library media center that has a professional collection of curriculum guides and educational journals containing ideas for classroom activities should have a copy of Turner's casebook.

Turner made a major contribution to the school library field with his publication of *Helping Teachers Teach* (Libraries Unlimited, 1985). The title itself states one of the least developed and most critical roles of the professional school media specialist. His casebook is a gathering of tested and successful learning activities which can be quickly planned and placed into action in most public school library situations. The lesson plans (not case studies) are written by practicing school librarians. They include "Improving Research Skills," "Images of Women: Past, Present, and Future" (an excellent outline for including oral histories), and "Along the Oregon Trail" (a common simulation experience which generates some interesting student papers).

The editor's comments for each lesson are very brief and add little to the text. The more creative teacher who has always thought in terms of using materials from the media center will probably not find this collection of lesson plans very unique or exciting. Those who need

some ideas to seed teachers who have not experienced the development of learning activities in the media center will find this collection from Turner to be very helpful.

Daniel Callison

REFERENCE BOOKS

475. **The Elementary School Library Collection: A Guide to Books and Other Media. Phases 1-2-3.** 16th ed. Lois Winkel with others, eds. Williamsport, Pa., Brodart, 1988. 1028p. index. $79.95. LC 87-24974. ISBN 0-87272-092-6.

The sixteenth edition of this important selection tool for school and public libraries continues its long-standing provision of a core book and audiovisual media collection. Books and other media of high quality available and/or published between 15 April 1985 and 15 April 1987 are included. As with previous editions, standards of quality including allegiance to certain "current trends of education" must be met before a title is listed. Arrangement is by Dewey Decimal Classification (eleventh abridged ed.) with author, title, and subject indexes.

ESLC has almost twice the titles as its competitor, *Children's Catalog* (see *ARBA* 87, entry 619), and contains audiovisual media that the H. W. Wilson list does not. Annotations in *ESLC* are descriptive for the most part, while the *Catalog* annotations contain excerpts of reviews. *ESLC* includes sections for reference, professional publications, and periodicals not included in the *Catalog*. Both tools have a heavy overlapping of titles and their revision policy is quite different. *ESLC* is published in its entirety annually, while the *Catalog* is published at five-year intervals with annual supplements. Each policy of revision has its own set of advantages for collection building.

In both lists, fiction and easy books predominate, biasing the lists toward literature and away from curricular nonfiction. This bias is as much a publisher's bias as a conscious one by the editors. Realizing this and other biases of basic lists such as "the best of what is in print," users who purchase and use the list must do so carefully, as instructed by the editor. School librarians will need to use the list to build more curriculum-oriented collections in contrast to public librarians who will want broader coverage of children's interests for the community as a whole. Purchasing the entire collection in phases for new schools or public libraries is not a wise practice where a focused collection matching local needs is desired. Use of the list for topical development of collections is a wiser practice.

While one may quibble with the selection of individual titles, the list is as current as the "in-print nightmare of U.S. publishing" will allow. The professional collection needs a thorough revision to reflect needs of both librarians and teachers in the school. Otherwise, the list is highly recommended for those who are beginning and building collections. Since the list is expensive, a system of cooperative purchase within a local area is recommended. [R: BL, July 88, p. 1844]　　David V. Loertscher

476. School Library Media Annual 1988. Volume Six. Jane Bandy Smith, ed. Englewood, Colo., Libraries Unlimited, 1988. 297p. index. $29.50. ISBN 0-87287-635-7; ISSN 0739-7712.

This volume was compiled by a team of editors who tried to follow the tradition of excellence established by the previous co-editors. The first concern of this book continues to be reading, but most recently this topic has come under new labels such as literacy, and has drawn the attention of a number of people and organizations. The school library media not being a classroom, the editors kept the practitioners in mind and geared their publication to current practice, dealing with such topics as continuing education, issues, research and studies, information, and publications.

The first part of the book reports on the "whole language approach," a student-centered, integrated language arts approach that requires an expanded role of library media personnel to assist students in their work. This also means that the library media center must have a wide assortment of quality literature to meet the needs of the students. It must develop active participation between teachers and media specialists.

Another section of the book looks at the publishing industry and its pressures and practices in the corporate political arena; its profit making business orientation is not always in line with pedagogical objectives. One California experience (the "whole language approach") and another in Georgia about the censorship issue in Gwinnett County are reported. Some attention is focused on research and the need for better bibliographical control. Concern is expressed for training, use, cost, and supervision in technology. In the field of automation, library media specialists are showing special interest in two areas: automated circulation and cataloging.

The last part of this volume is like an almanac dealing with information on a variety of topics. This book is a wealth of information

and the editors must be commended for their good work.　　Camille Côté

477. University Press Books for Secondary School Libraries. 20th ed. New York, for American Association of School Librarians, American Library Association by Association of American University Presses, 1988. 49p. index. free pa. ISSN 0887-1345.

Selected by secondary school librarians, this annotated list of over two hundred titles from university presses is intended to increase the awareness of titles which can add depth and breadth to a secondary school collection on topics less frequently published by commercial publishers. Titles are arranged in Dewey Decimal Classification order and each entry contains complete bibliographic information as well as an annotation taken from recognized reviewing sources or provided by members of the committee. Each entry is coded for level (high school or junior high school) and expected appeal (general, regional, or special, for those libraries with in-depth collections in the field). Titles were selected which enhance the curriculum, are of interest to young adults, are new editions of previously published works, or are scholarly titles that require a basic knowledge of the subject. A directory of contributing publishers with addresses is located on the inside covers. Author and title indexes are included.

The largest group of titles is in history, geography, and biography, with the next largest group in the social sciences. The literature section is the third largest group, and the pure sciences and the arts have about an equal number. The other subject areas of Dewey have a limited number of titles. While all secondary school libraries will find this a helpful selection aid, those in schools offering honors or advanced placement courses will find it particularly useful.　　Donald C. Adcock

Microcomputers

478. Herring, James E., ed. **The Microcomputer, the School Librarian, and the Teacher: An Introduction with Case Studies.** London, Clive Bingley; distr., Chicago, American Library Association, 1987. 150p. illus. bibliog. index. $22.95pa. ISBN 0-85157-399-1.

Although this work seems to be just another book for school librarians and teachers concerning the use of microcomputers in teaching and learning from a British viewpoint; this is a *special* source. The introduction presents microcomputers in light of a global English-speaking context. All types of microcomputers are mentioned and some specific English projects are highlighted. Four of the ten chapters were written by the editor. Other contributors are knowledgeable and seem to have extensive backgrounds.

Chapters are "Introduction," "Justification," "Administration," "Publicity and Information," "Issue (circulation) Systems," "Database Creation," "Information Skills," "Prestel (online) Access," "Criteria for Selecting Software," "In-service Training," and "Predictions for the Future." Significant appendices include a list of software mentioned in the book, a glossary of terms, a sample printout from the SIR (Schools Information Retrieval Project) Program, and conclude with a brief and easily used index.

The book is a useful source for gaining an understanding of the use of computers in British school libraries, built around case studies from fifteen schools and educational authorities where the microcomputer has become an integral part of their curriculum. Throughout the chapters there are simple, clear and effective graphics appropriately located to enhance the text. The $22.95 price seems high, but worth it for the computer aficionado. [R: BR, Nov/Dec 88, p. 45]   Thomas L. Hart

Programs

GENERAL WORKS

479. Information Power: Guidelines for School Library Media Programs. By the American Association of School Librarians and Association for Educational Communications and Technology. Washington, D.C., Association for Educational Communications and Technology and Chicago, American Library Association, 1988. 171p. illus. bibliog. index. $12.95pa. LC 88-3480. ISBN 0-8389-3352-1.

The latest national guidelines for school library media programs are primarily addressed to building-level school library media specialists. Separate chapters address the mission and challenges of school library media programs; the program itself; roles and responsibilities of the school library media specialist; leadership, planning, and management; personnel; resources and equipment; facilities; and district, regional, and state leadership. Appendices include quantitative results from a 1985-1986 survey of school library media centers; budget formulas; quantitative guidelines for library media facilities; policies and statements on access to information; and an annotated bibliography of pertinent research studies.

Typically, these guidelines tend to be idealistic as they attempt to provide guidance for school library media programs. As a result, they are a well-supported philosophical statement about the importance of school library media centers and their potential in the educational setting. The new standards stress the need for an active media specialist who is fully involved in educational activities and has leadership responsibilities. The increasing importance of information is acknowledged, and the media specialist is assigned responsibility for promoting effective access to information resources in all formats and for fully exploiting the new technologies. At the same time, the standards recognize that school library media programs will vary from school to school. All in all, the new guidelines can help media specialists clarify their own thinking, and help to explain the value of school library media programs to other educators and parents. It is hoped that schools and media specialists who are not yet attuned to these ideas will not be discouraged.

These standards are mostly qualitative. This could help dispel the notion that the "right" number of books "makes" a good media center. At the same time it will be more difficult to get support from administrators and school boards who are numbers oriented. More specific guidelines might have influenced those educators who are unresponsive to the philosophical ideas expressed here.

These guidelines should be of interest to school libraries and all academic libraries serving future media specialists, school administrators, or principals. [R: BL, 1 Apr 88, p. 1356; BR, Nov/Dec 88, pp. 44-45; VOYA, Dec 88, p. 257]   Carol A. Doll

480. Loertscher, David V. **Taxonomies of the School Library Media Program.** Englewood, Colo., Libraries Unlimited, 1988. 336p. illus. bibliog. index. $23.50pa. LC 87-35367. ISBN 0-87287-662-4.

In this book Loertscher defines and discusses the modern school library media center. Roles of the media specialist, teacher, student, and school administrator are detailed, with accompanying taxonomies based on the degree to which the media center is actively involved in all aspects of the school's instructional program. Classifications range from an isolated media center to one included in curriculum development at the school or district level. Examples are given of methods or units that can help increase the involvement of the media center in the school. It is also noted that technical aspects of the media center must operate smoothly to support this activity. Evaluation of the various parts of the school library media center and its program is encouraged. Appendices include evaluation forms for school library media specialists, the Purdue Self-Evaluation System for school media centers, and additional readings.

This book gives Loertscher an opportunity to develop and explore his personal philosophy that a school library media specialist should be actively involved in the school's instructional program. The book is supported by a partially annotated bibliography and numerous details, ranging from complete lesson plans to planning sheets for a cooperative teacher-media specialist unit to a chart comparing hand production times to computerized times for typical media center operations such as writing overdues. Furthermore, teachers, students, and administrators are all included in the development of the ideas, which is important because the school library media center does not exist in isolation. The strongest feature of this title is the continuous emphasis placed on evaluation. Many interesting, pertinent, evaluation questions have been included which should yield helpful data. While not all of the instruments are well designed (e.g., the student questionnaire seems to assume students do not come to the media center), it is vital that media specialists accept the concept of evaluation and incorporate it into media center management. This title can certainly help in that respect. It can also help in situations where media specialists are trying to convince administrators that teacher evaluation techniques are not suited to media specialists.

In general, this could be a useful book for working media specialists or for school library media center administration classes. [R: BL, July 88, p. 1823; BR, Sept/Oct 88, pp. 48-49; SLJ, Oct 88, p. 44; VOYA, Oct 88, pp. 208-9]

Carol A. Doll

481. **Toward Effective School Library Media Programs: A Resource Bank.** Compiled by the Committee for Library Media Planning. Burlingame, Calif., California Media and Library Education Association, c1986, 1987. 106p. illus. $5.00 looseleaf.

The purpose of this compilation of selected articles, reports, and documents regarding school library programs is to provide school media specialists, administrators, and other educational support groups with written rationales for justifying, developing, and maintaining effective school media programs. Arranged by order of suggested use, the first section supplies planners with the philosophical foundations for establishing and advocating a progressive school library program. Included in this part are reprintings of *The Alliance for Excellence: Librarians Respond to "A Nation at Risk,"* David Loertscher's 1982 article concerning taxonomic levels for school librarians' participation in the curriculum, and the compilers' statement of commitment to develop strong school media programs. Part 2 describes the background and current status of school library programs in California. Research studies on collection development as well as selections from the California Administrative Code, Title V, are furnished. The third part presents selected research results, articles, and checklists relating to program development, implementation, and evaluation. Criteria for selecting library personnel and designing a quality program comprise the last section.

Although most of the materials in this resource bank relate specifically to the problems and needs of California public schools, the articles and rationales are applicable to any state's school library media programs. Copyright release has been obtained for all articles and the masters have been printed on one side to permit easy duplication. School media specialists will find that this compilation contains most of the salient articles, research, and documents necessary for the justification of a forceful school library media program.

Kathleen W. Craver

482. McDonald, Frances Beck, comp. **The Emerging School Library Media Program: Readings.** Englewood, Colo., Libraries Unlimited, 1988. 328p. bibliog. index. $24.50pa. LC 88-6784. ISBN 0-87287-660-8.

In the past year, several very good publications on school library media have crossed my desk and this new work concentrates on different themes related to school library media. This collection illustrates MEDIA: "*M*edia specialists providing *E*xcellence in education through *D*esigning and *I*ntegrating learning *A*ctivities throughout the curriculum." Surveying the literature, one realizes quickly the lack of consensus concerning school library media programs and services. This book focuses on many important aspects such as learning, research, changing roles, media specialists, services, networks, and leadership. Library media specialists should facilitate the learning process of students through different services like access, reference, production, instruction, and consulting.

The second part of this book reports a U.S. study of 209 public schools entitled "'Exemplary Elementary Schools' and Their Library Media Centers." A position paper by Ken Haycock, a Canadian expert in school libraries, discusses the librarian as a professional teacher and educator. Then there is an excellent chapter on educating students to think. This method includes critical thinking skills allowing students to evaluate and use information in a way to become information-literate. If media specialists can accomplish their tasks well, the library media center will become a vital part of every school. Providing precepts and examples which will stimulate individual approaches to program development, this book will be a valuable addition to every school.   Camille Côté

483. Woolls, Blanche. **Managing School Library Media Programs.** Englewood, Colo., Libraries Unlimited, 1988. 181p. illus. index. (School Library Media Management Series). $21.50pa. LC 88-2689. ISBN 0-87287-590-3.

Members of the school library media profession have come to expect the work of Woolls to be comprehensive and complete. This work, the first in an anticipated series on school library media management and administration, is no exception. As stated in the preface, it "contains an overview of the tasks currently assigned to a person managing a library media program." The work begins with a brief history of school library media centers, the preparation of personnel and seeking of jobs, choosing and beginning the job, and the various aspects of management and administration, including a systems approach in planning. Especially useful will be such units as marketing, evaluation, networking, and professional associations. It ends with a look to the future.

The work is well researched, builds on the work of other leaders in the field (e.g., David V. Loertscher, James W. Liesener, etc.), and gives practical examples to implement the theory of good administration. Practicing library media professionals will find a range from very basic to very advanced methodology, and all will find the work helpful. The comprehensiveness of the work, and the inclusion of much basic information, may limit the ease with which the experienced school library media specialist can use the work, but sections like those on Loertscher's levels of curriculum integration, collection mapping, circulation systems, deselection, etc., will be especially useful. Future volumes in the series will be helpful in providing more detailed information in such areas as budget and facilities planning. An especially useful chapter is chapter 8, "On the Job: Managing Services."

The use of an overabundance of regional examples should be noted by those media professionals in other areas of the country, especially with regard to the training and preparation of media professionals and state licensing, which differ greatly in other parts of the country. The

work, however, is a significant addition to the literature of the school library media field. [R: BL, July 88, p. 1822; BL, July 88, p. 1844; BR, Nov/Dec 88, p. 45; VOYA, Oct 88, pp. 207-8]
                Anthony C. Schulzetenberg

ACTIVITIES

484. Kinghorn, Harriet R., and Fay Hill Smith. **At Day's End: Book-Related Activities for Small Groups.** Englewood, Colo., Libraries Unlimited, 1988. 235p. illus. maps. $19.50pa. LC 88-22491. ISBN 0-87287-654-3.

At Day's End is designed to alleviate the problems which frequently occur near the end of a typical school day: the time when both teachers and students are exhausted and ready to quit even though the clock shows another thirty minutes left in the school day. The authors have developed thirteen units which supplement or complement the elementary school curriculum. Units include such familiar topics as animals, birds, insects, the circus, and continents as well as humor and favorite books. Unit activities range from reading, writing, and calculating to drawing, craft projects, and research. Each unit also provides a bibliography of children's books on the topic covered. While units are designed to provide a creative use of the end of the school day, they could be equally useful at any time when the topic is being studied in the curriculum.

Elementary teachers will find this book another practical weapon in their arsenals of teaching tools. Recommended for elementary school professional collections and public libraries.   Carol J. Veitch

485. McElmeel, Sharron L. **An Author a Month (For Pennies).** Englewood, Colo., Libraries Unlimited, 1988. 224p. illus. index. $23.50pa. LC 88-15731. ISBN 0-87287-661-6.

Based on the author's belief in the value of good literature, this title presents activities designed to integrate reading with classroom teaching. The intent is to provide students with positive experiences related to good books. In-depth units are given for each of nine authors, and contain biographical information with comments on the author's/artist's work, initial instructions for the teacher or media specialist, and an "idea cupboard" full of suggested student activities. Shorter units are included on three additional authors.

The activities suggested are nicely detailed and should be easy to adapt to individual classes. One strength of this book lies in the variety of the book-based activities, which range from compare-and-contrast to keeping a journal to follow-up library research to studying an artist's style, to cooking to art activities, to creative drama and puppet shows. McElmeel also does a good job of identifying related works by other authors (such as Cinderella variants in the unit on Marcia Brown) and compiling pertinent bibliographies for topics such as friendship and hats. It is also helpful to find numerous titles listed for each author.

While it is indeed true that picture books can be effectively used with students in upper elementary and middle school, the authors included in this title tend to make it most useful for the primary grades. Marcia Brown, Eric Carle, Tomie dePaola, Dr. Seuss, and Steven Kellogg, for example, are less appealing to older students, although the techniques presented here could be used for authors of books for older children, too. The biographical sections on each author would be stronger if they were supported by a bibliography based on professional literature. The information seems to be based on McElmeel's personal files and interviews with the author. Also, it is sometimes hard to identify where activities for one title end and those for the next title start. The spacing and margins could have been used to highlight titles discussed.

The basic idea of this book is sound and the activities are worthwhile. It will be of most value to teachers or media specialists working with primary grades who can afford the price.

Carol A. Doll

486. Mohr, Carolyn, Dorothy Nixon, and Shirley Vickers. **Thinking Activities for Books Children Love: A Whole Language Approach.** Englewood, Colo., Teacher Ideas Press/Libraries Unlimited, 1988. 206p. illus. $17.50pa. LC 88-39450. ISBN 0-87287-697-7.

Here is a creative source for assisting library media specialists and teachers to introduce books that children love as the basis for a whole language curriculum. The authors state that "the most effective way to motivate children is to use experiences, materials and literature they love." The books included were selected by children as compiled in *Children's Books: Awards and Prizes* (Childrens Book Council, 1985), and are books consistently read and loved by students in grades three through six. The primary purpose of this source is to provide questions that encourage higher-level thinking skills which will be a major survival skill in our technological society.

Fifteen books are used for this guide. For each book there is a one-page summary and then for groups of chapters of these books there

are vocabulary words, knowledge questions, comprehension questions, application questions, analysis questions, synthesis questions, and evaluation questions. There is one brief appendix containing poetry formulas for the cinquain, diamante, and haiku forms.

Thomas L. Hart

487. Phillips, Kathleen C., and Barbara Steiner. **Catching Ideas: Activity Book for Creative Writing.** Englewood, Colo., Teacher Ideas Press/Libraries Unlimited, 1988. 163p. illus. index. $24.00pa. LC 88-26595. ISBN 0-87287-712-4.

As the activity book to accompany *Creative Writing: A Handbook for Teaching Young People* (Libraries Unlimited, 1985), this source contains eight chapters of practical suggestions for assisting elementary and middle schools in their efforts to teach writing to children. Each chapter contains various exercises on such topics as fun with words (e.g., word sounds and meanings, parts of speech, alphabet games, anagrams); expanding an idea into an actual story; writing a report, news story, magazine article, or peom; and different types of writing (e.g., mystery story, family history, interview, humorous story, letter). The audience perspective is included (writing for self, to entertain, or to inform), and numerous sample exercises are provided. Each chapter follows a similar structure in providing the purpose, suggested activities and exercises, expected results, and supplemental readings. Suggestions are appropriate for both group and individual work, and cover such standard (but difficult to find) lessons as teaching similes, metaphors, clichés to avoid, and onomatopoeia.

This source will prove to be a valuable time-saver for busy teachers and a solid addition to the shelves of curriculum and education libraries, as well as school instructional materials centers. It may easily be used with or without the accompanying textbook.

Ilene F. Rockman

488. Silverman, Eleanor. **Trash into Treasure: Recycling Ideas for Library/Media Centers: Containing 100 Easy-to-Do Ideas.** rev. ed. Metuchen, N.J., Scarecrow, 1988. 164p. illus. index. $22.50pa. LC 87-36449. ISBN 0-8108-2101-X.

The idea of recycling common household objects for school projects, while not new, still has merit. The seven chapters found in this book are arranged around traditional library activities or concerns including books, dramatics, facilities and resources, holiday creations, fun activities, puppetry and storytelling. Each begins with a list of collectibles for the projects, a do list of helpful hints, and suggested activities for using that media/format. The "recipe" outline format of the one hundred ideas (fourteen more than the 1982 edition) presented is especially helpful for the busy librarian who can quickly see the materials list, directions, and suggestions for making the idea more successful.

The puppet section includes an especially wide variety of puppet types. Although a few ideas, such as having students create their own cartoons, appear new, egg carton organizers, coat-hook mobiles, and using scrap paper sheets at the card catalog are fairly standard.

Some ideas do not appear related to either media center activities or curriculum (e.g., flower vase bottles), and librarians who have been using Print Shop signs for several years might not see much need for hand lettering recycled ditto sheets. A few illustrative photographs were blurred. One final concern is the legality of copying music cassette tapes for a "Music-Listening Station."

Probably the greatest strength of this book lies in the fact that few of the ideas require elaborate preparation and almost all could be adapted to tie in with ongoing library skills or content-area instruction by the creative librarian.

Perhaps its greatest fault lies in the fact that the current philosophy of integrating library skills begins with a focus on curriculum content, not the resources used, as this book does.

Carol Truett

Reading and Curriculum Instruction

489. Carlsen, G. Robert, and Anne Sherrill. **Voices of Readers: How We Come to Love Books.** Urbana, Ill., National Council of Teachers of English, 1988. 155p. $8.75pa. LC 87-37541. ISBN 0-8141-5639-8.

This new publication by the National Council of Teachers of English is unique in that it is concerned with the "why" rather than the "how" of reading. Carlsen, a veteran teacher-educator in the area of secondary English, collected over a thirty-year period of teaching literature for adolescents, thousands of student papers that were autobiographical accounts of the students' early experiences with reading and learning to read. Sherrill, who teaches courses in children's and adolescent literature, analyzed these autobiographies and categorized selected excerpts into several chapters: "Growing with Books"; "Learning to Read"; "Literature and

the Human Voice"; "Reading Habits and Attitudes"; "Sources for Books"; "Reading and Human Relations"; "What Books Do for Readers"; "Subliterature"; "Teachers and Teaching"; "Libraries and Librarians"; "The Reading of Poetry"; "The Classics"; and "Barriers: Why People Don't Read." More specific subdivisions are also provided within these chapters. The excerpts in each section are followed by what the editors call a reprise, which draws together and summarizes the contents of the excerpts in each subcategory.

The book concludes with a chapter called "Final Discussion," which does not include autobiographical excerpts, but rather a discussion of how to cultivate reading skill. It identifies the conditions that promote reading such as the availability of books and magazines; family members who read aloud; adults and peers who read; role models who value reading; sharing and discussing books; owning books; availability of libraries and librarians; social interaction; freedom of choice in reading material; personal experience; and school programs. The conditions that discourage reading include: growing up with nonreaders; traumatic learning experiences; obstacles during the teenage years; and educational methodology. A chart indicates the importance of these experiences as a function of age groups from preschool to eighteen years of age and older.

Hopefully, reading teachers, educators working with reluctant readers, and parents can find the analysis of these personal accounts helpful in providing an optimal environment that would encourage students to come to love books.

Lois Buttlar

490. Cuddigan, Maureen, and Mary Beth Hanson. **Growing Pains: Helping Children Deal with Everyday Problems through Reading.** Chicago, American Library Association, 1988. 165p. index. $17.50pa. LC 88-3451. ISBN 0-8389-0469-6.

Hanson, a pediatric nurse, and Cuddigan, a librarian, teamed up to review children's literature to help librarians, teachers, parents, and other caregivers come to terms with common problems of childhood and help children continue their growing process. The editors' objective is to highlight good children's literature. Most of the books cited in this annotated bibliography were published between 1976 and 1986 and their subjects cover thirteen areas divided in subcategories. As is demonstrated in this bibliography, "books can encourage children to express their thoughts and feelings" (p. 154), and help children cope with their anxieties. Books in many cases can facilitate channels of communication between the adults and children and help children cope with the problems surrounding them, be they family, school, illness, or problems of adaptation to society. Children's literature provides wonderful opportunities for children's developmental needs and progress in everyday life. Cuddigan's experience as librarian is a great asset in this case because for sixteen years she has had the unique experience of observing children responding to books.

The subjects covered in this bibliography range from the traditional concerns of family and schools to the more modern issues such as child abuse and sexual equality. Full bibliographic citation is provided for every book, with a short annotation (four to six lines) and in some instances a comment on the quality of the book (e.g., "highly recommended"). This bibliography can be an invitation for parents and caregivers to select literature to instill values formation in children. The editors remind the readers, though, that no book can be recommended with absolute certainty and that the final decision rests with the child and the parent or the caregiver.

This book should find its way to every family's library as well as public and school libraries. [R: BL, 1 Oct 88, pp. 330-31]

Camille Côté

491.   Davidson, Jane L., ed. **Counterpoint and Beyond: A Response to** *Becoming a Nation of Readers.* Urbana, Ill., National Council of Teachers of English, 1988. 112p. $6.25pa. LC 88-22541. ISBN 0-8141-0876-8.

This monograph serves as a forum for the responses of a number of reading authorities to *Becoming a Nation of Readers*, a federally sponsored 1985 report which offered a plan for solving persistent reading problems of U.S. students. Issues in the report that are considered to be controversial, incomplete, or inconsistent are addressed; reactions and alternative recommendations for the improvement of literacy are set forth. The purpose of the volume, stated by the editor, is to continue to dialogue about reading and the reading process.

Ten essays are provided by teacher educators and reading researchers. They bring a wide range of classroom experience, school administration, and community involvement to bear on their topics, which cover issues related to beginning reading instruction, literature and minorities, and an analysis of the metaphors employed in the report. A public school principal's reaction to the report is provided, along with an examination of the possible positive and negative outcomes for curricula were *Becoming a Nation of Readers'* recommendations implemented.

The volume's audience is expected to be local and state curriculum planners, education policymakers and administrators, teachers of English language arts, teachers of reading, and teacher educators. It should be purchased by any library whose patrons are interested in reading education and literacy.

Susan S. Baughman

492.   Lesquereux, John, and Helen Pain. **The Library and the Curriculum.** 2d ed. London, School Libraries Group, Library Association, 1987. 25p. (Studies in School Library Management, 3). £3.00pa. ISBN 0-948933-09-7.

This third pamphlet in a series on the management of school libraries focuses on the curriculum and its relationship to the library. Presented concisely, issues are followed by activities designed to reveal the situation in a particular school. Librarians are urged "at the risk of being strangled by your colleagues try asking about four or five of them: 'What do you think the school is for?' ... 'What do you think our library is for?'" From this general investigation into the philosophy of the school, librarians are guided into inquiring how the curriculum is organized, designed, and implemented. Attention then turns to the librarian's interaction with individual teachers and pupils. Although the background of the book is British, North American librarians may find that the ideas and activities suggested have practical value in any context. By the conclusion of its twenty-five pages, the librarian has been led to distinguish between "the curriculum at a level of policy or as an ideal, intended offering"; "the curriculum as it is taught by teachers"; and "the curriculum as pupils encounter it." A librarian who follows the activities suggested is likely to discover new insights into relationships between the library, the curriculum, and those engaged in teaching and learning.

Adele M. Fasick

493.   Reinking, David, ed. **Reading and Computers: Issues for Theory and Practice.** New York, Teachers College Press, 1987. 205p. illus. index. (Computers and Education Series). $22.95. LC 87-10053. ISBN 0-8077-2866-7.

Through eleven signed, scholarly essays this readable book boldly explores the present and future roles of computers in reading. Divided into three sections (theoretical, research, and instructional issues), contributors ponder such diverse topics as eye movements and computer-aided instruction, computer speech in reading instruction, and computer-simulated instruction to study preservice teachers' thought processes. Each section is preceded by an introduction to summarize and unify the ten to twenty-page essays which follow. A section noting the authors' credentials and an integrated author/subject index conclude the work.

The author clearly states that he chose "recognized scholars to share their insights, technological expertise, research, and innovative applications of computer technology in the area of reading." As a thought-provoking book highlighting significant research which extends beyond the mere use of software in reading classes, this work will be attractive to educational researchers, faculty members, graduate students, and reading practitioners. It is a fine addition to the field, and modestly priced for a hardbound book.   Ilene F. Rockman

494. Snoddon, Ruth V. **Ready-to-Use Library Skills Games: Reproducible Activities for Building Location and Literature Skills.** Englewood Cliffs, N.J., Center for Applied Research in Education, 1987. 1v. (various paging). illus. $22.95 spiralbound. LC 86-23308. ISBN 0-87628-721-6.

495. Snoddon, Ruth V. **Library Skills Activities for the Primary Grades: Ready-to-Use Projects and Activities for Grades 1-4.** Englewood Cliffs, N.J., Center for Applied Research in Education, 1987. 1v. (various paging). illus. $24.95 spiralbound. LC 87-13235. ISBN 0-87628-105-4.

Snoddon's *Ready to-Use Library Skills Games* consists of games designed to provide "reproducible activities for building location and literature skills" for grades 3-8 (subtitle). They include "Dooby Dewey," a bingo-like game which is supposed to familiarize students with Dewey classification as used in libraries; "Super Dooby," which provides "trivia" questions on books, the Dewey decimal system, the library, and the Newbery Awards; and "Alpha Dooby," which provides sets of book spines for alphabetizing fiction, and for organizing nonfiction.

Her *Library Skills Activities for Primary Grades* consists of "over 200 stimulating projects and activities which enhance, enrich and reinforce your classroom and library programs — all ready for immediate duplication and use with individual students, small groups or the entire class!" (cover). There are three sections, each relating to five "Research Reports," although the first few "reports" appear to be pictures drawn on blanks on some of the reproducible pages. Both the table of contents and the section introduction explain the grade level. For example, "Research Report # 4, 'Note-Taking Knacks,' ... is suitable for grades 3 and

4" (p. 2). Section 1 relates to using the library, alphabetical order, and note taking. Sections 2 and 3 provide exercises relating to maps, reference books, and other nonfiction books used while "researching" animals and countries. Each section has a series of loosely related "Activities Pages." Like Toor and Weisburg's *Sharks, Ships and Potato Chips* (Library Learning Resources, 1986) there is a strong emphasis on library skills activities.

The illustrations and charts in *Library Skills Activities* appear to have been drawn on a computer and printed with a dot matrix printer. Those in *Games* are standard black line drawings. The *Games* would be considerably easier to use and more appealing if they were prepared as full color games, boxed, ready for use. Busy teachers and school library media specialists may be put off by the amount of work needed to provide reinforced game cards, and other playing pieces, which will still be in basic black.

Neither book clearly relates to a K-12 library media skills curriculum, integrated with classroom instruction, which is the current emphasis in the field, and which is based on sounder reinforcement theory than repeated worksheets and games. However, since some school library media specialists and elementary school teachers seem to have an insatiable appetite for "one more" worksheet or game for teaching library skills, books like Snoddon's will probably find a ready market.

Betty Jo Buckingham

496. Strickland, Dorothy S., Joan T. Feeley, and Shelley B. Wepner. **Using Computers in the Teaching of Reading.** New York, Teachers College Press, 1987. 240p. illus. index. (Computers in the Curriculum Series). $16.95pa. LC 86-14567. ISBN 0-8077-2823-3.

With similar paperback texts on the market, what makes this book unique? It applies Robert Taylor's model — the computer as tutor, tool, and tutee — to the reading/language curriculum using currently available software. Written by three education professors, the books' eight chapters are aimed at "improving the teaching of reading" for the K-adult levels.

The "computer as tool" notes assistance programs such as word processors, reading assessment programs, and information retrieval databases; the "computer as tutor" chapters cover instructional programs such as drill and practice; and the "computer as tutee" includes skill development such as programming and problem solving. Concluding the work are chapters on organizing the computer curriculum and evaluating software, a nonevaluative guide to software, issues and trends (such as computer piracy), a glossary of terms, and a subject index.

This source is solid. Throughout the text are current research studies intended to offer specific, practical guidance to common classroom situations. Sorely missing, however, are discussions concerning the needs of bilingual, ESL, mainstreamed, or adult basic education students. Also omitted is the mention of public domain software.

Most competing texts cover similar territory—review sources, types of software, and the link between software and reading instruction—but do not include the application of scholarship to current practice. This is true for *Computer Applications in Reading* (International Reading Association, 1987), *Computers and Reading Instruction* (Addison-Wesley, 1983), *Microcomputers in Reading and Language Arts* (Prentice Hall, 1986), and *Teaching Reading Using Microcomputers* (Prentice Hall, 1986).

Students and professors of reading, computer specialists, reading teachers, school administrators, and parents will be interested in this modestly priced work.

Ilene F. Rockman

497. Strong, Gary E., comp. **On Reading—In the Year of the Reader.** Sacramento, Calif., California State Library Foundation, 1987. 122p. $15.75pa.

Compiled by California's state librarian in conjunction with the nationally proclaimed Year of the Reader (1987), *On Reading* is a collection of brief essays by various Californians relating their personal feelings about the value of reading. The contributors range from established scholars to newly literate participants in the adult literacy program and include such library and literary luminaries as Regina Minudri, Robert Vosper, David C. Weber, Robert M. Hayes, Ray Bradbury, Clifton Fadiman, and Irving Stone.

Following an introductory section, the essays are grouped into sections entitled "Reading in a Democracy," "Reading to Learn," "Reading to Create," "Librarians as Readers," "Reading for Enjoyment," and "Reading and Literacy." An "Afterword" by the compiler (who also wrote a portion of the introduction) concludes the book. In an anthology of this type, one does not expect, nor does one find, an index or a bibliography. However, a list of all of the books mentioned by the various contributors would have made an interesting and appropriate addition.

Essentially a celebration of reading, books, and libraries, this nicely done compilation will provide enjoyable reading and a wealth of wonderful quotations for those similarly captivated by the "joys of reading and the love of books." [R: BL, July 88, p. 1780; LJ, 15 May 88, p. 64]   Kristin Ramsdell

SERVICES TO SPECIAL USERS

498. **Guidelines for Libraries Serving Persons with a Hearing Impairment or a Visual Impairment.** By the Roundtable for Libraries Serving Special Populations, New York Library Association. New York, New York Library Association, 1987. 31p. $5.00pa. ISBN 0-931658-21-7.

This short monograph is essentially an application of the National Library Service for the Blind and Physically Handicapped publication, *Revised Standards and Guidelines of Service for the Library of Congress Network of Libraries for the Blind and Physically Handicapped 1984*, to the New York state environment. Prepared by the Roundtable for Libraries Serving Special Populations (RLSP) within the New York Library Association, this monograph is the result of a project initiated at the association's annual conference in 1984. The guidelines are intended to be updated periodically, and the authors do not pretend that it is a definitive document.

There are four major sections: two dealing with guidelines for serving persons with hearing and visual impairments, and two establishing self-assessment checklists for hearing and visual impairments. As is all too common, there is not mention or consideration of persons with learning disabilities; visual impairment continues to be narrowly defined as variations of blindness. These limitations, however, stretch back to the national scene and are not unique to New York state. Yet when configuring guidelines for local consumption, it would seem to be an excellent opportunity for states to build and *expand* upon previous work, rather than make simple adaptations. The monograph could be very useful—as far as it goes.   Darlene E. Weingand

499. Hoy, Stephen, and Sheila Hoy. **Reading for Elderly People: A Handbook for Those Working with the Elderly.** Bicester, England, Winslow Press, 1987. 49p. illus. £5.95pa. ISBN 0-863880-62-2.

This practical guide is intended to help professionals and volunteers who work with the elderly in hospitals, day centers, libraries, or residential care facilities promote reading and reading aloud sessions. The preliminary content deals with some myths about old age and the elderly and discusses benefits of reading aloud activities, places to obtain reading materials, and ways of making these materials accessible. Following this, the authors provide suggestions on how to run a reading aloud program. They address such factors as choosing appropriate topics and reading material, identifying an audience, and running the session; they supplement this discussion with a list of some popular readings. In addition, the authors make suggestions on how to use reading aloud to encourage reminiscing about historical events or periods and include a list of recommended sources. They also recommend follow-up activities, such as outings, displays, or guest lectures, which can capitalize upon the interest created by the reading aloud sessions. Other topics covered include making the sessions enjoyable for the confused elderly, choosing individuals to run the sessions, recruiting and involving volunteers, creating support for the program, and resolving problems.

This handbook was written for a British audience, so North American readers may want to reconsider some of the specific book titles recommended for reading aloud. However, the sincerity, experience, and practicality of Sheila and Stephen Hoy are evident throughout, and their insights and suggestions will be of value to those initiating and running reading aloud programs.   Stephen H. Aby

500. Kempson, Elaine, and Marianne Dee, eds. **A Future Age: A Practical Handbook for Librarians Working with Older Adults** Newcastle-under-Lyme, England, AAL Publishing; distr., Newcastle-under-Lyme, England, Remploy, 1987. 81p. £8.95pa. ISBN 0-900092-58-0.

The introduction establishes the rationale for this collection of nine brief essays from a British point of view by declaring that "librarians share, with society as a whole, a stereotype of 'old age' that stresses physical and mental infirmity." As a consequence, library services concentrate on book delivery to housebound or institutionalized people and small collections of books deposited in public housing facilities. In truth, the introduction continues, the diverse needs of the vast majority of senior citizens – those who are neither housebound nor publicly housed – are the most ignored. The first essay, discussing characteristics of the elderly, concludes that because of their very diversity the elderly deserves a library service which reflects their individuality and which takes full account of them as persons with needs for continuing education, information and advice, and leisure and recreation services. In the second essay, the coeditors explore a range of possibilities open to

British (and, by extension, other) public librarians wanting to develop services for the elderly – for example, a sympathetic staff, a suitable building, well-selected library media, and a variety of services (library clubs, lectures, film shows, practical courses, etc.), including those in which elders participated in their planning and development. This excellent overview chapter is followed by chapters that describe as case studies how different libraries addressed the needs of the elderly in their communities: the active elderly in Leicestershire; a grass roots movement (the University of the Third Age in Wakefield) giving elders an opportunity to develop their own intellectual, educational, and creative interests; ethnic minorities in Wandsworth; etc. The final chapter makes a strong case for the use of reading therapy (e.g., U.S. term: bibliotherapy) with elderly people restricted by their physical or mental frailty, or both.

Each essay (except the one on ethnic minorities) includes a selected bibliography of British (and occasionally U.S.) sources. U.S. library collections may find this brief British manual on working with older adults a fine complement to works such as Betty J. Turock's *Serving the Older Adult* (Bowker, 1982), Rhea Rubin's *Using Bibliotherapy* (Oryx Press, 1978), and Rubin's *Bibliotherapy Sourcebook* (Oryx Press, 1978). [R: LAR, 15 Aug 88, p. 472; RLR, Aug 88, p. 198]   Wiley J. Williams

501. Rubin, Rhea Joyce, and Gail McGovern. **Working with Older Adults: A Handbook for Libraries.** 2d ed. Sacramento, Calif., California State Library Foundation, 1988. 1v. (various paging). illus. $15.00 spiralbound. ISBN 0-929722-27-2.

Originally used as part of a workshop, this handbook is a collection of statistics, guidelines, policies, suggested readings, organizations, and other information intended to help librarians provide services to "older adults as they arrive at the next age of their lives" (preface). The material is arranged into four broad subject areas: "Identifying the Aging," "Materials and Services," "Public Relations," and "Resources." A fifth area mentioned in the table of contents, "Companion Packet," is not part of the book, but was probably part of the workshop.

Part 1 provides profiles of older adults and data on their health status and needs in the United States and particularly in California. It also includes both a telephone survey for identifying the information needs of older adults and a worksheet for profiling the elderly in a particular community. Part 2 includes some descriptions of the information needs of older adults and suggestions and policy guidelines for libraries serving that population. Part 3 provides some suggestions on, and examples of, how libraries can effectively promote their services for older adults. Part 4 contains not only bibliographies on various aspects of library services for older adults, but also lists of publications and organizations serving the aging.

While this handbook contains much useful information, librarians should be aware that at least some parts are not as complete as they otherwise might be; this is probably due to its originally having been part of a workshop where materials were complemented by oral presentations. For example, the statistical data are very selective and provide nowhere near the depth of other sources, such as *America's Elderly: A Sourcebook* (Center for Urban Policy Research, 1988). Similarly, while the section on "Public Relations" contains some detailed guidelines, it also includes pages which are cryptic. Still, librarians trying to improve older adult services may benefit from many of the practical suggestions, as well as the bibliographies and organizations listed in the "Resources" section.

Stephen H. Aby

502. A State of Change: California's Ethnic Future and Libraries. Conference and Awareness Forum Proceedings 1988. Nora Jacob, ed. Sacramento, Calif., California State Library Foundation, 1988. 344p. $15.00pa.

This volume contains the executive summary of the RAND Corporation report entitled *Public Libraries Face California's Ethnic and Racial Diversity*, the State of Change Conference proceedings, awareness forums repots, and recommendations for action. Included are speeches made by Mayor Henry Cisneros of San Antonio, Robert McNulty of Partners for Liveable Places, and Yvonne Brathwaite Burke, a member of the Board of Regents of the University of California.

Challenge session summaries comprise presentations by Willie B. Kennedy, two-term member of the San Francisco County Board of Supervisors; Sal B. Castro, prevention counselor at Belmont High School in Los Angeles; Peter M. Detwiler, principal consultant to the California State Senate's Committee on Local Government; Hardy Franklin, director of the District of Columbia Public Library; Henry L. Gardner, city manager of Oakland; and Harry H. L. Kitano, professor of social welfare and sociology at the University of California, Los Angeles. Topics addressed during the challenge sessions are change, community relations, finance, libraries, politics, and socioeconomic perspectives. Issues and recommendations regarding each topic are included.

This volume is must reading for library administrators serving diversified ethnic communities. It is valuable for long-range planning; goal setting involving services, personnel, and resources; and for identifying community needs.

Edmund F. SantaVicca

503. Turock, Betty J., ed. Information and Aging. Proceedings of the Twenty-fifth Annual Symposium of the Graduate Alumni and Faculty of the Rutgers School of Communication.... Jefferson, N.C., McFarland, 1988. 88p. bibliog. $9.95pa. LC 88-42569. ISBN 0-89950-358-6.

Information and Aging is a collection of symposium presentations on the information needs of, and the state of library services to, the United States' aging population. The papers cover the update of the 1971 *National Survey of Public Library Services for Older Adults*, the intellectual and learning abilities of the aged, a model of the information state of older Americans, information and referral services, literacy, and federal funding. There is also a section where experts on library services to the aged offer brief responses to the national survey update, as well as their recommendations for the future. In addition, there is a very selective annotated bibliography on library services for older adults. The two appendices reproduce the ALA's "Guidelines for Services to Older Adults" and "The Library's Responsibility to the Aging."

Though these presentations span a range of issues on information and aging, certain themes do recur. Most of the papers stress the importance of education in breaking the stereotypes about the aged; these stereotypes hinder the provision of quality service. Furthermore, many of the authors point out that fiscal constraints on public service institutions necessitate coalition building for the more effective and efficient provision of services to the aged. Finally, some of the papers present the argument that libraries must have designated budget lines and staff in order to serve the distinctive information needs of the aged.

This is a valuable collection for a number of reasons. First, as the articles point out, the aged are an increasingly important segment of the population; yet they have not received the library service they deserve. Second, because the articles span a range of topics and audiences, there should be something here to appeal to public service librarians, administrators, policymakers, and theorists. Third, since most of the articles are short and to-the-point, they are easy to absorb; this should make the collection accessible to those newly interested in the topic. While this book may not substitute for more systematic treatments of the subject, it should be a useful addition to collections on both social gerontology and library services to the elderly.

Stephen H. Aby

SPECIAL LIBRARIES AND COLLECTIONS

General Works

504. Directory of Special Libraries and Information Centers 1987: Colorado, South Dakota, Utah, Wyoming. Denver, Colo., Rocky Mountain Chapter, Special Libraries Association, 1987. 114p. index. $20.00pa.

Information on nearly three hundred special libraries and their resources has been gathered together in this very useful publication, described in its introduction as "the first attempt by the Rocky Mountain Chapter/Special Libraries Association to create a regional directory of special libraries." The book is not a comprehensive listing of all special libraries in the four-state region encompassed; some six hundred questionnaires were sent out, but many of the libraries (especially smaller ones) either did not respond or declined to be listed. However, for those who did respond, the directory provides just the right amount of concise and helpful information.

The entries are organized first by state, then within state alphabetically by parent organization. Elements of each entry include organization, library, and head librarians' names; address and telephone number; subjects; special collections; number of books, periodicals (bound volumes), and subscriptions; availability of public access, telephone reference, and interlibrary loan; computer databases, telecommunications, and systems in use; OCLC/RLIN symbol; and notes of other appropriate information supplied by the individual libraries. A check of selected entries indicates that they are both correct and current. (Special librarians must have a fairly low job-change rate!) Two indexes—geographic (by city/town) and subject (basic but complete)—round out the directory.

This publication will be a welcome resource for anyone looking for information in the four states covered, and will be especially useful to special librarians trying to find other information professionals in specific subject areas. The chapter and association are to be congratulated on the results of their collaboration, and encouraged to update the directory on a regular (biannual?) basis. G. Kim Dority

505. Tools of the Profession. Hilary Kanter, ed. Washington, D.C., Special Libraries Association, 1988. 129p. $15.00 spiralbound. ISBN 0-87111-338-4.

This collection of bibliographies is the product of members of seventeen divisions of the Special Libraries Association. As such, it represents the collective expertise of information professionals working in various special library settings. Each bibliography includes complete citations; and in some cases, annotations and/or classified groups by format are included. Seventeen subject areas are covered: advertising and marketing; aerospace; business and finance; chemistry; engineering; food, agriculture, and nutrition; insurance and employee benefits; metals/materials; natural resources; nuclear science; pharmaceuticals; physics, astronomy, mathematics (including statistics and computer science); public utilities; publishing; social science; telecommunications (broadcasting); and transportation. Each bibliography provides a sound base for reference, research, and collection development within the particular subject area.

This volume will be most beneficial to those conducting research in relevant fields, and to other information professionals who may be faced with the task of creating or developing a special library collection. Recommended for special library, academic library, and appropriate public library collections.

Edmund F. SantaVicca

506. Who's Who in Special Libraries 1988-89. Washington, D.C., Special Libraries Association, 1988. 298p. maps. index. $25.00pa. ISBN 0-87111-339-2.

The 1988-1989 membership directory of the Special Libraries Association remains substantially unchanged from those of previous years. The first section, which totals forty-seven pages, may be correctly termed an organizational handbook. Among other items of interest, this section includes names, addresses, and telephone numbers of the current board of directors, a list of association staff members, information about the organizational structure, the complete bylaws, history, honors and awards, and past presidents. This section also includes the locations and dates of future meetings, the location of SLA student groups with names and telephone numbers of faculty advisors, and the names and addresses of all division and state chapter officers.

As much routine information is repetitive and identical to the previous year, change is accomplished by inclusion of additional information as opposed to revision. The division, chapter, and business indexes are in reality alphabetical listings of the membership by subject division, state chapter affiliation, and organizational affiliation. The alphabetical listing of the more than twelve thousand members of the association includes organizational affiliation, addresses, and telephone numbers when known, and comprises one-half of the volume. Until 1980, *Who's Who in Special Libraries* was published as the annual directory issue of *Special Libraries*, the official journal of the association. A true name index with page references as in the earlier publications may have been deemed prohibitively expensive, but making a distinction between the handbook and the directory on the title page would not be. Nor does the title of the separate section reflect the true nature of the publication. Nonetheless, this is a useful and informative work. Mailed without charge to members of the association, *Who's Who in Special Libraries* would be of interest to vendors, suppliers, and all who have an interest in activities of the Special Libraries Association. Robert M. Ballard

Archival

507. **Automating Intellectual Access to Archives.** Anne J. Gilliland, ed. Champaign, Ill., Graduate School of Library and Information Science, University of Illinois, 1988. 1v. (various paging). (*Library Trends*, Vol. 36, No. 3). $15.00pa.

The past twenty years or so have seen the development of automated systems to accommodate the special needs of archives. We are now at a point where several options for the automation of archival holdings are available and the question has become not shall we automate but *when* shall we automate our collections. There are plenty of legitimate concerns that individual institutions must debate, but the overriding fact, which is beyond our control, is that many scholars are seeking information in different ways than they did in the past. There is a good chance that our collections will be overlooked by those who could best use them if we do not provide methods of access that are compatible with those of other information providers. The eight papers in this issue *Library Trends* provide a look at what has happened in the automation of archives and at the implications for the future. They approach the subject in rather broad terms, stressing the commonality between applications rather than describing details of specific systems or applications. The very real problem of coping with the change brought about by automation is dealt with in Lisa B. Weber's "Educating Archivists for Automation" and Anne J. Gilliland's "The

Developoment of Automated Archival Systems: Planning and Managing Change," placed, appropriately, first and second in the collection. The next three articles, those by Steven L. Hensen, H. Thomas Hickerson, and Patricia D. Cloud, deal with the use of the MARC AMC format while the next three, by Frederick L. Honhart, W. Theodore Dürr, and Matthew B. Gilmore, look at viable alternatives to the AMC-based systems. The articles are fully documented and these references provide the reader with an excellent guide to additional information. [R: JAL, Sept 88, p. 261]
Dean H. Keller

Art

508. **Art Libraries Society of North America. 15th Annual Conference, Washington, D.C., February 13-19, 1987. Conference Abstracts.** Tucson, Ariz., Art Libraries Society of North America, [1987]. 59p. $5.00pa.

This is a group of single page conference abstracts in conference handout format. Each abstract has been written before the presentation and while the name of the presenter is given and an affiliation is listed, a complete address is not. For art librarians looking for resource people in the arts who might be helpful on detailed topics, the publication might be of limited use; however, as a record of the conference, the publication is so brief that it is not useful as topical reading. Recommended only as an ephemeral reference list.
David V. Loertscher

509. Stam, Deirdre C., and Angela Giral, eds. **Linking Art Objects and Art Information.** Champaign, Ill., Graduate School of Library and Information Science, University of Illinois, 1988. 1v. (various paging). illus. (*Library Trends*, Vol. 37, No. 2). $15.00pa.

This issue examines the recent efforts by several institutions to design automated systems that will organize information concerning art objects to best serve the diverse needs and approaches of researchers, students, curators, and registrars. The editors point out that, due to the lack of a centralized source of information, projects developed by individual institutions rarely achieve wide recognition. Although many of the systems are based on bibliographic utilities, the important distinction is made between the advantages of shared records for cataloging books and the limited benefits for museums because of the uniqueness of records for individual art objects. The different articles in the journal examine various aspects of the automated systems: the capabilities different users need in a system to serve their research needs, the difficulties of linking object and information in a system, considerations in using iconographical research collections, theoretical discussions of art database design, and descriptions of actual systems developed by several museums and libraries (e.g., J. Paul Getty, Smithsonian, Avery Library, British Architectural Library, etc.). Since the contributors are librarians, art history and library science professors, and information specialists, the articles focus on theory and content rather than technical specifications. Editors Stam and Giral have done an admirable job of compiling essays which provide a comprehensive overview of the field, and their perceptive introduction highlights the issues and concerns in this area.

Judy Dyki

Community/School

510. Amey, L. J., ed. **Combining Libraries: The Canadian and Australian Experience.** Metuchen, N.J., Dalhousie University with Scarecrow, 1987. 433p. illus. maps. bibliog. (Dalhousie University, School of Library and Information Studies, No. 2). $39.50. LC 87-16678. ISBN 0-8108-2049-8.

The author, a member of the School of Library and Information Studies at Dalhousie University, has produced a most helpful guide for those librarians, college presidents, town officers, and library school students interested in school-housed public libraries. These essays are written by administrators responsible for developing combined libraries (school-public, junior college-public) and concentrate on administrative arrangements, contractual agreements, and social and geographical considerations. Emphasis is placed on sets of guidelines for the establishment and operation of these libraries. The discussion on contracts includes the wording of an actual contract. The editor's aim is for readers "to learn about the subsequent development of the library: how did it evolve through the years, what changes were made, what worked and what didn't?" The work serves to correct the belief that a combined library denies a community a fully developed public library. Often, these combined institutions provide superior reference collections, better reference services, and more varied film collections—highly popular items with the public.

The index is carefully prepared, complete with cross-references and good subject headings. A five-hundred-item bibliography is not limited geographically, but is international in

scope. [R: CLJ, Dec 88, pp. 398-400; EL, Nov-Dec 88, pp. 43-44; JAL, May 88, p. 114; LAR, 15 Aug 88, p. 470; LJ, 15 Apr 88, p. 62; RLR, Aug 88, pp. 189-90]   Milton H. Crouch

Genealogy

511. Filby, P. William, comp. **Directory of American Libraries with Genealogy or Local History Collections.** Wilmington, Del., Scholarly Resources, 1988. 319p. index. $75.00. LC 87-37109. ISBN 0-8420-2286-4.

More Americans are searching for their ancestors than ever before; genealogy is now outranked in popularity as a hobby in the United States only by stamp and coin collecting. The purpose of this directory is to help that horde of researchers to locate collections, identify what they contain, and discover how they may be accessed. The information is based on a mailing of over 4,000 questionnaires sent to U.S. and Canadian libraries; the return rate was 37 percent. Part 1 of the questionnaire contained fifteen questions concerning basic information on the collection, and part 2 asked respondents to indicate what items they owned from a checklist of twenty-six book titles and nine periodicals. As a result of the low rate of return many important collections have been omitted. A spot check of New Jersey reveals the omission of the state university collection, at least five county historical societies with substantial genealogical collections, and many town libraries that collect local history. The compiler's name is synonymous with genealogical research, and, therefore, it is a surprise to find him associated with this enterprise. Anyone seeking a genealogical or local history collection will be as well served by the *American Library Directory* (see entry 535) or the directory prepared by the American Association for State and Local History. This title is recommended for only the most definitive of genealogical collections. [R: Choice, Oct 88, p. 290; LJ, 1 Oct 88, p. 81; RBB, 15 Nov 88, p. 552; WLB, Sept 88, p. 95]   Robert F. Van Benthuysen

Government Publications

512. Hajnal, Peter I., ed. **International Information: Documents, Publications, and Information Systems of International Governmental Organizations.** Englewood, Colo., Libraries Unlimited, 1988. 339p. bibliog. index. $27.50. LC 88-2236. ISBN 0-87287-501-6.

Documents of Intergovernmental Organizations (IGO) are a valuable information resource on a wide range of subjects. Because access to them may be complex, they tend to be overlooked and are often underutilized. IGO document publishing output is overwhelming. Formal publication, which accounts for only about 35 percent of the output is of lower priority than a variety of other reports and publications, and IGOs are thus often out-of-date when received. The complex structure of the United Nations and of the European community, with their various publication groups, makes access to information difficult. In this volume, experts in the use of IGO documents outline the structure of these organizations and indicate those groups responsible for publication of documents. Ways in which documents are classified, the status of bibliographic control, issues in collection development, and availability of documents for research are discussed. The current status of efforts to develop online databases is discussed and a description of databases now available is provided. Bibliographies and notes at the end of each chapter provide useful added information.

The authors have provided a useful roadmap to an important information resource. They have clarified issues and have thus taken steps toward a better understanding of IGOs. Documents specialists will find this clearly written presentation most useful as a guide to all aspects of work with them. [R: Choice, Nov 88, p. 462; JAL, Sept 88, p. 266; RQ, Winter 88, p. 280]   Ann E. Prentice

513. Nurcombe, Valerie J., comp. **Directory of Specialists in Official Publications.** 2d ed. Winsford, England, Standing Committee on Official Publications, 1988. 56p. index. £6.00 pa. ISBN 0-9512011-1-5.

This directory lists 193 librarians in the British Isles (including the Republic of Ireland) who specialize in the publications of the central and local governments of the United Kingdom. Entries are arranged geographically by the regions of England, Scotland, Wales, Northern Ireland, and the Republic of Ireland, and within those regions by county. Each entry supplies the name and the address of the specialist along with any particular subject interests. Four appendices respectively list information: (1) for inquiring about the publications of various departments of the central government; (2) about Her Majesty's Stationery Office; (3) about explanatory memoranda produced concerning European commission proposals; and (4) about books on official publications. There are name and subject indexes for finding the appropriate librarian. Although this is a specialized publication with a narrow audience, it is also very well done. Library schools and individ-

uals interested in comparative librarianship and government publications, particularly those of the United Kingdom, will find this volume to be a useful resource.   Ronald H. Fritze

514. Schorr, Alan Edward. **Federal Documents Librarianship, 1879-1987.** Juneau, Alaska, Denali Press, 1988. 215p. index. $25.00pa. LC 87-73054. ISBN 0-938737-14-7.

Given the current level of concern in the library community about diminishing access to government information, Schorr's work should be gratefully received. Arranged alphabetically by first author within ten broad subject divisions, twenty-five hundred citations provide access to more than a hundred years of writings on government information policy and practice. Access is provided to journal articles, proceedings, theses, books, news articles, and chapters within monographs. The citations appear complete and cover the topics of administration; bibliographies, guides, indexes, and abstracts; collection development; depository library programs; government information policy; microform; public services; teaching and technical services; and general publications. Although these subdivisions may provide sufficiently precise subject access for those already familiar with government documents, a detailed subject index would increase this guide's usefulness. [R: JAL, July 88, p. 198; LJ, 15 June 88, p. 44]
                              Elizabeth D. Liddy

515. Schwarzkopf, LeRoy C., comp. **Government Reference Books 86/87: A Biennial Guide to U.S. Government Publications.** Tenth biennial volume. Englewood, Colo., Libraries Unlimited, 1988. 436p. index. $47.50. LC 76-146307. ISBN 0-87287-666-7.

This is the tenth biennial volume in this extremely useful series on government publications. The same general format used in previous editions is followed in this volume. Within four broad subject categories, such as general library reference and social sciences, nearly fifteen hundred items are listed in topical subgroupings. Each entry contains a full bibliographic citation, OCLC and *Monthly Catalog* numbers, LC card number, and, new with this edition, depository shipping list and item numbers and LC classification numbers. A descriptive, noncritical annotation is provided for each entry.

In addition to listing LC classification, depository list, and item numbers, this edition introduces several other changes. Most serial titles have been withdrawn and are now included in a new companion publication, *Government Reference Serials* (Libraries Unlimited, 1988), although some irregular or monographic series are still included. Microform titles are listed, reflecting the shift to dual formatting as part of the substantial economies and reductions in depository publication and distribution resulting from the Gramm-Rudman-Hollings deficit reduction bill of 1986. In addition, only items distributed to depository libraries by GPO itself are now listed, eliminating numerous publications now issued by privately contracted agencies in response to the deficit legislation and other Office of Management and Budget economy directives. Finally, the biennial period covered by this volume now represents the actual date of item distribution to the depository libraries, not the imprint date of the item. A more detailed author/title/subject index is included in this edition, an improvement on the limited subject access of earlier volumes.

Along with its companion volume on government serial publications, this work should continue to prove extremely helpful both to depository libraries and other libraries with large government publication collections. [R: Choice, Oct 88, p. 296]

Elizabeth Patterson

516. Schwarzkopf, LeRoy C., comp. **Government Reference Serials.** Englewood, Colo., Libraries Unlimited, 1988. 344p. index. $45.00. LC 87-37846. ISBN 0-87287-451-6.

This is a companion to *Government Reference Books*, the biennial guide to U.S. government publications published since 1968/69 by Libraries Unlimited (1988).

Included are government publications of reference value issued annually or biennially as well as quarterly, monthly, or even daily. Only items available for distribution through the Government Printing Office's depository library program are cited, as is the case for *Government Reference Books*. The same topical headings as found in *GRB* are used, with publications grouped under four main parts: "General Library Reference," "Social Sciences," "Science and Technology," and "Humanities."

The guide contains 583 numbered entries arranged alphabetically by title under each topic or subtopic. Entries consist of the citation, the history of the serial, and the annotation. To standard bibliographic elements used in *GRB*, the compiler has added the Library of Congress classification number, the Dewey Decimal number, the depository item number, and the GPO price list (no. 36) ID number. Separate indexes for titles, corporate authors, and subjects as well as a Superintendent of Documents (SuDocs) class number index complete the publication. The most valuable enhancement is the inclusion of the publishing history of the serial.

Details include the predecessor title(s), changes in SuDocs numbers and other variations, with information on the specific issue when the change occurred.

The amount of detail provided on the many U.S. government serials of reference use is truly remarkable. Including this information has only been possible with the issuance of a separate volume for serials. Some libraries may not need this much detail, especially for older titles not in their collections, but researchers in major libraries who often need to track down elusive older material should find the publication invaluable. All libraries with sizable government collections should have *Government Reference Serials* as well as *Government Reference Books*. [R: BR, Sept/Oct 88, p. 52; JAL, July 88, p. 198; LJ, 15 June 88, p. 44; RBB, 15 Oct 88, p. 388]

Robert W. Schaaf

517. Zwirn, Jerrold. **Congressional Publications and Proceedings: Research on Legislation, Budgets, and Treaties.** 2d ed. Englewood, Colo., Libraries Unlimited, 1988. 299p. bibliog. index. $27.50. LC 88-12395. ISBN 0-87287-642-X.

This is a classic example of a very good work that has been significantly improved by its author. The first edition of Zwirn's book was published a mere five years ago and remains a highly useful resource for research into the legislative process. Zwirn has retained the organizational structure of eleven chapters ranging from "The Congressional Agenda" to "United States Treaties." Each chapter includes charts, title pages of important documents, and a list of references (most twice as long as in the first edition). Nearly all of the chapters have been expanded, at least slightly, and several have been substantially reworked and lengthened (e.g., Zwirn placed more emphasis on legislative history and doubled in length the chapters on the federal budget and U.S. treaties).

Appendix A has been transformed from an alphabetical listing with dates and SuDocs classification numbers to a more useful series of charts—a classified listing of committee jurisdiction arranged by specific and general categories. For the second edition, Zwirn has added an appendix called "Legislative Information Resources." "Aimed at those who desire to explore congressional affairs, including the policy agenda, in greater depth or scope," the appendix is arranged by broad areas: background material, the legislative process, legislative history and status, the federal budget, U.S. treaties, and national issues. Each of these areas is broken down into congressional, other federal, and nonfederal sources. This appendix can serve well as a "pathfinder" for faculty or librarians not familiar with the legislative process.

Zwirn's work is similar in purpose to Robert Goehlert's book *Congress and Law-making: Researching the Legislative Process* (ABC-Clio, 1979), which will also appear in a second edition (in early 1989).

Thomas A. Karel

Hospital

518. Schlenther, Elizabeth. **Miffy and Others in Hospital: Library Service to a Children's Ward.** Manchester, England, Haigh & Hochland, 1988. 1v. (unpaged). $4.50pa. ISBN 1-869888-01-4.

Maintaining that library services to hospitalized children have been neglected, and that books should be used to offer reassurance, entertainment, and growth, the author reports on her project in the children's ward at Bronglais Hospital, Wales. She describes library operations (classification, selection, acquisition, and financing) as well as her special activities (ward visits, reading lists, and cooperative efforts). Following are an outline of the steps in establishing library services to children and an annotated list of selected titles for inclusion in such a collection. The inexpensive booklet is written in a clear, direct style that complements the practical hints and advice it offers.

This booklet is designed for service providers in British hospitals. The problem of quality library services for the institutionalized youngster has already attracted the attention of the health care community in the United States. The Association for the Care of Children's Health prepares numerous pamphlets and programs, and the Department of Pediatrics at Strong Memorial Hospital in Rochester, New York, distributes bibliographies of appropriate book selections. These printed materials are much more comprehensive and essential for practicing librarians. However, the new title offers hints and suggestions, plus an overall view of the needed service. It is therefore a worthwhile purchase for librarians establishing a new library.

Margaret K. Norden

Law

519. Dane, Jean, and Philip A. Thomas. **How to Use a Law Library.** 2d ed. London, Sweet & Maxwell; distr., Agincourt, Ont. and Buffalo, N.Y., Carswell, 1987. 274p. illus. index. $35.50; $16.50pa. ISBN 0-421-36030-5; 0-421-36040-2pa.

This is an excellent introductory text to British legal bibliography. The title is misleading—the book deals with significant British and related legal materials in a law library, and how to find and use these materials. An introductory chapter discusses using a library in general, and a law library in particular. British legal materials are comparable to American materials, and the following are discussed: current and older law reports; citators; indexes and digests; parliamentary legislation (including bills, acts, and statutes); delegated legislation including statutory instruments (comparable to American administrative law and regulations); periodicals and periodical indexes; government publications, including parliamentary and nonparliamentary publications together with their catalogs and indexes; legal encyclopedias and dictionaries, including compilations of words and phrases; and legal bibliographies. A separate chapter discusses two leading online legal databases available in Great Britain: Lexis and Lawtel. Separate chapters also discuss specialized legal materials of Scotland, Northern Ireland, Republic of Ireland, and the European communities as well as treaties and public international law. The text contains sample pages of a number of publications. Appendices include a selected list of abbreviations of law reports, series, and periodicals, and a list of legal words and abbreviations in English, Latin, and French.

LeRoy C. Schwarzkopf

520. Fraser, Joan N., ed. **Law Libraries in Canada: Essays to Honour Diana M. Priestly.** Agincourt, Ont. and Buffalo, N.Y., Carswell, 1988. 237p. bibliog. $46.25. ISBN 0-459-31321-5.

This is a collection of scholarly essays in honor of one of Canada's influential law librarians and educators, Diana M. Priestly. Of the eighteen contributors to this volume, most are Canadian law librarians or law school professors. The essays are arranged into four sections: "Law Libraries," "Research and Reading," "Issues and Events," and "Law Librarians." Among the topics covered in the essays are: collection development in academic law libraries, the history and development of law firm libraries in Canada, aspects of the Canadian legal system, computer-assisted legal research, and the development of library standards.

Several of the essays stand out. Balfour J. Halevy's "Adventures in Canadian Legal Bibliography" chronicles the process and pleasures of bibliographic detective work. There is a delightful biographical sketch by David Ricardo Williams on two eminent Canadian jurists, and Lyman R. Robinson contributes a position paper on "The Influence of a Law Library on a Law School." There is a lengthy exploration of the KE classification schedule (Canadian law) by E. Ann Rae. This essay is complemented by Judith Ginsberg's brief note on the KF classification and how it was modified for use in Canadian law libraries. Preservation enthusiasts will be intrigued by a case study of a devastating fire at the Dalhousie University Law Library in August 1985. The focus of the essay by Christian L. Wiktor and Louis Vagianos is on the aftermath of the fire, the salvage and restoration activity, and the reconstruction of the entire library system. Finally, there is a twenty-one page bibliography of writings by Canadian law librarians during the past forty-five years.

Several appendices provide a variety of reference information: addresses of academic law, courthouse, parliamentary, and legislative libraries, and government publishers; notes on Canadian usage and a short list of recommended reference books for a law library; and academic law library statistics for 1986-1987. While this collection is obviously of primary interest for Canadian law libraries, major American law school libraries might also benefit from some of the material included. [R: CLJ, Dec 88, pp. 397-98]   Thomas A. Karel

521.   Garson, Marjorie A., and others. **Reflections on Law Librarianship: A Collection of Interviews.** Littleton, Colo., Fred B. Rothman, 1988. 262p. illus. index. (AALL Publ. Series, No. 29). $35.00. LC 88-11434. ISBN 0-8377-0128-7.

Delightful, entertaining, and informative, this collection of interviews reveals the personalities, achievements, and contributions of twelve outstanding law librarians. Each interview is conducted in a question and response exchange, and at times is redirected by the interviewer. Distinct, divergent individuals emerge on the pages of this thoughtfully produced collection.

Each chapter features a separate law librarian. Following individual portaits, a brief biographical sketch giving the current and previous positions, educational background, and professional contributions introduces each person. The interview itself comprises the major portion of each chapter ranging in length from ten to thirty-five pages. If the librarian has changed positions since the interview, appropriate information is presented in a postscript. In addition to the personalities discussed, threads of library history, struggles of an expanding profession, and developing technologies are woven into the fabric of the text. A brief index concludes the publication.

Elizabeth Thweatt

522.   **Law Librarian's New Product Directory.** New York, Garland, 1988. 524p. illus. index. $125.00 looseleaf with binder.

This is one of those ideas that is destined to remain just that: a good idea and nothing more. Basically, the *New Product Directory* is supposed to be a convenient way of obtaining information about new law books and services. It is actually nothing more than an index of selected publishers' new book announcements along with reproductions of publishers' flyers and brochures. The concept of a new product directory is interesting. Since a law librarian is typically deluged with mailings announcing new publications, the idea for an organized arrangement of these mailings is thought to make the work of an acquisitions librarian easier. The reason that the execution of the concept fails is that in the end it does not actually serve its purpose effectively or efficiently.

First of all, the *New Product Directory* is not comprehensive. If it is not comprehensive it cannot serve as an efficient substitute for regularly reading the mailings from publishers. A diligent acquisitions librarian regularly reads all of the incoming mail for ideas of new books to add to his or her library. If the *New Product Directory* is meant to relieve the librarian of the burden of wading through the mail, then by using it the librarian should be able to ignore the mail and rely totally on the directory. Since it is obviously *not* comprehensive, the librarian cannot ignore the mail for fear of overlooking an announcement about a useful new title. Therefore, the librarian is stuck with reading the mail just as thoroughly as before, looking for materials that are not in the directory. Thus the *New Product Directory* becomes not a convenience but an additional burden. It is merely another thing to read on a regular basis when looking for announcements about new materials to purchase.

Second, even if it were comprehensive, the directory would fail to alleviate the burden of scanning the mail looking for announcements about new products and services. Undoubtedly librarians will receive more announcements about new materials in direct mail from publishers than they will through the directory.

Perhaps the only useful purpose that the *New Product Directory* serves is that it obviates the necessity for collecting the new product announcements in pamphlet boxes. Since all of the flyers are reproduced on three-hole-punched 8½-by-11-inch paper, they all fit neatly into a binder that one receives with a subscription. A dubious advantage over collectint the real thing.

Richard A. Leiter

Medical

523. Flower, M. A. **Libraries without Walls: Blueprint for the Future. Report of a Survey of Health Science Library Collections and Services in Canada.** Toronto, Canadian Health Libraries Association, 1987. 148p. bibliog. $10.00 spiral-bound.

The purpose of this study by the Special Resource Committee on Medical School Libraries of the Association of Canadian Medical Colleges and the Canadian Health Libraries Association has been to "gather and present information on health science libraries in Canada today" and to "recommend steps which need to be taken to improve health information service nation-wide" (p. 4). The report includes both narrative and tabular information. Part of the text, particularly that dealing with francophone libraries, is in French. The report looks at the standard problems facing medical libraries; recommendations focus on the use of technology, administration, interlibrary loan, and financing. Also included is a three-page bibliography of material on the current state of medical education, particularly in Canada. [R: CLJ, Apr 88, p. 123] Philip A. Metzger

524. **Medical Libraries: A User Guide.** By Stan Jenkins. London, British Medical Association, 1987. 110p. illus. bibliog. £7.95pa.; £9.50pa. (overseas). ISBN 0-7279-0215-6.

Of the making of library handbooks—whether of *individual* libraries or special collections, resources, services, or library systems—there appears to be no end. Just as there are variations in handbook titles—though *reader's* or *user/user's* guides, or *how to use*, are frequently included in titles—there are variations in the contents of such guides. They often give full identification of the library or collection, including the exact address, telephone number, days and hours of service, services provided (e.g., circulation, interlibrary loans, reference, online searching, regulations as to use), catalogs, indexes and abstracts, staff assistance, floor plans or directory information to the facility, a table of contents/index, and history of the institution.

Medical Libraries includes many of the above-mentioned sections. Its most striking difference in approach is that it is not a handbook to a single library but to a special type of library, and as such reminds librarians of, say, Leslie T. Morton's *How to Use a Medical Library* (6th ed. Heinemann Medical, c1979). *Medical Libraries* was published by the British Medical Association (BMA) in the centennial year of its library (the Nuffield Library) "with the principal aim of encouraging more effective use of libraries and literature among the medical profession, research workers, and students" in Great Britain and abroad. The text is expertly interspersed with photographs (e.g., of Ernest Hart, the BMA's first librarian, and of the new Nuffield Library, which opened in 1986), sample catalog entries, sample entries from medical reference works, and diagrams (e.g., a photocopier).

The guide opens with a brief history of the BMA library and a chapter on six types of British libraries with medical collections. The guide then simply and clearly describes both the practical aspects of using libraries—the catalogs, bibliographies, and guides to information sources—and the variety of services being rendered by librarians (bibliographic assistance, translations, current awareness bulletins, etc.). The chapters on computer searches and library technology are especially useful ones. The penultimate chapter is a selection of briefly annotated reference titles—dictionaries and encyclopedias, directories, drug information, etc.—of especial use for users who like to find information for themselves. The final chapter considers what the medical library of the future may be like. *Medical Libraries: A User Guide* will be of considerable interest to medical practitioners, librarians, and students as well as to library students. [R: LAR, 15 Mar 88, p. 173]

Wiley J. Williams

525. Poland, Ursula H., ed. **World Directory of Biological and Medical Sciences Libraries.** Munich, New York, K. G. Saur, 1988. 203p. (IFLA Publications, 42). $30.00. ISBN 3-598-21772-2.

This directory of 1,371 life sciences libraries from more than one hundred countries was compiled from responses to questionnaires. It was a project of the Biological and Medical Sciences Libraries Section of the Division of Special Libraries, International Federation of Library Associations and Institutions. Libraries with collections in biomedical sciences (including allied health), dentistry, veterinary sciences, and pharmaceutical sciences (nonprofit organizations only) are included. For developing countries all libraries with such collections are included; for developed countries, the twenty-five major resources (as selected by each country's organization of biomedical sciences librarians) are listed.

The directory is arranged alphabetically by country, and within country, alphabetically by city. Entries typically include the name of the library or parent institution; address, telephone and telex numbers; contact person at the library; subjects included in the collection;

number of titles in the collection; lending status; and names of union lists to which the library/ institution contributes.

The volume concludes with three appendices: a bibliography of national and regional directories of biological and medical libraries; a list of associations of biomedical librarians; and addresses of union lists and cooperative service centers. The limited coverage of libraries in developed countries (previously mentioned) makes it clear that the directories listed in the first appendix and others (such as the *American Library Directory* [see entry 535], *Directory of Special Libraries and Information Centers* [see *ARBA* 88, entry 644], and *Subject Directory of Special Libraries and Information Centers* [see *ARBA* 88, entry 64]—each covering U.S. and Canadian libraries) must be used to provide a truer picture of life sciences collections. Furthermore, users of this volume will not fail to note the attention that Ursula Poland, the editor, gives in the introduction to questions "that yielded inconsistent results." The final paragraph of the introduction states: "Nonetheless, the Working Group for this … project is pleased to present the results of this survey and expresses hope that … future editions will address the shortcomings of this work, as well as fill its gaps." It thus remains to be seen exactly how useful this directory will be.

Wiley J. Williams

Mental Health

526. **Standards & Guidelines for Client Library Services in Residential Mental Health Facilities.** By Standards for Client Library Services in Residential Mental Health Facilities Committee, Association of Specialized and Cooperative Library Agencies. Chicago, Association of Specialized and Cooperative Library Agencies, American Library Association, 1987. 29p. bibliog. $10.00 spiralbound. ISBN 0-8389-7137-7.

In the past few decades, professional librarians have reevaluated their role in providing information to a diverse society. They have identified new users and found a need for library service standard and accreditation requirements. Institutionalized persons, particularly those confined to a residential mental health facility, constitute one group of patrons whose newly acknowledged information requirements needed to be addressed. Stimulated by judicial decisions, popular concern for patients' rights, the attention of the Joint Commission on Accreditation of Hospitals, and other social developments, the Association of

Specialized and Cooperative Library Agencies (ASCLA) appointed a committee that published the standards here under review.

Beginning with an introduction on the history of client libraries and the development of standards, the book notes the purpose, scope, and audience. There follow detailed guidelines that pertain to library administration, budget, staffing, material, services, and facilities. Discussing the desirable cooperative relationship between client libraries and other facilities and services, the ASCLA states that the library community has a "responsibility to serve clients when they are resident in their service area." The book concludes with a glossary of terms and acronyms, a bibliography of background materials, the Bill of Rights for Mental Health Patients, and the American Library Association's Bill of Rights.

These comprehensive and realistic standards were written by experienced librarians and administrators. They do not break new ground but incorporate the needs of a discrete clientele into guidelines already formulated for information providers. This written policy belongs in all residential mental health facilities and major teaching institutions.

Margaret K. Norden

Museums

527. Chenhall, Robert G., and David Vance. **Museum Collections and Today's Computers.** Westport, Conn., Greenwood Press, 1988. 169p. illus. bibliog. index. $37.95. LC 88-3091. ISBN 0-313-25339-0.

For many years scholars have held that historic objects housed in museums can be read like library texts. But retrieval and referencing of the millions of objects in U.S. museums alone has been a problem. With the advent of the computer, electronic cataloging of museum collections is becoming a reality. This book is a useful guide to starting a computer cataloging project. It lays out the rudiments of computer retrieval, database organization, and image processing. It does not purport to dictate a particular computer system, since museums have individualized needs, but it offers case studies and examples to help museums make informed decisions. The glossary and bibliography of the book are also helpful. Museum libraries and academic collections supporting museum and computer studies will appreciate this introductory text.

Simon J. Bronner

National

528. Cole, John Y., ed. **Library of Congress: A Documentary History: Guide to the Microfiche Collection.** Bethesda, Md., Congressional Information Service, 1987. 86p. index. $1,365.00 pa. (with microfiche). LC 87-15511. ISBN 0-88692-122-8.

The Library of Congress, the world's largest library, is one of the United States's special cultural treasures. It is not only a great national resource, but also an institution which has become entwined with the fabric of our cultural history in such areas as Congress, government, authorship, printing, scholarship, literature and the arts, and librarianship. Scholars may now conveniently explore the Library of Congress and its evolution with the publication of a major microfiche collection (40,000 printed pages, 500 microfiche) consisting of general histories, annual reports, catalogs, and archival checklists and sources. The set contains documents which traverse the period from the administration of John Beckley, the first Librarian of Congress, to the tenure of Daniel Boorstin.

Access to the microfiche collection is facilitated by this guide edited by Cole, scholar of the Library of Congress and executive director of the Library's Center for the Book. His excellent introductory essay, "The Library of Congress and Its Multiple Missions," summarizes major developments in the library's history through a focus on the twelve Librarians of Congress. Subsequent sections detail the resources for the study of the library; the Librarians of Congress and their administrations; major functions and services; and the various buildings. An author and title index round out the volume.

Both publisher and editor deserve commendation for assembling the collection and for providing a thorough, readable guide to the many documents.

Arthur P. Young

Women's Studies

529. Jackson-Brown, Grace. **Libraries and Information Centers within Women's Studies Research Centers.** Washington, D.C., Special Libraries Association, 1988. 34p. bibliog. (SLA Research Series, No. 3). $7.00 spiralbound. ISBN 0-87111-333-3.

Jackson-Brown has written six essays on topics related to women's studies, women's studies research centers (WSRCs), their libraries, and affiliated information centers. Each essay in this contribution to the Special Librar-ies Association Research Series is well written and documented.

A definition of women's studies research centers is given in the opening essay, and this is followed by an overview that chronicles the women's studies movement. In the third essay, libraries and information centers within WSRCs are highlighted. The topics of advocacy and publishing are featured in the next two essays, and a national database is spotlighted in the last. Suggestions for additional study and reading are included in a selected bibliography section. In the appendix is a directory giving the names and addresses of forty-five women's studies research centers.

This concise look at women's studies and WSRCs provides a glimpse of this evolving field to interested onlookers while offering a means of further study to those who seriously pursue this topic.

Dianne Brinkley Catlett

STATISTICS

530. Simpson, I. S. **Basic Statistics for Librarians.** 3d ed. London, Library Association and Chicago, American Library Association, 1988. 242p. illus. index. $25.00. LC 87-17488. ISBN 0-8389-2100-0.

The audience of the third edition is primarily those taking courses of information and library studies and secondarily for practicing librarians and information scientists who need an introduction to statistical applications. The book will not make readers experts in statistics, but it gives them enough to be knowledgeable consumers of reported research. This is done through chapters which range from simple descriptions and presentation of data to analysis of variance, correlation, and regression, although the latter three topics receive only brief discussion. A new chapter on bibliometrics is helpful for its examples of library applications.

The chapter on computerization has been expanded and now includes three statistical packages: SPSS-S, Minitab, and VIEWSHEET. In this chapter the reader is given an example of what can be done with these packages, because operations commands are specific to computer brands used to create the examples: IBM 360/168 mainframe, Harris minicomputer, and BBC microcomputer. SPSS-X and Minitab are widely used in the United States and are good choices for inclusion. To do statistics today without a computer statistical package is almost unthinkable. [R: LAR, Apr 88, p. 235; RLR, Aug 88, pp. 209-10]

Nathan M. Smith

Part III
REVIEWS OF
PERIODICALS

Reviews of Periodicals

NATIONAL

531. Feliciter, Vol. 1- , No. 1- . Ottawa, Canadian Library Association, 1956- . monthly. free to members. ISSN 0014-9802.

Feliciter began life as a typical series of sheets of news about the Canadian Library Association. All back issues are available on microfilm from CLA, and the newspaper is indexed in *Library Literature* (to the amazement of the late Elizabeth Morton, CLA's first executive director, who told me twenty years ago that she did not understand why it was being indexed by *Library Literature* since *Feliciter* was only intended to be a chatty newsletter). It is now a tabloid, about twelve pages an issue, available eleven times a year upon payment of membership fees. As a newspaper, it has news of the association, its affiliates, other library groups, and government activities that impinge on Canadian "libraryland." Its editorial board lists six contributing editors who represent affiliated subassociations such as the CACUL (Canadian Association of College and University Libraries) and six regional correspondents covering the west, the east, and Quebec. Presumably material about Ontario is written in-house since the CLA is based in Ottawa, Ontario. An editor and one writer are listed on the masthead. The only advertisements are for available jobs, and these are either classified-style or boxed. There are also many boxes containing addresses for calls for nominations for officers or awards, resolutions, committee work, reports to be made, and so forth. No excuses here for the membership *not* to know who to write and where to send it!

There are five categories of news. They begin with the straightforward accounts such as "Retirement battle going to high court," "Library porn protest scores a direct hit," or "Canada's national archives in need of a new home." (All of these are from the January-March 1988 issues.) The second category is reports from the CLA Board on its discussions (but not the in-camera ones) usually about finances, and the CLA Council discussions, news, and motions; reports on upcoming CLA conferences in order to generate excitement about future expectations; reports from affiliated groups such as CASLIS, CAPL, CACUL, and CLTA; reports by and from committees and interest groups; reports of various provincial library association conferences; and reports on various surveys such as the one on literacy published in the January issue. In the third category are regular columns: from the president, from the members, from the editor, and from the exhibitors. The fourth category is a "coming events" section, while the fifth category comprises a "people" area: appointments, deaths, and profiles of association officers and distinguished librarians who are CLA members.

Nicely distributed among all these words are many photographs of buildings, interiors, portraits, and people at meetings. But some of them are too dark or hazy. About the only thing that is not here but should be is some kind of book note column for Canadians on materials on information science and libraries. Quite properly the *Canadian Library Journal* (the "academic" quarterly published by the CLA) has book reviews, but these are late and infrequent, too slow for today's hectic pace. *Feliciter* used to have these book notes; they should return to its pages.

Dean Tudor

532. Reference Reviews, Vol. 1- , No. 1- . Harlow, England, Longman Group, 1987- . quarterly. £50.00/yr. (United Kingdom); £55.00/

yr. (Europe); £60.00/yr. (other countries); £12.50 (single issue). ISSN 0950-4125.

In the 1986 *Library Science Annual* (Libraries Unlimited), a study by this reviewer of major reference-book review media drew several conclusions that ought to affect the way librarians responsible for reference collection development use those media. One of the conclusions was that there was far less overlap among the review journals than commonly believed and that therefore librarians had best not rely on just one or even two or three of the sources to keep themselves up to date on new reference titles. The study also concluded that there is a correlation between the length of a review and its value because longer reviews allow the space needed to make comparisons to similar works and to convey a full sense of the work under review. These considerations bear on an evaluation of *Reference Reviews*, a British quarterly that offers in each issue fifty to sixty reviews of new reference titles.

Aside from a three-paragraph "editorial," actually an editor's news note, and a list of contributors, *Reference Reviews* has no editorial content other than the reviews, all of them composed by librarians at public, academic, and special libraries in the United Kingdom. The author/title index cumulates for the four issues of each volume. The reviews are arranged in broad disciplinary groups (e.g., social sciences, technology, the arts), and are subdivided by narrower disciplines (e.g., astronomy, medicine, architecture). Most of the titles reviewed in the two issues examined bear a British imprint with U.S. imprints scattered among them. The signed reviews, each several hundred words in length, provide additional confirmation of the study conclusions noted above. They make appropriate comparisons; they evaluate the works from the point of view of reference practice; and they convey a good sense of the works' strengths and weaknesses, citing numerous examples. The length of the reviews is similar to the longer reviews published in ALA's *Reference Books Bulletin*. However, unlike the committee members who create *RBB*'s reviews, the *Reference Reviews* contributors seem to have a great deal of latitude in how they approach their assignments. The welcome result is lively, robust writing. For example, the review of Jeff Rovin's *The Encyclopedia of Super Villains* (Facts on File, 1987) is laced with sardonic humor, and the reviewer of a cumulation of the *British National Bibliography* (British Museum, 1950-) notes that "to explain [its] value to readers of this journal is to tell a drowning man that he needs a life jacket."

While a reference book selector cannot monitor too many reviewing sources, those sources have to be judged in a social context. Because most of the reference sources reviewed in *Reference Reviews* are British works addressing a British audience, its utility to librarians in the United States is fairly well limited to those working in large libraries whose interest in Britain is demonstrated by their need for British reference books. [R: Choice, Jan 88, p. 753; LAR, 15 Jan 88, p. 45]   James Rettig

SUBJECT

533. **Aslib Book List: A Monthly List of Selected Books Published in the Fields of Science, Technology, Medicine and the Social Sciences,** Vol. 1- , No. 1- . London, Aslib, 1935- . monthly. £50.00/yr. (United Kingdom); £55.00/yr. (foreign); £45.00/yr. (United Kingdom Aslib members); £50.00/yr. (foreign Aslib members). ISSN 0001-2521.

All books included in this monthly selection list have been "reviewed, rated, and recommended by a subject specialist" and are accompanied by an annotation averaging fifty to seventy words in length. Unless otherwise stated, London is the place of publication of each bibliographical reference. Approximately 25 to 35 percent of the books included are published in the United States. Arrangement of references is by Universal Decimal Classification. This simply means looking for a book on the subject of zoology under the 59 classification as opposed to 590 (Dewey). Page numbers are not used, but all references are numbered sequentially beginning with the first entry in the first issue of the volume year. Thus the number 78 behind an author's name in the index is a reference to the numerical sequence of that review and not to a page. Monthly issues average twenty-four to thirty-two pages in length, include approximately 90 to 120 annotations, and an alphabetical author index. A cumulative author, subject, and classification index for each volume is published separately.

Medicine and the social sciences have been included since 1973. There was a change in format to a bland and less attractive publication in 1982, but content remains substantially unchanged otherwise. Intended as a selection aid for public, academic, and special libraries and information units in the United Kingdom, books are rated by type of readership with a rating system that is outlined in each issue. The annotations are terse, but informative and the *Aslib Book List* serves its primary market well.

Use in a public or special library in the United States would be limited. It could be a useful selection aid for a large academic library in the United States, but the cost in relation to size and other selection aids available would serve as an inhibiting factor. Robert M. Ballard

534. **Australasian Public Libraries and Information Services,** Vol. 1- , No. 1- . Underdale, S.A., Aust., Auslib Press, 1988- . 3-4 issues/yr. $21.00/yr.; $30.00/yr. (institutions); (overseas, add $4.00). ISSN 1030-5033.

Started in April 1988, this journal, under the initial editorship of Alan Bundy, is an effort to provide a quarterly forum for publishing articles and short items on public libraries and other publicly accessible information services in Australia, New Zealand, and the South Pacific. The 1988 issues contain between sixty and seventy pages and eight to nine articles each and it appears as though that will be the pattern. The articles are well written and carefully edited but deal not so much with topics of burning contemporary interest as with historical topics (e.g., the manuscripts of Major-General Macquarie), descriptions of institutions (e.g., the Archives Authority of New South Wales), and subjects of broad general interest (e.g., what the community expects from a country library). The journal's format may reflect a different approach to librarianship, more nearly akin to the contents of the *Australian Library Journal* or *Australian Academic and Research Libraries* than *American Libraries* or *Library Journal*, but it makes for heavy reading. So far news items, book reviews, and similar shorter pieces, which might help give *APLIS* life, have been lacking although book reviews seem to be in the offing since reviewers are solicited. *APLIS* is indexed and abstracted in *Australian Library and Information Science Abstracts* and the *Australian Education Index*. If it garners enough subscribers to survive, it will undoubtedly be the best continuing source of information about public library developments in the South Pacific. [R: RLR, Aug 88, pp. 190-91]

Norman D. Stevens

535. **Bulletin of the Medical Library Association,** Vol. 1- , No. 1- . Chicago, Medical Library Association, 1911- . quarterly. $95.00/yr.; free with membership. ISSN 0025-7338.

The *Bulletin of the Medical Library Association* (*BMLA*) is the foremost scholarly journal in the field of health sciences librarianship. It contains articles and brief communications in all disciplines relevant to health sciences librarianship, proceedings of the Medical Library Association's (MLA) annual meeting, and reports of other official meetings and actions of the association.

Until the early 1960s, *BMLA* contained both lengthy articles and association news. Member dissatisfaction with a quarterly publication as a means for distributing current information led to the creation of the *MLA News* (Medical Library Association, 1961-) as a medium for ephemeral association news. *BMLA* concurrently limited its editorial focus to substantive articles of lasting interest.

Contributed articles are now heavily research oriented, although brief communications frequently address practical issues. Invited symposia on "hot topics" of general interest have also been featured since 1986. Lengthy book reviews focus primarily on information science publications. Special features include a regular "Journal Notes" column which provides one-sentence summaries of current articles in information science; the proceedings of the annual meeting published in the January issue; and the biennial update of a standard reference tool, "Selected List of Books and Journals for the Small Medical Library," by Alfred N. Brandon and Dorothy R. Hill, which is published in the April issue in odd-numbered years. A detailed subject index is published in the October issue.

BMLA's closest competitor in the field of health sciences librarianship is *Medical Reference Services Quarterly* (*MRSQ*), published by Haworth Press (1982-). There is a heavy overlap in authorship between the two publications. *MRSQ* is more informal in tone, has a less stringent refereeing process, and tends to publish more practical articles of interest primarily to public services personnel. *BMLA*'s more formal approach reflects its scholarly research focus covering all aspects of health sciences librarianship. The writing is of a consistently high quality and adheres to stringent editorial standards and policies.

Most health sciences librarians have ready access to *BMLA*, since it is received as a benefit of personal or institutional MLA membership. Librarians in other fields will also find it of interest, since articles often focus on new technological developments first introduced in health sciences libraries which later spread to the profession as a whole. Examples include IAIMS (Integrated Academic Information Management Systems) development, medical informations, and end-user database searching. Therefore, no general library science or information science collection can be considered complete without it. Carolyn G. Weaver

536. **Canadian Association of Law Libraries Newsletter/Bulletin. Association Canadienne**

des Bibliothèques de Droit, Vol. 1- , No. 1- . Downsview, Ont., Canadian Association of Law Libraries, 1970- . 5 issues/yr. $60.00/yr.

Published in English five times a year, this newsletter/bulletin is the official publication of the Canadian Association of Law Libraries (CALL). Each issue includes professional news and developments, articles, reports of committees and special interest groups, and book reviews. Statistical surveys prepared by CALL committees and special interest groups are periodically published. The proceedings of the annual conference are published yearly, as is an annual index.

The news and developments section informs CALL members of activities of the national and regional Canadian library associations and of other law library-related developments. Feature articles range from one thousand to five thousand words and address such disparate topics as public legal education in Canada and early courts in Alberta. Book reviews averaging about five hundred words critique scholarly legal treatises as well as literature on law librarianship. Surveys may be limited in scope (e.g., salaries of law firm librarians) or very broad (e.g., comprehensive data on academic, courthouse, and law association libraries). Each issue also lists CALL officers and chairs of committees and special interest groups.

The newsletter/bulletin has the dilemma of trying to be both a vehicle for informing the more than four hundred CALL members of professional activities and a scholarly journal. Compounding this problem is the historical difficulty the editors have had in getting publication copy from members. Recent changes, however, have led to a more professional and useful publication. Issues are now planned one year in advance, resulting in a tighter and better defined publication. Other recently implemented changes include regular columns on regional membership news and reviews of databases. Furthermore, contracting with a desktop publisher has improved the style and editorial oversight.

The newsletter/bulletin succeeds quite well as the sole publication of the Canadian Association of Law Libraries. Substantial progress has been made in the past year which should make it even more valuable to CALL members and to others wanting to keep abreast of developments in Canadian law libraries.

James S. Heller

537. **The Christian Librarian: The Journal of the Association of Christian Librarians,** Vol. 1- , No. 1- . Cedarville, Ohio, Association of Christian Librarians, 1957- . quarterly. $16.00/ yr. (U.S., Canada, and Mexico); $20.00/yr. (overseas). ISSN 0412-3131.

The Christian Librarian is a quarterly publication of the Association of Christian Librarians (ACL), an organization whose membership is comprised primarily of librarians working in evangelical colleges and universities. This nondenominational journal is the vehicle through which ACL members "communicate their interpretation of the profession." Articles, which are generally scholarly and appropriately documented, cover topics ranging from networking and budgeting (many of which may be of interest to professionals working in nonevangelical settings) to moral and ethical issues that underlie Christian ideology.

There are also opinion pieces written by both practitioners and administrators. These are thoughtfully conceived and appear to be more practical than theoretical in tone. Letters to the editor reflect a kinship among professionals working and sharing common goals in a relatively specialized branch of librarianship. Book reviews, which range in length from two hundred to three hundred words, tend to be critical from a theological standpoint. The journal also features annotations on topics of interest to ACL readers.

The journal is simple yet professional in appearance. Creative typesetting and variations in spacing add to its visual appeal and allow for easy browsing and reading.

Although this journal is aimed at improving communication among librarians in evangelical settings, other librarians (e.g., those working in libraries of liberal arts colleges) may find it useful as one of many selection aids for collection development in the area of religion.

Dianne Brinkley Catlett

538. **The Electronic Library,** Vol. 1- , No. 1- . Medford, N.J., Learned Information, 1983- . bimonthly. $79.00/yr. ISSN 0264-0473.

This journal is a mix of articles on technology, new developments, and new applications. International in scope, it is intended for managers, researchers, and applications specialists in information systems and science. The major portion of each issue reviewed consists of regular columns, one providing reviews of hardware and a second reviewing software. In some issues, a third column, "Technical Notes," provides an overview of the use of particular technologies. For each column, the reviewer and affiliation are listed. Articles cover a wide range of relevant topics. They may be very specific descriptions of the development and adaptation of a system, an overview of current thinking about a particular technology, or the report of a survey on the use of information technology. One issue reviewed featured an excellent overview of library networking in North America.

Additional regular features include a news section with brief reports on technology, people, and activities; book reviews, reviews of articles, chapters of books, and publications outside the regular information press; and a worldwide calendar of conferences of interest to those dealing with information in electronic formats.

This is a successful blend of pertinent information written by individuals knowledgeable about both technology and the environments in which it is used. Written for the well-informed generalist, it is useful current awareness reading.

Ann E. Prentice

539. Expert Systems for Information Management, Vol. 1- , No. 1- . London, Taylor Graham, 1988- . 3 issues/yr. $75.00/yr. ISSN 0953-5551.

Applications of expert systems and knowledge-based systems have affected many areas outside computer science and engineering including information science and management. The extent of commercial exploitation of these systems is rapidly growing and their acceptance as tools for information management is becoming widespread. The goal of this periodical is to provide a suitable forum for applications of artificial intelligence in the fields of information science, law, business, social sciences, arts, and humanities. The present periodical seeks to highlight the theory and practice of the expert systems approach in information management from a less technical standpoint for users and potential users and to promote interactions from researchers and practitioners in this area. In order to include a wide area of applications, the editorial board has been drawn from notable researchers in both the academic and the commercial sectors. Topics covered include expert systems tools such as intelligent front ends and natural language interfaces; systems such as text analysis and summary systems, referral systems, and legal and regulatory advisory systems; management concerns such as records management, portfolio management, and network management; and other related areas such as expertise directories, credit sanctioning, auditing, patent surveillance, resource allocation, stock control, information retrieval, and business intelligence. Many articles in the journal are reports of case studies and projects based on the expert systems approach. These articles are descriptive, nontechnical, well written, and easy to understand. Most can be understood by readers in managerial positions with minimum background in artificial intelligence. Additional features including

book reviews, bibliographies of recent literature, and lists of forthcoming meetings are of valuable service and provide useful information to readers. Compared to other technical journals, this periodical contains a large number of in-depth book reviews to introduce readers to the vast amount of available literature. A long list of recent literature is extremely useful in alerting readers to other up-to-date publications. This periodical is published three times a year and is highly recommended for acquisition in both professional and academic libraries.

John Y. Cheung

540. HCL Cataloging Bulletin, Vol. 1- , No. 1- . Minnetonka, Minn., Hennepin County Library, 1973- . bimonthly. $12.00/yr.; $1.50 (single issue). ISSN 0732-894X.

541. Library Automation News: A Current Awareness Service for the Hennepin County Library, Vol. 1- , No. 1- . Minnetonka, Minn., Hennepin County Library, 1983- . monthly. $15.00/yr.

Hennepin County's creative cataloging continues to make library news and generate lively discussion. Standard subject headings have traditionally been resistant to modification. Retrospective conversion was time-consuming and costly. New headings never evolved as rapidly as requests for information on the new topic. Hennepin County's catalogers fill this void. Their subject headings are often more detailed than a small library would need; however, as a former children's specialist, I find much satisfaction in the headings that are child oriented.

Each issue of the *HCL Cataloging Bulletin* contains the additions and revisions of subject headings that were made since the last issue. All cross-references are included for each entry. While many of the headings would have been considered too specific or ephemeral in our less automated past, library automation has created a climate where subject heading changes are easier and less time-consuming.

Library Automation News is a monthly abstract of online cataloging literature. The focus is limited to items of probable interest to HCL staff and has a public library bias. Abstracts are grouped by general subject. Source documents include library and general periodicals, books, and reports. The editors have expanded the service to include more items related to online planning/management, user interfaces, training methods, microcomputer hardware/software, and online circulation, acquisitions, and serials control. This publication would be especially useful to public libraries exploring library automation. [R: LJ, 15 May 88, p. 64]   Carol J. Veitch

542. **Input,** Vol. 1- , No. 1- . Guelph, Ont., Documentation and Media Resources, The Library, University of Guelph, 1977- . bimonthly. $20.00/yr. ISSN 0706-151X.

Input evolved from a periodical first published in 1977, titled *Input-CODOC Newsletter*, which was the communication medium of the Co-Operative Documents Project, the users of the government documents coding scheme known as CODOC. In its present form, *Input* was first published in May 1979 by the University of Waterloo. The University of Guelph took over publication in 1984. The purpose of the periodical is to provide information on Canadian publications, people, and programs of interest to government documents librarians. The periodical is pamphlet-sized (5¼ by 8¼ inches). Material is not typeset, but prepared on a word processor or typewriter, usually with flush right margins. Spacing varies between single and double space, and pages have either one or two columns. Issues average fourteen pages each. The materials in the past two volumes generally consist of four categories: announcements and short reports of Canadian Library Association-sponsored meetings related to government documents; short, annotated listings of interesting or significant new Canadian government publications; news items or short annotated bibliographies related to programs or publications of Statistics Canada, the Canadian government's general purpose statistical agency; and miscellaneous news items or short articles on Canadian government publications or documents librarianship. This is currently the only periodical of its kind in Canada devoted to government publications and documents librarianship. Comparable U.S. periodicals which are similar in purpose, but more detailed in coverage, are the newsletter published by the American Librarian Association's Government Documents Round Table (GODORT), *Documents to the People* and the Association of American Law Libraries' Government Documents Special Interest Section newsletter, *Jurisdocs*. With Canada lacking a large and active national library organization comparable to GODORT, the University of Guelph Library provides a useful service with this newsletter.

LeRoy C. Schwarzkopf

543. **The Laserdisk Professional,** Vol. 1- , No. 1- . Weston, Conn., Pemberton Press, 1988- . 6 issues/yr. $78.00/yr. (U.S. and Canada); $93.00/yr. (Mexico and Central America); $108.00/yr. (foreign airmail). ISSN 0896-4149.

Considering the recent proliferation of information related to compact disk technology, the logical questions to ask when evaluating yet another publication are whether it does something unique or whether it does what it does better than publications that already exist. Although *The Laserdisk Professional* (*LP*) is neither unparalleled nor clearly superior, it should be read widely and be available on library shelves.

LP, a bimonthly which first appeared in May 1988, entered a world of readers already comfortable with *CD-ROM Review* (CW Communications, 1987-), and *CD-ROM Librarian* (previously *Optical Information Systems Update/Library and Information Center Applications*, Meckler, 1987-). All three of these journals cover similar ground. *LP* does offer a couple of unique, useful, and entertaining columns: "Book Reviews — Recent Writings Reviewed" and "Q&A — Readers' Questions Are Answered" (e.g., How do you select a good, inexpensive — but quiet — printer for a library reference area … ?) that have no equivalents in the two older publications. But by and large, *LP* resembles its predecessors and includes in-depth articles on particular CD-ROM products as well as briefer reviews; reports of experience from the field (e.g., an article called "Compact Disks in an Academic Library: Developing an Evaluation Methodology," and a column called "Library Scene — Laserdisks in Libraries"); industry news; hardware, legislative, and market information and predictions; and interviews with industry leaders (e.g., Microsoft's Bill Gates).

Similarities in tables of contents disguise subtle differences in tone and perspective. *CD-ROM Review* complements the other two journals with its computer industry point of view. The "laserdisk" in *LP*'s title suggests broader coverage than the "CD-ROM" in *CD-ROM Librarian* but, in terms of the emphasis they place on library applications of compact disk technology, the two publications definitely compete. Is *LP* worth the annual subscription price it will take to put it on library shelves in addition to or instead of its competitor?

LP's publisher has aims for its fledging publication that will sound familiar to readers of its other successful efforts, *ONLINE* (1977-) and *Database* (1978-); it intends its newest journal to function as a "practical, useful reference tool," providing professional users of CD-ROM, videodiscs, and other media with "a 'hands-on' approach" to laserdisk products and services. If the first issue is any reliable indicator of what is to come, *LP* lives up admirably to these intentions.

Major developments in compact disk technology occur almost daily and have profound implications for library processing and services. Two well-designed, skillfully edited, and practically informative publications cannot be considered too many in such a dynamic environment. In a "do more with less" era, the prudent recommendation would be buy one or the other (and *LP* will serve you well if it is your primary source of library-related compact disk information). Libraries and individuals will be best served, however, with access to both.

Connie Miller

544. Library & Information Science Research: An International Journal, Vol. 5- , No. 1- . Norwood, N.J., Ablex, 1983- . $28.50/yr.; $57.50/yr. (institutions); add $12.00 for overseas. ISSN 0740-8188.

Although no statement of purpose is provided, this quarterly refereed journal (formerly known as *Library Research*, 1979-1982) is currently edited by Jane Robbins of the University of Wisconsin at Madison. Each issue contains four to six lengthy research articles, one to four signed dissertation reviews (with a separate editor), and one to four signed book reviews, including many by noted personalities, faculty members at the nation's top graduate schools, international scholars, or practitioners at large academic research institutions. The cover serves as the table of contents. Topics of recent articles have included the use of reserve readings and students' grades in courses, unobtrusive reference testing, and predictors of interlibrary loan turnaround times. A list of winners of the ALA Research Round Table Award is regularly published. Article formats follow the traditional scientific model, with abstracts preceding each article, and figures/tables accompanying the text. The volume ends with number 4 (October/December issue), which contains separate cumulative author and contents indexes, and a list of volume referees. This source will be of greatest value to professors, graduate students, and scholars who want to stay current with a broad span of the latest research. It is widely indexed in education, library science, social science, and computer science sources (paper and electronic), which aids in the accessibility of its articles. Of concern is the different pricing of subscriptions, with institutions charged twice as much as individuals.

Ilene F. Rockman

545. Library Materials Guide, Vol. 1- , No. 1- . Grand Rapids, Mich., Christian Schools International, 1964- . semiannual. $28.48/yr.; $22.78/yr. (members). ISBN 0-87463-054-1.

Library Materials Guide is a semiannual reviewing guide "designed to assist the Christian librarian in selecting materials that will help students grow in their knowledge of God's world and gain wisdom in evaluating it" (p. 7, Spring 1988). Approximately 450 to 500 books are reviewed in each issue in categories for beginning, intermediate, and older readers (subdivided by broad subject groups) and for professional books. An author/title index, a subject index, and a publisher's directory are provided.

The publisher is Christian Schools International (CSI), which apparently is related to the Christian Reformed Church although no theological position statement is given. Reviewers are listed and reviews are initialed but no credentials are given for the reviewers except for their relationship to Christian schools (53 percent) or colleges. Over 28 percent had no designation except a town and state or province. While the percentage has decreased since 1982, 31 percent still come from Grand Rapids. Reviewers evaluate books "based on a common set of evaluation guidelines," rating them as "highly recommended," "recommended," or "acceptable," but the criteria they follow are not included.

There appears to be considerable overlap with secular reviewing publications. A sample compared to *Booklist* showed 57.6 percent of the titles were reviewed in both sources. Nearly 75 percent of the publishers in *Library Materials Guide* were also listed in the Wilson catalog series.

While a semiannual publication cannot achieve the balance one would desire for a collection, the fall 1987 and spring 1988 guides placed a strong emphasis on fiction, 70 percent for lower elementary, 46 percent for middle grades, and 38 percent for older students — all considerably higher than the percentage in such reviewing sources as the Wilson catalog series. Science, technology, and biography, on the other hand, seem to be deemphasized. The expected expansion of the religion category occurs only at the upper grade level where over 10 percent of the items fell in the 200s.

Reviews frequently relate to the church-related-school emphasis of the publication. A review of a book of native American tales notes "as is true of any collection of myths, these necessitate discussion and placement within a Christian context" (p. 61, Spring 1988). A review of a series on visual geography states that "Religion is almost ignored. On the positive side, the volumes are up-to-date and deal frankly with issues such as basic justice and the disparity between rich and poor" (p. 62, Spring 1988). Of a picture book about a Vietnamese girl, the reviewer writes "not a Christian book.... However, the story does provide excellent insights and the opportunity to discuss another culture and its religion. A teacher's book" (p. 24, Spring 1988). Books in the religion category carry such reviews as "by contemporary evangelicals and fundamental Christians" and "practical, helpful, biblical" (p. 77, Spring 1988).

It appears that controversial authors and topics frequently may be omitted. For example, only one title by Judy Blume and one by Stephen King were found in the five issues examined. Books on sexuality were reviewed because of their "Christian perspective" or for teachers (p. 68, Fall 1987). Homosexuality and abortion were not indexed in the two issues with subject indexes. Of Taylor's book *Censorship* (Watts, 1986), the reviewer notes "the author dwells so strongly on the negative aspects and consequences of censorship that an impression is created that nothing positive can come out of censorship" (p. 80, Spring 1988).

Library Materials Guide probably is accepted widely by librarians serving schools associated with CSI. An explanation of its theological position, the criteria followed in selecting and reviewing titles, and the credentials of the reviewers would be helpful to other librarians in Christian and secular libraries who might wish to use a conservative selection source.

Betty Jo Buckingham

546. **Library Outreach Reporter,** Vol. 1- , No. 1- . Brooklyn, N.Y., Library Outreach Reporter, 1987- . bimonthly. $18.00/yr.; $24.00/yr. (foreign). ISSN 0895-1179.

Beginning in September/October 1987, this publication is designed to deliver "current information highlighting Service to the Aging, Disabled Persons, Literacy Programs, and Ethnic Library Service." Its editorial guidelines state an interest in "articles on all aspects of Outreach Service" including "reports on a current or ongoing program/project, current research, local/state/national conference reports, new materials and products, and publicity/funding ideas"—all limited to one typewritten page. The editors of *Library Outreach Reporter (LOR)* have reserved the producing of issue-based articles to themselves.

Each of the first issues from 1 to 4 displayed different format and typography, but issues 4 and 5 seem to have settled on a style. Further, the latest issues (May/June 1988) defines itself as "a professional publication that provides a forum for information, analysis, and evaluation of issues in Outreach and Special Services. Authors' opinions should be regarded as

their own." An occasional photograph has also been added. However, this publication retains the look and feel of a newsletter, a useful structure for its purpose, but not to be confused with more literary or scholarly journals.

Averaging twelve to twenty pages per issue (including advertisements), recent issues are considerably larger than the original eight-page issue, indicating a desire for growth and development. *LOR* attempts to reach an important market with its information exchange. Best wishes as it continues to try its wings.

Darlene E. Weingand

547. **Library Personnel News,** Vol. 1- , No. 1- . Chicago, Office of Library Personnel Resources, American Library Association, 1987- . quarterly. $20.00/yr.; $5.00 (single issue). ISSN 0891-2742.

The purpose of this quarterly publication is to help the library/information community to be aware of trends and issues in the personnel administration field. Each issue is approximately sixteen pages in length and usually deals with one or two main topics as well as including short articles, news notes, highlights from recent personnel literature, and notices of legislation and court cases applicable to libraries. Topics in the first seven issues include recruitment and selection, staff development, job satisfaction, AIDS, job sharing, performance appraisal, professional ethics, pay equity, volunteers, and work place health and safety. The first anniversary issue is a theme issue providing excellent coverage of the changing roles of professionals, paraprofessionals, and other staff in a variety of work settings. The editors ensure that articles are crisp and to-the-point but not dogmatic. *Library Personnel News* provides the most comprehensive coverage of personnel issues of any library periodical. A more frequent publication schedule would make it even more useful in providing a current awareness service. [R: LJ, 1 Mar 88, p. 50]

Helen Howard

548. **Library Systems Newsletter,** Vol. 1- , No. 1- . Chicago, *Library Technology Reports*, American Library Association, 1981- . monthly. $35.00/yr. (United States, Canada, Mexico); $50.00/yr. (other countries); $4.00 (single issue). ISSN 0277-0288.

Published since 1981, with the well-known consultant Richard W. Boss as contributing editor, the contents of this journal are usually news clippings of developments in information technology and corporate structure changes that affect library systems automation. On an annual basis the editor conducts a survey of automated library system vendors "to get an overview and

Part III—Reviews of Periodicals / Subject

to facilitate comparison among vendors." The vendors chosen for this survey are those who offer integrated, multifunction turnkey systems or software only. Besides the news coverage there is usually a feature article on some aspect of library systems automation, such as modems, CD-ROM, Open System Interconnection (OSI), interfacing computers, local area networks (LAN), and so on. For those involved in day-to-day library systems operations, this eight-page monthly newsletter might be a welcome change from scanning incoming unsolicited mail and picking up brochures at conferences. At its current price, it is a bargain.

Pauline A. Cochrane

549. Library Talk: The Magazine for Elementary School Librarians, Vol. 1- , No. 1- . Columbus, Ohio, Linworth Publishing, 1988- . bimonthly. $35.00/yr.; $38.00/yr. (Canadian); $7.00 (single issue).

Formatted in a *USA Today* style, *Library Talk* is produced by the publishers of *The Book Report* (1982-), the bimonthly magazine for junior and senior high librarians. In twenty-one pages one finds two feature articles: "Shop Talk," a two-page column filled with "glad tidings" snippets concerning successful, promotional library programs; and "Book Bag," a column featuring short reviews of miscellaneous elementary school level books and software. Approximately one-third of the magazine is devoted to reviews of fiction, reference, and paperback materials for elementary school students. Future issues are to be published on booktalks, bulletin boards, and working with classroom teachers.

Although *Library Talk* is directed to a highly specialized readership in need of subject-specific journals, its content, format, and style do not recommend it as a replacement for such periodicals as *Journal of Youth Services in Libraries* (formerly *Top of the News*) or *School Library Journal*. The feature articles, for example, are only one page each in length and as a result lack any meaningful discussion of the subject. The page limit also imposes a "recipe" format on the articles which in turn diminishes the quality of the writing. The overall style of *Library Talk* is testimonial. The hints and tips from librarians about their successes are bereft of the results of even a "quick and dirty" evaluation survey. Last, the reviews contained in this periodical are of materials that in some cases have been reviewed at least six months before in other acquisition journals. *Library Talk* should be regarded only as an additional periodical purchase for elementary school librarians.

Kathleen W. Craver

550. MLA News, No. 1- . Chicago, Medical Library Association, 1961- . 10 issues/yr. $33.00/yr.; free with membership. ISSN 0541-5489.

MLA News is the official newsletter of the Medical Library Association, containing brief articles and news items of interest to members, a list of employment opportunities, and a schedule of continuing education sessions. The *News* began in November 1961 as a medium for timely publication of association news and other ephemeral materials which had formerly been published in the *Bulletin of the Medical Library Association* (1911-). Although the content is focused specifically on association members, some articles and regular columns will appeal to a broader audience, since they address professional issues such as library legislation and publishing industry practices. Media hardware and software reviews are another feature with wide appeal. Articles are well written and quite current, with a deadline one month prior to the month of publication. News of MLA sections and chapters is also featured.

The "Employment Opportunities" column is the most popular feature of the publication, since it serves as a primary device for professional recruitment by virtually all health sciences libraries. Job seekers may subscribe to an advance mailing of "Employment Opportunities" at a minimal cost.

As an ephemeral publication, the *News* does not merit permanent retention by any but the most comprehensive library; but as a current awareness tool concerning the affairs of MLA and of health sciences librarianship in general, it is invaluable.

Carolyn G. Weaver

551. Rural Libraries, A Forum for Rural Library Service, Vol. 1- , No. 1- . Clarion, Pa., Center for the Study of Rural Librarianship, College of Library Science, Clarion University of Pennsylvania, 1980- . semiannual. $6.00/ yr.; $3.00 (single issue). ISSN 0276-2048.

In 1978 the College of Library Science of Clarion State College (Clarion University of Pennsylvania since July 1, 1983) organized the unique Center for the Study of Rural Librarianship "to extend the knowledge relative to the nature and the role of rural libraries in the United States." As part of an active publications program, the center began publication in winter 1980 of *Rural Libraries* as a "forum for the reporting of investigation, activities, and research related to rural library service." The practical and state-of-the-art research articles are the contributions of a variety of specialists—for example, college professors of marketing, sociology, history, and librarianship, and librarians in county/regional, state, and academic libraries. Many of the articles include notes and/or bibliography, tables, copies of survey instruments, and analyses of surveys. The diversity of the contents can be illustrated by mentioning a few selected titles: "A Survey of Rural Libraries in Continuing Education," "Public Relations and the Rural Library: A Bibliography," "Steps to Take: Marketing the Rural Library," "Folklore: Programming in the Rural Community," "Flagler Humanities Programs: Success in a Tiny Library," and "Public Libraries/Agricultural Extension Agencies Potential for Cooperation."

Rural Libraries, reproduced from justified typewritten copy, uses no color, relying instead on the quality of its contents. A cumulative index in three parts—author, title, and subject—to volumes one (the only quarterly volume) through the first number of volume six (thirteen issues, 1980-1986) appears in volume 7, number 1 (1987). This journal belongs in library schools/library education departments and in the large number of libraries in areas geographically removed from metropolitan centers.

Wiley J. Williams

552. The School Librarian's Workshop, Vol. 1- , No. 1- . Berkeley Heights, N.J., Library Learning Resources, 1980- . monthly (except July and August). $40.00/yr. ISSN 0271-3667.

Edited by the authors of two very well done guides for school librarians, *The Library Media Specialist's Daily Plan Book* (Center for Applied Research, 1982) and *Sharks, Ships and Potato Chips: Curriculum Integrated Library Instruction* (Library Learning Resources, 1986), this attractive and well-formatted two-color newsletter would appear to serve as an update or supplement to these earlier, but still useful, works. Issues come three-hole punched for notebook filing, and a subject index is provided in June for the previous school year. The journal covers the same sorts of materials found in the books, with an emphasis on the teaching of library skills through curriculum integration, but also including public relations tips, working with teachers, library enrichment activities, bulletin boards, library skills teaching units, annotated bibliographies, games, and other useful activities, plus professional development and networking ideas.

The "Poet's Corner" reviews a poetry book each month, and "Reference Question of the Month" is actually an entire set of questions relating to a particular theme which can be used for teaching reference skills. Recent themes have included military engagements and famous battles, Mexican miscellany, biblical animals, and

Australia. Besides the regular columns and features, special articles highlight current problems or issues in school librarianship and education. Some recent ones discussed the need to check answers to reference exercises each year, since reference tools change; the role of state media organizations in promoting the profession, and the application of the educational teaching theories of Madeline Hunter to the media center.

While the majority of articles are written by the authors/editors, each issue generally also includes several sent by readers, sharing their resources and successful ideas. Writing style is popular and columns and articles are brief, running from one paragraph to as many as two pages in length. Judging from volume numbering, the periodical has been in existence at least eight years as of 1988 and it is certainly hoped that the editors will continue publishing this extremely practical, relevant, and motivating newsletter. School librarians short on subscription funds should consider sharing issues with a neighboring library or asking their school district media center to make this title available to them. It is similar in scope and format to *School Library Media Center Activities Monthly* (LMS Associates, 1984-), which librarians may wish to compare it with before making a purchase decision.

Carol Truett

REGIONAL

553. High Roller, Vol. 14- , No. 5- . Reno, Nev., Nevada Library Association, 1977- . quarterly. $20.00/yr.; free with membership; $25.00/yr. (foreign). ISSN 0197-6044.

The *High Roller* began in the 1970s as a mimeograph published by the Nevada State Library, taking the place of another sporadically produced newsletter during the preceding decades as an organ of the Nevada Library Association (NLA). Modern library development in Nevada began in the 1940s, promoted by the University of Nevada at Reno, Washoe County, and the Nevada State Library. The Nevada Library Association waxed, waned, and waxed again in the 1950s and the 1960s, blooming under the guidance of public and university libraries and later by the newly developed community college libraries in the north, east, and south. The *High Roller* is a steadying influence upon the Nevada library community, emphasizing association activities, developments and promotions; it publishes excellent, scholarly white papers suggesting direction, goals, and guidelines toward which the library community can strive. At least two issues provide information on the annual NLA convention programs and personalities. Reports by NLA sections and interest groups are presented regularly as are book reviews and national library news in capsule form. The articles are well written, comprehensive, and detailed.

The format has double-column pages and readable type, and is explicitly captioned with many black-and-white advertisements. As a library publication, it is equal to productions done in Arizona, Oregon, Idaho, and Montana.

Jack I. Gardner

554. **Oregon Library News,** Vol. 1- , No. 1- . Portland, Oreg., Oregon Library Association, 1952- . monthly. $15.00/yr. ISSN 0030-4375.

This newsletter serves as the chief communication tool for Oregon librarians. It includes notes about people and events which will be of interest primarily within the state boundaries: for example, Oregon legislative action affecting libraries and the activities of the newsletter's parent body, the Oregon Library Association. It is also one channel of information about what is happening with other library groups (e.g., the American Library Association and the Pacific Northwest Library Association).

Businesslike in tone, with occasional illustrations, the *Oregon Library News* publishes short articles describing projects and programs of the state's libraries (especially public libraries) and has recently run a column featuring "What Works in Oregon Libraries." The newsletter includes announcements about continuing education workshops, association meetings, and elections. Notes on professional books and videos also appear sporadically.

This is a good, solid, informational tool. It fills its role adequately without pretensions toward being anything more.

Berniece M. Owen

555. **TL, Tennessee Librarian,** Vol. 29- , No. 2- . Nashville, Tenn., Tennessee Library Association, 1977- . quarterly. $10.00/yr.; free with membership; $12.00/yr. (foreign); $3.00 (single issue). ISSN 0162-1564.

All too often, professional librarians want to get into the big leagues immediately and attempt to do so by sending everything they write to *Library Journal* or *American Libraries*. Generally, unless those magazines have provided their *nihil obstat* to the writer, they are rejected. But as this journal shows, state magazines are lively, interesting, and a wonderful proving ground for the novice professional.

Tennessee Librarian, or as it has come to be called of late, *TL* (violating that sacred rule of title change), began publication in the summer of 1948. The journal was 6 by 9 inches and the cover displayed solid color stock. The articles from that time to this have changed very little over the years. Newsy items have occupied a good one-third to one-half of the journal. One to three articles appear in the journal, while library information and association meetings round out the content.

TL has been blessed with outstanding editors. In the forty years of its existence, fifteen editors have assumed the rank of proofkeeper, article-solicitor, make-up, layout, chief bottle-washer, and managing editor. About the only thing that *TL* editors have not had to do was set type themselves.

In 1953, the *TL* cover changed to white stock with pictures. The pictures were often of librarians, libraries, or state annual conventions. In 1969 the cover returned to color stock, some covers with pictures, most without. Even librarians are often guilty of doing what they complain about to others: *TL* changed its size in 1973 to 6½ by 10 inches, and again in 1982, to 8 by 11 inches. During this year the journal was not typeset, but duplicated from camera-ready, dot matrix printouts. The effect was disastrous, and wise heads prevailed in 1986, when the magazine returned to 6½ by 10 inches, typeset, and all issues in a volume number of the same color stock.

Traditionally, *TL* has focused on what is most useful to the practicing librarian. Recent issues provide good examples of this. An article describing the new University of Tennessee Library, the John C. Hodges $30 million facility, was showcased in the spring of 1987 and again in the winter of 1988. An article detailing the friends of the library organizations recounted the many successes and near misses of the Volunteer State's bookworms. Jud Barry, a librarian in Kingsport, described in the spring 1988 issue the Tennessee Library Association's (TLA) efforts to marry the library's confidentiality policy regarding circulating records with state law. Other articles have included a discussion of DIALOG, descriptions of upcoming ALA conferences, an article on end-user searching, hand-carried interlibrary loans for small libraries situated near a larger academic facility, and a union list of Tennessee library newsletters.

Most of the articles avoid the controversial, though such articles have not been entirely lacking during *TL*'s long run. Regular features include the column "P Slips," a column announcing news happenings in Tennessee libraries, the editorial, a letter from the Tennessee Library Association president, and "Tennessee Reviews," a column that reviews books by or about Tennesseeans or Tennessee, within and without the library discipline. This column also features an annual bibliography that is published in the journal. Candidates for TLA office appear when those elections are imminent, and reports from the various roundtables of TLA are published when necessary.

TLA executive members are considering a newsletter that would be published more frequently than the quarterly *TL*. But that idea has run into the usual financial hitches, along with some concern over whether it would ultimately detract from *TL*'s audience.

In an age that is seeing such ventures come rapidly to a screeching halt, *TL* remains one of the better state journals. The combination of devoted editors and concerned membership has managed to bring to the magazine the right mix of blood, sweat, and tears to make of *TL* something every librarian, Tennesseean or not, can rightly be proud of.   Mark Y. Herring

Part IV
ABSTRACTS OF LIBRARY SCIENCE DISSERTATIONS

Abstracts of Library Science Dissertations

Gail A. Schlachter

INTRODUCTION

Unlike the commercially produced monographs, reference books, and journals described elsewhere in this edition of *Library Science and Information Annual*, doctoral dissertations are cloaked by fragmented and sluggish bibliographic announcements and distribution channels. While it is possible to contact library schools at the end of each year to identify dissertations completed there during that year, the only way to learn about dissertations dealing with library and library-related topics that were prepared outside of library schools is to wait until they are listed in *Dissertation Abstracts International (DAI)*. However, dissertations completed in the third and fourth quarter of one year are frequently not included in *DAI* until the third or fourth quarter of the next year. As a result, it was impossible to review dissertations completed in 1988 and meet the manuscript submission date for this edition of *LISCA*. Thus, this volume provides a review of the 1987 dissertations and, similarly, each subsequent volume will cover dissertations completed in a previous year.

To date, 91 library, information, and related dissertations completed in 1987 have been identified. To place those doctoral studies in perspective, the following quantitative profile is modeled after the statistical analysis provided in Schlachter and Thomison's *Library Science Dissertations, 1925-1972: An Annotated Bibliography* (Libraries Unlimited, 1974) and

Library Science Dissertations, 1973-1981: An Annotated Bibliography (Libraries Unlimited, 1982).

Completion Data

On the average, 14 dissertations were completed each year between 1925 and 1972. From 1973 through 1981, the yearly average increased 800 percent, to 111 dissertations per year. The number of dissertations completed in 1987 (91) was down substantially from both the 1972 to 1981 yearly average but up from the totals reported in the last two editions of the *Annual*: 83 in 1985 and 74 in 1986.

Sponsoring Schools

The 91 dissertations reviewed for this edition of the *Annual* were completed at 36 private and public institutions of higher learning in the United States and Canada, less than one-third the number of schools involved in the total production of library and library-related dissertations between 1973 and 1981. The five "top" producing universities, responsible for more than 40 percent of the doctoral studies reviewed for 1987, are Florida State University (13 percent), Rutgers—The State University (8 percent), University of Illinois at Urbana-Champaign (8 percent), Texas Woman's University (7 percent), and University of Pittsburgh (5 percent). Only two of the schools—Florida State University and University of Pittsburgh—were also listed as top producers in this section of the *Annual* analysis last year.

Degrees Received

Following the pattern set between 1925 and 1981, the Ph.D. remained the most commonly earned degree (84 percent) in 1987, followed by the Ed.D. (12 percent), and the D.L. (4 percent). Although in past years other degrees (e.g., D.L.A., D.B.A.) were also represented in the dissertations reviewed, to date none have been reported for studies completed in 1987.

Methodology Employed

As in the analyses reported by Schlachter and Thomison in the two volumes of *Library Science Dissertations*, each of the 91 dissertations completed in 1987 was placed into one of seven research categories: citation/content analysis, experimental design, theoretical treatment, operations research (systems analysis and all forms of information storage and retrieval), survey research (case studies, mailed questionnaires, interviews), historical analysis (including biographies and bibliographies), and other (including those dissertations for which insufficient information was available to determine methodology employed). The ranking of research methodologies employed in the 91 dissertations completed during 1987, from most to least used, is survey research (40 percent), operations research (29 percent), historical analysis (12 percent), citation/content analysis (9 percent), experimental design (7 percent), theoretical treatment (2 percent), and other (1 percent). These rankings and percentages differed in two major ways from the approaches used in the 1986 dissertations: (1) while survey research remained the most commonly employed methodology, the percent of dissertations using that technique decreased from 48 percent in 1986 to 40 percent in 1987; and (2) the percentage of dissertations utilizing operations research more than doubled, from 12 percent in 1986 to 29 percent in 1987, making operations research the second-ranked methodology in 1987.

Sex

Although women have consistently constituted the majority of practicing librarians, they wrote only a minority of library, information, and related dissertations from 1925 to 1979. Since that time, however, the field has oscillated. From 1980 to 1982, women were responsible for the first time for over half the dissertations completed. In 1983, 1984, and 1985, the trend reversed; no more than 47 percent of the dissertations in any of those years were written by women. In 1986, the picture changed; women wrote 54 percent of the library, information, and related dissertations completed that year. In 1987, 53 percent of the dissertations were written by men and only 47 percent by women.

Summary

Using the results of this quantitative analysis, it is possible to develop a profile of the library, information, and related dissertations completed in 1987. The typical dissertation was written for the Ph.D. degree by a man, using survey research methods at one of a handful of major universities in the United States.

The following 45 dissertations have been chosen to be abstracted in the 1989 edition of *Library and Information Science Annual* because they represent the quality, interest, relevance, and/or subjects of the library, information, and related dissertations completed in 1987.

ABSTRACTS

556. Abdo, Mekhag B. (Ph.D., State University of New York at Buffalo, 1987). **The Academic Library in the Electronic Age: The Case of Six Arabian Peninsula Countries.** 354p. Order no. AAD87-10682.

PURPOSE: This study examined the current and potential impact of the electronic age on the structure and services of academic libraries in the following Arabian Peninsula countries: Bahrain, Kuwait, Oman, Qatar, Saudi Arabia, and United Arab Emirates.

PROCEDURE: A questionnaire sent to library directors and deans collected data on regional cooperation, automation activities, and organizational structure (in the present and projected for the future) at thirteen academic libraries in the Arabian Peninsula.

FINDINGS: The more technical/specialized the library, the more automation was present. The lack of trained librarians and the lack of standardized bibliographic tools for the control of Arabic bibliographic information proved to be basic problems for the automation of academic libraries. An additional problem: only two systems were available that could handle the automation of a bilingual collection.

RECOMMENDATIONS: Using the data collected in the study, Abdo developed automation guidelines for the University of Qatar Library and made recommendations on the regional level for the other libraries included in the study.

557. Adediji, Okanlawon Oladipo (Ph.D., University of Pittsburgh, 1987). **Identification of Priorities of Nigerian Academic Library Directors.** 138p. Order no. AAD88-10097.

PURPOSE: This study collected data from academic library directors in Nigeria to determine: (1) their current and future priorities; (2) their perceptions of library services, staff, and collection development programs; (3) their views on centrality, demand, and cost; and (4) the relationship between their projections of library funding and their perceptions of future library priorities.

PROCEDURE: Questionnaires were sent to directors in twenty-four Nigerian university libraries. Respondents were asked to evaluate twenty library services and programs. Data were analyzed using frequencies, percentages, measures of central tendency, rank ordering of means, and standard deviations.

FINDINGS: The library programs/activities considered most central to the missions and objectives of the surveyed Nigerian academic libraries were readers' services and technical services. Books and periodicals were the materials most in demand. Books were the most costly service offered in the surveyed libraries. Of most concern to the library directors (both now and in the future) was library service, followed by collection development; of least concern to the directors were staff-related issues.

558. Allen, Jean Short (Ph.D., University of North Carolina at Chapel Hill, 1987). **Information-Seeking Patterns and Resource Use by Baptist Leaders in Three Central American Countries.** 292p. Order no. AAD87-22258.

PURPOSE: In order to examine how individuals in developing countries obtain needed information, Allen collected data on the information-seeking behavior of Baptist leaders in Costa Rica, Guatemala, and Honduras.

PROCEDURE: Questionnaires were sent to 606 Baptist leaders (in a sample of seven groups). Responses were received from 57 percent. The collected data were analyzed using a SAS program.

FINDINGS: The factors found to relate to the use of print materials and/or libraries included sex, leadership responsibility, education, income, and urban residence. Baptist leaders with lower income and more routine jobs were most likely to turn to the radio or television for information gathering. When it came to the

informal interchange of information, the local pastor proved to be the most important source, but books were found to be most used for theological information.

CONCLUSIONS: Because the information-seeking behavior of Central Americans described in this study paralleled earlier findings reported for Americans, Allen concluded that the theory of information seeking may cut across national and cultural lines.

559. Al-Odeh, Abdul-Rahman Mahmoud (Ph.D., University of Missouri at Columbia, 1987). **Feasibility and Support for an Interlibrary Loan Network among the West Bank and Gaza Academic Libraries.** 131p. Order no. AAD87-28784.

PURPOSE: The purpose of this study was twofold: to determine the status of academic libraries in the West Bank and Gaza (Jordan) and to explore the degree of support for an interlibrary loan network among those libraries.

PROCEDURE: To collect data for this study, Al-Odeh conducted a literature search on interlibrary loan developments (particularly in developing countries) and sent questionnaires to academic library directors in the West Bank and Gaza.

FINDINGS: Al-Odeh found substantive differences in the level of holdings and staffing at the surveyed libraries. Most of the books, serials, and staff were concentrated in the major academic libraries. No formal interlibrary loan network existed, although some information borrowing and lending occurred. All but one of the library directors polled in this study supported the concept of an interlibrary loan network for the libraries in the West Bank and Gaza. In descending order, the greatest obstacles to participation in an interlibrary loan network were determined to be lack of advance planning, adequate resources, strong leadership, organizational support, adequate finances, a cooperative spirit, and effective communications.

560. Al-Sabbah, Imad A. (Ph.D., Florida State University, 1987). **The Evolution of the Interdisciplinarity of Information Science: A Bibliometric Study.** 275p. Order no. AAD87-13300.

PURPOSE: Using issues of the *Journal of the American Society for Information Science* (*JASIS*) published since 1970, Al-Sabbah examined the interdisciplinarity of information science as a discipline.

PROCEDURE: Al-Sabbah investigated the citation patterns in a randomly selected sample of 10 percent of the articles published in *JASIS* from January 1970 through December 1985. *JASIS* was chosen for this study because, in the opinion of experts, it best represented the information science literature. Descriptive statistics were used to analyze the data.

FINDINGS: In the citation analysis, thirty-two different disciplines were identified in the literature. The most important of these was information science, followed by computer science, library science, and general science. The contribution of computer science to the literature increased by 300 percent during the study period while the contribution of library science decreased by nearly 5 percent.

CONCLUSIONS: During the past fifteen years, the relationship between information science and computer science has been growing stronger, while the relationship between information science and library science has been weakening.

561. Awogbami, Popoola Akanni (Ph.D., University of Pittsburgh, 1987). **The Availability and Utilization of Microforms in Agricultural Libraries: A Case Study of Five U.S. Sites, with Implications for Nigerian Agricultural Libraries.** 122p. Order no. AAD88-07361.

PURPOSE: In this dissertation, Awogbami studied the availability and utilization of microforms in the agricultural libraries of five American academic institutions: Ohio State University, Pennsylvania State University, University of Illinois, University of Wisconsin, and University of Minnesota.

PROCEDURE: Awogbami conducted an extensive literature search and collected data from a population of heads of selected agricultural libraries and a randomly selected sample of agricultural scientists employed by the five universities under study. The following statistical methods were used to analyze the data: percentages, means, standard deviations, one-way analyses of variance, and Pearson Product Moment Correlation coefficients.

FINDINGS: The libraries investigated in this case study had neither separate microform acquisitions budgets nor microform specialists. Further, microforms were not covered in their selection policies. The majority of the agricultural scientists used microforms in their teaching and researching, but they complained that the medium strained their eyes and restricted their posture.

CONCLUSIONS: According to Awogbami, these findings have the following implications for Nigerian agricultural libraries: (1) agricultural librarians in Nigeria should acquire more microforms, (2) there should be microform specialists available in the libraries, (3)

funds should be set aside for the purchase of microforms and microform equipment, (4) Nigerian agricultural scientists should use microforms along with other information resources, and (5) there should be a national agricultural microform project.

562. Barez, Shohreh (Ph.D., University of California at Berkeley, 1987). **Seismic Safety in Existing Public Buildings: A Study of Library Facilities.** 178p. Order no. AAD88-13787.

PURPOSE: This study was conducted, first, to focus on the dangers of earthquakes and, second, to encourage a multidisciplinary approach to the planning, research, design, and construction necessary in the event of an earthquake disaster.

PROCEDURE: As part of this study, Barez (1) reviewed major areas of seismic deficiencies in older buildings (especially libraries), (2) detailed seismic safety points of concern in libraries, (3) proposed a qualitative process for evaluating safety in libraries, (4) covered the range of structural and architectural issues that must be considered in making seismic retrofitting decisions, and (5) discussed a number of factors affecting rehabilitation and seismic retrofit.

FINDINGS: Because of their unique combination of high occupancy, utilization, and incompatible structural subsystems, libraries are particularly vulnerable to earthquakes.

CONCLUSIONS: Preservationists and urban planners need to be involved in design decisions to protect the architectural character of older buildings.

RECOMMENDATIONS: A multidisciplinary approach should be taken to the retrofit construction and use of existing buildings.

563. Basu, Santi Gopal (Ph.D., Florida State University, 1987). **Public Library Services to Visually-Disabled Children in the United States.** 189p. Order no. AAD88-02814.

PURPOSE: This study focused on the services, materials, and special equipment available to visually disabled children in American public libraries.

PROCEDURE: Questionnaires were sent to children's librarians in two groups of public libraries: (1) all public libraries designated as subregional libraries by the Library of Congress's National Library Service for the Blind and Physically Handicapped (NLS) and (2) a sample of public libraries that are not subregional libraries.

FINDINGS: More general (Non-subregional) public libraries offered general services (e.g., storytelling, film programs, arts-and-crafts programs, puppetry) to visually disabled children than did subregional libraries. More subregional public libraries offered special services, specialized materials (talking books, braille books and magazines, large-print materials), and special equipment than did general libraries. Few public libraries in either group owned Kurzweil Reading Machines, Optacon Reading Machines, voice synthesizers, or computer (braille) output devices.

CONCLUSIONS: Neither library size nor geographic location related to the services, materials, or special equipment offered by public libraries to visually disabled children.

564.   Baum, Christina Diane (Ed.E., University of Kentucky, 1987). **The Impact of Feminist Thought on American Librarianship.** 274p. Order no. AAD87-15914.

PURPOSE: The purpose of this study was to use citation and content analysis to determine the impact of radical and liberal feminism on the writings and programs of female librarians between 1965 and the beginning of 1986.

PROCEDURE: Baum used three techniques to trace the impact of feminist thought on American librarianship. First, she analyzed the content of 250 articles and books written about library women by library women from 1965 to 1985. Next, she analyzed the 5,583 citations that appeared in that literature and classified the feminist authors outside of librarianship as either liberal or radical. Finally, she analyzed the content of the women's programs offered at the American Library Association annual conferences from 1965 to 1985.

FINDINGS: The content analysis of library literature revealed nineteen major liberal issues (wage discrimination was the predominant one), eight liberal issues (sexist terminology predominated), twelve liberal agendas (networking predominated), and five radical agendas (consciousness raising predominated). Of the 250 sources analyzed, 112 did not propose any agenda to address the issues they raised. Citation analysis identified twenty sources (of the 250 studied) that contained citations and a total of thirty-four citations to liberal or radical feminist authors outside of librarianship. Content analysis of the programs at the American Library Association annual conferences from 1965 to 1985 isolated ninety-one programs dealing with feminist issues, most of which were liberal in content (sixty-five programs) and sponsored by the Social Responsibilities Round Table (forty-eight programs).

CONCLUSIONS: During the period under study, the ideology and agendas put forth by women in librarianship reflected liberal feminist politics.

565.   Bodart, Joni (Ph.D., Texas Woman's University, 1987). **The Effect of a Booktalk Presentation of Selected Titles on the Attitude toward Reading of Senior High School Students and on the Circulation of These Titles in the High School Library.** 137p. Order no. AAD87-29673.

PURPOSE: In this experimental study, Bodart measured the effect of booktalks on (1) senior high school students' reading attitudes and (2) the circulation of materials.

PROCEDURE: A Solomon Four Group design was used to collect data on the 1984-1985 students at Emporia High School. A high school librarian there was trained to give booktalks and gave a presentation to half of the experimental (freshmen class) population during their English classes. The Lewis and Teale Reading Attitude Survey was administered to half the population as a pretest and to the whole population as a posttest. In order to determine if the booktalks had an effect on the other three grades at the high school as well as the experimental group, Bodart examined the circulation records for students in all grades.

FINDINGS: No significant difference was found (1) between the mean pretest and posttest scores, (2) among the mean scores of the four grades studied, or (3) between males and females and their attitudes toward reading. Significant differences were found among the teachers, indicating their students' attitudes toward reading and the number of books they checked out were affected by the booktalks. For a majority of the books covered in the talks, circulation stayled at above average levels for three months following the presentations. Freshmen students checked out more of the presented titles than students in the other three grades and girls (especially those at the higher reading levels) checked out far more of the titles than did boys at the school.

566.   Chauncey, Carole Agatha (Ph.D., Case Western Reserve University, 1987). **An Assessment of Index Term Ranking.** 252p. Order no. AAD88-02457.

PURPOSE: Concerned that index terms are not equally content bearing or equally dependable in promoting the retrieval of relevant documents, Chauncey examined indexing practices to determine (1) the degree of agreement in selected indexing terms, (2) when the most content-bearing terms are assigned, and (3) which terms have the highest agreement in specific parts of the indexed text.

PROCEDURE: To collect data for this study, Chauncey had indexers participate in two tests: exhaustivity-time experiment (productivity test) and inter-indexer consistency versus exhaustivity.

FINDINGS: Chauncey found (1) a direct relationship between selection time and exhaustivity and (2) an inverse relationship between inter-indexer consistency and exhaustivity. Specifically, as selection time increased, so did exhaustivity; but, as exhaustivity increased, inter-indexer consistency decreased.

567. Craver, Kathleen Woods (Ph.D., University of Illinois at Urbana-Champaign, 1987). **The Influence of the Availability of an Academic Online Catalog on the Use of Academic Libraries by College-Bound High School Seniors.** 241p. Order no. AAD87-21619.

PURPOSE: The purpose of this study was to measure the impact that access to an academic online catalog in a school library had on the use of library materials and facilities by college-bound high school seniors.

PROCEDURE: To collect data for this study, Craver looked at the research bibliographies prepared by 73 high school seniors who did not have access to an academic online catalog (pre-online catalog students), bibliographies prepared by 80 high school seniors who did have access (post-online catalog students), and questionnaires completed by 114 students in both these groups. To determine if there were any statistically significant differences in the library use of the pre- and post-online catalog groups, Carver calculated aggregate totals, t-tests, and analyses of variance.

FINDINGS: Post-online students cited more sources, particularly sources from an undergraduate academic library, more periodicals from the academic library, but fewer public library books and periodicals than did the pre-online catalog students.

CONCLUSIONS: Access to an academic online catalog in a school library significantly influenced the use of academic libraries by college-bound high school students.

RECOMMENDATIONS: School librarians should consider adding segments on online catalog use and use of other types of libraries to their library instruction units, and they should consider joining a multitype network that has computerized access to bibliographic materials.

568. Dalrymple, Prudence Ward (Ph.D., University of Wisconsin at Madison, 1987). **Retrieval by Reformulation in Two Library Catalogs: Toward a Cognitive Model of Searching Behavior.** 326p. Order no. AAD87-16512.

PURPOSE: Drawing on the model known as reformulation, first articulated by Williams and Tou in 1982, Dalrymple looked at an academic library to test the analogy between patterns of retrieval from human long-term memory and information retrieval from bibliographic databases.

PROCEDURE: Forty students at the University of Wisconsin were randomly assigned to two groups: one to use the card catalog and the other to use the online catalog. They were asked to complete a series of five searches on specific subjects.

FINDINGS: Students in the online group were more persistent and more frequently engaged in query reformulations, while students in the card catalog group obtained larger retrieval sets and had more favorable search assessments. When it came to attitudes, however, no significant differences between the two groups were discovered. While searching, the students were asked to "think aloud" during the process; Dalrymple analyzed the transcripts of these verbal protocols to identify reformulations, to further operationalize the concept of reformulation, and to assess the utility of protocol analysis in information retrieval research.

569. Davis, H. Scott (Ed.D., East Texas State University, 1987). **Library Instruction in Five Southern States.** 183p. Order no. AAD88-08005.

PURPOSE: In this dissertation, Davis collected data from schools in five southern states on the following topics: types of library instruction, format emphasis (print or nonprint), staffing used in process, evaluation procedures used, school administrator's perceptions of library instruction, and the role of state departments of education.

PROCEDURE: Questionnaires were sent to three groups: 593 school librarians (48 percent response rate), 593 school administrators (52 percent response rate), and the five state departments of education (100 percent response rate).

FINDINGS: Most schools (88 percent) offered a library instruction program, which was generally informal (61 percent), provided in English courses (90 percent), focused on print rather than nonprint materials (78 percent), conducted by librarians (77 percent), and periodically evaluated (72 percent). At least half of the school administrators surveyed reported they were familiar with library instruction as a library service and perceived it as important. Library instruction was required by three of the southern states studied and encouraged by the other two.

570.   DeVinney, Gemma (Ph.D., State University of New York at Buffalo, 1987). **The 1965-1974 Faculty Status Movement as a Professionalization Effort with Social Movement Characteristics: A Case Study of the State University of New York.** 332p. Order no. AAD87-27687.

PURPOSE: This historical case study was based on Bucher and Strauss's conceptualization of segmentation within professions and examined the faculty status movement among librarians at the State University of New York (SUNY) between 1965 and 1974.

PROCEDURES: DeVinney surveyed the literature, used historical research methods, and employed a case-study approach to collect data for this dissertation.

FINDINGS: While academic librarians have been attempting to achieve faculty status since the turn of the century, the movement accelerated between 1965 and 1975. At the State University of New York during this period, the activity was conducted in four distinct stages: (1) between 1965 and mid-1968, SUNY librarians successfully lobbied to receive academic rank, with voting privileges and a tenure system; (2) between mid-1968 and the end of 1970, SUNY librarians established the SUNY Librarians Association (SUNYLA) to extend the definition of faculty status to include academic year appointments and salary parity with classroom faculty members; (3) between the beginning of 1971 and mid-1973, SUNYLA attempted to convince the faculty bargaining agent (Senate Professional Association) to fight for full faculty status for librarians; (4) from mid-1973 through the end of 1974, SUNY librarians concluded that full faculty status for librarians was unlikely and concentrated on converting SUNYLA from a lobbying group to more of a professional association.

RECOMMENDATIONS: The findings in this case study can be used as the basis for future research on the history of the faculty status movement in the United States.

571.   Droessler, William Frederick (Ph.D., Florida State University, 1987). **The Relationship of Collection Development Policies and Microsoftware Collections in Small Academic Libraries: Six Case Studies.** 160p. Order no. AAD88-02817.

PURPOSE: This study was conducted to determine the effect collection development policies had on the development of microsoftware collections in six small academic libraries.

PROCEDURE: The study was conducted in two stages. First, 436 small academic institutions were surveyed, to collect data on the use of microcomputers in their libraries. Then, six libraries were selected from the survey group to be studied in-depth. Of these, three had small microsoftware collections and three had more extensive holdings.

FINDINGS: The majority of libraries (four) either had no collection policy for software programs or were in the process of revising their existing policies. The other two libraries had policies in place. Those libraries that planned for microcomputer collections and services in their collection development policies were more organized in projecting these services. Of the factors that related to the development of collection development policies and software collections, the most important were financial resources and library leadership.

CONCLUSIONS: Libraries with software collection development policies had software collections that "mirrored the collection development policy."

572.   Edyburn, Dave Lee (Ph.D., University of Illinois at Urbana-Champaign, 1987). **An Evaluation of the Information Retrieval Skills of Students with and without Learning Handicaps Using Printed and Electronic Encyclopedias.** 270p. Order no. AAD88-03029.

PURPOSE: In this experimental study, Edyburn compared (1) student use of printed and electronic encyclopedias, (2) student attitudes toward printed and electronic encyclopedias, and (3) effects of interface and task difficulty on information retrieval from the encyclopedias.

PROCEDURE: Using a repeated measures Latin square design, Edyburn randomly selected and assigned fifteen junior high school students without learning disabilities and thirteen junior high school students with learning disabilities to three different treatment groups (printed encyclopedias, electronic encyclopedias with menus, and electronic encyclopedias with commands). Data were collected on IQ, spelling ability, reference skills, keyboarding speed, and attitudes. A number of statistical methods were used to analyze the data, including regression analysis.

FINDINGS: Students using the menu driven electronic encyclopedia had greater information retrieval success than did students using the command driven version but not greater than using the printed encyclopedia. Greater success was also found on assigned versus self-selected tasks and on simple versus complex tasks. The best predictors of retrieval success proved to be reference skills and keyboarding speed. Although no relationship was found between attitudes and type of encyclopedia used, it was found that students with learning disabilities had more positive attitudes than the nonhandicapped students after each of the three treatments.

573. Engle, June Lester (D.L., Columbia University, 1987). **The State Library Agency as a Policy Actor: An Examination of the Role of the State Library Agency in the Development of Statewide Multitype Library Networks in Four Southeastern States.** 706p. Order no. AAD88-09346.

PURPOSE: Focusing on the period 1976 through 1982 and on the topic of statewide multitype library networks, Engle examined (1) the extent of leadership provided by library agencies in Georgia, Kentucky, Tennessee, and Alabama and (2) the players involved in the planning for the multitype library networks.

PROCEDURE: Document analysis, interviewing, and transient observation were the techniques used to collect the data for this study. A public policy framework was constructed to analyze the data.

FINDINGS: Engle found that the historical role of the state library agencies, their relative power and visibility in the public and academic library arenas, their willingness to use their resources to enhance a leadership role, and their success in creating permanent relationships with various library segments directly related to the balance of power between these agencies and other major "policy actors" in the library community. Other important factors she found to influence the agencies' ability to assume leadership roles included the political relationship between the agencies and their host environments, the perceived autonomy and power of the agencies, the extent of the legislative mandate, and an agency director's personality and style. When it came to the involvement of the various types of libraries, Engle found that structure and cohesion within the various library sectors and libraries' receptiveness to multitype planning/resource sharing were the major factors. As for the implementation of national policy in the library environment, Engle isolated four significant elements: policy consensus, policy priority, the implementation environment, and the available leadership.

CONCLUSIONS: Politics, power, and personality are the most important factors influencing the policy role of state library agencies.

574. Fenske, Ruth Elizabeth (Ph.D., University of Michigan, 1987). **Professional Socialization of Beginning Librarians as Measured by Involvement in Professional Activities.** 373p. Order no. AAD87-12112.

PURPOSE: The purpose of this study was to assess the degree of professional socialization of beginning librarians (who graduated in 1978) in Michigan and Illinois and to determine the relationship between their socialization and work environment.

PROCEDURE: Data were collected from 196 graduates of library schools at the University of Michigan and the University of Illinois as well as from a representative sample of their employing institutions. For the purposes of this study, professional socialization was defined as respondents' involvement in professional activities, and work environment was defined as organizational encouragement, supervisory encouragement, and supervisory level of socialization. Drawing on previous literature and social science theories, Fenske developed a model to use in examining the data, analyzed the data using numerous descriptive data techniques, and tested the study hypotheses by using Spearman's rho, Cramer's V, and asymmetric lambda.

FINDINGS: Fenske found weak relationships between (1) the supervisor's perception of organizational encouragement and the supervisor's desire to be active in the profession, (2) the beginning librarian's perception of organizational encouragement and desire of the librarian to be active in the profession, and (3) the supervisor's level of professional activity and the beginning librarian's level of professional activity. Of the various types of libraries/librarians studied here, academic libraries/librarians most closely fit the hypothesized model.

CONCLUSIONS: After an analysis of the open-ended question responses, Fenske concluded that the organization encouragement scale used in the study may have validity problems.

RECOMMENDATIONS: A coordinated series of case studies should be conducted to further explore reasons for the differences by type of library reported in this study.

575. Fleming, Lois Delavan (Ph.D., Florida State University, 1987). **Linkage Practices and Procedures Used by a Community-Based Educational Agency: Case Studies of Six Public Libraries.** 301p. Order no. AAD88-02818.

PURPOSE: Using the bond issue referendum as the medium, Fleming investigated the practices and procedures that public libraries use to link with their community.

PROCEDURE: To collect data on the practices and procedures used by six selected public libraries during bond referendum campaigns, Fleming reviewed community and library documents, checked local newspaper clippings, conducted on-site personal interviews, and performed direct observation.

FINDINGS: The most important factor in the successful passage of a bond issue turned out to be the status of the community's economy.

CONCLUSIONS: There were common linkage practices in both successful and unsuccessful referenda campaigns; they differed only in extensiveness. The kinds of linkages practiced were more important than the number used.

576. Goodin, M. Elspeth (Ph.D., Rutgers University, 1987). **The Transferability of Library Research Skills from High School to College.** 186p. Order no. AAD88-03480.

PURPOSE: This study was conducted to answer three research questions: (1) Can a library instruction program be developed that teaches high school seniors the search strategies/information skills that will be useful as college freshmen? (2) Can these skills be reflected in a research paper? and (3) Can the transferability of these skills be measured?

PROCEDURE: The library instruction program used in this experimental study was based on the recommendations of sixty-two college faculty members (who responded to a questionnaire requesting information on library-related course requirements). The 159 study participants came from college preparatory English classes at two comparable high schools and were divided into two groups, one control and one experimental. The experimental group was given first a pretest to measure basic college library information knowledge, next lessons on the research process, then a college-level research paper assignment, and finally a posttest on basic college library information knowledge. The control group received the pretest, the research paper assignment, and the posttest. In addition, all participants were given a Likert-type attitudinal questionnaire to complete.

FINDINGS: The experimental group participants received significantly higher posttest scores than did control group participants. The knowledge acquired was reflected in the research paper assignment. In fact, college students who had been in the experimental groups as high school seniors reported that they were able to utilize the research skills they had learned in the program on the college level. No significant difference was found in the attitudes of experimental and control group participants.

CONCLUSIONS: Goodin offered two major conclusions. First, because no significant difference between the groups was found on the attitude scale questionnaire, Goodin questioned the ability of the questionnaire to adequately measure the transferability of research skills from high school to college. Second, in Goodin's view, when high school librarians make the research setting approachable, they become a linking agent between high school and college libraries.

577. Gusts, Lilita Vija (D.L., Columbia University, 1987). **Oral History as an Information Source: A Descriptive Study of How Oral History Evolved in Fourteen North American Programs.** 521p. Order no. AAD88-09358.

PURPOSE: This study focused on oral history collections and examined how they were created, processed, and maintained.

PROCEDURE: Data were collected from a representative sample of twelve American and two Canadian oral history programs on their goals, governance, purposes, operational procedures, management, funding, and cooperative activities. Three instruments were used to collect the data: institutional profile questionnaire, interview schedule, and observation checklist.

FINDINGS: Leadership proved to be the most important factor in establishing and maintaining an oral history collection. The funding available influenced which subjects were documented and which methodologies were employed. Factors found to associate with the creation and processing of oral history interviews included the programs' personnel, purposes, and relationships with persons interviewed. The most important factor influencing the continuation of the oral history process was found to be the agreements entered into as a by-product of the joint creation of interviews. Considerable variation was found in the surveyed programs' application of oral history purposes to the interviews created, the format of the interviews deposited in a research collection, and the publicly available information about the circumstances of the interviews.

CONCLUSIONS: Users, librarians, and archivists need more education about the usefulness and usability of oral history resources.

578. Hjellvik, Jenny (Ph.D., Texas Woman's University, 1987). **Education for Librarianship in Norway: A Historical Survey.** 187p. Order no. AAD87-15008.

PURPOSE: The purpose of this study was to trace the establishment, growth, and development of library science education in Norway from 1905 (the date of Norway's independence) to 1985.

PROCEDURE: Data for this study were collected from primary and secondary sources.

FINDINGS: Library science education in Norway progressed through three clearly defined stages: (1) informal instruction that libraries provided for their own employees, (2) short courses offered by large academic libraries, and (3) formal training offered by the Norwegian School of Library and Information Science (Statens Bibliotekhøgskole). Although the need for formal library education was recognized early in the twentieth century, the economic problems of the 1920s and 1930s delayed the establishment of a national library school until 1940. Since that time, the organization and content of the program of study offered there have changed substantively, from an emphasis on the practical to the more theoretical. In 1984, the program was expanded to include computer/information science as well as library science.

579. Holmes, Gloria Price (Ph.D., Florida State University, 1987). **An Analysis of the Information-Seeking Behavior of Science Teachers in Selected Secondary Public Schools in Florida.** 203p. Order no. AAD87-11722.

PURPOSE: This study focused on the following information-seeking behaviors of selected secondary school science teachers in Duval County, Florida: information sources used, characteristics of information sources used, and factors related to selection of information resources.

PROCEDURE: Questionnaires were sent to eighty biology/chemistry teachers at selected senior high schools in Duval County, Florida (85 percent response rate). The hypotheses proposed in this study were tested using chi-square analysis at the .05 level of significance.

FINDINGS: The surveyed teachers relied extensively on textbooks, whatever the subject taught, the level of course taught, or the teacher's professional or personal characteristics. While the teachers tended to rate academic libraries as excellent, they used their personal libraries more (because it took less time to obtain the information). In the teachers' view, a model information system would provide convenience, accessibility, currency, relevance, automation, and appropriate staff.

CONCLUSIONS: School library/media specialists and other information providers could use the data collected in this study to plan, design, and maintain more efficient and effective information systems.

580. Hughes, Sue Margaret (Ph.D., Texas Woman's University, 1987). **A Study of the Elements Contributing to the Success of Regional**

Publishers in Texas, 1975-1985. 152p. Order no. AAD88-16796.

PURPOSE: In addition to looking at the factors that have contributed to the success of publishers in Texas between 1975 and 1985, Hughes examined the critical successes and number of copies printed/sold of individual titles.

PROCEDURE: Questionnaires were sent to publishers in Texas, collecting data on quality and quantity of monographs published, selection criteria and policies, marketing strategies, social value of books published, and book awards won.

FINDINGS: Compared to East Coast publishers, those in Texas had a late start. Hughes found that the most important element in successful publishing in Texas was the company's owner. There were few ownership changes in Texas in the period under study and that made for continuity and stability of publishing operations. Most owners started their publishing companies for one of four reasons: to make information available to a wider audience, to produce quality books, to support new authors, or to cover subjects not previously addressed. In general, the owners were motivated by the opportunity to control personally the publishing process. They enjoyed making decisions themselves and took great pride in the publishing results.

581. Maciuszko, Kathleen Lynn (Ph.D., Case Western Reserve University, 1987). **Hardcopy versus Online Searching: A Study in Retrieval Effectiveness.** 320p. Order no. AAD88-02459.

PURPOSE: Using an experimental design, Maciuszko compared the subject retrieval effectiveness of hard copy and online searching.

PROCEDURE: The methodology used in this study involved (1) a set of twenty-two questions submitted by six college students (covering the areas of biology, business, and popular interest) and (2) public and academic librarians searching the questions in the hard copy indexes and online counterparts (through WILSONLINE) of *Biological and Agricultural Index*, *Business Periodicals Index*, and *Readers' Guide to Periodical Literature* (sources chosen because they were intended for the general public rather than a specialized audience).

FINDINGS: There was little duplication of citations between the two searching modes. Retrieval results were low for both. One mode was not more effective than the other in subject searching for bibliographic information.

CONCLUSIONS: Regardless of which searching mode was used, the effectiveness of information retrieval systems was not adequate.

582. Mann, Carol Ann Pirrung (Ed.D., East Texas State University, 1987). **The Identification of Evaluation Criteria for Learning Resources Specialists in Texas.** 214p. Order no. AAD87-25306.

PURPOSE: Mann used input from school principals, district library supervisors, and learning resources specialists to consider appropriate evaluation criteria for learning resources specialists in Texas, including—for the first time—computer competencies.

PROCEDURE: Mann presented forty-one state certification competencies for learning resources specialists plus six validated microcomputer competencies to a panel of forty-two district library supervisors, fifty principals, and seventy-eight librarians working on the elementary or secondary school level in Texas. The participants were asked to rate the competencies on two scales: importance for evaluation and respondents' ability to evaluate. The data were analyzed using factor analyses, one-way analyses of variance, and t-tests.

FINDINGS: Two sets of factors were identified as important in the evaluation of school librarians' job performance (in order of importance): organization and management (four traditional library tasks, including record keeping, collection development, and reference service) and learning resources development (twelve tasks, most of which related to technological or research duties). The respondents indicated they were better able to evaluate librarians on learning resource development tasks than on organization or management functions.

CONCLUSIONS: The same items that the respondents chose as important for evaluating the job performance of school librarians (record keeping, materials selection, acquisitions, and circulation) were also chosen by the respondents as "evaluable." Audiovisual and computer-related job functions were not agreed upon as evaluation criteria.

583. McDonald, Joseph Andrew, Jr. (Ph.D., Drexel University, 1987). **Academic Library Effectiveness: An Organizational Perspective.** 259p. Order no. AAD88-06515.

PURPOSE: The purpose of this study was to establish criteria for measuring academic library organizational effectiveness. For the purposes of this study, effectiveness was defined as "successful organizational transactions as perceived by a group of specified library decision makers."

PROCEDURE: Effectiveness was studied from an organizational (rather than program, personal, or supra-organization) perspective.

Data were collected from 131 libraries in colleges or universities in six middle Atlantic states and the District of Columbia that did not offer a doctoral degree.

FINDINGS: Library effectiveness may be a multidimensional construct; at least thirteen major dimensions were identified in the study. Libraries varied considerably in their level of organizational effectiveness.

584. McKee, Nancy Carol (Ph.D., Florida State University, 1987). **The Depiction of the Physically Disabled in Preadolescent Contemporary Realistic Fiction: A Content Analysis.** 167p. Order no. AAD87-11730.

PURPOSE: Using content analysis, McKee examined the treatment of disabled characters in contemporary realistic fiction written for the preadolescent.

PROCEDURE: The depiction of disabled characters in fiction books written from 1965 through 1974 was compared with the depiction in books written from 1975 through 1984. A total of ninety-seven books was analyzed.

FINDINGS: From 1965 through 1974, most of the disabled characters were teenage white male students who were orthopedically impaired. When females were portrayed, they tended to be visually impaired. The stereotyped image portrayed was one of "Super Crip," an individual who excelled in all endeavors or had extraordinary abilities. From 1975 through 1984, the majority of disabled characters were females with health impairments (e.g., asthma, cancer, diabetes, and hemophilia). Male disabled characters, when presented, continued to be orthopedically impaired. The stereotyped image portrayed in the literature changed from "Super Crip" to "Own Worst Enemy."

CONCLUSIONS: During the twenty-year period under study, the number of stereotypes in the literature not only decreased but also became less negative. A greater variety of disabilities was portrayed in the literature published between 1975 and 1984 than in the earlier years covered in the study.

585. Mills, Emma Joyce White (Ph.D., Florida State University, 1987). **An Examination of Procedures and Practices in the Selection of Black Materials for Children's Collections of Public Libraries in the United States.** 227p. Order no. AAD88-05676.

PURPOSE: Mills conducted this survey to identify factors that could relate to the selection and/or acquisition of black materials for children.

PROCEDURE: To collect data for this study, Mills sent questionnaires to 202 public library employees (not just children's librarians). Frequency and percentage distributions, means, and standard deviations were used to analyze data on the following categories: selection cycle, types of materials selected (e.g., reference books, periodicals); holdings of black materials by subject categories; reviewing sources; problems in selecting black materials; budget allocations for types of library materials; and holdings in the libraries' children's collections.

FINDINGS: After looking at five factors that might influence the selection and purchase of children's materials (reviews, children, parents, teachers, and library staff), Mills found that there was no significant difference between long-term and short-term public library goals for the selection of books about minority groups. Generally, the respondents tended to exclude materials because they estimated patrons would never call for them, despite the fact that the literature shows that not every item in the library's collection will ever be consulted or circulated.

CONCLUSIONS: There may be a discrepancy between the concept of "cultural diversity" and librarians' willingness to select and purchase black materials.

586.   Mitchell, Eugene Stephen (Ph.D., Rugers University, 1987). **Leadership Style in Academic Libraries: A Test of Fiedler's Contingency Model of Leadership Effectiveness.** 185p. Order no. AAD87-23277.

PURPOSE: To test the validity of Fiedler's Contingency Model of Leadership Effectiveness, Mitchell examined the leadership style of academic library department heads.

PROCEDURE: The questionnaires sent to 278 academic library department heads in the areas of acquisitions, catalog maintenance and cataloging, circulation, collection development, processing, and reference (75 percent response rate) consisted of Fiedler's Least Preferred Co-Worker Scale and his situational control scales, to collect information on leader motivation, leader-member relations, task structure, and position power; Morse and Wagner's Managerial Performance Rating Scale, to determine the effectiveness of leader performance; and Bare's Group Effectiveness Scale, to determine effectiveness of group performances. Mitchell used analysis of variance and stepwise multiple regression analysis on the data collected through the questionnaires to test the hypotheses in the study.

FINDINGS: There were four major findings in the study: (1) academic library departments exhibited different types of situational control; (2) there was no relationship between leadership effectiveness and the type of leader motivation (task-motivated leaders versus relationship-motivated leaders); (3) when managerial performance was considered, situational demands varied with task structure, position power, and least preferred co-worker; and (4) when group performance measures were considered, situational demands varied with task structure and position power.

CONCLUSIONS: The contingency model, as tested in this study, did not extend to academic libraries.

RECOMMENDATIONS: A model based on the effect of task structure (and other factors) might be useful in predicting the effectiveness of academic library department heads.

587.   Murgai, Sarla R. (Ed.D., University of Tennessee, 1987). **Managerial Motivation and Career Aspirations of Library/Information Science Students.** 162p. Order no. AAD88-02687.

PURPOSE: This study examined the relationship between managerial achievement-motivation and such factors as gender, age, marital status, educational attainment, experience, mobility, professional development, and career commitment.

PROCEDURE: After reviewing the literature on the status of women in library and information service, Murgai mailed a questionnaire to students enrolled in eleven southeastern library/information science graduate schools.

FINDINGS: For the majority of motivation criteria studied, no significant differences were found between male and female respondents. Women did score significantly higher than males on future orientation, social need, and perserverance, and males scored significantly higher on achievement-motivation.

CONCLUSIONS: The differences in career attainment and salaries earned by males and females could not be explained by lack of motivation or desire to achieve.

588.   Oldenburg, Adele Louise (Ph.D., Florida State University, 1987). **The Role, Scope, and Nature of Archives in Two-Year Institutions of Higher Education in the Southeastern United States.** 210p. Order no. AAD88-05683.

PURPOSE: The purpose of this study was to trace the historical development of archives, particularly the role, scope, and nature of archival collections in two-year colleges.

PROCEDURE: In addition to collecting data through a modified historical research approach (using books, documents, articles, and database searches), Oldenburg conducted a two-stage survey, sending questionnaires (based on the instrument used by Burckel and Cook in 1982) to 320 public and private two-year colleges in eleven southeastern states.

FINDINGS: Neither public nor private two-year colleges put a high priority on archives. Further, the archive collections were never utilized to their fullest. Still, most of the surveyed institutions indicated an interest in expanding archival functions in the future.

CONCLUSIONS: The findings in this study corresponded to those reported by Burckel and Cook when they examined college and university archives in 1982.

RECOMMENDATIONS: Oldenburg put forward three major recommendations: (1) to conduct a follow-up study within ten-years that would chart the progress of archival activity in the United States; (2) to survey the remaining two-year colleges for archival activity, under the sponsorship of each state's archivist association; and (3) to see that the regional surveys are collected and published by the Society of American Archivists.

589. Ostrom, Janice Christine (Ph.D., Kansas State University, 1987). **Continuing Library Education: Practices and Preferences of Kansas School Librarians.** 192p. Order no. AAD87-15233.

PURPOSE: This study was conducted to determine the continuing education preferences of school librarians in Kansas during 1985-1986.

PROCEDURE: Ostrom constructed a twenty-nine-item questionnaire to collect data from 250 randomly selected school librarians in Kansas (half of whom belonged to the Kansas Association of School Librarians and half of whom did not) on the following topics: type of continuing education preferred, appropriate agency to provide continuing education, obstacles to participation in continuing education programs, benefits expected from participation in continuing education programs, perceived degree of support from employing districts, and appropriate role of professional associations in the continuing education process. Responses were received from 172 librarians (69 percent response rate). To analyze the collected data, Ostrom used frequencies, means, standard deviations, and t-tests.

FINDINGS: The respondents expressed strong interest in continuing education opportunities, particularly those offered during the summer or in the evening and those offered as workshops, institutes, seminars, short courses, professional conferences, off-campus semester courses, and in-service days. They did not perceive their school districts or immediate supervisors as sharing their degree of interest,

they felt constrained by time and finances, and they wished their employing districts would give them leave to attend continuing education programs. They looked to both academic institutions and the Kansas Association of School Librarians to provide their continuing education opportunities.

590. Ravelli, Joseph Louis (Ph.D., Rutgers University, 1987). **An Historical Analysis of Academic Library Development in the Late Nineteenth-Century: Case Studies of the Libraries of New Jersey's Universities with Colonial Origins.** 369p. Order no. AAD87-23299.

PURPOSE: Ravelli examined the critical forces at work during the late nineteenth century that affected the development of libraries at the two academic institutions in New Jersey with colonial origins: Princeton University and Rutgers University.

PROCEDURE: Primary and secondary sources were used to collect data on Frederick Vinton, Princeton librarian from 1873 to 1889 under university President James McCosh, and Irving S. Upson, Rutgers librarian from 1884 to 1906 under President Merrill Gates and President Austin Scott. As part of the methodology, Ravelli drew on the ideas and activities of Justin Winson and Melvil Dewey to develop a model of progressive academic library policies. He then used the model to examine the libraries and library policies of Upson and Vinton.

FINDINGS: The most important factors affecting the development of progressive academic librarianship in the late nineteenth century were found to be European ideology, institutional acceptance of new educational approaches, strong administrative leadership, and adequate financial resources. During the study period, Princeton enjoyed strong leadership and financial support from private benefactors. The school had a full-time professional librarian, a healthy budget for library materials, and a separate library building. In comparison, Rutgers had a weak leadership and limited financial support; it lacked the commitment, financial resources, and library quality that characterized Princeton's operations.

591. Rider, John Robert (Ed.D., University of Oregon, 1987). **A Film Selection Aid for Medium-Sized Academic Libraries: A Comparative Survey of Academic Film Collections.** 110p. Order no. AAD88-00550.

PURPOSE: In this citation study, Rider investigated the possibility that a core list of film titles could be prepared by analyzing the film collection lists issued by mid-sized academic institutions.

PROCEDURE: To identify basic holdings for a film collection, Rider calculated the frequency with which titles appeared in the film catalogs of fifty mid-sized educational institutions with similar structures, course offerings, populations, and educational purposes.

FINDINGS: By using citation analysis, Rider identified 122 of the most frequently listed film titles. In the bibliography included in the dissertation, Rider listed these titles in order of their frequency as well as by subject and also annotated their contents. In a separate section, Rider listed the other titles in the catalogs that had frequencies below the 122 cut-off point.

CONCLUSIONS: The average age of films in the academic library collections analyzed in this study was twenty-one years. The average size of the film/video collections was 818 titles.

592. Rieck, Donald Arthur (Ph.D., Iowa State University, 1987). **Video Format Influences and Trends in University Film Rental Libraries: An Investigation of Selection and Evaluation Procedures.** 392p. Order no. AAD88-05132.

PURPOSE: The focus of this study was on the evaluation and selection processes of film rental libraries in academic institutions.

PROCEDURE: A two-step data collection procedure was used. First, a fifteen-member delphi panel of experts (1) forecasted ten- and twenty-five-year trends for rental libraries and (2) assessed the importance of current and future evaluation criteria and selection approaches. Second, a questionnaire was sent to 204 film/video rental library directors (73 usable responses).

FINDINGS: Moderate changes were forecast for the next ten years and major changes for the next twenty-five years, including the obsolescence of the 16mm format, the utilization of electronic distribution methods, and the possible extinction of the film rental library.

CONCLUSIONS: These findings have implications for the distribution/production of media, the operation of rental libraries, and the conduct of collection development research.

593. Roy, Loriene (Ph.D., University of Illinois at Urbana-Champaign, 1987). **An Investigation of the Use of Weeding and Displays as Methods to Increase the Stock Turnover Rate in Small Public Libraries.** 267p. Order no. AAD87-21745.

PURPOSE: In this experimental study, Roy tested three hypotheses: (1) weeding will increase a variation of stock turnover rate (STR) referred to as STR A/B, (2) multiple displays will significantly increase STR A/B only if weeding is used, and (3) the greatest increase in STR A/B will occur only when both treatments happen simultaneously.

PROCEDURE: To test these hypotheses, Roy conducted the experiment at eight small public libraries in Illinois. In two of the libraries, weeding took place (11 percent of the adult circulating book collection was temporarily moved to storage); in two other libraries, up to five displays of adult circulating books were introduced simultaneously; in the third set of two libraries, both weeding and displays were instituted at the same time; and in the remaining pair of libraries (which served as the control group), neither weeding nor displays were attempted. Analyses of variance and paired t-tests were used to analyze the data collected.

FINDINGS: When weeding was used alone, there was a 9 percent increase in STR A/B; with weeding and displays together, STR A/B more than doubled, to 23 percent. Nevertheless, when analysis of variance tests was performed, no significant difference in STR A/B among the four pairs of libraries was found. However, simultaneous weeding and book displays resulted in significant increases in circulation. When paired t-tests were run, it was found that while the circulation of particular books increased when the books were displayed, overall book displays did not tend to increase total circulation.

CONCLUSIONS: The usefulness of STR as an in-house evaluation of performance might be in question. Libraries interested in increasing STR might try supplementing multiple displays with more stringent and continual weeding. Other approaches to increasing STR should also be attempted.

594. Ribin, Richard Evan (Ph.D., University of Illinois at Urbana-Champaign, 1987). **A Study of Employee Turnover of Full Time Public Librarians in Moderately-Large and Large Size Public Libraries in Seven Midwestern States.** 320p. Order no. AAD87-21746.

PURPOSE: Recognizing the value of turnover as a measure of organizational health, Rubin examined turnover activity in selected public libraries in the Midwest in order to establish baseline data on turnover rates for these libraries and to analyze the relationships between turnover rates, turnover behavior, and gender.

PROCEDURE: Rubin collected data on the characteristics of thirty-one public libraries (e.g., staff size, beginning salary, budget per capita) and 421 individual turnovers that occurred between 1980 and the beginning of 1985 (e.g., gender, salary, marital status, reason for leaving).

FINDINGS: Compared to other professions, the turnover rate in librarianship is low. Although females are stereotyped as having higher turnover rates (because of the conflicting demands of family and job), Rubin found no relationship between gender and turnover. However, the data did suggest that among librarians leaving their jobs, females were more likely to go for family reasons than were males.

CONCLUSIONS: Gender did not prove to be a good predictor of either turnover rate or why librarians leave their jobs.

595. Russell, Thyra Kaye (Ph.D., Southern Illinois University at Carbondale, 1987). **Job Sharing in Illinois Libraries.** 154p. Order no. AAD87-28299.

PURPOSE: In this study, Russell focused on the process of job sharing (where one full-time job is divided between two people who voluntarily share the responsibilities and benefits of the position) in order to identify the extent of job sharing in Illinois and to determine the reactions of job sharers and their directors to the arrangement.

PROCEDURE: To determine the number of job sharing arrangements in Illinois, questionnaires were sent to 1,277 directors in all types of libraries; 875 directors responded and identified 69 job sharing positions. Follow-up questionnaires were then sent to the 69 job sharers (61 percent response rate) and their library directors (84 percent response rate). Frequency distributions were used to analyze the data collected in the survey.

FINDINGS: In general, job sharers tended to be married women with children, to earn a salary of less than $5,000 per year, and to work without fringe benefits. Nevertheless, most job sharers reported they liked their work (particularly the "flexibility"), found the arrangement effective, and wanted to continue in a job sharing position. Similarly, library directors were satisfied with the job sharing arrangements in their libraries and believed the practice should be maintained. Both groups agreed the best area in which to develop job sharing positions is public services (especially in circulation departments).

596. Schmidt, Elizabeth Guinan (Ph.D., Florida State University, 1987). **A Quasi-Experimental Study of the Effects of Teacher Bibliographic Instruction on the Library Skills of College Bound High School Students.** 195p. Order no. AAD87-11740.

PURPOSE: Using a quasi-experimental design, Schmidt examined the effect that library instruction given to teachers had on their students' library skills.

PROCEDURE: College-bound high school students of English and mathematics were placed in experimental or control groups. The teachers of the experimental groups took a self-directed instruction unit on analyzing reference queries and selecting reference tools; the teachers of the control groups were not given any library instruction. Analyses of covariance were calculated to determine if the students in the experimental groups showed greater improvement in their library skills and library use than did students in the control groups. The .10 level of significance was used to test Schmidt's hypotheses.

FINDINGS: No significant relationship was found between teachers' library instruction and their students' library skills or use. However, the library skills of the experimental groups' teachers improved significantly after receiving library instruction. The improvement was greater for experimental English teachers than for mathematics teachers.

597. Scott, Willodene Alexander (Ph.D., George Peabody College for Teachers of Vanderbilt University, 1987). **A Comparison of Role Perceptions of the School Library Media Specialist among Library Media Educators, School Library Media Specialists, Principals, and Classroom Teachers.** 153p. Order no. AAD86-24212.

PURPOSE: Focusing on the role of school library media specialists, Scott collected data on the perceptions of them held by four groups of educators: library media educators, school library media specialists, principals, and classroom teachers.

PROCEDURE: Questionnaires (based on the Role Expectations of Library Media Specialists Instrument) were sent to education personnel in a large metropolitan public school system and in public/private institutions of higher education. One-way analysis of variance was used to measure differences in perceptions among the four educator groups as well as five teaching levels and five degree levels on the following dependent variables: technological media role, interpersonal relations role, leadership role, instructional role, and clerical role.

FINDINGS: The four groups studied held similar views on most of the school library media specialist's role indicators. However, when it came to the interpersonal and instructional roles, teachers held significantly different perceptions than did the other three groups. A direct relationship was found between education and role perception; the higher the academic degree earned, the less variance in role perception.

598.   Seavey, Charles Alden (Ph.D., University of Wisconsin at Madison, 1987). **Public Library Systems in Wisconsin, 1970-1980: An Evaluation.** 265p. Order no. AAD88-01500.

PURPOSE: This study was conducted to determine the impact of the 1971 Wisconsin enabling legislation creating public library systems on levels of community library service in the state.

PROCEDURE: Seavey measured five components of library service: circulation per capita, expenditures per capita, full-time employee rate, turnover rate, and a library service index (calculated by combining the first four factors).

FINDINGS: Statistical analysis supported the hypothesized increases in expenditures per capita, full-time employee rate, and the library service index during the 1970s. No relationship was found between levels of library service and (1) conditions of system administration, (2) time of adoption of the system structure, (3) number of counties, or (4) services offered (e.g., direct circulation services, direct financial support). Levels of library service were found to relate to the following socio-economic variables: urban population, gross local government revenues, and library expenditures (which together accounted for 66 percent of the variance in level of library service).

599.   Walls, Francine Elizabeth (Ed.D., Seattle University, 1987). **Current Perspective and Ethical Concerns of Information Intermediaries in the Pacific Northwest.** 152p. Order no. AAD87-20581.

PURPOSE: In this study, Walls focused on the characteristics and ethical concerns of information intermediaries (those who "search for, prepare or analyze information for others, on demand, and for a fee") in the Pacific Northwest.

PROCEDURE: Questionnaires were sent to information intermediaries in the Pacific Northwest (forty usable responses) and a telephone interview was conducted with a random sample of them (twelve usable responses).

FINDINGS: Most of the respondents were female, business owners, graduates of library schools, and ethical in intent. Most of the information intermediary firms were sole proprietorships (located in Washington or British Columbia) which were started with small monetary outlays, made modest incomes, and conducted mainly online and manual searches. The ethical areas of concern to the respondents included (1) online searchers who lacked adequate skills and (2) lack of performance standards for information intermediaries. The area of least concern was legal liability. In fact, most firms did not have written codes of ethics, written disclaimers for the delivery of incorrect secondary information, or any type of liability insurance.

600.   Whitlatch, Jo Bell (Ph.D., University of California at Berkeley, 1987). **Client/Service Provider Perceptions of Reference Service Outcomes in Academic Libraries: Effects of Feedback and Uncertainty.** 388p. Order no. AAD88-14115.

PURPOSE: Using a model based on boundary spanning theory, Whitlatch examined a set of variables (client socialization, service orientation, feedback, time constraints, task uncertainty, size, discipline paradigm, and type of assistance) that might relate to the following academic library reference service outcomes: librarian value of service, user value of service, and user success in locating needed materials.

PROCEDURE: A survey questionnaire was used to collect data on 257 reference transactions at five academic libraries in northern California.

FINDINGS: Significant relationships were found between service outcomes and the following four variables: service orientation, task uncertainty, feedback, and time constraints. Users and reference librarians differed in perception in three of the service outcomes studied: general quality of service, relevance of information, and amount of information. In 83 percent of the reference transactions, the librarian's judgment of service value was the same or lower than that of the user.

CONCLUSIONS: In a reference setting, users expect to be provided with quick and concise information. In many cases, librarian judgments of service value can adequately substitute for user service value judgments.

Author/Title Index

Unless otherwise indicated, reference is to entry number. References to page number are identified by a *p* (e.g., p.4).

Subject Index

Unless otherwise indicated, reference is to entry number. References to page number are identified by a *p* (e.g., p.4).